Programming
in C++

The Jones and Bartlett Series in Computer Science

Programming in C++

Nell Dale
University of Texas, Austin

Chip Weems
University of Massachusetts, Amherst

Mark Headington
University of Wisconsin—LaCrosse

Jones and Bartlett Publishers
Sudbury, Massachusetts

Boston   London   Singapore

Editorial, Sales, and Customer Service Offices
Jones and Bartlett Publishers
40 Tall Pine Drive
Sudbury, MA 01776
(978) 443-5000
info@jbpub.com
http://www.jbpub.com

Jones and Bartlett Publishers International
Barb House, Barb Mews
London W6 7PA
UK

Library of Congress Cataloging-in-Publication Data

Dale, Nell B.
    Programming in C++ / Nell Dale, Chip Weems, Mark Headington.
        p.   cm.
    Includes index.
    ISBN 0-7637-0537-3
    1. C++ (Computer program language)   I. Weems, Chip.
    II. Headington, Mark R.   III. Title.
    QA76.73.C153D35   1997
    005.13'3—dc21   97-32144
                                                                                           CIP

Acquisitions Editor and Vice President: David P. Geggis
Development Editor: Karen Jolie
Production Editor: Joan M. Flaherty
Manufacturing Buyer: Jane Brombeck
Design: George H. McLean
Editorial Production Service: Jennifer Bagdigian
Typesetting: BookMasters, Inc.
Cover Design: Marshall Henrichs
Printing and Binding: Courier Companies

Printed in the United States of America

02 01 00 99   10 9 8 7 6 5 4 3 2 1

PREFACE

Programming in C++ has been prepared in response to requests for a straight-forward no-frills introduction to C++. We have been very gratified by the wide use of its parent textbook, *Programming and Problem Solving with C++* and that book will, of course, continue to be available. However, many users have suggested that this briefer version might be more appropriate for their first course in computer science fundamentals.

Our experience has shown that topics once considered too advanced can be taught in the first course. For example, preconditions and postconditions are used in the context of the algorithm walk-through, in the development of testing strategies, and as interface documentation for user-written functions. Data abstraction and abstract data types are explained in conjunction with the C++ class mechanism, forming a natural lead-in to object-oriented programming.

In this book, we continue our commitment to presenting the material in a way that is precise yet accessible to the student. The chapters contain many exercises and examples that have been compiled and tested thoroughly. Most chapters conclude with a programming example. These longer examples appear after the chapter discussion, which is interrupted only by short examples.

The Use of C++

Some educators reject the C and C++ languages as too permissive and too conducive to writing cryptic, unreadable programs. Our experience does not support this view, *provided that the use of language features is modeled appropriately.* We have found that, with careful instruction in software engineering, students can learn to use C++ to produce clear, readable code.

Our choice of C++ over C was a very easy one. C++ enforces stronger type checking than C does. C++ all but eliminates the need for preprocessor macros. C++ provides reference types, with the result that parameter passage by reference does not require a premature exposure to pointers as in C. C++ stream I/O is simpler for students to use than the `printf` and `scanf` functions. C++ provides linguistic support for data abstraction, information hiding, and object-oriented programming. And, of course, learning the fundamental features of

C++ in the first course eliminates a transition from C to C++ in subsequent course work.

It must be emphasized that, although we use C++ as a vehicle for teaching computer science concepts, the book is not a language manual and does not attempt to cover all of C++. One example is our omission of the C++ template mechanism. Other language features—operator overloading, default parameters, and mechanisms for advanced forms of inheritance, to name a few—are omitted in an effort not to overwhelm the beginning student with too much too fast.

Design Approach

Currently, there are diverse opinions about when to introduce the topic of object-oriented programming (OOP). Some educators advocate an immersion in OOP from the very beginning, whereas others (for whom this book is intended) favor a more heterogeneous approach in which both structured design and object-oriented design are presented as design tools.

What some advocates refer to as OOP might more properly be called OBP—object-based programming. OBP entails the use of existing, externally supplied C++ classes, *as-is*. Although OBP is useful in allowing the student to construct programs with "interesting" (for example, graphical) objects, true OOP requires much more: design and implementation of abstract data types (ADTs), the analysis and design of inheritance hierarchies, and the use of polymorphism in the form of run-time binding of operations to objects.

The chapter organization of *Programming in C++* reflects a transitional approach to OOP. Although we provide an early preview of object-oriented design (Chapter 4), the sequence of topics in Chapters 1 through 15 mirrors our belief that OOP is best understood after a firm grounding in algorithm design, control abstraction, and data abstraction.

Features

Web Enhancement.   A new feature of this book is the C++ *links* for which selected key topics in each chapter are marked with a Web icon that prompts students to visit a special C++ links page on the Jones and Bartlett Web site by entering the URL **http://www.jbpub.com/C++/links** into a World Wide Web browser such as Netscape Navigator or Microsoft Internet Explorer. Brief descriptions are provided to place the links in context *before* the student connects to the sites of various organizations or individuals that currently supply information or additional instruction on a particular topic. This feature gives students instant access to some real-world applications of terms and concepts presented in the text. The site will be updated on a regular basis to ensure that students receive the most recent and pertinent information available on the Internet.

Goals. Each chapter begins with a list of learning objectives for the student. These goals are reinforced and tested in the end-of-chapter exercises.

Programming Examples. Included in most chapters, programming examples present a problem and discuss its solution. Then we code the solution in C++. We show sample test data and output and follow up with a discussion of testing the program.

Testing and Debugging. These sections consider the implications of the chapter material with regard to testing of programs. They conclude with testing and debugging hints.

Quick Checks. These questions test the student's recall of major points associated with the chapter's goals. Upon reading each question, the student immediately should know the answer, which he or she can then verify by glancing at the answers at the end of the section. The page number on which the concept is discussed appears at the end of each question so that the student can review the material in the event of an incorrect response.

Exam Preparation Exercises. To help the student prepare for tests, these questions usually have objective answers and are designed to be answerable with a few minutes of work.

Programming Warm-Up Exercises. To provide the student with experience in writing C++ code fragments or functions, he or she can practice the syntactic constructs without the burden of writing a complete program.

Programming Problems. These require the student to write complete programs.

Supplements

Instructor's Guide with Test Item File. Prepared by the authors, the *Instructor's Guide* features teaching notes, answers to the balance of the exercises, transparency masters, and a compilation of exam questions. The *Instructor's Guide* is available on request from Jones and Bartlett.

Instructor's CD-ROM. The CD-ROM contains a *PowerPoint®* presentation that provides a lecture outline for each chapter of the text for use in the classroom by the instructor and/or placed on hard drives for students to access and review. This CD-ROM also contains a computerized test bank. Additionally, *Web simulations* in many chapters illustrate the power of the Internet without having a live Internet connection in the classroom.

Program Disk.   The source for all the programs in the text is available through the URL **http://www.jbpub.com/disks** on the Jones and Bartlett World Wide Web site. Detailed instructions for downloading this code may be found on the page following the preface.

Acknowledgments

We would like to thank the many individuals who have helped us in the preparation of this text. We are indebted to the members of the faculties of the Computer Science Departments at the University of Texas at Austin, the University of Massachusetts at Amherst, and the University of Wisconsin—La Crosse.

We extend special thanks to Jeff Brumfield for developing the syntax template metalanguage and allowing us to use it in the text. Thanks also to Sylvia Sorkin of Essex Community College, Baltimore, MD, who developed the *PowerPoint®* for Windows 95 v7.0 soft transparencies that appear in the Instructor's CD-ROM.

For their many helpful suggestions, we thank the lecturers, teaching assistants, consultants, and student proctors who run the courses for which this book was written, and the students themselves.

We are grateful to the following faculty members who took the time to respond to a recent survey on CS1 conducted by our publisher: Elizabeth Alpert, Hartnell College; Hamid R. Arabnia, University of Georgia; Don Bailes, East Tennessee State University; Albert L. Baker, Iowa State University; Natasha Bozovic, San Jose State University; John Cigas, Rockhurst College; Bennett Clark, South Dakota School of Mines and Technology; Lee Cornell, Mankato State University; John Crenshaw, Western Kentucky University; David O. Edwards, Goldey-Beacom College; Anthony J. Farrell, Chestnut Hill College; Ann R. Ford, University of Michigan; Susan Gauch, University of Kansas; Randall Hock, Saginaw Valley State University; Jack Hodges, San Francisco State University; Hikyoo Koh, Lamar University; Pamela Lawhead, The University of Mississippi; Stephen P. Leach, Florida State University; Mark LeBlanc, Wheaton College; Mei-Ling L. Liu, California Polytechnic State University, San Luis Obispo; Andy Lopez, University of Minnesota, Morris; Marilyn Loser, Adams State College; E. Terry Magel, Kentucky State University; Patricia Nettnin, Finger Lakes Community College; Deborah Noonan, College of William and Mary; Lynn Olson, Wartburg College; Bobbie Ann Othmer, Westminster College of Salt Lake City; Parviz Partow, California State University, Los Angeles; Holly Patterson, Texas A&M University, Corpus Christi; Howard D. Pyron, University of Missouri, Rolla; Joseph T. Rears, The College of New

Jersey; Robert Strader, Stephen F. Austin State University; K. D. Summerhays, University of San Francisco.

We also thank Dave Geggis, our editor at Jones and Bartlett, Karen Jolie, our development editor, and Joan Flaherty and Jenny Bagdigian who managed the production of this book.

Anyone who has ever written a book—or is related to someone who has—can appreciate the amount of time involved in such a project. To our families—all the Dale clan and the extended Dale family (too numerous to name); to Lisa, Charlie, and Abby; to Anne, Brady, and Kari—thanks for your tremendous support and indulgence.

N. D.
C. W.
M. H.

PROGRAMMING IN C++
PROGRAM DISK

Jones and Bartlett Publishers offers free to students and instructors a program disk with all the complete programs found in *Programming in C++*. The program disk is available through the Jones and Bartlett World Wide Web site on the Internet.*

Download Instructions

1. First, connect to the Jones and Bartlett student diskette home page (http://www.jbpub.com/disks/).
2. Choose *Programming in C++*.
3. Follow the instructions for downloading and saving the *Programming in C++* data disk.
4. If you need assistance downloading a Jones and Bartlett student diskette, please send e-mail to help@jbpub.com.

*Downloading the *Programming in C++* program disk via the Jones and Bartlett home page requires access to the Internet and a World Wide Web browser such as Netscape Navigator or Microsoft Internet Explorer. Instructors at schools without Internet access may call 1-800-832-0034 and request a copy of the program disk. Jones and Bartlett grants adopters of *Programming in C++* the right to duplicate copies of the program disk or to store the files on any stand-alone computer or network.

CONTENTS

10 Simple Data Types: Built-In and User-Defined   *302*

14 Records (C++ Structs)   *457*

15 Classes, Data Abstraction, and Object-Oriented Software Development   *497*

Appendixes   *A1*

Glossary   *A15*

Answers to Selected Exercises   *A19*

Index   *A43*

Overview of Programming and Problem Solving

GOALS

- To understand what a computer program is
- To be able to list the basic stages involved in writing a computer program
- To understand what an algorithm is
- To learn what a high-level programming language is
- To be able to describe what a compiler is and what it does
- To understand the compilation and execution processes
- To learn what the major components of a computer are and how they work together
- To be able to distinguish between hardware and software
- To be able to choose an appropriate problem-solving method for developing an algorithmic solution to a problem

Overview of Programming

programming
Planning, scheduling, or performing a task or an event

computer
A programmable device that can store, retrieve, and process data

computer programming
The process of planning a sequence of steps for a computer to follow

computer program
A list of instructions to be performed by a computer

Much of human behavior and thought is characterized by logical sequences. Since infancy, you have been learning how to act, how to do things. And you have learned to expect certain behavior from other people.

On a broader scale, mathematics never could have been developed without logical sequences of steps for solving problems and proving theorems. Mass production never would have worked without operations taking place in a certain order. Our whole civilization is based on the order of things and actions.

We create order, both consciously and unconsciously, through a process we call **programming.** This book is concerned with the programming of one of our tools, the **computer.**

Just as a concert program lists the actions the players perform, a **computer program** lists the steps the computer performs. From now on, when we use the words *programming* and *program,* we mean **computer programming** and **computer program.**

The computer allows us to do tasks more efficiently, quickly, and accurately than we could by hand—if we could do them by hand at all. In order to use this

1

powerful tool, we must specify what we want done and the order in which we want it done. We do this through programming.

How Do We Write a Program? To write a program, we must go through a two-phase process: *problem solving* and *implementation* (see Figure 1-1).

Problem-Solving Phase

1. *Analysis and Specification.* Understand (define) the problem and what the solution must do.
2. *General Solution (Algorithm).* Develop a logical sequence of steps that solves the problem.
3. *Verify.* Follow the steps exactly to see if the solution really does solve the problem.

Implementation Phase

1. *Concrete Solution (Program).* Translate the algorithm into a programming language.
2. *Test.* Have the computer follow the instructions. Then manually check the results. If you find errors, analyze the program and the algorithm to determine the source of the errors, and then make corrections.

Once a program has been written, it enters a third phase: maintenance.

FIGURE 1-1

Programming Process

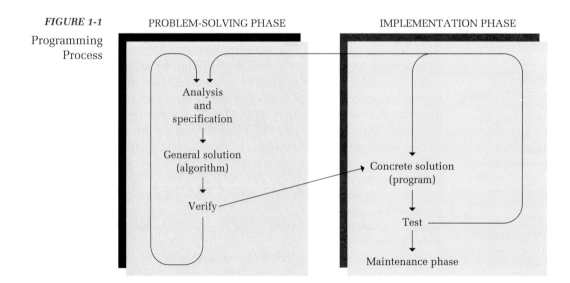

PROBLEM-SOLVING PHASE   IMPLEMENTATION PHASE

Analysis and specification

General solution (algorithm)

Verify

Concrete solution (program)

Test

Maintenance phase

Maintenance Phase

1. *Use.* Use the program.
2. *Maintain.* Modify the program to meet changing requirements or to correct any errors that show up in using it.

Each time the program is modified, it is necessary to repeat the problem-solving and implementation phases for those aspects of the program that change. Together, the problem-solving, implementation, and maintenance phases constitute the program's *life cycle.*

A computer is not intelligent. It cannot analyze a problem and come up with a solution. The programmer must analyze the problem, arrive at the solution, and then communicate it to the computer. What's the advantage of using a computer if it can't solve problems? Once we have prepared a solution for the computer, it can repeat the solution very quickly and consistently. The computer frees people from repetitive and boring tasks.

The programmer begins the programming process by analyzing the problem and developing a general solution called an **algorithm.** Understanding and analyzing a problem take up much more time than Figure 1-1 implies. They are the heart of the programming process.

Our definitions of a computer program and an algorithm look similar, because all programs are implementations of algorithms. A program is simply an algorithm for a computer.

An algorithm is a verbal or written description of a logical sequence of actions. We use algorithms every day. Recipes, instructions, and directions are all examples of algorithms that are not programs.

When you start your car, you follow a step-by-step procedure. The algorithm might look something like this:

1. Insert the key.
2. Make sure the transmission is in Park (or Neutral).
3. Depress the gas pedal.
4. Turn the key to the start position.
5. If the engine starts within six seconds, release the key to the ignition position.
6. If the engine doesn't start in six seconds, release the key, wait ten seconds, and repeat steps 3 through 6, but not more than five times.
7. If the car doesn't start, call the garage.

Without the phrase "but not more than five times" in step 6, you could be trying to start the car forever. Why? Because if something is wrong with the car, repeating steps 3 through 6 over and over again will not start it. This kind of never-ending situation is called an infinite loop. If we leave the phrase "but not more than five times" out of step 6, the procedure does not fit our definition of an algorithm. An algorithm must terminate in a finite amount of time for all possible conditions.

algorithm
A step-by-step procedure for solving a problem in a finite amount of time

Suppose a programmer needs an algorithm to determine an employee's weekly wages. The algorithm reflects what would be done by hand:

1. Look up the employee's pay rate.
2. Determine the number of hours worked during the week.
3. If the number of hours worked is less than or equal to 40, multiply the number of hours by the pay rate to calculate regular wages.
4. If the number of hours worked is greater than 40, multiply 40 by the pay rate to calculate regular wages, and then multiply the difference between the number of hours worked and 40 by one and a half times the pay rate to calculate overtime wages.
5. Add the regular wages to the overtime wages (if any) to determine total wages for the week.

The steps the computer follows are often the same steps you would use to do the calculations by hand.

After developing a general solution, the programmer tests the algorithm, "walking through" each step mentally or manually. If the algorithm doesn't work, the programmer repeats the problem-solving process, analyzing the problem again and coming up with another algorithm. Often the second algorithm is just a variation of the first. When the programmer is satisfied with the algorithm, he or she translates it into a **programming language.** We use the C++ programming language in this book.

**programming
language**
A set of rules, symbols, and special words used to construct a program

A programming language is a simplified form of English (with math symbols) that adheres to a strict set of grammatical rules. English is far too complicated a language for today's computers to follow. Programming languages, because they limit vocabulary, are much simpler.

Although a programming language is simple in form, it is not always easy to use. Try giving someone directions to the nearest airport using a vocabulary of no more than 45 words, and you'll begin to see the problem. Programming forces you to write very simple, exact instructions.

Translating an algorithm into a programming language is called *coding* the algorithm. The product of that translation—the program—is tested by running (*executing*) it on the computer. If the program fails to produce the desired results, the programmer must *debug* it—that is, determine what is wrong and then modify the program, or even the algorithm, to fix it. The combination of coding and testing an algorithm is called *implementation.*

Some people try to speed up the programming process by going directly from the problem definition to coding the program (see Figure 1-2). A shortcut here is very tempting and at first seems to save time. However, for many reasons that will become obvious to you as you read this book, this kind of shortcut actually takes *more* time and effort. Developing a general solution before you write a program helps you manage the problem, keep your thoughts straight, and avoid

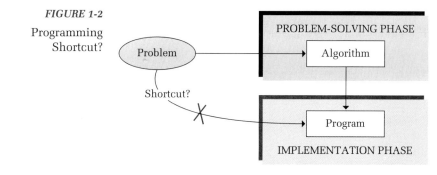

FIGURE 1-2

Programming
Shortcut?

mistakes. If you don't take the time at the beginning to think out and polish your algorithm, you'll spend a lot of extra time debugging and revising your program.

In addition to solving the problem, implementing the algorithm, and maintaining the program, **documentation** is an important part of the programming process. Documentation includes written explanations of the problem being solved and the organization of the solution, comments embedded within the program itself, and user manuals that describe how to use the program. Most programs are worked on by many people over a long period of time. Each of those people must be able to read and understand your code.

After you write a program, you must give the computer the information or data necessary to solve the problem. **Information** is any knowledge that can be communicated, including abstract ideas and concepts. **Data** are information in a form the computer can use—for example, numbers and letters.

documentation
The written text and comments that make a program easier for others to understand, use, and modify

information
Any knowledge that can be communicated

data
Information that has been put into a form a computer can use

What Is a Programming Language?

The only programming language that a computer can directly execute is the primitive instruction set built into it—the **machine language,** or *machine code.* For example:

machine language
The language, made up of binary-coded instructions, that is used directly by the computer

Instruction Name	Machine Language Form
Add	100101
Subtract	010011

Computer scientists develop high-level programming languages that are easier to use than machine code because they are closer to English and other natural languages (see Figure 1-3).

A program called a **compiler** translates programs written in a high-level language (such as C++, Pascal, FORTRAN, COBOL, Java, or Ada) into machine language. If you write a program in a high-level language, you can run it

compiler
A program that translates a high-level language into machine code

◼️ *Data Representation*

In a computer, data are represented electronically by pulses of electricity. Electric circuits, in their simplest form, are either on or off. Usually a circuit that is on is represented by the number 1; a circuit that is off is represented by the number 0. Any kind of data can be represented by combinations of enough 1s and 0s. We simply have to choose which combination represents each piece of data we are using. For example, we could arbitrarily choose the pattern 1101000110 to represent the name C++.

Data represented by 1s and 0s is in binary form. *The binary (base-2) number system uses only 1s and 0s to represent numbers. (The decimal [base-10] number system uses the digits 0 through 9.) The word* bit *(short for* binary digit) *often is used to refer to a single 1 or 0. So the pattern 1101000110 has 10 bits. A binary number with 10 bits can represent 2^{10} (1024) different patterns. A* byte *is a group of 8 bits; it can represent 2^8 (256) patterns. Inside the computer, each character (such as the letter A, the letter g, or a question mark) is usually represented by a byte. Groups of 16, 32, and 64 bits are gen-erally referred to as* words *(although the terms* short word *and* long word *are sometimes used to refer to 16-bit and 64-bit groups, respectively).*

The process of assigning bit patterns to pieces of data is called coding—*the same name we give to the process of translating an algorithm into a programming language. In the early days of computers, programming meant translating an algorithm into patterns of 1s and 0s because the only language the first computers could work with was binary in form.*

Fortunately, we no longer have to work with binary coding schemes. Today the process of coding is usually just a matter of writing down the data in letters, numbers, and symbols. The computer automatically converts these letters, numbers, and symbols into binary form. Still, as you work with computers, you will continually run into numbers that are related to powers of 2—numbers like 256, 32768, and 65536—reminders that the binary number system is lurking somewhere nearby.

source program

A program written in a high-level programming language

object program

The machine language version of a source program

on any computer that has the appropriate compiler. This is possible because most high-level languages are *standardized,* which means that an official description of the language exists.*

A program in a high-level language is called a **source program.** To the compiler, a source program is just input data. It translates the source program into a machine language program called an **object program.** Some compilers also

---

*Some programming languages—LISP, Prolog, and many versions of BASIC, for example—are translated into machine language by an *interpreter* rather than a compiler. The difference between a compiler and an interpreter is outside the scope of this textbook, which focuses only on compiled languages.

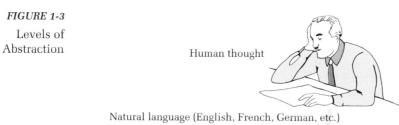

FIGURE 1-3

Levels of
Abstraction

Human thought

Natural language (English, French, German, etc.)

High-level language (C++, FORTRAN, COBOL, etc.)

Machine code (computer)

output a listing—a copy of the program with error messages and other information inserted.

A benefit of standardized high-level languages is that they allow you to write *portable* (or *machine-independent*) code. A C++ program can be run on different machines, whereas a program written in machine language is not portable from one computer to another.

It is important to understand that *compilation* and *execution* are two distinct processes. During compilation, the computer runs the compiler program. During execution, the object program is loaded into the computer's memory, replacing the compiler program. The computer then runs the object program, doing whatever the program instructs it to do (see Figure 1-4).

The instructions in a programming language reflect the operations a computer can perform. A computer can:

- transfer data from one place to another.
- input data from an input device (a keyboard, for example) and output data to an output device (a screen, for example).
- store data into and retrieve data from its memory and secondary storage.
- compare two data values for equality or inequality.
- perform arithmetic operations.

FIGURE 1-4
Compilation/
Execution

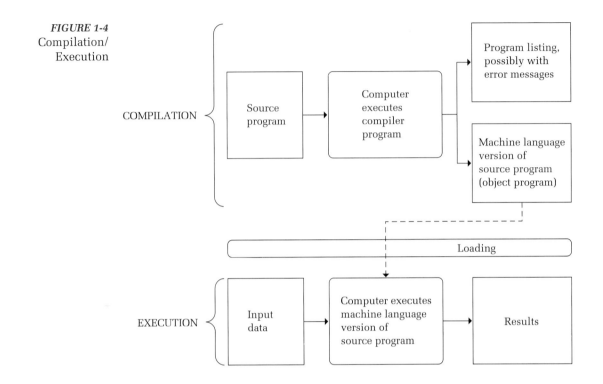

Programming languages require that we use certain structures to express algorithms as programs. There are four basic ways of structuring statements (instructions) in C++ and other languages: sequentially, conditionally, repetitively, and with subprograms (see Figure 1-5). A *sequence* is a series of statements that are executed one after another. *Selection,* the conditional structure, executes different statements depending on certain conditions. The repetitive structure, the *loop,* repeats statements while certain conditions are met. And the *subprogram* allows us to structure a program by breaking it into smaller units.

Assume you're driving a car. Going down a straight stretch of road is like following a *sequence* of instructions. When you come to a fork in the road, you must decide which way to go and then take one or the other branch of the fork. This is what the computer does when it encounters a *selection* (sometimes called a *branch* or *decision*) in a program. Sometimes you have to go around the block several times to find a place to park. The computer does the same sort of thing when it encounters a *loop* in a program.

A *subprogram* is a process that consists of multiple steps. Every day, for example, you follow a procedure to get from home to work. It makes sense, then, for someone to give you directions to a meeting by saying, "Go to the office, then go four blocks west," without listing all the steps you have to take to get to the

FIGURE 1-5   Basic Structures of Programming Languages

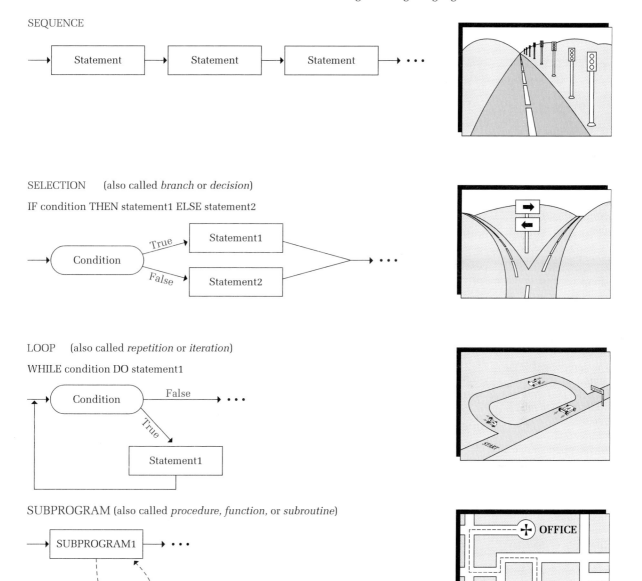

SEQUENCE

SELECTION   (also called *branch* or *decision*)

IF condition THEN statement1 ELSE statement2

LOOP   (also called *repetition* or *iteration*)

WHILE condition DO statement1

SUBPROGRAM (also called *procedure, function,* or *subroutine*)

office. Subprograms allow us to write parts of our programs separately and then assemble them into final form. They can greatly simplify the task of writing large programs.

What Is a Computer?

www.jbpub.com/C++links

memory unit
Internal data storage in a computer

central processing unit (CPU)
The part of the computer that executes the instructions (program) stored in memory; made up of the arithmetic/logic unit and the control unit

arithmetic/logic unit (ALU)
The component of the central processing unit that performs arithmetic and logical operations

control unit
The component of the central processing unit that controls the actions of the other components

input/output (I/O) devices
The parts of the computer that accept data to be processed (input) and present the results of that processing (output)

You can learn how to write programs without knowing much about computers. But if you know something about the parts of a computer, you can better understand the effect of each instruction in a programming language.

There are six basic components in most computers: the memory unit, the arithmetic/logic unit, the control unit, input devices, output devices, and auxiliary storage devices. Figure 1-6 is a stylized diagram of the basic components of a computer.

The **memory unit** is an ordered sequence of storage cells, each capable of holding a piece of data. Each memory cell has a distinct address to which we refer in order to store information into it or retrieve information from it. These storage cells are called *memory cells*, or *memory locations.** The memory unit holds both data and instructions, as shown in Figure 1-7.

The part of the computer that follows instructions is called the **central processing unit (CPU).** The CPU usually has two components. The **arithmetic/logic unit (ALU)** performs arithmetic operations (addition, subtraction, multiplication, and division) and logical operations (comparing two values). The **control unit** controls the actions of the other components so that program instructions are executed in the correct order.

For us to use computers, we must have some way of getting data into and out of them. **Input/output (I/O) devices** accept data to be processed (input) and present data that have been processed (output). A keyboard is a common input device. A video display is a common output device.

For the most part, computers simply move and combine data in memory. The differences among various computers basically involve the size of their memories and the speed with which data can be recalled, the efficiency with which data can be moved or combined, and limitations on I/O devices.

When a program is executing, the computer proceeds through a series of steps, the *fetch-execute cycle:*

1. The control unit retrieves (*fetches*) the next coded instruction from memory.
2. The instruction is translated into control signals.
3. The control signals tell the appropriate unit (arithmetic/logic unit, memory, I/O device) to perform (*execute*) the instruction.
4. The sequence repeats from step 1.

---

*The memory unit is also referred to as RAM, an acronym for **r**andom **a**ccess **m**emory (because we can access any location at random).

FIGURE 1-6

Basic Components
of a Computer

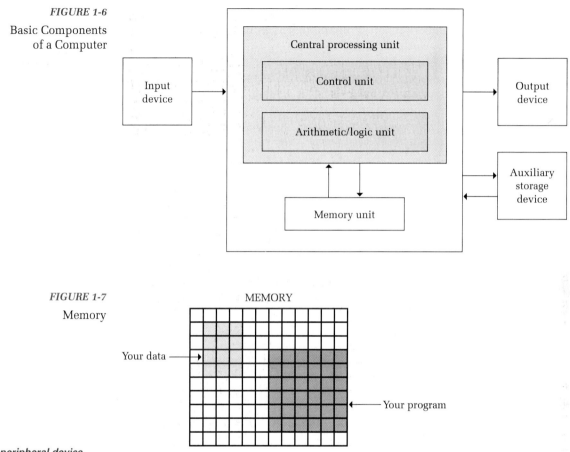

FIGURE 1-7

Memory

peripheral device
*An input, output, or
auxiliary storage de-
vice attached to a
computer*

**auxiliary storage
device**
*A device that stores
data in encoded form
outside the com-
puter's main memory*

hardware
*The physical compo-
nents of a computer*

software
*Computer programs;
the set of all pro-
grams available on a
computer*

Computers can have a wide variety of **peripheral devices** such as keyboards, printers, mice, and auxiliary storage devices. An **auxiliary storage device,** or *secondary storage device,* holds coded data for the computer until we actually want to use the data. Instead of inputting data every time, we can input it once and have the computer store it onto an auxiliary storage device. Typical auxiliary storage devices are magnetic tape drives and disk drives. A *magnetic tape drive* is like a tape recorder. A *disk drive* is a cross between a compact disk player and a tape recorder. It uses a thin disk made out of magnetic material. A read/write head (similar to the record/playback head in a tape recorder) travels across the spinning disk, retrieving or recording data.

Together, all of these physical components are known as **hardware.** The programs that allow the hardware to operate are called **software.** Hardware

interface
*A shared boundary
that allows indepen-
dent systems to meet
and act on or com-
municate with each
other*

operating system
*A set of programs that
manages all of the
computer's resources*

editor
*An interactive pro-
gram used to create
and modify source
programs or data*

usually is fixed in design; software is easily changed. In fact, the ease with which software can be manipulated is what makes the computer such a versatile, powerful tool.

In addition to our programs, there are programs in the computer, called *system software,* that are designed to simplify the user/computer **interface,** making it easier for us to use the machine.

The set of programs includes the compiler as well as the operating system and the editor (see Figure 1-8). The **operating system** manages all of the computer's resources. It can input programs, call the compiler, execute object programs, and carry out any other system commands. The **editor** is an interactive program used to create and modify source programs or data.

www.jbpub.com/C++links

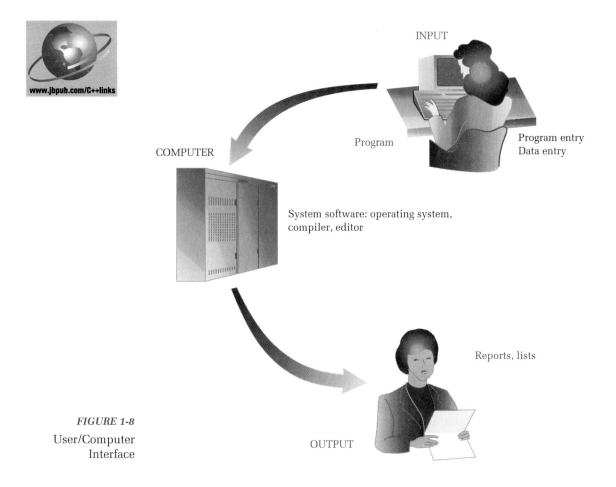

INPUT

COMPUTER

Program

Program entry
Data entry

System software: operating system,
compiler, editor

Reports, lists

FIGURE 1-8
User/Computer
Interface

OUTPUT

Problem-Solving Techniques

You solve problems every day, often unaware of the process you are going through. In a learning environment, you usually are given most of the information you need: a clear statement of the problem, the necessary input, and the required output. In real life, the process is not always so simple. You often have to define the problem yourself and then decide what information you have to work with and what the results should be.

After you understand and analyze a problem, you must come up with a solution—an algorithm. Most of your experience with algorithms is in the context of *following* them. In the problem-solving phase of computer programming, you will be *designing* algorithms. This means you will have to be conscious of the strategies you use to solve problems in order to apply them to programming problems.

Ask Questions

If you are given a task orally, you ask questions—When? Why? Where?—until you understand exactly what you have to do. If your instructions are written, you might put question marks in the margin or in some other way indicate that the task is not clear. Your questions may be answered by a later paragraph, or you might have to discuss them with the person who gave you the task.

These are some of the questions you will be asking in the context of programming:

- What do I have to work with—that is, what are my data?
- What do the data look like?
- How much data is there?
- How will I know when I have processed all the data?
- What should my output look like?
- How many times is the process going to be repeated?
- What special error conditions might come up?

Look for Things That Are Familiar

Never reinvent the wheel. If a solution exists, use it. If you've solved the same or a similar problem before, just repeat your solution. In programming, you will see certain problems again and again in different guises. A good programmer immediately recognizes a subtask he or she has solved before and plugs in the solution. For example, finding the daily high and low temperatures is really the same problem as finding the highest and lowest grades on a test. You want the largest and smallest values in a set of numbers (see Figure 1-9).

Solve by Analogy

Often a problem reminds you of a similar problem you have seen before. You may find solving the problem at hand easier if you remember how you solved the other problem. In other words, draw an analogy between the two problems. As you work your way through the new problem, you come across things that

FIGURE 1-9

Look for Things
That Are Familiar

LIST OF TEMPERATURES		LIST OF TEST SCORES
42		27
18		14
27		55
95		98
55		72
72	Use the same	66
33	method to	45
78	find these	12
86	values in	39
61	both cases.	70
58		68
91		
HIGHEST = 95		HIGHEST = 98
LOWEST = 18		LOWEST = 12

are different than they were in the old problem, but usually these are just details that you can deal with one at a time.

Analogy is really just a broader application of the strategy of looking for things that are familiar. When you are trying to find an algorithm for solving a problem, don't limit yourself to computer-oriented solutions. Step back and try to get a larger view of the problem. Don't worry if your analogy doesn't match perfectly—the only reason for starting with an analogy is that it gives you a place to start (see Figure 1-10). The best programmers are people who have broad experience solving all kinds of problems.

Means-Ends Analysis

Often the beginning state and the ending state are given; the problem is to define a set of actions that can be used to get from one to the other. Suppose you want to go from Boston, Massachusetts, to Austin, Texas. You know the beginning state (you are in Boston) and the ending state (you want to be in Austin). The problem is how to get from one to the other.

In this example, you have lots of choices. You can fly, walk, hitchhike, ride a bike, or whatever. The method you choose depends on your circumstances. If you're in a hurry, you'll probably decide to fly.

Once you've narrowed down the set of actions, you have to work out the details. It may help to establish intermediate goals that are easier to meet than the overall goal. Let's say there is a really cheap, direct flight to Austin out of Newark, New Jersey. You might decide to divide the trip into legs: Boston to Newark and then Newark to Austin. Your intermediate goal is to get from Boston to Newark. Now you only have to examine the means of meeting that intermediate goal (see Figure 1-11).

FIGURE 1-10
Analogy

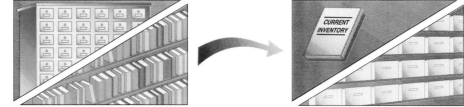

A library catalog system can give insight into how to organize a parts inventory.

The overall strategy of means-ends analysis is to define the ends and then to analyze your means of getting between them. The process translates easily to computer programming. You begin by writing down what the input is and what the output should be. Then you consider the actions a computer can perform and choose a sequence of actions that can transform the input into the output.

Divide and Conquer

We often break up large problems into smaller units that are easier to handle. Cleaning the whole house may seem overwhelming; cleaning the rooms one at a time seems much more manageable. The same principle applies to programming. We break up a large problem into smaller pieces that we can solve individually (see Figure 1-12). In fact, the functional decomposition methodology and the object-oriented methodology, which we describe in Chapter 4, are based on the principle of divide and conquer.

The Building-Block Approach

Another way of attacking a large problem is to see if there are any existing solutions for smaller pieces of the problem. It may be possible to put some of these solutions together end to end to solve most of the big problem. This strategy is

FIGURE 1-11   Means-Ends Analysis

Start: Boston **Goal:** Austin	**Means:** *Fly,* walk, hitchhike, bike, drive, sail, bus
Start: Boston **Goal:** Austin	**Revised Means:** Fly to Chicago and then Austin; *fly to Newark and then Austin;* fly to Atlanta and then Austin
Start: Boston **Intermediate Goal:** Newark **Goal:** Austin	**Means to Intermediate Goal:** *Commuter flight,* walk, hitchhike, bike, drive, sail, bus
Solution: Take commuter flight to Newark and then catch cheap flight to Austin	

FIGURE 1-12
Divide and Conquer

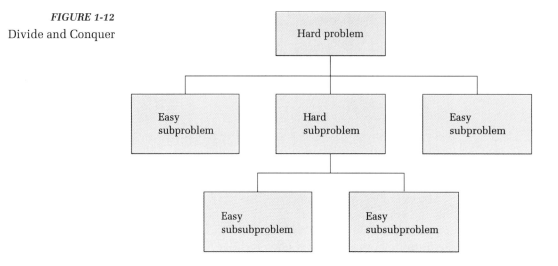

just a combination of the look-for-familiar-things and divide-and-conquer approaches. You look at the big problem and see that it can be divided into smaller problems for which solutions already exist. Solving the big problem is just a matter of putting the existing solutions together, like mortaring together blocks to form a wall (see Figure 1-13).

Merging
Solutions

Another way to combine existing solutions is to merge them on a step-by-step basis. For example, to compute the average of a list of values, we must both sum and count the values. If we already have separate solutions for summing values and for counting values, we can combine them. But if we first do the summing and then do the counting, we have to read the list twice. We can save steps if we merge these two solutions: read a value and then add it to the running total and add 1 to our count before going on to the next value. Whenever the solutions to subproblems duplicate steps, think about merging them instead of joining them end to end.

Mental Blocks:
The Fear of
Starting

Writers are all too familiar with the experience of staring at a blank page, not knowing where to begin. Programmers have the same difficulty when they first tackle a big problem. They look at the problem and it seems overwhelming.

Remember that you always have a place to begin solving any problem: Write it down on paper in your own words so that you understand it. Once you begin to try to paraphrase the problem, you can focus on each of the subparts individually instead of trying to tackle the entire problem at once. This process gives you a clearer picture of the overall problem. It helps you see pieces of the problem that look familiar or that are analogous to other problems you have

FIGURE 1-13   Building-Block Approach

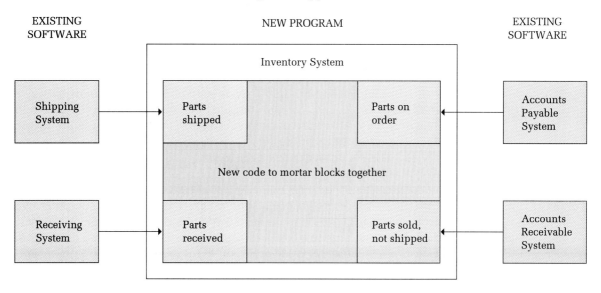

solved. And it pinpoints areas where something is unclear, where you need more information.

As you write down a problem, you tend to group things together into small, understandable chunks, which may be natural places to split the problem up— to divide and conquer. Your description of the problem may collect all of the information about data and results into one place for easy reference. Then you can see the beginning and ending states necessary for means-ends analysis.

Most mental blocks are caused by not really understanding the problem. Rewriting the problem in your own words is a good way to focus on the subparts of the problem, one at a time, and to understand what is required for a solution.

Algorithmic Problem Solving
Coming up with a step-by-step procedure for solving a particular problem is not always cut-and-dried. In fact, it is usually a trial-and-error process requiring several attempts and refinements. We test each attempt to see if it really solves the problem. If it does, fine. If it doesn't, we try again. You typically use a combination of the techniques we've described to solve any non-trivial problem.

Remember that the computer can only do certain things (see p. 9). Your primary concern, then, is how to make the computer transform, manipulate, calculate, or process the input data to produce the desired output. If you keep in mind the allowable instructions in your programming language, you won't design an algorithm that is difficult or impossible to code.

Summary

Computer programming is the process of planning a sequence of steps for a computer to follow. It involves a problem-solving phase and an implementation phase. After analyzing a problem, we develop and test a general solution (algorithm). This general solution becomes a concrete solution—our program—when we write it in a high-level programming language. The sequence of instructions that makes up our program is then compiled into machine code, the language the computer uses. After correcting any errors or "bugs" that show up during testing, our program is ready to use.

Data and instructions are represented as binary numbers (numbers consisting of just 1s and 0s) in electronic computers. The process of converting data and instructions into a form usable by the computer is called coding.

A programming language reflects the range of operations a computer can perform. The basic control structures in a programming language—sequence, selection, loop, and subprogram—are based on these fundamental operations. In this text, you will learn to write programs in the high-level programming language called C++.

Computers are composed of six basic parts: the memory unit, the arithmetic/logic unit, the control unit, input and output devices, and auxiliary storage devices. The arithmetic/logic unit and control unit together are called the central processing unit. The physical parts of the computer are called hardware. The programs that are executed by the computer are called software.

System software is a set of programs designed to simplify the user/computer interface. It includes the compiler, the operating system, and the editor.

We've said that problem solving is an integral part of the programming process. Although you may have little experience programming computers, you have lots of experience solving problems. The key is to stop and think about the strategies you use to solve problems, and then to use those strategies to devise workable algorithms. Among those strategies are asking questions, looking for things that are familiar, solving by analogy, applying means-ends analysis, dividing the problem into subproblems, using existing solutions to small problems to solve a larger problem, merging solutions, and paraphrasing the problem in order to overcome a mental block.

The computer is widely used today in science, engineering, business, government, and the arts. Learning to program in C++ can help you use this powerful tool effectively.

C++ Syntax and Semantics, and the Program Development Process

The Elements of C++ Programs

In this chapter, we start looking at the rules and symbols that make up the C++ programming language. We also review the steps required to create a program and make it work on a computer.

C++ Program Structure

function
A subprogram in C++

In Chapter 1, we said that subprograms allow us to write parts of our program separately and then assemble them into final form. In C++, all subprograms are referred to as **functions,** and a C++ program is a collection of one or more functions.

19

Each function performs some particular task, and collectively they solve the entire problem.

Every C++ program must have a function named `main`. Execution of the program begins with the `main` function. You can think of `main` as the master and the other functions as the servants. When `main` wants the function `Square` to perform a task, `main` *calls* (or *invokes*) `Square`. When the `Square` function completes execution of its statements, it obediently returns control to the master, `main`, so the master can continue executing.

Let's look at an example of a C++ program with three functions: `main`, `Square`, and `Cube`. Don't be too concerned with the details in the program—just observe its overall look and structure.

```cpp
#include <iostream.h>

int Square( int );
int Cube( int );

int main()
{
    cout << "The square of 27 is " << Square(27) << endl;
    cout << "and the cube of 27 is " << Cube(27) << endl;
    return 0;
}
```

PROGRAMMING EXAMPLE cont'd.

```
int Square( int n )
{
    return n * n;
}

int Cube( int n )
{
    return n * n * n;
}
```

In each of the three functions, the left brace ({) and right brace (}) mark the beginning and end of the statements to be executed. Statements appearing between the braces are known as the *body* of the function.

Execution of a program always begins with the first statement of the main function. In our program, the first statement is

```
cout << "The square of 27 is " << Square(27) << endl;
```

This is an output statement that causes information to be printed on the computer's screen. You will learn how to construct output statements like this later in the chapter. Briefly, this statement prints two items. The first is the message

```
The square of 27 is
```

The second item to be printed is the value obtained by calling (invoking) the Square function, with the value 27 as the number to be squared. As the servant, the Square function performs its task of squaring the number and sending the computed result (729) back to its *caller,* the main function. Now main can continue executing by printing the value 729 and proceeding to its next statement.

In a similar fashion, the second statement in main prints the message

```
and the cube of 27 is
```

and then invokes the Cube function and prints the result, 19683. The complete output produced by executing this program is, therefore,

```
The square of 27 is 729
and the cube of 27 is 19683
```

Both `Square` and `Cube` are examples of *value-returning functions*. A value-returning function returns a single value to its caller. The word `int` at the beginning of the first line of the `Square` function

```
int Square( int n )
```

states that the function returns an integer value.

Now look at the `main` function again. You'll see that the first line of the function is

```
int main()
```

The word `int` indicates that `main` is a value-returning function that should return an integer value. And it does. After printing the square and cube of 27, `main` executes the statement

```
return 0;
```

to return the value 0 to its caller. But who calls the `main` function? The answer is: the computer's operating system.

When you work with C++ programs, the operating system is considered to be the caller of the `main` function. The operating system expects `main` to return a value (the *exit status*) when `main` finishes executing. By convention, a return value of 0 means everything went OK. A return value of anything else (typically 1, 2, . . .) means something went wrong. Later in this book we look at situations in which you might want to return a value other than 0 from `main`. For the time being, we'll always conclude the execution of `main` by returning the value 0.

We have briefly examined the overall appearance of a C++ program—a collection of one or more functions, including `main`. And we have mentioned what is special about the `main` function—it is a required function, execution begins there, and it returns a value to the operating system. Now it's time to begin looking at the details of the C++ language.

Syntax and Semantics

syntax
The formal rules governing how valid instructions are written in a programming language

A programming language is a set of rules, symbols, and special words used to construct a program. There are rules for both **syntax** (grammar) and **semantics** (meaning).

Syntax is a formal set of rules that defines exactly what combinations of letters, numbers, and symbols can be used in a programming language. There is no room for ambiguity in the syntax of a programming language because the computer can't think; it doesn't "know what we mean."

semantics

The set of rules that determines the meaning of instructions written in a programming language

Syntax rules are the blueprints we use to "build" instructions in a program. They allow us to take the elements of a programming language—the basic building blocks of the language—and assemble them into *constructs,* syntactically correct structures. If our program violates any of the rules of the language—by misspelling a crucial word or leaving out an important comma, for instance—the program is said to have *syntax errors* and cannot compile correctly until we fix them.

■ *Metalanguages*

Metalanguage *is the word* language *with the prefix* meta, *which means "beyond" or "more comprehensive." A metalanguage is a language that goes beyond a normal language by allowing us to speak precisely about that language. It is a language for talking about languages.*

One of the oldest computer-oriented metalanguages is the Backus-Naur Form (BNF), *which is named for John Backus and Peter Naur, who developed it in 1960. BNF syntax definitions are written out using letters, numbers, and special symbols. For example, a decimal (base-10) integer number in C++ must be at least one digit, it may or may not be more than one digit, and the first digit must be nonzero. The BNF definition of a decimal integer number in C++ is*

```
<DecimalInteger> ::=
  <NonzeroDigit> | <NonzeroDigit>
    <DigitSequence>
<NonzeroDigit> ::= 1 | 2 | 3 | 4 | 5
  | 6 | 7 | 8 | 9
<DigitSequence> ::= <Digit> | <Digit>
  <DigitSequence>
<Digit> ::= 0 | <NonzeroDigit>
```

where the symbol ::= *is read "is defined as," the symbol* | *means "or," the symbols* < *and* > *are used to enclose words called* nonterminal symbols *(symbols that still need to be defined), and everything else is called a* terminal symbol.

The first part of the definition reads: "A decimal integer is defined as a nonzero digit or a nonzero digit followed by a digit sequence." This rule contains nonterminal symbols that must be defined. In the second part, the nonterminal symbol NonzeroDigit is defined as any one of the numeric characters 1 through 9, all of which are terminal symbols. The third part defines the nonterminal symbol DigitSequence as either a Digit or a Digit followed by another DigitSequence. The self-reference in the definition is a roundabout way of saying that a digit sequence can be a sequence of one or more digits. In the last line, Digit is defined as any one of the numeric characters 0 through 9.

BNF is an extremely simple language, but that simplicity leads to syntax definitions that can be long and difficult to read. In this text, we introduce another metalanguage, called a syntax template. *Syntax templates show at a glance the form a C++ construct takes.*

One final note: Metalanguages only show how to write instructions that the compiler can translate. They do not define what those instructions do (their semantics). Formal languages for defining the semantics of a programming language exist, but they are beyond the scope of this text. Throughout this book, we describe the semantics of C++ in English.

Syntax   In this book, we write the syntax rules for C++ using *syntax templates.* A syntax
Templates   template is a generic example of the C++ construct being defined. Graphic conventions show which portions are optional and which can be repeated. A **boldface** word or symbol is a literal word or symbol in the C++ language. A
nonboldface word can be replaced by another template.

Let's look at an example. This template defines a decimal integer in C++:

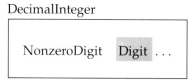

The shading indicates the part of the definition that is optional. The three dots
(. . .) mean that the preceding symbol or shaded block can be repeated. So a decimal integer in C++ must begin with a nonzero digit and is optionally followed
by one or more digits.

Remember that a word not in boldface type can be replaced with another template. These are the templates for NonzeroDigit and Digit:

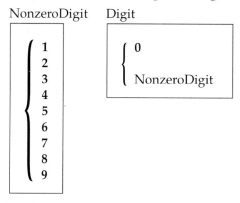

A brace indicates a list of items from which any one can be chosen. So a nonzero
digit can be any one of the numeric characters 1 through 9, and a digit can be either the character 0 or a nonzero digit.

Now let's look at the syntax template for the C++ `main` function:

MainFunction

```
int main()
{
    Statement
        .
        .
        .
}
```

The `main` function begins with the word `int`, followed by the word `main` and then left and right parentheses. This first line of the function is the *heading*. After the heading, the left brace signals the start of the statements in the function (its body). The shading and the three dots indicate that the function body consists of zero or more statements. (In this diagram we have placed the three dots vertically to suggest that statements usually are arranged vertically, one above the next.) Finally, the right brace indicates the end of the function.

In principle, the syntax template allows the function body to have no statements at all. In practice, however, the body should include a `return` statement because the word `int` in the function heading states that `main` returns an integer value. Thus, the shortest C++ program is

```
int main()
{
    return 0;
}
```

As you might guess, this program does nothing useful when executed!

As we introduce C++ language constructs throughout the book, we use syntax templates to display the proper syntax.

When you finish this chapter, you will know enough about the syntax and semantics of statements in C++ to write programs that perform calculations and print the results. But before we can write statements, we first must look at how names are written in C++ and at some of the elements of a program.

Naming Program Elements: Identifiers

Identifiers are used in C++ to name things. Identifiers are made up of letters (A–Z, a–z), digits (0–9), and the underscore character (_), but must begin with a letter or underscore.

Remember that an identifier *must* start with a letter or underscore:

Identifier

> LetterOrUnderscore   LetterOrDigitOrUnderscore   . . .

identifier
A name associated with a function or data object and used to refer to that function or data object

(Identifiers beginning with an underscore have special meanings in some C++ systems, so it is best to begin an identifier with a letter.)

Here are some examples of valid identifiers:

```
sum_of_squares J9 box_22A GetData Bin3D4 count
```

And here are some examples of invalid identifiers and the reasons why they are invalid:

Invalid Identifier	Explanation
40Hours	Identifiers cannot begin with a digit.
Get Data	Blanks are not allowed in identifiers.
box-22	The hyphen (−) is a math symbol (minus) in C++.
cost_in_$	Special symbols such as $ are not allowed.
int	The word int is predefined in the C++ language.

reserved word
A word that has special meaning in C++; it cannot be used as a programmer-defined identifier

The last identifier in the table, int, is an example of a **reserved word**. Reserved words have specific uses in C++; you cannot use them as programmer-defined identifiers. Appendix A lists all of the reserved words in C++.

> ■ *Using Meaningful, Readable Identifiers*
>
> *The names we use to refer to things in our programs are totally meaningless to the computer. The computer behaves in the same way whether we call the value* 3.14159265, pi, *or* cake, *as long as we always call it the same thing. However, it is much easier for somebody to figure out how a program works if we choose names that make sense.*
>
> *C++ is a* case-sensitive *language. Uppercase letters are different from lowercase letters. The identifiers*
>
> ```
> PRINTTOPPORTION  printtopportion
>  pRiNtToPpOrTiOn PrintTopPortion
> ```
>
> *are four distinct names and are not interchangeable in any way. As you can see, the last of these forms is the easiest to read. In this book, we use combinations of uppercase letters, lowercase letters, and underscores in identifiers. We explain our conventions for choosing between uppercase and lowercase as we proceed through this chapter.*

Now that we've seen how to write identifiers, we look at some of the things that C++ allows us to name.

Data and Data Types

Where does a program get the data it needs to operate? Data is stored in the computer's memory. Each memory location has a unique address that we refer to when we store or retrieve data. The "address" of each location in memory is a binary number in a machine language code. In C++ we use identifiers to name memory locations, then the compiler translates them for us. This is one of the advantages of a high-level programming language: It frees us from having to keep track of the actual memory locations in which our data and instructions are stored. In C++ each piece of data must be of a specific **data type.** The data type determines how the data are represented in the computer and the kinds of processing the computer can perform on them.

data type
A specific set of data values along with a set of operations on those values

Some types of data are used so frequently that C++ defines them for us. Also, programmers may define their own data types. We use the standard (built-in) data types until Chapter 10, where we show you how to define your own.

Overview of C++ Data Types. The C++ built-in data types are organized into simple types, structured types, and address types (see Figure 2-1). This chapter introduces you to the simple types. The structured types come much later in the book and the address types are beyond the scope of this text. First we look at the integral types (those used to represent integers), and then we consider the floating types (used to represent real numbers containing decimal points).

Integral Types. The data types `char`, `short`, `int`, and `long` are known as integral types because they refer to integer values—whole numbers with no fractional part. (We postpone talking about the fifth integral type—`enum`—until Chapter 10.)

FIGURE 2-1   C++ Data Types

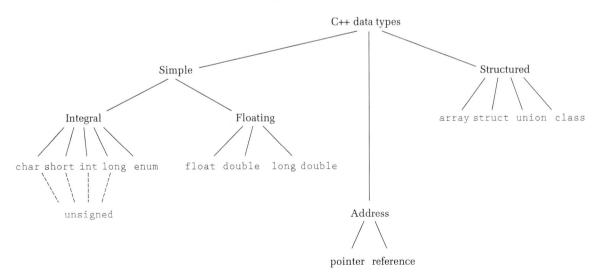

In C++ the simplest form of integer value is a sequence of one or more digits:

```
22   16   1   498   0   4600
```

Commas are not allowed.

In most cases, a minus sign preceding an integer value makes the integer negative:

```
-378   -912
```

The exception is when you explicitly add the reserved word `unsigned` to the data type name:

```
unsigned int
```

An `unsigned` integer value is assumed to be only positive or zero. You will only need to use `unsigned` types for very specialized, advanced problems. We rarely use `unsigned` in this book.

The data types `char`, `short`, `int`, and `long` are intended to represent different sizes of integers, from smaller (fewer bits) to larger (more bits).

`char` memory cell

`short` memory cell

`int` memory cell

`long` memory cell

The sizes are machine dependent (that is, they may vary from machine to machine). In general, the more bits there are in the memory cell, the larger the integer value that can be stored.

You nearly always use `int` for manipulating integer values, but sometimes you have to use `long` if your program requires values larger than the maximum `int` value. (On many personal computers, the range of `int` values is from -32768 through +32767. On larger machines, `int` typically ranges from -2147483648 through +2147483647.) If your program tries to compute a value larger than your machine's maximum value, the result is *integer overflow*. Some machines give you an error message when overflow occurs, but others don't. We talk more about overflow in later chapters.

One caution about integer values in C++: A value beginning with a zero is taken to be an octal (base-8) number instead of a decimal (base-10) number. If you write

015

the C++ compiler takes this to mean the decimal number 13. If you aren't familiar with the octal number system, don't worry about why an octal 15 is the same as a decimal 13. The important thing to remember is not to start a decimal integer value with a zero (unless you want the number 0, which is the same in both octal and decimal). In Chapter 10, we discuss the various integral types in more detail.

More About the `char` ***Type.*** We have seen that `char` is the "smallest" data type that can be used to represent integer values. A `char` value occupies less memory space than an `int` value, so programmers sometimes use the `char` data type to save memory in programs that use small integer values. But there is another, far more typical use of the `char` type: to describe data consisting of one alphanumeric character—a letter, a digit, or a special symbol:

'A'   'a'   '8'   '2'   '+'   '-'   '$'   '?'   '*'   ' '

Each machine uses a particular *character set,* the set of alphanumeric characters it can represent. (See Appendix D for some sample character sets.) Notice that each character is enclosed in single quotes (apostrophes). The C++ compiler needs the quotes to differentiate between the character data '8' and the integer value 8 because the two are stored differently inside the machine. Notice also that the blank, ' ', is a valid character.

You wouldn't want to add the character 'A' to the character 'B' or subtract the character '3' from the character '8', but you might want to compare character values. Each character set has a *collating sequence,* a predefined ordering of all the characters. Although this sequence varies from one character set to another, 'A' always compares less than 'B', 'B' less than 'C', and so forth. And '1' compares less than '2', '2' less than '3', and so on.

Floating Point Types. Floating point types (or floating types), the second major category of simple types in C++, are used to represent real numbers. Floating point numbers have an integer part and a fractional part, with a decimal point in between. Either the integer part or the fractional part, but not both, may be missing. Here are some examples:

18.0   127.54   0.57   4.   193145.8523   .8

Starting `0.57` with a 0 does not make it an octal number. It is only with integer values that a leading 0 indicates an octal number.

Just as the integral types in C++ come in different sizes (`char`, `short`, `int`, and `long`), so do the floating point types. In increasing order of size, the floating point types are `float`, `double` (meaning double precision), and `long double`. Each larger size gives us a wider range of values and more precision (the number of significant digits in the number), but at the expense of more memory space to hold the number.

Floating point values also can have an exponent, as in scientific notation. (In scientific notation, a number is written as a value multiplied by 10 to some power.) Instead of writing 3.504×10^{12}, in C++ we write `3.504E12`. The `E` means exponent of base 10. The number preceding the letter `E` doesn't need to include a decimal point. Here are some examples of floating point numbers in scientific notation:

```
1.74536E-12   3.652442E4   7E20
```

Most programs don't need the `double` and `long double` types. The `float` type usually provides sufficient precision and range of values for floating point numbers. Even personal computers provide `float` values with a precision of six or seven significant digits and a maximum value of about `3.4E+38`.

We talk more about floating point numbers in Chapter 10. But there is one more thing you should know about them now. Computers cannot always represent floating point numbers exactly. You learned in Chapter 1 that the computer stores all data in binary (base-2) form. Many floating point values can only be approximated in the binary number system. Don't be surprised if your program prints out the number 4.8 as 4.7999998. In most cases, slight inaccuracies in the rightmost fractional digits are to be expected and are not the result of programmer error.

Naming Elements: Declarations

declaration

A statement that associates an identifier with a data object, a function, or a data type so that the programmer can refer to that item by name

Identifiers can be used to name both constants and variables. In other words, an identifier can be the name of a memory location whose contents are not allowed to change or it can be the name of a memory location whose contents may change.

How do we tell the computer what an identifier represents? By using a **declaration,** a statement that associates a name (an identifier) with a description of an element in a C++ program (just as a dictionary definition associates a name with a description of the thing being named). In a declaration, we name an identifier and what it represents. For example, the declaration

```
int empNum;
```

announces that `empNum` is the name of a variable whose contents are of type `int`. When we declare a variable, the compiler picks a location in memory to be associated with the identifier and automatically keeps track of it for us.

In C++ each identifier can represent just one thing (except under special circumstances, which we talk about in Chapters 7 and 8). Every identifier you use in a program must be different from all others.

Constants and variables are collectively called *data objects*. Both data objects and the actual instructions in a program are stored in various memory locations. You have seen that a group of instructions—a function—can be given a name. Later on, you'll see that a name also can be associated with a programmer-defined data type, a data type that is not predefined in the C++ language.

In C++ you must declare every identifier before it is used. This allows the compiler to verify that the use of the identifier is consistent with what it was declared to be. If you declare an identifier to be a constant and later try to change its value, the compiler detects this inconsistency and issues an error message.

There is a different form of declaration statement for each kind of data object, function, or data type in C++. The forms of declarations for variables and constants are introduced here; others are covered in later chapters.

Variables. While a program is executing, different data values may be stored in the same memory location at different times. This kind of memory location is called a **variable,** and its contents are the *variable value*. The symbolic name that we associate with a memory location is the *variable name* or *variable identifier* (see Figure 2-2). In practice, we often refer to the variable name as the *variable*.

Declaring a variable means specifying both its name and its data type. This tells the compiler to associate a name with a memory location whose contents are of a specific type (for example, `int`, `float`, or `char`). The following statement declares `empNum` to be a variable of type `int`:

variable
A location in memory, referenced by an identifier, in which a data value that can be changed is stored

```
int empNum;
```

A declaration always ends with a semicolon. In C++ a variable can contain only data values of the type specified in its declaration; thus, the variable

FIGURE 2-2
Variable

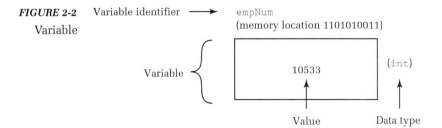

empNum can contain *only* int values. If the C++ compiler comes across an instruction that tries to store a float value into empNum, it generates extra instructions to convert the float value to an int. In Chapter 3, we examine how these conversions take place.

It is possible to declare several variables in one statement:

```
int studentCount, maxScore, sumOfScores;
```

Here, all three variables are declared to be int variables. Our preference, though, is to declare each variable with a separate statement:

```
int studentCount;
int maxScore;
int sumOfScores;
```

With this form it is easier, when modifying a program, to add new variables to the list or delete ones you no longer want.

Declaring each variable with a separate statement also allows you to attach comments for the human reader to the right of each declaration, as we do here:

```
float payRate;      // Employee's pay rate
float hours;        // Hours worked
float wages;        // Wages earned
float total;        // Total company payroll
int   empNum;       // Employee ID number
```

These declarations tell the compiler to set up locations in memory for four float variables—payRate, hours, wages, and total—and to set up one location for an int variable named empNum. The comments (the words written after the // on each line) explain to the reader what each variable represents.

Now that we've seen how to declare variables in C++, let's look at how to declare constants.

Constants. All numbers—integer and floating point—are constants. So are single characters (enclosed in single quotes) and sequences of characters, or *strings* (enclosed in double quotes).

```
16  32.3  'A'  "Howdy boys"
```

In C++ as in mathematics, a constant is something whose value never changes.

We use numeric constants as part of arithmetic expressions (as you will see later in this chapter). For example, we can write a statement that adds the constants 5 and 6 and places the result into a variable named sum. When we use the actual value of a constant in a program, we are using a **literal value** (or *literal*).

literal value
Any constant value written in a program

Notice that a char literal can have only one character within single quotes ('), whereas a string literal can have many characters and must be enclosed within double quotes ("). The use of quotes lets us differentiate between char or string literals and identifiers. "amount" (in double quotes) is the character string made up of the letters *a, m, o, u, n,* and *t* in that order. On the other hand, amount (without the quotes) is an identifier, perhaps the name of a variable.

Although character and string literals are put in quotes, literal integers and floating point numbers are not, because there is no chance of confusing them with identifiers. Why? Because identifiers must start with a letter or underscore, and numbers must start with a digit.

named constant
A location in memory, referenced by an identifier, where a data value that cannot be changed is stored

An alternative to the literal constant is the **named constant** (or *symbolic constant*), which is introduced in a declaration statement. A named constant is just another way of representing a literal value. Instead of using the literal value directly, we give it a name in a declaration statement, then use that name. For example, we can write an expression that multiplies the literal values 3.14159 and 4.5. Or we can define a constant in a declaration statement for each of those values, and then use the constant names in the instruction. For example, we can use either

3.14159*4.5 or PI*RADIUS

but the latter is more descriptive.

It may seem easier to use the literal value of a constant than to give the constant a name and then refer to it by that name. But, in fact, named constants make a program easier to read because they make the meaning of literal constants clearer. And named constants also make it easier to change a program later on.

Here we see some example constant declarations. Notice that the reserved word const begins the declaration, and an equal sign (=) appears between the identifier and the literal value.

```
const char   BLANK = ' ';
const float  PI = 3.14159;
const float  INTEREST_RATE = 0.12;
const float  TAX_RATE = 0.001;
const int    MAX = 20;
```

Many C++ programmers capitalize the entire identifier of a named constant and separate the English words with an underscore. The idea is to let the reader quickly distinguish between variable names and constant names in the middle of a program.

◾ Using Named Constants

It's a good idea to use named constants instead of literals. In addition to making your program more readable, it can make it easier to modify. C++ allows us to declare constants with different names but the same value. If a value has different meanings in different parts of a program, it makes sense to declare and use a constant with an appropriate name for each meaning.

Named constants also are reliable; they protect us from mistakes. If you mistype the name PI as PO, the C++ compiler will tell you that the name PO has not been declared. On the other hand, even though we recognize that the number 3.14149 is a mistyped version of pi (3.14159), the number is perfectly acceptable to the compiler. It won't warn us that anything is wrong.

It's a good idea to add comments to constant declarations as well as variable declarations. For example:

```
const float MAX_HOURS = 40.0;   // Maximum normal work hours
const float OVERTIME = 1.5;     // Overtime pay rate factor
```

Taking Action:
Executable
Statements

Up to this point we've looked at ways of declaring data objects in a program. Now we turn our attention to ways of performing operations on data.

Assignment. The value of a variable is changed through an **assignment statement.** For example,

assignment statement
A statement that stores the value of an expression into a variable

```
quizScore = 10;
```

assigns the value 10 to the variable quizScore (stores the value 10 into the memory location called quizScore). The semantics (meaning) of the assignment operator (=) is "store"; the value of the expression is *stored* into the variable. Any previous value in the variable is destroyed and replaced by the value of the expression.

Only one variable can be on the left-hand side of an assignment statement. An assignment statement is *not* like a math equation ($x + y = z + 4$); the expression (what is on the right-hand side of the assignment operator) is evaluated, and that value is stored into the single variable on the left of the assignment operator. A variable keeps its assigned value until another statement stores a new value into it.

■ *Capitalization of Identifiers*

Programmers often use capitalization as a visual clue to what an identifier represents. Different programmers adopt different conventions for using uppercase letters and lowercase letters. The convention we use in this book is the following:

- *For variables, we begin with a lowercase letter and capitalize each successive word.*

```
lengthInYards   sumOfSquares   hours
```

- *Names of programmer-written functions are capitalized the same way, but they begin with capital letters.*

```
CalcPay(payRate, hours, wages)   Cube(27)   MyDataType
```

However, C++ expects every program to have a function named main—*all in lowercase letters—so we cannot name it* Main. *Nor can we use* Int *for the built-in data type* int. *C++ reserved words use all lowercase letters.*

- *For named constants, we capitalize every letter and use underscores to separate the English words.*

```
UPPER_LIMIT   PI   MAX_LENGTH
```

C++ does not require this particular style of capitalizing identifiers. You may wish to capitalize in a different fashion, but be consistent throughout your program. It can be confusing or misleading if you use inconsistent capitalization.

Given the declarations

```
int   num;
int   alpha;
float rate;
char  ch;
```

we can make the following assignments:

Variable	Expression
alpha =	2856;
rate =	0.36;
ch =	'B';
num =	alpha;

However, the following assignment is not valid:

```
ch = "Hello";
```

A `char` variable can hold only one character.

Expressions are made up of constants, variables, and operators. The following are all valid expressions:

```
alpha + 2    rate - 6.0    4 - alpha    rate    alpha * num
```

The operators allowed in an expression depend on the data types of the constants and variables in the expression. The *arithmetic operators* are

+   Unary plus
-   Unary minus
+   Addition
-   Subtraction
*   Multiplication
/   {Floating point division (floating point result)
     {Integer division (no fractional part)
%   Remainder from integer division

unary operator
An operator that has
just one operand

binary operator
An operator that has
two operands

The first two operators are **unary operators**—they take just one operand. The remaining five are **binary operators,** taking two operands. Unary plus and minus are used as follows:

```
-54    +259.65    -rate
```

You almost never use the unary plus. Without any sign, a numeric constant is assumed to be positive anyway.

You may not be familiar with integer division and remainder (%). Let's look at them more closely. Note that % is used only with integers. When you divide one integer by another, you get an integer quotient and a remainder. Integer division gives only the integer quotient, and % gives only the remainder. (If either operand is negative, the result may vary from one C++ compiler to another.)

$$\begin{array}{ll} 3 & \leftarrow 6/2 \\ 2\overline{)6} & \\ \underline{6} & \\ 0 & \leftarrow 6 \ \% \ 2 \end{array} \qquad \begin{array}{ll} 3 & \leftarrow 7/2 \\ 2\overline{)7} & \\ \underline{6} & \\ 1 & \leftarrow 7 \ \% \ 2 \end{array}$$

In contrast, floating point division yields a floating point result. The expression

```
7.0 / 2.0
```

yields the value 3.5.

Here are some expressions using arithmetic operators and their values:

Expression	Value	Expression	Value
3 + 6	9	8 / 9	0
3.4 - 6.1	− 2.7	8 / 7	1
2 * 3	6	8 % 8	0
8 / 2	4	8 % 9	8
8.0 / 2.0	4.0	8 % 7	1
8 / 8	1	0 % 7	0
		5 % 2.3	error (both operands must be integers)

Be careful with division and remainder. The expressions 7.0/0.0, 7/0, and 7%0 all produce errors. The computer cannot divide by zero.

Because variables are allowed in expressions, the following are valid assignments:

```
alpha = num + 6;   num = alpha * 2;   alpha = alpha + 1;
alpha = num / 2;   num = 6 % alpha;   num = num + alpha;
```

Notice that the same variable can appear on both sides of the assignment operator. In the case of

```
num = num + alpha;
```

the value in `num` and the value in `alpha` are added together, then the sum of the two values is stored into `num`, replacing the previous value stored there. This example shows the difference between mathematical equality and assignment. The mathematical equality

```
num = num + alpha
```

is true only when `alpha` equals zero. The assignment statement

```
num = num + alpha;
```

is valid for *any* value of alpha.

In the examples of expressions so far, we have been careful not to mix integer and floating point values in the same expression. When mixed-type expressions occur, the compiler applies certain rules for converting operands from one type to another. In the next chapter, we discuss those rules.

Increment and Decrement.   In addition to the arithmetic operators, C++ provides *increment* and *decrement* operators:

++   Increment
- -   Decrement

These are unary operators that take a single variable name as an operand. For integer and floating point operands, the effect is to add 1 to (or subtract 1 from) the operand. If `num` currently contains the value 8, the statement

```
num++;
```

causes `num` to contain 9. You can achieve the same effect by writing the assignment statement

```
num = num + 1;
```

but C++ programmers typically prefer the increment operator.

The ++ and - - operators can be either *prefix operators*

```
++num;
```

or *postfix operators*

```
num++;
```

Both of these statements behave in exactly the same way; they add 1 to whatever is in num. The choice between the two is a matter of personal preference.

C++ allows the use of ++ and -- in the middle of a larger expression:

```
alpha = num++ * 3;
```

In this case, the postfix form of ++ gives a different result from the prefix form. In Chapter 10, we explain the ++ and -- operators in detail. In the meantime, you should use them only to increment or decrement a variable as a separate, stand-alone statement.

Output.   In C++ we write out the results of calculations by using a special variable name cout (pronounced "see-out") along with the *insertion operator* ($<<$):

```
cout << "Hello";
```

This statement displays the characters Hello on the *standard output device,* usually the screen.

The variable cout is predefined in C++ systems to denote an *output stream.* You can think of an output stream as an endless sequence of characters going to an output device. In the case of cout, the output stream goes to the standard output device.

The insertion operator $<<$ (often pronounced as "put to") takes two operands. Its left-hand operand is a stream expression (in the simplest case, just a stream variable such as cout). Its right-hand operand is either a string or an expression whose result is a simple type:

```
cout << "The answer is ";
cout << 3 * num;
```

The insertion operator converts its right-hand operand to a sequence of characters and inserts them into (or, more precisely, appends them to) the output stream. Notice how the $<<$ points in the direction the data are going—*from* the expression or string written on the right *to* the output stream on the left.

You can use the $<<$ operator several times in a single output statement. Each occurrence appends the next data item to the output stream. For example, we can write the preceding two output statements as

```
cout << "The answer is " << 3 * num;
```

If `num` contains the value 5, both versions produce the same output:

```
The answer is 15
```

The following output statements yield the output shown. These examples assume that the variable `i` contains the value 2, and `j` contains 6.

Statement	What Is Printed (□ means blank)
`cout << i;`	2
`cout << "i = " << i;`	i□=□2
`cout << "Sum = " << i + j;`	Sum□=□8
`cout << "ERROR MESSAGE";`	ERROR□MESSAGE
`cout << "Error=" << i;`	Error=2
`cout << "j:" << j << "i:" << i;`	j:6i:2
`cout << "j:" << j << ' ' << "i:" << i;`	j:6□i:2

An output statement prints string constants exactly as they appear within quotes. To let the computer know that you want to print a string constant—not a named constant or variable—you must use double quotes to enclose the string. If you don't put quotes around a string, you'll probably get an error message (like "UNDECLARED IDENTIFIER") from the C++ compiler. If you want to print a string that includes a double quote, you use a backslash (\) character and a double quote, with no space between them. For example, to print the string

```
Al "Butch" Jones
```

the output statement looks like this:

```
cout << "Al \"Butch\" Jones";
```

Normally, successive output statements cause the output to continue along the same line of the display screen. The sequence

```
cout << "Hi";
cout << "there";
```

writes the following to the screen, all on the same line:

```
Hithere
```

To print the two words on separate lines, we do this:

```
cout << "Hi" << endl;
cout << "there" << endl;
```

The output from these statements is

```
Hi
there
```

The identifier `endl` (meaning "end line") doesn't fit the pattern we gave. It is neither an expression whose result is a simple type nor a string. It is a special C++ feature called a *manipulator.* We discuss manipulators in the next chapter. For now, the important thing to note is that `endl` lets you finish an output line and go on to the next line whenever you wish.

Beyond Minimalism: Adding Comments to a Program

All you need to create a working program is the correct combination of declarations and executable statements. The compiler ignores comments, but they are of enormous help to anyone who must read the program. Comments can appear anywhere in a program.

C++ comments come in two forms. The first is any sequence of characters enclosed by the /* */ pair. The compiler ignores anything within the pair. Here's an example:

```
float fuelLoad;   /* The amount of fuel, entered in pounds */
```

The second, and more common, form begins with two slashes (//) and extends to the end of the line:

```
float fuelLoad;   // The amount of fuel, entered in pounds
```

The compiler ignores anything after the two slashes.

It is good programming style to write fully commented programs. A comment should appear at the beginning of a program to explain what the program does:

```
// This program computes the weight and balance of a Beechcraft
// Starship-1 airplane, given the amount of fuel, number of
// passengers, and weight of luggage in fore and aft storage.
// It assumes that there are two pilots and a standard complement
// of equipment, and that passengers weigh 170 pounds each
```

Another good place for comments is in constant and variable declarations, where the comments explain how each identifier is used. In addition, comments should introduce each major step in a long program and should explain anything that is unusual or difficult to read (for example, a lengthy formula).

It is important to make your comments concise and to arrange them in the program so that they are easy to see and it is clear what they refer to. If comments are too long or crowd the statements of the program, they make the program more difficult to read—just the opposite of what you intended!

Program Construction

We have looked at basic elements of C++ programs: identifiers, declarations, variables, constants, expressions, statements, and comments. Now let's see how to collect these elements into a program. As you saw earlier, C++ programs are made up of functions, one of which must be named `main`. A program also can have declarations that lie outside of any function. The syntax template for a program looks like this:

Program

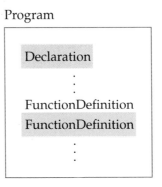

A function definition consists of the function heading and its body, which is delimited by left and right braces:

FunctionDefinition

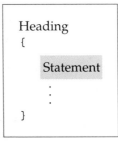

Here's an example of a program with just one function, the `main` function:

```
//*********************************************************************
// FreezeBoil program
// This program computes the midpoint between
// the freezing and boiling points of water
//*********************************************************************
#include <iostream.h>

const float FREEZE_PT = 32.0; // Freezing point of water
const float BOIL_PT = 212.0;  // Boiling point of water

int main()
{
    float avgTemp;            // Holds the result of averaging
                              //    FREEZE_PT and BOIL_PT

    cout << "Water freezes at " << FREEZE_PT << endl;
    cout << " and boils at " << BOIL_PT << " degrees." << endl;

    avgTemp = FREEZE_PT + BOIL_PT;
    avgTemp = avgTemp / 2.0;

    cout << "Halfway between is ";
    cout << avgTemp << " degrees." << endl;

    return 0;
}
```

The program begins with a comment that explains what the program does. Immediately after the comment, the line

```
#include <iostream.h>
```

instructs the C++ system to insert the contents of a file named `iostream.h` into our program. This file contains information that C++ requires to output values to a stream such as `cout`. We'll consider what is done by the `#include` line a little later.

Next come declarations of the constants `FREEZE_PT` and `BOIL_PT`. Comments explain how they are used. The rest of the program is the function definition for `main`. The first line is the function heading: the reserved word `int`, the name of the function, and then opening and closing parentheses. (The parentheses inform the compiler that `main` is a function, not a variable or named constant.) The body of the function includes a declaration of the variable `avgTemp` and then a list of executable statements. Our `main` function finishes by returning zero as the function value.

Notice how we use spacing in the program to make it easy to read. We use blank lines to separate statements into related groups, and we indent the body of the `main` function. The compiler doesn't require us to format the program this way; we do so only to make it more readable.

Blocks (Compound Statements)   The body of a function is an example of a *block* (or *compound statement*). This is the syntax template for a block:

Block

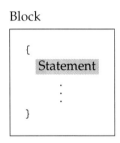

A block is just a sequence of zero or more statements enclosed (delimited) by a { } pair. We can thus redefine a function definition as a Heading followed by a Block. In later chapters, we'll define the syntax of Heading in detail. In the case of the `main` function, Heading is simply

```
int main()
```

Here is the syntax template for a statement, limited to the C++ statements discussed in this chapter:

Statement

NullStatement
Declaration
AssignmentStatement
IncrementStatement
DecrementStatement
OutputStatement
Block

A statement can be empty (the *null statement*). The null statement is just a semi-colon (;). It does absolutely nothing at execution time; execution just proceeds to the next statement. It is not used often.

As the syntax template shows, a statement also can be a declaration, an executable statement, or even a block. The latter means that you can use an entire block wherever a single statement is allowed. In later chapters where we introduce the syntax for branching and looping structures, you'll see that this fact is very important.

We use blocks often, especially as parts of other statements. Leaving out a { } pair can dramatically change the meaning as well as the execution of a program. This is why we always indent the statements inside a block—the indentation makes a block easy to spot in a long, complicated program.

Notice in the syntax templates for the block and the statement that there is no mention of semicolons. Yet the `FreezeBoil` program contains many semicolons. Each kind of statement is separately defined to include an ending semicolon. However, the syntax template for the block shows no semicolon after the right brace. The rule for using semicolons in C++, then, is quite simple: Terminate each statement *except* a compound statement (block) with a semicolon.

One more thing about blocks and statements: According to the syntax template for a statement, a declaration is officially considered to be a statement. A declaration, therefore, can appear wherever an executable statement can. In a block, we can mix declarations and executable statements if we wish:

```
{
    int i;
    i = 35;
    cout << i;
    float x;
    x = 14.8;
    cout << x;
}
```

It's far more common, though, for programmers to group the declarations together before the start of the executable statements:

```
{
    int i;
    float x;

    i = 35;
    cout << i;
    x = 14.8;
    cout << x;
}
```

The C++
Preprocessor

www.jbpub.com/C++links

Imagine that you are the C++ compiler. You are presented with the following program. You are to check it for syntax errors and, if there are none, translate it into machine language.

```
int main()
{
    cout << "Happy Birthday" << endl;
    return 0;
}
```

You, the compiler, recognize the identifier int as a C++ reserved word and the identifier main as the name of a required function. But what about the identifiers cout and endl? The programmer has not declared them as variables or named constants, and they are not reserved words. You have no choice but to issue an error message and give up.

The way to fix this program is to insert a line near the top that says

```
#include <iostream.h>
```

just as we did in the FreezeBoil program (as well as in the sample program at the beginning of this chapter).

The line says to insert the contents of a file named iostream.h into the program. This file contains declarations of cout, endl, and other items needed to perform stream input and output. The #include line is not handled by the C++ compiler but by a program known as the *preprocessor.*

The preprocessor concept is fundamental to C++. The preprocessor is a program that acts as a filter during the compilation phase. Your source program passes through the preprocessor on its way to the compiler (see Figure 2-3).

A line beginning with a pound sign (#) is not considered to be a C++ language statement (and thus is not terminated by a semicolon). It is called a *preprocessor directive.* The preprocessor expands an #include directive by physically inserting the contents of the named file into your source program. Files that appear in an #include directive usually have a file name ending in .h, meaning *header file.* Header files contain constant, variable, and function declarations needed by a program.

In the directive

```
#include <iostream.h>
```

FIGURE 2-3   C++ Preprocessor

▪ *Understanding Before Changing*

When you are in the middle of getting a program to run and you come across an error, it's tempting to start changing parts of the program to try to make it work. Don't! You'll nearly always make things worse. It's essential that you understand what is causing the error and carefully think through the solution. The only thing you should try is running the program with different input data to determine the pattern of behavior.

There is no magic trick—inserting an extra semicolon or right brace, for example—that can automatically fix a program. If the compiler tells you that a semicolon or a right brace is missing, you have to examine the program and determine precisely what the problem is. Perhaps you accidentally typed a

colon instead of a semicolon. Or maybe there's an extra left brace.

A good rule of thumb is: If the source of a problem isn't immediately obvious, leave the computer and go somewhere where you can quietly look over a printed copy of the program. Studies show that people who do all of their debugging away from the computer actually get their programs to work in less time and in the end produce better programs than those who continue to work on the machine—more proof that there is still no mechanical substitute for human thought. *

*Basili, V. R., Selby, R. W., "Comparing the Effectiveness of Software Testing Strategies," *IEEE Trans. on Software Engineering*, Vol. SE-13, No. 12, pp. 1278–1296, Dec. 1987.

the angle brackets $\langle \ \rangle$ are required. They tell the preprocessor to look for the file in the standard *include directory*—a location in the computer system that contains all the header files available to C++ programmers. In Chapter 3, you will see examples of including other header files.

PROGRAMMING EXAMPLE

Mileage

Problem: Write a program to calculate the miles per gallon a car gets on a trip, given the amounts in gallons of the fillups and the starting and ending mileage. The starting mileage was 67308.0; the ending mileage, 68750.5. During the trip, the car was filled up four times. The four amounts were 11.7, 14.3, 12.2, and 8.5 gallons. Assume that the tank was full initially and that the last fillup was at the end of the trip.

Output: The quantities on which the calculations are based and the computed miles per gallon, all appropriately labeled.

Discussion: If you calculated this by hand, you would add up the gallon amounts, then divide the sum into the mileage traveled. The mileage traveled is, of course, just the ending mileage minus the starting mileage. This is essentially the algorithm we use in the program. Let's make all of the numeric quantities named constants, so that it is easier to change the program later. Here is the algorithmic solution:

```
AMT1 = 11.7
AMT2 = 14.3
AMT3 = 12.2
AMT4 = 8.5
START_MILES = 67308.0
END_MILES = 68750.5
Set mpg = (END_MILES - START_MILES) / (AMT1 + AMT2 + AMT3 + AMT4)
Write the fillup amounts
Write the starting mileage
Write the ending mileage
Write the mileage per gallon
```

From the algorithm we can create tables of constants and variables that help us write the declarations in the program.

Constants

Name	Value	Description
AMT1	11.7	Number of gallons for fillup 1
AMT2	14.3	Number of gallons for fillup 2
AMT3	12.2	Number of gallons for fillup 3
AMT4	8.5	Number of gallons for fillup 4
START_MILES	67308.0	Starting mileage
END_MILES	68750.5	Ending mileage

Variables

Name	Data Type	Description
mpg	float	Computed miles per gallon

Now we're ready to write the program. Let's call it Mileage. We can take the declarations from the tables and create the executable statements from the algorithm. We must add comments and be sure to label the output.

PROGRAMMING EXAMPLE cont'd.

Here is the program:

```
//***********************************************************************
// Mileage program
// This program computes miles per gallon given four amounts
// for gallons used, and starting and ending mileage
//***********************************************************************
#include <iostream.h>

const float AMT1 = 11.7;              // Number of gallons for fillup 1
const float AMT2 = 14.3;              // Number of gallons for fillup 2
const float AMT3 = 12.2;              // Number of gallons for fillup 3
const float AMT4 = 8.5;               // Number of gallons for fillup 4
const float START_MILES = 67308.0;   // Starting mileage
const float END_MILES = 68750.5;     // Ending mileage

int main()
{
    float mpg;   // Computed miles per gallon

    mpg = (END_MILES - START_MILES) / (AMT1 + AMT2 + AMT3 + AMT4);

    cout << "For the gallon amounts " << endl;
    cout << AMT1 << ' ' << AMT2 << ' '
         << AMT3 << ' ' << AMT4 << endl;
    cout << "and a starting mileage of " << START_MILES << endl;
    cout << "and an ending mileage of " << END_MILES << endl;
    cout << "the mileage per gallon is " << mpg << endl;
    return 0;
}
```

The output from this program is

```
For the gallon amounts
11.7 14.3 12.2 8.5
and a starting mileage of 67308
and an ending mileage of 68750.5
the mileage per gallon is 30.888651
```

As the output of START_MILES shows, C++ does not display a decimal point and 0 when a floating point value is a whole number. Also, different versions of C++ may display either fewer or more decimal places (digits to the right of the decimal point) than the output shown here. In the next chapter, we discuss how the programmer can control the appearance of floating point numbers in the output.

Testing and Debugging Hints

1. Every identifier that isn't a C++ reserved word must be declared. If you use a name that hasn't been declared—either by your own declaration statements or by including a header file—you get an error message.
2. C++ is a case-sensitive language. Two identifiers that are capitalized differently are treated as two different identifiers. The word `main` and all C++ reserved words use only lowercase letters.
3. An `int` constant other than 0 should not start with a zero. If it starts with zero, it is an octal (base-8) number.
4. Watch out for integer division. The expression `47/100` yields 0, the integer quotient. This is one of the major sources of wrong output in C++ programs.
5. Check for mismatched quotes in `char` constants and strings. Each `char` constant begins and ends with an apostrophe (single quote). Each string begins and ends with a double quote.
6. Make sure your statements end in semicolons (except compound statements, which do not have a semicolon after the right brace).
7. If the cause of an error in a program is not obvious, leave the computer and study a printed copy. Change your program only after you understand the source of the error.

Summary

In this text, we write the syntax (grammar) rules of C++ using *syntax templates.* We describe the semantics (meaning) of C++ statements in English.

Identifiers are used in C++ to name things. Some identifiers, called *reserved words,* have predefined meanings in the language; others are created by the programmer. The identifiers you invent are restricted to those *not* reserved by the C++ language. Reserved words are listed in Appendix A.

Identifiers are associated with memory locations by declarations. A declaration may give a name to a location whose value does not change (a constant) or to one whose value does change (a variable). Every constant and variable has an associated data type. C++ provides many predefined data types, the most common of which are `int`, `float`, and `char`.

The assignment operator is used to change the value of a variable by assigning it the value of an expression. At execution time, the expression is evaluated and the result is stored into the variable. Another way to change the value of a variable is to add 1 to its value with the increment operator (++) or to subtract 1 from its value with the decrement operator (--).

Program output is accomplished by means of the output stream variable `cout`, along with the insertion operator (<<). Each insertion operation sends output data to the standard output device. When an `endl` manipulator appears instead of a data item, the computer terminates the current output line and goes on to the next line.

A C++ program is a collection of one or more function definitions (and optionally some declarations outside of any function). One of the functions *must* be named `main`. Execution of a program always begins with the `main` function. Collectively, the functions all cooperate to produce the desired results.

Quick Check

The Quick Check is intended to help you decide if you've met the goals set forth at the beginning of each chapter. If you understand the material in the chapter, the answer to each question should be fairly obvious. After reading a question, check your response against the answers listed at the end of the Quick Check. If you don't know an answer or don't understand the answer that's provided, turn to the page(s) listed at the end of the question to review the material.

1. Every C++ program consists of at least how many functions? (p. 19)
2. Use the following syntax template to decide whether your last name is a valid C++ identifier. (pp. 24–25)

Identifier

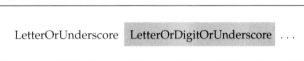

3. Write a C++ constant declaration that gives the name DELTA to the value 0.562. (pp. 30–32)
4. Which of the following words are reserved words in C++? (*Hint:* Look in Appendix A.)

```
const pi float integer sqrt
```

(p. 26)
5. Declare an `int` variable named `count`, a `float` variable named `sum`, and a `char` variable named `letter`. (pp. 30–32)
6. Assign the value 10 to the `int` variable `toes`. (pp. 34–36)
7. You want to divide 9 by 5.
   a. How do you write the expression if you want the result to be the floating point value 1.8?
   b. How do you write it if you want only the integer quotient? (pp. 36–37)
8. What is the value of the following C++ expression?

```
5 % 2
```

(pp. 36–37)
9. Write an output statement to print out the title of this book (*Programming in C++*). (pp. 39–40)

10. What does the following statement print out?

```
cout << "The answer is " << 2 + 2 << endl;z
```

(pp. 39–40)

11. The following program code is incorrect. Rewrite it, using correct syntax for the comment.

```
float annualReceiptsMA; / Total of monthly cash
                        / receipts in the
                        / Massachusetts store
```

(pp. 41–42)

12. Fill in the blanks in this program.

```
#include _____

const float PI = 3.14159;  // Ratio of circumference
                           //    to diameter

int _____ ()
_____

    float circumference;  // The computed circumference
                          //    of the circle

    circumference _____ PI * 7.8;

    _____ << "The circumference of a circle";

    _____ << " of diameter 7.8 is " _____ endl;

    _____ << circumference _____ endl;

    return _____;

_____
```

(pp. 42–44)

13. What should you do if a program fails to run correctly and the reason for the error is not immediately obvious? (p. 47)

Answers 1. A program must have at least one function—the `main` function. 2. Unless your last name is hyphenated, it probably is a valid C++ identifier.
3. `const float DELTA = 0.562;` 4. `const, float`
5. `int    count`
   `float sum;`
   `char  letter;`
6. `toes = 10;` 7. a. `9.0 / 5.0` b. `9 / 5` 8. 1
9. `cout << "Programming in C++" << endl;`
10. `The answer is 4`
11. `float annualReceiptsMA; // Total of monthly cash`
    `                       // receipts in the`
    `                       // Massachusetts store`

   or

   `float annualReceiptsMA; /* Total of monthly cash */`
   `                        /* receipts in the      */`
   `                        /* Massachusetts store  */`

12. ```
#include <iostream.h>
const float PI = 3.14159; // Ratio of circumference
                           //   to diameter

int main()
{
    float circumference;   // The computed circumference
                           //   of the circle
    circumference = PI * 7.8;
    cout << "The circumference of a circle";
    cout << " of diameter 7.8 is " << endl;
    cout << circumference << endl;
    return 0;
}
```

13. Get a fresh printout of the program, leave the computer, and study the program until you understand the cause of the problem. Then correct the algorithm and the program as necessary before you go back to the computer and make any changes in the program file.

## Exam Preparation Exercises

1. Mark the following identifiers either valid or invalid.

| | Valid | Invalid |
|---|---|---|
| a. `item#1` | _____ | _____ |
| b. `data` | _____ | _____ |
| c. `y` | _____ | _____ |
| d. `3Set` | _____ | _____ |
| e. `PAY_DAY` | _____ | _____ |
| f. `bin-2` | _____ | _____ |
| g. `num5` | _____ | _____ |
| h. `Sq Ft` | _____ | _____ |
```

2. Given these four syntax templates:

Dwit   Twitnit   Twit   Nit

mark the following "Dwits" either valid or invalid.

		Valid	Invalid
a.	XYZ	_____	_____
b.	123	_____	_____
c.	X1	_____	_____
d.	23Y	_____	_____
e.	XY12	_____	_____
f.	Y2Y	_____	_____
g.	ZY2	_____	_____
h.	XY23X1	_____	_____

3. Mark the following constructs either valid or invalid. Assume all variables are of type int.

		Valid	Invalid
a.	x * y = c;	_____	_____
b.	y = con;	_____	_____
c.	const int x : 10;	_____	_____
d.	int x;	_____	_____
e.	a = b % c;	_____	_____

4. Match each of the following terms with the correct definition (1 through 15) given below. There is only one correct definition for each term.

_____ a. program   _____ g. variable
_____ b. algorithm   _____ h. constant
_____ c. compiler   _____ i. memory
_____ d. identifier   _____ j. syntax
_____ e. compilation phase   _____ k. semantics
_____ f. execution phase   _____ l. block

(1) A symbolic name made up of letters, digits, and underscores but not beginning with a digit
(2) A place in memory where a data value that cannot be changed is stored
(3) A program that takes a program written in a high-level language and translates it into machine code
(4) An input device
(5) The time spent planning a program
(6) Grammar rules
(7) A sequence of statements enclosed by braces
(8) Meaning
(9) A program that translates assembly language instructions into machine code

    (10) When the machine code version of a program is being run

    (11) A place in memory where a data value that can be changed is stored

    (12) When a program in a high-level language is converted into machine code

    (13) The part of the computer that holds both program and data

    (14) A step-by-step procedure for solving a problem in a finite amount of time

    (15) A sequence of instructions that enables a computer to perform a particular task

5. Compute the value of each legal expression. Indicate whether the value is an integer or a floating point value. If the expression is not legal, explain why.

    a. `10 + 3`

    b. `-9.4 - 6.2`

    c. `10.0 / 3.0`

    d. `10 / 3`

    e. `10 % 3`

    f. `10.0 % 3.0`

    g. `4 / 8`

6. If `alpha` and `beta` are `int` variables and `alpha = 4` and `beta = 9`, what value is stored into `alpha` in each of the following? Answer each part independently of the others.

    a. `alpha = 3 * beta;`

    b. `alpha = alpha + beta;`

    c. `alpha++;`

    d. `alpha = alpha / beta;`

    e. `alpha--;`

    f. `alpha = alpha + alpha;`

    g. `alpha = beta % 6;`

7. Which of the following are reserved words and which are programmer-defined identifiers?

	Reserved	Programmer-Defined
a. `char`	___	___
b. `sort`	___	___
c. `INT`	___	___
d. `long`	___	___
e. `Float`	___	___

8. Reserved words can be used as variable names. (True or False?)

9. In a C++ program consisting of just one function, that function can be named either `main` or `Main`. (True or False?)

10. If a and b are `int` variables and a = 5 and b = 2, what output does each of the following statements produce?

    a. `cout << "a = " << a << "b = " << b << endl;`

    b. `cout << "Sum:" << a + b << endl;`

    c. `cout << "Sum:   " << a + b << endl;`

    d. `cout << a / b << " feet" << endl;`

11. What does the following program print?

```
#include <iostream.h>

const int LBS = 10;
```

```
int main()
{
    int price;
    int cost;
    char ch;

    price = 30;
    cost = price * LBS;
    ch = 'A';
    cout << "Cost is " << endl;
    cout << cost << endl;
    cout << "Price is " << price << "Cost is " << cost << endl;
    cout << "Grade " << ch << " costs " << endl;
    cout << cost << endl;
    return 0;
}
```

12. What is the advantage of using named constants instead of literal constants in the Mileage program?

Programming Warm-Up Exercises

1. Change the program in Exam Preparation Exercise 11 so that it prints the cost for 15 pounds.
2. Change the program in Exam Preparation Exercise 11 so that the price is a named constant rather than a variable.
3. Write three consecutive output statements that print the following three lines:

```
The moon
is
blue.
```

4. Enter the following program into your computer and run it. In the initial comments, replace the items within parentheses with your own information. (Omit the parentheses.)

```
//***********************************
// Programming Assignment One
// (your name)
// (date program was run)
// (description of the problem)
//***********************************
#include <iostream.h>

const float DEBT = 300.0; // Original value owed
const float PAYMT = 22.4; // Payment
const float INTR = 0.02;  // Interest rate
```

```
int main()
{
    float charg;    // Interest times debt
    float reduc;    // Amount debt is reduced
    float remain;   // Remaining balance

    charg = INTR * DEBT;
    reduc = PAYMT - charg;
    remain = DEBT - reduc;
    cout << "Payment: " << PAYMT
         << " Charge: " << charg
         << " Balance owed: " << remain << endl;
    return 0;
}
```

5. Enter the following program into your computer and run it. Add comments, using the pattern shown in Exercise 4 above. (Notice how hard it is to tell what the program does without the comments.)

```
#include <iostream.h>

const int T_COST = 1376;
const int POUNDS = 10;
const int OUNCES = 12;

int main()
{
    int   totOz;
    float uCost;

    totOz = 16 * POUNDS;
    totOz = totOz + OUNCES;
    uCost = T_COST / totOz;
    cout << "Cost per unit: " << uCost << endl;
    return 0;
}
```

6. Change the program in Exercise 5 above so that it prints the total cost and total weight (labeled appropriately) before printing the cost per unit.
7. Change the `Mileage` program to add a fifth gasoline fillup of 10.3 gallons. Assume that the starting and ending mileages remain the same.

Programming Problems

1. Write a C++ program that will print your initials in large block letters, each letter made up of the same character it represents. The letters should be a minimum of seven

printed lines high and should appear all in a row. For example, if your initials are DOW, your program should print out

```
DDDDDDD            OOOOO      W        W
D       D         O     O     W        W
D        D        O     O     W        W
D        D        O     O     W    W   W
D        D        O     O     W   W W  W
D        D        O     O     W W    W W
DDDDDDD            OOOOO       WW      WW
```

Be sure to include appropriate comments in your program, choose meaningful identifiers, and use indentation as we do in the programs in this chapter.

2. Many (but not all) C++ systems provide a header file `limits.h`. This header file contains declarations of constants related to the specific compiler and machine on which you are working. Two of these constants are `INT_MAX` and `INT_MIN`, the largest and smallest `int` values for your particular computer. Write a program to print out the values of `INT_MAX` and `INT_MIN`. The output should identify which value is `INT_MAX` and which value is `INT_MIN`. Be sure to include appropriate comments in your program, and use indentation as we do in the programs in this chapter.

3. Write a program that outputs three lines, labeled as follows:

```
7 / 4 using integer division equals  <result>
7 / 4 using floating point division equals  <result>
7 remainder 4 equals  <result>
```

where `<result>` stands for the result computed by your program. Use named constants for 7 and 4 everywhere in your program (including the output statements) to make the program easy to modify. Be sure to include appropriate comments in your program, choose meaningful identifiers, and use indentation as we do in the programs in this chapter.

Arithmetic Expressions, Function Calls, and Output

GOALS

- To be able to construct and evaluate expressions that include multiple arithmetic operations
- To understand implicit type coercion and explicit type conversion
- To be able to call (invoke) a value-returning function
- To be able to recognize and understand the purpose of parameters
- To be able to use C++ library functions in expressions
- To be able to call (invoke) a void function (one that does not return a function value)
- To be able to use C++ manipulators to format the output
- To be able to format the statements in a program in a clear and readable fashion

In Chapter 2, we introduced the elements of the C++ language and discussed how to construct and run very simple programs. In this chapter we revisit two topics in greater depth: writing arithmetic expressions and formatting the output. We also show how to make programs more powerful by using *library functions*—prewritten functions that are part of every C++ system.

Arithmetic Expressions

The expressions we've used so far have contained at most a single arithmetic operator. We also have been careful not to mix values of different data types in an expression. Now we look at more complicated expressions—ones that are composed of several operators and that contain mixed types.

Precedence Rules Arithmetic expressions can be made up of many constants, variables, operators, and parentheses. In what order are the operations performed? For example, in the assignment statement

```
avgTemp = FREEZE_PT + BOIL_PT / 2.0;
```

is `FREEZE_PT + BOIL_PT` calculated first or is `BOIL_PT / 2.0` calculated first?

The five basic arithmetic operators (+ for addition, - for subtraction, * for multiplication, / for division, and % for remainder) and parentheses are ordered the same way mathematical operators are, according to *precedence rules:*

Highest precedence: ()

                                     * / %

Lowest precedence: + -

In the example above, we divide `BOIL_PT` by 2.0 first and then add `FREEZE_PT` to the result.

You can change the order of evaluation with parentheses. In the statement

```
avgTemp = (FREEZE_PT + BOIL_PT) / 2.0;
```

`FREEZE_PT` and `BOIL_PT` are added first, and then their sum is divided by 2.0. We evaluate subexpressions in parentheses first and then follow the precedence of the operators.

When there are multiple arithmetic operators with the same precedence, their *grouping order* (or *associativity*) is from left to right. The expression

```
int1 - int2 + int3
```

means `(int1 - int2) + int3`, not `int1 - (int2 + int3)`. As another example, we would use the expression

```
(float1 + float2) / float1 * 3.0
```

to evaluate the expression in parentheses first, then divide the sum by `float1`, and multiply the result by 3.0. Here are some more examples.

Expression	Value
10 / 2 * 3	15
10 % 3 - 4 / 2	−1
5.0 * 2.0 / 4.0 * 2.0	5.0
5.0 * 2.0 / (4.0 * 2.0)	1.25
5.0 + 2.0 / (4.0 * 2.0)	5.25

Type Coercion
and Type
Casting

Integer values and floating point values are stored differently in memory. The pattern of bits that represents the constant 2 does not look at all like the pattern of bits representing the constant 2.0. What happens if we mix integer and floating point values together in an assignment statement or an expression? Let's look first at assignment statements.

Assignment Statements.   If you make the declarations

```
int    someInt;
float someFloat;
```

then `someInt` can hold *only* integer values, and `someFloat` can hold *only* floating point values. The assignment statement

```
someFloat = 12;
```

type coercion
The implicit (auto-matic) conversion of a value from one data type to another

appears to store the integer value 12 into `someFloat`. But the computer refuses to store anything other than a `float` value into `someFloat`. The compiler inserts extra instructions that first convert 12 into 12.0 and then store 12.0 into `someFloat`. This implicit (automatic) conversion of a value from one data type to another is known as **type coercion.**

The statement

```
someInt = 4.8;
```

also causes type coercion. When a floating point value is assigned to an `int` variable, the fractional part is truncated (cut off). As a result, `someInt` is assigned the value 4.

With both of the assignment statements above, the program would be less confusing for someone to read if we avoided mixing data types:

```
someFloat = 12.0;
someInt = 4;
```

More often, it is not just constants but entire expressions that are involved in type coercion. Storing the result of an `int` expression into a `float` variable doesn't cause loss of information; a whole number such as 24 can be represented in floating point form as 24.0. However, storing the result of a floating point expression into an `int` variable can cause loss of information because the fractional part is truncated. It is easy to overlook the assignment of a floating point expression to an `int` variable when we try to discover why our program is producing the wrong answers.

To make our programs as clear (and error-free) as possible, we use explicit **type casting** (or *type conversion*). A C++ *cast operation* consists of a data type name and then, within parentheses, the expression to be converted:

```
someFloat = float(3 * someInt + 2);
someInt = int(5.2 / someFloat - anotherFloat);
```

Both of the statements

```
someInt = someFloat + 8.2;
someInt = int(someFloat + 8.2);
```

produce identical results. The only difference is in clarity. With the cast opera-tion, it is perfectly clear to the programmer and to others reading the program that the mixing of types is intentional, not an oversight. Countless errors have resulted from unintentional mixing of types.

Note that there is a way to round off rather than truncate a floating point value before storing it into an `int` variable. Here's how:

```
someInt = int(someFloat + 0.5);
```

With pencil and paper, see for yourself what gets stored into `someInt` when `someFloat` contains 4.7. Now try it again, assuming `someFloat` con-tains 4.2. (This technique of rounding assumes that `someFloat` is a positive number.)

Arithmetic Expressions.   So far we have been talking about mixing data types across the assignment operator (=). It's also possible to mix data types within an expression:

```
someInt * someFloat
4.8 + someInt - 3
```

Such expressions are called **mixed type** (or **mixed mode**) **expressions.**

Whenever an integer value and a floating point value are joined by an oper-ator, implicit type coercion occurs as follows.

1. The integer value is temporarily coerced to a floating point value.
2. The operation is performed.
3. The result is a floating point value.

Let's examine how the machine evaluates the expression `4.8 + someInt - 3`, where `someInt` contains the value 2. First, the operands of the + operator have mixed types, so the value of `someInt` is coerced to 2.0. (This conversion is only temporary; it does not affect the value stored in `someInt`.) The addition takes place, yielding a value of 6.8. Next, the subtraction (-) operator joins a floating point value (6.8) and an integer value (3). The value 3 is coerced to 3.0, the subtraction takes place, and the result is the floating point value 3.8.

Just as with assignment statements, you can use explicit type casts within expressions to lessen the risk of errors. Writing expressions like

```
float(someInt) * someFloat
4.8 + float(someInt - 3)
```

makes it clear what your intentions are.

Not only are explicit type casts valuable for program clarity, they also can be mandatory for correct programming. Given the declarations

```
int    sum;
int    count;
float  average;
```

suppose that `sum` and `count` currently contain 60 and 80, respectively. If `sum` represents the sum of a group of integer values and `count` represents the number of values, let's find the average value:

```
average = sum / count;     // Wrong
```

Unfortunately, this statement stores the value 0.0 into `average`. Here's why. The expression to the right of the assignment operator is not a mixed type expression. Both operands of the / operator are of type `int`, so integer division is performed. Dividing 60 by 80 yields the integer value 0. Next, the machine implicitly coerces 0 to the value 0.0 before storing it into `average`. The way to find the average correctly, as well as clearly, is this:

```
average = float(sum) / float(count);
```

This statement gives us floating point division instead of integer division. As a result, the value 0.75 is stored into `average`.

As a final remark about type coercion and type conversion, you may have noticed that we have concentrated only on the `int` and `float` types. It is also possible to stir char values, short values, and double values into the pot. The results can be confusing and unexpected. In Chapter 10, we return to the topic with a more detailed discussion. In the meantime, you should avoid mixing values of these types within an expression.

Function Calls and Library Functions

Value-Returning Functions   At the beginning of Chapter 2, we showed a program consisting of three functions: main, Square, and Cube.

```
int main()
{
    cout << "The square of 27 is " << Square(27) << endl;
    cout << "and the cube of 27 is " << Cube(27) << endl;
    return 0;
}

int Square( int n )
{
    return n * n;
}

int Cube( int n )
{
    return n * n * n;
}
```

We said that all three functions are value-returning functions. Square returns a value to its caller—the square of the number sent to it. Cube returns a value—the cube of the number sent to it. And main returns a value to the operating system—the program's exit status.

Let's focus for a moment on the Cube function. The main function contains a statement

```
cout << "and the cube of 27 is " << Cube(27) << endl;
```

In this statement, the master (main) causes the servant (Cube) to compute the cube of 27 and give the result back to main. The sequence of symbols

function call (function invocation)
The mechanism that transfers control to a function

```
Cube(27)
```

is a **function call** or **function invocation.** The computer temporarily puts the main function on hold and starts the Cube function running. When Cube has finished doing its work, the computer goes back to `main` and picks up where it left off.

In the above function call, the number 27 is known as a *parameter* (or *argument*). Parameters make it possible for the same function to work on many different values. For example, we can write statements like these:

```
cout << Cube(4);
cout << Cube(16);
```

Here's the syntax template for a function call:

FunctionCall

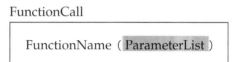

FunctionName (ParameterList)

parameter list
A mechanism by which functions communicate with each other

The **parameter list** is a way for functions to communicate with each other. Some functions, like `Square` and `Cube`, have a single parameter in the parameter list. Other functions, like `main`, have no parameters in the list. And some functions have two, three, or more parameters in the parameter list, separated by commas.

Value-returning functions are used in expressions in much the same way that variables and constants are. The value computed by a function simply takes its place in the expression. For example, the statement

```
someInt = Cube(2) * 10;
```

stores the value 80 into `someInt`. First the `Cube` function is executed to compute the cube of 2, which is 8. The value 8—now available for use in the rest of the expression—is multiplied by 10. Note that a function call has higher precedence than multiplication, which makes sense if you consider that the function result must be available before the multiplication takes place.

Here are several facts about value-returning functions:

- The function call is used within an expression; it does not appear as a separate statement.
- The function computes a value (*result*) that is then available for use in the expression.
- The function returns exactly one result—no more, no less.

The `Cube` function expects to be given (or *passed*) a parameter of type `int`. What happens if the caller passes a `float` parameter? The answer is that the compiler applies implicit `type` coercion. The function call `Cube(6.9)` computes the cube of 6, not 6.9.

Although we have been using literal constants as parameters to Cube, the parameter could just as easily be a variable or named constant. In fact, the parameter to a value-returning function can be any expression of the appropriate type. In the statement

```
alpha = Cube(int1 * int1 + int2 * int2);
```

the expression in the parameter list is evaluated first, and only its result is passed to the function. For example, if int1 contains 3 and int2 contains 5, the above function call passes 34 as the parameter to Cube.

An expression in a function's parameter list can even include calls to functions. For example, we could use the Square function to rewrite the above assignment statement as follows:

```
alpha = Cube(Square(int1) + Square(int2));
```

Library Functions

www.jbpub.com/C++links

Certain computations, such as square root or absolute value, are very common in programs. To make the programmer's life easier, every C++ system includes a *standard library*—a large collection of prewritten functions that perform such computations. Here is a small sample:

Header File	Function	Parameter Type(s)	Result Type	Result
`<stdlib.h>`	`abs(i)`	`int`	`int`	Absolute value of i
`<math.h>`	`cos(x)`	`float`	`float`	Cosine of x (x is in radians)
`<math.h>`	`fabs(x)`	`float`	`float`	Absolute value of x
`<stdlib.h>`	`labs(j)`	`long`	`long`	Absolute value of j
`<math.h>`	`pow(x, y)`	`float`	`float`	x raised to the power y (if x = 0.0, y must be positive; if x ≤ 0.0, y must be a whole number)
`<math.h>`	`sin(x)`	`float`	`float`	Sine of x (x is in radians)
`<math.h>`	`sqrt(x)`	`float`	`float`	Square root of x (x ≥ 0.0)

(Technically, the entries marked `float` should all say `double`. These functions perform their work using double precision floating point values. But because of type coercion, the functions still work when you pass `float` values to them.)

Using a library function is easy. First, you place an #include directive near the top of your program, specifying the appropriate header file. This directive causes the C++ preprocessor to insert declarations into your program that give the compiler some information about the function. Then, whenever you want to use the function, you just make a function call. Here's an example:

```
#include <iostream.h>
#include <math.h>          // For sqrt() and fabs()
      .
      .
      .

float alpha;
float beta;
      .
      .
      .

alpha = sqrt(7.3 + fabs(beta));
```

The C++ standard library provides dozens of functions for you to use. Appendix C lists a larger selection than we have presented here. You should glance briefly at this appendix now, keeping in mind that some of the terminology will make sense only after you have read further into the book.

Void Functions

Up to now we have looked only at **value-returning functions.** If you look at the following function definition for CalcPay you see that it begins with the word void instead of a data type like int or float:

value-returning function
A function that returns a single value to its caller and is invoked from within an expression

```
void CalcPay( . . . )
{
      .
      .
      .
}
```

CalcPay is an example of a function that doesn't return a value to its caller. Instead, it just performs some action and returns. We refer to such a function as a *non-value-returning function*, a *void-returning function*, or, simply, a **void function.** In many programming languages, a void function is known as a **procedure.**

void function (procedure)
A function that does not return a function value to its caller and is invoked as a separate statement

Void functions are invoked differently from value-returning functions. With a value-returning function, the function call appears in an expression. With a void function, the function call is a separate, stand-alone statement. Function main would call CalcPay like this:

```
CalcPay(payRate, hours, wages);
```

From the caller's perspective, a call to a void function has the flavor of a command or built-in instruction:

```
DoThis(x, y, z);
DoThat();
```

In contrast, a call to a value-returning function doesn't look like a command; it looks like a value in an expression:

```
y = 4.7 + Cube(x);
```

For the next few chapters, we won't be writing our own functions (except `main`). Instead, we'll be concentrating on how to use existing functions, including functions for performing stream input and output. Some of these functions are value-returning functions; others are void functions. Again, we emphasize the difference in how you invoke these two kinds of functions: A call to a value-returning function occurs in an expression, while a call to a void function occurs as a separate statement.

Formatting Output

To format a program's output means to control how it appears visually on the screen or on a printer. If the variables i, j, and k contain the values 15, 2, and 6, respectively, the statement

```
cout << "Results: " << i << j << k;
```

outputs the stream of characters

```
Results: 1526
```

Without spacing between the numbers, this output is difficult to interpret. Let's examine how we can control both the horizontal and vertical spacing of our output. We look first at vertical spacing.

Creating Blank Lines   You already have seen how to control vertical spacing by using the `endl` manipulator in an output statement. A sequence of output statements continues to write characters across the current line until an `endl` terminates the line. Here are some examples:

Statements	Output Produced

```cout << "Hi there, ";```
```cout << "Lois Lane. " << endl;```
```cout << "Have you seen ";```
```cout << "Clark Kent?" << endl;```
	Hi there, Lois Lane.
	
	Have you seen Clark Kent?

```cout << "Hi there, " << endl;```
```cout << "Lois Lane. " << endl;```
```cout << "Have you seen " << endl;```
```cout << "Clark Kent?" << endl;```
	Hi there,
	Lois Lane.
	Have you seen
	Clark Kent?

```cout << "Hi there, " << endl;```
```cout << "Lois Lane. ";```
```cout << "Have you seen " << endl;```
```cout << "Clark Kent?" << endl;```
	Hi there,
	
	Lois Lane. Have you seen
	Clark Kent?

What do you think the following statements print out?

```
cout << "Hi there, " << endl;
cout << endl;
cout << "Lois Lane." << endl;
```

The first output statement causes the words *Hi there,* to be displayed; the endl causes the cursor to go to the next line. The next statement prints nothing but goes on to the next line. The third statement prints the words *Lois Lane.* and terminates the line. The resulting output is the three lines

```
Hi there,

Lois Lane.
```

Whenever you use an endl immediately after another endl, a blank line is produced. As you might guess, three consecutive uses of endl outputs two blank lines, four consecutive uses outputs three blank lines, and so forth.

Note that we have a great deal of flexibility in how we write an output statement in a C++ program. We could combine the three preceding statements into two statements:

```
cout << "Hi there, " << endl << endl;
cout << "Lois Lane." << endl;
```

In fact, we could do it all in one statement. One possibility is

```
cout << "Hi there, " << endl << endl << "Lois Lane." << endl;
```

Here's another:

```
cout << "Hi there, " << endl << endl
     << "Lois Lane." << endl;
```

The last example shows that you can spread a single C++ statement onto more than one line of the program. The compiler treats the semicolon, not the physical end of a line, as the end of a statement.

Inserting Blanks Within a Line

To control the horizontal spacing of the output, one technique is to send extra blank characters to the output stream. (Remember that the blank character, generated by pressing the space bar on a keyboard, is a perfectly valid character in C++.)

To prevent the output of 15, 2, and 6 from looking like this:

```
Results: 1526
```

you could print a single blank (as a char constant) between the numbers:

```
cout << "Results: " << i << ' ' << j << ' ' << k;
```

This statement produces the output

```
Results: 15 2 6
```

If you want even more spacing between items, use string constants containing blanks:

```
cout << "Results: " << i << "   " << j << "   " << k;
```

Here, the resulting output is

```
Results: 15    2    6
```

As another example, to produce this output:

```
*  *  *  *  *  *  *  *

*  *  *  *  *  *  *  *  *

*  *  *  *  *  *  *  *
```

you would use these statements:

```
cout << " * * * * * * * *" << endl << endl;
cout << "* * * * * * * * *" << endl << endl;
cout << " * * * * * * * *" << endl;
```

All of the blanks and asterisks are enclosed in double quotes, so they print literally as they are written in the program. The extra `endl` manipulators give you the blank lines between the rows of asterisks.

If you want blanks to be printed, you *must* enclose them in quotes. The statement

```
cout << '*' <<                         '*';
```

produces the output

```
**
```

Despite all of the blanks we included in the output statement, the asterisks print side by side because the blanks are not enclosed by quotes.

Manipulators For some time now, we have been using the `endl` manipulator to terminate an output line. In C++ a manipulator is a rather curious thing that behaves like a function but travels in the disguise of a data object. Like a function, a manipulator causes some action to occur. But like a data object, a manipulator can appear in the midst of a series of insertion operations:

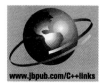

```
cout << someInt << endl << someFloat;
```

(Manipulators are used *only* in input and output statements.)

The C++ standard library supplies many manipulators, but for now we look at only three of them: `endl`, `setw`, and `setprecision`. The `endl` manipulator comes "for free" when we `#include` the header file `iostream.h` to perform I/O. The other two manipulators, `setw` and `setprecision`, require that we also `#include` the header file `iomanip.h`:

```
#include <iostream.h>
#include <iomanip.h>
    .
    .
    .
cout << setw(5) << someInt;
```

The manipulator `setw`—meaning "set width"—lets us control how many columns the next data item should occupy when it is output. (`setw` is only for formatting numbers and strings, not `char` data.) The parameter to `setw` is an integer expression called the *fieldwidth specification;* the desired number of columns is called the *field.* The next data item to be output is printed right-justified (filled with blanks on the left to fill up the field).

Let's look at some examples:

Statement	Output (□ means blank)
ans = 33 (Integer) num = 7132 (Integer)	
1. cout << setw(4) << ans << setw(5) << num << setw(4) << "Hi";	□□33□7132□□Hi 4 5 4
2. cout << setw(2) << ans << setw(4) << num << setw(2) << "Hi";	337132Hi 2 4 2
3. cout << setw(6) << ans << setw(3) << "Hi" << setw(5) << num;	□□□□33□Hi□7132 6 3 5

Statement	*Output (▢ means blank)*
4. `cout << setw(7) << "Hi"` `<< setw(4) << num;`	▢▢▢▢▢Hi 7132 $\underbrace{}_{7}$ $\underbrace{}_{4}$
5. `cout << setw(1) << ans` `<< setw(5) << num;`	33▢7132 $\underbrace{}$ $\underbrace{}_{5}$ Field automatically expands to fit the two-digit value

In (1), each of the values is specified to occupy enough columns so that there is at least one space separating them. In (2), the values all run together because the fieldwidth specified for each value is just large enough to hold the value. This output obviously is not very readable. It's better to make the fieldwidth larger than the minimum size required so that some space is left between values. In (3), there are extra blanks for readability; in (4), there are not. In (5), the fieldwidth is not large enough for the value in `ans`, so it automatically expands to make room for all of the digits.

Setting the fieldwidth is a one-time action. It holds only for the very next item to be output. After this output, the fieldwidth resets to 0, meaning "extend the field to exactly as many columns as are needed." In the statement

```
cout << "Hi" << setw(5) << ans << num;
```

the fieldwidth resets to 0 after `ans` is output. As a result, we get the output

```
Hi    337132
```

You can specify a fieldwidth for floating point values just as for integer values. But you must remember to allow for the decimal point in the column count. The value 4.85 occupies four output columns, not three. If x contains the value 4.85, the statement

```
cout << setw(4) << x << endl
     << setw(6) << x << endl
     << setw(3) << x << endl;
```

produces the output

```
4.85
 4.85
4.85
```

In the third line, a fieldwidth of 3 isn't sufficient, so the field automatically expands to accommodate the number.

There are several other issues involved with output of floating point numbers. First, large floating point values are printed in scientific (E) notation. The value 123456789.5 may print on some systems as

```
1.234567E+08
```

Second, if the number is a whole number, C++ doesn't print a decimal point. The value 95.0 prints as

```
95
```

Third, you often would like to control the number of decimal places (digits to the right of the decimal point) that are displayed. For example, if you are printing monetary values as dollars and cents, you would prefer the values 12.8 and 16.38753 to print as 12.80 and 16.39.

To address the first two issues, you can include the following two statements in your program before any floating point output takes place:

```
cout.setf(ios::fixed, ios::floatfield);   // Set up floating point
cout.setf(ios::showpoint);                //   output format
```

These two statements employ some very advanced C++ notation. It's way too early in our look at C++ to explain fully the meaning of all the symbols and identifiers. But here's the general idea. `setf` is a void function associated with the `cout` stream. (Note that the dot, or period, between `cout` and `setf` is required.) The first function call ensures that floating point numbers are always printed in decimal form rather than scientific notation. The second function call specifies that the decimal point should always be printed, even for whole numbers. Our advice is to use these statements just as you see them.

The third issue—the number of decimal places to be displayed—is handled by the `setprecision` manipulator:

```
cout << setprecision(3) << x;
```

The parameter to `setprecision` specifies the desired number of decimal places. Unlike `setw`, which applies only to the very next item printed, the value sent to `setprecision` remains in effect for all subsequent output (until you change it with another call to `setprecision`). Here are some examples of using `setprecision` in conjunction with `setw`:

Value of x	Statement	Output (□ means blank)
310.0	`cout << setw(10)` `<< setprecision(2) << x;`	□□□□310.00
310.0	`cout << setw(10)` `<< setprecision(5) << x;`	□310.00000
310.0	`cout << setw(7)` `<< setprecision(5) << x;`	310.00000 (expands to 9 columns)
4.827	`cout << setw(6)` `<< setprecision(2) << x;`	□□4.83 (last displayed digit is rounded off)
4.827	`cout << setw(6)` `<< setprecision(1) << x;`	□□□4.8 (last displayed digit is rounded off)

Here, too, the total number of columns is expanded if the specified fieldwidth is too narrow. However, the number of columns for fractional digits is controlled entirely by the parameter to `setprecision`.

The following table summarizes the three manipulators we have discussed in this section:

Header File	Manipulator	Parameter Type	Effect
`<iostream.h>`	`endl`	None	Terminates the current output line
`<iomanip.h>`	`setw(n)`	int	Sets fieldwidth to n*
`<iomanip.h>`	`setprecision(n)`	int	Sets floating point precision to n digits

*`setw` is only for numbers and strings, not `char` data. Also, `setw` applies only to the very next output item, after which the fieldwidth is reset to 0 (meaning "use only as many columns as are needed").

◾ *Program Formatting*

As far as the compiler is concerned, C++ statements are free format. However, it is extremely important that your programs be readable, both for your sake and for the sake of anyone else who has to use them. When you write an outline for an English paper, you follow certain rules of indentation to make it readable. Similar rules make your programs easier to read. Take a look at the following program for computing the cost per square foot of a house. It compiles and runs correctly, but does not conform to any formatting standards.

```
// HouseCost program
// This program computes the cost per square foot of
   // living space for a house, given the dimensions of
// the house, the number of stories, the size of the
// nonliving space, and the total cost less land
#include <iostream.h>
#include <iomanip.h>// For setw() and setprecision()
const float WIDTH = 30.0; // Width of the house
    const float LENGTH = 40.0; // Length of the house
const float STORIES = 2.5; // Number of full stories
const float NON_LIVING_SPACE = 825.0;// Garage, closets, etc.
const float PRICE = 150000.0; // Selling price less land
int main() { float grossFootage;// Total square footage
    float livingFootage;         // Living area
float costPerFoot;    // Cost/foot of living area
cout.setf(ios::fixed, ios::floatfield);  // Set up floating pt.
cout.setf(ios::showpoint);        // output format
grossFootage = LENGTH * WIDTH * STORIES; livingFootage =
 grossFootage - NON_LIVING_SPACE; costPerFoot = PRICE /
livingFootage; cout << "Cost per square foot is "
<< setw(6) << setprecision(2) << costPerFoot << endl;
return 0; }
```

Now look at the same program with proper formatting:

```
//*************************************************************
// HouseCost program
// This program computes the cost per square foot of
// living space for a house, given the dimensions of
// the house, the number of stories, the size of the
// nonliving space, and the total cost less land
//*************************************************************
#include <iostream.h>
#include <iomanip.h>     // For setw() and setprecision()
```

```
const float WIDTH = 30.0;              // Width of the house
const float LENGTH = 40.0;             // Length of the house
const float STORIES = 2.5;             // Number of full stories
const float NON_LIVING_SPACE = 825.0;  // Garage, closets, etc.
const float PRICE = 150000.0;          // Selling price less land

int main()
{
    float grossFootage;        // Total square footage
    float livingFootage;       // Living area
    float costPerFoot;         // Cost/foot of living area

    cout.setf(ios::fixed, ios::floatfield);   // Set up floating pt.
    cout.setf(ios::showpoint);                //    output format

    grossFootage = LENGTH * WIDTH * STORIES;
    livingFootage = grossFootage - NON_LIVING_SPACE;
    costPerFoot = PRICE / livingFootage;

    cout << "Cost per square foot is "
         << setw(6) << setprecision(2) << costPerFoot << endl;
    return 0;
}
```

Need we say more?
    Appendix E discusses programming style. Use it as a guide when you are writing programs.

PROGRAMMING EXAMPLE

Map Measurements

Problem: You're spending a day in the city. You plan to visit the natural history museum, a record store, a gallery, and a bookshop, and then go to a concert. You have a tourist map that shows where these places are located. The scale of the map is one quarter-inch equals one mile. You want to determine how far apart they are and how far you'll walk during the entire day. Then you can decide when it would be better to take a taxi. According to the map's legend, one inch on the map equals one quarter of a mile on the ground.

Output: The distance between each of the places and the total distance, rounded to the nearest tenth of a mile. The values on which the calculations are based also should be printed for verification purposes.

Discussion: You can measure the distances between two points on the map with a ruler. The program must output miles, so you need to multiply the number of inches by 0.25. You then write down the figure, rounded to the nearest tenth of a mile. When you've done this for each pair of places, you add the distances to get the total mileage. This is essentially the algorithm we use in the program.

The only tricky part is how to round a value to the nearest tenth of a mile. In the last chapter, we showed how to round a floating point value to the nearest integer by adding 0.5 and using a type cast to truncate the result:

```
int(floatValue + 0.5)
```

To round to the nearest tenth, we first multiply the value by 10, round the result to the nearest integer, and then divide by 10 again. For example, if `floatValue` contains 5.162, then

```
float(int(floatValue * 10.0 + 0.5)) / 10.0
```

gives 5.2 as its result.

Let's treat all of the quantities as named constants so that it is easier to change the program later. From measuring the map, you know that the distance from the museum to the record store is 1.5 inches, from the record store to the gallery is 2.3 inches, from the gallery to the bookshop is 5.9 inches, and from the bookshop to the concert is 4.0 inches.

Here is the program:

```
//*******************************************************************
// Walk program
// This program computes the mileage (rounded to tenths of a mile)
// for each of four distances between points in a city, given
// the measurements on a map with a scale of one inch equal to
// one quarter of a mile
//*******************************************************************
#include <iostream.h>
#include <iomanip.h>              // For setprecision()

const float DISTANCE1 = 1.5;     // Measurement for first distance
const float DISTANCE2 = 2.3;     // Measurement for second distance
const float DISTANCE3 = 5.9;     // Measurement for third distance
const float DISTANCE4 = 4.0;     // Measurement for fourth distance
const float SCALE = 0.25;         // Map scale
```

PROGRAMMING EXAMPLE cont'd.

```cpp
int main()
{
    float totMiles;         // Total of rounded mileages
    float miles;            // An individual rounded mileage

    cout.setf(ios::fixed, ios::floatfield);  // Set up floating pt.
    cout.setf(ios::showpoint);               //   output format

    totMiles = 0.0;

    // Compute miles for each distance on the map

    miles = float(int(DISTANCE1 * SCALE * 10.0 + 0.5)) / 10.0;
    cout << "For a measurement of " << setprecision(1) << DISTANCE1
        << " the first distance is " << miles << " mile(s) long."
        << endl;
    totMiles = totMiles + miles;

    miles = float(int(DISTANCE2 * SCALE * 10.0 + 0.5)) / 10.0;
    cout << "For a measurement of " << DISTANCE2
        << " the second distance is " << miles << " mile(s) long."
        << endl;
    totMiles = totMiles + miles;

    miles = float(int(DISTANCE3 * SCALE * 10.0 + 0.5)) / 10.0;
    cout << "For a measurement of " << DISTANCE3
        << " the third distance is " << miles << " mile(s) long."
        << endl;
    totMiles = totMiles + miles;

    miles = float(int(DISTANCE4 * SCALE * 10.0 + 0.5)) / 10.0;
    cout << "For a measurement of " << DISTANCE4
        << " the fourth distance is " << miles << " mile(s) long."
        << endl;
    totMiles = totMiles + miles;

    // Print the total miles

    cout << endl;
    cout << "Total mileage for the day is " << totMiles << " miles."
        << endl;
    return 0;
}
```

PROGRAMMING EXAMPLE cont'd.

The output from the program is

```
For a measurement of 1.5 the first distance is 0.4 mile(s) long.
For a measurement of 2.3 the second distance is 0.6 mile(s) long.
For a measurement of 5.9 the third distance is 1.5 mile(s) long.
For a measurement of 4.0 the fourth distance is 1.0 mile(s) long.

Total mileage for the day is 3.5 miles.
```

Testing and Debugging Hints

1. Double-check every expression according to the precedence rules to be sure that the operations are performed in the desired order.
2. Avoid mixing integer and floating point values in expressions. If you must mix them, consider using explicit type casts to reduce the chance of mistakes.
3. For each assignment statement, check that the expression result has the same data type as the variable to the left of the assignment operator (=). If not, consider using an explicit type cast for clarity and safety. And remember that storing a floating point value into an `int` variable truncates the fractional part.
4. For every library function you use in your program, be sure to `#include` the appropriate header file.
5. Examine each call to a library function to see that you have the right number of parameters and that the data types of the parameters are correct.

Summary

Much of the computation of a program is performed in arithmetic expressions. Expressions can contain more than one operator. The order in which the operations are performed is determined by precedence rules. In arithmetic expressions, multiplication, division, and remainder are performed first, then addition and subtraction. Multiple arithmetic operations of the same precedence are grouped from left to right. You can use parentheses to override the precedence rules.

Expressions may include function calls. C++ supports two kinds of functions: value-returning functions and void functions. A value-returning function is called by writing its name (and parameter list) as part of an expression. A void function is called by writing its name (and parameter list) as a complete C++ statement.

The C++ standard library is an integral part of every C++ system. The library contains many prewritten functions that are accessed by using #include directives to the C++ preprocessor.

Designing a program includes careful attention to the output format. Output should be clear, understandable, and neatly arranged. Messages in the output should describe the significance of values. Blank lines (produced by successive uses of the endl manipulator) and blank spaces within lines help to organize the output and improve its appearance.

The setw and setprecision manipulators control the appearance of values in the output. These manipulators do *not* affect the values actually stored in memory, only their appearance when output.

The format of the program itself should be clear and readable. C++ is a free-format language. A consistent style that uses indentation, blank lines, and spaces within lines helps you (and other programmers) understand and work with your programs.

Quick Check

1. What is the result of evaluating the expression

   ```
   (1 + 2 * 2) / 2 + 1
   ```

   (p. 60)
2. How would you write the following formula as a C++ expression that produces a floating point value as a result? (pp. 61–63)

   $$\frac{9}{5}c + 32$$

3. Add type casts to the following statements to make the type conversions clear and explicit. Your answers should produce the same results as the original statements. (pp. 62–63)

   ```
   a. someFloat = 5 + someInt;
   b. someInt = 2.5 * someInt / someFloat;
   ```

4. You want to compute the square roots and absolute values of some floating point numbers. (pp. 64–67)
   a. Which C++ library functions would you use?
   b. Which header file(s) must you #include in order to use these functions?
5. Which part of the following function call is its parameter list? (pp. 64–65)

   ```
   Square(someInt + 1)
   ```

6. In the statement

```
alpha = 4 * Beta(gamma, delta) + 3;
```

would you assume that `Beta` is a value-returning function or a void function? (pp. 67–68)

7. In the statement

```
Display(gamma, delta);
```

would you assume that `Display` is a value-returning function or a void function? (pp. 67–68)

8. If you want to print the word *Hello* on one line and then print a blank line, how many consecutive `endl` manipulators should you insert after printing "`Hello`"? (pp. 68–70)

9. Assume the `float` variable pay contains the value 327.66101. Using the `setw` and `setprecision` manipulators, what output statement would you use to print pay in dollars and cents with three leading blanks? (pp. 71–75)

10. Reformat the following program to make it clear and readable. (pp. 76–77)

```
//***************************************************************
               // SumProd program
    // This program computes the sum and product of two integers
//***************************************************************
#include <iostream.h>
const int INT1=20;const int INT2=8;int main() { cout <<
"The sum of " << INT1 << " and "
<< INT2 << " is " << INT1+INT2 << endl;cout
<< "Their product is " << INT1*INT2 << endl;return 0; }
```

Answers   1. The result is 3.   2. `9.0 / 5.0 * c + 32.0`
3. a. `someFloat = float(5 + someInt);`
   b. `someInt = int(2.5 * float(someInt) / someFloat);`   4. a. sqrt and fabs
b. `math.h`   5. `someInt + 1`   6. A value-returning function   7. A void function   8. Two consecutive `endl` manipulators are necessary.   9. `cout << setw(9) << setprecision(2) << pay;`
10. `//***************************************************************`
    `// SumProd program`
    `// This program computes the sum and product of two integers`
    `//***************************************************************`
    `#include <iostream.h>`

    `const int INT1 = 20;`
    `const int INT2 = 8;`

```
int main()
{
    cout << "The sum of " << INT1 << " and " << INT2
         << " is " << INT1 + INT2 << endl;
    cout << "Their product is " << INT1 * INT2 << endl;
    return 0;
}
```

Exam Preparation Exercises

1. Compute the value of each legal expression. Indicate whether the value is an integer or a floating point value. If the expression is not legal, explain why.
   a. `10.0 / 3.0 + 5 * 2`
   b. `10 % 3 + 5 % 2`
   c. `10 / 3 + 5 / 2`
   d. `12.5 + (2.5 / (6.2 / 3.1))`
   e. `-4 * (-5 + 6)`
   f. `13 % 5 / 3`
   g. `(10.0 / 3.0 % 2) / 3`

2. What value is stored into the `int` variable `result` in each of the following?
   a. `result = 15 % 4;`
   b. `result = 7 / 3 + 2;`
   c. `result = 2 + 7 * 5;`
   d. `result = 45 / 8 * 4 + 2;`
   e. `result = 17 + (21 % 6) * 2;`
   f. `result = int(4.5 + 2.6 * 0.5);`

3. Translate the following C++ code into algebraic notation. (All variables are `float` variables.)

   ```
   y = -b + sqrt(b * b - 4.0 * a * c);
   ```

4. Given the following program fragment:

   ```
   int   i;
   int   j;
   float z;

   i = 4;
   j = 17;
   z = 2.6;
   ```

determine the value of each expression below. If the result is a floating point value, include a decimal point in your answer.

a. `i / float(j)`
b. `1.0 / i + 2`
c. `z * j`
d. `i + j % i`
e. `(1 / 2) * i`
f. `2 * i + j - i`
g. `j / 2`
h. `2 * 3 - 1 % 3`
i. `i % j / i`
j. `int(z + 0.5)`

5. To use each of the following statements, a C++ program must #include which header file(s)?

a. `cout << x;`
b. `int1 = abs(int2);`
c. `y = sqrt(7.6 + x);`
d. `cout << y << endl;`
e. `cout << setw(5) << someInt;`

6. Evaluate the following expressions. If the result is a floating point number, include a decimal point in your answer.

a. `fabs(-9.1)`
b. `sqrt(49.0)`
c. `3 * int(7.8) + 3`
d. `pow(4.0, 2.0)`
e. `sqrt(float(3 * 3 + 4 * 4))`
f. `sqrt(fabs(-4.0) + sqrt(25.0))`

7. Show precisely the output of the following C++ program. Use a □ to indicate each blank.

```
#include <iostream.h>
#include <iomanip.h>  // For setw()

int main()
{
    char  ch;
    int   n;
    float y;
```

```
ch = 'A';
cout << ch;
ch = 'B';
cout << ch << endl;
n = 413;
y = 21.8;
cout << setw(5) << n << " is the value of n" << endl;
cout << setw(7) << y << " is the value of y" << endl;
return 0;
}
```

8. Given that x is a float variable and x = 14.3827, show the output of each statement below. Use a □ to indicate each blank.

```
a. cout << "x is" << setw(5) << setprecision(2) << x;
b. cout << "x is" << setw(8) << setprecision(2) << x;
c. cout << "x is" << setw(0) << setprecision(2) << x;
d. cout << "x is" << setw(7) << setprecision(3) << x;
```

9. Show precisely what is output by the following statement.

```
cout << "A rolling" << endl
     << "stone" << endl << endl
     << "gathers" << endl
     << endl << endl << endl << "no"
     << "moss" << endl;
```

10. Name two things that contribute to the readability of a program.
11. Formatting a program incorrectly causes an error. (True or False?)
12. In the Walk program, a particular pattern of statements is repeated four times with small variations. Identify the repeating pattern. Then circle those parts of the statements that vary with each repetition.

Programming Warm-Up Exercises

1. Write an assignment statement to calculate the sum of the numbers from 1 through n using Gauss's formula:

$$\text{sum} = \frac{n(n + 1)}{2}$$

Store the result into the int variable sum.

2. Given the declarations

```
int    i;
int    j;
float x;
float y;
```

write a valid C++ expression for each of the following algebraic expressions.

a. $\dfrac{x}{y} - 3$

b. $(x + y)(x - y)$

c. $\dfrac{1}{x + y}$

d. $\dfrac{1}{x} + y$

e. $\dfrac{i}{j}$ (the floating point result)

f. $\dfrac{i}{j}$ (the integer quotient)

g. $\dfrac{\dfrac{x + y}{3} - \dfrac{x - y}{5}}{4x}$

3. Given the declarations

```
int    i;
long   n;
float x;
float y;
```

write a valid C++ expression for each of the following algebraic expressions. Use calls to library functions wherever they are useful.

a. $|i|$ (absolute value)

b. $|n|$

c. $|x + y|$

d. $|x| + |y|$

e. $\dfrac{x^3}{y}$

f. $\sqrt{x^6 + y^5}$

g. $(x + \sqrt{y})^7$

4. Write expressions to compute both solutions for the quadratic formula. The formula is

$$\dfrac{-b \pm \sqrt{b^2 - 4ac}}{2a}.$$

The $\pm$ means "plus or minus" and indicates that there are two solutions to the equation: one in which the result of the square root is added to $-b$ and one in which the result is subtracted from $-b$. Assume all variables are `float` variables.

5. Complete the following C++ program. The program should find and output the perimeter and area of a rectangle, given the length and the width. Be sure to label the output. And don't forget to use comments.

```
//***************************************************
// Rectangle program
// This program finds the perimeter and the area
// of a rectangle, given the length and width
//***************************************************
#include <iostream.h>

int main()
{
    float length;      // Length of the rectangle
    float width;       // Width of the rectangle
    float perimeter;   // Perimeter of the rectangle
    float area;        // Area of the rectangle

    length = 10.7;
    width = 5.2;
```

6. Write C++ output statements that produce exactly the following output.

```
a. Four score
   and seven years ago
b. Four score
   and seven
   years ago
c. Four score
   and

   seven
   years ago
d. Four
      score
         and
   seven
      years
         ago
```

7. a. Modify the Walk program to include a roundoff factor so that the rounding of `miles` can be modified easily. Currently, the program uses a literal constant (10.0) in several places to round `miles` to the nearest tenth, requiring us to make multiple changes if we want a different roundoff factor.
   b. Should the roundoff factor be a constant or a variable? Explain.

Programming Problems

1. Write a C++ program that converts a Celsius temperature to its Fahrenheit equivalent. The formula is

$$\text{Fahrenheit} = \frac{9}{5}\,\text{Celsius} + 32.$$

Make the Celsius temperature a named constant so that its value can be changed easily. The program should print both the value of the Celsius temperature and its Fahrenheit equivalent, with appropriate identifying messages. Be sure to include appropriate comments in your program, choose meaningful identifiers, and use indentation as we do in the programs in this chapter.

2. Write a program to calculate the diameter, the circumference, and the area of a circle given a radius of 6.75. Assign the radius to a `float` variable, and then output the radius with an appropriate message. Declare a named constant PI with the value 3.14159. The program should output the diameter, the circumference, and the area, each on a separate line, with identifying labels. Print each value to five decimal places within a total fieldwidth of 10. Be sure to include appropriate comments in your program, choose meaningful identifiers, and use indentation as we do in the programs in this chapter.

3. You have bought a car, taking out a loan with an annual interest rate of 9%. You will make 36 monthly payments of $165.25 each. You want to keep track of the remaining balance you owe after each monthly payment. The formula for the remaining balance is

$$\text{bal}_k = \text{pmt} \left[\frac{1 - (1 + i)^{k-n}}{i} \right]$$

where

$\quad\quad\quad$ bal_k = balance remaining after the kth payment
$\quad\quad\quad\quad$ k = payment number (1, 2, 3, . . .)
$\quad\quad\quad$ pmt = amount of the monthly payment
$\quad\quad\quad\quad\quad$ i = interest rate per month (annual rate ÷ 12)
$\quad\quad\quad\quad$ n = total number of payments to be made

Write a program to calculate and print the balance remaining after the first, second, and third monthly car payments. Before printing these three results, the program should output the values on which the calculations are based (monthly payment, interest rate, and total number of payments). Label all output with identifying messages, and print all money amounts to two decimal places. Be sure to include appropriate comments in your program, choose meaningful identifiers, and use indentation as we do in the programs in this chapter.

4 Program Input and the Software Design Process

GOALS

- To be able to construct input statements to read values into a program
- To be able to determine the contents of variables assigned values by input statements
- To be able to write appropriate prompting messages for interactive programs
- To know when noninteractive input/output is appropriate and how it differs from interactive input/output

- To be able to write programs that use data files for input and output
- To be able to apply the functional decomposition methodology to solve a simple problem
- To be able to take a functional decomposition and code it in C++, using self-documenting code
- To understand the basic principles of object-oriented design

A program needs data on which to operate. We have been writing all of the data values in the program itself, in literal and named constants. If this were the only way we could enter data, we would have to rewrite a program each time we wanted to apply it to a different set of values. In this chapter, we look at ways of entering data into a program while it is running.

Once we know how to input data, process the data, and output the results, we can begin to think about designing more complicated programs. We have talked about general problem-solving strategies and writing simple programs. For a simple problem, it's easy to choose a strategy, write the algorithm, and code the program. But as problems become more complex, we have to use a more organized approach. In the second part of this chapter, we look at two general methodologies for developing software: functional decomposition and object-oriented design.

Getting Data into Programs

One of the biggest advantages of computers is that a program can be used with many different sets of data. To do so, we must keep the data separate from the program until the program is executed. Then instructions in the program copy values from the data set into variables in the program. After storing these values into the variables, the program can perform calculations with them.

The process of placing values from an outside data set into variables in a program is called *input*. In widely used terminology, the computer is said to *read* outside data into the variables. The data for the program can come from an input device or from a file on an auxiliary storage device. We look at file input later in this chapter; here we consider the *standard input device,* the keyboard.

Input Streams and the Extraction Operator (>>)

The concept of a stream is fundamental to input and output in C++. As we stated in Chapter 3, you can think of an output stream as an endless sequence of characters going from your program to an output device. Likewise, think of an *input stream* as an endless sequence of characters coming into your program from an input device.

The header file `iostream.h` contains, among other things, the definitions of two data types: `istream` and `ostream`. These are data types representing input streams and output streams, respectively. The header file also contains declarations that look approximately like this:

```
istream cin;
ostream cout;
```

(We say "approximately" because the actual declarations are slightly different in a way that does not concern us right now.) The first declaration says that `cin` (pronounced "see-in") is a variable of type `istream`. The second says that `cout` (pronounced "see-out") is a variable of type `ostream`. Furthermore, `cin` is associated with the standard input device (the keyboard), and `cout` is associated with the standard output device (usually the display screen).

As you have already seen, you can output values to `cout` by using the *insertion operator* (<<), which is sometimes pronounced "put to":

```
cout << 3 * price;
```

In a similar fashion, you can input data from `cin` by using the *extraction operator* (>>), sometimes pronounced "get from":

```
cin >> cost;
```

When the computer executes this statement, it inputs the next number you type on the keyboard (425, for example) and stores it into the variable `cost`.

The extraction operator `>>` takes two operands. Its left-hand operand is a stream expression (in the simplest case, just the variable `cin`). Its right-hand operand is a variable of a simple type (`char`, `int`, `float`, and so forth).

You can use the `>>` operator several times in a single input statement. Each occurrence extracts (inputs) the next data item from the input stream. For example, there is no difference between the statement

```
cin >> length >> width;
```

and the pair of statements

```
cin >> length;
cin >> width;
```

Using a sequence of extractions in one statement is a convenience for the programmer.

When you are new to C++, you may get the extraction operator (`>>`) and the insertion operator (`<<`) reversed. Here is an easy way to remember which one is which: Always begin the statement with either `cin` or `cout`, and use the operator that points in the direction in which the data is going. The statement

```
cout << someInt;
```

sends data from the variable `someInt` *to* the output stream. The statement

```
cin >> someInt;
```

sends data from the input stream *to* the variable `someInt`.

Unlike the items specified in an output statement, which can be constants, variables, or complicated expressions, the items specified in an input statement can *only* be variable names. Why? Because an input statement indicates where input data values should be stored. Only variable names refer to memory locations where we can store values while a program is running.

When you enter input data at the keyboard, you must be sure that each data value is appropriate for the data type of the variable in the input statement.

Data Type of Variable In an >> Operation	Valid Input Data
char	A single printable character other than a blank
int	An int literal constant, optionally preceded by a sign
float	An int or float literal constant (possibly in scientific, E, notation), optionally preceded by a sign

Notice that when you input a number into a float variable, the input value doesn't have to have a decimal point. An integer value is automatically coerced to a float value. Any other mismatches, such as trying to input a float value into an int variable or a char value into a float variable, can lead to unexpected and sometimes serious results. Later in this chapter we discuss what might happen.

When looking for the next input value in the stream, the >> operator skips any leading *whitespace characters.* Whitespace characters are blanks and certain nonprintable characters like the character that marks the end of a line. (We talk about this end-of-line character in the next section.) After skipping these characters, the >> operator proceeds to extract the data value from the input stream. If this data value is a char value, input stops as soon as a single character is input. If the data value is int or float, input of the number stops at the first character that is inappropriate for the data type, such as a whitespace character. Here are some examples, where i, j, and k are int variables, ch is a char variable, and x is a float variable:

Statement	Data	Contents after Input
1. cin >> i;	32	i = 32
2. cin >> i >> j;	4 60	i = 4, j = 60
3. cin >> i >> ch >> x;	25 A 16.9	i = 25, ch = 'A', x = 16.9
4. cin >> i >> ch >> x;	25	
	A	
	16.9	i = 25, ch = 'A', x = 16.9
5. cin >> i >> ch >> x;	25A16.9	i = 25, ch = 'A', x = 16.9
6. cin >> i >> j >> x;	12 8	i = 12, j = 8 (Computer waits for a third number)
7. cin >> i >> x;	46 32.4 15	i = 46, x = 32.4 (15 is held for later input)

Examples (1) and (2) are straightforward cases of integer input. Example (3) shows that you do not use quotes around character data values when they are input. Example (4) demonstrates how the process of skipping whitespace characters includes going on to the next line of input if necessary. Example (5) shows that the first character encountered that is inappropriate for a numeric data type ends the number. Input for the variable i stops at the input character A, after which the A is stored into ch, and then input for x stops at the end of the input line. Example (6) shows that if you are at the keyboard and haven't entered enough values to satisfy the input statement, the computer waits for more data. Example (7) shows that if more values are entered than there are variables in the input statement, the extra values remain waiting in the input stream until they are read by the next input statement. If there are extra values left when the program ends, the computer disregards them.

The Reading Marker and the Newline Character

To help explain stream input in more detail, we introduce the concept of the *reading marker*. The reading marker works like a bookmark, but, instead of marking a place in a book, it keeps track of the point in the input stream where the computer should continue reading. The reading marker indicates the next character waiting to be read. The extraction operator >> leaves the reading marker on the character following the last item input.

Each input line has an invisible end-of-line character (the *newline character*) that tells the computer where one line ends and the next begins. To find the next input value, the >> operator crosses line boundaries (newline characters) if it has to.

Where does the newline character come from? What is it? The answer to the first question is easy. When you are working at a keyboard, you generate a newline character each time you hit the Return or Enter key. Your program also generates a newline character when it uses the endl manipulator in an output statement. The endl manipulator outputs a newline, telling the cursor to go to the next line. The answer to the second question varies from computer system to computer system. The newline character is a nonprintable control character that the system recognizes as meaning the end of a line, whether it's an input line or an output line.

In a C++ program, you can refer directly to the newline character by using the symbols \n. Although \n consists of two symbols, it refers to a single character—the newline character. Just as you can store the letter *A* into a char variable ch like this:

```
ch = 'A';
```

you can store the newline character into a variable:

```
ch = '\n';
```

Let's look at some examples using the reading marker and the newline character. In the following table, i is an int variable, ch is a char variable, and x is a `float` variable. The input statements produce the results shown. The part of the input stream printed in color is what has been extracted by input statements. The reading marker, denoted by the shaded block, indicates the next character waiting to be read. The \n denotes the newline character.

Statements	Contents after Input	Marker Position in the Input Stream
1.		2̅5 A 16.9\n
cin >> i;	i = 25	25 ▮A 16.9\n
cin >> ch;	ch = 'A'	25 A▮16.9\n
cin >> x;	x = 16.9	25 A 16.9 \n̅
2.		2̅5\n A\n 16.9\n
cin >> i;	i = 25	25 \n̅ A\n 16.9\n
cin >> ch;	ch = 'A'	25\n A \n̅ 16.9\n
cin >> x;	x = 16.9	25\n A\n 16.9 \n̅
3.		2̅5A16.9\n
cin >> i;	i = 25	25 A̅ 16.9\n
cin >> ch;	ch = 'A'	25A 1̅6.9\n
cin >> x;	x = 16.9	25A16.9 \n̅

Reading Character Data with the `get` **Function**

As we have discussed, the >> operator skips leading whitespace characters in the input stream. Suppose that `ch1` and `ch2` are `char` variables and the program executes the statement

```
cin >> ch1 >> ch2;
```

If the input stream consists of

R 1

then the extraction operator stores 'R' into `ch1`, skips the blank, and stores '1' into `ch2`. (Note that the char value '1' is not the same as the `int` value 1. The two are represented differently in memory. The extraction operator interprets the same data in different ways, depending on the data type of the variable that's being filled.)

What if we had wanted to input *three* characters from the input line: the *R*, the blank, and the 1? With the extraction operator, it's not possible. Whitespace characters such as blanks are skipped over.

The `istream` data type provides a second way in which to read character data, in addition to the `>>` operator. You use the `get` function, which inputs the next character without skipping any whitespace. Its call looks like this:

```
cin.get(someChar);
```

You give the name of an `istream` variable (here, `cin`), then a dot (period), and then the function name and parameter list. Notice that the call to `get` uses the syntax for calling a void function, not a value-returning function. The function call is a complete statement; it is not part of a larger expression.

The effect of the above function call is to input the next character waiting in the stream—even if it is a whitespace character like a blank—and store it into the variable `someChar`. The parameter to the `get` function *must* be a variable.

Using `get`, we now can input all three characters of the input line

```
R 1
```

We can use three consecutive calls to the `get` function

```
cin.get(ch1);
cin.get(ch2);
cin.get(ch3);
```

or we can do it this way:

```
cin >> ch1;
cin.get(ch2);
cin >> ch3;
```

The first version is probably a bit clearer for someone to read and understand.

Here are some examples of character input using both the `>>` operator and `get`. All of `ch1`, `ch2`, and `ch3` are `char` variables.

Statements	Contents after Input	Marker Position in the Input Stream
1.		A B\n CD\n
cin >> ch1;	ch1 = 'A'	A B\n CD\n
cin >> ch2;	ch2 = 'B'	A B\n CD\n
cin >> ch3;	ch3 = 'C'	A B\n C D\n
2.		A B\n CD\n
cin.get(ch1);	ch1 = 'A'	A B\n CD\n
cin.get(ch2);	ch2 = ' '	A B\n CD\n
cin.get(ch3);	ch3 = 'B'	A B\n CD\n
3.		A B\n CD\n
cin >> ch1;	ch1 = 'A'	A B\n CD\n
cin >> ch2;	ch2 = 'B'	A B\n CD\n
cin.get(ch3);	ch3 = '\n'	A B\n C D\n

You may be puzzled about the peculiar syntax in a function call like

```
cin.get(ch1);
```

This statement uses a C++ notation called *dot notation.* There is a dot (period) between the variable name cin and the function name get. Certain predefined data types, like istream and ostream, have functions that are tightly associated with them, and dot notation is required in the function calls. If you forget to use dot notation by using

```
get(ch1);
```

you get a compile-time error message, something like "UNDECLARED IDEN-TIFIER." The compiler thinks you are trying to call an ordinary function named get, not the get function associated with the istream type.

Another example you saw in the last chapter is the function call that forces decimal points to appear in the output of all floating point numbers:

```
cout.setf(ios::showpoint);
```

(This statement uses even stranger syntax in the form of the double colon, whose purpose we won't attempt to discuss here.) Later in the chapter, we discuss the meaning behind dot notation.

Skipping Characters with the ignore *Function*

Most of us have a specialized tool lying in a kitchen drawer or in a toolbox. It gathers dust and cobwebs because we almost never use it. But when we suddenly need it, we're glad we have it.

The ignore function associated with the istream type is like this specialized tool. You rarely have occasion to use ignore; but when you need it, you're glad it's available.

The ignore function is used to skip (read and discard) characters in the input stream. It is a function with two parameters, called like this:

```
cin.ignore(200, '\n');
```

The first parameter is an int expression; the second, a char value. This particular function call tells the computer to skip the next 200 input characters *or* to skip characters until a newline character is read, whichever comes first.

Here are some examples that use a char variable ch and three int variables, i, j, and k:

Statements	*Contents after Input*	*Marker Position in the Input Stream*
1.		957 34 1235\n 128 96\n
cin >> i >> j;	i = **957**, j = **34**	957 34 1235\n 128 96\n
cin.ignore(100, '\n');		957 34 1235\n 128 96\n
cin >> k;	k = **128**	957 34 1235\n 128 96\n
2.		A 22 B 16 C 19\n
cin >> ch;	ch = **'A'**	A 22 B 16 C 19\n
cin.ignore(100, 'B');		A 22 B 16 C 19\n
cin >> i;	i = **16**	A 22 B 16 C 19\n
3.		A BCDEF\n
cin.ignore(2, '\n');		AB C DEF\n
cin >> ch;	ch = **'C'**	ABC D EF\n

Example (1) shows the most common use of the `ignore` function, which is to skip the rest of the data on the current input line. Example (2) demonstrates the use of a character other than '\n' as the second parameter. We skip over all input characters until a 'B' has been found, then read the next input number into `i`. In both (1) and (2), we are focusing on the second parameter to the `ignore` function, and we arbitrarily choose any large number like 100 for the first parameter. In (3), we change our focus and concentrate on the first parameter. Our intention is to skip the next two input characters on the current line.

Interactive Input/Output

An *interactive program* is one in which the user communicates directly with the computer. Many of the programs that you write will be interactive. There is a certain "etiquette" involved in writing interactive programs that has to do with instructions for the user (the person executing your program).

To get data into an interactive program, we begin with *input prompts,* printed messages that explain what the user should enter. Without these messages, the user has no idea what to type into a program. A program also should print out all of the data values typed in so that the user can verify that they were entered correctly. Printing out the input values is called *echo printing.* Here's a program segment showing the proper use of prompts:

```
cout << "Enter the part number:" << endl;            // Prompt
cin >> partNumber;
cout << "Enter the quantity of this part ordered:"   // Prompt
    << endl;
cin >> quantity;
cout << "Enter the unit price for this part:"        // Prompt
    << endl;
cin >> unitPrice;
totalPrice = quantity * unitPrice;
cout << "Part " << partNumber                        // Echo print
    << ", quantity " << quantity
    << ", at $ " << setprecision(2) << unitPrice
    << " each" << endl;
cout << "totals $ " << totalPrice << endl;
```

And here's the output, with the user's input shown in color:

```
Enter the part number:
4671
```

```
Enter the quantity of this part ordered:
10
Enter the unit price for this part:
27.25
Part 4671, quantity 10, at $ 27.25 each
totals $ 272.50
```

The amount of information you put into your prompts depends on who is going to be using a program. If you are writing a program for people who are not familiar with computers, your messages should be more detailed. For example, "Type a four-digit part number, then press the key marked RETURN." If the program is going to be used frequently by the same people, you could shorten the prompts: "Enter PN." and "Enter Qty." If the program is for very experienced users, you can prompt for several values at once and have them type all of the values on one input line:

```
Enter PN, Qty, Unit Price:
4176 10 27.25
```

In programs that use large amounts of data, this method saves the user keystrokes and time. However, it also makes it easier for the user to enter values in the wrong order.

Prompts are not the only way in which programs interact with users. It can be helpful to have a program print out some general instructions at the beginning ("Press RETURN after typing each data value. Enter a negative number when done."). When data are not entered in the correct form, a message that indicates the problem should be printed. For users who haven't worked much with computers, it's important that these messages be informative and "friendly." The message

```
ILLEGAL DATA VALUES!!!!!!!
```

is likely to upset an inexperienced user. Moreover, it doesn't offer any constructive information. A much better message would be

```
That is not a valid part number.
Part numbers must be no more than four digits long.
Please reenter the number in its proper form:
```

In Chapter 5, we introduce the statements that allow us to test for erroneous data.

Noninteractive Input/Output

Although we tend to use examples of interactive I/O in this text, many programs are written using noninteractive I/O. A common example of noninteractive I/O on large computer systems is *batch processing.* In batch processing, the user and the computer do not interact while the program is running. This method is most effective when a program is going to input or output large amounts of data. An example of batch processing is a program that inputs a file containing semester grades for thousands of students and prints grade reports to be mailed out.

When a program must read in many data values, the usual practice is to prepare them ahead of time, storing them into a file. This allows the user to go back and make changes or corrections to the data as necessary before running the program. When a program is designed to print lots of data, the output can be sent directly to a high-speed printer or another disk file. After the program has been run, the user can examine the data at leisure. In the next section, we discuss input and output with disk files.

Programs designed for noninteractive I/O do not print prompting messages for input. It is a good idea, however, to echo print each data value that is read. Echo printing allows the person reading the output to verify that the input values were prepared correctly. Because noninteractive programs tend to print large amounts of data, their output often is in the form of a table—columns with descriptive headings.

Most C++ programs are written for interactive use. But the flexibility of the language allows you to write noninteractive programs as well. The biggest difference is in the input/output requirements. Noninteractive programs are generally more rigid about the organization and format of the input and output data.

File Input and Output

In everything we've done so far, we've assumed that the input to our programs comes from the keyboard and that the output from our programs goes to the screen. We look now at input/output to and from files.

Files A file is a named area in secondary storage that holds a collection of information (for example, the program code we have typed into the editor). The information in a file usually is stored on an auxiliary storage device, such as a disk.

Our programs can read data from a file in the same way they read data from the keyboard. And they can write output to a disk file in the same way they write output to the screen.

Why would we want a program to read data from a file instead of the keyboard? If a program is going to read a large quantity of data, it is easier to enter the data into a file with an editor than to enter it while the program is running. With the editor, we can go back and correct mistakes. Also, we do not have to enter the data all at once; we can take a break and come back later. And if we want to rerun the program, having the data stored in a file allows us to do so without reentering the data.

Why would we want the output from a program to be written to a disk file? The contents of a file can be displayed on a screen or printed. This gives us the option of looking at the output over and over again without having to rerun the program. Also, the output stored in a file can be read into another program as input.

Using Files   If we want a program to use file I/O, we have to do four things:

1. Request the preprocessor to include the header file `fstream.h`
2. Use declaration statements to declare the files we are going to use
3. Prepare each file for reading or writing by using a function named `open`
4. Specify the name of the file in each input or output statement

Including the Header File `fstream.h`.   Suppose we want the Mileage program (page 49) to read data from a file and to write its output to a file. The first thing we must do is use the preprocessor directive

```
#include <fstream.h>
```

Through the header file `fstream.h`, the C++ standard library defines two data types, `ifstream` and `ofstream` (standing for *input file stream* and *output file stream*). Consistent with the general idea of streams in C++, the `ifstream` data type represents a stream of characters coming from an input file, and `ofstream` represents a stream of characters going to an output file.

All of the `istream` operations you have learned about—the extraction operator (`>>`), the `get` function, and the `ignore` function—are also valid for the `ifstream` type. And all of the `ostream` operations, like the insertion operator (`<<`) and the `endl`, `setw`, and `setprecision` manipulators, apply also to the `ofstream` type. To these basic operations, the `ifstream` and `ofstream` types add some more operations designed specifically for file I/O.

Declaring File Streams.   In a program, you declare stream variables the same way that you declare any variable—you specify the data type and then the variable name:

```
int      someInt;
float    someFloat;
ifstream inFile;
ofstream outFile;
```

(You don't have to declare the stream variables `cin` and `cout`. The header file `iostream.h` already does this for you.)

For our Mileage program, let's name the input and output file streams `inMPG` and `outMPG`. We declare them like this:

```
ifstream inMPG;    // Holds gallon amounts and mileages
ofstream outMPG;   // Holds miles per gallon output
```

Note that the `ifstream` type is for input files only, and the `ofstream` type is for output files only. With these data types, you cannot read from and write to the same file. If you wanted to do so, you would use a third data type named `fstream`, the details of which we don't explore in this book.

Opening Files.   The third thing we have to do is prepare each file for reading or writing, an act called *opening a file*. Opening a file causes the computer's operating system to perform certain actions that allow us to proceed with file I/O.

In our example, we want to read from the file stream `inMPG` and write to the file stream `outMPG`. We open the relevant files by using the statements.

```
inMPG.open("inmpg.dat");
outMPG.open("outmpg.dat");
```

which are both function calls. In each call, the parameter is a string enclosed by quotes. The first statement is a call to a function named `open`, which is associated with the `ifstream` data type. The second is a call to another function (also named `open`) associated with the `ofstream` data type. As we discussed earlier, we use dot notation (as in `inMPG.open`) to call certain library functions that are tightly associated with data types.

Exactly what does an open function do? First, it associates a stream variable used in your program with a physical file on disk. Our first function call creates a connection between the stream variable `inMPG` and the actual disk file, `inmpg.dat`. (Names of file streams must be identifiers; they are variables in your program. But some computer systems do not use this format for file names on disk. For example, many systems include a dot in file names.) Similarly, the second function call associates the stream variable `outMPG` with the disk file `outmpg.dat`. Associating a program's name for a file (`outMPG`) with the actual name for the file (`outmpg.dat`) is much the same as associating a program's name for the standard output device (`cout`) with the actual device (the screen).

The next thing the `open` function does depends on whether the file is an input file or an output file. With an input file, the `open` function sets the file reading marker to the first piece of data in the file. (Each input file has its own reading marker.)

With an output file, the `open` function checks to see whether the file already exists. If the file doesn't exist, `open` creates a new, empty file for you. If the file does exist, `open` erases the old contents of the file. Then the writing marker is set at the beginning of the empty file (see Figure 4-1). As output proceeds, each successive output operation advances the writing marker to add data to the end of the file.

Because the reason for opening files is to *prepare* the files for reading or writing, you must open the files before using any input or output statements that refer to the files. In a program, it's a good idea to open files right away to be sure that the files are prepared before the program attempts any file I/O.

```
        .
        .
        .
int main()
{
      :  ⎫  Declarations
         ⎬
         ⎭

   // Open the files

   inMPG.open("inmpg.dat");
   outMPG.open("outmpg.dat");
      .
      .
      .

}
```

Specifying Files in Input/Output Statements.   There is just one more thing we have to do in order to use files. As we said earlier, all `istream` operations are also valid for the `ifstream` type, and all `ostream` operations are valid for the

FIGURE 4-1

The Effect of
Opening
a File

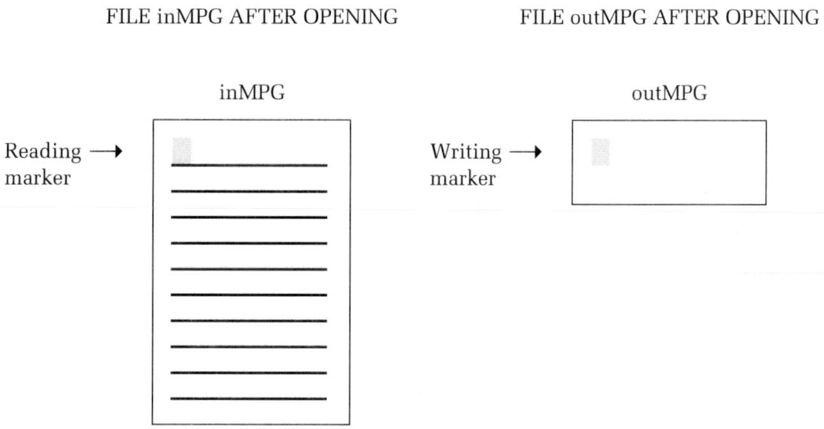

FILE inMPG AFTER OPENING

FILE outMPG AFTER OPENING

`ofstream` type. So, to read from or write to a file, all we need to do in our input and output statements is substitute the appropriate file stream variable for `cin` or `cout`. In our Mileage program, we would use a statement like

```
inMPG >> amt1 >> amt2 >> amt3 >> amt4 >> startMiles >> endMiles;
```

to instruct the computer to read data from the file `inMPG` instead of from `cin`. And all of the output statements that write to the file `outMPG` would specify `outMPG`, not `cout`, as the destination:

```
outMPG << "the mileage per gallon is " << mpg << endl;
```

What is nice about C++ stream I/O is that we have a uniform syntax for performing I/O operations, regardless of whether we're working with the keyboard and screen, with files, or with other I/O devices.

An Example Program Using Files   Here's the Mileage program reworked. Now it reads its input from the file `inMPG` and writes its output to the file `outMPG`. Compare this program with the original version on page 49 and notice that the constants have disappeared because the data are now input at execution time.

```
//*************************************************************
// Mileage program
// This program computes miles per gallon given four amounts
// for gallons used, and starting and ending mileage
//*************************************************************
#include <iostream.h>
#include <fstream.h>        // For file I/O

int main()
{
    float     amt1;         // Number of gallons for fillup 1
    float     amt2;         // Number of gallons for fillup 2
    float     amt3;         // Number of gallons for fillup 3
    float     amt4;         // Number of gallons for fillup 4
    float     startMiles;   // Starting mileage
    float     endMiles;     // Ending mileage
    float     mpg;          // Computed miles per gallon
    ifstream  inMPG;        // Holds gallon amounts and mileages
    ofstream  outMPG;       // Holds miles per gallon output

    // Open the files

    inMPG.open("inmpg.dat");
    outMPG.open("outmpg.dat");
```

```
// Get data

inMPG >> amt1 >> amt2 >> amt3 >> amt4 >> startMiles >> endMiles;

// Compute miles per gallon

mpg = (endMiles - startMiles) / (amt1 + amt2 + amt3 + amt4);

// Output results

outMPG << "For the gallon amounts" << endl;
outMPG << amt1 << ' ' << amt2 << ' '
       << amt3 << ' ' << amt4 << endl;
outMPG << "and a starting mileage of " << startMiles << endl;
outMPG << "and an ending mileage of " << endMiles << endl;
outMPG << "the mileage per gallon is " << mpg << endl;
return 0;
}
```

In this program, what happens if you mistakenly specify `cout` instead of `outMPG` in one of the output statements? Nothing disastrous; the output of that one statement merely goes to the screen instead of the output file. And what if, by mistake, you specify `cin` instead of `inMPG` in the input statement? The consequences are not as pleasant. When you run the program, the computer will appear to go dead (to *hang*). Here's the reason.

Execution reaches the input statement and the computer waits for you to enter the data from the keyboard. But you don't know that the computer is waiting. There's no message on the screen prompting you for input, and you are assuming (wrongly) that the program is getting its input from a data file. So the computer waits, and you wait, and the computer waits, and you wait. Every programmer at one time or another has had the experience of thinking the computer has hung, when, in fact, it is working just fine, silently waiting for keyboard input.

Input Failure

When a program inputs data from the keyboard or an input file, errors can occur. Let's suppose that we're executing a program. It prompts us to enter an integer value, but we absentmindedly type some letters. The input operation fails because of the invalid data. In C++ terminology, the `cin` stream has entered the *fail state*. Once a stream has entered the fail state, any further I/O operations using that stream are considered to be null operations—that is, they have no effect at all. Unfortunately for us, *the computer does not halt the program or give any error message.* The computer just continues executing the program, silently ignoring each additional attempt to use that stream.

Invalid data is the most common reason for input failure. When your program inputs an int value, it is expecting to find only digits in the input stream, possibly preceded by a plus or minus sign. If there is a decimal point somewhere within the digits, does the input operation fail? Not necessarily; it depends on where the reading marker is. Let's look at an example.

Assume that a program has int variables i, j, and k, whose contents are currently 10, 20, and 30, respectively. The program now executes the following two statements:

```
cin >> i >> j >> k;
cout << "i: " << i << " j: " << j << " k: " << k;
```

If we type these characters for the input data:

```
1234.56 7 89
```

then the program produces this output:

```
i: 1234 j: 20 k: 30
```

Let's see why.

When reading int or float data, the extraction operator stops reading at the first character that is inappropriate for the data type. In our example, the input operation for i succeeds. The computer extracts the first four characters from the input stream and stores the integer value 1234 into i. The reading marker is now on the decimal point:

```
1234▮56 7 89
```

The next input operation (for j) fails; an int value cannot begin with a decimal point. The cin stream is now in the fail state, and the current value of j (20) remains unchanged. The third input operation (for k) is ignored, as are all the rest of the statements in our program that read from cin.

Another way to make a stream enter the fail state is to try to open an input file that doesn't exist. Suppose that you have a data file on your disk named myfile.dat. In your program you have the following statements:

```
ifstream inFile;

inFile.open("myfil.dat");
inFile >> i >> j >> k;
```

In the call to the `open` function, you misspelled the name of your disk file. At run time, the attempt to open the file fails, so the stream `inFile` enters the fail state. The next three input operations (for `i`, `j`, and `k`) are null operations. Without issuing any error message, the program proceeds to use the (unknown) contents of `i`, `j`, and `k` in calculations. The results of these calculations are certain to be puzzling.

The point of this discussion is not to make you nervous about I/O but to make you aware. The Testing and Debugging section at the end of this chapter offers suggestions for avoiding input failure. And in Chapters 5 and 6, you will learn about program statements that let you test the state of a stream.

Software Design

The programs we have written thus far were short and straightforward because the problems to be solved were simple. We are almost ready to write more complicated programs, but first we need to step back and look at the overall process of programming.

As you learned in Chapter 1, the programming process consists of a problem-solving phase and an implementation phase. The problem-solving phase includes *analysis* (analyzing and understanding the problem to be solved) and *design* (designing a solution to the problem). Given a complex problem—one that results in a 10,000-line program, for example—it's simply not reasonable to skip the design process and go directly to writing C++ code. What we need is a systematic way of designing a solution to a problem, no matter how complicated it is.

In the remainder of this chapter, we describe two important design methodologies: *functional decomposition* and *object-oriented design.* These methodologies help you create solutions that can be easily implemented as C++ programs. The resulting programs are readable, understandable, and easy to debug and modify.

Functional Decomposition

functional decomposition
A technique for developing a program in which the problem is divided into more easily handled subproblems, the solutions of which create a solution to the overall problem

The design technique we'll be using for the next several chapters is **functional decomposition.** It allows us to use the divide-and-conquer approach, which we talked about in Chapter 1.

In functional decomposition, we work from the abstract (a list of the major steps in our solution) to the particular (algorithmic steps that can be translated directly into C++ code). You can also think of this as working from a high-level solution, leaving the details of implementation unspecified, down to a fully detailed solution.

The easiest way to solve a problem is to give it to someone else and say, "Solve this problem." This is the most abstract level of a problem solution: a

single-statement solution that encompasses the entire problem without specifying any of the details. It's at this point that we programmers are called in. Our job is to turn the abstract solution into a concrete solution, a program.

We start by breaking the solution into a series of major steps. In the process, we move to a lower level of abstraction—that is, some of the implementation details (but not too many) are now specified. Each of the major steps becomes an independent subproblem that we can work on separately. In a very large project, one person (the *chief architect* or *team leader*) formulates the subproblems and then gives them to other members of the programming team, saying, "Solve this problem." In the case of a small project, we give the subproblems to ourselves. Then we choose one subproblem at a time and break it into another series of steps that, in turn, become smaller subproblems. The process continues until each subproblem cannot be divided further or has an obvious solution.

Why do we work this way? Why not simply write out all of the details? Because it is much easier to focus on one problem at a time. For example, suppose you are working on a program to print out certain values and discover that you need a complex formula to calculate an appropriate fieldwidth for printing one of the values. Calculating fieldwidths is not the purpose of the program. If you shift your focus to the calculation, you are more likely to forget some detail of the overall printing process. What you do is write down an abstract step— "Calculate the fieldwidth required"—and go on with the problem at hand. Once you've completed the general solution, you can go back to solving the step that does the calculation.

By subdividing the problem, you create a hierarchical structure called a *tree structure*. Each level of the tree is a complete solution to the problem that is less abstract (more detailed) than the level above it. Figure 4-2 shows a generic solution tree for a problem. Steps that are shaded have enough implementation details to be translated directly into C++ statements. These are *concrete steps*. Those that are not shaded are *abstract steps;* they reappear as subproblems in the next level down. Each box in the figure represents a *module*. Modules are the basic building blocks in functional decomposition. The diagram in Figure 4-2 is also called a *module structure chart*.

Modules   A module begins life as an abstract step in the next higher level of the solution tree. It is completed when it solves a given subproblem—that is, when it specifies a series of steps that does the same thing as the higher-level abstract step.

In a properly written module, all of the concrete steps should directly address the given subproblem; abstract steps are used only for significant new subproblems. Each module should do just one thing and do it well. Knowing which details to make concrete and which to leave abstract is a matter of experience, circumstance, and personal style. For example, you might decide to include a fieldwidth calculation in a printing module if there isn't so much detail in the rest of the module that it becomes confusing. On the other hand, if the

FIGURE 4-2   Hierarchical Solution Tree

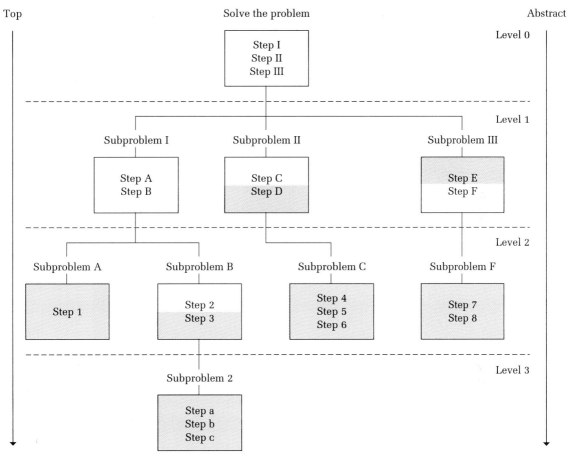

calculation is performed several times, it makes sense to write it as a separate module and just refer to it each time you need it.

Writing Modules.   Here's one approach to writing modules:

1. Think about how you would solve the subproblem by hand.
2. Begin writing down the major steps.
3. If a step is simple enough so that you can see how to implement it directly in C++, it is at the concrete level; it doesn't need any further refinement.
4. If you have to think about implementing a step as a series of smaller steps or as several C++ statements, it is still at an abstract level.

5. If you are trying to write a series of steps and start to feel overwhelmed by details, you probably are bypassing one or more levels of abstraction. Stand back and look for pieces that you can write as more abstract steps.

As you work your way down the solution tree, you make a series of design decisions. If a decision proves awkward or wrong (and many times it will), you can backtrack (go back up the tree to a higher-level module) and try something else. You don't have to scrap your whole design—only the small part you are working on.

Pseudocode.   You'll find it easier to implement a design if you write the steps in pseudocode. *Pseudocode* is a mixture of English statements and C++-like control structures that can be translated easily into C++. (We show an example of using pseudocode in the programming example at the end of this chapter.) When a concrete step is written in pseudocode, it should be possible to rewrite it directly as a C++ statement in a program.

Remember that the problem-solving phase of the programming process takes time. If you spend the bulk of your time analyzing and designing a solution, coding and implementing the program will take very little time.

Object-Oriented Design

object-oriented design
A technique for developing a program in which the solution is expressed in terms of objects—self-contained entities composed of data and operations on that data

A second software design methodology is known as **object-oriented design (OOD)**. In this section, we present only a preview of OOD. A thorough treatment requires additional C++ language features that are introduced in Chapter 15 of this text. Even though we won't be using OOD, it's important to recognize that functional decomposition is not the only technique used by programmers.

Let's begin our look at OOD by making an observation about functional decomposition. Functional decomposition can be thought of as the design of a problem solution by focusing on actions and algorithms. In functional decomposition, data play a secondary role in support of actions to be performed.

In contrast, OOD focuses on entities ("objects") and operations on those objects. For example, a banking problem may require a `checkingAccount` object with associated operations `OpenAccount`, `WriteCheck`, `MakeDeposit`, and `IsOverdrawn`. The `checkingAccount` object consists of both data (the account number and the current balance, for example) and operations, all bundled together.

The first step in OOD is to identify the major objects in the problem, together with their associated operations. The final problem solution is ultimately expressed in terms of these objects and operations. In OOD, data play a leading role. Algorithms are used to implement operations on the objects and to guide the interaction of objects with each other.

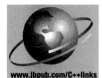

Like functional decomposition, OOD uses the divide-and-conquer approach to problem solving. Both techniques break up large problems into smaller units that are easier to handle. The difference is that in functional decomposition the units are modules representing algorithms, whereas the units in OOD are objects.

Several programming languages, called *object-oriented programming languages,* have been created specifically to support OOD. Examples are C++, Java, Smalltalk, CLOS, Eiffel, and Object-Pascal. In these languages, a *class* is a programmer-defined data type from which objects are created. Although we did not say it at the time, we have been using classes and objects to perform input and output in C++. cin is an object of a data type (class) named istream, and cout is an object of a class ostream.

In C++, the operations associated with a class are written as functions and are called *member functions.* A member function is invoked by giving the name of the class object, then a dot, and then the function name and parameter list:

```
cin.ignore(100, '\n');
cin.get(someChar);
```

OOD leads to programs that are collections of objects. Each object is responsible for one part of the entire solution, and the objects communicate with each other by calling one another's member functions. OOD is especially suitable for large software projects for three reasons. First, objects within a program often model real-life objects in the problem to be solved. Second, with the expanding use of OOD, more and more individuals and software companies are supplying libraries of prewritten classes and objects. Putting existing pieces together is an excellent example of the building-block approach we discussed in Chapter 1. Third, OOD employs a concept called *inheritance,* which allows you to adapt an existing class to meet your particular needs without having to inspect and modify the source code for that class. Together, OOD, class libraries, and inheritance can dramatically reduce the time and effort required to design, implement, and maintain large software systems.

In this section, we have presented only an introduction to OOD. A more complete discussion requires knowledge of topics that we explore in later chapters. Until then, our programs are relatively small and we use functional decomposition to arrive at our problem solutions.

An important perspective to keep in mind is that functional decomposition and object-oriented design are not separate, disjoint techniques. OOD decomposes a problem into objects. Objects not only contain data; they also have associated operations. The operations on objects require algorithms. Sometimes the algorithms are complicated and must be decomposed into subalgorithms by using functional decomposition. Experienced programmers are familiar with both methodologies and know when to use one or the other, or a combination of the two.

Now let's look at an example that demonstrates functional decomposition.

◼ *Documentation*

As you create your functional decomposition or object-oriented design, you are developing documentation for your program. Documentation *includes the written problem specifications, design, development history, and actual code of a program.*

Good documentation helps other programmers read and understand a program and is invaluable when software is being debugged and modified (maintained). If you haven't looked at your program for six months and need to change it, you'll be happy that you documented it well. Of course, if someone else has to use and modify your program, documentation is indispensable.

*Documentation is both external and internal to the program. External documentation includes the specifications, the development history, and the design documents. Internal documentation includes the program format and **self-documenting code**—meaningful identifiers and comments. You can use the pseudocode from your functional decomposition as comments in your program.*

This kind of documentation may be sufficient for someone reading or maintaining your programs. However, if a program is going to be used by people who are not programmers, you must provide a user's manual as well.

Be sure to keep documentation up-to-date. Indicate any changes you make in a program in all of the pertinent documentation. Use self-documenting code to make your programs more readable.

self-documenting code
Program code containing meaningful identifiers as well as judiciously used clarifying comments

◼◼ PROGRAMMING EXAMPLE

Weighted Average of Test Scores

Problem: Find the weighted average of three test scores. The data for each test is a score (an integer number) followed by its associated weight (a floating point number); each pair of numbers is on a separate line. The data are stored in a file called `scoreFile`.

Input: Three lines of data, each listing a test score (integer) and weight (floating point).

Output: Print the input data with headings (echo printing). Print the weighted average with an explanation. All floating point values are to be displayed to two decimal places.

PROGRAMMING EXAMPLE cont'd.

Discussion: It is common to give different weights to tests in order to arrive at a student's grade in a course. For example, if two tests are worth 30 percent each and a final exam is worth 40 percent, we multiply the first test grade by 0.30, the second test grade by 0.30, and the final grade by 0.40. We then add these three values to get a weighted average. We use this by-hand algorithm to solve the problem.

Because the data are going to be read from a file, we have to #include the header file fstream.h, declare an input file stream, prepare the file for reading (open it), and remember to use the file stream instead of cin in the input statements.

Assumptions: The three weights add up to 1.00, and the input data are correct (checking for erroneous input data is not done).

Functional Decomposition in Pseudocode

Main Module   *Level 0*

> Prepare file for reading
> Get data
> Print data
> Find weighted average
> Print weighted average

Prepare File for Reading   *Level 1*

> Open scoreFile

Get Data

> Read test1, weight1 from scoreFile
> Read test2, weight2 from scoreFile
> Read test3, weight3 from scoreFile

PROGRAMMING EXAMPLE cont'd.

Print Data

Print heading
Print test1, weight1
Print test2, weight2
Print test3, weight3

Find Weighted Average

Set ave = test1 * weight1
    + test2 * weight2 + test3 * weight 3

Print Weighted Average

Print blank line
Print "Weighted average = ", ave

Print Heading   *Level 2*

Print "Test Score   Weight"
Print blank line

Module Structure Chart:

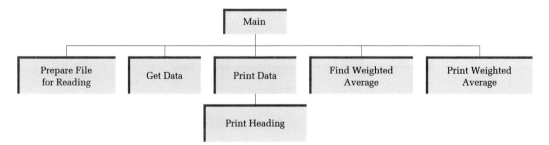

PROGRAMMING EXAMPLE cont'd.

Here is the complete program. There are no prompting messages because the input is taken from a file.

```cpp
//****************************************************************
// TestAverage program
// This program finds the weighted average of three test scores
//****************************************************************
#include <iostream.h>
#include <fstream.h>     // For file I/O
#include <iomanip.h>     // For setw() and setprecision()

int main()
{
    int      test1;                          // Score for first test
    int      test2;                          // Score for second test
    int      test3;                          // Score for third test
    float    weight1;                        // Weight for first test
    float    weight2;                        // Weight for second
                                             //   test
    float    weight3;                        // Weight for third test
    float    ave;                            // Weighted average of
                                             //   the tests
    ifstream scoreFile;                      // Input data file
    cout.setf(ios::fixed, ios::floatfield);  // Set up floating pt.
    cout.setf(ios::showpoint);               //   output format

    // Prepare file for reading

    scoreFile.open("scores.dat");

    // Get data

    scoreFile >> test1 >> weight1;
    scoreFile >> test2 >> weight2;
    scoreFile >> test3 >> weight3;

    // Print heading

    cout << "Test Score  Weight" << endl << endl;

    // Print data

    cout << setw(7) << test1
         << setw(11) << setprecision(2) << weight1 << endl;
    cout << setw(7) << test2 << setw(11) << weight2 << endl;
    cout << setw(7) << test3 << setw(11) << weight3 << endl;
```

PROGRAMMING EXAMPLE cont'd.

```
// Find weighted average

ave = test1 * weight1 + test2 * weight2 + test3 * weight3;

// Print weighted average

cout << endl;
cout << "Weighted average = " << ave << endl;
return 0;
}
```

If the file `scoreFile` (that is, the physical disk file `scores.dat`) contains this data:

```
90 0.30
85 0.25
78 0.45
```

the output from the program looks like this:

```
Test Score    Weight

      90        0.30
      85        0.25
      78        0.45

Weighted average = 83.35
```

Testing and Debugging

An important part of implementing a program is testing it (checking the results). From here on, these Testing and Debugging sections offer tips on how to test your programs and what to do if a program doesn't work the way you expect. But don't wait until you've found a bug to read the Testing and Debugging sections. It's much easier to prevent bugs than it is to fix them.

When testing programs that input data values, input operations can fail. When input fails, the computer doesn't issue a warning message, but simply continues, ignoring any further input operations. The two most common reasons for input failure are invalid data and the *end-of-file error.*

An end-of-file error occurs when the program has read all of the input data available in a file and needs more data to fill the variables in its input statements.

It might be that the data file simply was not prepared properly. Perhaps it contains fewer data items than the program requires. Or perhaps the format of the input data is wrong. Leaving out whitespace between numeric values is guaranteed to cause trouble. For example, we may want a data file to contain three integer values—25, 16, and 42. Look what happens with this data:

```
2516    42
```

and this code:

```
inFile >> i >> j >> k;
```

The first two input operations use up the data in the file, leaving the third with no data to read. The stream `inFile` enters the fail state, so `k` isn't assigned a new value and the computer quietly continues executing.

If the data file is prepared correctly and there is still an end- of-file error, the problem is in the program logic. For some reason, the program is attempting too many input operations. It could be a simple oversight such as specifying too many variables in a particular input statement. It could be a misuse of the `ignore` function, causing values to be skipped inadvertently. Or it could be a serious flaw in the algorithm. You should check all of these possibilities.

The other major source of input failure, invalid data, happens when numeric and character data are mixed inappropriately in the input. The input stream fails if it is supposed to read a numeric value, but the reading marker is positioned at a character that isn't allowed in the number.

There are several possible causes of invalid data. The most common is an error in the data. Another cause is using the wrong variable name (which happens to be of the wrong data type) in an input statement. Declaring a variable to be of the wrong data type is a variation on the problem. Last, leaving out a variable (or including an extra one) in an input statement can leave the reading marker positioned on the wrong type of data.

Another oversight, one that doesn't cause input failure but causes programmer frustration, is to use `cin` or `cout` in an I/O statement when you meant to specify a file stream. If you mistakenly use `cin` instead of an input file stream, the program stops and waits for input from the keyboard. If you mistakenly use `cout` instead of an output file stream, you get unexpected output on the screen.

By giving you a framework that can help you organize and keep track of the details involved in designing and implementing a program, functional decomposition (and, later, object-oriented design) should help you avoid these errors in the first place.

Testing and Debugging Hints

1. Input and output statements always begin with the name of a stream variable, and the $>>$ and $<<$ operators point in the direction in which the data is going. The statement

   ```
   cout << n;
   ```

   sends data *to* the output stream `cout`, and the statement

   ```
   cin >> n;
   ```

   sends data *to* the variable n.
2. When a program inputs from or outputs to a file, be sure each I/O statement from or to the file uses the name of the file stream, not `cin` or `cout`.
3. When you open a data file for input, make sure that the parameter to the `open` function supplies the correct name of the file as it exists on disk.
4. Be sure that each input statement specifies the correct number of variables and that each of those variables is of the correct data type.
5. If your input data is mixed (character and numeric values), be sure to deal with intervening blanks.
6. Echo print the input data to verify that each value is where it belongs and is in the proper format. (This is crucial because an input failure in C++ doesn't produce an error message or terminate the program.)
7. Remember that the extraction operator $(>>)$ skips whitespace characters. If you need to input these characters, you must use the `get` function.

Summary

Programs operate on data. If data and programs are kept separate, the same program can be run with multiple sets of input data.

The extraction operator $(>>)$ inputs data from the keyboard or a file, storing it into its right-hand operand. The extraction operator skips any leading whitespace characters to find the next data value in the input stream. The `get` function does not skip leading whitespace characters; it inputs the next character and stores it into the `char` variable specified in its parameter list. Both $>>$ and `get` leave the reading marker positioned at the next character to be read. The next input operation begins at the point indicated by the marker.

The newline character (denoted by \n in a C++ program) marks the end of a line. You create a newline when you press the Return or Enter key. Your program generates a newline each time you use the `endl` manipulator or explicitly output the \n character. Newline does not print; it controls the movement of the cursor or the position of a line on a printer.

Interactive programs prompt the user for data entry and directly inform the user of results and errors. Designing interactive dialogue is an exercise in the art of communication.

Noninteractive input/output allows data to be prepared in advance and allows the program to run again with the same data in the event of a problem during processing.

Data files often are used for noninteractive processing. There are four things you have to do to use files: (1) include `fstream.h`; (2) declare the file streams; (3) prepare the files for reading or writing by calling `open`; and (4) specify the name of the file stream in each statement that uses it.

Functional decomposition and object-oriented design are methods for tackling large programming problems. Functional decomposition begins with an abstract solution that then is divided into major steps. Each step becomes a subproblem that is analyzed and subdivided further. A concrete step is one that can be translated directly into C++; those that need more refining are abstract steps. A module is a collection of concrete and abstract steps that solves a subproblem.

Object-oriented design produces a problem solution by focusing on objects and their associated operations. The first step is to identify the major objects in the problem and choose appropriate operations on those objects. The result of the design process is a program consisting of self-contained objects that manage their own data and communicate by invoking each other's operations.

Careful attention to program design, program formatting, and documentation produces highly structured and readable programs.

Quick Check

1. Write a C++ statement that inputs values from the standard input stream into two `float` variables, x and y. (pp. 90–91)
2. Your program is reading from the standard input stream. The next three characters waiting in the stream are a blank, a blank, and the letter *A*. Indicate what character is stored into the `char` variable `ch` by each of the following statements. (Assume the same initial stream contents for each.)
   a. `cin >> ch;`
   b. `cin.get(ch);`
   (pp. 94–95)
3. Input prompts should acknowledge the user's experience.
   a. What sort of message would you have a program print to prompt a novice user to input a social security number?
   b. How would you change the wording of the prompting message for an experienced user? (pp. 98–99)
4. If a program is going to input 1000 numbers, is interactive input appropriate? (p. 100)
5. What are the four things that you have to remember to do in order to use data files in a C++ program? (pp. 101–104)
6. How many levels of abstraction are there in a functional decomposition before you reach the point at which you can begin coding a program? (pp. 107–110)
7. Modules are the building blocks of functional decomposition. What are the building blocks of object-oriented design? (pp. 110–111)

Answers 1. `cin >> x >> y`; 2. a. 'A' b. ' ' (a blank) 3. a. `Please type a nine-digit social security number, then press the key marked RETURN.` b. `Enter SSN.` 4. No. Batch input is more appropriate for programs that input large amounts of data. 5. (1) Include the header file `fstream.h`. (2) Declare the file streams along with your other variable declarations. (3) Call the `open` function to prepare each file for reading or writing. (4) Specify the name of the file stream in each I/O statement that uses it. 6. There is no fixed number of levels of abstraction. You keep refining the solution through as many levels as necessary until the steps are all concrete. 7. The building blocks are objects, each of which has associated operations.

Exam Preparation Exercises

1. What is the main advantage of having a program input its data rather than writing all the data values as constants in the program?
2. Given these two lines of data:

   ```
   17 13
   7 3 24 6
   ```

   and this input statement:

   ```
   cin >> int1 >> int2 >> int3;
   ```

   a. What is the value of each variable after the statement is executed?
   b. What happens to any leftover data values in the input stream?
3. The newline character signals the end of a line.
   a. How do you generate a newline character from the keyboard?
   b. How do you generate a newline character in a program's output?
4. When reading `char` data from an input stream, what is the difference between using the `>>` operator and using the `get` function?
5. Integer data values can be read into `float` variables. (True or False?)
6. You may use either spaces or newlines to separate numeric data values being entered into a C++ program. (True or False?)
7. Consider this input data:

   ```
   14 21 64
   19 67 91
   73 89 27
   23 96 47
   ```

   What are the values of the `int` variables a, b, c, and d after the following program segment is executed?

   ```
   cin >> a;
   cin.ignore(200, '\n');
   cin >> b >> c;
   cin.ignore(200, '\n');
   cin >> d;
   ```

8. Given the input data

```
123W 56
```

what is printed by the output statement when the following code segment is executed?

```
int1 = 98;
int2 = 147;
cin >> int1 >> int2;
cout << int1 << ' ' << int2;
```

9. Given the input data

```
11 12.35 ABC
```

what is the value of each variable after the following statements are executed? Assume that i is of type int, x is of type float, and ch1 is of type char.
   a. cin >> i >> x >> ch1 >> ch1;
   b. cin >> ch1 >> i >> x;

10. Define the following terms as they apply to interactive input/output.
    a. Input prompt
    b. Echo printing

11. Correct the following program so that it reads a value from the file inData and writes it to the file outData.

```
#include <iostream.h>

int main()
{
    int     n;
    ifstream inData;

    outData.open("results.dat");
    cin >> n;
    outData << n << endl;
    return 0;
}
```

12. Use your corrected version of the program in Exercise 11 to answer the following questions.
    a. If the file inData initially contains the value 144, what does it contain after the program is executed?
    b. If the file outData is initially empty, what are its contents after the program is executed?

13. List three characteristics of programs that are designed using a highly organized methodology such as functional decomposition or object-oriented design.
14. In the TestAverage programming example, look at the module structure chart and identify each module as abstract or concrete.
15. Redraw the module structure chart for the TestAverage example using Prepare File for Reading, Get and Echo Data, Find Weighted Average, and Print Weighted Average as level 1 modules. Add any appropriate modules at levels below these modules.

Programming Warm-Up Exercises

1. Your program has three `char` variables: `ch1`, `ch2`, and `ch3`. Given the input data

   ```
   A   B   C\n
   ```

   write the input statement(s) required to store the *A* into `ch1`, the *B* into `ch2`, and the *C* into `ch3`. Note that each pair of input characters is separated by two blanks.
2. Change your answer to Exercise 1 so that the *A* is stored into `ch1` and the next two blanks are stored into `ch2` and `ch3`.
3. Write a single input statement that reads the input lines

   ```
   10.25    7.625\n
   8.5\n
   1.0\n
   ```

   and stores the four values into the `float` variables `length1`, `height1`, `length2`, and `height2`.
4. Write a series of statements that input the first letter of each of the following names into the `char` variables `chr1`, `chr2`, and `chr3`.

   ```
   Peter\n
   Kitty\n
   Kathy\n
   ```

5. Write a set of variable declarations and a series of input statements to read the following lines of data into variables of the appropriate type. You can make up the variable names. Notice that the values are separated from one another by a single blank and that there are no blanks to the left of the first character on each line.

   ```
   A 100 2.78 g 14\n
   207.98 w q 23.4 92\n
   R 42 L 27 R 63\n
   ```

6. Write a program segment that reads nine integer values from a file and writes them to the screen, three numbers per output line. The file is organized one value to a line.

7. Write a code segment for an interactive program to input values for a person's age, height, and weight, and the initials of their first and last names. The numeric values are all integers. Assume that the person using the program is a novice user. How would you rewrite the code for an experienced user?

8. Fill in the blanks in the following program, which should read four values from the file dataIn and output them to the file resultsOut.

```
#include _____
#include _____

int main()
{
    int        val1;
    int        val2;
    int        val3;
    int        val4;
    _____     dataIn;
    ofstream _____;
    _____ ("myinput.dat");
    _____ ("myoutput.dat");
    _____ >> val1 >> val2 >> val3 >> val4;
    _____ << val1 << val2 << val3 << val4 << endl;
    return 0;

}
```

9. Use functional decomposition to write an algorithm for starting the engine of an automobile with a manual transmission.

10. Use functional decomposition to write an algorithm for logging on to your computer system, and entering and running a program. The algorithm should be simple enough for a novice user to follow.

11. The quadratic formula is

$$x = \frac{-b \pm \sqrt{b^2 - 4ac}}{2a}$$

Use functional decomposition to write an algorithm to read the three coefficients of a quadratic polynomial from a file (inQuad) and write the two floating point solutions to another file (outQuad). Assume that the discriminant (the portion of the formula inside the square root) is nonnegative. You may use the standard library function sqrt. (Express your solution as pseudocode, not as a C++ program.)

Programming Problems

1. Write a functional decomposition and a C++ program to read an invoice number, the quantity ordered, and the unit price (all integers), and compute the total price. The program should write out the invoice number, quantity, unit price, and total price with identifying phrases. Format your program with consistent indentation, and use appropriate comments and meaningful identifiers. If you are using an

interactive system, write the program to be run interactively, with informative prompts for each data value.

2. How tall is a rainbow? Because of the way in which light is refracted by water droplets, the angle between the level of your eye and the top of a rainbow is always the same. If you know the distance to the rainbow, you can multiply it by the tangent of that angle to find the height of the rainbow. The magic angle is 42.3333333 degrees. The C++ standard library works in radians, however, so you have to convert the angle to radians with this formula:

$$\text{radians} = \text{degrees} \times \frac{\pi}{180}$$

where π equals 3.14159265.

Through the header file `math.h`, the C++ standard library provides a tangent function named `tan`. This is a value-returning function that takes a floating point parameter and returns a floating point result:

```
x = tan(someAngle);
```

If you multiply the tangent by the distance to the rainbow, you get the height of the rainbow.

Write a functional decomposition and a C++ program to read a single floating point value—the distance to the rainbow—and compute the height of the rainbow. The program should print the distance to the rainbow and its height with phrases that identify which number is which. Display the floating point values to four decimal places. Format your program with consistent indentation, and use appropriate comments and meaningful identifiers. If you are using an interactive system, write the program so that it prompts the user for the input value.

3. Sometimes you can see a second, fainter rainbow outside a bright rainbow. This second rainbow has a magic angle of 52.25 degrees. Modify the program in Problem 2 so that it prints the height of the main rainbow, the height of the secondary rainbow, and the distance to the main rainbow, with a phrase identifying each of the numbers.

Conditions, Logical Expressions, and Selection Control Structures

GOALS

- To be able to construct a simple logical (Boolean) expression to evaluate a given condition

- To be able to construct a complex logical expression to evaluate a given condition

- To be able to construct an If-Then-Else statement to perform a specific task

- To be able to construct an If-Then statement to perform a specific task

- To be able to construct a set of nested If statements to perform a specific task

- To be able to determine preconditions and postconditions for modules, and use them to perform an algorithm walk-through

- To be able to trace the execution of a C++ program

- To be able to test and debug a C++ program

So far, the statements in our programs have been executed in their physical order. But what if we want the computer to execute the statements in some other order? Suppose we want to check the validity of input data and then perform a calculation *or* print an error message, not both. To do so, we must be able to ask a question and then, based on the answer, choose one or another course of action.

The If statement allows us to execute statements in an order that is different from their physical order. We can ask a question with it and do one thing if the answer is yes (true) or another if the answer is no (false). In the first part of this chapter, we deal with asking questions; in the second part, we deal with the If statement itself.

Flow of Control

The order in which statements are executed in a program is called the *flow of control.* In a sense, the computer is under the control of one statement at a time. When a statement has been executed, control is turned over to the next statement (like a baton being passed in a relay race).

control structure
A statement used to alter the normally sequential flow of control

Flow of control is normally sequential (see Figure 5-1). Where we want the flow of control to be nonsequential, we use **control structures,** special statements that transfer control to a statement other than the one that physically comes next.

Selection   We use a selection (or branching) control structure when we want the computer to choose between alternative actions. We make an assertion, a claim that is either true or false. If the assertion is true, the computer executes one statement. If it is false, it executes another (see Figure 5-2).

FIGURE 5-1   Sequential Control   *FIGURE 5-2*   Selection (Branching) Control Structure

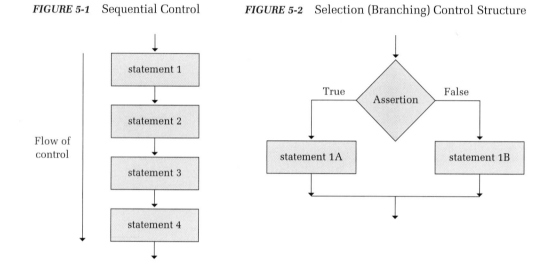

Suppose the computer must decide whether or not a worker has earned overtime pay. It does this by testing the assertion that the person has worked more than 40 hours. If the assertion is true, the computer follows the instructions for computing overtime pay. If the assertion is false, the computer simply computes the regular pay. Before we examine selection control structures in C++, let's look closely at how we get the computer to make decisions.

Conditions and Logical Expressions

To ask a question in C++, we make an assertion that is either true or false. The computer *evaluates* the assertion, checking it against some internal condition (the values stored in certain variables, for instance) to see whether it is true or false.

Logical Expressions   In C++, assertions take the form of *logical expressions* (also called *Boolean expressions**). A logical expression is made up of logical values and operations. Here are some examples of logical expressions:

- A Boolean variable or constant
- An expression followed by a relational operator followed by an expression
- A logical expression followed by a logical operator followed by a logical expression

Let's look at each of these in detail.

www.jbpub.com/C++links

Boolean Data.   Some programming languages include a data type named Boolean, which has only two literal constants: *true* and *false*. In these languages, if you declare a variable `dataOK` to be of type `Boolean`, you can store either the value *true* or the value *false* into the variable:

```
dataOK = true;
```

The C++ language doesn't have a Boolean data type. In C++, the value 0 represents *false*, and any nonzero value represents *true*. Programmers usually use the `int` type to represent Boolean data:

```
int dataOK;
   .
   .
   .
dataOK = 1; // Store "true" into dataOK
   .
   .
   .
dataOK = 0; // Store "false" into dataOK
```

Many C++ programmers prefer to define their own Boolean data type by using a *Typedef statement*. This statement allows you to introduce a new name for an existing data type. Here's an example:

```
typedef int Boolean;
```

---

*The word Boolean ('bo͞ol-ē-un) is a tribute to George Boole, a nineteenth-century English mathematician who described a system of logic using just two values, true and false.

All this statement does is cause the compiler to substitute the word `int` for every occurrence of the word `Boolean` in the rest of the program. If a program uses these statements:

```
typedef int Boolean;
   .
   .
   .
Boolean dataOK;
```

then the compiler substitutes `int` for `Boolean` in the declaration:

```
int  dataOK;
```

Notice that we have capitalized the identifier `Boolean` according to the style we described in Chapter 2.

To complete the construction of our own Boolean type in C++, we define two named constants, `true` and `false`:

```
typedef int Boolean;
const Boolean true = 1;
const Boolean false = 0;
   .
   .
   .
Boolean dataOK;
   .
   .
   .
dataOK = true;
   .
   .
   .
dataOK = false;
```

Normally we would write these named constants in all uppercase, but because there is a proposed standard that would include a Boolean type as part of the C++ library, we have chosen to break our convention to be compatible with the proposed standard. As you can see, we haven't *really* created a new data type. `Boolean` is just a synonym for `int`, and `true` and `false` are synonyms for 1 and 0. Why do we go to the trouble of doing this? First, it helps us to mentally separate `int` data from Boolean data as we design and implement programs.

Second, someone looking at our programs can see right away that the identifiers `Boolean`, `true`, and `false` refer to logical data and not integer values.

Throughout the rest of this text, whenever we need Boolean data in a C++ program, we incorporate the following statements into the program:

```
typedef int Boolean;
const Boolean true = 1;
const Boolean false = 0;
```

Relational Operators.   One way of assigning values to Boolean variables is to use an assignment statement, like this:

```
itemFound = true;
```

We also can assign values to Boolean variables by setting them equal to the result of comparing two expressions with a *relational operator*. Relational operators test a relationship between two values.

Let's look at an example. In this program fragment, `lessThan` is a Boolean variable and `i` and `j` are `int` variables:

```
cin >> i >> j;
lessThan = (i < j); // Assigns true to lessThan if i < j
```

By comparing two values, we assert that a relationship (like "less than") exists between them. If the relationship does exist, the assertion is true; if not, it is false. These are the relationships we can test for in C++:

`==` Equal to	`>` Greater than	`>=` Greater than or equal to
`!=` Not equal to	`<` Less than	`<=` Less than or equal to

In C++, the result of a comparison is the `int` value 1 (meaning `true`) or 0 (meaning `false`). For example, if x is 5 and y is 10, the following expressions all have the value 1 (`true`):

`x == 5`	`y > x`	`y >= x`
`x != y`	`x < y`	`x <= y`

If x is the character 'M' and y is 'R', the expressions are still `true` because the relational operator `<`, used with letters, means "comes before in the alphabet," or, more properly, "comes before in the collating sequence of the character set." For example, in the widely used ASCII character set, all of the uppercase letters are in alphabetical order, as are the lowercase letters, but all of the uppercase letters come before the lowercase letters. So

```
'M' < 'R'     and     'm' < 'r'
```

are `true`, but

```
'm' < 'R'
```

is `false`.

Of course, we have to be careful about the data types of things we compare. The safest approach is always to compare `ints` with `ints`, `floats` with `floats`, and `chars` with `chars`. If you mix data types in a comparison, implicit type coercion takes place just as in arithmetic expressions. If an `int` value and a `float` value are compared, the computer temporarily coerces the `int` value to its `float` equivalent before making the comparison. As with arithmetic expressions, it's wise to use explicit type casting to make your intentions known:

```
someFloat >= float(someInt)
```

Until you learn more about the `char` type in Chapter 10, be careful to compare `char` values only with other `char` values. For example, the comparisons

```
'0' < '9'     and     0 < 9
```

are appropriate, but

```
'0' < 9
```

generates an implicit type coercion and a result that probably isn't what you expect.

We can use relational operators not only to compare variables or constants, but also to compare the values of arithmetic expressions. In the following table, we compare the results of adding 3 to x and multiplying y by 10 for different values of x and y:

Value of x	Value of y	Expression	Result
12	2	x + 3 <= y * 10	1 (true)
20	2	x + 3 <= y * 10	0 (false)
7	1	x + 3 != y * 10	0 (false)
17	2	x + 3 == y * 10	1 (true)
100	5	x + 3 > y * 10	1 (true)

Caution: It's easy to confuse the assignment operator (=) and the == relational operator. These two operators have very different effects in a program. Some people pronounce the relational operator as "equals-equals" to remind themselves of the difference.

Logical Operators.   In mathematics, the *logical operators* AND, OR, and NOT take logical expressions as operands. C++ uses special symbols for the logical operators: && (for AND), || (for OR), and ! (for NOT). By combining relational operators with logical operators, we can make more complex assertions. For example, suppose we want to determine whether a final score is greater than 90 *and* a midterm score is greater than 70. In C++, we would write the expression this way:

```
finalScore > 90 && midtermScore > 70
```

The AND operation (&&) requires both relationships to be `true` in order for the overall result to be `true`. If either or both of the relationships are `false`, the entire result is `false`.

The OR operation (||) takes two logical expressions and combines them. If *either* or *both* are `true`, the result is `true`. Both values must be `false` for the result to be `false`. Now we can determine whether the midterm grade is an A *or* the final grade is an A. If either the midterm grade or the final grade equals A, the assertion is `true`. In C++, we write the expression like this:

```
midtermGrade == 'A' || finalGrade == 'A'
```

The NOT operator (!) precedes a single logical expression and gives its opposite as the result. If (grade == 'A') is `false`, then !(grade == 'A') is `true`. NOT gives us a convenient way of reversing the meaning of an assertion. For example,

```
!(hours > 40)       is the equivalent of     hours <= 40
```

In some contexts, the first form is clearer; in others, the second makes more sense.

The following pairs of expressions are equivalent:

Expression	Equivalent Expression
`!(a == b)`	`a != b`
`!(a == b || a == c)`	`a != b && a != c`
`!(a == b && c > d)`	`a != b || c <= d`

Take a close look at these expressions to be sure you understand why they are equivalent. It may help to try evaluating them with some values for a, b, c, and d. Notice the pattern here: The expression on the left is just the one to its right with ! added and the relational and logical operators reversed (for example, == instead of != and || instead of &&). Remember this pattern. It allows you to rewrite expressions in the simplest form.*

Logical operators can be applied to the results of comparisons. They also can be applied directly to variables of type Boolean. For example, instead of writing

```
isElector = (age >= 18 && district == 23);
```

to assign a value to Boolean variable isElector, we could use two intermediate Boolean variables, isVoter and isConstituent:

```
isVoter = (age >= 18);
isConstituent = (district == 23);
isElector = isVoter && isConstituent;
```

The two tables that follow summarize the results of applying && and || to a pair of logical expressions (represented here by Boolean variables x and y).

Value of x	Value of y	Value of x && y
true	true	true
true	false	false
false	true	false
false	false	false

---

*In Boolean algebra, the pattern is formalized by a theorem called *DeMorgan's Law.*

Value of x	Value of y	Value of $x \;||\; y$
true	true	true
true	false	true
false	true	true
false	false	false

The following table summarizes the results of applying the ! operator to a logical expression (represented by Boolean variable x).

Value of x	Value of $!x$
true	false
false	true

Technically, the C++ operators !, &&, and || are not required to have logical expressions as operands. Their operands can be of any simple data type, even floating point types. Throughout this text, we apply the logical operators *only* to logical expressions, not to arithmetic expressions.

Caution: It's easy to confuse the logical operators && and || with two other C++ operators, & and |. We don't discuss the & and | operators here, but we'll tell you that they are used for a role quite different from that of the logical operators. If you accidentally use & instead of &&, or | instead of ||, you won't get an error message from the compiler. But your program probably will compute wrong answers. Some programmers pronounce && as "and-and" and || as "or-or" to avoid making mistakes.

Short-Circuit Evaluation.   Consider the logical expression

```
i == 1 && j > 2
```

short-circuit (condi-tional) evaluation Evaluation of a logical expression in left-to-right order with evaluation stopping as soon as the final truth value can be determined

C++ uses **short-circuit** (or **conditional**) **evaluation** of logical expressions. Evaluation proceeds from left to right, and the computer stops evaluating subexpressions as soon as possible—that is, as soon as it knows the value of the entire expression. How can the computer know if a lengthy logical expression is true or false if it doesn't examine all the subexpressions? Let's look first at the AND operation.

An AND operation yields the value `true` only if both of its operands are `true`. In the expression above, suppose that the value of `i` happens to be 95. The first subexpression is `false`, so it isn't necessary even to look at the second subexpression. The computer stops evaluation and produces the final result of `false`.

With the OR operation, the left-to-right evaluation stops as soon as a `true` subexpression is found. Remember that an OR produces a result of `true` if either one or both of its operands are `true`. Given this expression:

```
c <= d || e == f
```

if the first subexpression is `true`, evaluation stops and the entire result is `true`. The computer doesn't waste time with an unnecessary evaluation of the second subexpression.

Precedence of Operators In Chapter 3, we discussed the rules of precedence that govern the evaluation of arithmetic expressions. C++'s rules of precedence also govern relational and logical operators. Here's a list showing the order of precedence for the arithmetic, relational, and logical operators (with the assignment operator thrown in as well):

```
!                       Highest precedence
*    /    %
+    -
<    <=   >   >=
==   !=
&&
||
=                       Lowest precedence
```

Operators on the same line in the list have the same precedence. If multiple operators have the same precedence in an expression, most of the operators group (associate) from left to right. For example, the expression

```
a / b * c
```

means `(a / b) * c`, not `a / (b * c)`. However, the `!` operator groups from right to left. Although you'd never have occasion to use this expression:

```
!!badData
```

the meaning of it is `!(!badData)` rather than the meaningless `(!!)badData`. Appendix B, Precedence of Operators, lists the order of precedence for all operators in C++.

Parentheses are used to override the order of evaluation in an expression. If you're not sure whether parentheses are necessary, use them anyway. The compiler disregards unnecessary parentheses. So if they clarify an expression, use them.

One final comment about parentheses: C++, like other programming languages, requires that parentheses always be used in pairs. Whenever you write a complicated expression, take a minute to go through and pair up all of the opening parentheses with their closing counterparts.

■ *Common Mistakes*

Many errors in logical expressions stem from our tendency to take shortcuts in English. We might ask whether the midterm grade or the final grade is an A, but if we write this directly in C++ as

```
midtermGrade || finalGrade == 'A'
```

we get erroneous results because we are trying to apply the logical `||` operator to a `char` variable. We have to write

```
midtermGrade == 'A' || finalGrade == 'A'
```

Similarly, asking if `i` equals 3 or 4 must be written

```
i == 3 || i == 4
```

Mathematicians use the notation

```
12 < y < 24
```

to mean "y is between 12 and 24," but translating this directly to C++ has a different effect. First, 12 and Y are compared, and then the Boolean result (0 or 1) is compared to 24, so that the final result is always `true`. The correct C++ translation is

```
12 < y && y < 24
```

Relational Operators with Floating Point Types

The relational operators can be applied to any of the three basic data types: `int`, `float`, and `char`. We've talked about comparing `int` and `char` values. Here we look at `float` values.

Do not compare floating point numbers for equality. Because small errors in the rightmost decimal places are likely to arise when calculations are performed on floating point numbers, two `float` values rarely are exactly equal. For example, consider the following code that uses two `float` variables named `oneThird` and `x`:

```
oneThird = 1.0 / 3.0;
x = oneThird + oneThird + oneThird;
```

We would expect `x` to contain the value 1.0, but it probably doesn't. The first assignment statement stores an *approximation* of $\frac{1}{3}$ into `oneThird`, perhaps 0.333333. The second statement stores a value like 0.999999 into `x`. If we now ask the computer to compare `x` with 1.0, the comparison yields `false`.

Instead of testing floating point numbers for equality, we test for *near* equality. To do so, we compute the difference between the two numbers and test to see if the result is less than some maximum allowable difference. For example, we often use comparisons like this:

```
fabs(r - s) < 0.00001
```

where `fabs` is the floating point absolute value function from the C++ standard library. The expression `fabs(r - s)` computes the difference between two `float` variables `r` and `s`. If the difference is less than 0.00001, the two numbers are close enough to call them equal. We discuss this problem with floating point accuracy in more detail in Chapter 10.

The If Statement

Now that we've seen how to write logical expressions, let's use them to alter the normal flow of control in a program. The *If statement* allows branches in the flow of control. With it, we can ask a question and choose a course of action: *If* a certain condition exists, *then* perform one action, *else* perform a different action.

The If-Then-Else Form

In C++, the If statement comes in two forms: the *If-Then-Else* form and the *If-Then* form. Let's look first at the If-Then-Else. Here is its syntax template:

IfStatement (the If-Then-Else form)

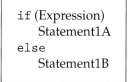

```
if (Expression)
        Statement1A
else
        Statement1B
```

The expression in parentheses can be of any simple data type. Almost without exception, this will be a logical (Boolean) expression. If the value of the expression is nonzero (`true`), the computer executes Statement1A. If the value of the expression is zero (`false`), Statement1B is executed. Statement1A often is called the *then-clause;* Statement1B, the *else-clause.* Figure 5-3 illustrates the flow of control of the If-Then-Else. In the figure, Statement2 is the next statement in the program after the entire If statement.

Notice that a C++ If statement uses the reserved words `if` and `else` but does not include the word *then.* Still, we use the term *If-Then-Else* because it corresponds to how we say things in English: "*If* something is true, *then* do this, *else* do that."

The code fragment at the top of page 138 shows how to write an If statement in a program. Observe the indentation of the then-clause and the else-clause, which makes the statement easier to read. And notice the placement of the statement following the If statement.

FIGURE 5-3

If-Then-Else Flow
of Control

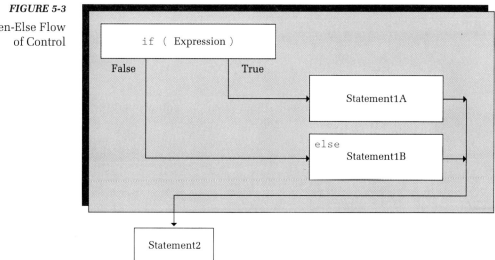

```
if (hours <= 40.0)
    pay = rate * hours;
else
    pay = rate * (40.0 + (hours - 40.0) * 1.5);
cout << pay;
```

In terms of instructions to the computer, the above code fragment says, "If hours is less than or equal to 40.0, compute the regular pay and then go on to execute the output statement. But if hours is greater than 40, compute the regular pay and the overtime pay, and then go on to execute the output statement."

Before we look any further at If statements, take another look at the syntax template for the If-Then-Else. According to the template, there is no semicolon at the end of an If statement, yet in the program fragment there seems to be a semicolon at the end of the If statement. The explanation is that the semicolon belongs to the assignment statement in the else-clause. The If statement doesn't have its own semicolon at the end.

Blocks   In checking to avoid division-by-zero in an expression, suppose that when the divisor is equal to zero we want to do *two* things: print an error message *and* set a variable named `result` equal to a special value like 9999. We would need two statements in the same branch, but the syntax template seems to limit us to one.

What we really want to do is turn the else-clause into a *sequence* of statements. This is easy. Remember from Chapter 2 that the compiler treats the block

```
{
    .
    .
    .
}
```

like a single statement. If you put a { } pair around the sequence of statements you want in a branch, the statements become a single block. For example:

```
if (divisor != 0)
    result = dividend / divisor;
else
{
    cout << "Division by zero is not allowed." << endl;
    result = 9999;
}
```

If the value of `divisor` is zero, the computer both prints the error message and sets the value of `result` to 9999 before continuing with whatever statement follows the If statement.

Blocks can be used in both branches of an If-Then-Else. For example:

```
if (divisor != 0)
{
    result = dividend / divisor;
    cout << "Division performed." << endl;
}
else
{
    cout << "Division by zero is not allowed." << endl;
    result = 9999;
}
```

When you use blocks in an If statement, there's a rule of C++ syntax to remember: *Never use a semicolon after the right brace of a block.* Semicolons are used only to terminate simple statements such as assignment statements, input statements, and output statements. In the examples above, there is no semicolon after the right brace that signals the end of each block.

The If-Then Form

Sometimes you run into a situation where you want to say, "*If* a certain condition exists, *then* perform some action; otherwise, don't do anything." In other words, you want the computer to skip a sequence of instructions if a certain condition isn't met. You could do this by leaving the `else` branch empty, using only the null statement:

```
if (a <= b)
    c = 20;
else
    ;
```

Better yet, you could simply leave off the `else` part. The resulting statement is the If-Then form of the If statement. This is its syntax template:

If Statement (the If-Then form)

```
if (Expression)
    Statement
```

Here's an example of an If-Then. Notice the indentation and the placement of the statement that follows the If-Then.

```
if (age < 18)
    cout << "Not an eligible ";
cout << "voter." << endl;
```

This statement means that if `age` is less than 18, first print "Not an eligible " and then print "voter." If age is not less than 18, skip the first output statement and go directly to print "voter."

As in an If-Then-Else, the branch in an If-Then can be a block. For example, let's say you are writing a program to compute income taxes. One of the lines on the tax form says, "Subtract line 23 from line 17 and enter result on line 24; if result is less than zero, enter zero and check box 24A." You can use an If-Then to do this in C++:

```
result = line17 - line23;
if (result < 0.0)
{
    cout << "Check box 24A" << endl;
    result = 0.0;
}
line24 = result;
```

This code does exactly what the tax form says it should. It computes the result of subtracting line 23 from line 17. Then it looks to see if `result` is less than zero. If it is, the computer outputs a message telling the user to check box 24A and then sets `result` to zero. Finally, the calculated result (or zero, if the result is less than zero) is stored into a variable named `line24`.

What happens if we leave out the left and right braces in the code fragment above? Let's look at it:

```
result = line17 - line23;              // Incorrect version
if (result < 0.0)
    cout << "Check box 24A" << endl;
    result = 0.0;
line24 = result;
```

Despite the way we have indented the code, the compiler takes the then-clause to be a single statement—the output statement. If `result` is less than zero, the computer executes the output statement, then sets `result` to zero, and then stores `result` into `line24`. So far, so good. But if `result` is initially greater than or equal to zero, the computer skips the then-clause and proceeds to the statement following the If statement—the assignment statement that sets `result` to zero. The outcome is that `result` ends up as zero no matter what its initial value was! The moral here is not to rely on indentation alone; you can't fool the compiler. If you want a compound statement for a then- or else-clause, you must include the left and right braces.

A Common
Mistake

Earlier we warned against confusing the = operator and the == operator. Here is an example of a mistake that every C++ programmer is guaranteed to make at least once in his or her career:

```
cin >> n;
if (n = 3)                         // Wrong
    cout << "n equals 3";
else
    cout << "n doesn't equal 3";
```

This code segment *always* prints out

```
n equals 3
```

no matter what was input for n. Here is the reason.

We've used the wrong operator in the If test. The expression n = 3 is not a logical expression; it's called an *assignment expression.* (If an assignment is written as a separate statement ending with a semicolon, it's an assignment *statement.*) An assignment expression has a *value* (above, it's 3) and a *side effect* (storing 3 into n). In the If statement of our example, the computer finds the value of the tested expression to be 3. Because 3 is a nonzero (`true`) value, the then-clause is executed, no matter what the value of n is. Worse yet, the side effect of the assignment expression is to store 3 into n, destroying what was there.

Our intention is not to focus on assignment expressions; we discuss their use later in the book. What's important now is that you see the effect of using = when you meant to use ==. The program compiles correctly but runs incorrectly. When debugging a faulty program, always look at your If statements to see whether you've made this particular mistake.

Nested If Statements

There are no restrictions on what the statements in an If can be. Therefore, an If within an If is okay. In fact, an If within an If within an If is legal. The only limitation here is that people cannot follow a structure that is too involved. And readability is one of the marks of a good program.

When we place an If within an If, we are creating a *nested control structure.* Control structures nest much like mixing bowls do, smaller ones tucked inside larger ones. Here's an example, written in pseudocode:

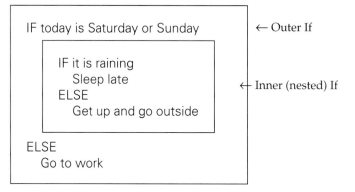

In general, any problem that involves a *multi-way branch* (more than two alternative courses of action) can be coded using nested If statements. For example, to print out the name of a month given its number, we could use a sequence of If statements (unnested):

```
if (month == 1)
    cout << "January";
if (month == 2)
    cout << "February";
if (month == 3)
    cout << "March";
    .
    .
    .
if (month == 12)
    cout << "December";
```

But the equivalent nested If structure,

```
if (month == 1)
    cout << "January";
else
    if (month == 2)              // Nested If
        cout << "February";
    else
        if (month == 3)          // Nested If
            cout << "March";
```

```
else
    if (month == 4)              // Nested If
        .
        .
        .
```

is more efficient because it makes fewer comparisons. The first version—the sequence of independent If statements—always tests every condition (all 12 of them), even if the first one is satisfied. In contrast, the nested If solution skips all remaining comparisons after one alternative has been selected.

In the last example, notice how the indentation of the then- and else-clauses causes the statements to move continually to the right. We use a special indentation style with deeply nested If-Then-Else statements to indicate that the complex structure is just choosing one of a set of alternatives. This general multi-way branch is known as an *If-Then-Else-If* control structure:

```
if (month == 1)
    cout << "January";
else if (month == 2)            // Nested If
    cout << "February";
else if (month == 3)            // Nested If
    cout << "March";
else if (month == 4)            // Nested If
    .
    .
    .
else
    cout << "December";
```

This style prevents the indentation from marching continuously to the right. But, more importantly, it visually conveys the idea that we are using a 12-way branch based on the variable month.

It's important to note one difference between the sequence of If statements and the nested If: More than one alternative can be taken by the sequence of Ifs, but the nested If can select only one. To see why this is important, consider the analogy of filling out a questionnaire. Some questions are like a sequence of If statements, asking you to circle all the items in a list that apply to you (such as all your hobbies). Other questions ask you to circle only one item in a list (your age group, for example) and are thus like a nested If structure. Both kinds of questions occur in programming problems. Being able to recognize which type of question is being asked permits you to immediately select the appropriate control structure.

Another particularly helpful use of the nested If is when you want to compare a series of consecutive ranges of values. For example, the following program shown below involves printing different messages for different ranges of temperatures.

```
//*********************************************************************
// Activity program
// This program outputs an appropriate activity
// for a given temperature
//*********************************************************************
#include <iostream.h>
int main()
{
    int temperature;    // The outside temperature

    // Get temperature

    cout << "Enter the outside temperature:" << endl;
    cin >> temperature;
    cout << "The current temperature is " << temperature << '.'
        << endl;

    // Print activity

    cout << "The recommended activity is ";
    if (temperature > 85)
        cout << "swimming." << endl;
    else if (temperature > 70)
        cout << "tennis." << endl;
    else if (temperature > 32)
        cout << "golf." << endl;
    else if (temperature > 0)
        cout << "skiing." << endl;
    else
        cout << "dancing." << endl;

    return 0;
}
```

The Dangling Else   When If statements are nested, you may find yourself confused about the if-else pairings: To which if does an else belong? For example, suppose that if a student's average is below 60, we want to print "Failing"; if it is at least 60 but less than 70, we want to print "Passing but marginal"; and if it is 70 or greater, we don't want to print anything.

We code this information with an If-Then-Else nested within an If-Then:

```
if (average < 70.0)
    if (average < 60.0)
        cout << "Failing";
    else
        cout << "Passing but marginal";
```

How do we know to which `if` the `else` belongs? Here is the rule that the C++ compiler follows: In the absence of braces, an `else` is always paired with the closest preceding `if` that doesn't already have an `else` paired with it. We indented the code to reflect this pairing.

Suppose we write the fragment like this:

```
if (average >= 60.0)        // Incorrect version
    if (average < 70.0)
        cout << "Passing but marginal";
else
    cout << "Failing";
```

Here we want the `else` branch attached to the outer If statement, not the inner, so we indent the code as you see it. But indentation does not affect the execution of the code. Even though the `else` aligns with the first `if`, the compiler pairs it with the second `if`. An `else` that follows a nested If-Then is called a *dangling else*. It doesn't logically belong with the nested If but is attached to it by the compiler.

To attach the `else` to the first `if`, not the second, you can turn the outer then-clause into a block:

```
if (average >= 60.0)        // Correct version
{
    if (average < 70.0)
        cout << "Passing but marginal";
}
else
    cout << "Failing";
```

The { } pair indicates that the inner If statement is complete, so the `else` must belong to the outer `if`.

Testing the State of an I/O Stream

In Chapter 4, we talked about the concept of input and output streams in C++. We introduced the data types istream, ostream, ifstream, and ofstream. We said that any of the following can cause an input stream to enter the fail state:

- Invalid input data
- An attempt to read beyond the end of a file
- An attempt to open a nonexistent file for input

C++ provides a way in which to determine if a stream is in the fail state. In a logical expression, you simply use the name of the stream variable as if it were a Boolean variable:

```
if (cin)
    .
    .
    .
if ( !inFile )
    .
    .
    .
```

testing the state of a stream
The act of using a C++ stream variable in a logical expression as if it were a Boolean variable; the result is nonzero (true) *if the last I/O operation on that stream succeeded, and zero* (false) *otherwise*

When you do this, you are said to be **testing the state of a stream.** The result of the test is either a nonzero value (meaning the last I/O operation on that stream succeeded) or zero (meaning the last I/O operation failed).

Conceptually, you should think of a stream variable in a logical expression as a Boolean variable with a value true (the stream state is okay) or false (the state isn't okay).

In an If statement, the way you phrase the logical expression depends on what you want the then-clause to do. The statement

```
if (inFile)
    .
    .
    .
```

executes the then-clause if the last I/O operation on inFile succeeded. The statement

```
if ( !inFile )
    .
    .
    .
```

executes the then-clause if `inFile` is in the fail state. (And remember that once a stream is in the fail state, it remains so. Any further I/O operations on that stream are null operations.)

Here's an example that shows how to check whether an input file was opened successfully:

```
#include <iostream.h>
#include <fstream.h>      // For file I/O

int main()
{
    int      height;
    int      width;
    ifstream inFile;

    inFile.open("mydata.dat");            // Attempt to open input file
    if ( !inFile )                        // Was it opened?
    {
        cout << "Can't open the input file.";   // No--print message
        return 1;                                // Terminate program
    }
    inFile >> height >> width;
       .
       .
       .

    return 0;
}
```

In this program, we begin by attempting to open the disk file `mydata.dat` for input. Immediately, we check to see whether the attempt succeeded. If it was successful, the value of the expression `!inFile` in the If statement is zero (`false`) and the then-clause is skipped. The program proceeds to read data from the file.

Let's trace through the program, assuming we weren't able to open the input file. Upon return from the `open` function, the stream `inFile` is in the fail state. In the If statement, the value of the expression `!inFile` is nonzero (`true`). Thus, the then-clause is executed. The program prints an error message to the user and then terminates, returning an exit status of 1 to inform the operating system of an abnormal termination of the program. (Our choice of the value 1 for the exit status is arbitrary. Programmers sometimes use different values to signal different reasons for termination. But most people just use the value 1.)

Whenever you open a data file for input, be sure to test the stream state before proceeding. If you don't, and the computer cannot open the file, your program continues executing and ignores any input operations on the file.

PROGRAMMING EXAMPLE

Warning Notices

Problem: Write a program that calculates the average of three test grades and prints out a student's ID number, average, and whether or not the student is passing. Passing is a 60-point average or better. If the student is passing with less than a 70 average, the program should indicate that he or she is marginal.

Input: Student ID number (of type `long`) followed by three test grades (of type `int`). On many personal computers, the maximum `int` value is 32767. The student ID number is of type `long` to accommodate larger values such as nine-digit Social Security numbers.

Output:

A prompt for input
The input values (echo print)
Student ID number, average grade, passing/failing message, marginal indica-
   tion, and error message if any of the test scores are negative

Discussion: To calculate the average, we have to read in the three test scores, add them, and divide by 3.

   To print the appropriate message, we have to determine whether or not the average is below 60. If it is at least 60, we have to determine if it is less than 70.

   If you were doing this by hand, you probably would notice if a test grade was negative and question it. If the semantics of your data imply that the values should be nonnegative, then your program should test to be sure they are. We test to make sure each grade is nonnegative, using a Boolean variable to report the result of the test. Here is the algorithm, which we will also refer to in our discussion of testing and debugging.

Main Module

```
Get data
Test data
IF data OK
    Calculate average
    Print message indicating status
ELSE
    Print "Invalid Data: Score(s) less than zero."
```

Which of these steps require(s) expansion? *Get data, Test data,* and *Print message indicating status* all require multiple statements in order to solve their particular subproblem. On the other hand, we can translate *Print "Invalid Data: . . ."* directly into a C++ output statement. What about the step *Calculate average*? We can write it as a single C++ statement, but there's another level of detail that we must fill in— the actual formula to be used. Because the formula is at a lower level of detail than the rest of the main module, we chose to expand *Calculate average* as a Level 1 module.

Get Data

```
Prompt for intput
Read studentID, test1, test2, test3
Print student ID, test1, test2, test3
```

Test Data

```
IF test1 < 0 OR test2 < 0 OR test3 < 0
    Set dataOK to false
ELSE
    Set dataOK to true
```

Calculate Average

```
Set average to (test1 + test2 + test3) / 3.0
```

Print Message Indicating Status

```
Print average
IF average >= 60.0
    Print "Passing"
    IF average < 70.0
        Print " but marginal"
    Print '.'
ELSE
    Print "Failing."
```

PROGRAMMING EXAMPLE cont'd.

```cpp
//**********************************************************************
// Notices program
// This program determines (1) a student's average based on three
// test scores and (2) the student's passing/failing status
//**********************************************************************
#include <iostream.h>
#include <iomanip.h>    // For setprecision()

typedef int Boolean;
const Boolean true = 1;
const Boolean false = 0;

int main()
{
    float    average;      // Average of three test scores
    long     studentID;    // Student's identification number
    int      test1;        // Score for first test
    int      test2;        // Score for second test
    int      test3;        // Score for third test
    Boolean dataOK;        // TRUE if data is correct

    cout.setf(ios::fixed, ios::floatfield);  // Set up floating pt.
    cout.setf(ios::showpoint);               //    output format

    // Get data

    cout << "Enter a Student ID number and three test scores:"
         << endl;
    cin >> studentID >> test1 >> test2 >> test3;
    cout << "Student number: " << studentID << " Test Scores: "
         << test1 << ", " << test2 << ", " << test3 << endl;

    // Test data

    if (test1 < 0 || test2 < 0 || test3 < 0)
        dataOK = false;
    else
        dataOK = true;

    if (dataOK)
    {
        // Calculate average

        average = float(test1 + test2 + test3) / 3.0;

        // Print message

        cout << "Average score is "
             << setprecision(2) << average << "--";
        if (average >= 60.0)
        {
```

PROGRAMMING EXAMPLE cont'd

```
            cout << "Passing";              // Student is passing
            if (average < 70.0)
                cout << " but marginal";    // But marginal
            cout << '.' << endl;
        }
        else                                // Student is failing
            cout << "Failing." << endl;
    }
    else                                    // Invalid data
        cout << "Invalid Data: Score(s) less than zero." << endl;

    return 0;
}
```

Here's a sample run of the program. Again, the input is in color.

```
Enter a Student ID number and three test scores:
9483681  73  62  68
Student Number: 9483681 Test Scores: 73, 62, 68
Average score is 67.67--Passing but marginal.
```

And here's a sample run with invalid data:

```
Enter a Student ID number and three test scores:
9483681  73  -10  62
Student Number: 9483681 Test Scores: 73, -10, 62
Invalid Data: Score(s) less than zero.
```

Testing and Debugging

In Chapter 1, we discussed the problem-solving and implementation phases of computer programming. Testing is an integral part of both phases. Here we test both phases of the process used to develop the Notices program. Testing in the problem-solving phase is done after the solution is developed but before it is implemented. In the implementation phase, we test after the algorithm is translated into a program, and again after the program has compiled successfully. The compilation itself constitutes another stage of testing that is performed automatically.

The Problem-Solving Phase: The Algorithm Walk-Through

To test at the problem-solving phase, we do a *walk-through* of the algorithm. For each module in the functional decomposition, we establish a set of assertions that must be true, called preconditions and postconditions. **Preconditions** are assertions that must be true before a module is executed in order for the module to execute correctly. **Postconditions** are assertions that must be true after the module has executed, if it has done its job correctly. To test a module, we

precondition
An assertion that must be true before a module begins executing

postcondition
An assertion that must be true after a module has executed

www.jbpub.com/C++links

manually walk through the algorithmic steps to confirm that they produce the required postconditions given the stated preconditions.

Our Warning Notices algorithm has five modules: the main module, Get Data, Test Data, Calculate Average, and Print Message. Usually there are no preconditions for the main module. Our main module's postcondition is that it outputs the correct result given the correct input. More specifically, the postconditions for the main module are

- the computer has read four integer values into `studentID`, `test1`, `test2`, and `test3`.
- the input values have been echo printed.
- the average of the last three input values has been printed if the values are valid.
- Either an error message or a message indicating the student's status has been printed. The message is "Passing." if the average is $>= 70.0$. The message is "Passing but marginal." if the average is < 70.0 and $>= 60.0$. The message is "Failing." if the average is < 60.0.

Because Get Data is the first module executed in the algorithm and because it does not depend on the contents of the variables it is about to manipulate, it has no preconditions. Its postconditions are that it has input an integer into `studentID`, and integer values into `test1`, `test2`, and `test3`.

The preconditions for module Test Data are that `test1`, `test2`, and `test3` contain integer values. Its postcondition is that `dataOK` contains `true` if the values in `test1`, `test2`, and `test3` are non-negative, otherwise `dataOK` contains `false`.

The preconditions for module Calculate Average are that `test1`, `test2`, and `test3` contain non-negative integer values. Its postcondition is that the mean of `test1`, `test2`, and `test3` has been computed from those values.

The precondition for module Print Message is that average contains the mean of the values in `test1`, `test2`, and `test3`. Its postcondition is that the value in average has been printed and a message indicating the status of the student has been printed. The message is "Passing." if the average is $>= 70.0$. The message is "Passing but marginal." if the average is < 70.0 and $>= 60.0$. The message is "Failing." if the average is < 60.0.

Now that we've established the preconditions and postconditions, we *walk through* the main program. At this point, we are concerned only with the steps in the main program, so for now we assume that each lower-level module executes correctly. At each step, we must determine the current conditions. If the step is a reference to another module, we have to verify that the preconditions of that module are met by the current conditions.

Get Data does not have any preconditions. At this level, we must assume that Get Data satisfies its postconditions—that it correctly inputs four integer values into `studentID`, `test1`, `test2`, and `test3`.

The preconditions for module Test Data are that `test1`, `test2`, and `test3` contain integer values. This must be the case if Get Data's postconditions are satisfied. Again, because we are concerned only with the step at level 0, we assume that Test Data satisfies its postcondition; that `dataOK` contains `true` or `false`, depending on the input values.

The If statement checks to see if `dataOK` is `true`. If it is, we take the Then branch. Assuming that Calculate Average correctly calculates the mean of `test1`, `test2`, and `test3` and that Print Message prints the average and the appropriate message, then that branch of the If statement is correct. If the value in `dataOK` is `false`, we take the Else branch and an error message is printed.

The next step is to examine each module at level 1 and answer this question: If the level-2 modules are assumed to be correct, does this module do what it is supposed to do? We simply repeat the walk-through process for each module, starting with its particular preconditions. In this example there are no level-2 modules, so the level-1 modules must be complete.

Get Data correctly reads in four values—`studentID`, `test1`, `test2`, and `test3`—which satisfies its postconditions. (The next refinement is coding this instruction. Whether or not it is coded correctly is *not* the problem at this phase; we deal with the code when we perform testing in the implementation phase.)

Test Data checks that all three of the variables containing scores are nonnegative. The OR operators combine the results so that if any of them are `true` the Else branch is taken. The If thus assigns `false` to `dataOK` if any of the numbers are negative, otherwise it assigns `true`. It therefore satisfies its postcondition.

Calculate Average sums the three test scores, divides the sum by 3.0, and assigns the result to average. The correct order of the operations in the formula is ensured by the parentheses enclosing the summation.

Print Message Indicating Status writes the value in average. It then tests whether average is greater than or equal to 60.0. If so, "Passing" is printed and it then tests whether average is less than 70. If average is less than 70, the words "but marginal." are added after "Passing"; otherwise Passing is ended with a period. If average is less than 60.0, the message "Failing." is printed. Thus the module satisifes its postconditions.

Once we've completed the algorithm walk-through, we have to correct any discrepancies and repeat the process. When we know that the modules do what they are supposed to do, we start translating the algorithm into our programming language.

A standard postcondition for any program is that the user has been notified of invalid data. You should *validate* every input value for which any restrictions apply. A data validation If statement tests an input value and outputs an error message if the value is not acceptable. (We validated the data when we tested for negative scores in program Notices.) The best place to validate data is immediately after it is input. In order to satisfy the data validation postcondition, the Warning Notices algorithm also should test the input values to ensure that they aren't too large.

For example, if the maximum score on a test is 100, then module Test Data should check for values in `test1`, `test2`, and `test3` that are greater than 100. The printing of the error message also should be modified to indicate the particular error condition that occurred. It would be best if it also specified the score that is invalid. Such a change makes it clear that Test Data should be the module to print the error messages. If Test Data prints the error message, then the If-Then-Else in the main module can be rewritten as an If-Then.

The Implementation Phase

Now that we've talked about testing in the problem-solving phase, we can turn to testing in the implementation phase. Testing is done here at several points.

www.jbpub.com/C++links

Code Walk-Through. After the code is written, you should go over it line by line to be sure that you've faithfully reproduced the algorithm, a process known as a *code walk-through.* In a team programming situation, you ask other team members to walk through the algorithm and code with you to double-check the design and code.

Execution Trace. You also should take some actual values and hand-calculate what the output should be by doing an *execution trace.* When the program is executed, you can use these same values as input and check the results.

The computer is a very literal device—it does exactly what we tell it to do, which may or may not be what we want it to do. We try to make sure that a program does what we want by tracing the execution of the statements.

We use the nonsense program below to demonstrate the technique. We keep track of the values of the program variables on the right-hand side. Variables with undefined values are indicated with a dash. When a variable is assigned a value, that value is listed in the appropriate column.

	Value of		
Statement	*a*	*b*	*c*
`const int x = 5;`			
`int main()`			
`{`			
`    int a, b, c;`	-	-	-
`    b = 1;`	-	1	-
`    c = x + b;`	-	1	6
`    a = x + 4;`	9	1	6
`    a = c;`	6	1	6
`    b = c;`	6	6	6
`    a = a + b + c;`	18	6	6
`    c = c % x;`	18	6	1
`    c = c * a;`	18	6	18
`    a = a % b;`	0	6	18
`    cout << a << b << c;`	0	6	18
`}`			

Now that we've seen how the technique works, let's apply it to the Notices program. We just list the statement section here, with most of the comments removed to save space. The input data are 9483, 73, 62, 60.

Statement	test1	test2	test3	average	dataOK	studentID
// Get Data						
cout << "Enter a Student ID number "	--	--	--	--	--	--
<< "and three test scores" << endl;						
cin >> studentID >> test1 >> test2 >> test3;	73	62	60	--	--	9483
cout << "Student Number: " << studentID						
<< " Test Scores: " << test1						
<< ", " test2 << ", " << test3 << endl;	73	62	60	--	--	9483
//Test Data						
if (test1 < 0 || test2 < 0 || test3 < 0)	73	62	60	--	--	9483
dataOK = FALSE;						
else						
dataOK = TRUE;	73	62	60	--	true	9483
if (dataOK)	73	62	60	--	true	9483
{						
// Calculate Average						
average = (test1 + test2 + test3) / 3.0;	73	62	60	67.67	true	9483
// Print Message						
cout << "Average score is " << setprecision (2)						
<< average << "--");	73	62	60	67.67	true	9483
if (average >= 60.0)	73	62	60	67.67	true	9483
{						
cout << "Passing";	73	62	60	67.67	true	9483
if (average < 70.0)	73	62	60	67.67	true	9483
cout << " but marginal.";	73	62	60	67.67	true	9483
cout << '.' << endl;	73	62	60	67.67	true	9483
}						
else						
cout << "Failing." << endl;						
}						
else						
cout << "Invalid Data: Score(s) less than zero."						
<< endl;						
return 0;						

The Then branch of the first If statement is not executed for this input data, so we do not fill in any of the variable columns to its right. The same situation occurs with the Else branches in the other If statements. The test data causes only their Then branches to be executed.

We always create columns for all of the variables in a program, even if we know that some stay empty. Why? Because it's possible to encounter an error that refers to an empty variable; having a column for the variable reminds us to check for just such an error.

When a program contains branches, we should retrace its execution with different input data so that each branch is traced at least once. In the next section, we describe how to develop data sets that test each of the program's branches.

Testing Selection Control Structures. To test a program with branches, we have to execute each branch at least once and verify the results. For example, in the Notices program, there are four If-Then-Else statements (see Figure 5-4). We need a series of data sets to test the different branches. For example, we could use the following sets of data for the input values of `test1`, `test2`, and `test3`:

FIGURE 5-4

Branching Structure
for Notices Program

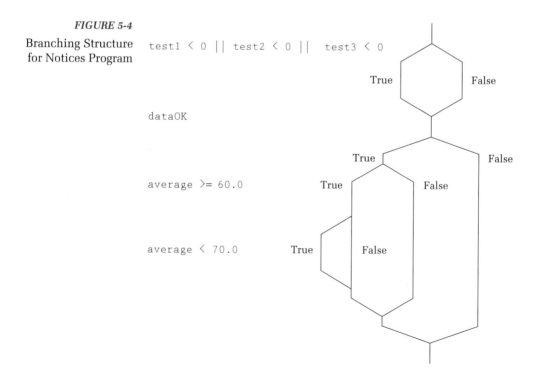

	test1	test2	test3
Set 1	100	100	100
Set 2	60	60	63
Set 3	50	50	50
Set 4	−50	50	50

Figure 5-5 shows the flow of control through the branching structure of the Notices program for each of these data sets. Set 1 is valid and gives an average of 100, which is passing and not marginal. Set 2 is valid and gives an average of 61, which is passing but marginal. Set 3 is valid and gives an average of 50, which is failing. Set 4 has an invalid test grade, which generates an error message.

The approach to testing that we've used here is called *code coverage* because the test data are designed by looking at the code of the program. Another approach to testing, *data coverage*, attempts to test as many allowable data values as possible without regard to the program code. Complete data coverage is impractical for many programs.

Often, testing is a combination of these two strategies. Instead of trying every possible data value, we examine the code and look for ranges of values for which processing is identical. Then we test the values at the boundaries and,

FIGURE 5-5 Flow of Control Through Notices Program for Each of Four Data Sets

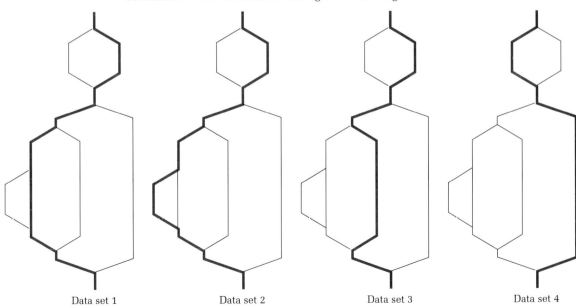

Data set 1   Data set 2   Data set 3   Data set 4

sometimes, a value in the middle of each range. For example, a simple condition, such as

```
alpha < 0
```

divides the integers into two ranges:

INT_MIN through -1
0 through INT_MAX

Thus, we should test the four values INT_MIN, -1, 0, and INT_MAX. A compound condition, such as

```
alpha >= 0 && alpha <= 100
```

divides the integers into three ranges:

INT_MIN through -1
0 through 100
101 through INT_MAX

Thus, we have six values to test.

Conditional branches are only one factor in developing a testing strategy. We consider more of these factors in later chapters.

Tests
Performed
Automatically
During
Compilation
and Execution

Once a program is coded and test data have been prepared, it is ready for compiling. The compiler has two responsibilities: to report any errors and (if there are no errors) to translate the program into object code.

Errors can be syntactic or semantic. The compiler finds syntactic errors. For example, the compiler warns you when reserved words are misspelled, identifiers are undeclared, semicolons are missing, and operand types are mismatched. But it won't find all of your typing errors. If you type > instead of <, you won't get an error message. It's up to you to design test data and carefully check the code to detect semantic errors.

Semantic errors (also called *logic errors*) are mistakes that give you the wrong answer. They are more difficult to locate than syntactic errors and usually surface when a program is executing. C++ detects only the most obvious semantic errors—those that result in an invalid operation (dividing by zero, for example). Although semantic errors sometimes are caused by typing errors, they are more often a product of faulty design.

By walking through the algorithm and the code, tracing the execution of the program, and developing a thorough test strategy, you should be able to avoid, or at least quickly locate, semantic errors in your programs.

Testing and Debugging Hints

1. C++ has three pairs of operators that are similar in appearance but very different in effect: == and =, && and &, and || and |. Double-check all of your logical expressions to be sure you're using the "equals-equals," "and-and," and "or-or" operators.

2. If you use extra parentheses for clarity, be sure that the opening and closing parentheses match up. To verify that parentheses are properly paired, start with the innermost pair and draw a line connecting them. Do the same for the others, working your way out to the outermost pair. For example,

```
if (((total/scores) > 50) && ((total/(scores - 1)) < 100))
```

And here is a quick way to tell whether you have an equal number of opening and closing parentheses. The scheme uses a single number (the "magic number"), whose value initially is 0. Scan the expression from left to right. At each opening parenthesis, add 1 to the magic number; at each closing parenthesis, subtract 1. At the final closing parenthesis, the magic number should be 0. For example,

```
if (((total/scores) > 50) && ((total/(scores - 1)) < 100))
   0   123                2   1    23      4         32      10
```

3. Don't use =< to mean "less than or equal to"; only the symbol <= works. Likewise, => is invalid for "greater than or equal to"; you must use >= for this operation.

4. In an If statement, remember to use a { } pair if the then-clause or else-clause is a sequence of statements. And be sure not to put a semicolon after the right brace.

5. Echo print all input data. This way you know that your input data are what they are supposed to be.

6. Test for bad data. If a data value must be positive, use an If statement to test the value. If the value is negative or 0, an error message should be printed; otherwise processing should continue. For example, the Activity program could have the following statement inserted after the second output statement (the echo print):

```
if (temperature > 120 || temperature < -35)
    cout << "Temperature data is in error." << endl;
else
{
    .
    .
    .
```

This If statement tests the limits of reasonable temperatures and executes the rest of the program only if the data value is reasonable.

7. Take some sample values and try them by hand as we did for the Notices program. (There's more on this in Chapter 6.)

8. If your program reads data from an input file, it should verify that the file was opened successfully. Immediately after the call to the `open` function, an If statement should test the state of the file stream.

9. If your program produces an answer that does not agree with a value you've calculated by hand, try these suggestions:
   a. Redo your arithmetic.
   b. Recheck your input data.
   c. Carefully go over the section of code that does the calculation. If you're in doubt about the order in which the operations are performed, insert clarifying parentheses.
   d. Check for integer overflow. The value of an `int` variable may have exceeded `INT_MAX` in the middle of a calculation. Some systems give an error message when this happens, but most do not.
   e. Check the conditions in branching statements to be sure that the correct branch is taken under all circumstances.

Summary

Using logical expressions is a way of asking questions while a program is running. The program evaluates each logical expression, producing a nonzero value if the expression is true or the value zero if the expression is not true.

The If statement allows you to take different paths through a program based on the value of a logical expression. The If-Then-Else is used to choose between two courses of action; the If-Then is used to choose whether or not to take a particular course of action. The branches of an If-Then or If-Then-Else can be any statement, simple or compound. They can even be another If statement.

The algorithm walk-through requires us to define preconditions and postconditions for each module in an algorithm. Then we have to verify that those assertions are true at the beginning and end of each module. By testing our design in the problem-solving phase, we can eliminate errors that can be more difficult to detect in the implementation phase.

An execution trace is a way of finding program errors once we've entered the implementation phase. It's a good idea to trace a program before you run it, so that you have some sample results against which to check the program's output.

Quick Check

1. Write a C++ expression that compares the variable `letter` to the constant 'Z' and yields `true` if `letter` is less than 'Z'. (pp. 129–130)

2. Write a C++ expression that yields `true` if `letter` is between 'A' and 'Z' inclusive. (pp. 130–132)
3. What form of the If statement would you use to make a C++ program print out "Is a letter" if the value in `letter` is between 'A' and 'Z' inclusive, and print out "Is not a letter" if the value in `letter` is outside that range? (pp. 136–138)
4. What form of the If statement would you use to make a C++ program print out "Is a letter" only if the value in `letter` is between 'A' and 'Z' inclusive? (pp. 139–140)
5. On a telephone, each of the digits 2 through 9 has a segment of the alphabet associated with it. What kind of control structure would you use to decide which segment a given letter falls into and to print out the corresponding digit? (pp. 142–143)
6. What is one postcondition that every program should have? (pp. 151–153)
7. In what phase of the program development process should you carry out an execution trace? (pp. 153–156)
8. You've written a program that prints out the corresponding digit on a phone given a letter of the alphabet. Everything seems to work right except that you can't get the digit '5' to print out; you keep getting the digit '6'. What steps would you take to find and fix this bug? (pp. 156–158)

Answers 1. `letter < 'Z'` 2. `letter >= 'A' && letter <= 'Z'` 3. The If-Then-Else form 4. The If-Then form 5. A nested If statement 6. The user has been notified of invalid data values. 7. The implementation phase 8. Carefully review the section of code that should print out '5'. Check the branching condition and the output statement there. Try some sample values by hand.

Exam Preparation Exercises

1. Given these values for Boolean variables x, y, and z:

   ```
   x = true, y = false, z = true
   ```

   evaluate the following logical expressions. In the blank next to each expression, write a T if the result is `true` or an F if the result is `false`.
   _____ a. `x && y || x && z`
   _____ b. `x || !y) && (!x || z)`
   _____ c. `x || y && z`
   _____ d. `!(x || y) && z`

2. Given these values for variables i, j, p, and q:

   ```
   i = 10, j = 19, p = true, q = false
   ```

   add parentheses (if necessary) to the expressions below so that they evaluate to `true`.
   a. `i == j || p`
   b. `i >= j || i <= j && p`
   c. `!p || p`
   d. `!q && q`

3. Given these values for the `int` variables i, j, m, and n:

i = 6, j = 7, m = 11, n = 11

what is the output of the following code?

```
cout << "Madam";
if (i < j)
    if (m != n)
        cout << "How";
    else
        cout << "Now";
cout << "I'm";
if (i >= m)
    cout << "Cow";
else
    cout << "Adam";
```

4. Given the `int` variables x, y, and z, where x is 3, y is 7, and z is 6, what is the output from each of the following code fragments?

a. ```
if (x <= 3)
        cout << x + y << endl;
    cout << x + y << endl;
```

b. ```
if (x != -1)
        cout << "The value of x is " << x << endl;
    else
        cout << "The value of y is " << y << endl;
```

c. ```
if (x != -1)
    {
        cout << x << endl;
        cout << y << endl;
        cout << z << endl;
    }
    else
        cout << "y" << endl;
        cout << "z" << endl;
```

**5.** Given this code fragment:

```
if (height >= minHeight)
    if (weight >= minWeight)
        cout << "Eligible to serve." << endl;
    else
        cout << "Too light to serve." << endl;
else
    if (weight >= minWeight)
        cout << "Too short to serve." << endl;
    else
        cout << "Too short and too light to serve." << endl;
```
```

  a. What is the output when `height` exceeds `minHeight` and `weight` exceeds `minWeight`?

  b. What is the output when `height` is less than `minHeight` and `weight` is less than `minWeight`?

6. Match each logical expression in the left column with the logical expression in the right column that tests for the same condition.

  _____ a. x < y && y < z   (1) !(x != y) && y == z
  _____ b. x > y && y >= z   (2) !(x <= y || y < z)
  _____ c. x != y || y == z   (3) (y < z || y == z) || x == y
  _____ d. x == y || y <= z   (4) !(x >= y) && !(y >= z)
  _____ e. x == y && y == z   (5) !(x == y && y != z)

7. The following expressions make sense but are invalid according to C++'s rules of syntax. Rewrite them so that they are valid logical expressions. (All the variables are of type `int`.)

  a. x < y <= z

  b. x, y, and z are greater than 0

  c. x is equal to neither y nor z

  d. x is equal to y and z

8. Given these values for Boolean variables x, y, and z:

  x = true, y = true, z = false

  indicate whether each expression is `true` (T) or `false` (F).

  _____ a. !(y || z) || x
  _____ b. z && x && y
  _____ c. ! y || (z || !x)
  _____ d. z || (x && (y || z))
  _____ e. x || x && z

9. For each of the following problems, decide which is more appropriate, an If-Then-Else or an If-Then. Explain your answers.

  a. Students who are candidates for admission to a college submit their SAT scores. If a student's score is equal to or above a certain value, print a letter of acceptance for the student. Otherwise, print a rejection notice.

  b. For employees who work more than 40 hours a week, calculate overtime pay and add it to their regular pay.

  c. In solving a quadratic equation, whenever the value of the discriminant (the quantity under the square root sign) is negative, print out a message noting that the roots are complex (imaginary) numbers.

  d. In a computer-controlled sawmill, if a cross section of a log is greater than certain dimensions, adjust the saw to cut 4-inch by 8-inch beams; otherwise, adjust the saw to cut 2-inch by 4-inch studs.

10. What causes the error message "UNEXPECTED ELSE" when this code fragment is compiled?

```
if (mileage < 24.0)
{
    cout << "Gas ";
    cout << "guzzler.";
};
else
    cout << "Fuel efficient.";
```

11. The following code fragment is supposed to print "Type AB" when Boolean variables typeA and typeB are both true, and print "Type O" when both variables are false. Instead, it prints "Type O" whenever just one of the variables is false. Insert a { } pair to make the code segment work the way it should.

```
if (typeA || typeB)
    if (typeA && typeB)
        cout << "Type AB";
else
    cout << "Type O";
```

12. The nested If structure below has five possible branches depending on the values read into char variables ch1, ch2, and ch3. To test the structure, you need five sets of data, each set using a different branch. Create the five test data sets.

```
cin >> ch1 >> ch2 >> ch3;
if (ch1 == ch2)
    if (ch2 == ch3)
        cout << "All initials are the same." << endl;
    else
        cout << "First two are the same." << endl;
else if (ch2 == ch3)
    cout << "Last two are the same." << endl;
else if (ch1 == ch3)
    cout << "First and last are the same." << endl;
else
    cout << "All initials are different." << endl;
```

a. Test data set 1: ch1 = _____ ch2 = _____ ch3 = _____
b. Test data set 2: ch1 = _____ ch2 = _____ ch3 = _____
c. Test data set 3: ch1 = _____ ch2 = _____ ch3 = _____
d. Test data set 4: ch1 = _____ ch2 = _____ ch3 = _____
e. Test data set 5: ch1 = _____ ch2 = _____ ch3 = _____

13. If x and y are Boolean variables, do the following two expressions test the same condition?

```
x != y
(x || y) && !(x && y)
```

14. The following If condition is made up of three relational expressions:

```
if (i >= 10 && i <= 20 && i != 16)
    j = 4;
```

If `i` contains the value 25 when this If statement is executed, which relational expression(s) will the computer evaluate? (Remember that C++ uses short-circuit evaluation.)

Programming Warm-Up Exercises

1. Declare `eligible` to be a Boolean variable, and assign it the value `true`.
2. Write a statement that sets the Boolean variable `available` to `true` if `numberOrdered` is less than or equal to `numberOnHand` minus `numberReserved`.
3. Write a statement containing a logical expression that assigns `true` to the Boolean variable `isCandidate` if `satScore` is greater than or equal to 1100, `gpa` is not less than 2.5, and `age` is greater than 15. Otherwise, `isCandidate` should be `false`.
4. Given the declarations

   ```
   Boolean leftPage;
   int     pageNumber;
   ```

   write a statement that sets `leftPage` to `true` if `pageNumber` is even. (*Hint:* Consider what the remainders are when you divide different integers by two.)
5. Write an If statement (or a series of If statements) that assigns to the variable `biggest` the greatest value contained in variables `i`, `j`, and `k`. Assume the three values are distinct.
6. Rewrite the following sequence of If-Thens as a single If-Then-Else.

   ```
   if (year % 4 == 0)
       cout << year << " is a leap year." << endl;
   if (year % 4 != 0)
   {
       year = year + 4 - year % 4;
       cout << year << " is the next leap year." << endl;
   }
   ```

7. Simplify the following program segment, taking out unnecessary comparisons. Assume that `age` is an `int` variable.

   ```
   if (age > 64)
       cout << "Senior voter";
   if (age < 18)
       cout << "Under age";
   if (age >= 18 && age < 65)
       cout << "Regular voter";
   ```

8. The following program fragment is supposed to print out the values 25, 60, and 8, in that order. Instead, it prints out 50, 60, and 4. Why?

```
length = 25;
width = 60;
if (length = 50)
    height = 4;
else
    height = 8;
cout << length << ' ' << width << ' ' << height << endl;
```

9. The following C++ program segment is almost unreadable because of the inconsistent indentation and the random placement of left and right braces. Fix the indentation and align the braces properly.

```
// This is a nonsense program
if (a > 0)
if (a < 20)
        {
    cout << "A is in range." << endl;
b = 5;
        }
            else
                    {
cout << "A is too large." << endl;
        b = 3;
}
        else
cout << "A is too small." << endl;
                cout << "All done." << endl;
```

10. Given the `float` variables x1, x2, y1, y2, and m, write a program segment to find the slope of a line through the points (x1, y1) and (x2, y2). Use the formula

$$m = \frac{(y1 - y2)}{(x1 - x2)}$$

to determine the slope of the line. If x1 equals x2, the line is vertical and the slope is undefined. The segment should write the slope with an appropriate label. If the slope is undefined, it should write the message "Slope undefined."

11. Given the `float` variables a, b, c, root1, root2, and discriminant, write a program segment to determine whether the roots of a quadratic polynomial are real or complex (imaginary). If the roots are real, find them and assign them to root1 and root2. If they are complex, write the message "No real roots."

    The formula for the solution to the quadratic equation is

$$\frac{-b \pm \sqrt{b^2 - 4ac}}{2a}$$

The ± means "plus or minus" and indicates that there are two solutions to the equation: one in which the result of the square root is added to −b and one in which the result is subtracted from $-b$. The roots are real if the discriminant (the quantity under the square root sign) is not negative.

12. The following program reads data from an input file without checking to see if the file was opened successfully. Insert statements that will print an error message and terminate the program if the file cannot be opened.

```cpp
#include <iostream.h>
#include <fstream.h>        // For file I/O

int main()
{
    int m;
    int n;
    ifstream info;
    info.open("indata.dat");
    info >> m >> n;
    cout << "The sum of " << m << " and " << n
         << " is " << m + n << endl;
    return 0;
}
```

13. In the Activity program, the `endl` manipulator appears five times, once in each output statement. Show how to eliminate this duplication of code by using `endl` just once after the appropriate message is printed.

14. For the Activity program, insert validation tests to exclude temperatures beyond 125 degrees and below -40 degrees. Provide constructive error messages to the user.

15. How would you modify the prompt in the Activity program so that the user avoids violating the constraints in Question 14?

Programming Problems

1. Using a functional decomposition, write a C++ program that inputs a single letter and prints out the corresponding digit on the telephone. The letters and digits on a telephone are grouped this way:

2 = ABC	4 = GHI	6 = MNO	8 = TUV
3 = DEF	5 = JKL	7 = PRS	9 = WXY

   No digit corresponds to either Q or Z. For these two letters, your program should print a message indicating that they are not used on a telephone.

   The program might operate like this:

```
Enter a single letter, and I will tell you what the corresponding
digit is on the telephone.
R
The digit 7 corresponds to the letter R on the telephone.
```

Here's another example:

```
Enter a single letter, and I will tell you what the corresponding
digit is on the telephone.
Q
There is no digit on the telephone that corresponds to Q.
```

Your program should print a message indicating that there is no matching digit for any nonalphabetic character the user enters. Also, the program should recognize only uppercase letters. Include the lowercase letters with the invalid characters.

Prompt the user with an informative message for the input value, as shown above. The program should echo print the input letter as part of the output.

Use proper indentation, appropriate comments, and meaningful identifiers throughout the program.

2. People who deal with historical dates use a number called the Julian day to calculate the number of days between two events. The Julian day is the number of days that have elapsed since January 1, 4713 B.C. For example, the Julian day for October 16, 1956, is 2435763. There are formulas for computing the Julian day from a given date and vice versa.

One very simple formula computes the day of the week from a given Julian day:

Day of the week = (Julian day + 1) % 7

where % is the C++ remainder operator. This formula gives a result of 0 for Sunday, 1 for Monday, and so on up to 6 for Saturday. For Julian day 2435763, the result is 2 (a Tuesday). Your job is to write a C++ program that inputs a Julian day, computes the day of the week using the formula, and then prints out the name of the day that corresponds to that number. If the maximum `int` value on your machine is small (32767, for instance), use the `long` data type instead of `int`. Be sure to echo print the input data and to use proper indentation and comments.

Your output might look like this:

```
Enter a Julian day number:
2451545
Julian day number 2451545 is a Saturday.
```

3. You can compute the date for any Easter Sunday from 1982 to 2048 as follows (all variables are of type `int`):*

```
a is year % 19
b is year % 4
c is year % 7
d is (19 * a + 24) % 30
e is (2 * b + 4 * c + 6 * d + 5) % 7
Easter Sunday is March (22 + d + e)
```

---

*Notice that this formula can give a date in April.

Write a program that inputs the year and outputs the date (month and day) of Easter Sunday for that year. Echo print the input as part of the output. For example:

```
Enter the year (for example, 1997):
1985
Easter is Sunday, April 7, in 1985.
```

4. The algorithm for computing the date of Easter can be extended easily to work with any year from 1900 to 2099. There are four years, 1954, 1981, 2049, and 2076, for which the algorithm gives a date that is seven days later than it should be. Modify the program for Problem 3 to check for these years and subtract 7 from the day of the month. This correction does not cause the month to change. Be sure to change the documentation for the program to reflect its broadened capabilities.

5. Write a C++ program that calculates and prints the diameter, the circumference, or the area of a circle, given the radius. The program inputs two data items. The first is a character—'D' (for diameter), 'C' (for circumference), or 'A' (for area)—to indicate the calculation needed. The next data value is a floating point number with two digits after the decimal point indicating the radius of the particular circle.

The program should echo print the input data. The output should be appropriately labeled and formatted to two decimal places. For example, if the input is

```
A 6.75
```

your program should print something like this:

```
The area of a circle with radius 6.75 is 143.14.
```

Here are the formulas you'll need:

Diameter = $2r$
Circumference = $2\pi r$
Area of a circle = πr^2

where r is the radius. Use 3.14159265 for π.

6 *Looping*

GOALS

- To be able to construct syntactically correct While loops

- To be able to construct count-controlled loops with a While statement

- To be able to construct event-controlled loops with a While statement

- To be able to use the end-of-file condition to control the input of data

- To be able to use flags to control the execution of a While statement

- To be able to construct counting loops with a While statement

- To be able to construct summing loops with a While statement

- To be able to choose the correct type of loop for a given problem

- To be able to construct nested While loops

- To be able to choose data sets that test a looping program comprehensively

loop

A control structure that causes a sequence of statements to be executed repeatedly

In Chapter 5, we saw how to select different statements for execution using the If statement. A **loop** executes the same statement (simple or compound) over and over, as long as a condition or set of conditions is met.

In this chapter, we discuss different types of loops and how they are constructed using the While statement. We also discuss *nested loops* (loops that contain other loops).

The While Statement

The While statement, like the If statement, tests a condition. Here is the syntax template for the While statement:

WhileStatement

```
while ( Expression )
   Statement
```

and this is an example of one:

```
while (inputVal != 25)
    cin >> inputVal;
```

The While statement is a looping control structure. The statement to be executed each time through the loop is called the *body* of the loop. In the example above, the body is the statement that reads in a value for `inputVal`.

Just like the condition in an If statement, the condition in a While statement can be an expression of any simple data type. Nearly always, it is a logical (Boolean) expression. The While statement says, "If the value of the expression is nonzero (true), execute the body and then go back and test the expression again. If the expression's value is zero (false), skip the body." So the loop body is executed over and over as long as the expression is true when it is tested. When the expression is false, the program skips the body and execution continues at the statement immediately following the loop. Of course, if the expression is false to begin with, the body is not even executed. Figure 6-1 shows the flow of control of the While statement, where Statement1 is the body of the loop and Statement2 is the statement following the loop.

The body of a loop can be a compound statement (block), which allows us to execute any group of statements repeatedly. Most often you'll use While loops in the following form:

```
while (Expression)
{
    .
    .
    .
}
```

FIGURE 6-1

While Statement
Flow of Control

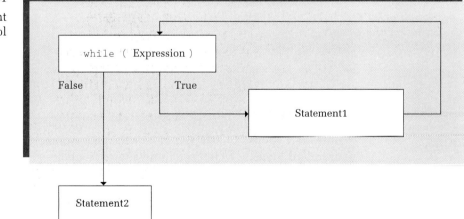

In this structure, if the expression is true, the entire sequence of statements in the block is executed, and then the expression is checked again. If it is still true, the statements are executed again. The cycle continues until the expression becomes false.

Phases of Loop Execution

loop entry
The point at which the flow of control reaches the first statement inside a loop

iteration
An individual pass through, or repetition of, the body of a loop

loop test
The point at which the While expression is evaluated and the decision is made either to begin a new iteration or skip to the statement immediately following the loop

termination condition
The condition that causes a loop to be exited

loop exit
The point at which the repetition of the loop body ends and control passes to the first statement following the loop

The body of a loop is executed in several phases:

- The moment that the flow of control reaches the first statement inside the loop body is the **loop entry.**
- Each time the body of a loop is executed, a pass is made through the loop. This pass is called an **iteration.**
- Before each iteration, control is transferred to the **loop test** at the beginning of the loop.
- When the last iteration is complete and the flow of control has passed to the first statement following the loop, the program has exited the loop. The condition that causes a loop to be exited is the **termination condition.** In the case of a While loop, the **loop exit** occurs when the expression is zero (`false`) at the point that the loop test is performed.

Notice that even though the termination condition may become satisfied midway through the execution of the loop, the current iteration is completed before the computer checks the While expression again. The loop exits only if the termination condition is still satisfied when the loop test is performed.

The concept of looping is fundamental to programming. In this chapter, we spend some time looking at typical types of loops and ways of implementing them with the While statement. These looping situations come up again and again when you are analyzing problems and doing functional decompositions.

Loops Using the While Statement

count-controlled loop
A loop that executes a specified number of times

event-controlled loop
A loop that terminates when something happens inside the loop body to signal that the loop should be exited

In solving problems, you will come across two major types of loops: **count-controlled loops,** which repeat a specified number of times, and **event-controlled loops,** which repeat until something happens within the loop.

If you are making an angel food cake and the recipe reads, "Beat the mixture 300 strokes," you are executing a count-controlled loop. If you are making a pie crust and the recipe reads, "Cut with a pastry blender until the mixture resembles coarse meal," you are executing an event-controlled loop; you don't know ahead of time the exact number of loop iterations.

***Count-
Controlled
Loops***

A count-controlled loop uses a variable we call the *loop control variable* in the loop test. Before we enter a count-controlled loop, we have to *initialize* (set the initial value of) the loop control variable and then test it. Then, as part of each iteration of the loop, we must *increment* (increase by 1) the loop control variable. Here's an example:

```
loopCount = 1;              // Initialization
while (loopCount <= 10)     // Test
{
         .
         .                  // Repeated actions
         .
    loopCount++;            // Incrementation
}
```

Here `loopCount` is the loop control variable. It is set to 1 before loop entry. The While statement tests the expression

```
loopCount <= 10
```

and executes the loop body as long as the expression is `true`. The dots inside the compound statement represent a sequence of statements to be repeated. The last statement in the loop body increments `loopCount`. Variables that are used this way are called *counters*. In our example, `loopCount` is incremented with each iteration of the loop—we use it to count the iterations. The loop control variable of a count-controlled loop is always a counter.

When designing loops, it is the programmer's responsibility to see that the condition to be tested is set correctly (initialized) before the While statement begins. The programmer also must make sure the condition changes within the loop so that it becomes `false` at some point; otherwise, the loop is never exited.

A loop that does not exit is called an *infinite loop* because, in theory, the loop executes forever. In the code above, omitting the incrementation of `loopCount` at the bottom of the loop would lead to an infinite loop; the While expression would always be `true` because the value of `loopCount` is forever 1. If your program goes on running for much longer than you expect it to, chances are that you've created an infinite loop. You may have to issue an operating system command to stop the program.

***Event-
Controlled
Loops***

In event-controlled loops, the termination condition depends on some event occurring while the loop body is executing. We'll look at two kinds of event-controlled loops here: sentinel-controlled and end-of-file-controlled.

Sentinel-Controlled Loops.   Loops often are used to read in and process long lists of data. Each time the loop body is executed, a new piece of data is read and processed. Often a special data value, called a *sentinel* or *trailer value,* is used to signal the program that there are no more data to be processed. Looping continues as long as the data value read is *not* the sentinel. In other words, reading the sentinel value is the event that controls the looping process.

A sentinel value must be something that never shows up in the normal input to a program. For example, if a program reads calendar dates, we could use February 31 as a sentinel value:

```
cin >> month >> day;                    // Get a date--priming read
while ( !(month == 2 && day == 31) )
{
        .
        .
        .                               // Process it
    cin >> month >> day;                // Get the next date
}
```

This segment reads the first data set prior to entering the loop (we refer to this as a *priming read*); if it is not the sentinel, it gets processed. At the end of the loop, the next data set is read in, and we go back to the beginning of the loop. If the new data set is not the sentinel, it gets processed just like the first. When the sentinel value is read, the While expression becomes `false`, and the loop exits (*without* processing the sentinel).

Many times the problem dictates the value of the sentinel. For example, if the problem does not allow data values of 0, then the sentinel value should be 0. When you process `char` data, one line of input at a time, the newline character (`'\n'`) often serves as the sentinel. Here's a code segment that reads and prints all of the characters on an input line (`inChar` is of type `char`):

```
cin.get(inChar);                        // Get first character
while (inChar != '\n')
{
    cout << inChar;                     // Echo it
    cin.get(inChar);                    // Get next character
}
```

(Notice that for this particular task we must use the `get` function, not the `>>` operator, to input a character. Remember that the `>>` operator skips whitespace characters—including blanks and newlines—to find the next data value in the input stream. In this example, we want to input *every* character, even a blank and especially the newline character.)

What happens if you forget to enter the sentinel value? In an interactive program, the loop executes again, prompting for input. At that point, you can enter the sentinel value. If the input to the program is from a file, once all the data have been read from the file, the loop body is executed again. However, there aren't any data left—because the computer has reached the end of the file—so the file stream enters the fail state. In the next section, we describe a way to use the end-of-file situation as an alternative to using a sentinel.

Before we go on, we mention an issue that is related not to the design of loops but to C++ language usage. In Chapter 5, we talked about the common mistake of using the assignment operator (=) instead of the relational operator (==) in an If condition. This same mistake can happen when you write While statements. See what happens when we use the wrong operator in the previous example:

```cpp
cin >> dataValue >> sentinel;
while (sentinel = 1)            // Whoops
{
    .
    .
    .

cin >> dataValue >> sentinel;
}
```

This mistake creates an infinite loop. The While expression is now an assignment expression, not a relational expression. The expression's value is 1 (interpreted by the computer as `true`), and its side effect is to store the value 1 into `sentinel`, replacing the value that was just input into the variable. Because the While expression is always `true`, the loop never stops.

End-of-File-Controlled Loops. After a program has read the last piece of data from an input file, the computer is at the end of the file (EOF, for short). At this moment, the stream state is all right. But if we try to input even one more data value, the stream goes into the fail state. We can use this fact to our advantage. To write a loop that inputs an unknown number of data items, we can use the failure of the input stream as a "sentinel."

In Chapter 5, we described how to test the state of an I/O stream. In a logical expression, we use the name of the stream as though it were a Boolean variable:

```cpp
if (inFile)
    .
    .
    .
```

In a test like this, the result is nonzero (`true`) if the most recent I/O operation succeeded, or zero (`false`) if it failed. In a While statement, testing the state of a stream works the same way. Suppose we have a data file containing integer values. If `inData` is the name of the file stream in our program, here's a loop that reads and echoes all of the data values in the file:

```
inData >> intVal;               // Get first value
while (inData)                  // While the input succeeded . . .
{
    cout << intVal << endl;     // Echo it
    inData >> intVal;           // Get next value
}
```

Let's trace this code, assuming there are three values in the file: 10, 20, and 30. The priming read inputs the value 10. The While condition is `true` because the input succeeded. Therefore, the computer executes the loop body. First the body prints out the value 10, and then it inputs the second data value, 20. Looping back to the loop test, the expression `inData` is `true` because the input succeeded. The body executes again, printing the value 20 and reading the value 30 from the file. Looping back to the test, the expression is `true`. Even though we are at the end of the file, the stream state is still okay—the previous input operation succeeded. The body executes a third time, printing the value 30 and executing the input statement. This time, the input statement fails; we're trying to read beyond the end of the file. The stream `inData` enters the fail state. Looping back to the loop test, the value of the expression is zero (`false`) and we exit the loop.

When we write EOF-controlled loops like the one above, we are expecting that end-of-file is the reason for stream failure. But keep in mind that *any* input error causes stream failure. The above loop terminates, for example, if input fails because of invalid characters in the input data. This fact emphasizes again the importance of echo printing. It helps us verify that all the data were read correctly before EOF was encountered.

Is it possible to use an EOF-controlled loop when we read from the standard input device (via the `cin` stream) instead of a data file? On many systems, yes. With the UNIX operating system, you can type Ctrl/D (that is, you hold down the Ctrl key and tap the D key) to signify end-of-file during interactive input. With the MS-DOS operating system, the end-of-file keystrokes are Ctrl/Z. Other systems use similar keystrokes.

Looping Subtasks   We have been looking at ways to use loops to affect the flow of control in programs. Looping by itself does nothing. The loop body must perform a task in order for the loop to accomplish something. In this section, we look at three tasks—counting, summing, and keeping track of a previous value—that often are used in loops.

Counting. A common task in a loop is to keep track of the number of times the loop has been executed. For example, the program fragment below reads and counts input characters until it comes to a period. (inChar is of type char; count is of type int.) The loop in this example has a counter variable; but the loop is not a count-controlled loop because the variable is not being used as a loop control variable.

```
count = 0;                  // Initialize counter
cin.get(inChar);            // Read the first character
while (inChar != '.')
{
    count++;                // Increment counter
    cin.get(inChar);        // Get the next character
}
```

After the loop is finished, count contains one less than the number of characters read. That is, it counts the number of characters up to, but not including, the sentinel value (the period). Notice that if a period is the first character, the loop body is not entered and count contains a zero, as it should. We use a priming read here because the loop is sentinel-controlled.

The counter variable in this example is called an **iteration counter** because its value equals the number of iterations through the loop. According to our definition, the loop control variable of a count-controlled loop is an iteration counter. However, as you've just seen, not all iteration counters are loop control variables.

iteration counter
A counter variable that is incremented with each iteration of a loop

Summing. Another common looping task is to sum a set of data values. Notice in the example below that the summing operation is written the same way, regardless of how the loop is controlled.

```
sum = 0;                    // Initialize the sum
count = 1;
while (count <= 10)
{
    cin >> number;          // Input a value
    sum = sum + number;     // Add the value to sum
    count++;
}
```

We initialize sum to 0 before the loop starts so that the first time the loop body executes, the statement

```
sum = sum + number;
```

adds the current value of sum (0) to number to form the new value of sum. After the entire code fragment has executed, sum contains the total of the 10 values read, count contains 11, and number contains the last value read.

Keeping Track of a Previous Value. Sometimes we want to remember the previous value of a variable. Suppose we want to write a program that counts the number of not-equal operators (!=) in a file that contains a C++ program. We can do so by simply counting the number of times an exclamation mark (!) followed by an equal sign (=) appears in the input. One way in which to do this is to read the input file one character at a time, keeping track of the two most recent characters, the current value and the previous value. In each iteration of the loop, the old current value becomes the previous value and a new current value is read. When EOF is reached, the loop is finished. Here's a loop that counts not-equal operators this way:

```
count = 0;                    // Initialize counter
inFile.get(prevChar);         // Initialize previous value
inFile.get(currChar);         // Initialize current value
while (inFile)                // While previous input succeeded . . .
{
    if (currChar == '=' &&    // Test for event
        prevChar == '!')
        count++;              // Increment counter
    prevChar = currChar;      // Replace previous value
                              //    with current value
    inFile.get(currChar);     // Get next value
}
cout << count << " != operators were found." << endl;
```

The counter in this example is an **event counter;** it is initialized to 0 and incremented only when a certain event occurrs. The counter in the previous example was an *iteration counter;* it was initialized to 1 and incremented during each iteration of the loop.

Study this loop carefully. It's going to come in handy. There are many times when you must keep track of the last value read in addition to the current value.

How to Design Loops

It's one thing to understand how a loop works when you look at it and something else again to design a loop that solves a given problem. In this section, we look at how to design loops. We divide the design process into two tasks: designing the control flow and designing the processing within the loop. We break each task into three phases: the task itself, initialization, and update. It's also important to specify the state of the program when it exits the loop.

There are seven different points to consider in designing a loop:

1. What is the condition that ends the loop?
2. How should the condition be initialized?
3. How should the condition be updated?
4. What is the process being repeated?
5. How should the process be initialized?
6. How should the process be updated?
7. What is the state of the program on exiting the loop?

We use these questions as a checklist. The first three help us design the parts of the loop that control its execution. The next three help us design the processing within the loop. The last question reminds us to make sure that the loop exits in an appropriate manner.

Designing the Flow of Control   The most important step in loop design is deciding what should make the loop stop. So here is our first question:

- What is the condition that ends the loop?

This question is answered through examination of the problem statement. For example:

Key Phrase in Problem Statement	Termination Condition
"Sum 365 temperatures"	The loop ends when a counter reaches 365 (count-controlled loop).
"Process all the data in the file"	The loop ends when EOF occurs (EOF-controlled loop).

Now we are ready to ask the next two questions:

- How should the condition be initialized?
- How should the condition be updated?

The answers depend on the type of termination condition.

For count-controlled loops that use an iteration counter, these are the answers to the questions:

- Initialize the iteration counter to 1.
- Increment the iteration counter at the end of each iteration.

When a loop uses an event counter, these are the answers to the questions:

- Initialize the event counter to 0.
- Increment the event counter each time the event occurs.

For sentinel-controlled loop, we answer our questions this way:

- Open the file, if necessary, and input a value before entering the loop (priming read).
- Input a new value for processing at the end of each iteration.

EOF-controlled loops require the same initialization as sentinel-controlled loops. Updating the loop condition means the loop must keep reading data.

Designing the Process Within the Loop

Next, we fill in the details of the process. In designing the process, we first must decide what we want a single iteration to do.

- What is the process being repeated?

To answer this question, we have to take another look at the problem statement. The definition of the problem may require the process to sum up data values or to keep a count of data values that satisfy some test. For example:

Count the number of integers in the file howMany.

This statement tells us that the process to be repeated is a counting operation.

We can now design the parts of the process that are necessary for it to be repeated correctly. We add steps to take into account the fact that the loop executes more than once. This part of the design typically involves initializing certain variables before the loop and then reinitializing or updating them before each subsequent iteration.

- How should the process be initialized?
- How should the process be updated?

For example, if the process within a loop requires that several different counts and sums be performed, each must have its own statements to initialize variables, increment counting variables, or add values to sums. Just deal with each counting or summing operation by itself—that is, first write the initialization statement, and then write the incrementing or summing statement. After you've done this for one operation, you go on to the next.

The Loop Exit

Now we have to consider the consequences of our design and double-check its validity.

- What is the state of the program on exiting the loop?

For example, suppose we've used an event counter and later processing depends on the number of events. It's important to be sure (with an algorithm walk-through) that the value left in the counter is the exact number of events—that it is not off by 1.

Designing correct loops depends as much on experience as it does on the application of design methodology. At this point, you may want to read through the programming example at the end of the chapter to see how the loop design process is applied to a real problem.

Nested Logic

www.jbpub.com/C++links

In Chapter 5, we described nested If statements. It's also possible to nest While statements. Both While and If statements contain statements and are themselves statements. So the body of a While statement or the branch of an If statement can contain other While and If statements. By nesting, we can create complex control structures.

Suppose we want to extend our code for counting commas on one line, repeating it for all the lines in a file. We put an EOF-controlled loop around it:

```
cin.get(inChar);              // Initialize outer loop
while (cin)                   // Outer loop test
{
    commaCount = 0;           // Initialize inner loop
                              //  (Priming read is taken care of
                              //   by outer loop's priming read)
    while (inChar != '\n')    // Inner loop test
    {
        if (inChar == ',')
            commaCount++;
        cin.get(inChar);      // Update inner termination condition
    }
    cout << commaCount << endl;
    cin.get(inChar);          // Update outer termination condition
}
```

In this code, notice that we have omitted the priming read for the inner loop. The priming read for the outer loop has already "primed the pump." It would be a mistake to include another priming read just before the inner loop; the character read by the outer priming read would be destroyed before we could test it.

Let's examine the general pattern of a simple nested loop:

```
Initialize outer loop
while (Outer loop condition)
{
    .
    .
    .
    Initialize inner loop
    while (Inner loop condition)
    {
        Inner loop processing and update
    }
    .
    .
    .
    Outer loop update
}
```

Notice that each loop has its own initialization, test, and update. The dots represent places where processing may take place in the outer loop. It's possible for an outer loop to do no processing other than to execute the inner loop repeatedly. On the other hand, the inner loop might be just a small part of the processing done by the outer loop; there could be many statements preceding or following the inner loop.

Let's look at another example. For nested count-controlled loops, the pattern looks like this (where `outCount` is the counter for the outer loop, `inCount` is the counter for the inner loop, and `limit1` and `limit2` are the number of times each loop should be executed):

```
outCount = 1;                     // Initialize outer loop counter
while (outCount <= limit1)
{
    .
    .
    .
    inCount = 1;                  // Initialize inner loop counter
    while (inCount <= limit2)
    {
        .
        .
        .
        inCount++;                // Increment inner loop counter
    }
    .
    .
    .
    outCount++;                   // Increment outer loop counter
}
```

Here, both the inner and outer loops are count-controlled loops, but the pattern can be used with any combination of loops.

Designing Nested Loops   To design a nested loop, we begin with the outer loop. The process being repeated includes the nested loop as one of its steps. Because that step is more complex than a single statement, our functional decomposition design methodology tells us to make it a separate module. We can come back to it later and design the nested loop just as we would any other loop.

Of course, nested loops themselves can contain nested loops (called *doubly nested loops*), which can contain nested loops (*triply nested loops*), and so on. You can use this design process for any number of levels of nesting. The trick is to defer details using the functional decomposition methodology—that is, focus on the outermost loop first, and treat each new level of nested loop as a module within the loop that contains it.

It's also possible for the process within a loop to include more than one loop. For example, here's an algorithm that reads and prints people's names from a file, omitting the middle name in the output:

Read and print first name (ends with a comma)
WHILE NOT EOF
    Read and discard characters from middle name (ends with a comma)
    Read and print last name (ends at newline)
    Output newline
    Read and print first name (ends with a comma)

The steps for reading the first name, middle name, and last name require us to design three separate loops. All of these loops are sentinel-controlled.

This kind of complex control structure would be difficult to read if written out in full. There are simply too many variables, conditions, and steps to remember at one time. In the next two chapters, we examine the control structure that allows us to break programs down into more manageable chunks—the subprogram.

As a final note about nested loops, it is important to keep in mind that the time it takes the computer to execute a deeply nested loop will be proportional to the product of the number of iterations at each level of the nested structure. For example, if we nest loops that count from 1 to 1000 four levels deep, the innermost loop body will execute 1,000,000,000,000 times. Such a loop would take several hours to execute on a typical computer.

PROGRAMMING EXAMPLE

Average Income by Gender

Problem: You've been hired by a law firm that is working on a sex discrimination case. Your firm has obtained a file of income data. As a first pass in the analysis of the data, you've been asked to compute the average income for females and the average income for males.

Input: A file, incFile, of floating point salary amounts, with one amount per line. Each amount is preceded by a character ('F' for female, 'M' for male). This code is the first character on each input line and is followed by a blank, which separates the code from the amount.

Output:

All the input data (echo print)
The number of females and their average income
The number of males and their average income

PROGRAMMING EXAMPLE cont'd

Discussion: The problem breaks down into three main steps. First, we have to process the data, counting and summing the salary amounts for each sex. Next, we compute the averages. Finally, we have to print the calculated results.

The first step is the most difficult. It involves a loop with several subtasks. We'll use our checklist of questions to develop these subtasks in detail.

1. *What is the condition that ends the loop?* The termination condition is EOF on the file `incFile`. It leads to the pseudocode While statement

   WHILE NOT EOF on incFile

2. *How should the condition be initialized?* We must open the file for input, and a priming read must take place.
3. *How should the condition be updated?* We must input a new data line with a gender code and amount at the end of each iteration. Here's the resulting algorithm:

   Open incFile for input (and verify the attempt)
   Read sex and amount from incFile
   WHILE NOT EOF on incFile

       .
       .
       . (Process being repeated)
       Read sex and amount from incFile

4. *What is the process being repeated?* From our knowledge of how to compute an average, we know that we have to count the number of amounts and divide this number into the sum of the amounts. Because we have to do this separately for females and males, the process consists of four parts: counting the females and summing their incomes, and then counting the males and summing their incomes. We develop each of these in turn.
5. *How should the process be initialized?* `femaleCount` and `femaleSum` should be set to zero. `maleCount` and `maleSum` also should be set to zero.
6. *How should the process be updated?* When a female income is input, `femaleCount` is incremented, and the income is added to `femaleSum`. Otherwise, an income is assumed to be for a male, so `maleCount` is incremented, and the amount is added to `maleSum`.
7. *What is the state of the program on exiting the loop?* The file stream `incFile` is in the fail state; `femaleCount` contains the number of input values preceded by 'F'; `femaleSum` contains the sum of the values preceded by 'F'; `maleCount` contains the number of values not preceded by 'F'; and `maleSum` holds the sum of those values.

PROGRAMMING EXAMPLE cont'd

From the description of how the process is updated, we can see that the loop must contain an If-Then-Else structure, with one branch for female incomes and the other for male incomes. Each branch must increment the correct event counter and add the income amount to the correct total. After the loop has exited, we have enough information to compute and print the averages, dividing each total by the corresponding count.

Assumptions: There is at least one male and one female among all the data sets. The only gender codes in the file are 'M' and 'F'—any other codes are counted as 'M'. (This last assumption invalidates the results if there are any illegal codes in the data.

Now we can write the program:

```
//*******************************************************************
// Incomes program
// This program reads a file of income amounts classified by
// gender and computes the average income for each gender
//*******************************************************************
#include <iostream.h>
#include <iomanip.h>    // For setprecision()
#include <fstream.h>    // For file I/O

int main()
{
    char      sex;              // Coded 'F' = female, 'M' = male
    int       femaleCount;     // Number of female income amounts
    int       maleCount;       // Number of male income amounts
    float     amount;          // Amount of income for a person
    float     femaleSum;       // Total of female income amounts
    float     maleSum;         // Total of male income amounts
    float     femaleAverage;   // Average female income
    float     maleAverage;     // Average male income
    ifstream  incFile;         // File of income amounts

    cout.setf(ios::fixed, ios::floatfield);   // Set up floating pt.
    cout.setf(ios::showpoint);                //    output format
    cout << setprecision(2);

    // Separately count females and males, and sum incomes

    // Initialize ending condition
    incFile.open("incfile.dat");              // Open input file
    if ( !incFile )                           //   and verify attempt
```

PROGRAMMING EXAMPLE cont'd

```
    {
        cout << "** Can't open input file **" << endl;
        return 1;
    }
    incFile >> sex >> amount;                    // Perform priming read

    // Initialize process

    femaleCount = 0;
    femaleSum = 0.0;
    maleCount = 0;
    maleSum = 0.0;

    while (incFile)
    {
        // Update process

        cout << "Sex: " << sex << " Amount: " << amount << endl;
        if (sex == 'F')
        {
            femaleCount++;
            femaleSum = femaleSum + amount;
        }
        else
        {
            maleCount++;
            maleSum = maleSum + amount;
        }

        // Update ending condition

        incFile >> sex >> amount;
    }

    // Compute average incomes

    femaleAverage = femaleSum / float(femaleCount);
    maleAverage = maleSum / float(maleCount);

    // Output results

    cout << "For " << femaleCount << " females, the average "
        << "income is " << femaleAverage << endl;
    cout << "For " << maleCount << " males, the average "
        << "income is " << maleAverage << endl;
    return 0;
}
```

PROGRAMMING EXAMPLE cont'd

Testing: With an EOF-controlled loop, the obvious test cases are a file with data and an empty file. We should test input values of both 'F' and 'M' for the gender, and try some typical data (so we can compare the results with our hand-calculated values) and some atypical data (to see how the process behaves). An atypical data set for testing a counting operation is an empty file, which should result in a count of zero. Any other result for the count indicates an error. For a summing operation, atypical data might include negative or zero values.

The Incomes program is not designed to handle empty files or negative income values. An empty file causes both `femaleCount` and `maleCount` to equal zero at the end of the loop. Although this is correct, the statements that compute average income cause the program to crash because they divide by zero. And a negative income would be treated like any other value, even though it is probably a mistake.

To correct these problems, we should insert If statements to test for the error conditions at the appropriate points in the program. When an error is detected, the program should print an error message instead of carrying out the usual computation.

Testing and Debugging

Loop Testing Strategy

www.jbpub.com/C++links

Even if a loop has been properly designed and verified, it is still important to test it rigorously, because there is always the chance of an error creeping in during the implementation phase. Because loops allow us to input many data sets in one run, and because there is the potential for each iteration to be affected by preceding ones, the test data for a looping program are usually more extensive than for a program with just sequential or branching statements. To test a loop thoroughly, we have to check for the proper execution of both a single iteration and multiple iterations.

Remember that a loop has seven parts (corresponding to the seven questions in our checklist). A test strategy must test each part. Although all seven parts aren't implemented separately in every loop, the checklist reminds us that some loop operations may serve multiple purposes, each of which should be tested. For example, the incrementing statement in a count-controlled loop may be updating both the process and the ending condition. So it's important to verify that it performs both actions properly with respect to the rest of the loop.

To test a loop, we try to devise data sets that could cause the variables to go out of range or leave the files in improper states that violate either the loop post-condition or the postcondition of the module containing the loop.

It's also good practice to test a loop for four special cases: (1) when the loop is skipped entirely, (2) when the loop body is executed just once, (3) when the loop executes some normal number of times, and (4) when the loop fails to exit.

Statements following a loop often depend on its processing. If a loop can be skipped, those statements may not execute correctly. If it's possible to execute a single iteration of a loop, the results can show whether the body performs correctly in the absence of the effects of previous iterations, which can be very helpful when you're trying to isolate the source of an error. Obviously, it's important to test a loop under normal conditions, with a wide variety of inputs. If possible, you should test the loop with real data in addition to mock data sets. Count-controlled loops should be tested to be sure they execute exactly the right number of times. And finally, if there is any chance that a loop might never exit, your test data should try to make that happen.

Testing and Debugging Hints

1. Plan your test data carefully to test all sections of a program.
2. Beware of infinite loops, where the expression in the While statement never becomes `false`. The symptom: The program doesn't stop.

    If you have created an infinite loop, check your logic and the syntax of your loops. Be sure there's no semicolon immediately after the right parenthesis of the While condition:

    ```
    while (Expression);
    Statement
    ```

    This causes an infinite loop in most cases; the compiler thinks the loop body is the null statement (the do-nothing statement terminated by a semicolon). In a count-controlled loop, make sure the loop control variable is incremented within the loop. In a flag-controlled loop, make sure the flag eventually changes.

    As always, watch for the = versus == problem in While conditions as well as in If conditions. The line

    ```
    while (someVar = 5)    // Wrong—should be ==
    ```

    produces an infinite loop. The value of the expression is always 5, which is interpreted as `true`.
3. Check the loop termination condition carefully, and be sure that something in the loop causes it to be met. Watch closely for values that cause one iteration too many or too few (the "off-by-1" syndrome).
4. Remember to use the `get` function rather than the extraction operator in loops that are controlled by detection of a newline character.
5. Perform an algorithm walk-through to verify that all of the appropriate preconditions and postconditions occur in the right places.

6. Trace the execution of the loop by hand with a code walk-through. Simulate the first few passes and the last few passes very carefully to see how the loop really behaves.
7. Use a *debugger* if your system provides one. A debugger is a program that runs your program in "slow motion," allowing you to execute one instruction at a time and to examine the contents of variables as they change. If you haven't already, check to see if a debugger is available on your system.
8. If all else fails, use *debug output statements*—output statements inserted into a program to help debug it. They output a message that indicates the flow of execution in the program or reports the values of variables at certain points in the program.

   For example, if you want to know the value of variable beta at a certain point in a program, you could insert this statement:

```
cout << "beta = " << beta << endl;
```

   If this output statement is in a loop, you will get as many values of beta as there are iterations of the body of the loop.

   After you have debugged your program, you can remove the debug output statements or just precede them with // so that they'll be treated as comments. (This practice is referred to as *commenting out* a piece of code.) You can remove the double slashes if you need to use the statements again.
9. An ounce of prevention is worth a pound of debugging. Use the checklist questions to design your loop correctly at the outset. It may seem like extra work, but it pays off in the long run.

Summary

The While statement is a looping construct that allows the program to repeat a statement as long as an expression is true. When the expression becomes false, the statement is skipped, and execution continues with the first statement following the loop.

With the While statement you can construct several types of loops that you will use again and again. These types of loops fall into two categories: count-controlled loops and event-controlled loops.

In a count-controlled loop, the loop body is repeated a specified number of times. Event-controlled loops continue executing until something inside the body signals that the looping process should stop. Event-controlled loops include those that test for a sentinel value in the data, end-of-file, or a change in a flag variable.

Sentinel-controlled loops are input loops that use a special data value as a signal to stop reading. EOF-controlled loops are loops that continue to input (and process) data values until there is no more data. In a flag-controlled loop, you must set a flag before the While, test it in the expression, and change it somewhere in the body of the loop.

A counter is a variable that is used for counting. It may be the loop control variable in a count-controlled loop, an iteration counter in a counting loop, or an event counter that counts the number of times a particular condition occurs in a loop. Summing is a looping operation that keeps a running total of certain values.

When you design a loop, there are seven points to consider: How the termination condition is initialized, tested, and updated; how the process in the loop is initialized, performed, and updated; and the state of the program upon loop exit. By answering the checklist questions, you can bring each of these points into focus.

To design a nested loop structure, begin with the outermost loop. When you get to where the inner loop must appear, make it a separate module and come back to its design later.

The process of testing a loop is based on the answers to the checklist questions and the patterns it might encounter (for example, executing a single iteration, multiple iterations, an infinite number of iterations, or no iterations at all).

Quick Check

1. Write the first line of a While statement that loops until the value of Boolean variable `done` becomes `true`. (pp. 170–171)
2. What are the four parts of a count-controlled loop? (p. 173)
3. Should you use a priming read with an EOF-controlled loop? (pp. 175–176)
4. What is the difference between a counting operation in a loop and a summing operation in a loop? (pp. 177–178)
5. What is the difference between a loop control variable and an event counter? (pp. 177–178)
6. What kind of loop would you use in a program that reads the closing price of a stock for each day of the week? (pp. 179–180)
7. How would you extend the loop in Question 7 to make it read prices for 52 weeks? (pp. 181–183)
8. How would you test a program that is supposed to count the number of females and the number of males in a data set? (Assume that females are coded with 'F' in the data; males, with 'M'.) (pp. 187–189)

Answers   1. `while ( !done )`   2. The process being repeated, plus initializing, testing, and incrementing the loop control variable.   3. Yes.   4. A counting operation increments by a fixed value with each iteration of the loop; a summing operation adds unknown values to the total.   5. A loop control variable controls the loop; an event counter simply counts certain events during execution of the loop. 6. Because there are five days in a business week, you would use a count-controlled loop that runs from 1 to 5.   7. Nest the original loop inside a count-controlled loop that runs from 1 to 52.   8. Run the program with data sets that have a different number of females and males, only females, only males, illegal values (other characters), and an empty input file.

Exam Preparation Exercises

1. In one or two sentences, explain the difference between loops and branches.
2. What does the following loop print out? (`number` is of type `int`.)

```
number = 1;
while (number < 11)
{
    number++;
    cout << number << endl;
}
```

3. By rearranging the order of the statements (don't change the way they are written), make the loop in Exercise 2 print the numbers from 1 through 10.
4. When the following code is executed, how many iterations of the loop are performed?

```
number = 2;
done = false;
while ( !done )
{
    number = number * 2;
    if (number > 64)
        done = true;
}
```

5. What is the output of this nested loop structure?

```
i = 4;
while (i >= 1)
{
    j = 2;
    while (j >= 1)
    {
        cout << j << ' ';
        j--;
    }
    cout << i << endl;
    i--;
}
```

6. The following code segment is supposed to write out the even numbers between 1 and 15. (n is an `int` variable.) It has two flaws in it.

```
n = 2;
while (n != 15)
{
    n = n + 2;
    cout << n << ' ';
}
```

a. What is the output of the code as written?

b. Correct the code so that it works as intended.

7. The following code segment is supposed to copy one line from the standard input device to the standard output device.

```
cin.get(inChar);
while (inChar != '\n')
{
    cin.get(inChar);
    cout << inChar;
}
```

a. What is the output if the input line consists of the characters ABCDE?

b. Rewrite the code so that it works properly.

8. Does the following program segment need any priming reads? If not, explain why. If so, add the input statement(s) in the proper place. (letter is of type char.)

```
while (cin)
{
    while (letter != '\n')
    {
        cout << letter;
        cin.get(letter);
    }
    cout << endl;
    cout << "Another line read . . . " << endl;
    cin.get(letter);
}
```

9. What sentinel value would you choose for a program that reads telephone numbers as integers?

10. Consider this program:

```
#include <iostream.h>

typedef int Boolean;
const Boolean true = 1;
const Boolean false = 0;
```

```
const int LIMIT = 8;

int main()
{
    int     sum;
    int     i;
    int     number;
    Boolean finished;

    sum = 0;
    i = 1;
    finished = false;
    while (i <= LIMIT && !finished)
    {
        cin >> number;
        if (number > 0)
            sum = sum + number;
        else if (number == 0)
            finished = true;
        i++;
    }
    cout << "End of test. " << sum << ' ' << number << endl;
    return 0;
}
```

and these data values:

```
5 6 -3 7 -4 0 5 8 9
```

    a. What are the contents of sum and number after exit from the loop?
    b. Do the data fully test the program? Explain your answer.
11. Here is a simple count-controlled loop:

```
count = 1;
while (count < 20)
    count++;
```

    a. List three ways of changing the loop so that it executes 20 times instead of 19.
    b. Which of those changes makes the value of count range from 1 through 21?
12. What is the output of the following program segment? (All variables are of type int.)

```
i = 1;
while (i <= 5)
```

```
{
    sum = 0;
    j = 1;
    while (j <= i)
    {
        sum = sum + j;
        j++;
    }
    cout << sum << ' ';
    i++;
}
```

Programming Warm-Up Exercises

1. Write a program segment that sets a Boolean variable `dangerous` to `true` and stops reading in data if `pressure` (a `float` variable being read in) exceeds 510.0. Use `dangerous` as a flag to control the loop.
2. Write a program segment that counts the number of times the integer 28 occurs in a file of 100 integers.
3. Write a nested loop code segment that produces this output:

```
1
1 2
1 2 3
1 2 3 4
```

4. Write a program segment that reads a file of student scores for a class (any size) and finds the class average.
5. a. Write a statement that prints the following headings in the format shown.

```
        Sales

Week1   Week2   Week3
```

   b. Write a statement that lines values up under each week's heading. The values are stored in the `int` variables `week1`, `week2`, and `week3`. The last digit of each number should fall under the 1, 2, or 3 of its column heading.
6. Write a program segment that reads in integers and then counts and prints out the number of positive integers and the number of negative integers. If a value is zero, it should not be counted. The process should continue until end-of-file occurs.
7. Write a program segment that adds up the even integers from 16 through 26, inclusive.

8. Write a program segment that prints out the sequence of all the hour and minute combinations in a day, starting with 1:00 A.M. and ending with 12:59 A.M.

9. Rewrite the code segment for Exercise 8 so that it prints the times in 10-minute intervals, arranged as a table with six columns and 24 rows.

10. Change program Incomes (page 185) so that it
    a. prints an error message when a negative income value is input and then goes on processing any remaining data. The erroneous data should not be included in any of the calculations. Thoroughly test the modified program with your own data sets.
    b. does not crash when there are no males in the input file or no females (or the file is empty). However, it should print an appropriate error message. Test the revised program with your own data sets.
    c. rejects data sets that are coded with a letter other than 'F' or 'M' and prints an error message before continuing to process the remaining data.

11. Develop a thorough set of test data for program Incomes as modified in Exercise 10.

Programming Problems

1. Write a functional decomposition and a C++ program that inputs an integer and a character. The output should be a diamond composed of the character and extending the width specified by the integer. For example, if the integer is 11 and the character is an asterisk (*), the diamond would look like this:

```
          *
        * * *
       * * * * *
      * * * * * * *
     * * * * * * * * *
    * * * * * * * * * * *
     * * * * * * * * *
      * * * * * * *
       * * * * *
        * * *
          *
```

If the input integer is an even number, it should be increased to the next odd number. Use meaningful variable names, proper indentation, appropriate comments, and good prompting messages.

2. Write a functional decomposition and a C++ program that inputs an integer larger than 1 and calculates the sum of the squares from 1 to that integer. For example, if the integer equals 4, the sum of the squares is 30 (1 + 4 + 9 + 16). The output should be the value of the integer and the sum, properly labeled. A negative input value signals the end of the data.

3. Using functional decomposition, write a program that prints out the approximate number of words in a file of text. For our purposes, this is the same as the number of gaps following words. A *gap* is defined as one or more spaces in a row, so a sequence of spaces counts as just one gap. The newline character also counts as a gap. Anything other than a space or newline is considered to be part of a word. For example, there are 19 words in the following hint, according to our definition. (*Hint:* Only count a space as a gap if the previous character read is something other than a space.) The program should echo print the data.

Use meaningful variable names, proper indentation, and appropriate comments. Thoroughly test the program with your own data sets.

7 *Functions*

GOALS

- To be able to write a program that uses functions to reflect the structure of your functional decomposition
- To be able to write a module of your own design as a void function
- To be able to define a void function to do a specified task
- To be able to distinguish between value and reference parameters
- To be able to use actual and formal parameters correctly.
- To be able to write a program that uses multiple calls to a single function
- To be able to define and use local variables correctly

- To be able to do the following tasks, given a functional decomposition of a problem:

  Determine what the formal parameter list should be for each module

  Determine which formal parameters should be reference parameters and which should be value parameters

  Code the program correctly

You have been using C++ functions since we introduced standard library routines such as `sqrt` and `abs` in Chapter 3. So far, we have not considered how the programmer can create his or her own functions other than `main`. That is the topic of this chapter and the next.

You might wonder why we waited until now to look at user-defined subprograms. The reason, and the major purpose for writing our own functions and void functions is to help organize and simplify large and complex programs. Until now, our programs have been relatively small and simple, so we didn't need to write subprograms. Now, we are ready to introduce subprograms so we can begin writing larger and more complex programs.

Functional Decomposition with Void Functions

www.jbpub.com/C++links

Recall from Chapter 3 that there are two kinds of subprograms that the C++ language works with: value-returning functions and void functions. In this chapter, we concentrate exclusively on creating our own void functions. In Chapter 8, we examine how to write value-returning functions.

From the early chapters on, you have been designing your programs as collections of modules. Many of these modules are naturally implemented as *user-defined void functions.* We now look at how to turn the modules in your algorithms into user-defined void functions.

Writing Modules as Void Functions

It is quite simple to turn a module into a void function in C++. Basically, a void function looks like the `main` function except that the function heading uses `void` rather than `int` as the data type. Additionally, a void function does not use a statement like

```
return 0;
```

as does `main`. A void function does not return a function value to its caller.

Let's look at a program using void functions. A friend of yours is returning from a long trip, and you want to write a program that prints the following message:

```
* * * * * * * * * * * * * *
* * * * * * * * * * * * * *
 Welcome Home!
* * * * * * * * * * * * * *
* * * * * * * * * * * * * *
* * * * * * * * * * * * * *
* * * * * * * * * * * * * *
```

Here is a design for the program, following the style we introduced in the Programming Example in Chapter 4.

Main   *Level 0*

```
Print two lines of asterisks
Print "Welcome Home!"
Print four lines of asterisks
```

Print 2 Lines   *Level 1*

```
Print "**************"
Print "**************"
```

Print 4 Lines

```
Print "**************"
Print "**************"
Print "**************"
Print "**************"
```

If we write the two Level 1 modules as void functions, the `main` function is simply

```
int main()
{
    Print2Lines();
    cout << " Welcome Home!" << endl;
    Print4Lines();
    return 0;
}
```

Notice how similar this code is to the main module of our functional decomposition. It contains two function calls—one to a function named `Print2Lines` and another to a function named `Print4Lines`. Both of these functions are *parameterless*—that is, they have no parameters within the parentheses.

The following code should look familiar to you, but look carefully at the function heading.

```
void Print2Lines()                         // Function heading
{
    cout << "****************" << endl;
    cout << "****************" << endl;
}
```

This segment is a *function definition.* A function definition is the code that extends from the function heading to the end of the block that is the body of the function. The function heading begins with the word `void`, signalling the compiler that this is not a value-returning function. The body of the function executes some ordinary statements and does *not* finish with a return statement to return a function value.

Now look again at the function heading. Following the function name is an empty parameter list—that is, there is nothing between the parentheses. Later we'll see what goes inside the parentheses if a function uses parameters. Now let's put main and the other two functions together to form a complete program.

```cpp
//*******************************************************************
// Welcome program
// This program prints a "Welcome Home" message
//*******************************************************************
#include <iostream.h>

void Print2Lines();                         // Function prototypes
void Print4Lines();

int main()
{
    Print2Lines();                          // Function call
    cout << " Welcome Home!" << endl;
    Print4Lines();                          // Function call
    return 0;
}

//*******************************************************************

void Print2Lines()                          // Function heading

// This function prints two lines of asterisks

{
    cout << "****************" << endl;
    cout << "****************" << endl;
}

//*******************************************************************

void Print4Lines()                          // Function heading

// This function prints four lines of asterisks

{
    cout << "****************" << endl;
    cout << "****************" << endl;
    cout << "****************" << endl;
    cout << "****************" << endl;
}
```

C++ function definitions can appear in any order. We could have chosen to place the main function last instead of first, but C++ programmers typically put main first and any supporting functions after it.

In the Welcome program, the two statements just before the main function are called *function prototypes.* These declarations are necessary because of the C++ rule requiring you to declare an identifier before you can use it. Our main function uses the identifiers Print2Lines and Print4Lines, but the definitions of those functions don't appear until later. We must supply the function prototypes to inform the compiler in advance that Print2Lines and Print4Lines are the names of functions, that they do not return function values, and that they have no parameters. We say more about function prototypes later in the chapter.

Because the Welcome program is so simple to begin with, it may seem more complicated with its modules written as functions. However, it is clear that it much more closely resembles our functional decomposition. This is especially true of the main function. As our programs grow to include many modules nested several levels deep, the ability to read a program in the same manner as a functional decomposition greatly aids in the development and debugging process.

Syntax and Semantics of Void Functions

Function Call (Invocation)

To call (or invoke) a void function, we use its name as a statement, with the parameters in parentheses following the name. A **function call** in a program results in the execution of the body of the called function. This is the syntax template of a function call to a void function:

function call (to a void function)
A statement that transfers control to a void function. In C++, this statement is the name of the function, followed by a list of actual parameters

actual parameter
A variable or expression listed in a call to a function

formal parameter
A variable declared in a function heading

FunctionCall (to a void function)

```
FunctionName ( ActualParameterList );
```

The parameters in the call to a function are the **actual parameters.** The parameters listed in the function heading are the **formal parameters.** (Some programmers use the terms *actual argument* and *formal argument* instead of *actual parameter* and *formal parameter*. Others use the term *argument* in place of *actual parameter,* and *parameter* in place of *formal parameter.*)

According to the syntax template for a function call, the parameter list is optional. A function is not required to have parameters. However, as the syntax template also shows, the parentheses are required even if the parameter list is empty.

If there are two or more parameters in the parameter list, you must separate them with commas. Here is the syntax template for ActualParameterList:

ActualParameterList

```
Expression , Expression  . . .
```

When a function call is executed, the actual parameters are passed to the formal parameters according to their positions, left to right, and then control transfers to the first executable statement in the function body. When the last statement in the function has executed, control returns to the point from which the function was called.

Function Declarations and Definitions

In C++, you must declare every identifier before it can be used. In the case of functions, a function's declaration must physically precede any function call.

A function declaration announces to the compiler the name of the function, the data type of the function's return value (either `void` or a data type like `int` or `float`), and the data types of the parameters it uses. The Welcome program shows a total of three function declarations. The first declaration (the statement labeled "Function prototype") does not include the body of the function. The remaining two declarations—for `main` and `PrintLines`—include bodies for the functions.

function prototype
A function declaration without the body of the function

In C++ terminology, a function declaration that omits the body is called a **function prototype,** and a declaration that does include the body is a **function definition.** Note that all definitions are declarations, but not all declarations are definitions.

function definition
A function declaration that includes the body of the function

Function Prototypes.   We have said that the definition of the `main` function usually appears first in a program, followed by the definitions of all other functions. To satisfy the requirement that identifiers be declared before they are used, C++ programmers typically place all function prototypes near the top of the program, before the definition of `main`.

A function prototype (known as a *forward declaration* in some languages) specifies in advance the data type of the function value to be returned (or the word `void`) and the data types of the parameters. A prototype for a void function has the following form:

FunctionPrototype (for a void function)

```
void FunctionName ( FormalParameterList ) ;
```

As you can see in the syntax template, no body is included for the function, and a semicolon terminates the declaration. The formal parameter list is optional and has the form

FormalParameterList (in a function prototype)

DataType**&** VariableName , DataType**&** VariableName ...

The ampersand (&) attached to the name of a data type is optional and has a special significance that we cover later in the chapter.

In a function prototype, the formal parameter list must specify the data types of the parameters, but their names are optional. You could write either

```
void DoSomething( int, float );
```

or

```
void DoSomething( int velocity, float angle );
```

It's useful for documentation purposes to supply names for the parameters, but the compiler ignores them.

Function Definitions.   You learned in Chapter 2 that a function definition consists of two parts: the function heading and the function body, which is syntactically a block (compound statement). Here's the syntax template for a function definition, specifically for a void function:

FunctionDefinition (for a void function)

```
void FunctionName ( FormalParameterList )
{
    Statement
        .
        .
        .
}
```

Notice that the function heading does *not* end in a semicolon the way a function prototype does. It is a common syntax error to put a semicolon at the end of the line.

The syntax of the parameter list differs slightly from that of a function prototype in that you *must* specify the names of all the formal parameters. Also, it's our style preference (but not a language requirement) to declare each formal parameter on a separate line:

FormalParameterList (in a function definition)

```
DataType& VariableName ,
DataType& VariableName
         .
         .
         .
```

Local Variables

local variable
A variable declared within a block and not accessible outside of that block

Because a function body is a block, any function—not only the `main` function—can include variable declarations within its body. These variables are **local variables** because they are accessible only within the block in which they are declared. As far as the calling code is concerned, they don't exist. If you tried to print the contents of a local variable from another function, a compile-time error such as "UNDECLARED IDENTIFIER" would occur.

In contrast to local variables, variables declared outside of all the functions in a program are called *global variables.* We return to the topic of global variables in Chapter 8.

Local variables occupy memory space only while the function is executing. At the moment the function is called, memory space is created for its local variables. When the function returns, its local variables are destroyed.* Therefore, every time the function is called, its local variables start out with their values undefined. Because every call to a function is independent of every other call to that same function, you must initialize the local variables within the function itself. And because local variables are destroyed when the function returns, you cannot use them to store values between calls to the function.

The following code segment illustrates each of the parts of the function declaration and calling mechanism that we have discussed.

---

*We'll see an exception to this rule in the next chapter.

```
#include <iostream.h>

void TryThis( int, int, float );    // Function prototype

int main()                          // main definition
{
    int   int1;                     // Variables local to main
    int   int2;
    float someFloat;
    .
    .
    .

    TryThis(int1, int2, someFloat); // Function call with three
                                    //   actual parameters
    .
    .
    .
}
void TryThis( int   param1,         // Function definition with
              int   param2,         //   three formal parameters
              float param3 )
{
    int   i;                        // Variables local to TryThis
    float x;
    .
    .
    .
}
```

The Return Statement   The main function uses the statement

```
return 0;
```

to return the value 0 (or 1 or some other value) to its caller, the operating system. Every value-returning function must return its function value this way.

A void function does not return a function value. Control returns from the function when it "falls off" the end of the body—that is, after the final statement has executed.

Alternatively, there is a second form of the `return` statement. It looks like this:

```
return;
```

This statement is valid *only* for void functions. It can appear anywhere in the body of the function; it causes control to exit the function immediately and return to the caller.

■ *Naming Void Functions*

When you choose a name for a void function, keep in mind how calls to it will look. A call is written as a statement; therefore, it should sound like an action. Try to choose a name that is a verb or has a verb as part of it. For example, the verb Print *in the function name makes the following call sound like an action:*

```
PrintLines(3);
```

Header Files From the very beginning we have been using `#include` directives such as:

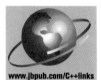

www.jbpub.com/C++links

```
#include <iostream.h>
#include <math.h>       // For sqrt() and fabs()
#include <fstream.h>    // For file I/O
#include <limits.h>     // For INT_MAX and INT_MIN
```

Exactly what are in these header files?

It turns out that there is nothing magical about header files. Their contents are just a series of C++ declarations. There are declarations of named constants such as `INT_MAX` and `INT_MIN`, and stream variables like `cin` and `cout`. But most of the items in a header file are function prototypes.

Suppose that your program needs to use the library function `sqrt` in a statement like this:

```
y = sqrt(x);
```

Every identifier must be declared before it can be used. If you forget to `#include` the header file `math.h`, the compiler gives you an "UNDECLARED IDENTIFIER" error message. The file `math.h` contains function prototypes for `sqrt` and all of the other math-oriented library functions. With this header file included in your program, the compiler not only knows that the identifier `sqrt` is the name of a function but it also can verify that your function call is correct with respect to the number of parameters and their data types.

Header files save you the trouble of specifying all of the library function prototypes yourself at the beginning of your program. With just one line—the #include directive—you cause the preprocessor to go out and find the header file and insert the prototypes into your program.

Parameters

value parameter
A formal parameter that receives a copy of the contents of the corresponding actual parameter

reference parameter
A formal parameter that receives the location (memory address) of the caller's actual parameter

When a function is executed, it uses the actual parameters given to it in the function call. How is this done? The answer to this question depends on the nature of the formal parameters. C++ supports two kinds of formal parameters: **value parameters** and **reference parameters.** With a value parameter, which is declared without an ampersand (&) at the end of the data type name, the function receives a copy of the actual parameter's value. With a reference parameter, which is declared by adding an ampersand to the data type name, the function receives the location (memory address) of the actual parameter. Before we examine in detail the difference between these two kinds of parameters, let's look at an example of a function heading with a mixture of reference and value parameter declarations.

```
void Example( int& param1,    // A reference parameter
              int param2,     // A value parameter
              float param3 )  // Another value parameter
```

With simple data types—int, char, float, and so on—a value parameter is the default (assumed) kind of parameter. In other words, if you don't do anything special (add an ampersand), a parameter is assumed to be a value parameter. To specify a reference parameter, you have to go out of your way to do something extra (attach an ampersand).

The following table summarizes the different kinds of parameters that we've seen.

Kind of Parameter	Usage
Actual parameter	Appears in a function *call*. The corresponding formal parameter may be either a reference or a value parameter.
Formal value parameter	Appears in a function *heading*. Receives a *copy* of the value stored in the corresponding actual parameter.
Formal reference parameter	Appears in a function *heading*. Receives the *address* of the corresponding actual parameter.

There must be the same number of actual parameters in a function call as there are formal parameters in the function heading.* Also, each actual parameter should have the same data type as the formal parameter in the same position. Notice how each formal parameter in the following example is matched to the actual parameter in the same position (the data type of each actual parameter is what you would assume from its name):

Function heading: `void ShowMatch(float num1,    int num2,   char letter)`

Function call: `ShowMatch(floatVariable, intVariable, charVariable);`

If the matched parameters are not of the same data type, implicit type coercion takes place. For example, if a formal parameter is of type `int`, an actual parameter that is a `float` expression is coerced to an `int` value before it is passed to the function. As usual in C++, you can avoid unintended type coercion by using an explicit type cast or, better yet, by not mixing data types at all.

Let's look at both kinds of parameters, starting with value parameters.

Value Parameters

Because value parameters are passed copies of their actual parameters, anything that has a value may be passed to a value parameter. This includes constants, variables, and even arbitrarily complicated expressions. (The expression is simply evaluated and a copy of the result is sent to the corresponding value parameter.)

Because a value parameter does not receive the location of the actual parameter, the actual parameter cannot be directly accessed or changed. When a function returns, the contents of any value parameters are destroyed, along with the contents of the local variables. The difference between value parameters and local variables is that the values of local variables are undefined when a function starts to execute, whereas value parameters are automatically initialized to the values of the corresponding actual parameters.

Because the contents of value parameters are destroyed when the function returns, they cannot be used to return information to the calling code. What if we *do* want to return information by modifying the actual parameters? We must use the second kind of parameter available in C++: reference parameters. Let's look at these now.

Reference Parameters

A reference parameter is one that you declare by attaching an ampersand to the name of its data type. It is called a reference parameter because the called function can refer to the corresponding actual parameter directly. Specifically, the function is allowed to inspect *and modify* the caller's actual parameter.

---

*This statement is not the whole truth. C++ has a special language feature—*default parameters*—that lets you call a function with fewer actual parameters than formal parameters. We do not cover default parameters in this book.

When a function is invoked using a reference parameter, it is the *location* (memory address) of the actual parameter, not its value, that is passed to the function. There is only one copy of the information, and it is used by both the caller and the called function. When a function is called, the actual parameter and formal parameter become synonyms for the same location in memory. Whatever value is left by the called function in this location is the value that the caller will find there. Therefore, you must be careful using a formal reference parameter because any change made to it affects the actual parameter in the calling code.

Only a variable can be passed as an actual parameter to a reference parameter because a function can assign a new value to the actual parameter. (In contrast, remember that an arbitrarily complicated expression can be passed to a value parameter.) Suppose that we have a function with the following heading:

```
void DoThis( float val,    // Value parameter
             int&  count ) // Reference parameter
```

Then the following function calls are all valid.

```
DoThis(someFloat, someInt);
DoThis(9.83, intCounter);
DoThis(4.9 * sqrt(y), myInt);
```

In the DoThis function, the first parameter is a value parameter, so any expression is allowed as the actual parameter. The second parameter is a reference parameter, so the actual parameter *must* be a variable name. The statement

```
DoThis(y, 3);
```

generates a compile-time error because the second parameter isn't a variable name.

There is another important difference between value and reference parameters when it comes to matching actual parameters with formal parameters. With value parameters, we said that implicit type coercion occurs if the matched parameters have different data types (the value of the actual parameter is coerced to the data type of the formal parameter). With reference parameters, if the matched parameters have different data types, a curious thing happens. C++ copies the value of the actual parameter into a temporary variable of the correct type and passes the address of the *temporary variable* to the formal parameter. When the function returns, the temporary variable is discarded. Any changes that you expected the function to make to your actual parameter were not made at all. To avoid this unpleasant result, always verify that the actual parameter has exactly the same data type as the formal parameter.

The following table summarizes the appropriate forms of actual parameters.

Formal Parameter	Actual Parameter
Value	A variable, constant, or arbitrary expression (type coercion may take place)
Reference	A variable only, of exactly the same data type as the formal parameter

Finally, it is up to the programmer to make sure that the formal and actual parameter lists match up semantically as well as syntactically. Similarly, if a function has two formal parameters of the same data type, you must be careful that the actual parameters are in the right order. If they are in the wrong order, no syntax error will result, but the answers will be wrong.

■ Parameter-Passing Mechanisms

There are three major ways of passing parameters to and from subprograms. C++ supports only two of these mechanisms; however, it's useful to know about all three in case you have occasion to use them in another language.

C++ reference parameters employ a mechanism called pass-by-address or pass-by-location. A memory address is passed to the function. Another name for this is pass-by-reference because the function can refer directly to the actual parameter.

C++ value parameters are an example of pass-by-value. The function receives a copy of the value of the actual parameter. Pass-by-value can be less efficient than pass-by-address because the value of a parameter may occupy many memory locations (as we see in Chapter 11), whereas an address usually occupies only a single location. For the simple data types int, char, and float, the efficiency of either mechanism is about the same.

A third method of passing parameters is called pass-by-name. The actual parameter is passed to the function as a character string that must be interpreted by special run-time support software (called a thunk) supplied by the compiler. Pass-by-name is the least efficient of the three parameter-passing mechanisms and is supported by the ALGOL and LISP programming languages, but not by C++.

There are two different ways of matching actual parameters with formal parameters, although C++ supports only one of them. Most programming languages, C++ among them, match actual and formal parameters by their relative positions in the two parameter lists. This is called positional matching, relative matching, or implicit matching. A few languages, such as Ada, also support explicit or named matching. In explicit matching, the actual parameter list specifies the name of the formal parameter to be associated with each actual parameter.

Explicit matching allows actual parameters to be written in any order in the function call. The real advantage is that each call documents precisely which values are being passed to which formal parameters.

Designing Functions

We've looked at some examples of functions and defined the syntax of function prototypes and function definitions. But how do we design functions? First, we need to be more specific about what functions do. We've said that they allow us to organize our programs more like our functional decompositions, but what really is the advantage of doing that?

The body of a function is like any other segment of code, except that it is contained in a separate block within the program. Isolating a segment of code in a separate block means that its implementation details can be "hidden" from view. As long as you know how to call a function and what its purpose is, you can use it without knowing how it actually works. For example, you don't know how the code for a library function like sqrt is written (its implementation is hidden from view), yet you still can use it effectively.

The specification of what a function does and how it is invoked defines its **interface** (see Figure 7-1). By hiding a module implementation, or **encapsulating** the module, we can make changes to it without changing the main function, as long as the interface remains the same. For example, you might rewrite the body of a function using a more efficient algorithm.

Encapsulation is what we do in the functional decomposition process when we postpone the solution of a difficult subproblem. We write down its purpose and what information it takes and returns, and then we write the rest of our design as if the subproblem already had been solved. We could hand this interface specification to someone else, and that person could develop a function for us that solves the subproblem. We needn't be concerned about how it works, as long as it conforms to the interface specification. Interfaces and encapsulation are the basis for *team programming,* in which a group of programmers work together to solve a large problem.

Thus, designing a function can (and should) be divided into two tasks: designing the interface and designing the implementation. We already know how to design an implementation—it is a segment of code that corresponds to an

www.jbpub.com/C++links

interface
A shared boundary that permits independent systems to meet and act on or communicate with each other. Also, the formal description of the purpose of a subprogram and the mechanism for communicating with it

encapsulation
Hiding a module implementation in a separate block with a formally specified interface

FIGURE 7-1

Function Interface (Visible) and Implementation (Hidden)

Heading: `void PrintActivity ( int temp )`
Precondition: `temp` is a temperature value in a valid range
Postcondition: A message has been printed indicating an appropriate activity given temperature `temp`

Implementation

algorithm. To design the interface, we focus on the *what*, not the *how*. We must define the behavior of the function (what it does) and the mechanism for communicating with it.

You already know how to specify formally the behavior of a function. Because a function corresponds to a module, its behavior is defined by the preconditions and postconditions of the module. All that remains is to define the mechanism for communicating with the function. To do so, make a list of the following items:

1. *Incoming values* that the function receives from the caller
2. *Outgoing values* that the function produces and returns to the caller
3. *Incoming/outgoing values*—values the caller has that the function changes (receives and returns)

Decide which identifiers inside the module match the values in this list. These identifiers become the variables in the formal parameter list for the function. Then the formal parameters are declared in the function heading. All other variables that the function needs are local and must be declared within the body of the function. This process may be repeated for all the modules at each level.

Let's look more closely at designing the interface. First we examine function preconditions and postconditions. After that, we consider in more detail the notion of incoming, outgoing, and incoming/outgoing parameters.

Writing Assertions as Program Comments   We have been writing module preconditions and postconditions as informal, English-language assertions. From now on, we include preconditions and postconditions as comments to document the interfaces of C++ functions. Here's an example:

```
void PrintAverage( float sum,
                   int   count )

// Precondition:
//     sum is assigned  &&  count > 0
// Postcondition:
//     The average sum/count has been output on one line

{
    cout << "Average is " << sum / float(count) << endl;
}
```

The precondition is an assertion describing everything that the function requires to be true at the moment the caller invokes the function. The postcondition describes the state of the program at the moment the function finishes executing.

You can think of the preconditions and postconditions as a contract. The contract states that if the preconditions are true at function entry, then the postconditions must be true at function exit. The *caller* is responsible for ensuring the preconditions, and the *function code* must ensure the postconditions. If the caller fails to satisfy its part of the contract (the preconditions), the contract is off; the function cannot guarantee that the postconditions will be true.

Above, the precondition warns the caller to make sure that `sum` has been assigned a meaningful value and to be sure that `count` is positive. If this precondition is true, the function guarantees it will satisfy the postcondition. If `count` isn't positive when `PrintAverage` is invoked, the effect of the function is undefined. (For example, if `count` equals zero, the postcondition surely isn't satisfied—the program crashes!)

Sometimes the caller doesn't need to satisfy any precondition before calling a function. In this case, the precondition can be written as the value TRUE or simply omitted. In the following example, no precondition is necessary:

```
void Get2Ints( int& int1,
               int& int2 )

// Postcondition:
//     User has been prompted to enter two integers
//   && int1 == first input value
//   && int2 == second input value

{
    cout << "Please enter two integers: ";
    cin >> int1 >> int2;
}
```

In assertions written as C++ comments, we use either `&&` or AND to denote the logical AND operator; either `||` or OR to denote a logical OR; either `!` or NOT to denote a logical NOT; and `==` to denote "equals." (Notice that we do *not* use `=` to denote "equals." Even when we write program comments, we want to keep C++'s `==` operator distinct from the assignment operator.)

There is one final notation we use when we express assertions as program comments. Preconditions implicitly refer to values of variables at the moment the function is invoked. Postconditions implicitly refer to values at the moment the function returns. But sometimes you need to write a postcondition that refers to parameter values that existed at the moment the function was invoked. To signify "at the time of entry to the function," we attach the symbols `@entry` to the end of the variable name. The following code segment is an example of the use of this notation. The `Swap` function exchanges, or swaps, the values of its two parameters.

```
void Swap( int& firstInt,
           int& secondInt )

// Precondition:
//     firstInt and secondInt are assigned
// Postcondition:
//     firstInt == secondInt@entry
// && secondInt == firstInt@entry

{
    int temporaryInt;
    temporaryInt = firstInt;
    firstInt = secondInt;
    secondInt = temporaryInt;
}
```

Documenting the Direction of Data Flow

Another helpful piece of documentation in a function interface is the direction of **data flow** for each parameter in the parameter list. Data flow is the flow of information between the function and its caller. We said earlier that each parameter can be classified as an *incoming* parameter, an *outgoing* parameter, or an *incoming/outgoing* parameter. (Some people refer to these as *input* parameters, *output* parameters, and *input/output* parameters.)

For an incoming parameter, the direction of data flow is one-way—into the function. The function inspects and uses the current value of the parameter but does not modify it. In the function heading, we attach the comment

data flow
The flow of information from the calling code to a function and from the function back to the calling code

```
/* in */
```

to the declaration of the formal parameter. (Remember that C++ comments, in the form that encloses a comment between /* and */, allow us to embed a comment within a line.) Here is the PrintAverage function with comments added to the formal parameter declarations:

```
void PrintAverage( /* in */ float sum,
                   /* in */ int   count )
// Precondition:
//     sum is assigned  &&  count > 0
// Postcondition:
//     The average sum/count has been output on one line

{
    cout << "Average is " << sum / float(count) << endl;
}
```

Pass-by-value is appropriate for each parameter that is incoming only. As you can see in the function body, `PrintAverage` does not modify the values of the parameters `sum` and `count`. It merely uses their current values. The direction of data flow is one-way—into the function.

The data flow for an outgoing parameter is one-way—out of the function. The function produces a new value for the parameter without using the old value in any way. The comment `/* out */` identifies an outgoing parameter. Here we've added comments to the `Get2Ints` function heading:

```
void Get2Ints( /* out */ int& int1,
               /* out */ int& int2 )
```

Pass-by-reference must be used for an outgoing parameter. If you look back at the body of `Get2Ints`, you'll see that the function stores new values into the two variables (by means of the input statement), replacing whatever values they originally contained.

Finally, the data flow for an incoming/outgoing parameter is two-way—into and out of the function. The function uses the old value and also produces a new value for the parameter. We use `/* inout */` to document this two-way direction of data flow. Here is an example of a function that uses two parameters, one of them incoming only and the other one incoming/outgoing:

```
void Calc( /* in */    int  alpha,
           /* inout */ int& beta  )

// Precondition:
//     alpha and beta are assigned
// Postcondition
//     beta == beta@entry * 7 - alpha

{
    beta = beta * 7 - alpha;
}
```

This function first inspects the incoming value of `beta` so that it can evaluate the expression to the right of the equal sign. Then it stores a new value into `beta` by using the assignment operation. The data flow for `beta` is therefore considered a two-way flow of information. Pass-by-value is appropriate for `alpha` (it's incoming only), but pass-by-reference is required for `beta` (it's an incoming/outgoing parameter).

■ *Formatting Function Headings*

*From here on, we follow a specific style when coding our function head-ings. Comments appear next to the formal parameters to explain how each parameter is used. Also, embedded comments indicate which of the three data flow categories each parameter belongs to (*in, out, *or* inout*).*

```
void Print( /* in */    float val,   // Value to be printed
            /* inout */ int& count ) // Number of lines printed
                                     //  so far
```

We use comments in the form of rows of asterisks (or dashes or some other character) before and after a function to make the function stand out from the surrounding code. Each function also has its own block of in-troductory comments, just like those at the start of a program, as well as its precondition and postcondition.

It's important to put as much care into documenting each function as you would into the documentation at the beginning of a program.

The following table summarizes the correspondence between a parameter's data flow and the appropriate parameter-passing mechanism.

Data Flow for a Parameter	*Parameter-Passing Mechanism*
Incoming	Pass-by-value
Outgoing	Pass-by-reference
Incoming/outgoing	Pass-by-reference

There are exceptions to the guidelines in this table. C++ requires that I/O stream variables be passed by reference because of the way streams and files are implemented. We encounter one more exception in Chapter 11.

PROGRAMMING EXAMPLE

Comparison of Furniture-Store Sales

Problem: A new regional sales manager for the Chippendale Furniture Stores
has just come into town. She wants to see a monthly, department-by-department
comparison, in the form of bar graphs, of the two Chippendale stores in town.
The daily sales for each department are kept in each store's accounting files.
Data on each store are stored in the following form:

Department ID number
Number of business days for the department
Daily sales for day 1
Daily sales for day 2
.
.
.
Daily sales for last day in period
Department ID number
Number of business days for the department
Daily sales for day 1
.
.
.

The bar graph to be printed is of the following form:

```
Bar Graph Comparing Departments of Store#1 and Store#2

Store Sales in 1,000s of dollars
    #   0          5         10        15        20        25
        |.........|.........|.........|.........|.........|

        Dept 1030
    1   * * * * * * * * * * * * * * * * * * * * *
        Dept 1030
    2   * * * * * * * * * * * * * * * * * * * * * * * * * * * * * * * * * * * * * *


        Dept 1210
    1   * * * * * * * * * * * * * * * * * * * * * * * * * * * * * * * * * * * * * * * * * * * * * *
        Dept 1210
    2   * * * * * * * * * * * * * * * * * * * * * * * * * * * * * * * * * * * * *
```

PROGRAMMING EXAMPLE cont'd

```
      Dept 2040
   1  * * * * * * * * * * * * * * * * * * * * * * * * * * * * * * * * * * * * * * * * * * * * * * * * * *   .
      Dept 2040
   2  * * * * * * * * * * * * * * * * * * * * * * * * * * * *
```

As you can see from the bar graph, each star represents $500 in sales. No stars are printed if a department's sales are less than or equal to $250.

Input: Two data files (`store1` and `store2`), each containing

Department ID number (`int`)
Number of business days (`int`)
Daily sales (several `float` values)

repeated for each department.

Output: A bar graph showing total sales for each department.

Discussion: Reading the input data from both files is straightforward. We need to open the files (let's call them `store1` and `store2`) and read a department ID number, the number of business days, and the daily sales for that department. After processing each department, we can read the data for the next department, continuing until we run out of departments (EOF is encountered). Because the process is the same for reading `store1` and `store2`, we can use one function for reading both files. All we have to do is pass the file name as a parameter to the function. We want total sales for each department, so this function has to sum the daily sales for a department as they are read. A function can be used to print the output heading. Another function can be used to print out each department's sales for the month in graphic form.

There are three loops in this program: one in the `main` function (to read and process the file data), one in the function that gets the data for one department (to read all the daily sales amounts), and one in the function that prints the bar graph (to print the stars in the graph). The loop for the `main` function tests for EOF on *both* `store1` and `store2`. One graph for each store must be printed for each iteration of this loop.

The loop for the `GetData` function requires an iteration counter that ranges from 1 through the number of days for the department. Also, a summing operation is needed to total the sales for the period.

At first glance, it might seem that the loop for the `PrintData` function is like any other counting loop, but let's look at how we would do this process by hand. Suppose we wanted to print a bar for the value 1850. We first would make sure the number was greater than 250, then print a star and subtract 500 from the original value. We would check again to see if the new value was greater than 250, then print a star and subtract 500. This process would repeat until the resulting value was less than or equal to 250. Thus, the loop requires a counter that

PROGRAMMING EXAMPLE cont'd

is decremented by 500 for each iteration, with a termination value of 250 or less. A star is printed for each iteration of the loop.

Function `PrintHeading` does not receive any values from `main`, nor does it return any. Thus, its parameter list is empty.

Function `GetData` receives the data file from `main` and returns it, modified, after having read some values. The function returns the values of the department ID and its sales for the month to `main`. Thus, `GetData` has three formal parameters: the data file (with data flow Inout), department ID (data flow Out), and department sales (data flow Out).

Function `PrintData` must receive the department ID, store number, and department sales from the `main` function to print the bar graph for an input record. Therefore, the function has those three items as its formal parameters, all with data flow In.

Assumptions: Each file is in order by department ID. The same departments are in each store.

Module Structure Chart:

Because we are expressing our modules as C++ functions, when we draw a module structure chart it now includes the names of parameters and uses arrows to show the direction of data flow.

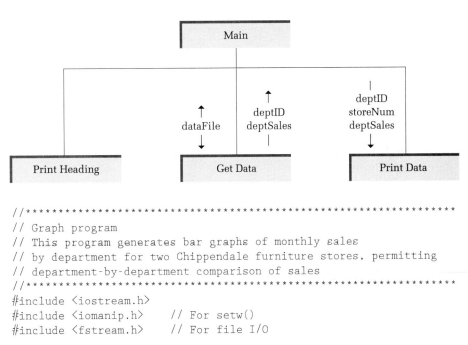

```
//****************************************************************************
// Graph program
// This program generates bar graphs of monthly sales
// by department for two Chippendale furniture stores, permitting
// department-by-department comparison of sales
//****************************************************************************
#include <iostream.h>
#include <iomanip.h>      // For setw()
#include <fstream.h>      // For file I/O
```

PROGRAMMING EXAMPLE cont'd

```cpp
void GetData( ifstream&, int&, float& );
void PrintData( int, int, float );
void PrintHeading();

int main()
{
    int      deptID1;        // Department ID number for Store 1
    int      deptID2;        // Department ID number for Store 2
    float    sales1;         // Department sales for Store 1
    float    sales2;         // Department sales for Store 2
    ifstream store1;         // Accounting file for Store 1
    ifstream store2;         // Accounting file for Store 2

    store1.open("store1.dat");
    store2.open("store2.dat");
    if ( !store1 || !store2 )                  // Make sure files
    {                                          //    were opened
        cout << "** Can't open input file(s) **" << endl;
        return 1;
    }


    PrintHeading();
    GetData(store1, deptID1, sales1);          // Priming reads
    GetData(store2, deptID2, sales2);
    while (store1 && store2)                    // While not EOF...
    {
        cout << endl;
        PrintData(deptID1, 1, sales1);         // Process Store 1
        PrintData(deptID2, 2, sales2);         // Process Store 2
        GetData(store1, deptID1, sales1);
        GetData(store2, deptID2, sales2);
    }
    return 0;
}


//**********************************************************************

void PrintHeading()

// Prints the title for the bar chart, a heading, and the numeric
// scale for the chart.  The scale uses one mark per $500
```

PROGRAMMING EXAMPLE cont'd

```
//   Postcondition:
//       The heading for the bar chart has been printed

{
    cout
        << "Bar Graph Comparing Departments of Store #1 and Store #2"
        << endl << endl
        << "Store  Sales in 1,000s of dollars" << endl
        << "  #      0         5        10        15        20        25"
        << endl
        << "         |.........|.........|.........|.........|........|"
        << endl;
}

//****************************************************************

void GetData( /* inout */ ifstream& dataFile,    // Input file
              /* out */    int&       deptID,     // Department number
              /* out */    float&     deptSales)  // Department's
                                                  //   monthly sales

// Takes an input accounting file as a parameter, reads the
// department ID number and number of days of sales from that file,
// then reads one sales figure for each of those days, computing a
// total sales figure for the month.  This figure is returned in
// deptSales.  (If input of the department ID fails due to
// end-of-file, deptID and deptSales are undefined.)
// Precondition:
//     dataFile has been successfully opened
//  && For each department, the file contains a department ID,
//     number of days, and one sales figure for each day
// Postcondition:
//     IF input of deptID failed due to end-of-file
//         deptID and deptSales are undefined
//     ELSE
//         The data file reading marker has advanced past one
//         department's data
//       && deptID == department ID number as read from the file
//       && deptSales == sum of the sales values for the department

{
    int   numDays;  // Number of business days in the month
    int   day;      // Loop control variable for reading daily sales
    float sale;     // One day's sales for the department
```

PROGRAMMING EXAMPLE cont'd

```
        dataFile >> deptID;
        if ( !dataFile )               // Check for EOF
            return;                    // If so, exit the function

        dataFile >> numDays;
        deptSales = 0.0;
        day = 1;                       // Initialize loop control variable
        while (day <= numDays)
        {
            dataFile >> sale;
            deptSales = deptSales + sale;
            day++;                     // Update loop control variable
        }
    }


//*********************************************************************


void PrintData( /* in */ int   deptID,      // Department ID number
                /* in */ int   storeNum,    // Store number
                /* in */ float deptSales )  // Total sales for the
                                            //    department

// Prints the department ID number, the store number, and a
// bar graph of the sales for the department.  The bar graph
// is printed at a scale of one mark per $500
// Precondition:
//     deptID contains a valid department number
//   && storeNum contains a valid store number
//   && 0.0 <= deptSales <= 25000.0
// Postcondition:
//     A line of the bar chart has been printed with one * for
//     each $500 in sales, with fractions over $250 rounded up
//   && No stars have been printed for sales <= $250


{
    cout << setw(12) << "Dept " << deptID << endl;
    cout << setw(3) << storeNum << "       ";
    while (deptSales > 250.0)
    {
        cout << '*' ;                        // Print '*' for each $500
        deptSales = deptSales - 500.0;       // Update loop control
    }                                        //   variable
    cout << endl;
}
```

PROGRAMMING EXAMPLE cont'd

Testing: We should test this program with data files that contain the same number of data sets for both stores and with data files that contain different numbers of data sets for both stores. The case where one or both of the files are empty also should be tested. The test data should include a set that generates a monthly sales figure of $0.00 and one that generates more than $25,000 in sales. We also should test the program to see what it does with negative days, negative sales, and mismatched department IDs. This series of tests would reveal that, for this program to work correctly for the furniture-store employees who are to use it, we should add several checks for invalid data.

The `main` function of the Graph program not only reflects our functional decomposition, it calls both `GetData` and `PrintData` twice. The result is a program that is shorter and more readable than one in which the code for each function is physically repeated.

Testing and Debugging

The combination of the formal parameters declared by a function and the actual parameters that are passed to the function by the caller constitutes the interface between the two functions. Errors that occur with the use of functions usually are due to an incorrect interface between the calling code and the called function.

One source of errors is mismatched actual and formal parameter lists. The C++ compiler ensures that the lists have the same number of parameters and that they are compatible in type. It's the programmer's responsibility, however, to verify that each actual parameter list contains the correct items. This is a matter of comparing the formal parameter declarations to the actual parameter list in every call to the function. This job is much easier if you give each formal parameter a distinct name and describe its purpose in a comment. You can avoid mistakes in writing an actual parameter list by using descriptive variable names in the calling code to suggest exactly what information is being passed to the function.

Another source of error is the failure to ensure that the preconditions for a function are met before it is called. For example, if a function assumes that the input file is not at EOF when it is called, then the calling code must ensure that this is true before calling the function. If a function behaves incorrectly, review its preconditions, then trace the program execution up to the point of the call to verify the preconditions. You can waste a lot of time trying to locate a bug in a correct function when the error is really in the part of the program prior to the call.

If the parameters match and the preconditions are correctly established, then the source of the error is most likely in the function itself. Trace the function to verify that it transforms the preconditions into the proper postconditions. Check that all local variables are initialized properly. Parameters that are supposed to return data to the caller must be declared as reference parameters (with a "&" attached to the data type name).

One helpful technique for debugging a function is to use your system's debugger, if one is available, to step through the execution of the function. Alternatively, you can insert debug output statements to print the values of the parameters immediately before and after calls to the function. It also may help to print the values of all local variables at the end of the function. This information provides a "snapshot" of the function (a picture of its status at a particular moment in time) at its two most critical points, and it is useful in verifying traces.

To test a function thoroughly, you must arrange the input data so that the preconditions are pushed to their limits; then the postconditions must be verified. For example, if a function requires a parameter to be within a certain range, try calling the function with values in the middle of that range and at its extremes.

Testing a function also involves trying to arrange the data to *violate* its preconditions. If the preconditions can be violated, then errors may crop up that appear to be in the function being tested, when they are really in the `main` function or another function. For example, function `PrintData` in the Graph program assumes that a department's sales will not exceed $25,000. If a figure of $250,000 is entered by mistake, the `main` function does not check this number before the call, and the function thus tries to print a row of 500 stars. When this happens, you might assume that `PrintData` has gone haywire, but it's the `main` function's fault for not checking the validity of the data. (The program should perform this test in function `GetData`.) Thus, a side effect of one function can multiply and give the appearance of errors elsewhere in a program. We take a closer look at the concept of side effects in the next chapter.

The `assert`
Library
Function

We have discussed how function preconditions and postconditions are useful for debugging (by checking that the preconditions of each function are true prior to a function call, and by verifying that each function correctly transforms the preconditions into the postconditions) and for testing (by pushing the preconditions to their limits and even violating them). To state the preconditions and postconditions for our functions, we've been writing the assertions as program comments:

```
// Precondition:
//    studentCount > 0
```

All comments, of course, are ignored by the compiler. They are not executable statements; they are for humans to examine.

On the other hand, the C++ standard library gives us a way in which to write *executable assertions*. Through the header file `assert.h`, the library provides a void function named `assert`. This function takes a logical (Boolean) expression as a parameter and halts the program if the expression is false. Here's an example:

```
#include <assert.h>
    .
    .
    .
assert(studentCount > 0);
average = sumOfScores / studentCount;
```

The parameter to the `assert` function must be a valid C++ logical expression. If its value is nonzero (`true`), nothing happens; execution continues on to the next statement. If its value is zero (`false`), execution of the program terminates immediately with a message stating the assertion as it appears in the parameter list, the name of the file containing the program source code, and the line number in the program. In the example above, if the value of `studentCount` is less than or equal to zero, the program halts after printing a message like this:

```
Assertion failed: studentCount > 0, file myprog.cpp, line 48
```

(This message is potentially confusing. It doesn't mean that `studentCount` *is* greater than zero. In fact, it's just the opposite. The message tells you that the assertion `studentCount > 0` is `false`.)

Executable assertions have an advantage over assertions expressed as comments: the effect of a false assertion is highly visible (the program terminates with an error message). The `assert` function is therefore valuable in software testing. A program under development might be filled with calls to the `assert` function to help identify where errors are occurring. If an assertion is false, the error message gives the precise line number of the failed assertion.

Additionally, there is a way to remove the assertions without really removing them. If you use the preprocessor directive #define NDEBUG before including the header file `assert.h`, like this:

```
#define NDEBUG
#include <assert.h>
    .
    .
    .
```

then all calls to the `assert` function are ignored when you run the program. (NDEBUG stands for "No debug," and a #define directive is a preprocessor feature that we don't discuss right now.) After program testing and debugging, programmers often like to "turn off" debugging statements yet leave them physically present in the source code in case they need the statements later. Inserting the line #define NDEBUG turns off assertion checking without having to remove the assertions.

As useful as the `assert` function is, it has two limitations. First, the parameter to the function must be expressed as a C++ logical expression. We can turn the comment

```
//  0.0 <= deptSales <= 25000.0
```

into an executable assertion with the statement

```
assert(0.0 <= deptSales && deptSales <= 25000.0);
```

But there is no easy way to turn the comment

```
//  For each department, the file contains a department ID,
//  number of days, and one sales figure for each day
```

into a C++ logical expression.

The second limitation is that the `assert` function is appropriate only for testing a program that is under development. A production program (one that has been completed and released to the public) must be robust and must furnish helpful error messages to the user of the program. You can imagine how baffled a user would be if the program suddenly quit and displayed an error message like

```
Assertion failed: sysRes <= resCount, file newproj.cpp, line 298
```

Despite these limitations, you'll want to use the `assert` function as a regular tool for testing and debugging your programs.

Testing and Debugging Hints

1. Follow documentation guidelines carefully when writing functions (see Appendix E). As your programs become more complex and prone to errors, it becomes increasingly important to adhere to documentation and formatting standards.
2. Provide a function prototype near the top of your program for each function you've written. Make sure that the prototype and its corresponding function heading are an *exact* match (except for the absence of parameter names in the prototype).
3. Be sure to put a semicolon at the end of a function prototype. But do *not* put a semicolon at the end of the function heading in a function definition.

Because function prototypes look so much like function headings, it's common to get one of them wrong.

4. Be sure the formal parameter list gives the data type of each parameter.

5. Use value parameters unless a result is to be returned through a parameter.

6. In a formal parameter list, be sure the data type of each reference parameter ends with an ampersand (&).

7. Make sure that the actual parameter list of every function call matches the formal parameter list in number and order of items, and be very careful with their data types. The compiler will trap any mismatch in the number of parameters. But if there is a mismatch in data types, there is no compile-time error. With pass-by-reference, the compiler creates a temporary variable whose address is passed to the function, and the results may not be what you expect. With pass-by-value, implicit type coercion takes place.

8. Remember that a reference parameter requires a variable as an actual parameter, whereas a value parameter can have any expression that supplies a value of the same data type (except as noted in hint 7) as an actual parameter.

Summary

C++ allows us to write programs in modules expressed as functions. The structure of a program, therefore, can parallel its functional decomposition even when the program is complicated. To make your `main` function look exactly like Level 0 of your functional decomposition, simply write each lower-level module as a function. The `main` function then executes these other functions in logical sequence.

An important means of communication between two functions is the use of two parameter lists: the formal parameter list (which includes the data type of each identifier) in the function heading, and the actual parameter list in the calling code. The items in these lists must agree in number and position, and they should agree in data type.

Part of the functional decomposition process involves determining what data must be received by a lower-level module and what information must be returned from it. The names of these data values, together with the preconditions and postconditions of a module, define its interface. The names of the data values become the formal parameter list, and the module name becomes the name of the function. With void functions, a call to the function is accomplished by writing the function's name as a statement, enclosing the appropriate actual parameters in parentheses.

C++ has two kinds of formal parameters: reference and value. Reference parameters have data types ending in "&" in the formal parameter list, whereas value parameters do not. Parameters that return values from a function should be reference parameters; all others should be value parameters. This minimizes the risk of errors, because only a copy of the value of an actual parameter is passed to a value parameter, and thus the original value cannot be changed.

In addition to the variables declared in its formal parameter list, a function may have local variables declared within it. These variables are accessible only within the block in which they are declared. Local variables must be initialized each time the function containing them is called because their values are destroyed when the function returns.

You may call functions from more than one place in a program. The positional matching mechanism allows the use of different variables as actual parameters to the same function. Multiple calls to a function, from different places and with different actual parameters, can be used to simplify greatly the coding of many complex programs.

Quick Check

1. If a design has one Level 0 module and three Level 1 modules, how many C++ functions is the program likely to have? (pp. 198–201)
2. Does a C++ function have to be declared before it can be used in a function call? (p. 201)
3. What is the difference between a function declaration and a function definition in C++? (pp. 202–204)
4. Given the function heading

```
void QuickCheck( int    size,
                 float& length,
                 char   initial )
```

   indicate which parameters are value parameters and which are reference parameters. (pp. 207–210)
5. a. What would a call to the `QuickCheck` function look like if the actual parameters were the variables `radius` (a `float`), `number` (an `int`), and `letter` (a `char`)? (p. 201)
   b. How is the matchup between these actual parameters and the formal parameters made? What information is actually passed from the calling code to the `QuickCheck` function, given these actual parameters? (pp. 207–208)
   c. Which of these actual parameters is (are) protected from being changed by the `QuickCheck` function? (pp. 208–210)
6. Where in a function are local variables declared, and what are their initial values equal to? (pp. 204–205)
7. Assume that you are designing a program and you need a void function that reads any number of floating point values and returns their average. The number of values to be read is in an integer variable named `dataPoints`, declared in the calling code.
   a. How many parameters will there be in the formal parameter list, and what will their data type(s) be? (pp. 211–212)

     b. Which of the formal parameters should be passed by reference and which should be passed by value? (pp. 211–212)

8. Describe one way in which you can use a function to simplify the coding of an algorithm. (pp. 218–219)

Answers   1. Four (including `main`)   2. Yes   3. A definition is a declaration that includes the function body.   4. `length` is a reference parameter; `size` and `initial` are value parameters. 5. a. `QuickCheck(number, radius, letter);`   b. The matchup is done on the basis of the parameters' positions in each list. Copies of the values of `size` and `initial` are passed to the function; the location (memory address) of `length` is passed to the function. c. `size` and `initial` are protected from change because it is only copies of their values that are sent to the function.   6. In the block that forms the body of the function. Their initial values are undefined. 7. a. There will be two parameters: an `int` containing the number of values to be read and a `float` containing the computed average. b. The `int` should be a value parameter; the `float` should be a reference parameter.   8. The coding may be simplified if the function is called from more than one place in the program.

Exam Preparation Exercises

1. Define the following terms:

function call	formal parameter
parameter list	actual parameter
parameterless function	local variable

2. Identify the following items in the program fragment shown below.

function prototype	function definition
function heading	formal parameters
actual parameters	function call
local variables	function body

```
void Test( int, int, int );

int main()
{
    int a;
    int b;
    int c;
    .

    .

    .
    Test(a, c, b);
    Test(b, a, c);
    .

    .

    .
}
```

```
void Test( int d,
           int e,
           int f )
{
    int g;
    int h;
    .
    .
    .
}
```

3. For the program in Exercise 2, fill in the blanks with variable names to show the matching that takes place between the actual and the formal parameter lists in each of the two calls to the Test function.

<table>
<tr><td colspan="2">First Call to Test</td><td colspan="2">Second Call to Test</td></tr>
<tr><td>Formal</td><td>Actual</td><td>Formal</td><td>Actual</td></tr>
<tr><td>1. _____</td><td>_____</td><td>1. _____</td><td>_____</td></tr>
<tr><td>2. _____</td><td>_____</td><td>2. _____</td><td>_____</td></tr>
<tr><td>3. _____</td><td>_____</td><td>3. _____</td><td>_____</td></tr>
</table>

4. What is the output of the following program?

```
#include <iostream.h>

void Print( int, int );

int main()
{
    int n;

    n = 3;
    Print(5, n);
    Print(n, n);
    Print(n * n, 12);
    return 0;
}

void Print( int a,
            int b )
{
    int c;

    c = 2 * a + b;
    cout << a << ' ' << b << ' ' << c << endl;
}
```

5. Using a reference parameter (passing by reference), a function can obtain the initial value of an actual parameter as well as change the value of the actual parameter. (True or False?)

6. Using a value parameter, the value of a variable can be passed to a function and used for computation there, without any modification of the actual parameter. (True or False?)

7. Given the declarations

   ```
   const int ANGLE = 90;

   char letter;
   int  number;
   ```

   indicate whether each of the following actual parameters would be valid using pass-by-value, pass-by-reference, or both.

   a. `letter`
   b. `ANGLE`
   c. `number`
   d. `number + 3`
   e. `23`
   f. `ANGLE * number`
   g. `abs(number)`

8. A variable named `widgets` is stored in memory location 13571. When the statements

   ```
   widgets = 23;
   Drop(widgets);
   ```

   are executed, what information is passed to the formal parameter in function `Drop`? (Assume the formal parameter is a reference parameter.)

9. Assume that, in Exercise 8, the formal parameter for function `Drop` is named `clunkers`. After the function body performs the assignment

   ```
   clunkers = 77;
   ```

   what is the value in `widgets`? in `clunkers`?

10. Using the data values

    ```
    3 2 4
    ```

    show what is printed by the following program.

    ```
    #include <iostream.h>

    void Test( int&, int&, int& );

    int main()
    {
        int a;
        int b;
        int c;
    ```

```
    Test(a, b, c);
    b = b + 10;
    cout << "The answers are " << b << ' ' << c << ' ' << a;
    return 0;
}

void Test( int& z,
           int& x,
           int& a )
{

    cin >> z >> x >> a;
    a = z * x + a;
}
```

11. The program below has a function named `Change`. Fill in the values of all variables before and after the function is called. Then fill in the values of all variables after the return to the `main` function. (If any value is undefined, write *u* instead of a number.)

```
#include <iostream.h>

void Change( int, int& );

int main()
{
    int a;
    int b;

    a = 10;
    b = 7;
    Change(a, b);
    cout << a << ' ' << b << endl;
    return 0;
}

void Change( int  x,
             int& y )
{
    int b;

    b = x;
    y = y + b;
    x = y;
}
```

Variables in `main` just before `Change` is called:

a _____
b _____

Variables in `Change` at the moment control enters the function:

x _____
y _____
b _____

Variables in `main` after return from `Change`:

a _____
b _____

12. Show the output of the following program.

```cpp
#include <iostream.h>

void Test( int&, int );

int main()
{
    int d;
    int e;

    d = 12;
    e = 14;
    Test(d, e);
    cout << "In the main function after the first call, "
        << "the variables equal " << d << ' ' << e << endl;
    d = 15;
    e = 18;
    Test(e, d);
    cout << "In the main function after the second call, "
        << "the variables equal " << d << ' ' << e << endl;
    return 0;
}

void Test( int& s,
           int  t )
{
    s = 3;
    s = s + 2;
    t = 4 * s;
    cout << "In function Test, the variables equal "
        << s << ' ' << t << endl;
}
```

13. Number the marked statements in the following program to show the order in which they are executed (the logical order of execution).

```
#include <iostream.h>

void DoThis( int&, int& );

int main()
{
    int number1;
    int number2;

____    cout << "Exercise ";
____    DoThis(number1, number2);
____    cout << number1 << ' ' << number2 << endl;
        return 0;
}

void DoThis( int& value1,
             int& value2 )
{
    int value3;

____    cin >> value3 >> value1;
____    value2 = value1 + 10;
}
```

14. If the program in Exercise 13 were run with the data values 10 and 15, what would be the values of the following variables just before execution of the `return` statement in the `main` function?

```
number1 _____   number2 _____   value3 _____
```

Programming Warm-Up Exercises

1. Write the function heading for a void function named `PrintMax` that accepts a pair of integers and prints out the greater of the two. Document the data flow of each parameter with `/* in */`, `/* out */`, or `/* inout */`.

2. Write the heading for a void function that corresponds to the following list.

   Module Rocket Simulation

Incoming	thrust (floating point)
Incoming/Outgoing	weight (floating point)
Incoming	timeStep (integer)
Incoming	totalTime (integer)
Outgoing	velocity (floating point)
Outgoing	outOfFuel (Boolean)

3. Write a void function that reads in a specified number of `float` values and returns their average. A call to this function might look like

```
GetMeanOf(5, mean);
```

where the first parameter specifies the number of values to be read, and the second parameter contains the result. Document the data flow of each parameter with `/* in */`, `/* out */`, or `/* inout */`.

4. Given the function heading

```
void Halve( /* inout */ int& firstNumber,
            /* inout */ int& secondNumber )
```

write the body of the function so that when it returns, the original values in `firstNumber` and `secondNumber` are halved.

5. Add comments to the preceding `Halve` function that state the function preconditions and postconditions.

6. a. Write a single void function to replace the repeated pattern of statements you identified in Exam Preparation Exercise 12 of Chapter 3. Document the data flow of the formal parameters with `/* in */`, `/* out */`, or `/* inout */`. Include comments giving the function preconditions and postconditions.
   b. Show the function calls with actual parameters.

7. a. Write a void function that reads in data values of type `int` (`heartRate`) until a normal heart rate (between 60 and 80) is read or EOF occurs. The function has one parameter, named `normal`, that contains `true` if a normal heart rate was read or `false` if EOF occurred. (Assume that a data type `Boolean` has already been defined.)
   b. Write a statement that invokes your function. You may use the same variable name for the actual and formal parameters.

8. Consider the following function definition.

```
void Rotate( /* inout */ int& firstValue,
             /* inout */ int& secondValue,
             /* inout */ int& thirdValue  )
{
    int temp;

    temp = firstValue;
    firstValue = secondValue;
    secondValue = thirdValue;
    thirdValue = temp;
}
```

   a. Add comments to the function that tell a reader what the function does and what is the purpose of each parameter and local variable.
   b. Write a program that reads three values into variables, echo prints them, calls the `Rotate` function with the three variables as parameters, and then prints the parameters after the function returns.

9. Modify the function in Exercise 8 to perform the same sort of operation on four values. Modify the program you wrote for part (b) of Exercise 8 to work with the new version of this function.

10. Write a void function named `CountUpper` that counts the number of uppercase letters on one line of input. The function should return this number to the calling code in a parameter named `upCount`.

11. Write a void function named `AddTime` that has three parameters: `hours`, `minutes`, and `elapsedTime`. `elapsedTime` is an integer number of minutes to be added to the starting time passed in through `hours` and `minutes`. The resulting new time is returned through `hours` and `minutes`. For example:

Before Call *to* `AddTime`	*After Call* *to* `AddTime`
`hours = 12`	`hours = 16`
`minutes = 44`	`minutes = 2`
`elapsedTime = 198`	`elapsedTime = 198`

12. Write a void function named `GetNonBlank` that returns the first nonblank character it encounters in the standard input stream. In your function, use the `cin.get` function to read each character. (This `GetNonBlank` function is just for practice. It's unnecessary because you could use the `>>` operator, which skips leading blanks, to accomplish the same result.)

13. Write a void function named `SkipToBlank` that skips all characters in the standard input stream until a blank is encountered. In your function, use the `cin.get` function to read each character. (This function is just for practice. There's already a library function, `cin.ignore`, that allows you to do the same thing.)

14. Modify the function in Exercise 13 so that it returns a count of the number of characters that were skipped.

15. Write a separate function for the Graph program that prints a bar of asterisks, given the department sales value. Then rewrite the existing `PrintData` function so that it calls your new function.

Programming Problems

1. Using functions, rewrite the program developed for Programming Problem 4 in Chapter 6.

   Develop a functional decomposition and write a C++ program to determine the number of words encountered in the input stream. For the sake of simplicity, we define a word to be any sequence of characters except whitespace characters (blanks and newlines). Words may be separated by any number of whitespace characters. A word may be any length, from a single character to an entire line of characters. If you are writing the program to read data from a file, then it should echo print the input. For an interactive implementation, you do not need to echo print for this program.

   For example, for the following data, the program would indicate that 26 words were entered.

```
This isn't exactly an example of g00d english, but it
does demonstrate that a w0rd is just a se@uence of
characters              with0u+ any blank$.   #####   .......
```

(*Hint:* One way to solve this problem involves turning the `SkipToBlank` function of Programming Warm-Up Exercise 13 into a `SkipToWhitespace` function.)

Now that your programs are becoming more complex, it is even more important for you to use proper indentation and style, meaningful identifiers, and plenty of comments.

2. Write a C++ program that reads characters representing binary (base 2) numbers from a data file and translates them to decimal (base 10) numbers. The decimal numbers should be output in a column with an appropriate heading. Each binary number has been placed "backwards" in the file. That is, the rightmost digit is the first encountered, the second digit from the right is encountered next, and so on. The program reads the digits one at a time. As each digit is read, the program should translate that digit into the corresponding decimal value by multiplying it by the appropriate power of 2 (depending on where the digit was in the number). There is only one number per input line, but there is an arbitrary number of blanks before each number. The program should check for bad data; if it encounters anything except a zero or a one, it should output the message "Bad integer on input."

As always, use plenty of comments, proper documentation and coding style, and meaningful identifiers throughout this program. You must decide which of your design modules should be coded as functions to make the program easier to understand.

3. Develop a functional decomposition and write a C++ program to print a calendar for one year, given the year and the day of the week that January 1 falls on. It may help to think of this task as printing 12 calendars, one for each month, given the day of the week on which a month starts and the number of days in the month. Each successive month starts on the day of the week that follows the last day of the preceding month. Days of the week should be numbered 0 through 6 for Sunday through Saturday. Years that are divisible by 4 are leap years. (Determining leap years actually is more complicated than this, but for this program it will suffice.) Here is a sample run for an interactive program:

```
What year do you want a calendar for?
2002
What day of the week does January 1 fall on?
(Enter 0 for Sunday, 1 for Monday, etc.)
2
        2002

      January
  S  M  T  W  T  F  S
  _____

         1  2  3  4  5
  6  7  8  9 10 11 12
 13 14 15 16 17 18 19
 20 21 22 23 24 25 26
 27 28 29 30 31
```

```
            February
   S  M  T  W  T  F  S
   ─────────────────────
                     1  2
   3  4  5  6  7  8  9
  10 11 12 13 14 15 16
  17 18 19 20 21 22 23
  24 25 26 27 28

              .

              .

              .


            December
   S  M  T  W  T  F  S
   ─────────────────────
   1  2  3  4  5  6  7
   8  9 10 11 12 13 14
  15 16 17 18 19 20 21
  22 23 24 25 26 27 28
  29 30 31
```

When writing your program, be sure to use proper indentation and style, meaningful identifiers, and plenty of comments.

4. In this problem you are to design and implement a Roman numeral calculator. The subtractive Roman numeral notation commonly in use today (such as IV, meaning "4") was used only rarely during the time of the Roman Republic and Empire. For ease of calculation, the Romans most frequently used a purely additive notation in which a number was simply the sum of its digits (4 equals IIII, in this notation). Each number starts with the digit of highest value and ends with the digit of smallest value. This is the notation we use in this problem.

Your program inputs two Roman numbers and an arithmetic operator and prints out the result of the operation, also as a Roman number. The values of the Roman digits are as follows:

```
I        1
V        5
X        10
L        50
C        100
D        500
M        1000
```

Thus, the number MDCCCCLXXXXVI represents 1996. The arithmetic operators that your program should recognize in the input are +, -, *, and /. These should perform the C++ operations of integer addition, subtraction, multiplication, and division.

One way of approaching this problem is to convert the Roman numbers into integers, perform the required operation, and then convert the result back into a Roman number for printing. The following might be a sample run of the program:

```
Enter the first number:
MCCXXVI
The first number is 1226
Enter the second number:
LXVIIII
The second number is 69
Enter the desired arithmetic operation:
+
The sum of MCCXXVI and LXVIIII is MCCLXXXXV (1295)
```

Your program should use proper style and indentation, appropriate comments, and meaningful identifiers. It also should check for errors in the input, such as illegal digits or arithmetic operators, and take appropriate actions when these are found. The program also may check to ensure that the numbers are in purely additive form—that is, digits are followed only by digits of the same or lower value.

8 Scope, Lifetime, and More on Functions

GOALS

- To be able to do the following tasks, given a C++ program composed of several functions

  Determine whether a variable is being referenced globally

  Determine which variables are local variables

  Determine which variables are accessible within a given block

- To be able to determine the lifetime of each variable in a program

- To understand and be able to avoid unwanted side effects

- To know when to use a value-returning function

- To be able to design and code a value-returning function for a specific task

- To be able to invoke a value-returning function properly

As programs get larger, the number of identifiers increases. Some of these identifiers we declare inside blocks. Other identifiers—function names, for example—we declare outside of any block. This chapter examines the C++ rules by which a function may access identifiers declared outside its own block. Using these rules, we return to the discussion of interface design that we began in Chapter 7.

Finally, we look at the second kind of subprogram provided by C++: the *value-returning function*. A value-returning function returns a single result—the function value—to the expression from which it was called. In this chapter, you learn how to write such functions.

Scope and Lifetime

Scope of Identifiers As we saw in Chapter 7, local variables are those declared inside a block, such as the body of a function. Recall that local variables cannot be accessed outside the block that contains them. The same access rule applies to local named constants: they can be accessed only in the block in which they are declared.

Any block, not only a function body, can contain variable and constant declarations. For example, this If statement contains a block that declares a local variable n:

```
if (alpha > 3)
{
    int n;

    cin >> n;
    beta = beta + n;
}
```

As a local variable, n cannot be accessed by any statement outside the block.

If we list all the places from which an identifier could be accessed legally, we would describe that identifier's *scope of visibility* or *scope of access,* often just called its **scope.**

scope
The region of program code where it is legal to reference (use) an identifier

C++ defines three categories of scope for any identifier.*

1. **Class scope.** This term refers to the data type called a *class,* which we described briefly in Chapter 4. We postpone a detailed discussion of class scope until Chapter 15.
2. **Local scope.** The scope of an identifier declared inside a block extends from the point of declaration to the end of that block.
3. **Global** (or **file**) **scope.** The scope of an identifier declared outside all functions and classes extends from the point of declaration to the end of the entire file containing the program code.

C++ function names have global scope. (There is an exception to this rule, which we discuss in Chapter 15 when we examine C++ classes.) Once a function name has been declared, it can be invoked by any other function in the rest of the program. In C++ there is no such thing as a local function—that is, you cannot nest a function definition inside another function.

Global variables and constants are those declared outside all functions. When a function declares a local identifier with the same name as a global identifier, the local identifier takes precedence within the function. This principle is called **name precedence** or **name hiding.**

name precedence
The precedence that a local identifier in a function has over a global identifier with the same name in any references that the function makes to that identifier; also called name hiding

Here's an example that uses both local and global declarations:

```
#include <iostream.h>

void SomeFunc( float );
```

---

*Technically, C++ defines four scope categories. The fourth relates to a statement called a goto statement, which we do not discuss in this book.

```
const int a = 17;      // A global constant
int b;                 // A global variable
int c;                 // Another global variable

int main()
{
    b = 4;                          // Assignment to global b
    c = 6;                          // Assignment to global c
    SomeFunc(42.8);
    return 0;
}

void SomeFunc( float c )            // Prevents access to global c
{
    float b;                        // Prevents access to global b

    b = 2.3;                        // Assignment to local b
    cout << "a = " << a;            // Output global a (17)
    cout << " b = " << b;           // Output local b (2.3)
    cout << " c = " << c;           // Output local c (42.8)
}
```

In this example, function `SomeFunc` accesses global constant `a` but declares its own local variables `b` and `c`. Thus, the output would be

```
a = 17 b = 2.3 c = 42.8
```

Local variable `b` takes precedence over global variable `b`, effectively hiding global `b` from the statements in function `SomeFunc`. Formal parameter `c` also blocks access to global variable `c` from within the function. Formal parameters act just like local variables in this respect.

Scope Rules

scope rules
The rules that determine where in the program an identifier may be accessed, given the point where that identifier is declared

nonlocal identifier
Any identifier declared outside a given block is said to be nonlocal with respect to that block

When you write C++ programs, you rarely declare global variables. There are negative aspects to using global variables, which we discuss later. But when a situation crops up where you have a compelling need for global variables, it pays to know how C++ handles these declarations. The rules for accessing identifiers that aren't declared locally are called **scope rules.**

In addition to local and global access, the C++ scope rules define what happens when blocks are nested within other blocks. Anything declared in a block that contains a nested block is **nonlocal** to the inner block. (Global identifiers are nonlocal with respect to all blocks in the program.) If a block accesses any identifier declared outside its own block, it is a *nonlocal access.*

Here are the detailed scope rules, excluding class scope and certain language features we have not yet discussed:

www.jbpub.com/C++links

1. A function name has global scope. Function definitions cannot be nested within function definitions.
2. The scope of a formal parameter is identical to the scope of a local variable declared in the outermost block of the function body.
3. The scope of a global variable or constant extends from its declaration to the end of the file, except as noted in rule 5.
4. The scope of a local variable or constant extends from its declaration to the end of the block in which it is declared. This scope includes any nested blocks, except as noted in rule 5.
5. The scope of an identifier does not include any nested block that contains a locally declared identifier with the same name (local identifiers have name precedence).

Here is a sample program that demonstrates C++ scope rules. To simplify the example, only the declarations and headings are spelled out. Note how the While-loop body labeled Block3, declared within function Block2, contains its own local variable declarations.

```
// ScopeRules program

#include <iostream.h>

void Block1( int, char& );
void Block2();

int  a1;        // One global variable
char a2;        // Another global variable

int main()
{
    .
    .
    .
}

//******************************************************************

void Block1( int   a1,        // Prevents access to global a1
             char& b2 )       // Has same scope as c1 and d2
{
    int c1;        // A variable local to Block1
    int d2;        // Another variable local to Block1
    .
    .
    .
}
```

```
//*****************************************************************

void Block2()
{
    int a1;         // Prevents access to global a1
    int b2;         // Local to Block2; no conflict with b2 in Block1

    while (...)
    {               // Block3
        int c1;     // Local to Block3; no conflict with c1 in Block1
        int b2;     // Prevents nonlocal access to b2 in Block2; no
                    //   conflict with b2 in Block1

        .
        .
        .

    }
}
```

Let's look at the ScopeRules program in terms of the blocks it defines and see just what these rules mean. Figure 8-1 shows the headings and declarations in the ScopeRules program with the scopes of visibility indicated by boxes.

Anything inside a box can refer to anything in a larger surrounding box, but outside-in references aren't allowed. Thus, a statement in Block3 could access any identifier declared in Block2 or any global variable. A statement in Block3 could not access identifiers declared in Block1 because it would have to enter the Block1 box from outside.

Notice that the formal parameters for a function are inside the function's box, but the function name itself is outside. If the name of the function were inside the box, no function could call another function. This demonstrates merely that function names are globally accessible.

Imagine the boxes in Figure 8-1 as rooms whose walls are made of two-way mirrors, with the reflective side facing out and the see-through side facing in. If you stood in the room for Block3, you would be able to see out through all the surrounding rooms to the declarations of the global variables (and anything between). You would not be able to see into any other rooms (such as Block1), however, because their mirrored outer surfaces would block your view. Because of this analogy, the term *visible* is often used in describing a scope of access. For example, variable a2 is visible throughout the program, meaning that it can be accessed from anywhere in the program.

Figure 8-1 does not tell the whole story; it represents only scope rules 1 through 4. We also must keep rule 5 in mind. Variable a1 is declared in two different places in the ScopeRules program. Because of name precedence, Block2 and Block3 access the a1 declared in Block2 rather than the global a1. Similarly, the scope of the variable b2 declared in Block2 does *not* include the "shadow" created by the local variable b2 declared in Block3.

FIGURE 8-1

Scope Diagram for
ScopeRules
Program

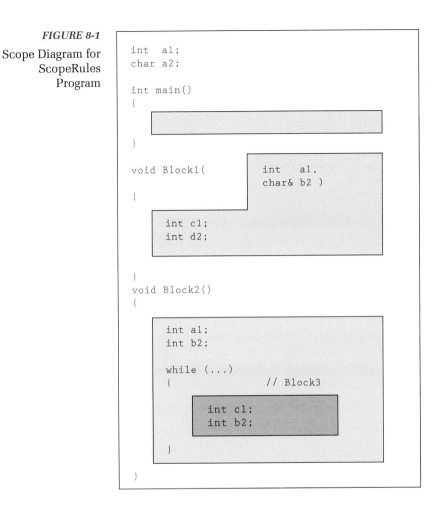

Name precedence is implemented by the compiler as follows. When a statement refers to an identifier, the compiler first checks the local declarations. If the identifier isn't local, the compiler works its way outward through each level of nesting until it finds an identifier with the same name. There it stops. If there is an identifier with the same name declared at a level even further out, it is never reached. If the compiler reaches the global declarations (including identifiers inserted by #include directives) and still can't find the identifier, an error message such as "UNDECLARED IDENTIFIER" will result.

Such a message most likely indicates a misspelling or an incorrect capitalization, or it could mean that the identifier was not declared before the reference to it or was not declared at all. It may also indicate, however, that the blocks are nested so that the identifier's scope doesn't include the reference.

Variable Declarations and Definitions

In Chapter 7, you learned that C++ terminology distinguishes between a function declaration and a function definition. C++ applies the same terminology to variable declarations. All of the variable declarations we have used from the beginning have been variable definitions. What would a variable declaration look like if it were *not* also a definition?

As we discuss later in the book, C++ allows you to create a multifile program, a program that physically occupies several files containing individual pieces of the program. C++ has a reserved word `extern` that lets you reference a global variable located in another file. A "normal" declaration such as

```
int someInt;
```

causes the compiler to reserve a memory location for `someInt`. On the other hand, the declaration

```
extern int someInt;
```

is an *external declaration*. It states that `someInt` is a global variable located in another file and that no additional storage should be reserved for it. Header files such as `iostream.h` contain external declarations so that user programs can access important variables defined in other files. For example, `iostream.h` includes declarations such as

```
extern istream cin;
extern ostream cout;
```

that allow you to reference `cin` and `cout` as global variables in your program. The variable definitions are located in another file supplied by the C++ system.

In C++ terminology, the statement

```
extern int someInt;
```

is merely a declaration of `someInt`. It associates a variable name with a data type so that the compiler can perform type checking. But the statement

```
int someInt;
```

is both a declaration and a definition of `someInt`. It is a definition because it reserves memory for `someInt`. In C++, you can declare a variable or a function many times, but there can be only one definition.

Except when it's important to distinguish between declarations and definitions of variables, we'll continue to use the phrase *variable declaration* instead of the more specific *variable definition.*

Lifetime of a Variable

A concept related to but separate from the scope of a variable is its **lifetime**—the period of time during program execution when an identifier actually has memory allocated to it. We have said that storage for local variables is allocated at the moment control enters a function. Then the variables are "alive" while the function is executing, and finally the storage is deallocated when the function exits. In contrast, the lifetime of a global variable is the lifetime of the entire program. Global memory space is allocated only once, when the program begins executing, and is deallocated only when the entire program terminates. Observe that scope is a *compile-time* issue, but lifetime is a *run-time* issue.

lifetime
The period of time during program execution when an identifier has memory allocated to it

automatic variable
A variable for which memory is allocated and deallocated when control enters and exits the block in which it is declared

static variable
A variable for which memory remains allocated throughout the execution of the entire program

In C++, each variable has a *storage class* that determines its lifetime. An **automatic variable** is one whose storage is allocated at block entry and deallocated at block exit. A **static variable** is one whose storage remains allocated for the duration of the entire program. All global variables are static variables. By default, variables declared within a block are automatic variables. However, you can use the reserved word `static` when you declare a local variable. If you do so, the variable is a static variable and its lifetime persists from function call to function call:

```
void SomeFunc()
{
    float   someFloat;      // Destroyed when function exits
    static int someInt;     // Retains its value from call to call
    .
    .
    .
}
```

It is usually better to declare a local variable as `static` than to use a global variable. Like a global variable, its memory remains allocated throughout the lifetime of the entire program. But unlike a global variable, its local scope prevents other functions in the program from accessing it.

Initializations in Declarations. One of the most common things we do in programs is first declare a variable and then, in a separate statement, assign an initial value to the variable. Here's a typical example:

```
int sum;
sum = 0;
```

C++ allows you to combine these two statements into one. The result is known as an *initialization in a declaration.* Here we initialize sum in its declaration:

```
int sum = 0;
```

In a declaration, the expression that specifies the initial value is called an *initializer.* Above, the initializer is the constant 0.

An automatic variable is initialized to the specified value each time control enters the block:

```
void SomeFunc( int someParam )
{
    int i = 0;                    // Initialized each time
    int n = 2 * someParam + 3;    // Initialized each time
    .
    .
    .
}
```

In contrast, initialization of a static variable (either a global variable or a local variable explicitly declared static) occurs once only, the first time control reaches its declaration. Furthermore, the initializer must be a constant expression (one with only constant values as operands). Here's an example:

```
void AnotherFunc( int param )
{
    static char ch = 'A';       // Initialized once only
    static int  m  = param + 1; // Illegal. Constant expression
                                //    required
    .
    .
    .
}
```

Although an initialization gives a variable an initial value, it is perfectly acceptable to reassign it another value during program execution.

The following table summarizes initialization of static and automatic variables.

	Automatic Variables	*Static Variables*
Initialized when?	Each time control reaches the declaration	Once only, the first time control reaches the declaration
Initializer	Any expression*	Constant expression only*

*Implicit type coercion takes place if the data type of the initializer is different from the data type of the variable.

There are differing opinions about initializing a variable in its declaration. Some programmers never do it, preferring to keep an initialization close to the executable statements that depend on that variable. For example,

```
int loopCount;
    .
    .
    .
loopCount = 1;
while (loopCount <= 20)
{
    .
    .
    .
}
```

If this loop was also nested inside another loop, then initialization of `loopCount` must be done before the `while`. Otherwise the loop's termination condition would not be reinitialized on subsequent iterations of the outer loop. Relying on initialization in the declaration in this situation is a common source of errors.

Other programmers maintain that a frequent cause of bugs is forgetting to initialize variables before using their contents; initializing each variable in its declaration eliminates these bugs. Most programmers seem to take a position somewhere between these two extremes.

Interface Design

We return now to the issue of interface design, which we first discussed in Chapter 7. Recall that the data flow through a function interface can take three forms: incoming only, outgoing only, and incoming/outgoing. Any item that can be classified as purely incoming should be coded as a value parameter. Items in the remaining two categories (outgoing and incoming/outgoing) must be reference parameters; the only way the function can deposit results into the caller's actual parameters is to have the addresses of those parameters. For emphasis, we repeat the following table from Chapter 7.

Data Flow for a Parameter	Parameter-Passing Mechanism
Incoming	Pass-by-value
Outgoing	Pass-by-reference
Incoming/outgoing	Pass-by-reference

Sometimes it is tempting to skip the interface design step when writing a function, letting it communicate with other functions by referencing global variables. Don't! Without the interface design step, you would actually be creating a poorly structured and undocumented interface. Except in well-justified circumstances, the use of global variables is a poor programming practice that can lead to program bugs. These bugs are extremely hard to locate and usually take the form of unwanted side effects.

Side Effects

Suppose you made a call to the `sqrt` library function in your program:

```
y = sqrt(x);
```

You expect that the call to `sqrt` will compute the square root of the variable x. You'd be surprised if `sqrt` also changed the value of your variable x because `sqrt`, by definition, does not make such changes. This would be an example of an unexpected and unwanted **side effect.**

side effect
Any effect of one function on another that is not a part of the explicitly defined interface between them

Side effects are sometimes caused by a combination of reference parameters and careless coding in a function. Perhaps an assignment statement in the function stores a temporary result into one of the reference parameters, accidentally changing the value of an actual parameter back in the calling code. As we mentioned before, using value parameters avoids this type of side effect by preventing the change from reaching the actual parameter.

Side effects can also occur when a function accesses a global variable. An error in the function might cause the value of a global variable to be changed in an unexpected way, causing an error in other functions that access that variable.

The symptoms of a side effect error are misleading because the trouble appears in one part of the program when it really is caused by something in another part. To avoid such errors, the only external effect that a function should have is to transfer information through the well-structured interface of the parameter list (see Figure 8-2). If functions access nonlocal variables *only* through

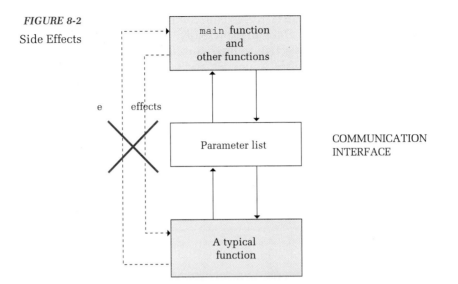

FIGURE 8-2

Side Effects

main function
and
other functions

e   effects

Parameter list

COMMUNICATION
INTERFACE

A typical
function

their parameter lists, and if all incoming-only parameters are value parameters, then each function is essentially isolated from other parts of the program and there are no side effects.

When a function is free of side effects, we can treat it as an independent module and reuse it in other programs. We cannot reuse functions with side effects.

Global Constants Contrary to what you might think, it is acceptable to reference named constants globally. Because the values of global constants cannot be changed while the program is running, no side effects can occur.

There are two advantages to referencing constants globally: (1) ease of change and (2) consistency. If we have to change the value of a constant, it's easier to change only one global declaration than to change a local declaration in every function. By declaring a constant in only one place, we also ensure that all parts of the program use exactly the same value.

This is not to say that you should declare *all* constants globally. If a constant is needed in only one function, then it makes sense to declare it locally within that function.

Value-Returning Functions

Up to now we have been writing void functions. We now turn our attention to value-returning functions. You already know several value-returning functions supplied by the C++ standard library: sqrt, abs, fabs, and others. From the caller's perspective, the difference between void and value-returning functions is that a call to a void function is a complete statement; a call to a value-returning function is part of an expression.

From a design perspective, value-returning functions are used when there is only one result returned by a function and that result is to be used directly in an expression. For example, suppose we are writing a program that calculates a prorated refund of tuition for students who withdraw in the middle of a semester.

As part of this program we must calculate the day number which is the number associated with each day of the year if you count sequentially from January 1. December 31 has the day number 365, except in leap years, when it is 366.

Let's write the calculation of the day number as a value-returning function named Day that returns the day number of a date in a given year.

Here's the function definition for Day. Don't worry about how Day works; for now, we are concerned mainly with its syntax and structure.

```
int Day( /* in */ int month,          // Month number, 1 - 12
         /* in */ int dayOfMonth,     // Day of month, 1 - 31
         /* in */ int year       )    // Year. For example, 1997

// This function computes the day number within a year, given
// the date. It accounts correctly for leap years.

{
    int correction;    // Correction factor to account for leap year
                       //   and months of different lengths

    // Test for leap year

    if (year % 4 == 0 && (year % 100 != 0 || year % 400 == 0))
    {
        if (month >= 3)         // If date is after February 29
            correction = 1;     //    then add one for leap year
    }
    else
        correction = 0;

    // Correct for different length months

    if (month == 3)
        correction = correction - 1;
    else if (month == 2 || month == 6 || month == 7)
        correction = correction + 1;
    else if (month == 8)
        correction = correction + 2;
    else if (month == 9 || month == 10)
        correction = correction + 3;
    else if (month == 11 || month == 12)
        correction = correction + 4;
    return (month - 1) * 30 + correction + dayOfMonth;
}
```

The first thing to note about the function definition is that it looks like a void function, except for the fact that the heading begins with the data type `int` instead of the word `void`. The second thing to observe is the `return` statement at the end, which includes an integer expression between the word `return` and the semicolon.

A value-returning function returns one value, not through a parameter but by means of a `return` statement. The data type at the beginning of the heading declares the type of value that the function will return. This data type is called the *function type,* although a more proper term is **function value type** (or *function return type* or *function result type*).

function value type
The data type of the result value returned by a function

The last statement in the `Day` function evaluates the expression

```
(month - 1) * 30 + correction + dayOfMonth
```

and returns the result as the function value.

You now have seen two forms of the `return` statement. The form

```
return;
```

is valid *only* in void functions. It causes control to exit the function immediately and return to the caller. The second form is

```
return Expression;
```

This form is valid *only* in a value-returning function. It returns control to the caller, sending back the value of Expression as the function value. (If the data type of Expression is different from the declared function type, its value is coerced to the correct type.)

In Chapter 7, we presented a syntax template for the function definition of a void function. We now update the syntax template to cover both void functions and value-returning functions:

FunctionDefinition

DataType FunctionName (FormalParameterList)
{
    Statement
       .
       .
       .
}

If DataType is void, the function is a void function; otherwise, it is a value-returning function. Notice from the shading in the syntax template that DataType is optional. If you omit the data type of a function, int is assumed. We mention this point only because you sometimes encounter programs where DataType is missing from the function heading. Many programmers do not consider this practice to be good programming style.

The formal parameter list for a value-returning function has exactly the same form as for a void function: a list of parameter declarations, separated by commas. Also, a function prototype for a value-returning function looks just like the prototype for a void function except that it begins with a data type instead of void.

Let's look at another example of a value-returning function. The C++ standard library provides a power function, pow, that raises a floating point number to a floating point power. The library does not supply a power function for int values, so we'll build one of our own. The function receives two integers, x and n (where $n \geq 0$), and computes x^n. We use a simple approach, multiplying repeatedly by x. Because the number of iterations is known in advance, a count-controlled loop is appropriate. The loop counts down to 0 from the initial value of n. For each iteration of the loop, x is multiplied by the previous product.

```
int Power( /* in */ int x,      // Base number
           /* in */ int n )     // Power to raise base to

// This function computes x to the n power

{
    int result;      // Holds intermediate powers of x

    result = 1;
    while (n > 0)
    {
        result = result * x;
        n--;
    }
    return result;
}
```

Boolean Functions Value-returning functions are not restricted to returning numerical results. We can also use them to evaluate a condition and return a Boolean result. Boolean functions can be useful when a branch or loop depends on some complex condition. Rather than code the condition directly into the If or While statement, we can call a Boolean function to form the controlling expression.

The C++ standard library provides a number of helpful Boolean functions that let you test the contents of char variables. To use them, you #include the header file ctype.h. Here are some of the available functions; Appendix C contains a more complete list.

Header File	Function	Function Type	Function Value
`<ctype.h>`	`isalpha(ch)`	`int`	Nonzero, if ch is a letter ('A'–'Z', 'a'–'z'); 0, otherwise
`<ctype.h>`	`isalnum(ch)`	`int`	Nonzero, if ch is a letter or a digit ('A'–'Z', 'a'–'z', '0'–'9'); 0, otherwise
`<ctype.h>`	`isdigit(ch)`	`int`	Nonzero, if ch is a digit ('0'–'9'); 0, otherwise
`<ctype.h>`	`islower(ch)`	`int`	Nonzero, if ch is a lowercase letter ('a'–'z'); 0, otherwise
`<ctype.h>`	`isspace(ch)`	`int`	Nonzero, if ch is a whitespace character (blank, newline, tab, carriage return, form feed); 0, otherwise
`<ctype.h>`	`isupper(ch)`	`int`	Nonzero, if ch is an uppercase letter ('A'–'Z'); 0, otherwise

Although Boolean is not a built-in data type in C++, the "is ... " functions behave like Boolean functions. They return an int value that is nonzero (true) or zero (false). These functions are convenient to use and make programs more readable. For example, the test

```
if (isalnum(inputChar))
```

is easier to read and less prone to error than if you coded the test the long way:

```
if (inputChar >= 'A' && inputChar <= 'Z' ||
    inputChar >= 'a' && inputChar <= 'z' ||
    inputChar >= '0' && inputChar <= '9'   )
```

In fact, this expression doesn't work correctly on some machines. We'll see why when we examine character data in Chapter 10.

> ■ *Naming Value-Returning Functions*
>
> *In Chapter 7, we said that it's good style to use verbs when naming void functions. With a value-returning function, the function call represents a value within an expression. Things that represent values, such as variables and value-returning functions, are best given names that are nouns or, occasionally, adjectives. Examples of names that suggest values rather than actions are* SquareRoot, Cube, Factorial, StudentCount, SumOfSquares, *and* SocialSecurityNum. *As you see, they are all nouns or noun phrases.*
>
> *Boolean value-returning functions are often named using adjectives or phrases beginning with* Is. *A few examples are* Valid, Odd, *and* IsTriangle.

Interface Design for Value-Returning Functions

The interface to a value-returning function is designed in much the same way as for a void function. We simply write down a list of what the function needs and what it must return. Because value-returning functions return only one value, there is only one item labeled "outgoing" in the list (the function return value). Everything else in the list is labeled "incoming," and there aren't any "incoming/outgoing" parameters.

Returning more than one value from a value-returning function (by modifying the actual parameters) is an unwanted side effect and should be avoided. If your interface design calls for multiple values to be returned or for the values of actual parameters to be changed, then you should use a void function.

A rule of thumb is never to use reference parameters in the formal parameter list of a value-returning function, but to use value parameters exclusively. An exception is the case where an I/O stream variable is passed to a value-returning function; remember, C++ allows a stream variable to be passed only to a reference parameter. Within a value-returning function, the only operation that should be performed is testing the state of the stream (for EOF or I/O errors). A value-returning function should not perform input or output operations. Such operations are considered to be side effects of the function.

> ■ *Ignoring a Function Value*
>
> *The C++ language lets you ignore the value returned by a value-returning function. For example, you could write the following statement in your program without any complaint from the compiler:*
>
> ```
> sqrt(x);
> ```

When this statement is executed, the value returned by sqrt *is promptly discarded. This call has no effect except to waste time by calculating a value that isn't used.*

Clearly, the above call to sqrt *is a mistake. But C++ programmers occasionally write value-returning functions that allow the caller to ignore the function value. Such a function is sort of a hybrid between a void function and a value-returning function.*

In this book, we don't write hybrid functions. We prefer to keep the concept of void function distinct from value-returning function. But there are two reasons why you should know about the topic of ignoring a function value. First, if you accidentally call a value-returning function as if it were a void function, the compiler won't prevent you from making the mistake. Second, you sometimes encounter this style of coding in other people's programs and in the C++ standard library. Several of the library functions are technically value-returning functions, but the function value is used merely to return something of secondary importance like a status value.

When to Use Value- Returning Functions

There aren't any formal rules for determining when to use a void function and when to use a value-returning function, but here are some guidelines:

1. If the module must return more than one value or modify any actual parameters, do not use a value-returning function.
2. If the module must perform I/O, do not use a value-returning function.
3. If there is only one value returned from the module and it is a Boolean value, a value-returning function is appropriate.
4. If there is only one value returned and that value is to be used immediately in an expression, a value-returning function is appropriate.
5. When in doubt, use a void function. You can recode any value-returning function as a void function by adding an extra outgoing parameter to carry back the computed result.
6. If both a void function and a value-returning function are acceptable, use the one you feel more comfortable implementing.

Value-returning functions were included in C++ to provide a way of simulating the mathematical concept of a function. The C++ standard library supplies a set of commonly used mathematical functions through the header file math.h. A list of these appears in Appendix C.

PROGRAMMING EXAMPLE

Starship Weight and Balance

www.jbpub.com/C++links

Problem: The company you work for has just upgraded its fleet of corporate aircraft by adding the Beechcraft Starship-1. As with any airplane, it is essential that the pilot know the total weight of the loaded plane at takeoff and its center of gravity. If the plane weighs too much, it won't be able to lift off. If its center of gravity is outside the limits established for the plane, it might be impossible to control. Either situation can lead to a crash. You have been asked to write a program that determines the weight and center of gravity of this new plane, based on the number of crew members and passengers as well as the weight of the baggage, closet contents, and fuel.

Input: Number of crew members, number of passengers, weight of closet contents, baggage weight, fuel in gallons.

Output: Total weight, center of gravity.

Discussion: As with most real-world problems, the basic solution is simple but is complicated by special cases. We use value-returning functions to hide the complexity so that the `main` function remains simple.

The total weight is basically the sum of the empty weight of the airplane plus the weight of each of the following: crew members, passengers, baggage, contents of the storage closet, and fuel. We use the standard average weight of a person, 170 pounds, to compute the total weight of the people. The weight of the baggage and the contents of the closet are given. Fuel weighs 6.7 pounds per gallon. Thus, the total weight is

$$\text{totalWeight} = \text{emptyWeight} + (\text{crew} + \text{passengers}) * 170 + \text{baggage} + \text{closet} + \text{fuel} * 6.7$$

To compute the center of gravity, each weight is multiplied by its distance from the front of the airplane, and the products—called *moment arms* or simply *moments*—are then summed and divided by the total weight (see Figure 8-3).

The formula is thus

$$\text{centerOfGravity} = (\text{emptyMoment} + \text{crewMoment} + \text{passengerMoment} + \text{cargoMoment} + \text{fuelMoment})/\text{totalWeight}$$

The Starship-1 manual gives the distance from the front of the plane to the crew's seats, closet, baggage compartment, and fuel tanks. There are four rows of

PROGRAMMING EXAMPLE cont'd

FIGURE 8-3 A Passenger Moment Arm

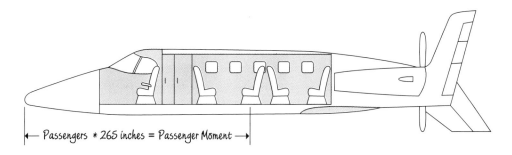

Passengers ∗ 265 inches = Passenger Moment

passenger seats, so this calculation depends on where the individual passengers sit. We have to make some assumptions about how passengers arrange themselves. Each row has two seats. The most popular seats are in row 2 because they are near the entrance and face forward. Once row 2 is filled, passengers usually take seats in row 1, facing their traveling companions. Row 3 is usually the next to fill up, even though it faces backward, because row 4 is a fold-down bench seat that is less comfortable than the armchairs in the forward rows. The following table gives the distance from the nose of the plane to each of the "loading stations."

Loading Station	Distance from Nose (inches)
Crew seats	143
Row 1 seats	219
Row 2 seats	265
Row 3 seats	295
Row 4 seats	341
Closet	182
Baggage	386

The distance for the fuel varies because there are several tanks, and the tanks are in different places. As fuel is added to the plane, it automatically flows into the different tanks so that the center of gravity changes as the tanks are filled. There are four formulas for computing the distance from the nose to the "center" of the fuel tanks, depending on how much fuel is being loaded into the plane. The following table lists these distance formulas.

PROGRAMMING EXAMPLE cont'd

Gallons of Fuel (G)	Distance (D) Formula
0–59	$D = 314.6 * G$
60–360	$D = 305.8 + (-0.01233 * (G - 60))$
361–520	$D = 303.0 + (0.12500 * (G - 361))$
521–565	$D = 323.0 + (-0.04444 * (G - 521))$

We define one value-returning function for each of the different moments, and we name these functions `CrewMoment`, `PassengerMoment`, `CargoMoment`, and `FuelMoment`. The center of gravity is then computed with the formula we gave earlier and the following parameters:

centerOfGravity = (CrewMoment(crew) + PassengerMoment(passengers) + CargoMoment(closet, baggage) + FuelMoment(fuel) + emptyMoment) /totalWeight

The empty weight of the Starship is 9887 pounds, and its empty center of gravity is 319 inches from the front of the airplane. Thus, the empty moment is 3,153,953 inch-pounds.

We now have enough information to write the algorithm to solve this problem. We'll use a void function to get the data. The `main` function then computes the total weight and uses our value-returning functions in its calculation of the center of gravity. It then prints these two results. In addition to printing the results, we'll also print a warning message that states the assumptions of the program and tells the pilot to double-check the results by hand if the weight or center of gravity is near the allowable limits. The warning message is printed by another void function.

Module Structure Chart:

The following chart introduces a new notation. The box corresponding to each value-returning function has an upward arrow originating at its right side. This arrow signifies the function value that is returned.

PROGRAMMING EXAMPLE cont'd

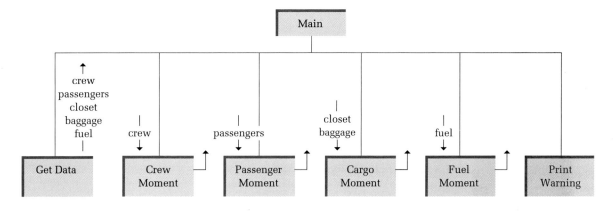

Here is the program that implements our algorithm.

```
//*********************************************************************
// Starship program
// This program computes the total weight and center of gravity
// of a Beechcraft Starship-1
//*********************************************************************
#include <iostream.h>
#include <iomanip.h>        // For setw() and setprecision()
const float PERSON_WT = 170.0;        // Average person weighs
                                      //    170 lbs.
const float LBS_PER_GAL = 6.7;        // Jet-A weighs 6.7 lbs.
                                      //    per gal.
const float EMPTY_WEIGHT = 9887.0;    // Standard empty weight
const float EMPTY_MOMENT = 3153953.0; // Standard empty moment

float CargoMoment( int, int );
float CrewMoment( int );
float FuelMoment( int );
void  GetData( int&, int&, int&, int&, int& );
float PassengerMoment( int );
void  PrintWarning();
```

PROGRAMMING EXAMPLE cont'd

```cpp
int main()
{
    int    crew;           // Number of crew on board (1 or 2)
    int    passengers;     // Number of passengers (0 through 8)
    int    closet;         // Weight in closet (160 lbs. maximum)
    int    baggage;        // Weight of baggage (525 lbs. max.)
    int    fuel;           // Gallons of fuel (10 through 565 gals.)
    float  totalWt;        // Total weight of the loaded Starship
    float  centerOfGravity; // Center of gravity of loaded Starship

    cout.setf(ios::fixed, ios::floatfield);   // Set up floating pt.
    cout.setf(ios::showpoint);                //    output format

    GetData(crew, passengers, closet, baggage, fuel);

    totalWt =
        EMPTY_WEIGHT + float(passengers + crew) * PERSON_WT +
        float(baggage + closet) + float(fuel) * LBS_PER_GAL;
    centerOfGravity =
        (CrewMoment(crew) + PassengerMoment(passengers) +
        CargoMoment(closet, baggage) + FuelMoment(fuel) +
        EMPTY_MOMENT) / totalWt;

    cout << "Total weight is " << setprecision(2) << totalWt
        << " pounds." << endl;
    cout << "Center of gravity is " << centerOfGravity
        << " inches from the front of the plane." << endl;
    PrintWarning();
    return 0;
}


//*******************************************************************

void GetData( /* out */ int& crew,         // Number of crew members
              /* out */ int& passengers,   // Number of passengers
              /* out */ int& closet,       // Weight of closet cargo
              /* out */ int& baggage,      // Weight of baggage
              /* out */ int& fuel       )  // Gallons of fuel

// Prompts for input and returns five values

// Postcondition:
//     All parameters (crew, passengers, closet, baggage, and fuel)
//     have been prompted for, input, and echo printed
```

PROGRAMMING EXAMPLE cont'd

```cpp
{
    cout << "Enter the number of crew members." << endl;
    cin >> crew;
    cout << "Enter the number of passengers." << endl;
    cin >> passengers;
    cout << "Enter the weight, in pounds, of cargo in the" << endl
        << " closet, rounded up to the nearest whole number."
        << endl;
    cin >> closet;
    cout << "Enter the weight, in pounds, of cargo in the" << endl
        << " aft baggage compartment, rounded up to the" << endl
        << " nearest whole number." << endl;
    cin >> baggage;
    cout << "Enter the number of U.S. gallons of fuel" << endl
        << " loaded, rounded up to the nearest whole number."
        << endl;
    cin >> fuel;
    cout << endl;
    cout << "Starship loading data as entered:" << endl
        << "    Crew:           " << setw(6) << crew << endl
        << "    Passengers:     " << setw(6) << passengers << endl
        << "    Closet weight:  " << setw(6) << closet << " pounds"
        << endl
        << "    Baggage weight: " << setw(6) << baggage << " pounds"
        << endl
        << "    Fuel:           " << setw(6) << fuel << " gallons"
        << endl << endl;
}


//*********************************************************************

float CrewMoment( /* in */ int crew )    // Number of crew members

// Computes the crew moment arm in inch-pounds

// Global constant PERSON_WT is used

// Precondition:
//    crew == 1  OR  crew == 2
// Postcondition:
//    Function value == Crew moment arm, based on the crew parameter

{
    const float CREW_DISTANCE = 143.0;  // Distance to crew seats
                                        //    from front
```

PROGRAMMING EXAMPLE cont'd

```
        return float(crew) * PERSON_WT * CREW_DISTANCE;
}


//***************************************************************

float PassengerMoment( /* in */ int passengers )   // Number of
                                              //   passengers


// Computes the passenger moment arm in inch-pounds
// Global constant PERSON_WT is used as the weight

// Precondition:
//     0 <= passengers <= 8
// Postcondition:
//     Function value == Passenger moment arm, based on the
//                       passengers parameter

{
    const float ROW1_DIST = 219.0;  // Distance to row 1 seats
                                    //   from front
    const float ROW2_DIST = 265.0;  // Distance to row 2 seats
    const float ROW3_DIST = 295.0;  // Distance to row 3 seats
    const float ROW4_DIST = 341.0;  // Distance to row 4 seats

    float moment = 0.0;             // Running total of moment as
                                    //   rows are added

    if (passengers > 6)                     // For passengers 7 and 8
    {
        moment = moment +
                float(passengers - 6) * PERSON_WT * ROW4_DIST;
        passengers = 6;                 // 6 remain
    }
    if (passengers > 4)                     // For passengers 5 and 6
    {
        moment = moment +
                float(passengers - 4) * PERSON_WT * ROW3_DIST;
        passengers = 4;                 // 4 remain
    }
    if (passengers > 2)                     // For passengers 3 and 4
    {
        moment = moment +
                float(passengers - 2) * PERSON_WT * ROW1_DIST;
        passengers = 2;                 // 2 remain
    }
```

PROGRAMMING EXAMPLE cont'd

```
        if (passengers > 0)                    // For passengers 1 and 2
            moment = moment +
                      float(passengers) * PERSON_WT * ROW2_DIST;
        return moment;
    }


//*****************************************************************


float CargoMoment( /* in */ int closet,     // Weight in closet
                   /* in */ int baggage )   // Weight of baggage

// Computes the total moment arm for cargo

// Precondition:
//     0 <= closet <= 160   &&   0 <= baggage <= 525
// Postcondition:
//     Function value == Cargo moment arm, based on the closet and
//                       baggage parameters

{
    const float CLOSET_DIST = 182.0;     // Distance from front
                                         //   to closet
    const float BAGGAGE_DIST = 386.0;    // Distance from front
                                         //   to bagg. comp.


    return float(closet) * CLOSET_DIST +
           float(baggage) * BAGGAGE_DIST;
}


//*****************************************************************


float FuelMoment( /* in */ int fuel )   // Fuel in gallons

// Computes the moment arm for fuel on board.
// Uses the global constant LBS_PER_GAL

// Precondition:
//     10 <= fuel <= 565
// Postcondition:
//     Function value == Fuel moment arm, based on the
//                       fuel parameter

{
    float fuelWt;            // Weight of fuel in pounds
    float fuelDistance;      // Distance from front of plane
```

PROGRAMMING EXAMPLE cont'd

```
    fuelWt = float(fuel) * LBS_PER_GAL;
    if (fuel < 60)
        fuelDistance = float(fuel) * 314.6;
    else if (fuel < 361)
        fuelDistance = 305.8 + (-0.01233 * float(fuel - 60));
    else if (fuel < 521)
        fuelDistance = 303.0 + ( 0.12500 * float(fuel - 361));
    else
        fuelDistance = 323.0 + (-0.04444 * float(fuel - 521));
    return fuelDistance * fuelWt;
}


//********************************************************************

void PrintWarning()

// Warns the user when to double check the results

// Postcondition:
//      An informational warning message has been printed

{
    cout << endl
        << "Notice:  This program assumes that passengers" << endl
        << "  fill the seat rows in order 2, 1, 3, 4, and" << endl
        << "  that each passenger and crew member weighs "
        << PERSON_WT << " pounds." << endl
        << "  It also assumes that Jet-A fuel weighs "
        << LBS_PER_GAL << " pounds" << endl
        << "  per U.S. gallon.  The center of gravity" << endl
        << "  calculations for fuel are approximate.  If" << endl
        << "  the aircraft is loaded near its limits, the" << endl
        << "  pilot's operating handbook should be used" << endl
        << "  to compute weight and center of gravity" << endl
        << "  with more accuracy." << endl;
}
```

Testing: Because someone could use the output of this program to make decisions that could result in property damage, injury, or death, it is essential to test the program thoroughly. In particular, it should be checked for maximum and minimum input values in different combinations. In addition, a wide range of test cases should be tried and verified against results calculated by hand. If possible, the program's output should be checked against sample calculations done by experienced pilots for actual flights.

Notice that the main function neglects to guarantee any of the function preconditions before calling the functions. If this program were actually to be used by pilots, it should have validation checks added in GetData.

Testing and Debugging

One of the advantages of a modular design is that you can test it long before the code has been written for all of the modules. If we test each module individually, then we can assemble the modules into a complete program with much greater confidence that the program is correct. In this section, we introduce a technique for testing a module separately.

Stubs and Drivers

Suppose you were given the code for a module and your job was to test it. How would you test a single module by itself? First of all, it must be called by something (unless it is the `main` function). Second, it may have calls to other modules that aren't available to you. To test the module, you must fill in these missing links.

stub

A dummy function that assists in testing part of a program. A stub has the same name and interface as a function that actually would be called by the part of the program being tested, but it is usually much simpler

When a module contains calls to other modules, we can write dummy functions called **stubs** to satisfy those calls. A stub usually consists of an output statement that prints a message like, "Function such-and-such just got called." Even though the stub is a dummy, it allows us to determine whether the function is called at the right time.

A stub can also be used to print the set of values that are passed to it; this tells us whether or not the module under test is supplying the proper information. Sometimes the stub will assign new values to its reference parameters to simulate data being read or results being computed to give the module something to keep working on. Because we can choose the values that are returned by the stub, we have better control over the conditions of the test run.

driver

A simple `main` function that is used to call a function being tested. The use of a driver permits direct control of the testing process

In addition to supplying a stub for each call within the module, you must provide a dummy program—a **driver**—to call the module itself. A driver program contains the bare minimum of code required to call the module being tested.

By surrounding a module with a driver and stubs, you gain complete control of the conditions under which it executes. This allows you to test different situations and combinations that may reveal errors.

Testing and Debugging Hints

1. Make sure that variables used as actual parameters to a function are declared in the block where the function call is made.
2. Carefully define the preconditions, postconditions, and parameter list to eliminate side effects. Variables used only in a function should be local. *Do not* use global variables in your programs. (*Exception:* It is acceptable to reference the global variables `cin` and `cout`.)
3. If the compiler displays a message such as "UNDECLARED IDENTIFIER," check that identifiers aren't misspelled, that they are declared, that their declaration precedes any references, and that the scope of each identifier includes the references to it.

4. If you intend to use a local name that is the same as a nonlocal name, a misspelling in the local declaration will wreak havoc. The C++ compiler won't complain, but will cause every reference to the local name to go to the nonlocal name instead.

5. Remember that the same identifier cannot be used in both the formal parameter list and the outermost local declarations of a function.

6. With a value-returning function, be sure the function heading and prototype begin with the correct data type for the function return value.

7. With a value-returning function, don't forget to use a statement

```
return Expression;
```

to return the function value. Make sure the expression is of the correct type, or implicit type coercion will occur.

8. Remember that a call to a value-returning function is part of an expression, whereas a call to a void function is a separate statement. (But C++ lets you call a value-returning function as if it were a void function, ignoring the return value. Be careful here.)

9. In general, don't use reference parameters in the formal parameter list of a value-returning function. A reference parameter must be used, however, when an I/O stream variable is passed as a parameter.

10. If necessary, use debug output statements to indicate when a function is called and if it is executing correctly. The values in the actual parameters can be printed immediately before (to show the incoming values) and immediately after (to show the outgoing values) the call to the function. You may want to use debug output statements in the function itself to indicate what happens each time it is called.

Summary

The scope of an identifier refers to the parts of the program in which it is visible. C++ functions have global scope, as do variables and constants that are declared outside all functions. Variables and constants declared within a block have local scope; they are not visible outside the block. The formal parameters of a function have the same scope as local variables declared in the outermost block of a function.

With rare exceptions, it is considered poor practice to declare global variables and reference them directly from a function. All communication between the modules of a program should be through the formal and actual parameter lists (and via the function value sent back by a value-returning function). The use of global constants, on the other hand, is considered to be an acceptable programming practice because it adds consistency and makes a program easier to change while avoiding the pitfalls of side effects. Well-designed and well-documented functions that are free of side effects can often be reused in other programs. Many programmers keep a library of functions that they use repeatedly.

The lifetime of a variable is the period of time during program execution when memory is allocated to it. Global variables have static lifetime (memory remains allocated for the duration of the program's execution). By default, local variables have automatic lifetime (memory is allocated and deallocated at block entry and block exit). A local variable may be given static lifetime by using the word `static` in its declaration. This variable has the lifetime of a global variable but the scope of a local variable.

C++ allows a variable to be initialized in its declaration. For a static variable, the initialization occurs once only—when control first reaches its declaration. An automatic variable is initialized each time control reaches the declaration.

C++ provides two kinds of subprograms, void functions and value-returning functions. A value-returning function is called from within an expression and returns a single result that is used in the evaluation of the expression. For the function value to be returned, the last statement executed by the function must be a `return` statement containing an expression of the appropriate data type.

All the scope rules, as well as the rules about reference and value parameters, apply to both void functions and value-returning functions. It is considered poor programming practice, however, to use reference parameters in a value-returning function declaration. Doing so increases the potential for side effects. (I/O stream variables are an exception.)

We can use stubs and drivers to test functions in isolation from the rest of a program. They are particularly useful in the context of team-programming projects.

Quick Check

1. a. How can you tell if a variable that is referenced inside a function is local or global? (pp. 240–242)
   b. Where are local variables declared? (pp. 240–242)
   c. When does the scope of an identifier declared in block A exclude a block nested within block A? (pp. 242–243)
2. A program consists of two functions, `main` and `DoCalc`. A variable x is declared outside both functions. `DoCalc` declares two variables, a and b, within its body; b is declared as `static`. In what function(s) are each of a, b, and x visible, and what is the lifetime of each variable? (pp. 242–245, 247–249)
3. Why should you use value parameters whenever possible? Why should you avoid the use of global variables? (pp. 249–251)
4. For each of the following, decide whether a value-returning function or a void function is the most appropriate implementation. (pp. 257–258)
   a. Selecting the larger of two values for further processing in an expression.
   b. Printing a paycheck.
   c. Computing the area of a hexagon.
   d. Testing whether an incoming value is valid and returning `true` if it is.
   e. Computing the two roots of a quadratic equation.

5. What would the heading for a value-returning function named `Min` look like if it had two `float` parameters, `num1` and `num2`, and returned a `float` result? (pp. 251–254)
6. What would a call to `Min` look like if the actual parameters were a variable named `deductions` and the literal `2000.0`? (pp. 251–254)

Answers 1. a. If the variable is not declared in either the body of the function or its formal parameter list, then the reference is global. b. Local variables are declared within a block (compound statement). c. When the nested block declares an identifier with the same name. 2. `x` is visible to both functions, but `a` and `b` are visible only within `DoCalc`. `x` and `b` are static variables; once memory is allocated to them, they are "alive" until the program terminates. `a` is an automatic variable; it is "alive" only while `DoCalc` is executing. 3. Both using value parameters and avoiding global variables will minimize side effects. Also, pass-by-value allows the actual parameters to be arbitrary expressions. 4. a. Value-returning function b. Void function c. Value-returning function d. Value-returning function e. Void function

```
5. float Min( float num1,
              float num2 )
6. smaller = Min(deductions, 2000.0);
```

Exam Preparation Exercises

1. If a function contains a locally declared variable with the same name as a global variable, no confusion results because references to variables in functions are first interpreted as references to local variables. (True or False?)
2. Variables declared at the beginning of a block are accessible to all statements in that block, including those in nested blocks (assuming the nested blocks don't declare local variables with the same names). (True or False?)
3. Define the following terms.

local variable	scope
global variable	side effects
lifetime	name precedence (name hiding)

4. What is the output of the following C++ program? (This program is an example of poor interface design practices.)

```
#include <iostream.h>

void DoGlobal();
void DoLocal();
void DoReference( int& );
void DoValue( int );

int x;
```

```
int main()
{
    x = 15;
    DoReference(x);
    cout << "x = " << x << " after the call to DoReference."
        << endl;
    x = 16;
    DoValue(x);
    cout << "x = " << x << " after the call to DoValue."
        << endl;
    x = 17;
    DoLocal();
    cout << "x = " << x << " after the call to DoLocal."
        << endl;
    x = 18;
    DoGlobal();
    cout << "x = " << x << " after the call to DoGlobal."
        << endl;
    return 0;
}


void DoReference( int& a )
{
    a = 3;
}


void DoValue( int b )
{
    b = 4;
}


void DoLocal()
{
    int x;

    x = 5;
}


void DoGlobal()
{
    x = 7;
}
```

5. What is the output of the following program?

```
#include <iostream.h>

void Test();

int main()
{
    Test();
    Test();
    Test();
    return 0;
}

void Test()
{
    int i = 0;
    static int j = 0;

    i++;
    j++;
    cout << i << ' ' << j << endl;
}
```

6. The following function calculates the sum of the numbers from 1 through n. However, it has an unintended side effect. What is it?

```
void SumInts( int& n,
              int& sum )
{
    sum = 0;
    while (n >= 1)
    {
        sum = sum + n;
        n = n - 1;
    }
}
```

7. Given the function heading

```
Boolean HighTaxBracket( int inc,
                        int ded )
```

is the following statement a legal call to the function if `income` and `deductions` are of type `int`?

```
if (HighTaxBracket(income, deductions))
    cout << "Upper Class";
```

8. The statement

```
Power(k, 1, m);
```

is a call to the following void function. Rewrite the function as a value-returning function, then write a function call that assigns the function value to the variable m.

```
void Power( float  base,
            int    exponent,
            float& answer   )
{
    int i;

    answer = 1.0;
    i = 1;
    while (i <= exponent)
    {
        answer = answer * base;
        i++;
    }
}
```

9. You are given the following Test function and a C++ program in which the variables a, b, c, and result are declared to be of type float. In the calling code, a = −5.0, b = 0.1, and c = 16.2. What is the value of result when each of the following calls returns?

```
float Test( float x,
            float y,
            float z )
{
    if (x > y || y > z)
        return 0.5;
    else
        return -0.5;
}
```

a. result = Test(5.2, 5.3, 5.6);
b. result = Test(fabs(a), b, c);

10. What is wrong with each of the following C++ function definitions?

a. ```
void Test1(int m,
            int n)
{
    return 3 * m + n;
}
```
b. ```
float Test2( int    i,
             float x )
{
    i = i + 7;
    x = 4.8 + float(i);
}
```

11. Explain why it is risky to use a reference parameter as a formal parameter of a value-returning function.

Programming Warm-Up Exercises

1. The following program is written with very poor style. For one thing, global variables are used in place of parameters. Rewrite it without global variables, using good programming style.

```
#include <iostream.h>
void MashGlobals();
int a, b, c;
int main()
{
cin >> a >> b >> c;
MashGlobals();
cout << "a=" << a << ' ' << "b=" << b << ' '
<< "c=" << c << endl;
return 0;
}
void MashGlobals()
{
int temp;
temp = a + b;
a = b + c;
b = temp;
}
```

2. Write the heading for a value-returning function Epsilon that receives two float parameters named high and low and returns a float result.

3. Write the heading for a value-returning function named `NearlyEqual` that receives three `float` parameters—num1, num2, and `difference`—and returns a Boolean result.

4. Given the heading you wrote in Exercise 3, write the body of the function. The function returns `true` if the absolute value of the difference between num1 and num2 is less than the value in `difference` and returns `false` otherwise.

5. Write a value-returning function named `CompassHeading` that returns the sum of its four `float` parameters: `trueCourse`, `windCorrAngle`, `variance`, and `deviation`.

6. Write a value-returning function named `FracPart` that receives a floating point number and returns the fractional part of that number. Use a single parameter named x. For example, if the incoming value of x is 16.753, the function return value is 0.753.

7. Write a value-returning function named `Circumf` that finds the circumference of a circle given the radius. The formula for calculating the circumference of a circle is π multiplied by twice the radius. Use 3.14159 for π.

8. Given the function heading

```
float Hypotenuse( float side1,
                  float side2 )
```

write the body of the function to return the length of the hypotenuse of a right triangle. The formal parameters represent the lengths of the other two sides. The formula for the hypotenuse is

$$\sqrt{side1^2 + side2^2}$$

9. Write a value-returning function named `FifthPow` that returns the fifth power of its `float` parameter.

10. Write a value-returning function named `Min` that returns the smallest of its three integer parameters.

11. The following If conditions work correctly on most, but not all, machines. Rewrite them using the "is ..." functions from the C++ standard library (header file `ctype.h`).

```
a. if (inChar >= '0' && inChar <= '9')
       DoSomething();
b. if (inChar >= 'A' && inChar <= 'Z' ||
       inChar >= 'a' && inChar <= 'z'  )
       DoSomething();
c. if (inChar >= 'A' && inChar <= 'Z' ||
       inChar >= '0' && inChar <= '9'  )
       DoSomething();
d. if (inChar < 'a' || inChar > 'z')
       DoSomething();
```

12. Write a Boolean value-returning function `IsPrime` that receives an integer parameter n, tests it to see if it is a prime number, and returns `true` if it is. (A prime number

is an integer greater than or equal to 2 whose only divisors are 1 and the number it-self.) A call to this function might look like this:

```
if (IsPrime(n))
    cout << n << " is a prime number.";
```

(*Hint:* If n is not a prime number, it is exactly divisible by an integer in the range 2 through √n.)

13. Write a value-returning function named `Postage` that returns the cost of mailing a package, given the weight of the package in pounds and ounces and the cost per ounce.

14. In the Starship program, the `main` function neglects to guarantee any of the function preconditions before calling the functions. Modify the `GetData` function to validate the input data. When control returns from `GetData`, the `main` function should be able to assume that all the data values are within the proper ranges.

Programming Problems

1. If a principal amount (P), for which the interest is compounded Q times per year, is placed in a savings account, then the amount of interest earned after N years is given by the following formula, where I is the annual interest rate as a floating point number:

amount $= P * (1 + I/Q)^{N*Q}$

Write a C++ program that inputs the values for P, I, Q, and N and outputs the inter-est earned for each year up through year N. You should use a value-returning func-tion to compute the amount of interest. Your program should prompt the user appropriately, label output values, and have good style.

2. The distance to the landing point of a projectile, launched at an angle `angle` (in radi-ans) with an initial velocity of `velocity` (in feet per second), ignoring air resistance, is given by the formula

$$\text{distance} = \frac{\text{velocity}^2 * \sin(2 * \text{angle})}{32.2}$$

Write a C++ program that implements a game in which the user first enters the dis-tance to a target. The user then enters the angle and velocity for launching a projectile. If the projectile comes within a tenth of one percent of the distance to the target, the user wins the game. If the projectile doesn't come close enough, the user is told how far off the projectile is and is allowed to try again. If after five tries there isn't a win-ning input, then the user loses the game.

To simplify input for the user, your program should allow the angle to be input in degrees. The formula for converting degrees to radians is

$$\text{radians} = \frac{\text{degrees} * 3.14159265}{180.0}$$

Each of the formulas in this problem should be implemented as a C++ value-returning function in your program. Your program should prompt the user for input appropriately, label the output values, and have proper programming style.

3. Write a program that computes the number of days between two dates. One way of doing this is to have the program compute the Julian day number for each of the dates and subtract one from the other. The Julian day number is the number of days that have elapsed since noon on January 1, 4713 B.C. The following algorithm may be used to calculate the Julian day number.

Given `year` (an integer, such as 1997), `month` (an integer from 1 through 12), and `day` (an integer from 1 through 31), if `month` is 1 or 2, then subtract 1 from `year` and add 12 to `month`.

If the date comes from the Gregorian calendar (later than October 15, 1582), then compute an intermediate result with the following formula (otherwise, let `intRes1` equal 0):

intRes1 = 2 − year / 100 + year / 400   (integer division)

Compute a second intermediate result with the formula

intRes2 = int(365.25 ∗ year)

Compute a third intermediate result with the formula

intRes3 = int(30.6001 ∗ (month + 1))

Finally, the Julian day number is computed with the formula

julianDay = intRes1 + intRes2 + intRes3 + day + 1720994.5

Your program should make appropriate use of value-returning functions in solving this problem. These formulas require nine significant digits; you may have to use the floating point type `double` or `long double`. Your program should prompt appropriately for input (the two dates). You should use proper style with plenty of comments.

9 Additional Control Structures

GOALS

- To be able to write a Switch statement for a multi-way branching problem
- To be able to write a Do-While statement and contrast it with a While statement
- To be able to write a For statement as an alternative to a While statement
- To understand the purpose of the `break` and `continue` statements
- To be able to choose the most appropriate looping statement for a given problem

In the preceding chapters, we introduced C++ statements for sequence, selection, loop, and subprogram. In some cases, we introduced more than one way of implementing these structures. For example, selection may be implemented by an If-Then statement or an If-Then-Else statement. The If-Then is sufficient to implement any selection structure, but C++ provides the If-Then-Else for convenience because the two-way branch is frequently used in programming.

This chapter introduces five new statements that are also nonessential to, but nonetheless convenient for, programming. One, the Switch statement, makes it easier to write selection structures that have many branches. Two new looping statements, For and Do-While, make it easier to program certain types of loops. The other two statements, `break` and `continue`, are control statements that are used as part of larger looping and selection structures.

The Switch Statement

switch expression
The expression whose value determines which switch label is selected. It cannot be a floating point expression

The Switch statement is a control structure for multi-way branches, similar to nested If statements. The value of the **switch expression**—an expression whose value is matched with a label attached to a branch—determines which one of the branches is executed. For example, in the following statement,

```
switch (letter)
{
    case 'X' : Statement1;
               break;
    case 'L' :
    case 'M' : Statement2;
               break;
    case 'S' : Statement3;
               break;
    default  : Statement4;
}
Statement5;
```

`letter` is the switch expression. The statement means "If `letter` is 'X', execute Statement1. If `letter` is 'L' or 'M', execute Statement2. If `letter` is 'S', execute Statement3. If `letter` is none of the above, execute Statement4." The `break` statement causes control to skip to the statement immediately after the Switch statement (Statement5). If we omit the `break` statements, then all of the statements following the selected branch are also executed. For example, if `letter` is 'M', in the following erroneous code,

```
switch (letter)
{
    case 'X': Statement1;
    case 'L':
    case 'M': Statement2;
    case 'S': Statement3;
    default : Statement4;
}
Statement5;
```

then execution skips to Statement2 and then continues uninterrupted with Statement3, Statement4, and Statement 5. Normal practice in writing a Switch statement is to end each branch with a `break` statement. Forgetting a `break` statement in a case alternative is a very common source of errors in C++ programs.

A Switch expression is an expression of an integral type—`char`, `short`, `int`, `long`, or `enum` (we discuss `enum` in the next chapter). The optional label in front of each branch is either a *case* label or *default.*

A case label expression is an integral expression whose operands must be literal or named constants. The following are examples of constant integral expressions (`CLASS_SIZE` is a named constant of type `int`):

```
3
CLASS_SIZE
'A'
2 * CLASS_SIZE + 1
```

The data type of a case label expression is coerced, if necessary, to match the type of the switch expression.

In our opening example that tests the value of `letter`, the following are case labels:

```
case 'X' :
case 'L' :
case 'M' :
case 'S' :
```

As the example shows, a single statement may be preceded by more than one case label. Each case constant may appear only once in a given Switch statement. If a value appears more than once, a syntax error results. Also, there can be only one default label in a Switch statement.

The flow of control through a Switch statement goes like this. First, the switch expression is evaluated. If the value matches one of the constants in a case label, control branches to the statement following that case label. From there, control proceeds sequentially until either a `break` statement or the end of the Switch statement is encountered. If the value of the switch expression doesn't match any case constant, then one of two things happens. If there is a default label, control branches to the statement following that label. If there is no default label, all statements within the Switch are skipped and control simply proceeds to the statement following the entire Switch statement.

The following Switch statement prints an appropriate comment based on a student's grade (`grade` is of type `char`):

```
switch (grade)
{
    case 'A' :
    case 'B' : cout << "Good Work";
               break;
    case 'C' : cout << "Average Work";
```

```
                break;
      case 'D' :
      case 'F' : cout << "Poor Work";
                 numberInTrouble++;
                 break;              // Unnecessary, but a good habit
    }
```

Notice that the final break statement is unnecessary. But programmers often include it because it's easier to insert another case label at the end if there is already a break statement present.

If grade does not contain one of the specified characters, none of the statements within the Switch is executed. Unless a precondition of the Switch statement is that grade is definitely one of 'A', 'B', 'C', 'D', or 'F', it would be wise to include a default label to account for an invalid grade:

```
switch (grade)
{
    case 'A' :
    case 'B' : cout << "Good Work";
               break;
    case 'C' : cout << "Average Work";
               break;
    case 'D' :
    case 'F' : cout << "Poor Work";
               numberInTrouble++;
               break;
    default  : cout << grade << " is not a legal letter grade.";
               break;
}
```

A Switch statement with a break statement after each case alternative behaves exactly like an If-Then-Else-If control structure. For example, our Switch statement is equivalent to the following code:

```
if (grade == 'A' || grade == 'B')
    cout << "Good Work";
else if (grade == 'C')
    cout << "Average Work";
else if (grade == 'D' || grade == 'F')
{
    cout << "Poor Work";
    numberInTrouble++;
}
else
    cout << grade << " is not a legal letter grade.";
```

The Do-While Statement

The Do-While statement is a looping control structure in which the loop condition is tested at the end (bottom) of the loop, which guarantees that the loop body is executed at least once.

Here is an example of a Do-While statement:

```
do
{
    Statement1 ;
    Statement2 ;
       .
       .
       .
    StatementN ;
} while (Expression) ;
```

This statement executes the compound statement between `do` and `while` as long as Expression is still nonzero (`true`) at the end of the loop.

Let's compare a While loop and a Do-While loop that do the same task: they find the first period in a file of data. Assume that there is at least one period in the file.

While Solution

```
dataFile >> inputChar;
while (inputChar != '.')
    dataFile >> inputChar;
```

Do-While Solution

```
do
    dataFile >> inputChar;
while (inputChar != '.');
```

The While solution requires a priming read so that `inputChar` has a value before the loop is entered. This isn't required for the Do-While solution because the input statement within the loop is executed before the loop condition is evaluated.

Let's look at another example. Suppose a program needs to read a person's age interactively. The program requires that the age be positive. The following loops ensure that the input value is positive before the program proceeds any further.

While Solution

```
cout << "Enter your age: ";
cin >> age;
while (age <= 0)
{
    cout << "Your age must be positive." << endl;
    cout << "Enter your age: ";
    cin >> age;
}
```

Do-While Solution

```
do
{
    cout << "Enter your age: ";
    cin >> age;
    if (age <= 0)
        cout << "Your age must be positive." << endl;
} while (age <= 0);
```

Notice that the Do-While solution does not require the prompt and input steps to appear twice—once before the loop and once within it—but it does test the input value twice.

We can also use the Do-While to implement a count-controlled loop *if* we know in advance that the loop body is always executed at least once. Below are two versions of a loop to sum the integers from 1 through n.

While Solution	*Do-While Solution*
| ```
sum = 0;
counter = 1;
while (counter <= n)
{
    sum = sum + counter;
    counter++;
}
``` | ```
sum = 0;
counter = 1;
do
{
    sum = sum + counter;
    counter++;
} while (counter <= n);
``` |

If n is a positive number, both of these versions are equivalent. But if n is 0 or negative, the two loops give different results. In the While version, the final value of `sum` is 0 because the loop body is never entered. In the Do-While version, the final value of `sum` is 1 because the body executes once and *then* the loop test is made.

Because the While statement tests the condition before executing the body of the loop, it is called a *pretest loop*. The Do-While statement does the opposite and thus is known as a *posttest loop*. Figure 9-1 compares the flow of control in the While and Do-While loops.

FIGURE 9-1

Flow of Control:
While and
Do-While

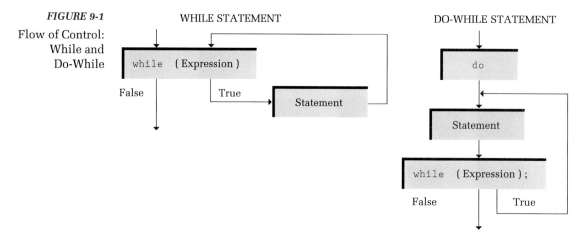

After we look at two other new looping constructs, we offer some guidelines for determining when to use each type of loop.

The For Statement

The For statement is designed to simplify the writing of count-controlled loops. The following statement prints out the integers from 1 through n:

```
for (count = 1; count <= n; count++)
    cout << count << endl;
```

This For statement means "Initialize the loop control variable `count` to 1. While `count` is less than or equal to n, execute the output statement and increment `count` by 1."

In C++, a For statement is merely a compact notation for a While loop. In fact, the compiler essentially translates a For statement into an equivalent While loop as follows:

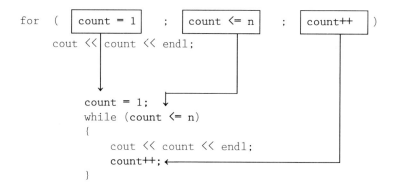

The syntax template for a For statement is

ForStatement

> for (InitStatement Expression1 ; Expression 2)
>   Statement

Expression1 is the While condition. InitStatement is a statement that always ends in a semicolon. Therefore, there is always a semicolon before Expression1. (You don't see a semicolon in the syntax template. If we included one, you would have to use *two* semicolons—one to terminate InitStatement and another before Expression1.)

Most often, a For statement is written such that InitStatement initializes a loop control variable and Expression2 increments or decrements the loop control variable. Here are two loops that execute the same number of times (50):

```
for (loopCount = 1; loopCount <= 50; loopCount++)
    .
    .
    .


for (loopCount = 50; loopCount >= 1; loopCount--)
    .
    .
    .
```

Just like While loops, Do-While and For loops may be nested. For example, the nested For structure

```
for (lastNum = 1; lastNum <= 7; lastNum++)
{
    for (numToPrint = 1; numToPrint <= lastNum; numToPrint++)
        cout << numToPrint;
    cout << endl;
}
```

prints the following triangle of numbers.

```
1
12
123
1234
12345
123456
1234567
```

The Break and Continue Statements

www.jbpub.com/C++links

The break statement, which we introduced with the Switch statement, can also be used with loops. A break statement causes an immediate exit from the innermost Switch, While, Do-While, or For statement in which it appears. Notice the word *innermost*. If break is in a loop that is nested inside another loop, control exits the inner loop but not the outer.

One of the more common ways of using break with loops is to set up an infinite loop and use If tests to exit the loop. Suppose we want to input 10 pairs of integers, performing data validation and computing the square root of the sum of each pair. For data validation, assume that the first number must be less than 100 and the second must be greater than 50. Also, after each input, we want to test the state of the stream for EOF. Here's a loop using break statements to accomplish the task (assume true has been defined as the integer 1):

```
loopCount = 1;
while (true)
{
    cin >> num1;
    if ( !cin || num1 >= 100)
        break;
    cin >> num2;
    if ( !cin || num2 <= 50)
        break;
    cout << sqrt(float(num1 + num2)) << endl;
    loopCount++;
    if (loopCount > 10)
        break;
}
```

Note that we could have used a For loop to count from 1 to 10, breaking out of it as necessary. However, this loop is both count-controlled and event-controlled, so we prefer to use a While loop.

The above loop contains three distinct exit points. Some people oppose this style of programming, because having multiple exit points from a long block can make the code hard to follow. Is there any advantage to using an infinite loop in conjunction with break? To answer this question, let's rewrite the loop without using break statements. The loop must terminate when num1 is invalid or num2 is invalid or loopCount exceeds 10. We'll use Boolean flags to signal invalid data in the While condition:

```
num1Valid = true;
num2Valid = true;
loopCount = 1;
```

```
while (num1Valid && num2Valid && loopCount <= 10)
{
    cin >> num1;
    if ( !cin || num1 >= 100)
        num1Valid = false;
    else
    {
        cin >> num2;
        if ( !cin || num2 <= 50)
            num2Valid = false;
        else
        {
            cout << sqrt(float(num1 + num2)) << endl;
            loopCount++;
        }
    }
}
```

One could argue that the first version is easier to follow and understand than this second version. The primary task of the loop body—computing the square root of the sum of the numbers—is more prominent in the first version. In the second version, the computation is obscured by being buried within nested Ifs. The second version also has a more complicated control flow.

The disadvantage of using `break` with loops is that it can become a crutch for those who are too impatient to think carefully about loop design. It's easy to overuse (and abuse) the technique. Here's an example, printing the integers 1 through 5:

```
i = 1;
while (true)
{
    cout << i;
    if (i == 5)
        break;
    i++;
}
```

There is no real justification for setting up the loop this way. Conceptually, it is a pure count-controlled loop, and a simple For loop does the job:

```
for (i = 1; i <= 5; i++)
    cout << i;
```

The For loop is easier to understand and is less prone to error.

A good rule of thumb is: Use break within loops only as a last resort. Specifically, use it only to avoid baffling combinations of multiple Boolean flags and nested Ifs.

Another statement that alters the flow of control in a C++ program is the continue statement. This statement, valid only in loops, terminates the current loop iteration (but not the entire loop). It causes an immediate branch to the bottom of the loop—skipping the rest of the statements in the loop body—in preparation for the next iteration. Here is an example of a reading loop in which we want to process only the positive numbers in an input file:

```
for (dataCount = 1; dataCount <= 500; dataCount++)
{
    dataFile >> inputVal;
    if (inputVal <= 0)
        continue;
    cout << inputVal;
    .
    .
    .

}
```

If inputVal is less than or equal to 0, control branches to the bottom of the loop. Then, as with any For loop, the computer increments dataCount and performs the loop test before going on to the next iteration.

The continue statement is not used often, but we present it for completeness (and because you may run across it in other people's programs). Its primary purpose is to avoid obscuring the main process of the loop by indenting it within an If statement. For example, the above code would be written without a continue statement as follows:

```
for (dataCount = 1; dataCount <= 500; dataCount++)
{
    dataFile >> inputVal;
    if (inputVal > 0)
    {
        cout << inputVal;
        .
        .
        .

    }
}
```

Be sure to note the difference between `continue` and `break`. The `continue` statement means "Abandon the current iteration of the loop, and go on to the next iteration." The `break` statement means "Exit the entire loop immediately."

Guidelines for Choosing a Looping Statement

Here are some guidelines to help you decide when to use each of the three looping statements (While, Do-While, and For).

1. If the loop is a simple count-controlled loop, the For statement is a "natural." Concentrating the three loop control actions—initialize, test, and increment/decrement—into one location (the heading of the For statement) reduces the chances of forgetting to include one of them.
2. If the loop is an event-controlled loop whose body is always executed at least once, a Do-While statement is appropriate.
3. If the loop is an event-controlled loop and nothing is known about the first execution, use a While statement.
4. When in doubt, use a While statement.
5. An infinite loop with `break` statements sometimes clarifies the code but more often reflects an undisciplined loop design. Use it only after careful consideration of While, Do-While, and For.

PROGRAMMING EXAMPLE

Monthly Rainfall Averages

Problem: Meteorologists have recorded monthly rainfall amounts at several sites throughout a region of the country. You have been asked to write an interactive program that lets the user enter one year's rainfall amounts at a particular site and prints out the average of the 12 values. After the data for a site are processed, the program asks whether the user would like to repeat the process for another recording site. A user response of 'y' means yes and 'n' means no. The program must trap erroneous input data (negative values for rainfall amounts and invalid responses to the "Do you wish to continue?" prompt).

Input: For each recording site, 12 floating point rainfall amounts. For each "Do you wish to continue?" prompt, either a 'y' or an 'n'.

PROGRAMMING EXAMPLE cont'd

Output: For each recording site, the floating point average of the 12 rainfall amounts, displayed to two decimal places.

Discussion: A solution to this problem requires several looping structures. At the topmost level of the design, we need a loop to process the data from all the sites. Each iteration must process one site's data, then ask the user whether to continue with another recording site. The program does not know in advance how many recording sites there are, so the loop cannot be a count-controlled loop. Although we can make either While or Do-While work correctly, we'll use a Do-While under the assumption that the user wants to process at least one site's data.

Another loop is required to input 12 monthly rainfall amounts and form their sum. A For loop is appropriate for this task, because we know that exactly 12 iterations must occur.

We'll need two more loops to perform data validation—one loop to ensure that a rainfall amount is negative and another to verify that the user types only 'y' or 'n' when prompted to continue. As we saw earlier in the chapter, Do-While loops are well suited to this kind of data validation. We want the loop body to execute at least once, reading an input value and testing for valid data. As long as the user keeps entering invalid data, the loop continues. Control exits the loop only when the user finally gets it right.

Assumptions: The user processes data for at least one site.

```
//*******************************************************************
// Rainfall program
// This program inputs 12 monthly rainfall amounts from a
// recording site and computes the average monthly rainfall.
// This process is repeated for as many recording sites as
// the user wishes.
//*******************************************************************
#include <iostream.h>
#include <iomanip.h>      // For setprecision()

void Get12Amounts( float& );
void GetOneAmount( float& );
void GetYesOrNo( char& );

int main()
{
    float sum;           // Sum of 12 rainfall amounts
    char  response;      // User response ('y' or 'n')

    cout.setf(ios::fixed, ios::floatfield);   // Set up floating pt.
    cout.setf(ios::showpoint);                //    output format
    cout << setprecision(2);
```

PROGRAMMING EXAMPLE cont'd

```cpp
        do
        {
            Get12Amounts(sum);
            cout << "Average rainfall is " << sum / 12.0
                << " inches" << endl << endl;
            cout << "Do you have another recording site? (y or n) ";
            GetYesOrNo(response);
        } while (response == 'y');
        return 0;
    }


    //*******************************************************************


    void Get12Amounts( /* out */ float& sum )    // Sum of 12 rainfall
                                                 // amounts

    // Inputs 12 monthly rainfall amounts and returns their sum

    // Postcondition:
    //     12 rainfall amounts have been read and verified to be
    //     nonnegative
    //  && sum == sum of the 12 input values

    {
        int   count;      // Loop control variable
        float amount;     // Rainfall amount for one month

        sum = 0;
        for (count = 1; count <= 12; count++)
        {
            cout << "Enter rainfall amount " << count << ':' << endl;
            GetOneAmount(amount);
            sum = sum + amount;
        }
    }


    //*******************************************************************


    void GetYesOrNo( /* out */ char& response )    // User response char

    // Inputs a character from the user

    // Postcondition:
    //     response has been input (repeatedly, if necessary, along
    //     with an error message)
    //  && response == 'y' or 'n'
```

PROGRAMMING EXAMPLE cont'd

```
{
    do
    {
        cin >> response;
        if (response != 'y' && response != 'n')
            cout << "Please type y or n: ";
    } while (response != 'y' && response != 'n');
}


//*********************************************************************

void GetOneAmount( /* out */ float& amount )    // Rainfall amount
                                                // for one month

// Inputs one month's rainfall amount

// Postcondition:
//     amount has been input (repeatedly, if necessary, along
//     with an error message)
//  && amount >= 0.0

{
    do
    {
        cin >> amount;
        if (amount < 0.0)
            cout << "Amount cannot be negative. Enter again:"
                    << endl;
    } while (amount < 0.0);
}
```

Testing: We should test two separate aspects of the Rainfall program. First, we should verify that the program works correctly given valid input data. Supplying arbitrary rainfall amounts of zero or greater, we must confirm that the program correctly adds up the values and divides by 12 to produce the average. Also, we should make sure that the program behaves correctly whether we type 'y' or 'n' when prompted to continue.

   The second aspect to test is the data validation code that we included in the program. When entering a particular rainfall amount, we should type negative numbers repeatedly to verify that an error message is printed and that we are unable to escape the Do-While loop until we eventually type a non-negative number. Similarly, when prompted to type 'y' or 'n' to process another recording site, we must press several incorrect keys to exercise the loop in the GetYesOrNo function. Here's a sample run showing the testing of the data validation code:

PROGRAMMING EXAMPLE cont'd

```
Enter rainfall amount 1:
0
Enter rainfall amount 2:
0
Enter rainfall amount 3:
0
Enter rainfall amount 4:
3.4
Enter rainfall amount 5:
9.6
Enter rainfall amount 6:
1.2
Enter rainfall amount 7:
-3.4
Amount cannot be negative. Enter again:
-9
Amount cannot be negative. Enter again:
1.3
Enter rainfall amount 8:
0
Enter rainfall amount 9:
0
Enter rainfall amount 10:
0
Enter rainfall amount 11:
0
Enter rainfall amount 12:
0
Average rainfall is 1.29 inches

Do you have another recording site? (y or n) d
Please type y or n: Y
Please type y or n: n
```

Testing and Debugging

The same testing techniques we used with While loops apply to Do-While and For loops. There are, however, a few additional considerations with these loops.

The body of a Do-While loop always executes at least once. Thus, you should try data sets that show the result of executing a Do-While loop the minimal number of times. With a data-dependent For loop, it is important to test for proper results when the loop executes zero times. This occurs when the starting value is greater than the ending value (or less than the ending value if the loop control variable is being decremented).

When a program contains a Switch statement, you should test it with enough different data sets to ensure that each branch is selected and executed correctly. You should also test the program with a switch expression whose value is not in any of the case labels.

Testing and Debugging Hints

1. In a Switch statement, make sure there is a `break` statement at the end of each case alternative. Otherwise, control "falls through" to the code in the next case alternative.
2. Case labels in a Switch statement are made up of values, not variables. They may, however, include named constants and expressions involving only constants.
3. A switch expression cannot be a floating point expression, and case constants cannot be floating point constants.
4. If there is a possibility that the value of the switch expression might not match one of the case constants, it's best to provide a `default` alternative.
5. Double-check long Switch statements to make sure that you haven't omitted any branches.
6. The Do-While loop is a posttest loop. If there is a possibility that the loop body should be skipped entirely, use a While statement.
7. The For statement heading (the first line) always has three pieces within the parentheses. Most often, the first piece initializes a loop control variable, the second piece tests the variable, and the third piece increments or decrements the variable. The three pieces must be separated by semicolons.
8. With nested control structures, the `break` statement can exit only one level of nesting—the innermost Switch or loop in which the `break` is located.

Summary

The Switch statement is a multi-way selection statement. It allows the program to choose among a set of branches. A Switch containing `break` statements can always be simulated by an If-Then-Else-If structure. If a Switch can be used, however, it often makes the code easier to read and understand. A Switch statement cannot be used with floating point values as labels.

The Do-While is a general-purpose looping statement. It is like the While loop except that its test occurs at the end of the loop, guaranteeing at least one execution of the loop body. As with a While loop, a Do-While continues as long as the loop condition is nonzero (true).

The For statement is used to implement count-controlled loops. The initialization, testing, and incrementation (or decrementation) of the loop control variable are centralized in one location, the first line of the For statement.

The For, Do-While, and Switch statements are the ice cream and cake of C++. We can live without them if we must, but they are nice to have.

Quick Check

1. Given a switch expression that is the `int` variable `nameVal`, write a Switch statement that prints your first name if `nameVal = 1`, your middle name if `nameVal = 2`, and your last name if `nameVal = 3`. (pp. 279–281)
2. How would you change the answer to Question 1 so that it prints an error message if the value is not 1, 2, or 3? (pp. 279–281)
3. What is the primary difference between a While loop and a Do-While loop? (pp. 282–284)
4. A certain problem requires a count-controlled loop that starts at 10 and counts down to 1. Write the heading (the first line) of a For statement that controls this loop. (pp. 284–285)
5. Within a loop, how does a `continue` statement differ from a `break` statement? (pp. 286–288)
6. What C++ looping statement would you choose for a loop that is both count-controlled and event-controlled and whose body might not execute even once? (p. 289)

Answers

```
1. switch (nameVal)
   {
        case 1 : cout << "Mary";
                break;
        case 2 : cout << "Lynn";
                break;
        case 3 : cout << "Smith";
                break;   // Not required
   }
2. switch (nameVal)
   {
        case 1  : cout << "Mary";
                break;
        case 2  : cout << "Lynn";
                break;
        case 3  : cout << "Smith";
                break;
        default : cout << "Invalid name value.";
                break;   // Not required
   }
```

3. The body of a Do-While always executes at least once; the body of a While may not execute at all.
4. `for (count = 10; count >= 1; count--)`   5. A `continue` statement terminates the current iteration and goes on to the next iteration (if possible). A `break` statement causes an immediate loop exit.   6. A While statement.

Exam Preparation Exercises

1. Define the following terms:

   switch expression
   pretest loop
   posttest loop

2. A switch expression may be an expression that results in a value of type `int`, `float`, or `char`. (True or False?)
3. The values in case labels may appear in any order, but duplicate case labels are not allowed within a given Switch statement. (True or False?)
4. All possible values for the switch expression must be included among the case labels for a given Switch statement. (True or False?)
5. Rewrite the following code fragment using a Switch statement.

```
if (n == 3)
    alpha++;
else if (n == 7)
    beta++;
else if (n == 10)
    gamma++;
```

6. What is printed by the following code fragment if n equals 3?

```
switch (n + 1)
{
    case 2  : cout << "Bill";
    case 4  : cout << "Mary";
    case 7  : cout << "Joe";
    case 9  : cout << "Anne";
    default : cout << "Whoops!";
}
```

7. If a While loop whose condition is `delta <= alpha` is converted into a Do-While loop, the loop condition of the Do-While loop is `delta > alpha`. (True or False?)
8. A Do-While statement always ends in a semicolon. (True or False?)
9. What is printed by the following program fragment, assuming the input value is 0? (All variables are of type `int`.)

```
cin >> n;
i = 1;
do
{
    cout << i;
    i++;
} while (i <= n);
```

10. What is printed by the following program fragment, assuming the input value is 0? (All variables are of type `int`.)

```
cin >> n;
for (i = 1; i <= n; i++)
      cout << i;
```

11. What is printed by the following program fragment? (All variables are of type int.)

```
for (i = 4; i >= 1; i--)
{
    for (j = i; j >= 1; j--)
        cout << j << ' ';
    cout << i << endl;
}
```

12. What is printed by the following program fragment? (All variables are of type int.)

```
for (row = 1; row <= 10; row++)
{
    for (col = 1; col <= 10 - row; col++)
        cout << '*';
    for (col = 1; col <= 2*row - 1; col++)
        cout << ' ';
    for (col = 1; col <= 10 - row; col++)
        cout << '*';
    cout << endl;
}
```

13. A `break` statement located inside a Switch statement that is within a While loop causes control to exit the loop immediately. (True or False?)

14. Given the For statement

```
for (count = 3; count <= 20; count++)
    cout << "Hello" << endl;
```

which one of the following assertions about `count` is correct just prior to the loop test?

a. $1 \leq$ count ≤ 20
b. $3 \leq$ count ≤ 20
c. $2 <$ count < 20
d. $3 <$ count < 21
e. $3 \leq$ count ≤ 21

Programming Warm-Up Exercises

1. Write a Switch statement that does the following:

   If the value of grade is
   'A', add 4 to sum
   'B', add 3 to sum
   'C', add 2 to sum
   'D', add 1 to sum
   'F', print "Student is on probation"

2. Modify the code for Exercise 1 so that an error message is printed if grade does not equal one of the five possible grades.

3. Rewrite the Day function of Chapter 8 (page 252), replacing the If-Then-Else-If structure with a Switch statement.

4. Write a program segment that reads and sums until it has summed 10 data values or until a negative value is read, whichever comes first. Use a Do-While loop for your solution.

5. Rewrite the following code segment using a Do-While loop instead of a While loop.

```
cout << "Enter 1, 2, or 3: ";
cin >> response;
while (response != 1 && response != 2 && response != 3)
{
    cout << "Enter 1, 2, or 3: ";
    cin >> response;
}
```

6. Rewrite the following code segment using a While loop.

```
cin >> ch;
if (cin)
    do
    {
        cout << ch;
        cin >> ch;
    } while (cin);
```

7. Rewrite the following code segment using a For loop.

```
sum = 0;
count = 1;
while (count <= 1000)
{
    sum = sum + count;
    count++;
}
```

8. Rewrite the following For loop as a While loop.

```
for (m = 93; m >= 5; m--)
    cout << m << ' ' << m * m << endl;
```

9. Rewrite the following For loop using a Do-While loop.

```
for (k = 9; k <= 21; k++)
    cout << k << ' ' << 3 * k << endl;
```

10. Write a value-returning function that accepts two int parameters, base and exponent, and returns the value of base raised to the exponent power. Use a For loop in your solution.

11. Make the logic of the following loop easier to understand by using an infinite loop with break statements.

```
sum = 0;
count = 1;
do
{
    cin >> int1;
    if ( !cin || int1 <= 0)
        cout << "Invalid first integer.";
    else
    {
        cin >> int2;
        if ( !cin || int2 > int1)
            cout << "Invalid second integer.";
        else
        {
            cin >> int3;
            if ( !cin || int3 == 0)
                cout << "Invalid third integer.";
            else
            {
                sum = sum + (int1 + int2) / int3;
                count++;
            }
        }
    }
} while (cin && int1 > 0 && int2 <= int1 && int3 != 0 &&
        count <= 100);
```

12. Rewrite the GetYesOrNo and GetOneAmount functions in the Monthly Rainfall Averages case study, replacing the Do-While loops with While loops.

Programming Problems

1. Develop a C++ program that inputs a two-letter abbreviation for one of the 50 states and prints out the full name of the state. If the abbreviation isn't valid, the program should print an error message and ask for an abbreviation again. The names of the 50 states and their abbreviations are:

State	Abbreviation	State	Abbreviation
Alabama	AL	Montana	MT
Alaska	AK	Nebraska	NE
Arizona	AZ	Nevada	NV
Arkansas	AR	New Hampshire	NH
California	CA	New Jersey	NJ
Colorado	CO	New Mexico	NM
Connecticut	CT	New York	NY
Delaware	DE	North Carolina	NC
Florida	FL	North Dakota	ND
Georgia	GA	Ohio	OH
Hawaii	HI	Oklahoma	OK
Idaho	ID	Oregon	OR
Illinois	IL	Pennsylvania	PA
Indiana	IN	Rhode Island	RI
Iowa	IA	South Carolina	SC
Kansas	KS	South Dakota	SD
Kentucky	KY	Tennessee	TN
Louisiana	LA	Texas	TX
Maine	ME	Utah	UT
Maryland	MD	Vermont	VT
Massachusetts	MA	Virginia	VA
Michigan	MI	Washington	WA
Minnesota	MN	West Virginia	WV
Mississippi	MS	Wisconsin	WI
Missouri	MO	Wyoming	WY

(*Hint:* Use nested Switch statements, where the outer statement uses the first letter of the abbreviation as its switch expression.)

2. Write a C++ program that reads a date in numeric form and prints it in English. For example:

```
Enter a date in the form mm dd yy.
10  27  42
October twenty-seventh, nineteen hundred forty-two.
```

Here is another example:

```
Enter a date in the form mm dd yy.
12  10  10
December tenth, nineteen hundred ten.
```

The program should work for any date in the twentieth century and should print an error message for any invalid date, such as 2 29 83 (1983 wasn't a leap year).

3. Write a C++ program that reads full names from an input file and writes the *initials* for the names into an output file named `initials`. For example, the input

```
John James Henry
```

should produce the output

```
JJH
```

The names are stored in the input file first name first, then middle name, then last name, separated by an arbitrary number of blanks. There is only one name per line. The first name or the middle name could be just an initial, or there may not be a middle name.

4. Write a C++ program that converts letters of the alphabet into their corresponding digits on the telephone. The program should let the user enter letters repeatedly until a Q or a Z is entered. (Q and Z are the two letters that are not on the telephone.) An error message should be printed for any nonalphabetic character that is entered.

The letters and digits on the telephone have the following correspondence.

ABC = 2	DEF = 3	GHI = 4
JKL = 5	MNO = 6	PRS = 7
TUV = 8	WXY = 9	

Here is an example:

```
Enter a letter: P
The letter P corresponds to 7 on the telephone.
Enter a letter: A
The letter A corresponds to 2 on the telephone.
Enter a letter: D
The letter D corresponds to 3 on the telephone.
Enter a letter: 2
Invalid letter. Enter Q or Z to quit.
Enter a letter: Z
Quit.
```

10 Simple Data Types: Built-In and User-Defined

GOALS

- To be able to identify all of the simple data types provided by the C++ language

- To become familiar with specialized C++ operators and expressions

- To be able to distinguish between external and internal representations of character data

- To understand how floating point numbers are represented in the computer

- To understand how the limited numeric precision of the computer can affect calculations

- To be able to select the most appropriate simple data type for a given variable

- To be able to declare and use an enumeration type

- To be able to use the For and Switch statements with user-defined enumeration types

- To be able to distinguish a named user-defined type from an anonymous user-defined type

- To be able to create a user-written header file

- To understand the concepts of type promotion and type demotion

Until now, we have worked primarily with the data types `int`, `char`, and `float`. These three data types are adequate for solving a wide variety of problems. But certain programs need other kinds of data. In this chapter, we take a closer look at all of the simple data types that are part of the C++ language. As part of this look, we discuss the limitations of the computer in doing calculations. We examine how these limitations can cause numerical errors and how to avoid such errors.

There are times when even the built-in data types cannot adequately represent all the data in a program. C++ has several mechanisms for creating *user-defined* data types; that is, we can define new data types ourselves. This chapter introduces one of these mechanisms, the enumeration type. In fact, the remainder of this book is devoted largely to introducing additional user-defined data types.

Built-In Simple Types

In Chapter 2, we defined a data type as a specific set of data values (which we call the *domain*) along with a set of operations on those values. For the `int` type, the domain is the set of whole numbers from INT_MIN through INT_MAX, and the allowable operations are +, -, *, /, %, ++, --, and the relational and logical operators. The domain of the `float` type is the set of all real numbers that a particular computer is capable of representing, and the operations are the same as those for the `int` type except that modulus (%) is excluded.

The `int` and `float` (and `char`) types have a property in common. Each data type is made up of indivisible, or atomic, data values. Data types with this property are called **simple** (or **atomic**) **data types.** When we say that a value is atomic, we mean that it has no component parts that can be accessed individually. For example, a single character of type `char` is atomic, but the string "Good Morning" is not (it is composed of several values of type `char`).

simple (atomic) data type
A data type in which each value is atomic (indivisible)

Another way of describing a simple type is to say that only one value can be associated with a variable of that type. In contrast, a *composite data type* is one in which an entire collection of values can be associated with a single variable of that type. Beginning in Chapter 11, we look at composite data types.

Figure 10-1 displays the simple types that are built into the C++ language. In this figure, one of the types—`enum`—is not actually a single data type in the sense that `int` and `float` are data types. Instead, it is a mechanism by

FIGURE 10-1

C++ Simple Data Types

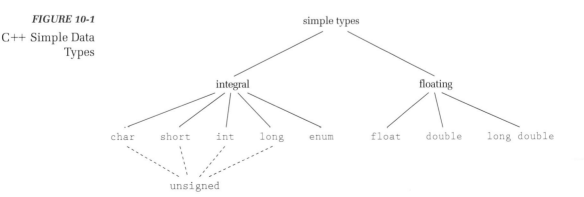

which we can define our own simple data types. We look at `enum` later in the chapter.

The integral types `char`, `short`, `int`, and `long` represent nothing more than integers of different sizes. Similarly, the floating point types `float`, `double`, and `long double` simply refer to floating point numbers of different sizes. What do we mean by *sizes*?

In C++, sizes are measured in multiples of bytes. Recall from Chapter 1 that a byte is a group of 8 consecutive bits (1s or 0s) in a computer's memory. By definition, the size of a C++ `char` value is 1 byte.

Let's use the notation *sizeof*(SomeType) to denote the size in bytes of a value of type SomeType. Then, by definition, *sizeof*(`char`) = 1. Other than `char`, the sizes of data objects in C++ are highly machine-dependent. On one machine it might be the case that

sizeof(`char`) = 1,
sizeof(`short`) = 2,
sizeof(`int`) = 4, and
sizeof(`long`) = 8

On another machine it might be that

sizeof(`char`) = 1,
sizeof(`short`) = 2,
sizeof(`int`) = 2, and
sizeof(`long`) = 4

The only guarantee made by the C++ language is that

$$1 = sizeof(\text{char}) \leq sizeof(\text{short}) \leq sizeof(\text{int}) \leq sizeof(\text{long})$$

and

$$sizeof(\text{float}) \leq sizeof(\text{double}) \leq sizeof(\text{long double})$$

range of values
The interval within which values of a numeric type must fall, specified in terms of the largest and smallest allowable values

For numeric data, the size of a data object determines its **range of values.** Let's look in more detail at the sizes, ranges of values, and constants for each of the built-in types.

Integral Types

Before looking at how the sizes of integral types affect their possible values, we remind you that the reserved word `unsigned` may precede the name of an integral type—`unsigned char`, `unsigned short`, `unsigned int`, `unsigned long`. Values of these types are nonnegative integers with values from 0 through some machine-dependent maximum value. Although we rarely use unsigned types in this book, we include them in this discussion for thoroughness.

Ranges of Values. The following table displays sample ranges of values for the char, short, int, and long data types and their unsigned variations:

Type	Size in Bytes*	Minimum Value*	Maximum Value*
char	1	−128	127
unsigned char	1	0	255
short	2	−32,768	32,767
unsigned short	2	0	65,535
int	2	−32,768	32,767
unsigned int	2	0	65,535
long	4	−2,147,483,648	2,147,483,647
unsigned long	4	0	4,294,967,295

* These values are for one particular machine. Your machine's values may be different.

Most C++ environments provide the header file limits.h, from which you can determine the maximum and minimum values for your machine. This header file defines the constants CHAR_MAX and CHAR_MIN, SHRT_MAX and SHRT_MIN, INT_MAX and INT_MIN, and LONG_MAX and LONG_MIN. The unsigned types have a minimum value of zero and maximum values defined by UCHAR_MAX, USHRT_MAX, UINT_MAX, and ULONG_MAX. To find out the values specific to your computer you could print them out like this:

```
#include <limits.h>
  .
  .
  .
cout << "Max. long = " << LONG_MAX << endl;
cout << "Min. long = " << LONG_MIN << endl;
  .
  .
  .
```

Constants. In C++, integer constants can be specified in three different number bases: decimal (base-10), octal (base-8), and hexadecimal (base-16). The uses of octal and hexadecimal values are outside the scope of this book.

The following table shows examples of integer constants in C++. Notice that an L or a U (either uppercase or lowercase) can be added to the end of a constant to signify long or unsigned, respectively.

Constant	Type	Remarks
1658	int	Decimal (base-10) integer.
65535U	unsigned int	Unsigned constants end in U or u.
421L	long	Explicit long constant. Ends in L or l.
53100	long	Implicit long constant, assuming the machine's maximum int is, say, 32767.
389123487UL	unsigned long	Unsigned long constants end in UL or LU in any combination of uppercase and lowercase letters.

You'll notice that this table presents only numeric constants for the integral types. We discuss char constants later in a separate section.

Floating Point Types

Ranges of Values.   Below is a table that gives sample ranges of values for the three floating point types, float, double, and long double. In this table we show, for each type, the maximum positive value and the minimum positive value (a tiny fraction that is very close to zero). Negative numbers have the same range but the opposite sign. Ranges of values are expressed in exponential (scientific) notation, where 3.4E+38 means 3.4×10^{38}.

Type	Size in Bytes*	Minimum Positive Value*	Maximum Positive Value*
float	4	3.4E–38	3.4E+38
double	8	1.7E–308	1.7E+308
long double	10	3.4E–4932	1.1E+4932

* These values are for one particular machine. Your machine's values may be different.

The standard header file float.h defines the constants FLT_MAX and FLT_MIN, DBL_MAX and DBL_MIN, and LDBL_MAX and LDBL_MIN. To determine the ranges of values for your machine, you could write a short program that prints out these constants.

Constants.   When you use a floating point constant like 5.8 in a C++ program, its type is assumed to be double (double precision). If you store the value into a `float` variable, the computer coerces its type from `double` to `float` (single precision). If you insist on a constant being of type `float` rather than `double`, you can append an F or an f at the end of the constant. Similarly, a suffix of L or l signifies a `long double` constant. Here are some examples of floating point constants in C++:

Constant	Type	Remarks
6.83	double	By default, floating point constants are of type double.
6.83F	float	Explicit float constants end in F or f.
6.83L	long double	Explicit long double constants end in L or l.
4.35E-9	double	Exponential notation, meaning 4.35×10^{-9}.

Additional C++ Operators

C++ has a rich, sometimes bewildering, variety of operators that allow you to manipulate values of the simple data types. Operators you have learned about so far include the assignment operator (=), the arithmetic operators (+, -, *, /, %), the increment and decrement operators (++, --), the relational operators (==, !=, <, <=, >, >=), and the logical operators (!, &&, ||). Another operator—at least the compiler formally treats it as an operator—is the pair of symbols ( ). This is either the function call operator, as in

```
ComputeSum(x, y);
```

or the type cast operator, as in

```
y = float(someInt);
```

C++ also has operators that are more specialized and seldom found in other programming languages. Here is a table of these additional operators. As you inspect the table, don't panic—a quick scan will do. We won't be using most of these operators in this text, and we discuss them only briefly so that you will have some familiarity with them if you should encounter them in other people's programs.

Operator		*Remarks*
Combined assignment operators		
+=	Add and assign	
-=	Subtract and assign	
*=	Multiply and assign	
/=	Divide and assign	
Increment and decrement operators		
++	Pre-increment	Example: `++someVar`
++	Post-increment	Example: `someVar++`
--	Pre-decrement	Example: `--someVar`
--	Post-decrement	Example: `someVar--`
Bitwise operators		Integer operands only
<<	Left shift	
>>	Right shift	
&	Bitwise AND	
|	Bitwise OR	
^	Bitwise EXCLUSIVE OR	
~	Complement (invert all bits)	
More combined assignment operators		Integer operands only
%=	Modulus and assign	
<<=	Shift left and assign	
>>=	Shift right and assign	
&=	Bitwise AND and assign	
|=	Bitwise OR and assign	
^=	Bitwise EXCLUSIVE OR and assign	
Other operators		
()	Cast	
`sizeof`	Size of operand in bytes	Form: `sizeof` Expr or `sizeof`(Type)
?:	Conditional operator	Form: Expr1 ? Expr2 : Expr3

The operators in this table, along with those you are already familiar with, comprise most—but not all—of the C++ operators. We introduce a few more operators in later chapters as the need arises.

Assignment Operators and Assignment Expressions

C++ has several assignment operators. The equal sign (=) is the basic assignment operator. When combined with its two operands, it forms an **assignment expression** (*not* an assignment statement). In C++, any expression becomes an **expression statement** when it is terminated by a semicolon. We use the term *assignment statement* to refer to an expression statement that contains an assignment expression.

assignment
expression
A C++ expression
with (1) a value and
(2) the side effect of
storing the expres-
sion value into a
memory location

expression statement
A statement formed
by appending a
semicolon to an
expression

Because an assignment is an expression, not a statement, you can use it anywhere an expression is allowed. Here is a statement that stores the value 20 into `firstInt`, the value 30 into `secondInt`, and the value 35 into `thirdInt`:

```
thirdInt = (secondInt = (firstInt = 20) + 10) + 5;
```

Some C++ programmers use this style of coding, but others find it hard to read and error-prone.

In Chapter 5, we cautioned against the mistake of using the = operator in place of the == operator:

```
if (alpha = 12)   // Wrong
    .
    .
    .
```

In addition to the = operator, C++ has several combined assignment operators (+=, *=, and the others listed in our table of operators). These operators have the following semantics:

Statement	*Equivalent Statement*
`i += 5;`	`i = i + 5;`
`pivotPoint *= n + 3;`	`pivotPoint = pivotPoint * (n + 3);`

The combined assignment operators are another example of "icing on the cake." They are sometimes convenient for writing a line of code more compactly, but you can do just fine without them.

Increment and Decrement Operators

The increment and decrement operators (++ and --) operate only on variables, not on constants or arbitrary expressions. Suppose a variable `someInt` contains the value 3. The expression `++someInt` denotes pre-incrementation. The side effect of incrementing `someInt` occurs first, so the resulting value of the expression is 4. In contrast, the expression `someInt++` denotes post-incrementation. The value of the expression is 3, and *then* the side effect of incrementing `someInt` takes place. The following code illustrates the difference between pre- and post-incrementation:

```
int1 = 14;
int2 = ++int1;  // Increments int1 then assigns 15 to int2

int1 = 14;
int2 = int1++;  // Assigns 14 to int2, then increments int1
```

Using side effects in the middle of larger expressions is always a bit danger-ous. It's easy to make semantic errors, and the code may be confusing to read. Look at this example:

```
a = (b = c++) * --d / (e += f++);
```

Some people make a game of seeing how much they can do in as few keystrokes as possible. But they should remember that serious software development re-quires writing code that other programmers can read and understand. Overuse of side effects hinders this goal. By far, the most common use of the ++ and -- operators is to do the incrementation or decrementation as a separate expres-sion statement:

```
count++;
```

Here, the value of the expression is unused, but we get the desired side effect of incrementing `count`.

Bitwise Operators

The bitwise operators listed in the operator table ($<<$, $>>$, &, |, and so forth) are used for manipulating individual bits within a memory cell. This book does not explore the use of these operators; the topic of bit-level operations is beyond an introduction to computer science and computer programming. However, be-ware that if you mistakenly write & for && or | for ||, that your program will probably compile successfully but will produce erroneous results. Like writing = when you mean to write ==, this is a very common mistake in C++ programs.

The Cast Operator

You have seen that C++ is very liberal about letting the programmer mix data types. Instead of relying on implicit type coercion we have recommended using an explicit type cast to show that type conversion is intentional:

```
intVar = int(floatVar);
```

In C++, the cast operation comes in two forms:

```
intVar = int(floatVar);     // Functional notation
intVar = (int) floatVar;    // Prefix notation--parentheses required
```

The first form is called functional notation because it looks like a function call. It isn't really a function call (there is no subprogram named `int`), but it has the appearance of a function call. The second form, prefix notation, is the only form available in the C language; C++ added the functional notation.

Although most C++ programmers use the functional notation for the cast operation, there is one restriction on its use. The data type name must be a single identifier. If the type name consists of more than one identifier, you *must* use prefix notation. For example,

```
myVar = unsigned int(someFloat);    // Not valid
myVar = (unsigned int) someFloat;   // Valid
```

The sizeof **Operator**

The sizeof operator is a unary operator that yields the size, in bytes, of its operand. The operand can be a variable name, as in

```
sizeof someInt
```

or the operand can be the name of a data type, enclosed in parentheses:

```
sizeof(float)
```

You could find out the size of a data type on your machine by using code like this:

```
cout << "Size of a short is " << sizeof(short) << " bytes." << endl;
```

The ? : **Operator**

The last operator in our operator table is ? :, which is a three-operand operator with the following syntax:

ConditionalExpression

> Expression1 ? Expression2 : Expression3

The computer evaluates Expression1. If it is nonzero (true), then the value of the expression is Expression2; otherwise, the value of the expression is Expression3. We do not use this unusual operator further in this text. It is mentioned here so that you will be familiar with it should you ever encounter it in a program.

Operator Precedence

On the next page is a summary of operator precedence for the C++ operators that we have encountered so far, excluding the bitwise operators. (Appendix B contains the complete list.)

Precedence (highest to lowest)

	Operator	*Associativity*
	( )	Left to right
unary:	++ -- ! + - (cast) sizeof	Right to left
	* / %	Left to right
	+ -	Left to right
	< <= > >=	Left to right
	== !=	Left to right
	&&	Left to right
	||	Left to right
	? :	Right to left
	= += -= etc.	Right to left

The column labeled *Associativity* describes grouping order. Within a precedence level, most operators group from left to right. For example,

```
a - b + c
```

means

```
(a - b) + c
```

Certain operators, though, group from right to left. Look at the assignment operators, for example. The expression

```
sum = count = 0
```

means

```
sum = (count = 0)
```

This associativity makes sense because the assignment operation is naturally a right-to-left operation.

Working with Character Data

Because char is an integral type and sizeof(char) equals 1, a char variable can store a small (one-byte) integer constant. For example,

```
char counter;
    .
    .
    .
counter = 3;
```

On computers with a very limited amount of memory space, programmers sometimes use the `char` type to save memory when they are working with small integers. But it is far more common to use `char` variables to store character data, such as the character 'A' or 'e' or '+':

```
char someChar;
    .
    .
    .
someChar = 'A';
```

A natural question to ask is, How does the computer know the difference between integer data and character data when the data is sitting in a memory cell? The answer is, The computer *can't* tell the difference! To explain this surprising fact, we have to look more closely at how character data are stored in a computer.

Character Sets

www.jbpub.com/C++links

external representation
The printable (character) form of a data value

internal representation
The form in which a data value is stored inside the memory

Each computer uses a particular character set, the set of all possible characters with which it is capable of working. There are two character sets widely in use today: the ASCII character set and the EBCDIC character set. ASCII is used by virtually all personal computers and minicomputers, and EBCDIC is found primarily on IBM mainframe computers. ASCII consists of 128 different characters, and EBCDIC has 256 characters. Appendix D shows the characters that are available in these two character sets.

Each character has an **external representation**—the way it looks on an I/O device like a printer—and an **internal representation**—the way it is stored inside the computer's memory. If you use the `char` constant 'A' in a C++ program, its external representation is the letter *A*. That is, if you print it out you see an *A*, as you would expect. Its internal representation, though, is an integer value. For example, the ASCII character 'A' has internal representation 65.

Let's look again at the statement

```
someChar = 'A';
```

Assuming our machine uses the ASCII character set, the compiler translates the constant 'A' into the integer 65. We could also have written the statement as

```
someChar = 65;
```

Both statements have exactly the same effect—that of storing 65 into `someChar`. However, the second version is *not* recommended. It is not as understandable as the first version, and it is nonportable (the program won't work correctly on a machine that uses EBCDIC, which uses a different internal representation—193—for 'A').

Earlier we mentioned that the computer cannot tell the difference between character and integer data in memory. Both are stored internally as integers. However, when we perform I/O operations, the computer does the right thing—it uses the external representation that corresponds to the data type of the expression being printed.

C++ `char` *Constants*   In C++, `char` constants come in two different forms. The first form, which we have been using regularly, is a single printable character enclosed by apostrophes (single quotes):

```
'A'  '8'  ')'  '+'
```

Notice that we said *printable* character. Character sets include both printable characters and *control characters* (or *nonprintable characters*). Control characters are not meant to be printed but are used to control the screen, printer, and other hardware devices. If you look at the ASCII character table, you see that the printable characters are those with integer values 32–126. The remaining characters (with values 0–31 and 127) are nonprintable control characters.

To accommodate control characters, C++ provides a second form of `char` constant: the *escape sequence*. An escape sequence is one or more characters preceded by a backslash (\). You are familiar with the escape sequence \n, which represents the newline character. Here is the complete description of the two forms of `char` constant in C++:

1. A single printable character—except an apostrophe (') or backslash (\)—enclosed by apostrophes.
2. One of the following escape sequences, enclosed by apostrophes:

       `\n`   Newline (Line feed in ASCII)
       `\t`   Horizontal tab
       `\v`   Vertical tab
       `\b`   Backspace
       `\r`   Carriage return
       `\f`   Form feed
       `\a`   Alert (a bell or beep)
       `\\`   Backslash

\' Single quote (apostrophe)
\" Double quote (quotation mark)
\0 Null character (all zero bits)

Even though an escape sequence consists of two or more characters, each escape sequence represents a single character in the character set.

Note that you can use an escape sequence within a string just as you can use any printable character within a string. The statement

```
cout << "\aWhoops!\n";
```

beeps the beeper, displays Whoops!, and terminates the output line. The statement

```
cout << "She said \"Hi\"";
```

outputs She said "Hi" and does not terminate the output line.

Programming Techniques What kinds of things can we do with character data in a program? The possibilities are endless and depend, of course, on the particular problem we are solving. But several techniques are so widely used that it's worth taking a look at them.

Comparing Characters. In previous chapters, you have seen examples of comparing characters for equality. We have used tests such as

```
if (ch == 'a')    and    while (inputChar != '\n')
```

Characters can also be compared by using $<$, $<=$, $>$, and $>=$. For example, if the variable firstLetter contains the first letter of a person's last name, we can test to see if the last name starts with *A* through *H* by using this test:

```
if (firstLetter >= 'A' && firstLetter <= 'H')
```

On one level of thought, a test like this is reasonable if you think of $<$ as meaning "comes before" in the character set and $>$ as meaning "comes after." On another level, the test makes even more sense when you consider that the underlying representation of a character is an integer number. The machine literally compares the two integer values using the mathematical meaning of less than or greater than.

When you write a logical expression to check whether a character lies within a certain range of values, you have to keep in mind the character set your machine uses. A test like

```
if (ch >= 'a' && ch <= 'z')
```

works correctly on some machines that use ASCII, but not on machines that use EBCDIC because the ordering of letters in EBCDIC intersperses control characters. A better approach, though, is to take advantage of the "is . . ." functions supplied by the standard library through the header file `ctype.h`. If you replace the above If test with this one:

```
if (islower(ch))
```

then your program is more portable; the test works correctly on any machine, regardless of its character set. It's a good idea to become well acquainted with these character-testing library functions (Appendix C). They can save you time and help you to write more portable programs.

Converting Digit Characters to Integers. Suppose you want to convert a digit that is read in character form to its numeric equivalent. Because the digit characters '0' through '9' are consecutive in both the ASCII and EBCDIC character sets, subtracting '0' from any digit in character form gives the digit in numeric form:

```
'0' - '0' == 0
'1' - '0' == 1
'2' - '0' == 2
    .
    .
    .
```

Why would you want to do this? Recall that when the extraction operator (>>) reads data into an `int` variable, the input stream fails if an invalid character is encountered. (And once the stream has failed, no further input will succeed). Suppose you're writing a program that prompts an inexperienced user to enter a number from 1 through 5. If the input variable is of type `int` and the user

Working with Character Data   **317**

accidentally types a letter of the alphabet, the program is in trouble. To defend against this possibility, you might read the user's response as a character and convert it to a number, performing error checking along the way. Here's a code segment that demonstrates the technique:

```cpp
#include <ctype.h>    // For isdigit()

typedef int Boolean;
const Boolean true = 1;
const Boolean false = 0;
    .
    .
    .

void GetResponse( /* out */ int& response )

{
    char    inChar;
    Boolean badData = false;

    do
    {
        cout << "Enter a number from 1 through 5: ";
        cin >> inChar;
        if ( !isdigit(inChar) )
            badData = true;                    // It's not a digit
        else
        {
            response = int(inChar - '0');
            if (response < 1 || response > 5)
                badData = true;                // It's a digit, but
        }                                      // it's out of range
        if (badData)
            cout << "Please try again." << endl;
    } while (badData);
}
```

Converting to Lowercase and Uppercase. When working with character data, you sometimes find that you need to convert a lowercase letter to uppercase, or vice versa. Fortunately, the programming technique required to do these conversions is easy—a simple call to a library function is all it takes. Through the header file `ctype.h`, the standard library provides not only the "is . . ." functions we have discussed, but also two value-returning functions named `toupper` and `tolower`. Here are their descriptions:

Header File	Function	Function Type	Function Value
`<ctype.h>`	`toupper(ch)`	`char`*	Uppercase equivalent of `ch`, if `ch` is a lowercase letter; `ch`, otherwise
`<ctype.h>`	`tolower(ch)`	`char`	Lowercase equivalent of `ch`, if `ch` is an uppercase letter; `ch`, otherwise

* Technically, both the parameter and the return value are of type `int`. But conceptually, the functions operate on character data.

Notice that the value returned by each function is just the original character if the condition is not met. For example, `tolower('M')` returns the character 'm', whereas `tolower('+')` returns '+'.

A common use of these two functions is to let the user respond to certain input prompts by using either uppercase or lowercase letters. For example, if you want to allow either *Y* or *y* for a "Yes" response from the user, and either *N* or *n* for "No," you might do this:

```
cout << "Enter Y or N: ";
cin >> inputChar;
if (toupper(inputChar) == 'Y')
{
    .
    .
    .

}
else if (toupper(inputChar) == 'N')
{
    .
    .
    .

}
else
    PrintErrorMsg();
```

More on Floating Point Numbers

We have used floating point numbers off and on since they were introduced in Chapter 2, but we have not examined them in depth. Floating point numbers have some special properties when used on the computer. Thus far, we've almost ignored these properties, but now it's time to consider them in detail.

Representation of Floating Point Numbers

Let's assume we have a computer where each memory location is the same size and is divided into a sign plus five decimal digits. When a variable or constant is defined, the location assigned to it consists of five digits and a sign. When an `int` variable or constant is defined, the interpretation of the number stored in that place is quite straightforward. When a `float` variable or constant is defined, the number stored there has both a whole number part and a fractional part, so it must be coded to represent both parts.

Let's see what such coded numbers might look like. The range of whole numbers we can represent with five digits is $-99{,}999$ through $+99{,}999$:

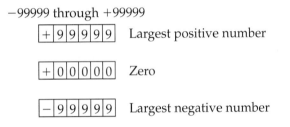

-99999 through $+99999$

| + | 9 | 9 | 9 | 9 | 9 | Largest positive number

| + | 0 | 0 | 0 | 0 | 0 | Zero

| - | 9 | 9 | 9 | 9 | 9 | Largest negative number

precision
The maximum number of significant digits

Our **precision** (the number of digits we can represent) is five digits, and each number within that range can be represented exactly.

What happens if we allow one of those digits (the leftmost one, for example) to represent an exponent?

| + | 8 | 2 | 3 | 4 | 5 |

Exponent

Then $+82345$ represents the number $+2345 * 10^8$. The range of numbers we now represent is much larger:

$-9999 * 10^9$ through $9999 * 10^9$

or

$-9{,}999{,}000{,}000{,}000$ through $+9{,}999{,}000{,}000{,}000$

However, our precision is now only four digits; that is, any four-digit number can be represented exactly in our system. But what happens to numbers with more digits? The four leftmost digits are represented correctly, and the rightmost

significant digits
Those digits from the first nonzero digit on the left to the last nonzero digit on the right (plus any zero digits that are exact)

digits, or least **significant digits,** are lost (assumed to be 0). Figure 10-2 shows what happens. Note that 1,000,000 can be represented exactly but −4,932,416 cannot, because this coding scheme limits us to four significant (nonzero) digits.

To extend our coding scheme to represent floating point numbers, we must be able to represent negative exponents. As examples,

$$7394 * 10^{-2} = 73.94$$

and

$$22 * 10^{-4} = 0.0022$$

Because our scheme does not allow for a sign for the exponent, we shall change it slightly. The sign that we have will be the sign of the exponent, and a sign can be added to the far left to represent the sign of the number itself (see Figure 10-3).

All the numbers between $9999 * 10^{-9}$ and $9999 * 10^9$ can now be represented accurately to four digits. Adding negative exponents to our scheme has allowed representation of fractional numbers.

Arithmetic with Floating Point Numbers

When we use integer arithmetic, our results are exact. Floating point arithmetic, however, is seldom exact. We can illustrate this by adding three floating point numbers, x, y, and z, using our coding scheme.

First, we add x to y and then we add z to the result. Next, we perform the operations in a different order, adding y to z, and then adding x to that result. The associative law of arithmetic says that the two answers should be the same—but are they? Let's use the following values for x, y, and z:

$$x = -1324 * 10^3 \qquad y = 1325 * 10^3 \qquad z = 5424 * 10^0$$

FIGURE 10-2
Coding Using Positive Exponents

NUMBER	POWER OF TEN NOTATION	CODED REPRESENTATION						VALUE
		Sign	Exp					
+99,999	$+9999 * 10^1$	+	1	9	9	9	9	+99,990
		Sign	Exp					
−999,999	$-9999 * 10^2$	−	2	9	9	9	9	−999,900
		Sign	Exp					
1,000,000	$+1000 * 10^3$	+	3	1	0	0	0	+1,000,000
		Sign	Exp					
4,932,416	$-4932 * 10^3$	−	3	4	9	3	2	−4,932,000

FIGURE 10-3

Coding Using
Positive and
Negative Exponents

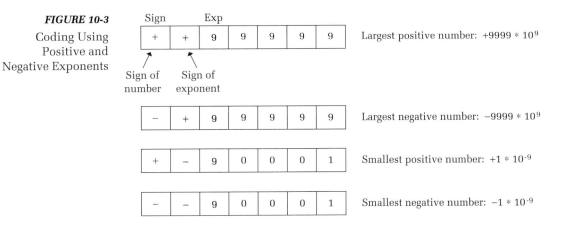

Largest positive number: +9999 * 10⁹

Largest negative number: −9999 * 10⁹

Smallest positive number: +1 * 10⁻⁹

Smallest negative number: −1 * 10⁻⁹

We first add z to the sum of x and y.

(x)	$-1324 * 10^3$
(y)	$\underline{1325 * 10^3}$
	$1 * 10^3$ $= 1000 * 10^0$

$(x + y)$	$1000 * 10^0$
(z)	$\underline{5424 * 10^0}$
	$6424 * 10^0$ $\leftarrow (x + y) + z$

Now here is the result of adding x to the sum of y and z:

(y)	$1325000 * 10^0$
(z)	$\underline{5424 * 10^0}$
	$1330424 * 10^0$ $= 1330 * 10^3$ (truncated to four digits)

$(y + z)$	$1330 * 10^3$
(x)	$\underline{-1324 * 10^3}$
	$6 * 10^3$ $= 6000 * 10^0 \leftarrow x + (y + z)$

These two answers are the same in the thousands place, but different thereafter. The error behind this discrepancy is called **representational error.**

representational error
Arithmetic error that occurs when the precision of the true result of an arithmetic operation is greater than the precision of the machine

Because of representational errors, it is unwise to use a floating point number as a loop control variable. Because precision may be lost in calculations involving floating point numbers, it is difficult to predict when (or even *if*) a loop control variable of type `float` (or `double` or `long double`) will become equal to the termination value. A count-controlled loop with a floating point control variable may behave in an unpredictable fashion.

Also because of representational errors, we should never compare floating point numbers for exact equality. Rarely are two floating point numbers exactly equal, and thus they should be compared only for near equality. If the difference between the two numbers is less than some acceptable small value, we can consider them equal for the purposes of the given problem.

Underflow and Overflow.   In addition to representational errors, there are two other problems to watch out for in floating point arithmetic: *underflow* and *overflow.*

Underflow is the condition that arises when the value of a calculation is too small to be represented. Going back to our decimal representation, let's look at a calculation involving small numbers:

$$
\begin{array}{r}
4210 * 10^{-8} \\
*\quad 2000 * 10^{-8} \\
\hline
8420000 * 10^{-16} \quad = 8420 * 10^{-13}
\end{array}
$$

This value cannot be represented in our scheme because an exponent of -13 is too small. Our minimum is -9. One way to resolve the problem is to set the result of the calculation to 0.0. Obviously, any answer depending on this calculation will not be exact.

Overflow is a more serious problem because there is no logical recourse when it occurs. For example, the result of the calculation

$$
\begin{array}{r}
9999 * 10^{9} \\
*\quad 1000 * 10^{9} \\
\hline
9999000 * 10^{18} \quad = 9999 * 10^{21}
\end{array}
$$

cannot be stored, so what should we do? To be consistent with our response to underflow, we could set the result to $9999 * 10^{9}$ (the maximum representable value in this case). Yet this seems intuitively wrong. The alternative is to stop with an error message.

C++ does not define what should happen in the case of overflow or underflow. Different implementations of C++ solve the problem in different ways. You might try to cause an overflow with your system and see what happens. Some systems print a run-time error message such as "FLOATING POINT OVERFLOW". On other systems, you may get the largest number that can be represented.

We have been discussing problems with floating point numbers, but integer numbers also can overflow both negatively and positively. Most implementations of C++ ignore integer overflow. To see how your system handles the situation, you should try adding 1 to `INT_MAX` and -1 to `INT_MIN`. On most systems, adding 1 to `INT_MAX` sets the result to `INT_MIN`, a negative number.

> ◾ *Choosing a Numeric Data Type*
>
> *A first encounter with all the numeric data types of C++ may leave you feeling overwhelmed. To help in choosing among them, here are some guidelines:*
>
> **1.** *Use floating point types only when you definitely need fractional values.*
>
> **2.** *For ordinary integer data, use* `int` *instead of* `char` *or* `short`. *It's easy to make overflow errors with these smaller data types.*
>
> **3.** *Use* `long` *only if the range of* `int` *values on your machine is too restrictive.*
>
> **4.** *Use* `double` *and* `long double` *only if you need enormously large or small numbers, or if your machine's* `float` *values do not carry enough digits of precision.*
>
> **5.** *Avoid the* `unsigned` *forms of integral types.*
>
> *By following these guidelines, you'll find that the simple types you use most often are* `int` *and* `float`, *along with* `char` *for character data. Only rarely do you need the longer and shorter variations of these fundamental types.*

User-Defined Simple Types

The concept of a data type is fundamental to all of the widely used programming languages. One of the strengths of the C++ language is that it allows programmers to create new data types, tailored to meet the needs of a particular program. Much of the remainder of this book is about user-defined data types. In this section, we examine how to create our own simple types.

Names of user-defined types obey the same scope rules that apply to identifiers in general. Most types are defined globally, although it is reasonable to define a new type within a subprogram if that is the only place it is used.

Enumeration Types

C++ allows the user to define a new simple type by listing (enumerating) the literal values that make up the domain of the type. These literal values must be *identifiers,* not numbers. The identifiers are separated by commas, and the list is enclosed in braces. Data types defined in this way are called **enumeration types.** Here's an example:

enumeration type
A user-defined data type whose domain is an ordered set of literal values expressed as identifiers

```
enum Days {SUN, MON, TUE, WED, THU, FRI, SAT};
```

This declaration creates a new data type named `Days`. Whereas Typedef merely creates a synonym for an existing type, an enumeration type like `Days` is a new type and is distinct from any existing type.

enumerator

One of the values in the domain of an enumeration type

The values in the `Days` type are called **enumerators.** The enumerators are *ordered*, in the sense that `SUN < MON < TUE . . . < FRI < SAT`. When applying relational operators to enumerators the relation that is tested is "comes before" or "comes after" in the ordering of the data type.

If there is some reason that you want different internal representations for the enumerators, you can specify them explicitly like this:

```
enum Days {SUN = 4, MON = 18, TUE = 9, . . . };
```

There is rarely any reason to assign specific values to enumerators. With the `Days` type, we are interested in the days of the week, not in the way the machine stores them internally.

Because enumerators are, in essence, named constants, we capitalize the entire identifier. This is purely a style choice. Many C++ programmers use both uppercase and lowercase letters in enumerators.

The identifiers used as enumerators must follow the rules for any C++ identifier. For example,

```
enum Vowel {'A', 'E', 'I', 'O', 'U'};    // Not legal
```

is not legal because the items are not identifiers. In the declaration

```
enum Places {1st, 2nd, 3rd};    // Not legal
```

type `Places` is not legal because identifiers cannot begin with digits. In the declarations

```
enum Starch {CORN, RICE, POTATO, BEAN};
enum Grain {WHEAT, CORN, RYE, BARLEY, SORGHUM};    // Not legal
```

type `Starch` and type `Grain` are legal by themselves, but together they are not. Identifiers in the same scope must be unique. `CORN` cannot be defined twice.

Suppose you are writing a program for a veterinary office. The program must keep track of different kinds of animals. The following enumeration type might be used for this purpose.

Type identifier   Literal values in the domain

```
enum Animals {RODENT, CAT, DOG, BIRD, REPTILE, HORSE, BOVINE, SHEEP};

Animals inPatient;
Animals outPatient;    } Creation of two variables of type Animals
```

RODENT is a literal, one of the values in the data type Animals. Be sure you understand that RODENT is not a variable name. Instead, RODENT is one of the values that can be stored into the variables inPatient and outPatient. Let's look at the kinds of operations we might want to perform on variables of enumeration types.

Assignment.   The assignment statement

```
inPatient = DOG;
```

does not assign to inPatient the character string "DOG", nor the contents of a variable named DOG. It assigns the *value* DOG, which is one of the values in the domain of the data type Animals.

   Assignment is a valid operation, as long as the value being stored is of type Animals. Both of the statements

```
inPatient = DOG;
outPatient = inPatient;
```

are acceptable. Each expression on the right-hand side is of type Animals—DOG is a literal of type Animals, and inPatient is a variable of type Animals. Although we know that the underlying representation of DOG is the integer 2, the compiler prevents us from using this assignment:

```
inPatient = 2;
```

Here is the precise rule: *Implicit type coercion is defined from an enumeration type to* int *but not from* int *to an enumeration type.* Applying this rule to the statements

```
someInt = DOG;     // Valid
inPatient = 2;     // Error
```

we see that the first statement stores 2 into someInt (because of implicit type coercion), but the second produces a compile-time error. The restriction against storing an int value into a variable of type Animals is to keep you from accidentally storing an out-of-range value:

```
inPatient = 65;    // Not legal, out of range
```

Incrementation.   Suppose you want to "increment" the value in `inPatient` so that it becomes the next value in the domain:

```
inPatient = inPatient + 1;   // Not legal
```

This statement is illegal for the following reason. The right-hand side is okay because implicit type coercion lets you add `inPatient` to 1; the result is an `int` value. But the assignment operation is not valid because you can't store an `int` value into `inPatient`. However, you can escape the type coercion rule by using an *explicit* type conversion—a type cast—as follows:

```
inPatient = Animals(inPatient + 1);   // Yes
```

When you use the type cast, the compiler assumes that you know what you are doing and allows it.

Incrementing a variable of enumeration type is very useful in loops. Sometimes we need a loop that processes all the values in the domain of the type. We might try the following For loop:

```
Animals patient;

for (patient=RODENT; patient <= SHEEP; patient++) // Not legal
   .
   .
   .
```

However, the compiler will complain about the expression `patient++`. To increment `patient`, we must use an assignment expression and a type cast:

```
for (patient=RODENT; patient <= SHEEP; patient=Animals(patient + 1))
   .
   .
   .
```

The only caution here is that when control exits the loop, the value of `patient` is one *greater than* the largest value in the domain (`SHEEP`). If you want to use `patient` outside the loop, you must reassign it a value that is within the appropriate range for the `Animals` type.

Comparison. The most common operation performed on values of enumeration types is comparison. When you compare two values, their ordering is determined by the order in which you listed the enumerators in the type declaration. For instance, the expression

```
inPatient <= BIRD
```

is true if inPatient contains the value RODENT, CAT, DOG, or BIRD.

You can also use values of an enumeration type in a Switch statement. Because RODENT, CAT, and so on are literals, they can appear in case labels:

```
switch (inPatient)
{
    case RODENT  :
    case CAT     :
    case DOG     :
    case BIRD    : cout << "Cage ward";
                     break;
    case REPTILE : cout << "Terrarium ward";
                     break;
    case HORSE   :
    case BOVINE  :
    case SHEEP   : cout << "Barn";
}
```

Input and Output. Stream I/O is defined only for the basic built-in types (int, float, and so on), not for enumeration types. Values of enumeration types must be input or output indirectly.

To input values, the usual strategy is to read a number or a letter code and translate it to one of the identifiers in the enumeration type. For example, the veterinary office program could read the kind of animal as a series of characters, then assign one of the values of type Animals to that patient. The following program fragment reads in an animal represented by its first two letters and converts it to one of the values in type Animals.

```
cin >> ch1 >> ch2;
switch (ch1)
{
    case 'R' : if (ch2 == 'o')
                      inPatient = RODENT;
                else
```

```
                        inPatient = REPTILE;
                break;
    case 'C' : inPatient = CAT;
                break;
    case 'D' : inPatient = DOG;
                break;
    case 'B' : if (ch2 == 'i')
                    inPatient = BIRD;
                else
                    inPatient = BOVINE;
                break;
    case 'H' : inPatient = HORSE;
                break;
    default : inPatient = SHEEP;
}
```

Enumeration type values cannot be printed directly either. Printing is done by using a Switch statement that prints a character string corresponding to the value.

```
switch (inPatient)
{
    case RODENT  : cout << "Rodent";
                    break;
    case CAT     : cout << "Cat";
                    break;
    case DOG     : cout << "Dog";
                    break;
    case BIRD    : cout << "Bird";
                    break;
    case REPTILE : cout << "Reptile";
                    break;
    case HORSE   : cout << "Horse";
                    break;
    case BOVINE  : cout << "Bovine";
                    break;
    case SHEEP   : cout << "Sheep";
}
```

You might ask, Why not use just a pair of letters or an integer number as a code to represent each animal in a program? We use enumeration types to make our programs more readable; they are another way to make code self-documenting.

Returning a Function Value. We have been using value-returning functions to compute and return values of built-in types such as `int`, `float`, and `char`:

```
int Factorial( int );
float CargoMoment( int );
```

C++ allows a function return value to be of *any* data type—built-in or user-defined—except an array (a data type we introduce in the next chapter).

Named and Anonymous Data Types

The enumeration types we have looked at, `Animals` and `Days`, are called **named types** because their declarations included names for the types. Variables of these new data types are declared separately using the type identifiers `Animals` and `Days`.

C++ also lets us introduce a new type directly in a variable declaration. Instead of the declarations

named type
A user-defined type whose declaration includes a type identifier that gives a name to the type

```
enum CoinType {NICKEL, DIME, QUARTER, HALF_DOLLAR};
enum StatusType {OK, OUT_OF_STOCK, BACK_ORDERED};

CoinType    change;
StatusType status;
```

we could write

```
enum {NICKEL, DIME, QUARTER, HALF_DOLLAR} change;
enum {OK, OUT_OF_STOCK, BACK_ORDERED} status;
```

anonymous type
A type that does not have an associated type identifier

A new type declared in a variable declaration is called an **anonymous type** because it does not have a name—that is, it does not have a type identifier associated with it.

If we can create a data type in a variable declaration, why bother with a separate type declaration that creates a named type? Named types, like named constants, make a program more readable, more understandable, and easier to modify. Also, declaring a type and declaring a variable of that type are two distinct concepts; it is better to keep them separate. In addition, assignment of one enumeration type variable to another is valid only if they are both of the same *named* type. In the following code segment, the assignment statement is not allowed:

```
enum {NICKEL, DIME, QUARTER, HALF_DOLLAR} amount;
enum {NICKEL, DIME, QUARTER, HALF_DOLLAR} thisCoin;
  .
  .
  .
amount = thisCoin;   // Not allowed
```

Even though the two anonymous data types have the same domain, the compiler considers them to be two distinct data types and won't let you assign `thisCoin` to `amount`. In fact, it first complains because the second declaration duplicates the identifiers in the first declaration.

User-Written Header Files   As you create your own user-defined data types, you sometimes find that a data type can be useful in more than one program. An example is the `Boolean` type we have been using in several programs. Instead of typing the statements

```
typedef int Boolean;
const Boolean true = 1;
const Boolean false = 0;
```

at the beginning of every program that uses the `Boolean` type, we can put these three statements into a separate file named, say, `bool.h`. Then we use `bool.h` just as we use system-supplied header files such as `iostream.h` and `math.h`. By using an #include directive, we ask the C++ preprocessor to insert physically the contents of the file into our program. (Although many C++ systems use `.h` to denote header files, other systems use `.hpp` or `.hxx`.)

When you enclose the name of a header file in angle brackets, as in

```
#include <iostream.h>
```

the preprocessor looks for the file in the standard *include directory,* a directory that contains all the header files supplied by the C++ system. On the other hand, you can enclose the name of a header file in double quotes, like this:

```
#include "bool.h"
```

In this case, the preprocessor looks for the file in the programmer's current directory. This mechanism allows us to write our own header files that contain type declarations and constant declarations. We can use a simple #include directive instead of retyping the declarations in every program that makes use of them (see Figure 10-4).

From now on, the program examples in this book use the directive

```
#include "bool.h"
```

instead of explicitly defining the `Boolean` type each time it is needed.

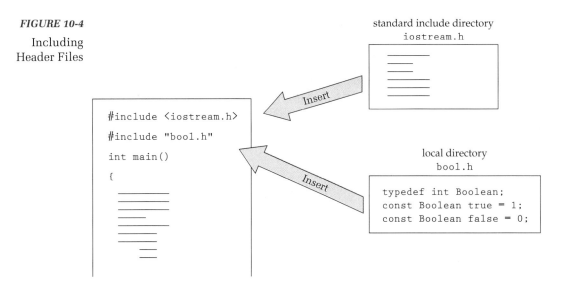

FIGURE 10-4

Including
Header Files

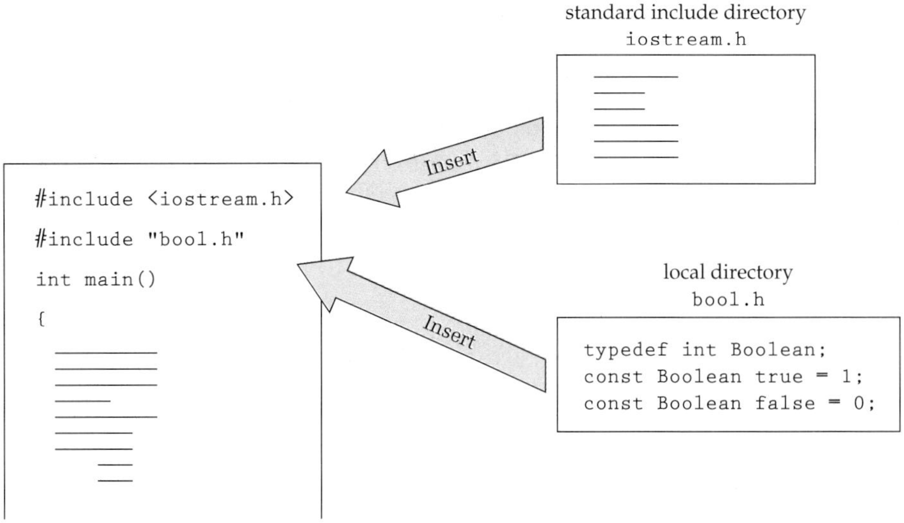

More on Type Coercion

As you have learned over the course of several chapters, C++ performs implicit
type coercion whenever values of different data types are used in

1. arithmetic and relational expressions
2. assignment operations
3. parameter passage
4. return of the function value from a value-returning function

For item 1—mixed-type expressions—the C++ compiler follows one set of rules
for type coercion. For items 2, 3, and 4, the compiler follows a second set of rules.
Let's examine each of these sets of rules.

Type Coercion in Arithmetic and Relational Expressions

Suppose that an arithmetic expression consists of one operator and two
operands—for example, `3.4*sum` or `var1/var2`. If the two operands are of different data types, then one of them is temporarily **promoted** (or **widened**) to
match the data type of the other. To understand exactly what promotion means,
let's look at the rule for type coercion in an arithmetic expression.

promotion (widening)
*The conversion of a
value from a "lower"
type to a "higher"
type according to a
programming lan-
guage's precedence
of data types*

Step 1: Each `char`, `short`, or enumeration value is promoted (widened) to `int`.
If both operands are now `int`, the result is an `int` expression.

Step 2: If step 1 still leaves a mixed-type expression, the following precedence of
types is used:

lowest ⟶ highest

`int, unsigned int, long, unsigned long, float, double, long double`

The value of the operand of "lower" type is promoted to that of the "higher" type, and the result is an expression of that type.

A simple example is the expression `someFloat+2`. This expression has no `char`, `short`, or enumeration values in it, so step 1 still leaves a mixed-type expression. In step 2, `int` is a "lower" type than `float`, so the value 2 is coerced temporarily to the `float` value, say, 2.0. Then the addition takes place, and the type of the entire expression is `float`.

This description of type coercion also holds for relational expressions such as

```
someInt <= someFloat
```

The value of `someInt` is temporarily coerced to floating point representation before the comparison takes place. The only difference between arithmetic expressions and relational expressions is that the resulting type of a relational expression is always `int`—the value 1 (true) or 0 (false).

Type Coercion in Assignments, Parameter Passage, and Return of a Function Value

In general, promotion of a value from one type to another does not cause loss of information. On the other hand, **demotion** (or **narrowing**) of data values can potentially cause loss of information.

Consider an assignment operation

$$v = e$$

where v is a variable and e is an expression. Regarding the data types of v and e, there are three possibilities:

demotion (narrowing)
The conversion of a value from a "higher" type to a "lower" type according to precedence of data types

1. If the types of v and e are the same, no type coercion is necessary.
2. If the type of v is "higher" than that of e (using the type precedence we explained with promotion), then the value of e is promoted to v's type before being stored into v.
3. If the type of v is "lower" than that of e, the value of e is demoted to v's type before being stored into v.

Demotion has the following effects:

- Demotion from a longer integral type to a shorter integral type (such as `long` to `int`) results in discarding the leftmost (most significant) bits in the binary number representation. The result may be a drastically different number.
- Demotion from a floating point type to an integral type causes truncation of the fractional part (and an undefined result if the whole-number part will not fit into the destination variable). The result of truncating a negative number is machine-dependent.
- Demotion from a longer floating point type to a shorter floating point type (such as `double` to `float`) may result in a loss of digits of precision.

Our description of type coercion in an assignment operation also holds for parameter passage (the mapping of actual parameters onto formal parameters) and for returning a function value with a `return` statement. For example, assume that INT_MAX on your machine is 32767 and that you have the following function:

```
void DoSomething( int n )
{
    .
    .
    .
}
```

If the function is called with the statement

```
DoSomething(50000);
```

then the value 50000 (which is implicitly of type `long` because it is larger than INT_MAX) is demoted to a completely different, smaller value that fits into an `int` location. In a similar fashion, execution of the function

```
int SomeFunc( float x )
{
    .
    .
    .
    return 70000;
}
```

causes demotion of the value 70000 to a smaller `int` value because `int` is the declared type of the function return value.

PROGRAMMING EXAMPLE

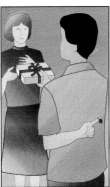

Birthday Reminder

Problem: Let's write a program that prints the names of friends who have a birthday in a given month.

Input: A month entered from the keyboard, with first letter capitalized.

Output: The names (and birthdays) of all friends with a birthday in that month.

Discussion: If we were solving this problem by hand, we would turn our calendar to the month in question and list the names written there. That is exactly what our program does: it recognizes which month is being requested and calls

PROGRAMMING EXAMPLE cont'd

a function that writes out the information for that month. The information for each month is represented as a series of output statements.

We represent the months as an enumeration type whose domain is the values JANUARY, FEBRUARY, MARCH, . . . DECEMBER. Thus, we must convert the month as input in character form into this type. We can perform the conversion by checking just the first one, two, or three characters of the input string. February, September, October, November, and December have unique first characters. April, August, and January can be distinguished by their first two characters. June, July, March, and May require three characters to distinguish them.

Assumptions: None.

```
//****************************************************************
// BirthdayReminder program
// This program takes a month as input and prints the
// list of birthdays associated with that month
//****************************************************************
#include <iostream.h>

enum Months
{
    JANUARY, FEBRUARY, MARCH, APRIL, MAY, JUNE,
    JULY, AUGUST, SEPTEMBER, OCTOBER, NOVEMBER, DECEMBER
};

Months A_Month( char );
Months J_Month( char, char );
Months M_Month( char );
void GetMonth( Months& );
void PrintJanuary();
void PrintFebruary();
void PrintMarch();
void PrintApril();
void PrintMay();
void PrintJune();
void PrintJuly();
void PrintAugust();
void PrintSeptember();
void PrintOctober();
void PrintNovember();
void PrintDecember();

int main()
{
    Months month;
```

PROGRAMMING EXAMPLE cont'd

```
        GetMonth(month);
        switch (month)
        {
            case JANUARY    : PrintJanuary();
                              break;
            case FEBRUARY   : PrintFebruary();
                              break;
            case MARCH      : PrintMarch();
                              break;
            case APRIL      : PrintApril();
                              break;
            case MAY        : PrintMay();
                              break;
            case JUNE       : PrintJune();
                              break;
            case JULY       : PrintJuly();
                              break;
            case AUGUST     : PrintAugust();
                              break;
            case SEPTEMBER  : PrintSeptember();
                              break;
            case OCTOBER    : PrintOctober();
                              break;
            case NOVEMBER   : PrintNovember();
                              break;
            case DECEMBER   : PrintDecember();
        }
        return 0;
    }


//********************************************************************

void GetMonth( /* out */ Months& month )    // User's desired month

// Inputs a month after prompting the user

// Postcondition:
//      User has been prompted to enter a month
//   && Only the characters needed to determine the month are read
//      (the remaining characters on the input line are read and
//      discarded)
//   && month == value of type Months corresponding to user's input
{
    char firstChar;
    char secondChar;
    char thirdChar;
```

PROGRAMMING EXAMPLE cont'd

```
        cout << "Please enter month, capitalizing first letter."
            << endl;
        cin.get(firstChar);
        cin.get(secondChar);
        cin.get(thirdChar);
        cin.ignore(500, '\n');      // Skip remaining characters
                                    //   through newline
        switch (firstChar)
        {
            case 'F': month = FEBRUARY;
                    break;
            case 'S': month = SEPTEMBER;
                    break;
            case 'O': month = OCTOBER;
                    break;
            case 'N': month = NOVEMBER;
                    break;
            case 'D': month = DECEMBER;
                    break;
            case 'J': month = J_Month(secondChar, thirdChar);
                    break;
            case 'A': month = A_Month(secondChar);
                    break;
            case 'M': month = M_Month(thirdChar);
                    break;
        }
}


//*******************************************************************


Months J_Month( /* in */ char secondChar,    // 2nd input char
                /* in */ char thirdChar  )    // 3rd input char

// Determines month beginning with J

// Precondition:
//     secondChar and thirdChar are assigned
// Postcondition:
//     Function value == JANUARY, if secondChar == 'a'
//                    == JULY, if thirdChar == 'l'
//                    == JUNE, otherwise
{
    if (secondChar == 'a')
        return JANUARY;
    else if (thirdChar == 'l')
        return JULY;
```

PROGRAMMING EXAMPLE cont'd

```
        else
            return JUNE;
    }

//***********************************************************************

Months A_Month( /* in */ char secondChar )    // 2nd input char

// Determines month beginning with A

// Precondition:
//     secondChar is assigned
// Postcondition:
//     Function value == APRIL, if secondChar == 'p'
//                    == AUGUST, otherwise

    {
        if (secondChar == 'p')
            return APRIL;
        else
            return AUGUST;
    }

//***********************************************************************

Months M_Month( /* in */ char thirdChar )    // 3rd input char

// Determines month beginning with M

// Precondition:
//     thirdChar is assigned
// Postcondition:
//     Function value == MARCH, if thirdChar == 'r'
//                    == MAY, otherwise

    {
        if (thirdChar == 'r')
            return MARCH;
        else
            return MAY;
    }

//***********************************************************************

void PrintJanuary()
{
```

PROGRAMMING EXAMPLE cont'd

```
        cout << "January printed" << endl;
}

//*********************************************************************

void PrintFebruary()
{
    cout << "February printed" << endl;
}

//*********************************************************************

void PrintMarch()
{
    cout << "March printed" << endl;
}
        .
        .
        .

//*********************************************************************

void PrintDecember()
{
    cout << "December printed" << endl;
}
```

Testing: To test this program, we must run it 12 times. For each run, a different month is used as input, the appropriate print function is called, and the corresponding message is printed. If you want to use this program, you have to create the output statements to print the data for your friends. The stubs we use to test the rest of the program merely show that each print function is called correctly. We have more to say about testing this program in the Testing and Debugging section that follows.

Testing and Debugging

Floating Point Data

When a problem requires the use of floating point numbers that are extremely large, small, or precise, it is important to keep in mind the limitations of the particular system you are using. When testing a program that performs floating point calculations, determine the acceptable margin of error beforehand, and then design your test data to try to push the program beyond those limits. Carefully check the accuracy of the computed results. (Remember that when you "hand calculate" the correct results, a pocket calculator may have *less* precision than your computer system.) If the program produces acceptable results when given worst-case data, it probably performs correctly on typical data.

Coping with Input Errors

Several times in this book we had our programs test for invalid data and write an error message. Writing an error message is certainly necessary, but it is only the first step. We must also decide what the program should do next. The problem itself and the severity of the error should determine what action is taken in any error condition. The approach taken also depends on whether or not the program is being run interactively.

In a program that reads its data only from an input file, there is no interaction with the person who entered the data. The program, therefore, should try to adjust for the bad data items, if at all possible.

If the invalid data item is not essential, the program can skip it and continue; for example, if a program averaging test grades encounters a negative test score, it could simply skip the negative score. A message should be written stating that an invalid data item was encountered and outlining the steps that were taken. Such messages form an *exception report.*

If the data item is essential and no guess is possible, processing should be terminated. A message should be written to the user with as much information as possible about the invalid data item.

In an interactive environment, the program can prompt the user to supply another value. The program should indicate to the user what is wrong with the original data. Another possibility is to write out a list of actions and ask the user to choose among them.

These suggestions on how to handle bad data assume that the program recognizes when bad data have been entered. There are two approaches to error detection: passive and active. Passive error detection leaves it to the system to detect errors. This may seem easier, but the programmer relinquishes control of processing when an error occurs. An example of passive error detection is the system's division-by-zero error.

Active error detection means having the program check for possible errors and determine an appropriate action if an error is encountered. An example of active error detection would be to read a value and use an If statement to see if the value is zero before dividing it into another number.

The BirthdayReminder program uses *no* error detection. If the input is typed incorrectly, the program either produces no output at all (if the first character of the month is invalid) or erroneous output (if the second or third characters are invalid). The `GetMonth`, `J_Month`, `A_Month`, and `M_Month` functions should be rewritten to incorporate active error detection. The first character must be checked to see whether it is one of the valid first letters. If not, the error must be reported. If the first character is an 'A', a 'J', or an 'M', the second or third character (or both) must be checked.

Testing and Debugging Hints

1. Avoid using unnecessary side effects in expressions. The test

```
if ((x = y) < z)
```

is less clear and more prone to error than the equivalent sequence of statements

```
x = y;
if (y < z)
```

Also, if you accidentally omit the parentheses around the assignment, like this:

```
if (x = y < z)
```

then, according to C++ operator precedence, x is *not* assigned the value of y. It is assigned either the value 1 (if $y < z$) or 0 (if $y \geq z$).

2. Programs that rely on a particular machine's character set may not run on another machine. Check to see what character-handling functions are supplied by the standard library. Functions like `tolower`, `toupper`, `isalpha`, and `iscntrl` automatically account for the character set being used.

3. Don't directly compare floating point values for equality. Instead, check them for near equality. The tolerance for near equality depends on the particular problem you are solving.

4. Use integers if you are dealing with whole numbers only. Any integer can be represented exactly by the computer, as long as it is within the machine's allowable range of values. Also, integer arithmetic is faster than floating point arithmetic on most machines.

5. Be aware of representational, overflow, and underflow errors. If possible, try to arrange calculations in your program to keep floating point numbers from becoming too large or too small.

6. If your program increases the value of a positive integer and the result suddenly becomes a negative number, you should suspect integer overflow. On most computers, adding 1 to INT_MAX yields INT_MIN, a negative number.

7. Avoid mixing data types in expressions, assignment operations, parameter passage, and the return of a function value. If you must mix types, explicit type casts can prevent unwelcome surprises caused by implicit type coercion.

8. Consider using enumeration types to make your programs more readable, understandable, and modifiable.

9. Avoid anonymous data typing. Give each user-defined type a name.
10. Enumeration type values cannot be input or output directly.
11. Type demotion can lead to decreased precision or corruption of data.

Summary

A data type is a set of values (domain) along with the operations that can be applied to those values. Simple data types are data types whose values are atomic (indivisible).

The integral types in C++ are `char`, `short`, `int`, `long`, and `enum`. The most commonly used integral types are `int` and `char`. The `char` type can be used for storing small (one-byte) numeric integers or, more often, for storing character data. Character data include both printable and nonprintable characters. Nonprintable characters—those that control the behavior of hardware devices—are expressed in C++ as escape sequences such as `\n`. Each character is represented internally as a nonnegative integer according to the particular character set (such as ASCII or EBCDIC) that a computer uses.

The floating point types built into the C++ language are `float`, `double`, and `long double`. Floating point numbers are represented in the computer with a mantissa and an exponent. This permits the use of numbers that are much larger or much smaller than those that can be represented with the integral types. Floating point representation also allows us to perform calculations on numbers with fractional parts.

Representational errors can affect the accuracy of a program's computations. When using floating point numbers, keep in mind that if two numbers are vastly different from each other in size, adding or subtracting them may give inaccurate results. Remember, also, that the computer has a limited range of numbers that it can represent. If a program tries to compute a value that is too large or too small, an error message may result when the program executes.

C++ allows the programmer to define additional data types. An enumeration type, created by listing the identifiers that make up the domain, is a new data type that is distinct from any existing type. Values of an enumeration type may be assigned, compared in relational expressions, used as case labels in a Switch statement, and returned as function values. Enumeration types are extremely useful in the writing of clear, self-documenting programs.

Quick Check

1. The C++ simple types are divided into integral types and floating point types. What are the five integral types (ignoring the `unsigned` variations) and the three floating point types? (pp. 303–305)

2. What is the difference between an expression and an expression statement in C++? (pp. 308–309)
3. Assume that the following code segment is executed on a machine that uses the ASCII character set. What is the final value of the char variable someChar? Give both its external and internal representations. (pp. 313–315)

```
someChar = 'T';
someChar = someChar + 4;
```

4. Why is it inappropriate to use a variable of a floating point type as a loop control variable? (pp. 319–322)
5. If a computer has four digits of precision, what would be the result of the following addition operation? (pp. 319–322)

400400.000 + 199.9

6. When choosing a data type for a variable that stores whole numbers only, why should int be your first choice? (p. 323)
7. Declare an enumeration type named AutoMakes, consisting of the names of five of your favorite car manufacturers. (pp. 323–325)
8. Given the type declaration

```
enum VisibleColors
{
    RED, ORANGE, YELLOW, GREEN, BLUE, INDIGO, VIOLET
};
```

write the first line of a For statement that "counts" from RED through VIOLET. Use a loop control variable named rainbow that is of type VisibleColors. (pp. 325–326)
9. Why is it better to use a named type than an anonymous type? (pp. 329–330)
10. Suppose that many of your programs need an enumeration type named Days and another named Months. If you place the type declarations into a file named calendar.h, what would an #include directive look like that inserts these declarations into a program? (pp. 330–331)
11. In arithmetic and relational expressions, which of the following could occur: type promotion, type demotion, or both? (pp. 331–333)

Answers 1. The integral types are char, short, int, long, and enum. The floating point types are float, double, and long double. 2. An expression becomes an expression statement when it is terminated by a semicolon. 3. The external representation is the letter *X*; the internal representation is the integer 88. 4. Because representational errors can cause the loop termination condition to be evaluated with unpredictable results. 5. 400500.000 (Actually, 4.005E + 5) 6. Floating point arithmetic is subject to numerical inaccuracies and is slower than integer arithmetic on most machines. Use of the smaller integral types, char and short, can more easily lead to overflow errors. The long type usually requires more memory than int, and the arithmetic is usually slower.
7. enum AutoMakes {SAAB, JAGUAR, CITROEN, CHEVROLET, FORD};
8. for (rainbow = RED; rainbow <= VIOLET; rainbow = VisibleColors(rainbow + 1))

9. Named types make a program more readable, more understandable, and easier to modify. Also, a variable of an anonymous enumeration type cannot be assigned to a variable of a named enumeration type, even if the domains of the types are the same.   10. `#include "calendar.h"` 11. Type promotion

Exam Preparation Exercises

1. Every C++ compiler guarantees that `sizeof(int) < sizeof(long)`. (True or False?)
2. Classify each of the following as either an expression or an expression statement.
   a. `sum = 0`
   b. `sqrt(x)`
   c. `y = 17;`
   d. `count++`
3. Rewrite each statement as described.
   a. Using the += operator, rewrite the statement

   ```
   sumOfSquares = sumOfSquares + x * x;
   ```

   b. Using the decrement operator, rewrite the statement

   ```
   count = count - 1;
   ```

   c. Using a single assignment statement that uses the ? : operator, rewrite the statement

   ```
   if (n > 8)
       k = 32;
   else
       k = 15 * n;
   ```

4. What is printed by each of the following program fragments? (In both cases, ch is of type `char`.)

   a. ```
   for (ch = 'd'; ch <= 'g'; ch++)
       cout << ch;
   ```

   b. ```
   ch = 'F';
   cout << ch << ' ' << int(ch);      // Assume ASCII
   ```

5. What is printed by the following output statement?

   ```
   cout << "Notice that\nthe character \\ is a backslash.\n";
   ```

6. If a system supports 10 digits of precision for floating point numbers, what are the results of the following computations?
   a. 1.4E+12 + 100.0
   b. 4.2E–8 + 100.0
   c. 3.2E–5 + 3.2E+5

7. Define the following terms:

   mantissa   significant digits
   exponent   overflow
   representational error

8. Given the type declaration

   ```
   enum Agents {SMITH, JONES, GRANT, WHITE};
   ```

   does the expression JONES > GRANT have the value true or false?

9. Given the following declarations,

   ```
   enum Perfumes {POISON, DIOR_ESSENCE, CHANEL_NO_5, COTY};
   Perfumes sample;
   ```

   indicate whether each statement below is valid or invalid.
   a. `sample = POISON;`
   b. `sample = 3;`
   c. `sample++;`
   d. `sample = Perfumes(sample + 1);`

10. Using the declarations

   ```
   enum SeasonType {WINTER, SPRING, SUMMER, FALL};
   SeasonType season;
   ```

   indicate whether each statement below is valid or invalid.
   a. `cin >> season;`
   b. `if (season >= SPRING)`
      .
      .
      .
   c. `for (season = WINTER; season <= SUMMER; season =`
                                `SeasonType(season + 1))`
      .
      .
      .

11. Consider the following program fragment:

   ```
   enum Colors {RED, GREEN, BLUE};

   Colors myColor;
   enum {RED, GREEN, BLUE} yourColor;
   ```

```
yourColor = GREEN;
myColor = yourColor;
```

a. The data type of `myColor` is a named type, and the data type of `yourColor` is an anonymous type. (True or False?)

b. The last assignment statement is valid because both enumeration types have the same domain. (True or False?)

12. If you have written your own header file named `mytypes.h`, then the preprocessor directive

```
#include <mytypes.h>
```

is the correct way to insert the contents of the header file into a program. (True or False?)

13. In each of the following situations, indicate whether promotion or demotion occurs. (The names of the variables are meant to suggest their data types.)

a. Execution of the assignment operation `someInt = someFloat`

b. Evaluation of the expression `someFloat + someLong`

c. Passing the actual parameter `someDouble` to the formal parameter `someFloat`

d. Execution of the statement

```
return someShort;
```

within an `int` function.

14. Active error detection leaves error hunting to C++ and the operating system, whereas passive error detection requires the programmer to do the error hunting. (True or False?)

Programming Warm-Up Exercises

1. Find out the maximum and minimum values for each of the C++ simple types on your machine. On most systems, these values are declared as named constants in the files `limits.h` and `float.h` in the standard include directory.

2. Using a combination of printable characters and escape sequences within *one* string, write a single output statement that does the following in the order shown:

   ▪ Prints `Hello`
   ▪ Prints a (horizontal) tab character
   ▪ Prints `There`
   ▪ Prints two blank lines
   ▪ Prints "`Ace`" (including the double quotes)

3. Write a While loop that copies all the characters (including whitespace characters) from an input file `inFile` to an output file `outFile`, except that every lowercase letter is converted to uppercase. Assume that both files have been opened successfully before the loop begins. The loop should terminate when end-of-file is detected.

4. Given the following declarations

```
int n;
char ch1;
char ch2;
```

and given that n contains a two-digit number, translate n into two single characters where ch1 holds the higher-order digit, and ch2 holds the lower-order digit. For example, if n = 59, ch1 would equal '5', and ch2 would equal '9'. Then output the two digits as characters in the same order as the original numbers. (*Hint:* Consider how you might use the / and % operators in your solution.)

5. In a program you are writing, a float variable beta may potentially contain a very large number. Before multiplying beta by 100.0, you want the program to test whether it is safe to do so. Write an If statement that tests for a possible overflow *before* multiplying by 100.0. Specifically, if the multiplication would lead to overflow, print a message and don't perform the multiplication; otherwise, go ahead with the multiplication.

6. Declare an enumeration type for the course numbers of computer courses at your school.

7. Declare an enumeration type for the South American countries.

8. Declare an enumeration type for the work days of the week (Monday through Friday).

9. Write a value-returning function that converts the first two letters of a work day into the type declared in Exercise 8.

10. Write a void function that prints a value of the type declared in Exercise 8.

11. Using a loop control variable today of the type declared in Exercise 8, write a For loop that prints out all five values in the domain of the type. To print each value, invoke the function of Exercise 10.

12. Below is a function that is supposed to return the average of two integers, rounded to the nearest integer.

```
int Avg( /* in */ int1,
         /* in */ int2 )
{
    return float(int1) / float(int2);
}
```

Sometimes this function returns an incorrect result. Describe what the problem is in terms of type promotion or demotion, and fix the problem.

13. Write the print functions for the BirthdayReminder program for a few of your friends and family.

14. Expand the BirthdayReminder program to read in a month and a date. The input data should be converted into a value in an enumeration type whose enumerators are FIRST_WEEK, SECOND_WEEK, THIRD_WEEK, and FOURTH_WEEK using the following formula:

Dates 1–7:   FIRST_WEEK
Dates 8–14:   SECOND_WEEK
Dates 15–21: THIRD_WEEK
Dates 22+ :   FOURTH_WEEK

Each monthly print function should take the week as a parameter and print the following message heading:

`Reminders for the` (first, second, third, fourth) `week of` (January ...) `are:`

Programming Problems

1. Read in the lengths of the sides of a triangle and determine whether the triangle is an isosceles triangle (two sides are equal), an equilateral triangle (three sides are equal), or a scalene triangle (no sides are equal). Use an enumeration type whose enumerators are `ISOSCELES`, `EQUILATERAL`, and `SCALENE`.

   The lengths of the sides of the triangle are to be entered as integer values. For each set of sides, print out the kind of triangle or an error message saying that the three sides do not make a triangle. (For a triangle to exist, any two sides together must be longer than the remaining side.) Continue analyzing triangles until end-of-file occurs.

2. Write a C++ program that reads a single character from 'A' through 'Z' and produces output in the shape of a pyramid composed of the letters up to and including the letter that is input. The top letter in the pyramid should be 'A', and on each level, the next letter in the alphabet should fall between the letter that was introduced in the level above it. For example, if the input is 'E', the output looks like the following:

```
    A
   ABA
  ABCBA
 ABCDCBA
ABCDEDCBA
```

3. Read in a floating point number character by character, ignoring any characters other than digits and a decimal point. Convert the valid characters into a single floating point number, and print the result. Your algorithm should convert the whole number part to an integer and the fractional part to an integer, and combine the two integers as follows:

   Set result = wholePart + fractionalPart$/(10^{\text{number of digits in fraction}})$

   For example, `3A4.21P6` would be converted into 34 and 216, and the result would be the sum

   $$34 + \frac{216}{1000}$$

   You may assume that the number has at least one digit on either side of the decimal point.

11 One-Dimensional Arrays

- To be able to declare a one-dimensional array for a given problem
- To be able to choose an appropriate component type for a one-dimensional array
- To be able to assign a value to an array component
- To be able to access a value stored in an array component
- To be able to fill an array with data, and process the data in the array
- To be able to initialize an array in its declaration
- To be able to pass arrays as parameters to functions
- To be able to apply subarray processing to a given problem
- To be able to use parallel arrays
- To be able to declare and use an array with index values that have semantic content

In the last chapter, we examined the concept of a data type and looked at how to define simple data types. In this chapter, we expand the definition of a data type to include structured types, which are collections of components given a single name.

Sometimes it is necessary to show relationships among different variables or to store and reference variables as a group. This is difficult to do if each variable is named individually. For example, if a set of individually named values must be printed in reverse order, all the values must be read and saved before the last one can be printed. If there were 1000 values, we would have to declare 1000 individual variables to hold the values, and write 1000 different I/O statements to input and output the values—an incredibly tedious task! A one-dimensional array is a structured data type that allows us to program operations of this kind with ease.

In this chapter, we discuss structured data types in general and examine the one-dimensional array data type in detail.

Simple Versus Composite Data Types

composite data type
(also called
structured*)*
A collection of compo-
nents whose organiza-
tion is characterized
by the method used
to access individual
components. The al-
lowable operations on
a composite data type
include the storage
and retrieval of indi-
vidual components

In Chapter 10, we examined simple, or atomic, data types. A value in a simple type is a single data item; it cannot be broken down into component parts. For example, each `int` value is a single integer number and cannot be further decomposed. In contrast, a **composite data type** is one in which each value is a *collection* of component data items. The entire collection is given a single name, yet each component can still be accessed individually. An example of a structured data type in C++ is the `ifstream` type, used for creating and manipulating input file streams. When you declare a variable `inFile` to be of type `ifstream`, `inFile` does not represent just one data value; it represents an entire collection of data items in an input file. But each of the components in the file can be accessed individually (by performing an input operation).

Simple data types, both built-in and user-defined, are the building blocks for composite types. A composite type gathers together a set of component values and imposes a specific arrangement on them (see Figure 11-1). The method used to access the individual components of a structured type depends on how the components are arranged. As we discuss various ways of structuring data, we'll look at the corresponding access mechanisms.

Figure 11-2 shows the composite types available in C++. This figure is a portion of the complete diagram presented in Figure 2-1.

FIGURE 11-1

Atomic (Simple) and Composite Data Types

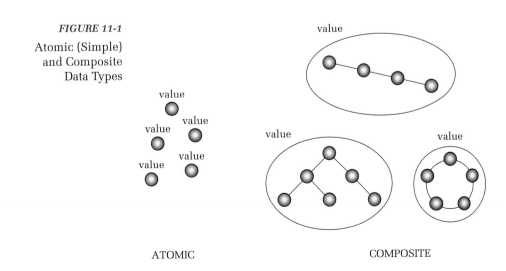

ATOMIC   COMPOSITE

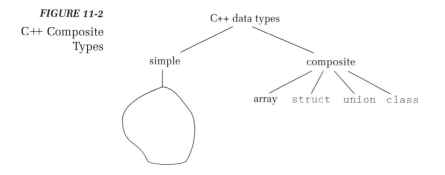

FIGURE 11-2

C++ Composite Types

In this chapter and the next two chapters, we examine array data types. The `struct` and `union` types are the topic of Chapter 14, and Chapter 15 explores a very powerful structured type—the `class`.

One-Dimensional Arrays

If we wanted to read a list of 1000 values and print them in reverse order, we could write a program of this form:

```
//***************************
// ReverseList program
//***************************
#include <iostream.h>

int main()
{
    int value0;
    int value1;
    int value2;

        .
        .
        .

    int value999;

    cin >> value0;
    cin >> value1;
    cin >> value2;
        .
        .
        .

    cin >> value999;
```

```
    cout << value999 << endl;
    cout << value998 << endl;
    cout << value997 << endl;
        .
        .
        .
    cout << value0 << endl;
    return 0;
}
```

This program is over 3000 lines long, and we have to use 1000 separate variables. Note that all the variables have the same name except for an appended number that distinguishes them. Wouldn't it be convenient if we could put the number into a counter variable and use For loops to go from 0 through 999, and then from 999 back down to 0? For example, if the counter variable were number, we could replace the 2000 original input/output statements with the following four lines of code (we enclose number in brackets to set it apart from value):

```
for (number = 0; number < 1000; number++)
    cin >> value[number];
for (number = 999; number >= 0; number--)
    cout << value[number] << endl;
```

This code fragment is correct in C++ *if* we declare value to be a *one-dimensional array*—that is, a collection of variables, all of the same type, where the first part of each variable name is the same, and the last part is an *index value* enclosed in square brackets. In our example, the value stored in number is called the *index.*

The declaration of a one-dimensional array is similar to the declaration of a simple variable (a variable of a simple data type), with one exception: you must also declare the size of the array. To do so, you indicate within brackets the number of components in the array:

```
int value[1000];
```

This declaration creates an array with 1000 components, all of type int. The first component has index value 0, the second component has index value 1, and the last component has index value 999.

Here is the complete ReverseList program, using array notation. This is certainly much shorter than our first version of the program.

```
//****************************
// ReverseList program
//****************************
#include <iostream.h>

int main()
{
    int value[1000];
    int number;

    for (number = 0; number < 1000; number++)
        cin >> value[number];
    for (number = 999; number >= 0; number--)
        cout << value[number] << endl;
    return 0;
}
```

Now that we have demonstrated how useful one-dimensional arrays can be, we define them formally and explain how individual components are accessed.

Declaring Arrays

one-dimensional array *A structured collection of components, all of the same type, that is given a single name. Each component (array element) is accessed by an index that indicates the component's position within the collection*

A **one-dimensional array** is a structured collection of components (often called *elements*) that can be accessed individually by specifying the position of a component with a single index value. (In Chapter 13, we introduce multidimensional arrays, arrays that have more than one index value.) Here is a syntax template describing the simplest form of a one-dimensional array declaration:

ArrayDeclaration

> DataType ArrayName [ConstIntExpression] ;

In the syntax template, DataType describes what is stored in each component of the array. Array components may be of almost any type, but for now we limit our discussion to atomic components. ConstIntExpression is an integer expression composed only of literal or named constants. This expression, which specifies the number of components in the array, must have a value greater than zero. If the value is n, the range of index values is 0 through $n - 1$, not 1 through n. For example, the declarations

```
float angle[4];
int   testScore[10];
```

create the arrays shown in Figure 11-3. The `angle` array has four components, each capable of holding one `float` value. The `testScore` array has a total of 10 components, all of type `int`.

Accessing Individual Components

To access an individual array component, we write the array name, followed by an expression, called an index expression, enclosed in square brackets. The expression specifies which component to access, and may be as simple as a constant or a variable name or as complex as a combination of variables, operators, and function calls. Whatever the form of the expression, it must result in an integral value. Index expressions can be of type `char`, `short`, `int`, `long`, or enumeration types because these are all integral types.

The simplest form of index expression is a constant. Using our `angle` array, the sequence of assignment statements

```
angle[0] = 4.93;
angle[1] = -15.2;
angle[2] = 0.5;
angle[3] = 1.67;
```

fills the array components one at a time (see Figure 11-4).

FIGURE 11-3

`angle` and `testScore` Arrays

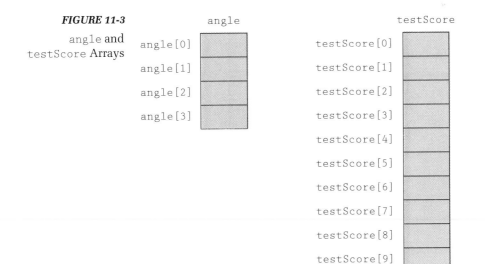

FIGURE 11-4

angle Array with
Values

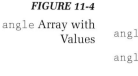

Each array component—angle[2], for instance—can be treated exactly the same as a simple variable. We can assign it a value

```
angle[2] = 9.6;
```

or read a value into it

```
cin >> angle[2];
```

or write its contents

```
cout << angle[2];
```

or pass it as a parameter

```
y = sqrt(angle[2]);
```

or use it in an arithmetic expression.

```
x = 6.8 * angle[2] + 7.5;
```

Let's look at index expressions that are more complicated than constants. Suppose we declare a 1000-element array of int values with the statement

```
int value[1000];
```

and execute the following two statements.

```
value[counter] = 5;
if (value[number+1] % 10 != 0)
    .
    .
    .
```

In the first statement, 5 is stored into an array component. If counter is 0, 5 is stored into the first component of the array. If counter is 1, 5 is stored into the second place in the array, and so forth.

In the second statement, an array component is selected by the expression number+1. The specific array component accessed is divided by 10 and checked to see if the remainder is nonzero. If number+1 is 0, the value in the first component is being tested; if number+1 is 1, the second place is tested; and so on. Figure 11-5 shows the indexing expression as a constant, a variable, and a more complex expression.

Out-of-Bounds Array Indices   Given the declaration

```
float alpha[100];
```

the valid range of index values is 0 through 99. What happens if we execute the statement

```
alpha[i] = 62.4;
```

FIGURE 11-5

An Index as a Constant, a Variable, and an Arbitrary Expression

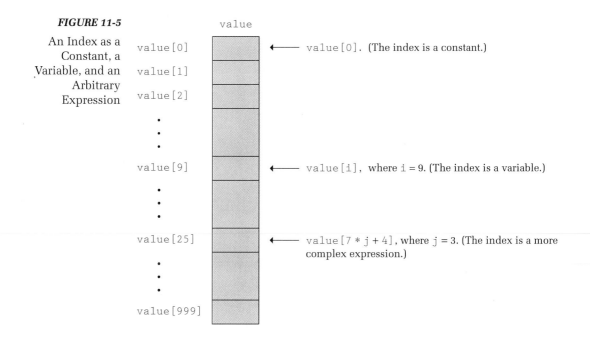

when i < 0 or when i > 99? The result is that a memory location outside the array is accessed. C++ does not check for **out-of-bounds** array indices (invalid indices) either at compile time or at run time. If i happens to be 100 in the statement above, the computer stores 62.4 into the next memory location past the end of the array, destroying whatever value was contained there. It is entirely the programmer's responsibility to make sure that an array index does not step off either end of the array.

Array-processing algorithms often use For loops to step through the array elements one at a time. Here is a loop to zero out our 100-element `alpha` array (i is an `int` variable):

```
for (i = 0; i < 100; i++)
    alpha[i] = 0.0;
```

We could also write the first line as

```
for (i = 0; i <= 99; i++)
```

However, C++ programmers commonly use the first version so that the number in the loop test (100) is the same as the array size. With this pattern, it is important to remember to test for *less-than*, not less-than-or-equal.

Initializing Arrays in Declarations

You learned in Chapter 8 that C++ allows you to initialize a variable in its declaration:

```
int delta = 25;
```

The value 25 is called an initializer. You also can initialize an array in its declaration, and the initializer has a special syntax. You specify a list of initial values for the array elements, separate them with commas, and enclose the list within braces:

```
int age[5] = {23, 10, 16, 37, 12};
```

In this declaration, `age[0]` is initialized to 23, `age[1]` is initialized to 10, and so on. There must be at least one initial value between the braces. If you specify too many initial values, you get a syntax error. If you specify too few, the remaining array elements are initialized to zero. It's always a good idea to specify exactly the right number of initial values.

Arrays follow the same rule as simple variables about the time(s) at which initialization occurs. A static array (one that is either global or declared as `static` within a block) is initialized once only, when control reaches its declaration. An automatic array (one that is local and not declared as `static`) is reinitialized each time control reaches its declaration.

An interesting feature of C++ is that you are allowed to omit the size of an array when you initialize it in a declaration:

```
float temperature[] = {0.0, 112.37, 98.6};
```

The compiler figures out the size of the array (here, 3) according to how many initial values are listed. In general, this feature is not particularly useful. In Chapter 12, though, we'll see that it can be convenient for initializing certain kinds of `char` arrays called strings.

Examples of Declaring and Accessing Arrays

We now look in detail at some specific examples of declaring and accessing arrays. Here are some declarations that a program might use to analyze occupancy rates in an apartment building:

```
const int BUILDING_SIZE = 350;   // Number of apartments

int occupants[BUILDING_SIZE];    // occupants[i] is the number of
                                 //   occupants in apartment i
int totalOccupants;              // Total number of occupants
int counter;                     // Loop control and index variable
```

`occupants` is a 350-element array of type `int` (see Figure 11-6).
`occupants[0]` = 3 if the first apartment has three occupants;
`occupants[1]` = 5 if the second apartment has five occupants; and so on. If

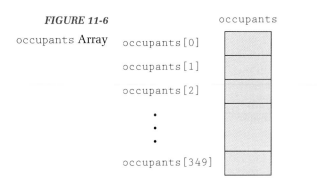

FIGURE 11-6

`occupants` Array

values have been stored into the array, then the following code totals the number of occupants in the building.

```
totalOccupants = 0;
for (counter = 0; counter < BUILDING_SIZE; counter++)
    totalOccupants = totalOccupants + occupants[counter];
```

The first time through the loop, `counter` is 0. We add the contents of `totalOccupants` (which is 0) to the contents of `occupants[0]`, storing the result into `totalOccupants`. Next, `counter` becomes 1 and the loop test occurs. The second loop iteration adds the contents of `totalOccupants` to the contents of `occupants[1]`, storing the result into `totalOccupants`. Now `counter` becomes 2 and the loop test is made. Eventually, the loop adds the contents of `occupants[349]` to the sum and increments `counter` to 350. At this point, the loop condition is false, and control exits the loop.

Note how we used the named constant `BUILDING_SIZE` in both the array declaration and the For loop. When constants are used in this manner, changes can be made easily. If the number of apartments changes from 350 to 400, only the `const` declaration of `BUILDING_SIZE` needs to be changed. If the literal value 350 were used in place of `BUILDING_SIZE`, several of the statements in the code above, and probably many more throughout the rest of the program, would have to be changed.

Because an array index is an integer value, we can access the components by their position in the array—that is, the first, the second, the third, and so on, until the last. Using an `int` index is the most common way of thinking about an array. C++, however, provides more flexibility by allowing an index to be of any integral type. (The index expression still must evaluate to an integer in the range from 0 through one less than the array size.) The next example shows an array where the indices are values of an enumeration type.

```
enum Drink {ORANGE, COLA, ROOT_BEER, GINGER_ALE, CHERRY, LEMON};

float salesAmt[6];  // Array of 6 floats, to be indexed by Drink type
Drink flavor;       // Variable of the index type
```

`Drink` is an enumeration type in which the enumerators ORANGE, COLA, ..., LEMON have internal representations 0 through 5, respectively. `salesAmt` is a group of six `float` components representing dollar sales figures for each kind of drink (see Figure 11-7). The following code prints the values in the array (see Chapter 10 to review how to increment values of enumeration types in For loops).

```
for (flavor = ORANGE; flavor <= LEMON; flavor = Drink(flavor + 1))
    cout << salesAmt[flavor] << endl;
```

FIGURE 11-7

salesAmt Array

salesAmt[ORANGE] (i.e., salesAmt[0])

salesAmt[COLA] (i.e., salesAmt[1])

salesAmt[ROOT_BEER] (i.e., salesAmt[2])

salesAmt[GINGER_ALE] (i.e., salesAmt[3])

salesAmt[CHERRY] (i.e., salesAmt[4])

salesAmt[LEMON] (i.e., salesAmt[5])

Here is one last example.

```
const int NUM_STUDENTS = 10;

char grade[NUM_STUDENTS];    // Array of 10 student letter grades
int  idNumber;               // Student ID number (0 through 9)
```

The grade array is pictured in Figure 11-8. Values are shown in the components, which implies that some processing of the array has already occurred. Following are some simple examples showing how the array may be used.

FIGURE 11-8

grade Array with Values

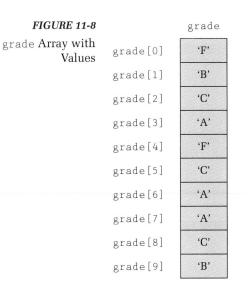

grade[0] 'F'

grade[1] 'B'

grade[2] 'C'

grade[3] 'A'

grade[4] 'F'

grade[5] 'C'

grade[6] 'A'

grade[7] 'A'

grade[8] 'C'

grade[9] 'B'

```
cin >> grade[2];
```

reads the next nonwhitespace character from the input stream and stores it into the component in `grade` indexed by 2;

```
grade[3] = 'A';
```

assigns the character 'A' to the component in `grade` indexed by 3;

```
idNumber = 5;
```

assigns 5 to the index variable `idNumber`;

```
grade[idNumber] = 'C';
```

assigns the character 'C' to the component of `grade` indexed by `idNumber` (that is, by 5); and

```
for (idNumber = 0; idNumber < NUM_STUDENTS; idNumber++)
    cout << grade[idNumber];
```

loops through the `grade` array, printing each component. For this loop, the output would be FBCAFCAACB. And, finally,

```
for (idNumber = 0; idNumber < NUM_STUDENTS; idNumber++)
    cout << "Student " << idNumber
         << " Grade " << grade[idNumber] << endl;
```

loops through `grade`, printing each component in a more readable form. `idNumber` is used as the index, but it also has semantic content—it is the student's identification number. The output would be

```
Student 0 Grade F
Student 1 Grade B
     .
     .
Student 9 Grade B
```

Passing Arrays as Parameters

In Chapter 8, we said that if a variable is passed to a function and it is not to be changed by the function, then the variable should be passed by value instead of by reference. We specifically excluded stream variables (such as those representing data files) from this rule and said that there would be one more exception. Arrays are this exception.

By default, C++ simple variables are always passed by value. To pass a simple variable by reference, you must append an ampersand (&) to the data type name in the formal parameter list:

```
int SomeFunc( float param1,    // Passed by value
              char& param2 )   // Passed by reference
{
   .
   .
   .
}
```

base address
The memory address of the first element of an array

It is impossible to pass a C++ array by value; arrays are *always* passed by reference. Therefore, you never use & when declaring an array as a formal parameter. When an array is passed as a parameter, its **base address**—the memory address of the first element of the array—is sent to the function. The function then knows where the caller's actual array is located and can access any element of the array.

Here is a C++ function that will zero out a one-dimensional float array of any size:

```
void ZeroOut( /* out */ float arr[],
              /* in  */ int   numElements )
{
    int i;

    for (i = 0; i < numElements; i++)
        arr[i] = 0.0;
}
```

In the formal parameter list, the declaration of arr does not include a size within the brackets. If you include a size, the compiler ignores it. The compiler only wants to know that it is a float array, not a float array of any particular size. Therefore, you must include a second parameter—the number of array elements—in order for this function to work correctly.

The calling code can invoke the ZeroOut function for a float array of any size. The following code fragment makes function calls to zero out two arrays of different sizes. Notice how an array parameter is declared in a function prototype.

```
void ZeroOut( float[], int );     // Function prototype
      .
      .
      .
int main()
{
    float velocity[30];
    float refractionAngle[9000];

      .

      .

    ZeroOut(velocity, 30);
    ZeroOut(refractionAngle, 9000);
      .

      .

      .
}
```

With simple variables, pass-by-value prevents a function from modifying the caller's actual parameter. You cannot pass arrays by value in C++, but you can still prevent the function from modifying the caller's array. To do so, you use the reserved word `const` in the declaration of the formal parameter. Below is a function that copies one `int` array into another. The first parameter—the destination array—is expected to be modified, but the second array is not.

```
void Copy( /* out */          int destination[],
           /* in */    const int source[],
           /* in */          int size          )
{
    int i;

    for (i = 0; i < size; i++)
        destination[i] = source[i];
}
```

The word `const` guarantees that any attempt to modify the `source` array within the `Copy` function results in a compile-time error.

One final remark about parameter passage: It is a common mistake to pass an array *element* to a function when passing the entire array was intended. For example, our `ZeroOut` function expects the base address of a `float` array to be sent as the first parameter. In the following code fragment, the function call is an error.

```
float velocity[30];
    .
    .
    .
ZeroOut(velocity[30], 30);    // Error
```

First of all, `velocity[30]` denotes a single array element—one floating point number—and not an entire array. Worse yet, there is no array element with an index of 30. The indices for the `velocity` array run from 0 through 29.

Processing Arrays

Three types of array processing occur especially often: using part of the declared array (a subarray), using two or more arrays in parallel (parallel arrays), and using index values that have specific meaning within the problem (indices with semantic content). We describe each of these methods briefly here.

Subarray Processing   The *size* of an array—the declared number of array components—is established at compile time. We have to declare it to be as big as it would ever need to be. Because the exact number of values to be put into the array is often dependent on the data itself, however, we may not fill all of the array components with values. The problem is that, to avoid processing empty ones, we must keep track of how many components are actually filled.

As values are put into the array, we keep a count of how many components are filled. We then use this count to process only components that have values stored in them. Any remaining places are not processed. For example, if there are 250 students in a class, a program to analyze test grades would set aside 250 locations for the grades. However, some students will surely be absent on the day of the test. So the number of test grades is counted, and that number, rather than 250, is used to control the processing of the array.

We often refer to the actual number of values in an array as its *length*. If the length is less than an array's declared size, functions that use array parameters should also have the length passed as a parameter. For example,

```
void Print( /* in */ const char grade[],    // Array for up to
                                             //    250 students
            /* in */        int length  )    // Number of grades
                                             //    actually in array
```

The programming example at the end of this chapter demonstrates the technique of subarray processing.

Parallel Arrays   In many problems, there are several pieces of information that go together. For example, we might have ID numbers and grades for a particular group of students. We can set up an int (or long) array for the ID numbers and a char array for the grades. We can then access the components in the arrays in parallel. A particular ID number goes with a particular grade because they have the same position in their respective arrays; that is, they have the same index value. In Figure 11-9, the grade in grade[0] is the grade for the student whose ID number is in idNum[0]; the grade in grade[1] is the grade for the student whose ID number is in idNum[1]; and so on.

Indices with
Semantic
Content   In some problems, the index has meaning beyond simple position; that is, the index has *semantic content*. An example is the salesAmt array we showed earlier. This array is indexed by a value of enumeration type Drink. The index of a specific sales amount is the kind of soft drink sold; for example, sales-Amt[ROOT_BEER] is the dollar sales figure for root beer.

FIGURE 11-9

Parallel Arrays

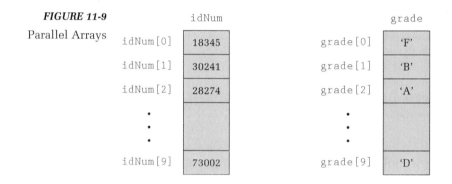

PROGRAMMING EXAMPLE

Comparison of Two Lists

Problem: You are writing a program for an application that does not tolerate erroneous input data. Therefore, the data are prepared by entering them twice into one file. The file contains two lists of positive integer numbers, separated by a negative number. These two lists of numbers should be identical; if they are not, then a data entry error has occurred. For example, if the input file contains the sequence of numbers 17, 14, 8, −5, 17, 14, 8, then the two lists of three numbers are identical. However, the sequence 17, 14, 8, −5, 17, 12, 8 shows a data entry error.

PROGRAMMING EXAMPLE cont'd

You decide to write a separate program to compare the lists and print out any pairs of numbers that are not the same. The exact number of integers in each list is unknown, but each list has no more than 500.

Input: A file (`dataFile`) containing two lists of positive integers. The lists are separated by a negative integer and are of equal length.

Output: The statement that the lists are identical, or a list of the pairs of values that do not match.

Discussion: Because the lists are in the same file, the first list has to be read and stored until the negative number is read. Then the second list can be read and compared with the first list.

If we were checking the lists by hand, we would write the numbers from the first list on a pad of paper, one per line. The line number would correspond to the number's position in the list; that is, the first number would be on the first line, the second number on the second line, and so on. The first number in the second list would then be compared to the number on the first line, the second number to the number on the second line, and so forth.

We use an array named `firstList` to represent the pad of paper. Its declaration looks like this:

```
const int MAX_NUMBER = 500;    // Maximum in each list

int firstList[MAX_NUMBER];     // Holds first list
```

Because the first array component has index 0, we must think of our pad of paper as having its lines numbered from 0, not 1.

Assumption: The two lists to be compared are of equal length.

Data Structures: A one-dimensional `int` array (`firstList`) to hold the first list of numbers. See Figure 11-10.

```
//***************************************************************************
// CheckLists program
// This program compares two lists of integers in a data file
// Assumption: The lists are of equal length
//***************************************************************************
#include <iostream.h>
#include <iomanip.h>     // For setw()
#include <fstream.h>     // For file I/O
#include "bool.h"        // For Boolean type
```

PROGRAMMING EXAMPLE cont'd

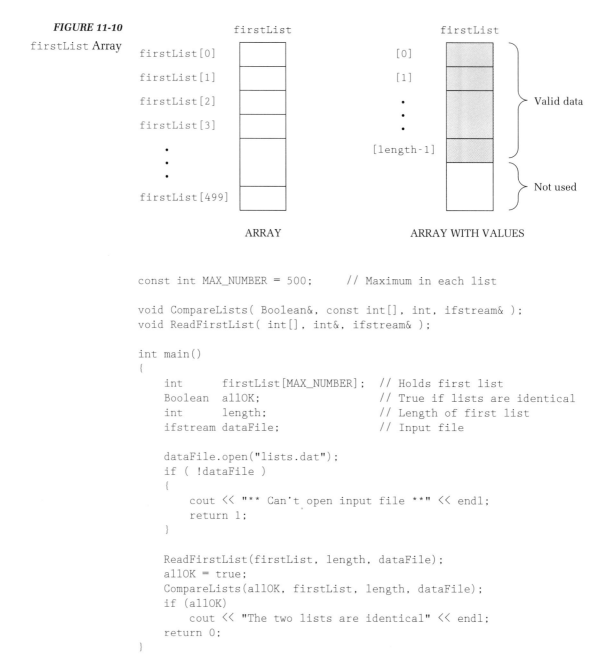

FIGURE 11-10

firstList Array

```
const int MAX_NUMBER = 500;      // Maximum in each list

void CompareLists( Boolean&, const int[], int, ifstream& );
void ReadFirstList( int[], int&, ifstream& );

int main()
{
    int      firstList[MAX_NUMBER];  // Holds first list
    Boolean  allOK;                  // True if lists are identical
    int      length;                 // Length of first list
    ifstream dataFile;               // Input file

    dataFile.open("lists.dat");
    if ( !dataFile )
    {
        cout << "** Can't open input file **" << endl;
        return 1;
    }

    ReadFirstList(firstList, length, dataFile);
    allOK = true;
    CompareLists(allOK, firstList, length, dataFile);
    if (allOK)
        cout << "The two lists are identical" << endl;
    return 0;
}
```

PROGRAMMING EXAMPLE cont'd

```
//******************************************************************

void ReadFirstList(
            /* out */ int         firstList[],   // Filled first list
            /* out */ int&        length,        // Number of values
            /* inout */ ifstream& dataFile   )   // Input file

// Precondition:
//     dataFile has been successfully opened for input
//   && The no. of input values in the first list <= MAX_NUMBER
// Postcondition:
//     length == number of input values in the first list
//   && firstList[0..length-1] contain the input values

{
    int counter;    // Index variable
    int number;     // Variable used for reading

    counter = 0;
    dataFile >> number;
    while (number >= 0)
    {
        firstList[counter] = number;
        counter++;
        dataFile >> number;
    }
    length = counter;
}


//******************************************************************

void CompareLists(
            /* inout */ Boolean&   allOK,        // True if lists match
            /* in */    const int  firstList[],  // 1st list of numbers
            /* in */    int        length,       // Length of 1st list
            /* inout */ ifstream&  dataFile   )  // Input file

// Precondition:
//     allOK is assigned
//   && length <= MAX_NUMBER
//   && firstList[0..length-1] are assigned
//   && The two lists are of equal length
// Postcondition:
//     The second list has been read
```

PROGRAMMING EXAMPLE cont'd

```
//   && IF all values in the two lists match
//         allOK == allOK@entry
//      ELSE
//         allOK == false
//        && The positions and contents of mismatches have been
//         printed

{
    int counter;    // Loop control and index variable
    int number;     // Variable used for reading

    for (counter = 0; counter < length; counter++)
    {
        dataFile >> number;
        if (number != firstList[counter])
        {
            allOK = false;
            cout << "Position " << counter << ": "
                << setw(4) << firstList[counter] << " != "
                << setw(4) << number << endl;
        }
    }
}
```

Testing: The program is run with two sets of data, one in which the two lists are identical and one in which there are errors. The data and the results from each are shown below.

Data Set One	*Data Set Two*
21	21
32	32
76	76
22	22
21	21
-4	-4
21	21
32	32
76	176
22	12
21	21

Output:	*Output:*
The two lists are identical.	Position 3: 76 != 176
	Position 4: 22 != 12

Testing and Debugging

We add a word of caution about the choice of looping structure to use when processing arrays. The most common error in processing arrays is an out-of-bounds array index. That is, the program attempts to access a component using an index that is either less than zero or greater than the array size minus one. For example, given the declarations

```
char line[100];
int  counter;
```

the following For statement would print the 100 elements of the line array and then print a 101st value—the value that resides in memory immediately beyond the end of the array.

```
for (counter = 0; counter <= 100; counter++)
    cout << line[counter];
```

This example is easy to debug; 101 characters get printed instead of 100. The loop test should be counter < 100. But you won't always use a simple For statement in accessing arrays. Suppose we read data into the line array in another part of the program. Let's use a While statement that reads to the newline character:

```
counter = 0;
cin.get(ch);
while (ch != '\n')
{
    line[counter] = ch;
    counter++;
    cin.get(ch);
}
```

This code seems reasonable enough, but what if the input contains a line with more than 100 characters? After the hundredth character is read and stored into the array, the loop continues to execute with the array index out of bounds. Characters are stored into memory locations past the end of the array, wiping out other data values (or even machine language instructions in the program!).

The moral is: When processing arrays, give special attention to the design of loop termination conditions. Always ask yourself if there is any possibility that the loop could keep running after the last array component has been processed.

Whenever an array index goes out of bounds, the first suspicion should be a loop that fails to terminate properly. The second thing to check is any array access involving an index that is based on input data or a calculation. When an array index is input as data, then a data validation check is an absolute necessity.

Testing and Debugging Hints

1. When an individual component of an array is accessed, the index must be within the range 0 through the array size minus one. Attempting to use an index value that is not within this range causes your program to access memory locations outside the array.
2. The individual components of an array are themselves variables of the component type. When values are stored into an array, they should either be of the component type or be explicitly converted to the component type; otherwise, implicit type coercion occurs.
3. Omitting the size of an array in its declaration is permitted only in two cases: (1) when an array is declared as a formal parameter and (2) when an array is initialized in its declaration. In all other declarations, you *must* specify the size of the array with a constant integer expression.
4. If an array parameter is incoming-only, declare the formal parameter as `const` to prevent the function from modifying the parameter accidentally.
5. Don't pass an individual array component as an actual parameter when the function expects to receive the base address of an entire array.
6. The size of an array is determined at compile time, but the number of values stored there (length) is determined at run time. This means that an array must be declared to be as large as it could ever be for the particular problem. Subarray processing is used to process only the components that have data in them.
7. Pass the length as well as the name of the array to functions when subarray processing is to take place.

Summary

In addition to being able to create user-defined atomic data types, we can create composite data types. In a composite data type, a name is given to a group of components that have a specific arrangement. With many structured types, the group can be accessed as a whole, or each individual component can be accessed separately.

The one-dimensional array gives a name to a sequential group of components. Each component can be accessed by its relative position within the group, and each component is a variable of the component type. To access a particular component, we give the name of the array and an index that specifies which component of the group we want. The index can be an expression of any integral type, as long as it evaluates to an integer from 0 through the array size minus one. Array components can be accessed in random order directly, or they can be accessed sequentially by stepping through the index values one at a time.

Quick Check

1. Declare an array named `quiz` that contains 12 components indexed by the integers 0 through 11. The component type is Boolean. (Assume that type `Boolean` has already been defined.) (pp. 352–353)
2. If an array is to hold the number of correct answers given by students to each question on a 20-question true/false quiz, what data type should be used for the components of the array? (pp. 352–353)
3. Given the declarations

```
const int MAX_LENGTH = 30;

char firstName[MAX_LENGTH];
```

   write an assignment statement that stores 'A' into the first component of array `firstName`. (pp. 353–355)
4. Given the declarations in Question 3, write an output statement that prints the value of the fourteenth component of array `firstName`. (pp. 353–355)
5. Given the declarations in Question 3, write a For statement that fills array `firstName` with blanks. (pp. 357–360)
6. Declare a five-element `int` array named `oddNums`, and initialize it (in its declaration) to contain the first five odd integers, starting with 1. (pp. 356–357)
7. Give the function heading for a void function named `SomeFunc`, where
   a. `SomeFunc` has a single parameter: a `float` array `x` that is an Inout parameter.
   b. `SomeFunc` has a single parameter: a `float` array `x` that is an In parameter.
   (pp. 361–363)
8. Given the declarations in Question 3 and the following program fragment, which reads characters into array `firstName` until a blank is encountered, write a For statement that prints out the portion of the array that is filled with input data. (pp. 363–364)

```
length = 0;
do
{
    cin.get(letter);
    if (letter != ' ')
    {
        firstName[length] = letter;
        length++;
    }
} while (letter != ' ');
```

9. Declare two parallel arrays indexed by the integers 0 through 99. One of the arrays will contain student ID numbers (type `long`); the other will consist of values of the enumeration type defined by

```
enum GenderType {FEMALE, MALE};
```

(pp. 363–364)

10. Define an enumeration type for the musical notes A through G (excluding sharps and flats). Then declare an array in which the index values represent musical notes, and the component type is `float`. Finally, show an example of a For loop that prints out the contents of the array. (pp. 363–364)

Answers

```
1. Boolean quiz[12];
2. int (or perhaps short)
3. firstName[0] = 'A';
4. cout << firstName[13];
5. for (index = 0; index < MAX_LENGTH; index++)
       firstName[index] = ' ';
6. int oddNums[5] = {1, 3, 5, 7, 9};
7. a. void SomeFunc( float x[] )
   b. void SomeFunc( const float x[] )
8. for (index = 0; index < length; index++)
       cout << firstName[index];
9. long number[100];         // Student numbers for 100 students
   GenderType gender[100];   // Genders for the same 100 students
10. enum NoteType {A, B, C, D, E, F, G};
    float noteVal[7];
    NoteType index;

    for (index = A; index <= G; index = NoteType(index + 1))
        cout << noteVal[index] << endl;
```

Exam Preparation Exercises

1. Every component in an array must have the same type, and the number of components is fixed at compile time. (True or False?)
2. The components of an array must be of an integral type. (True or False?)
3. Declare one-dimensional arrays according to the following descriptions.
   a. A 24-element `float` array
   b. A 500-element `int` array
   c. A 50-element double precision floating point array
   d. A 10-element `char` array
4. Write a code fragment to do the following tasks:
   a. Declare a constant named `CLASS_SIZE` representing the number of students in a class.
   b. Declare an array `quizAvg` of size `CLASS_SIZE` whose components will contain quiz score averages (floating point).

5. Write a code fragment to do the following tasks:
   a. Declare an enumeration type `BirdType` made up of bird names.
   b. Declare an `int` array `sightings` that is to be indexed by `BirdType`.
6. Given the declarations

```
const int MAX_LENGTH = 100;

enum Colors
{
    BLUE, GREEN, GOLD, ORANGE, PURPLE, RED, WHITE, BLACK
};
int     count[8];
Colors cIndex;                  // Index for count array
Colors rainbow[MAX_LENGTH];
int     rIndex;                 // Index for rainbow array
```

write code fragments to do the following tasks:
   a. Set `count` to all zeros.
   b. Set `rainbow` to all WHITE.
   c. Count the number of times GREEN appears in `rainbow`.
   d. Print the value in `count` indexed by BLUE.
   e. Total the values in `count`.
7. What is the output of the following program? The data for the program are given below it.

```
#include <iostream.h>

int main()
{
    int a[100];
    int b[100];
    int j;
    int m;
    int sumA = 0;
    int sumB = 0;
    int sumDiff = 0;

    cin >> m;
    for (j = 0; j < m; j++)
    {
        cin >> a[j] >> b[j];
        sumA = sumA + a[j];
        sumB = sumB + b[j];
        sumDiff = sumDiff + (a[j] - b[j]);
    }
```

```
    for (j = m - 1; j >= 0; j--)
        cout << a[j] << ' ' << b[j] << ' '
            << a[j] - b[j] << endl;
    cout << endl;
    cout << sumA << ' ' << sumB << ' ' << sumDiff << endl;
    return 0;
}
```

Data:

```
    5
11  15
19  14
 4   2
17   6
 1   3
```

8. A person wrote the following code fragment, intending to print 10 20 30 40.

```
int arr[4] = {10, 20, 30, 40};
int index;

for (index = 1; index <= 4; index++)
    cout << ' ' << arr[index];
```

Instead, the code printed 20 30 40 24835. Explain the reason for this output.

9. Given the declarations

```
int sample[8];
int i;
int k;
```

show the contents of the array sample after the following code segment is executed. Use a question mark to indicate any undefined values in the array.

```
for (k = 0; k < 8; k++)
    sample[k] = 10 - k;
```

10. Using the same declarations given for Exercise 9, show the contents of the array sample after the following code segment is executed.

```
for (i = 0; i < 8; i++)
    if (i <= 3)
        sample[i] = 1;
    else
        sample[i] = -1;
```

11. Using the same declarations given for Exercise 9, show the contents of the array `sample` after the following code segment is executed.

```
for (k = 0; k < 8; k++)
    if (k % 2 == 0)
        sample[k] = k;
    else
        sample[k] = k + 100;
```

Programming Warm-Up Exercises

Use the following declarations in Exercises 1–8. Assume the data type `Boolean` already has been defined. You may declare any other variables that you need.

```
const int MAX_STUD = 100;   // Max. number of students

Boolean failing[MAX_STUD];
Boolean passing[MAX_STUD];
int     grade;
int     length;
int     score[MAX_STUD];
```

1. Write a C++ function that initializes all components of `failing` to `false`. Pass `failing` and `length` as parameters.
2. Write a C++ function that has `failing`, `score`, and `length` as parameters. Set the components of `failing` to `true` wherever the parallel value of `score` is less than 60.
3. Write a C++ function that has `passing`, `score`, and `length` as parameters. Set the components of `passing` to `true` wherever the parallel value of `score` is greater than or equal to 60.
4. Write a C++ value-returning function `PassTally` that takes `passing` and `length` as parameters, and returns the count of components in `passing` that are `true`.
5. Write a C++ value-returning function `Error` that takes `passing`, `failing`, and `length` as parameters. `Error` returns `true` if any parallel components are the same.
6. Write a C++ function that takes `score`, `passing`, `grade`, and `length` as parameters. The function should set the components of `passing` to `true` wherever the parallel value of `score` is greater than `grade`.
7. Write a C++ value-returning function that takes `grade`, `length`, and `score` as parameters. The function should return the count of values in `score` that are greater than or equal to `grade`.
8. Write a C++ function that takes `score` and `length` as parameters, and reverses the order of the components in `score`; that is, `score[0]` goes into `score[length-1]`, `score[1]` goes into `score[length-2]`, and so on.
9. For the Comparison of Two Lists programming example, rewrite the program by eliminating the assumption that the two lists are of equal length. If one list is longer than the other, print a message indicating which is longer, and stop the comparison.

Programming Problems

1. The local baseball team is computerizing its records. You are to write a program that computes batting averages. There are 20 players on the team, identified by the numbers 1 through 20. Their batting records are coded in a file as follows. Each line contains four numbers: the player's identification number and the number of hits, walks, and outs he or she made in a particular game. Here is a sample:

   ```
   3 2 1 1
   ```

   The example above indicates that during a game, player number 3 was at bat four times and made 2 hits, 1 walk, and 1 out. For each player there are several records in the file. Each player's batting average is computed by adding the player's total number of hits and dividing by the total number of times at bat. A walk does not count as either a hit or a time at bat when the batting average is being calculated. Your program prints a table showing each player's identification number, batting average, and number of walks. (Be careful: The players' identification numbers are 1 through 20, but C++ array indices start at 0.)

2. An advertising company wants to send a letter to all its clients announcing a new fee schedule. The clients' names are on several different lists in the company. The various lists are merged to form one file, `clientNames`, but obviously, the company does not want to send a letter twice to anyone.

   Write a program that removes any names appearing on the list more than once. On each line of data, there is a four-digit code number, followed by a blank and then the client's name. For example, Amalgamated Steel is listed as

   ```
   0231 Amalgamated Steel
   ```

   Your program should output each client's code and name, but no duplicates should be printed.

3. Write a program that calculates the mean and standard deviation of integers stored in a file. The output should be of type `float` and should be properly labeled and formatted to two decimal places. The formula for calculating the mean of a series of integers is to add all the numbers, then divide by the number of integers. Expressed in mathematical terms, the mean $\overline{X}$ of N numbers $X_1, X_2, \ldots, X_N$ is

   $$\overline{X} = \frac{\sum_{i=1}^{N} X_i}{N}$$

   To calculate the standard deviation of a series of integers, subtract the mean from each integer (you may get a negative number) and square the result, add all these squared differences, divide by the number of integers minus one, then take the square root of the result. Expressed in mathematical terms, the standard deviation S is

   $$S = \sqrt{\frac{\sum_{i=1}^{N} (X_i - \overline{X})^2}{N - 1}}$$

4. One of the local banks is gearing up for a big advertising campaign and would like to see how long its customers are waiting for service at drive-up windows. Several employees have been asked to keep accurate records for the 24-hour drive-up service. The collected information, which is read from a file, consists of the time when the customer arrived in hours, minutes, and seconds; the time when the customer actually was served; and the ID number of the teller. Write a program that does the following:

   a. Reads in the wait data.
   b. Computes the wait time in seconds.
   c. Calculates the mean, standard deviation (defined in Programming Problem 3), and range.
   d. Prints a single-page summary showing the values calculated in part (c).

   Input:

   The first data line contains a title.
   The remaining lines each contain a teller ID, an arrival time, and a service time.
   The times are broken up into integer hours, minutes, and seconds according to a 24-hour clock.

   Processing:

   Calculate the mean and the standard deviation.
   Locate the shortest wait time and the longest wait time for any number of records up to 100.

   Output:

   The input data (echo print).
   The title.
   The following values, all properly labeled: number of records, mean, standard deviation, and range (minimum and maximum).

5. Your history professor has so many students in her class that she has trouble determining how well the class does on exams. She has discovered that you are a computer whiz and has asked you to write a program to perform some simple statistical analyses on exam scores. Your program must work for any class size up to 100 ($0 < N \leq 100$). Write and test a computer program that does the following:

   a. Reads the test grades from file `inData`.
   b. Calculates the class mean, standard deviation (defined in Programming Problem 3), and percentage of the test scores falling in the ranges <10, 10–19, 20–29, 30–39, . . . , 80–89, and ≥ 90.
   c. Prints a summary showing the mean and the standard deviation, as well as a histogram showing the percentage distribution of test scores.

   Input:

   The first data line contains the number of exams to be analyzed and a title for the report.
   The remaining lines have ten test scores on each line until the last, and one to ten scores on the last. The scores are all integers.

   Output:

   The input data as they are read.
   A report consisting of the title that was read from data, the number of scores, the mean, the standard deviation (all clearly labeled), and the histogram.

6. A small postal system ships packages within your state. Acceptance of parcels is subject to the following constraints:
   a. Parcels are not to exceed a weight of 50 pounds.
   b. Parcels are not to exceed 3 feet in length, width, or depth, and may not have a combined length and girth exceeding 6 feet. (The girth of a package is the circumference of the package around its two smallest sides; the mathematical formula is

   $$girth = 2 * (s1 + s2 + s3 - largest)$$

   where *largest* is the largest of the three parcel dimensions, s1, s2, and s3.)

   Your program should process a transaction file containing one entry for each box mailed during the week. Each entry contains a transaction number, followed by the weight of the box and its dimensions (the dimensions can be in any order). The program should print the transaction number, weight, and postal charge for all accepted packages, and the transaction number and weight for all rejected packages. At the end of the report, the program must print the number of packages processed and the number rejected.

   Input:

   Parcel post table—weight and cost (contains 25 pairs of values). This table should be stored in two one-dimensional arrays. You can determine the postal cost of each parcel by first searching the `weight` array and then using the corresponding element in the `cost` array. If a package weight falls between weight categories in the table, your program should use the cost for the higher weight.

   Transaction file—transaction number, weight, and three dimensions for an arbitrary number of transactions. Assume that all weights are whole numbers, and that all dimensions are given to the nearest inch.

   Output:

   First line—appropriate headings.
   Next *n* records—transaction number, whether accepted or rejected; weight; and cost.
   Last line—number of packages processed, number of packages rejected.

7. The final exam in your psychology class consists of 30 multiple-choice questions. Your instructor says that if you write the program to grade the finals, you won't have to take the exam.

   Input:

   The first data line contains the key to the exam. The correct answers are the first 30 characters; they are followed by an integer number that says how many students took the exam (call it *n*).
   The next *n* lines contain student answers in the first 30 character positions, followed by the student's name in the next 10 character positions.

   Output:

   For each student—the student's name; followed by the number of correct answers; followed by PASS if the number correct is 60 percent or better, or FAIL otherwise.

Applied Arrays: Lists and Strings

GOALS

- To be able to search a list for a component with a given value
- To be able to sort the components of a list into ascending or descending order
- To be able to insert a value into an ordered list
- To be able to search an ordered list using the binary search algorithm
- To be able to declare and use character strings

Chapter 11 introduced the concept of a one-dimensional array, a data structure that is a collection of components of the same type given a single name. In general, a one-dimensional array is a structure used to represent a list of items. In this chapter, we examine some common algorithms that are applied again and again to data stored as a list in a one-dimensional array. These are implemented as general-purpose functions that can be modified easily to work with many kinds of lists.

We also consider the *string*, a special kind of one-dimensional array that is used to process character information like words or names. We use strings to rewrite the GetMonth function in the BirthdayReminder program, discussed in Chapter 10.

Lists and List Algorithms

In Chapter 11, we noted that a list may contain fewer values than the number of places reserved in the array. We used a variable length to keep track of the number of values currently stored in the array, and we employed subarray processing to prevent processing array components that were not part of the list of values. That is, the number of places in the array is fixed, but the number of values in the list stored there may vary.

list
A variable-length, linear collection of homogeneous components

For a moment, let's think of the concept of a list not in terms of arrays but as a separate data type. We can define a **list** as a varying-length, linear collection of homogeneous components. That's quite a mouthful. By *linear* we mean that each component (except the first) has a unique component that comes before it and each component (except the last) has a unique component that comes after it. By *homogeneous* we mean that all the components are of the same data type. The **length** of a list—the number of values currently stored in the list—can vary during the execution of the program.

length
The actual number of values stored in a list

Like any data type, a list must have associated with it a set of allowable operations. What kinds of operations would we want to define for a list? Here are some possibilities: create a list, add an item to a list, delete an item from a list, print a list, search a list for a particular value, sort a list into alphabetical or numerical order, and so on. When we define a data type formally—by specifying its properties and the operations that preserve those properties—we are creating an *abstract data type*. In this chapter, we focus on lists and—later—strings as abstract data types. In Chapter 15, we explore the concept of abstract data types in greater detail.

Defining an abstract data type is a paper-and-pencil activity. We conceive of the properties we want the data values to have, and we choose a useful set of operations that manipulate those data values. But to use an abstract data type in a computer program, we must *implement* the abstract data type by using existing data types. In this chapter, we implement lists by using arrays. But an array is not the only way to implement a list. In Chapter 15, we introduce a new C++ type—the `class`—which is a tool for implementing abstract data types.

Using arrays to implement lists is a widely used technique. The remainder of this section is devoted to developing a set of general-purpose operations for creating and manipulating lists that are stored in arrays.

Sequential Search in an Unordered List

Scanning a list to find a particular value is part of many everyday tasks. We scan the television guide to see what time a program is aired. We scan a course syllabus to locate the current reading assignment.

Scanning a list is an example of a *sequential search*—an algorithm in which we start at the beginning of the list and look at each item in sequence. We stop the search as soon as we find the item we are looking for (or when we reach the end of the list, concluding that the desired item is not present in the list).

We'll code a general-purpose sequential search function that can be used in any program that uses a list. The following declarations are assumed to be global declarations.

```
const int MAX_LENGTH = ⬜ ;        // Maximum possible number of
                                   //    components needed
typedef ⬜ ItemType;               // Type of each component
                                   //    (some simple type)
```

The general-purpose search function needs five parameters:

1. The array containing the list to be searched
2. The length of the list
3. The item being searched for
4. A flag telling whether or not the search was successful
5. The index indicating where the item was located (if found)

The array containing the list is made up of components of type ItemType.

We call the array list and the item being searched for item. The variables length, found, and index serve the following purposes: length is the number of filled components in the list array, found tells whether the item is in list, and index gives the location of item if it is present in list.

Note that the two outgoing parameters, index and found, are redundant. The index parameter would be sufficient because the calling routine could check to see if index is greater than length−1. If it is, then item was not found. We keep this redundancy, however, for clarity.

```
#include "bool.h"    // For Boolean type
    .
    .
    .
void Search(
        /* in */ const ItemType list[],    // List to be searched
        /* in */        ItemType item,      // Item to be found
        /* in */        int      length,    // Length of list
        /* out */       int&     index,     // Location of item if found
        /* out */       Boolean& found  )   // True if item is found

// Searches list for item, returning the index
// of item if item was found

{
    index = 0;
    while (index < length && item != list[index])
        index++;

    found = (index < length);
}
```

To see how the While loop and the subsequent assignment statement work, let's look at the two possibilities: either item is in the list or it is not. If item is in the list, the loop terminates when the expression index < length is true and the expression item != list[index] is false. After loop exit, the variable found is therefore assigned the value of the expression index < length, which is true. On the other hand, if item is not in the list, the loop terminates when the expression `index < length` is `false`—that is, when `index` becomes equal to `length`. Subsequently, the value assigned to `found` is `false`.

We can use this sequential search function in any program requiring a list search. In the form shown, it searches a list of `ItemType` components, provided that `ItemType` is an integral type. When the function is used with a list of floating point values, it must be modified so that the While statement tests for near equality (for the reasons discussed in Chapter 10). In the following statement, `fabs` is the floating point absolute value function and it is assumed that `EPSILON` is defined as a global constant.

```
while (index < length && fabs(item - list[index]) >= EPSILON)
    index++;
```

The sequential search algorithm finds the first occurrence of the searched-for item. How would we modify it to find the last occurrence? We would initialize `index` to `length−1` and decrement `index` each time through the loop, stopping when we found the item we wanted or when `index` became −1.

Sorting

www.jbpub.com/C++links

The `Search` algorithm assumes that the list to be searched is unordered. A drawback to searching an unordered list is that we must scan the entire list to discover that the search item is not there. Think what it would be like if your city telephone book contained people's names in random rather than alphabetical order. To look up Mary Anthony's phone number, you would have to start with the first name in the phone book and scan sequentially, page after page, until you found it. In the worst case, you might have to examine tens of thousands of names only to find out that Mary's name is not in the book.

Of course, telephone books *are* alphabetized, and the alphabetical ordering makes searching easier. If Mary Anthony's name is not in the book, you discover this fact quickly by starting with the A's and stopping the search as soon as you have passed the place where her name should be. In software development, arranging list items into order is a very common operation on lists. For example, we might want to put a list of stock numbers into either ascending or descending order, or we might want to put a list of words into alphabetical order. Arranging values into order is known as **sorting.**

sorting
Arranging the components of a list into order (for instance, words into alphabetical order or numbers into ascending or descending order)

If you were given a sheet of paper with a column of 20 numbers on it and were asked to write the numbers in ascending order, you would probably:

1. Make a pass through the list, looking for the smallest number.
2. Write it on the paper in a second column.
3. Cross the number off the original list.

4. Repeat the process, always looking for the smallest number remaining in the original list.
5. Stop when all the numbers have been crossed off.

We can implement this algorithm directly in C++, but we need two arrays—one for the original list and a second for the ordered list. If the list is large, we might not have enough memory for two copies of it. Also, it is difficult to "cross off" an array component. We would have to simulate this with some dummy value like INT_MAX. We would set the value of the crossed-off variable to something that would not interfere with the processing of the rest of the components. A slight variation of this hand-done algorithm allows us to sort the components *in place.* This means that we do not have to use a second array; we can put a value into its proper place in the original list by having it swap places with the component that is there.

If our array is called list and contains length values, we can state the algorithm as follows:

FOR count going from 0 through length–2
    Find minimum value in list[count] . . list [length–1]
    Swap minimum value with list[count]

Figure 12-1 illustrates how this algorithm works.

Observe that we make length−1 passes through the list, with count running from 0 through length−2. The loop does not need to be executed when count equals length−1 because the last value, list[length−1], is in its proper place after the preceding components have been sorted.

This sort, known as *straight selection,* belongs to a class of sorts called selection sorts. There are many types of sorting algorithms. Selection sorts are characterized by swapping one component into its proper place on each pass through the

FIGURE 12-1   Straight Selection Sort

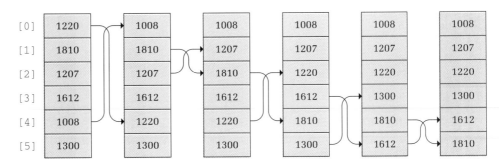

list. Swapping the contents of two variables—two components in an array—requires a temporary variable so that no values are lost (see Figure 12-2).

Two parameters are needed for the selection sort function: the array containing the list to be sorted and the length of the list. The code for this sorting algorithm is:

```
void SelSort( /* inout */ ItemType list[],    // List to be sorted
                /* in */    int      length )  // Length of list

// Sorts list into ascending order

{
    ItemType temp;              // Temporary variable
    int      passCount;         // Loop control variable
    int      placeCount;        // Loop control variable
    int      minIndex;          // Index of minimum so far

    for (passCount = 0; passCount < length - 1; passCount++;)
    {
        minIndex = passCount;

        // Find the index of the smallest component
        // in list[passCount..length-1]

        for (placeCount = passCount + 1; placeCount < length;
                                                placeCount++)
            if (list[placeCount] < list[minIndex])
                minIndex = placeCount;
```

FIGURE 12-2

Exchanging the Contents of Two Variables, x and y

Step 2: Contents of y goes into x

Step 1: Contents of x goes into temp

Step 3: Contents of temp goes into y

```
                    // Swap list[minIndex] and list[passCount]

                    temp = list[minIndex];
                    list[minIndex] = list[passCount];
                    list[passCount] = temp;
                }
            }
```

Note that with each pass through the inner loop, we are looking for the minimum value in the rest of the list (`list[passCount]` through `list[length -1]`). Therefore, `minIndex` is initialized to `passCount` and the inner loop runs from `placeCount` equal to `passCount+1` through `length−1`.

Note also that we may swap a component with itself, which occurs if no value in the remaining list is smaller than `list[passCount]`. We could avoid such an unnecessary swap by checking to see if `minIndex` is equal to `passCount`. Because this comparison would have to be made during each iteration of the loop, it is more efficient not to check for this possibility and just to swap something with itself occasionally. If the components we are sorting are much more complex than simple numbers, we might reconsider this decision.

This algorithm sorts the components into ascending order. To sort them into descending order, we need to scan for the maximum value instead of the minimum value. Simply changing the relational operator in the inner loop from "<" to ">" effects this change. Of course, `minIndex` would no longer be a meaningful identifier and should be changed to `maxIndex`.

Sequential Search in a Sorted List

When we search for an item in an unordered list, we won't discover that the item is missing until we reach the end of the list. If the list is ordered, we know that an item is missing when we pass its correct place in the list. For example, if a list contains the values

7
11
13
76
98
102

and we are looking for 12, we need only compare 12 with 7, 11, and 13 to know that 12 is not in the list.

If the search item is greater than the current list component, we move on to the next component. If the item is equal to the current component, we have found what we are looking for. If the item is less than the current component, then we know that it is not in the list. In either of the last two cases, we stop looking. We can restate this algorithmically as follows.

Set current position to beginning of list
WHILE item > current component in list AND more places to look
    Increment current position
Set found = (item equals current component)

We can make this algorithm more efficient by removing the compound condition ("AND more places to look"). We instead store `item` as a sentinel into `list[length]`. On exit from the loop, we can set `found` to `true` if `item` is equal to the current component and the current position does not equal length.

Store a copy of item beyond end of list
Set current position to beginning of list
WHILE item > current component in list
    Increment current position
Set found = (current position < length AND item equals current component)

This search function needs the same parameters as the previous one. To the function precondition we must add the requirement that the list is already sorted.

```
void SearchOrd(
        /* inout */ ItemType list[],      // List to be searched
        /* in    */ ItemType item,        // Item to be found
        /* in    */ int      length,      // Length of list
        /* out   */ int&     index,       // Location of item if found
        /* out   */ Boolean& found  )     // True if item is found

// Searches list for item, returning its index

{
    index = 0;

    // Store item at position beyond end of list

    list[length] = item;

    // Exit loop when item is found, perhaps as sentinel

    while (item > list[index])
        index++;

    // Determine whether item was found prior to sentinel

    found = (index < length && item == list[index]);
}
```

On average, searching an ordered list in this way takes the same number of iterations to find an item as searching an unordered list. The advantage of this new algorithm is that we find out sooner if an item is missing. Thus, it is slightly more efficient; however, it works only on a sorted list.

Inserting into an Ordered List   What if we want to add a new value to an already sorted list? We can store the new value at `list[length]`, increment `length`, and sort the array again. However, such a solution is *not* efficient. Inserting five new items results in five separate sorting operations. Let's build another list operation, named `Insert`, that inserts a value into a sorted list.

If we were to insert a value by hand into a sorted list, we would write the new value out to the side and draw a line showing where it belongs. We do so by scanning the list until we find a value greater than the one we are inserting. The new value goes in the list just before that point.

We can do something similar in our function. We can find the proper place in the list using the by-hand algorithm. Instead of writing the value to the side, we have to shift all the values larger than the new one down one place to make room for it. The main algorithm is expressed as follows, where `item` is the value being inserted.

```
WHILE place not found AND more places to look
    IF item > current component in list
        increment current place
    ELSE
        place found
Shift remainder of list down
Insert item
Increment length
```

Assuming that `index` is the place where `item` is to be inserted, the algorithm for Shift List Down is

```
Set list[length]     = list[length–1]
Set list[length–1]   = list[length–2]
        .                    .
        .                    .
        .                    .
Set list[index+1]    = list[index]
```

We can use a For loop that decrements the control variable to shift the components in the list down one position. We can code the modules Insert Item and Increment Length directly. This algorithm is illustrated in Figure 12-3. There is something familiar about the While loop in our algorithm: it is logically like the While loop in `SearchOrd`. In `SearchOrd`, we leave the loop either when we find `item` or when we pass the place in the list where `item` belongs.

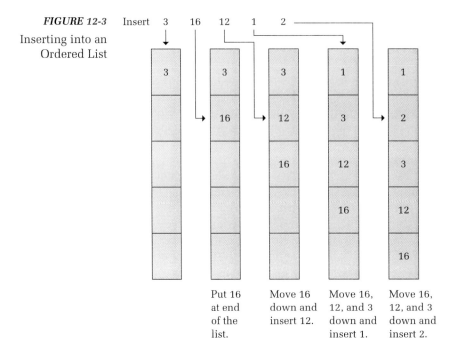

FIGURE 12-3

Inserting into an
Ordered List

We can simply use SearchOrd to find the insertion place for us. On return from SearchOrd, if found is false, index is the place in list where item should be inserted. If found is true, we can either insert a second copy or skip the insertion, as we choose, as long as we clearly document what is done. Inserting a second copy seems more reasonable. Therefore, index is the insertion point, whether or not item already exists in the list.

This function needs three parameters: the array containing the list, the number of components in the list, and the item being inserted. Again, we use the variable names list, item, and length. This time, both list and length must be incoming/outgoing parameters because they are changed each time the function is invoked.

```
void Insert( /* inout */ ItemType list[],    // List to be changed
             /* inout */ int&     length,    // Length of list
             /* in */    ItemType item  )     // Item to be inserted

// Inserts item into its proper place in the sorted list

{
    Boolean placeFound;    // True if item is already in the list
    int     index;         // Position where item belongs
    int     count;         // Loop control variable
```

```
            SearchOrd(list, item, length, index, placeFound);

            // Shift list[index..length-1] down one

            for (count = length - 1; count >= index; count--)
                list[count+1] = list[count];

            // Insert item

            list[index] = item;

            // Increment length of list

            length++;
}


//***********************************************************************

void SearchOrd(
            /* inout */ ItemType list[],      // List to be searched
            /* in */    ItemType item,        // Item to be found
            /* in */    int      length,      // Length of list
            /* out */   int&     index,       // Location of item if found
            /* out */   Boolean& found  )     // True if item is found
{
        .
        .       // Same as before
        .
}
```

Notice that the Insert function works even if the list is empty. SearchOrd stores item into list[0], where it is immediately found. On return from SearchOrd, index is 0. Because index is greater than the value of length−1 (which is −1), the body of the For loop is not executed. item is then stored into the first position in list, and length is set to 1. This algorithm also works if item is larger than any component in the list. When this happens, index equals length, and item is placed at the end of the list.

This algorithm is the basis for another sorting algorithm—an *insertion sort.* In an insertion sort, values are inserted one at a time into a list that was originally empty. An insertion sort is often used when input data must be sorted; each value is put into its proper place as it is read.

Binary Search in an Ordered List   There is a second search algorithm on a sorted list that is considerably faster both for finding an item and for discovering that an item is missing. This algorithm is called a *binary search.* A binary search is based on the principle of successive approximation. The algorithm divides the list in half (divides by 2—that's why it's called *binary* search) and decides which half to look in next. Division of the selected portion of the list is repeated until the item is found or it is determined that the item is not in the list.

This method is analogous to the way in which we look up a word in a dictionary. We open the dictionary in the middle and compare the word with one on the page that we turned to. If the word we're looking for comes before this word, we continue our search in the left-hand section of the dictionary. Otherwise, we continue in the right-hand section of the dictionary. We repeat this process until we find the word. If it is not there, we realize that either we have misspelled the word or our dictionary isn't complete.

The algorithm for a binary search is given below. The list of values is called list, and the value being looked for is called item (see Figure 12-4).

1. Compare item to list[middle]. If item = list[middle], then we have found it. If item < list[middle], then look in the first half of list. If item > list[middle], then look in the second half of list.
2. Redefine list to be the half of list that we look in next, and repeat the process in step 1.
3. Stop when we have found item or know it is missing. We know it's missing when there is nowhere else to look and we still have not found it.

With each comparison, at best, we find the item for which we are searching; at worst, we eliminate half of the remaining list from consideration.

We need to keep track of the first possible place to look (first) and the last possible place to look (last). At any one time, we are looking only in list[first] through list[last]. When the function begins, first is set to 0 and last is set to length−1.

This function needs the same five parameters as the previous search functions.

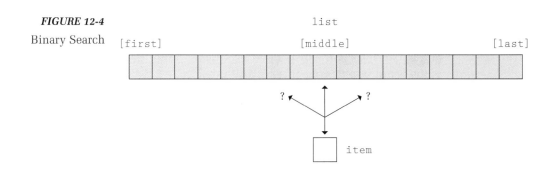

FIGURE 12-4

Binary Search

```
void BinSearch(
    /* in */ const ItemType list[],      // List to be searched
    /* in */         ItemType item,       // Item to be found
    /* in */         int      length,     // Length of list
    /* out */        int&     index,      // Location of item if found
    /* out */        Boolean& found )     // True if item is found

// Searches list for item, returning its index

{
    int first = 0;              // Lower bound on list
    int last = length - 1;      // Upper bound on list
    int middle;                 // Middle index

    found = false;
    while (last >= first && !found)
    {
        middle = (first + last) / 2;
        if (item < list[middle])
            // Assert: item is not in list[middle..last]
            last = middle - 1;
        else if (item > list[middle])
            // Assert: item is not in list[first..middle]
            first = middle + 1;
        else
            // Assert: item == list[middle]
            found = true;
    }
    index = middle;
}
```

Let's do a code walk-through of this algorithm. The value being searched for is 24. Figure 12-5(a) shows the values of first, last, and middle during the first iteration. In this iteration, 24 is compared with 103, the value in list[middle]. Because 24 is less than 103, last becomes middle−1 and first stays the same. Figure 12-5(b) shows the situation during the second iteration. This time, 24 is compared with 72, the value in list[middle]. Because 24 is less than 72, last becomes middle−1 and first again stays the same.

In the third iteration (Figure 12-5c), middle and first are both 0. The value 24 is compared with 12, the value in list[middle]. Because 24 is greater than 12, first becomes middle+1. In the fourth iteration (Figure 12-5d), first, last, and middle are all the same. Again, 24 is compared with the value in list[middle]. Here 24 is less than 64, so last becomes middle−1. Now that last is less than first, the process stops; found is false.

The binary search algorithm is the most complex algorithm that we have examined so far. The table below shows first, last, middle, and list[middle]

FIGURE 12-5

Code Walk-Through of `BinSearch` Function (Search Item Is 24)

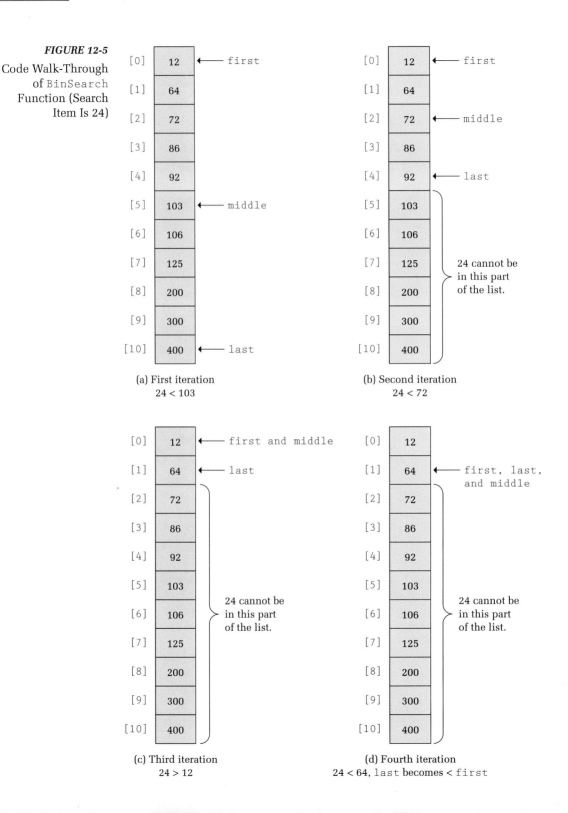

(a) First iteration
24 < 103

(b) Second iteration
24 < 72

(c) Third iteration
24 > 12

(d) Fourth iteration
24 < 64, `last` becomes < `first`

for searches of 106, 400, and 406, using the same data as in the previous example. Go over the results shown in this table carefully.

item	first	last	middle	list[middle]	Termination of Loop
106	0	10	5	103	
	6	10	8	200	
	6	7	6	106	found = true
400	0	10	5	103	
	6	10	8	200	
	9	10	9	300	
	10	10	10	400	found = true
406	0	10	5	103	
	6	10	8	200	
	9	10	9	300	
	10	10	10	400	
	11	10			last < first
					found = false

The calculation

```
middle = (first + last) / 2;
```

requires us to specify that one of the preconditions of the function restricts the value of length to INT_MAX/2. If the item being searched for happens to reside in the last position of the list (for example, when item equals 400 in our sample list), then first + last equals length + length. If length is greater than INT_MAX/2, the sum length + length would produce an integer overflow.

Notice in the table that whether we searched for 106, 400, or 406, the loop never executed more than four times. It never executes more than four times in a list of 11 components because the list is being cut in half each time through the loop. The table below compares a sequential search and a binary search in terms of the average number of iterations needed to find an item.

Length of List	Average Number of Iterations	
	Sequential Search	Binary Search
10	5.5	2.9
100	50.5	5.8
1,000	500.5	9.0
10,000	5000.5	12.4

If the binary search is so much faster, why not use it all the time? It certainly is faster in terms of the number of times through the loop, but more computations are performed within the binary search loop than in the other search algorithms. This means that if the number of components in the list is small (say, less than 20), the sequential search algorithms are faster because they do less work at each iteration. As the number of components in the list increases, the binary search algorithm becomes relatively more efficient. Remember, however, that the binary search requires the list to be sorted, and sorting itself takes time. Keep three factors in mind when you are deciding which search algorithm to use:

1. The length of the list to be searched
2. Whether or not the list already is ordered
3. The number of times the list is to be searched

Now let's turn our attention to a second application of arrays—a special kind of array that is useful when working with alphanumeric data.

Working with Character Strings

www.jbpub.com/C++links

In Chapter 2, we introduced string constants. Syntactically, a string constant is a sequence of characters enclosed by double quotes:

```
"Hi"
```

A string constant is stored as a `char` array with enough components to hold each specified character plus one more—the *null character.* The null character, which is the first character in both the ASCII and EBCDIC character sets, has internal representation 0. In C++, the escape sequence \0 stands for the null character. When the compiler encounters the string "Hi" in a program, it stores the three characters 'H', 'i', and '\0' into a three-element, anonymous (unnamed) `char` array as follows:

Unnamed array

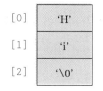

string
A collection of charac-ters interpreted as a single item; in C++, a null-terminated se-quence of characters stored in a `char` *array*

The **string** is the only kind of C++ array for which there exists an aggregate constant—the string constant. Notice that in a C++ program, the symbols 'A' denote a single character, whereas the symbols "A" denote two: the character 'A' and the null character.

In addition to string constants, we can create string *variables.* To do so, we explicitly declare a `char` array and store into it whatever characters we want to, finishing with the null character. Here's an example:

```
char myStr[8];     // Room for 7 significant characters plus '\0'

myStr[0] = 'H';
myStr[1] = 'i';
myStr[2] = '\0';
```

In C++, all strings (constants or variables) are assumed to be null-terminated. This convention is agreed upon by all C++ programmers and standard library functions. The null character serves as a sentinel value; it allows algorithms to locate the end of the string. For example, here is a function that determines the length of any string, not counting the terminating null character:

```
int StrLength( /* in */ const char str[] )
{
    int i = 0;     // Index variable

    while (str[i] != '\0')
        i++;
    return i;
}
```

The value of `i` is the correct value for this function to return. If the array being examined is

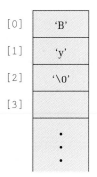

then `i` equals 2 at loop exit. The string length is therefore 2.

The actual parameter to the StrLength function can be a string variable, as in the function call

```
cout << StrLength(myStr);
```

or it can be a string constant:

```
cout << StrLength("Hello");
```

In the first case, the base address of the myStr array is sent to the function, as we discussed in Chapter 11. In the second case, a base address is also sent to the function—the base address of the unnamed array that the compiler set aside for the string constant.

There is one more thing we should say about our StrLength function. A C++ programmer would not actually write this function. The standard library supplies several string-processing functions, one of which is named strlen and does exactly what our StrLength function does. Later in the chapter, we look at strlen and other library functions.

Thinking of a string as an abstract data type, what kinds of operations might we find useful? Here are a few:

Create and initialize a string
Input a string
Output a string
Determine the length of a string
Compare two strings
Copy one string to another

We could come up with many other operations as well, but let's look at these particular ones.

Initializing Strings   In Chapter 11, we showed how to initialize an array in its declaration, by specifying a list of initial values within braces, like this:

```
int delta[5] = {25, -3, 7, 13, 4};
```

To initialize a string variable in its declaration, you could use the same technique:

```
char message[8] = {'W', 'h', 'o', 'o', 'p', 's', '!', '\0'};
```

However, C++ allows a more convenient way to initialize a string. You can simply initialize the array by using a string constant:

```
char message[8] = "Whoops!";
```

This shorthand notation is unique to strings because there is no other kind of array for which there are aggregate constants.

We said in Chapter 11 that you can omit the size of an array when you initialize it in its declaration (in which case, the compiler determines its size). This feature is often used with strings because it keeps you from having to count the number of characters. For example,

```
char promptMsg[] = "Enter a positive number:";
char errMsg[] = "Value must be positive.";
```

Be very careful about one thing: C++ treats initialization (in a declaration) and assignment (in an assignment statement) as two distinct operations. Different rules apply. Array initialization is legal, but aggregate array assignment is not.

```
char myStr[20] = "Hello";    // OK
  .
  .
  .
myStr = "Howdy";             // Not allowed
```

String Input and Output

There is no aggregate assignment, aggregate comparison, or aggregate arithmetic on arrays. Aggregate input/output of arrays is also not possible, with one exception: strings. Let's look first at output.

To output the contents of an array that is *not* a string, you aren't allowed to do this:

```
int alpha[100];
  .
  .
  .
cout << alpha;  // Not allowed
```

Instead, you must write a loop and print the array elements one at a time. However, aggregate output of a null-terminated char array (that is, a string) is valid. The string can be a string constant (as we've been doing since Chapter 2):

```
cout << "Results are:";
```

or it can be a string variable:

```
char msg[8] = "Welcome";
  .
  .
  .
cout << msg;
```

In both cases, the insertion operator (<<) outputs each character in the array until the null character is found. It is up to you to double-check that the terminating null character is present in the array. If not, the << operator will march through the array and into the rest of memory, printing out bytes until—just by chance— it encounters a byte whose integer value is 0.

To input strings, we have several options in C++. The first is to use the extraction operator (>>). When reading input characters into a string variable, the >> operator skips any leading whitespace characters such as blanks and newlines. It then reads successive characters into the array, stopping at the first *trailing* whitespace character (which is not consumed, but remains as the first character waiting in the input stream). The >> operator also takes care of adding the null character to the end of the string. For example, assume we have the following code:

```
char firstName[31];   // Room for 30 characters plus '\0'
char lastName[31];

cin >> firstName >> lastName;
```

Suppose that the input stream initially looks like this (where □ denotes a blank):

□□Mary□Smith□□□18

Then our input statement stores 'M', 'a', 'r', 'y', and '\0' into `firstName[0]` through `firstName[4]`; stores 'S', 'm', 'i', 't', 'h', and '\0' into `lastName[0]` through `lastName[5]`; and leaves the input stream as

□□□18

Although the >> operator is widely used for string input, it has two potential drawbacks.

1. If your string variable isn't large enough to hold the sequence of input characters (and the '\0'), the >> operator will continue to store characters into memory past the end of the array.
2. The >> operator cannot be used to input a string that has blanks within it. (It stops reading as soon as it encounters the first whitespace character.)

To deal with these facts, we use a variation of the `get` function. We have used the `get` function to input a single character, even if it is a whitespace character:

```
cin.get(inputChar);
```

The `get` function also can be used to input string data, in which case the function call requires two parameters. The first is a string variable and the second is an `int` expression.

```
cin.get(myStr, charCount + 1);
```

The `get` function does not skip leading whitespace characters and continues until it either has read `charCount` characters or it reaches the newline character '\n', whichever comes first. It then appends the null character to the end of the string. With the statements

```
char oneLine[81];   // Room for 80 characters plus '\0'
    .
    .
    .
cin.get(oneLine, 81);
```

the `get` function reads and stores an entire input line (to a maximum of 80 characters), embedded blanks and all. If the line has fewer than 80 characters, reading stops at '\n' but does not consume it. The newline character is now the first one waiting in the input stream. To read two consecutive lines worth of strings, it is necessary to consume the newline character:

```
char dummy;
    .
    .
    .
cin.get(string1, 81);
cin.get(dummy);          // Eat newline before next "get"
cin.get(string2, 81);
```

The first function call reads characters up to, but not including, '\n'. If the input of dummy were omitted, then the input of string2 would read *no* characters because '\n' would immediately be the first character waiting in the stream.

Finally, the ignore function—introduced in Chapter 4—can be useful in conjunction with the get function. Recall that the statement

```
cin.ignore(200, '\n');
```

says to skip at most 200 input characters but stop if a newline was read. (The newline character *is* consumed by this function.) If a program inputs a long string from the user but only wants to retain the first four characters of the response, here is a way to do it:

```
char response[5];        // Room for 4 characters plus '\0'

cin.get(response, 5);    // Input at most 4 characters
cin.ignore(100, '\n');   // Skip remaining chars up to and
                         // including '\n'
```

The value 100 in the last statement is arbitrary. Any "large enough" number will do.

Here is a table that summarizes the differences between the >> operator and the get function when reading string data:

Statement	Skips Leading Whitespace?	Stops Reading When?
cin >> inputStr;	Yes	At the first trailing whitespace character (which is *not* consumed)
cin.get(inputStr, 21);	No	When either 20 characters are read or '\n' is encountered (which is *not* consumed)

Run-Time Input of File Names   Until now, our programs that have read from input files and written to output files have included code similar to this:

```
ifstream inFile;    // Input file to be analyzed

inFile.open("datafile.dat");
if ( !inFile )
{
    cout << "** Can't open input file **" << endl;
    return 1;
}
    .
    .
    .
```

The open function associated with the ifstream data type requires a string parameter that specifies the name of the actual data file on disk. By using a string constant, as in the above example, the file name is fixed at compile time. That is, the program works only for this one particular disk file.

We often want to make a program more flexible by allowing the file name to be determined at *run time.* A common technique is to prompt the user for the name of the file, read the user's response into a string variable, and pass the string variable as a parameter to the open function. The following code fragment, which is another example of the use of the get and ignore functions, demonstrates the run-time input of a file name.

```
ifstream inFile;            // Input file to be analyzed
char     fileName[51];      // Max. 50 characters plus '\0'

cout << "Enter the input file name: ";
cin.get(fileName, 51);              // Read at most 50 characters
cin.ignore(100, '\n');              // Skip rest of input line

inFile.open(fileName);
if ( !inFile )
{
    cout << "** Can't open input file **" << endl;
    return 1;
}
    .
    .
    .
```

From now on, our end-of-chapter case studies use this technique of reading a file name at run time.

String Library Routines   Through the header file `string.h`, the C++ standard library provides a large assortment of string operations that people have found to be useful. In this section, we discuss three of these library functions: `strlen`, which returns the length of a string; `strcmp`, which compares two strings using the relations less-than, equal, and greater-than; and `strcpy`, which copies one string to another. Here is a summary of `strlen`, `strcmp`, and `strcpy`:

Header File	Function	Function Value	Effect
`<string.h>`	`strlen(str)`	Integer length of `str` (excluding `'\0'`)	Computes length of `str`.
`<string.h>`	`strcmp(str1, str2)`	An integer < 0, if `str1 < str2` The integer 0, if `str1 = str2` An integer > 0, if `str1 > str2`	Compares `str1` and `str2`.
`<string.h>`	`strcpy(toStr, fromStr)`	Base address of `toStr` (usually ignored)	Copies `fromStr` (including `'\0'`) to `toStr`, overwriting what was there; `toStr` must be large enough to hold the result.

The `strlen` function is similar to the `StrLength` function we wrote earlier. It returns the number of characters in a string prior to the terminating `'\0'`. Here's an example of a call to the function:

```
#include <string.h>
    .
    .
    .
char subject[] = "Computer Science";

cout << strlen(subject);   // Prints 16
```

The `strcpy` routine is important because aggregate assignment with the `=` operator is not allowed. In the following code fragment, we show the wrong way and the right way to perform a string copy.

```
#include <string.h>
  .
  .
  .
char myStr[100];
  .
  .
  .
myStr = "Abracadabra";            // Not legal
strcpy(myStr, "Abracadabra");     // Legal
```

In strcpy's parameter list, the destination string is the one on the left, just as an assignment operation transfers data from right to left. It is the caller's responsibility to make sure that the destination array is large enough to hold the result.

The strcpy function is technically a value-returning function; it not only copies one string to another, it also returns as a function value the base address of the destination array. The reason why the caller would want to use this function value is not at all obvious, and we don't discuss it here. Programmers nearly always ignore the function value and simply invoke strcpy as if it were a void function (as we did above).

The strcmp function is used for comparing two strings. The function receives two strings as parameters and compares them in *lexicographic* order (the order in which they would appear in a dictionary). Specifically, corresponding characters in the strings are compared one by one, starting with the first. The first unequal pair of characters determines the order. For example, "Hello" compares less than "Helvetica". The first three characters are the same in both strings, but 'l' compares less than 'v' in both ASCII and EBCDIC. Given the function call strcmp(str1, str2), the function returns one of the following int values: a negative integer, if str1 < str2 lexicographically; the value 0, if str1 = str2; or a positive integer, if str1 > str2. The precise values of the negative integer and the positive integer are unspecified. You simply test to see if the result is less than zero, zero, or greater than zero. Here is an example:

```
if (strcmp(str1, str2) < 0)     // If str1 is less than str2 . . .
  .
  .
  .
```

Given the declarations

```
char word1[6] = "Small";
char word2[6] = "Small";
```

the following function calls would return the results indicated.

Function Call	Function Value	
strcmp(word1, word2)	0	(They are equal.)
strcmp(word1, "Tree")	Negative number	('S' comes before 'T'.)
strcmp("Smile", word1)	Positive number	('i' comes after 'a'.)
strcmp("S", word1)	Negative number	('\0' comes before 'm'.)

The preceding results would be the same with any character set. Different character sets give different results, however, if an uppercase letter and a lower-case letter are compared. Uppercase letters come before lowercase letters in ASCII and after lowercase letters in EBCDIC. Also, special symbols, such as punctuation marks, are ordered differently with respect to each other in the two sets.

We have described only three of the string-handling routines provided by the standard library. These three are the most commonly needed, but there are many more. If you are designing programs that use strings extensively, you should read the documentation on strings for your C++ system.

Using Typedef with Arrays   In Chapter 10, we discussed the Typedef statement as a way of giving an additional name to an existing data type. The most familiar example is

```
typedef int Boolean;
```

We can also use Typedef to give a name to an array type. Here's an example:

```
typedef float FloatArr[100];
```

This statement says that the type FloatArr is the same as the type "100-element array of float." (Notice that the array size in brackets comes at the very end of the statement.) We can now declare variables to be of type FloatArr:

```
FloatArr angle;
FloatArr velocity;
```

The compiler essentially translates these declarations into

```
float angle[100];
float velocity[100];
```

Up to this point, we haven't used Typedef to give names to array types. We tend to picture an integer or floating point array as a group of individual, separate components. On the other hand, we often visualize a string as a complete unit, almost as if it were a simple data type. Using Typedef to give a name to a string type gives us some consistency in that vision:

```
typedef char String20[21];
  .
  .
  .
String20 firstName;
String20 lastName;

cin >> firstName >> lastName;
if (strcmp(lastName, "Jones") > 0)
  .
  .
  .
```

Notice how the identifier String20 suggests a maximum of 20 significant characters, and the physical size we use is 21 to allow room for the terminating null character.

The Programming Example that follows uses many of the concepts we have described in this section: string initialization, string I/O, string-handling library functions, and Typedef to define string types.

PROGRAMMING EXAMPLE

Birthday Reminder Revisited

Problem: Rewrite the GetMonth function, from the Birthday Reminder program in Chapter 10, so that it uses strings to convert the input month to a value of enumeration type Months. Rerun the program without making any other changes.

Discussion: The BirthdayReminder program inputs a month and prints the names and birthdays of friends who have birthdays that month. In the original program, the characters in the month's name are read one at a time until the

PROGRAMMING EXAMPLE cont'd

program recognizes the month, and any remaining characters in the month are ignored. Now that we know how to use strings, we can read the entire name of the month into a string variable and process it as a whole word rather than decoding it character by character.

We use an array of strings containing the months of the year. A month is read into a string variable. The Search function is used to search the array for the input string. If it is found at location index, we use index to access a parallel array containing the values of the enumeration type Months. In other words, we convert a month in string form to the equivalent month in the enumeration type by using parallel arrays, one containing strings and the other containing the enumeration equivalents. If the string is not found, the program can issue an error message and prompt the user to reenter the month.

Data Structures:

An array of strings containing the months of the year.
An array containing enumeration type values for the months of the year.

The two arrays look like those in Figure 12-6. Although these two arrays look similar, they have quite different representations in the computer. One contains the months in character form; the other contains the months in the form of an enumeration type.

FIGURE 12-6

Data Structures for GetMonth Function

[0]	"January"	[0]	JANUARY
[1]	"February"	[1]	FEBRUARY
[2]	"March"	[2]	MARCH
[3]	"April"	[3]	APRIL
[4]	"May"	[4]	MAY
[5]	"June"	[5]	JUNE
[6]	"July"	[6]	JULY
[7]	"August"	[7]	AUGUST
[8]	"September"	[8]	SEPTEMBER
[9]	"October"	[9]	OCTOBER
[10]	"November"	[10]	NOVEMBER
[11]	"December"	[11]	DECEMBER

PROGRAMMING EXAMPLE cont'd

Let's call the string representation of a month strMonth and the enumeration version month, as it is called in the BirthdayReminder program. The array of strings can be called strMonthAry, and the parallel array can be called monthAry.

Now we can code the new function GetMonth. We must remember to initialize the arrays strMonthAry and monthAry. We also need to modify the Search function to make it work on string data.

```cpp
#include <string.h>            // For strcmp()
    .
    .
    .
typedef char String9[10];    // Room for 9 characters plus '\0'
    .
    .
    .


//******************************************************************

void GetMonth( /* out */ Months& month )    // User's desired month

// Inputs a month after prompting the user

// Postcondition:
//     User has been prompted to enter a month
//  && On invalid input, the user has been repeatedly prompted to
//     type a correct month
//  && month == value of type Months corresponding to user's input

{
    String9 strMonth;                       // Input month in string form
    Months  monthAry[12] =                  // Table of months in enum form
    {
        JANUARY, FEBRUARY, MARCH, APRIL,
        MAY, JUNE, JULY, AUGUST,
        SEPTEMBER, OCTOBER, NOVEMBER, DECEMBER
    };

    String9 strMonthAry[12] =               // Parallel table in string form
    {
        "January", "February", "March", "April",
        "May", "June", "July", "August",
        "September", "October", "November", "December"
    };
    int     index;                          // Index of located month
    Boolean found;                          // True if month is valid
```

PROGRAMMING EXAMPLE cont'd

```
    do
    {
        cout << "Please enter month, capitalizing first letter."
            << endl;
        cin.get(strMonth, 10);          // Input at most 9 chars and
                                        //    leave room for '\0'
        cin.ignore(100, '\n');          // Consume '\n' because the
                                        //    "get" routine does not
        Search(strMonthAry, strMonth, 12, index, found);
        if (found)
            month = monthAry[index];
        else
            cout << "Month is misspelled." << endl << endl;
    } while ( !found );
}


//**********************************************************************

void Search(
    /* in */   const String9 strMonthAry[],  // List to be searched
    /* in */   const String9 strMonth,       // Search value
    /* in */   int           length,         // Length of list
    /* out */  int&          index,          // Location if found
    /* out */  Boolean&      found      )    // True if value found

// Searches strMonthAry for strMonth, returning the index
// of strMonth if strMonth was found

// Precondition:
//     length <= 12
// && strMonthAry[0..length-1] are assigned
// && strMonth is assigned
// Postcondition:
//     IF strMonth is in strMonthAry
//         found == true  &&  strMonthAry[index] contains strMonth
//     ELSE
//         found == false  &&  index == length

{
    index = 0;
    while (index < length &&
            strcmp(strMonth, strMonthAry[index]) != 0)
        index++;
    found = (index < length);
}
```

PROGRAMMING EXAMPLE cont'd

Because the BirthdayReminder program is so long, it is not repeated here. However, we guarantee that this function `GetMonth` was substituted for the one in Chapter 10 and the program was rerun. Notice that `strMonthAry` is an array of arrays, making it a *two-dimensional array*. We return to this subject in Chapter 13.

Testing and Debugging

In this chapter, we have discussed and coded five general-purpose functions: two sequential searches, a binary search, a selection sort, and an insertion into an ordered list (which can also be used as a sort). We can test these functions by embedding them in driver programs. The drivers should read in data, call the function, and print out the results. Following is the algorithm for a driver to test the `Search` function:

```
Get list of components
WHILE more items to be searched for
    Get item
    Search(list, item, length, index, found)
    IF found
        Print item, "found at position", index
    ELSE
        Print item, "not found in list"
```

The driver would have to be run with several sets of test data to test the `Search` function thoroughly. The minimum set of lists of components would be:

1. A list of no components
2. A list of one component
3. A list of `MAX_LENGTH` − 1 components
4. A list of more than one but less than `MAX_LENGTH` − 1 components

The minimum set of items being searched for would be:

1. `item` in `list[0]`
2. `item` in `list[length-1]`
3. `item between list[0] and list[length-1]`
4. `item < list[0]`
5. `item > list[length-1]`
6. `item` value between `list[0]` and `list[length-1]` but not there

Because `ItemType` can be any data type that the relational operators can be applied to, function `Search` should be tested with components of several different types.

We leave the coding of this driver program and the creation of the test data as an exercise (see Programming Problem 6). All of our general purpose functions should be tested in a similar manner.

In the `SearchOrd` function, we stored the value being searched for in `list[length]`. The assumption that `length` would be less than `MAX_LENGTH` (the number of places in the array) is written into the documentation. This could lead to a potential error if the calling module fails to check that `length` is less than `MAX_LENGTH`.

If the precondition listed in the function documentation is that `length` < `MAX_LENGTH`, then the calling module must make sure that the function is not called with `length` ≥ `MAX_LENGTH`. Another way of dealing with the case where `length` ≥ `MAX_LENGTH` is to add an error flag to the functions' formal parameter lists and have the functions themselves check for `length` ≥ `MAX_LENGTH`. If `length` ≥ `MAX_LENGTH`, the error flag is set to `true` and the search is terminated. This approach changes the preconditions of the functions so that they can be called even when `length` ≥ `MAX_LENGTH`.

Either way of handling the problem is acceptable. The important point is that it must be clearly stated whether the calling routine or the called function is to check for the error condition.

Testing and Debugging Hints

1. Review the Testing and Debugging Hints for Chapter 11. They apply to all one-dimensional arrays, including strings.
2. Make sure that every string is terminated with the null character. String constants are automatically null-terminated by the compiler. On input, the >> operator and the `get` function automatically add the null character. If you store characters into a string variable individually or manipulate the array in any way, be sure to account for the null character.
3. Remember that C++ treats string initialization (in a declaration) as different from string assignment. Initialization is allowed but assignment is not.
4. Aggregate input/output is allowed for strings but not for other array types.
5. If you use the >> operator to input into a string variable, be sure the array is large enough to hold the null character plus the longest sequence of (non-whitespace) characters in the input stream.
6. With string input, the >> operator stops at, *but does not consume,* the first trailing whitespace character. Likewise, if the `get` function stops reading early because it encounters a newline character, the newline character is not consumed.
7. When you use the `strcpy` library function, ensure that the destination array is at least as large as the array from which you are copying.
8. General-purpose functions should be tested outside the context of a particular program, using a driver.
9. Test data should be chosen carefully to test all end conditions and some in the middle. End conditions are those that reach the limits of the structure used

to store them. For example, in a one-dimensional array, there should be test data items in which the number of components is 0, 1, and MAX_LENGTH (MAX_LENGTH − 1 in the case of SearchOrd), as well as between 1 and MAX_LENGTH.

Summary

This chapter has provided practice in working with lists represented by one-dimensional arrays. We have examined algorithms that search and sort data stored in a list, and we have written functions to implement these algorithms. We can use these functions again and again in different contexts because we have written them in a general fashion.

In the searching and sorting functions, the components in the array are of type ItemType. ItemType can be defined as any simple data type, although slight modifications may be required to accommodate floating point types.

Strings are a special case of char arrays in C++. The last significant character must be followed by a null character to mark the end of the string. Strings are useful in working with character information. Because strings can be copied and compared using standard library functions, our general-purpose list operations can be adapted easily to work with arrays of strings.

Quick Check

1. In a sequential search of an unordered array of 1000 values, what is the average number of loop iterations required to find a value? What is the maximum number of iterations that may be required to find a value? (pp. 380–382)
2. The following program fragment sorts a list into ascending order. Change it to sort into descending order. (pp. 382–385)

```
for (passCount = 0; passCount < length - 1; passCount++)
{
    minIndex = passCount;
    for (placeCount = passCount + 1; placeCount < length;
                                              placeCount++)
        if (list[placeCount] < list[minIndex])
            minIndex = placeCount;
    temp = list[minIndex];              // Swap
    list[minIndex] = list[passCount];
    list[passCount] = temp;
}
```

3. Describe how the list insertion operation can be used to build a sorted list from unordered input data. (pp. 387–389)

4. Describe the basic principle behind the binary search algorithm. (pp. 389–394)
5. Using Typedef, define an array data type that holds a string of 15 characters plus the null character. Declare an array variable of this type, initializing it to your first name. Then use a library function to replace the contents of the variable with your last name. (pp. 402–405)

Answers   1. The average number is 500 iterations. The maximum is 1000 iterations.   2. The only required change is to replace the "<" symbol in the inner loop with a ">". As a matter of style, `minIndex` should be changed to `maxIndex`.   3. The list initially has a length of 0. Each time a data value is read, insertion adds the value to the list in its correct position. When all the data have been read, they are in the array in sorted order.   4. The binary search takes advantage of ordered list values, looking at a component in the middle of the list and deciding whether the search value precedes or follows the midpoint. The search is then repeated on the appropriate half, quarter, eighth, and so on, of the list until the value is located.

5. `typedef char String15[16];`

   `String15 name = "Anna";`

   `strcpy(name, "Rodriguez");`

Exam Preparation Exercises

1. What three factors should you consider when you are deciding which search algorithm to use on a list?
2. The following values are stored in an array in ascending order.

   28 45 97 103 107 162 196 202 257

   Applying function `Search` to this array, search for the following values and indicate how many comparisons are required to either find the number or find that it is not in the list.
   a. 28
   b. 32
   c. 196
   d. 194
3. Repeat Exercise 2 using the `SearchOrd` function.
4. The following values are stored in an array in ascending order.

   29 57 63 72 79 83 96 104 114 136

   Apply function `BinSearch` with `item = 114` to this list, and trace the values of `first`, `last`, and `middle`. Indicate any undefined values with a *U*.
5. A binary search is always better to use than a sequential search. (True or False?)
6. a. Define a data type `NameType` to be a string of at most 40 characters plus the null character.
   b. Declare a variable `oneName` to be of type `NameType`.
   c. Declare `employeeName` to be a 100-element array variable whose elements are strings of type `NameType`.

7. Given the declarations

```
typedef char NameString[21];
typedef char WordString[11];

NameString firstName;
NameString lastName;
WordString word;
```

mark the following statements valid or invalid. (Assume the header file `string.h` has been included.)

a. ```
   i = 0;
   while (firstName[i] != '\0')
   {
       cout << firstName[i];
       i++;
   }
   ```
b. `cout << lastName;`
c. ```
   if (firstName == lastName)
       n = 1;
   ```
d. ```
   if (strcmp(firstName, lastName) == 0)
       m = 8;
   ```
e. `cin >> word;`
f. `lastName = word;`
g. ```
   if (strcmp(NameString, "Hi") < 0)
       n = 3;
   ```
h. ```
   if (firstName[2] == word[5])
       m = 4;
   ```

8. Given the declarations

```
typedef char String20[21];
typedef char String30[31];

String20 rodent;
String30 mammal;
```

write code fragments for the following tasks. (If the task is not possible, say so.)
a. Store the string "Moose" into `mammal`.
b. Copy whatever string is in `rodent` into `mammal`.
c. If the string in `mammal` is greater than "Opossum" lexicographically, increment a variable count.
d. If the string in `mammal` is less than or equal to "Jackal", decrement a variable `count`.
e. Store the string "Grey-tipped field shrew" into `rodent`.
f. Print the length of the string in `rodent`.
```

9. Given the declarations

```
const int NUMBER_OF_BOOKS = 200;

typedef     char BookName[31];
typedef     char PersonName[21];
BookName    bookOut[NUMBER_OF_BOOKS];
PersonName  borrower[NUMBER_OF_BOOKS];
BookName    bookIn;
PersonName  name;
```

mark the following statements valid or invalid. (Assume the header file `string.h` has been included.)

a. `cout << bookIn;`

b. `cout << bookOut;`

c. `for (i = 0; i < NUMBER_OF_BOOKS; i++)`
       `cout << bookOut[i] << endl;`

d. `if (bookOut[3] > bookIn)`
       `cout << bookIn;`

e. `for (i = 0; i < NUMBER_OF_BOOKS; i++)`
     `if (strcmp(bookIn, bookOut[i]) == 0)`
       `cout << bookIn << ' ' << borrower[i] << endl;`

f. `bookIn = "Don Quixote";`

g. `cout << name[2];`

10. Write code fragments to perform the following tasks, using the declarations given in Exercise 9. Assume that the books listed in `bookOut` have been borrowed by the person listed in the corresponding position of `borrower`.

a. Write a code fragment to print each book borrowed by `name`.

b. Write a code fragment to count the number of books borrowed by `name`.

c. Write a code fragment to count the number of copies of `bookIn` that have been borrowed.

d. Write a code fragment to count the number of copies of `bookIn` that have been borrowed by `name`.

Programming Warm-Up Exercises

1. Write a C++ value-returning function `Index` that searches an `int` array `list` for a value `item` and returns its place in the array. There are `length` values in `list`. If `item` is not in the array, `Index` should return −1.

2. Write a C++ value-returning function `Count` that counts the occurrences of a value `item`, of simple type `ItemType`, in an unsorted array `numList`. There are `length` items in `numList`.

3. Write a C++ value-returning function that receives two `int` arrays (`arr1` and `arr2`) of length `length`. This function should return the product of all components of `arr2` for which the corresponding components of `arr1` are negative.

4. Write a C++ value-returning function `Found` that searches a `float` array `list` for a `float` value greater than the value of `item`. If such a value is found, the function returns `true`; otherwise, `false` is returned. The number of components in `list` is passed as a parameter.

5. Rewrite SearchOrd to give it an additional formal parameter overflow. If length is greater than or equal to MAX_LENGTH, overflow is true, an appropriate error message is printed, and the search is not made. Otherwise, overflow is false. The constant MAX_LENGTH may be accessed globally. Change the function documentation to reflect this change.

6. Rewrite function SearchOrd so that it searches a text file instead of an array.

7. Write a C++ function that searches a list list of length length for item. If item is found, it is deleted and the list is compacted (that is, all the components below item are moved up one place). Adjust length appropriately. item is of simple type ItemType.

8. Repeat Exercise 7, assuming that item is of string type StrType and list contains components of type StrType.

9. Write a C++ function that removes all occurrences of item in a list list of length length. Adjust length appropriately. item is of simple type ItemType.

10. Write a C++ function that takes two parallel arrays, isAbsent (Boolean) and score (float), and length as parameters. This function should store a zero into each position of score for which false is in the parallel position of isAbsent. The other components of score should be left alone.

11. Write a C++ value-returning function that returns the sum of the products of parallel components in two int arrays, data and weight. Pass length as a parameter.

12. Modify function BinSearch so that index is where item should be inserted when found is false.

13. Modify function Insert so that it uses function BinSearch rather than function SearchOrd to find the insertion point. (Assume that BinSearch has been modified as in Exercise 12.)

14. Given the declarations

```
const int MAX_LEN = 200;
typedef int ItemType;

ItemType list1[MAX_LEN];
ItemType list2[MAX_LEN];
int       length1;         // Length of list1
int       length2;         // Length of list2
ItemType item;
```

and viewing a list as an abstract data type, implement the following operations on a list.

a. A function named Empty that returns true if a given list is empty. (*Hint:* Pass the length of the list to the function.)

b. A function named Full that returns true if no more space is left in the array containing the list.

c. A function named Equal that takes two lists as parameters and returns true if they are of the same length and each element in one list equals the corresponding element in the second list.

d. A function named Delete that takes a list and an item and searches the list for an instance of the item. If the item is found, it is removed from the list, and succeeding items are moved up to fill the empty space.

e. A function named `DeleteAll` that removes all instances of an item from a list without leaving gaps in the array.

f. A function named `Component` that returns a component of the list if a given position number (index value) is in the range 0 through `length`−1. The function should also return a Boolean flag named `valid` that is `false` if the index is outside this range.

15. In the Birthday Reminder Revisited programming example, the `GetMonth` function declares and initializes two local arrays, `monthAry` and `strMonthAry`. These are automatic variables, so they are created and initialized every time the function is called, and they are destroyed each time the function returns. Improve the function by ensuring that the arrays are created and initialized only once and remain "alive" for the duration of the entire program. (*Hint:* Review the description in Chapter 8 of lifetimes of variables.)

Programming Problems

1. A company wants to know the percentages of total sales and total expenses attributable to each salesperson. Each has a data line giving his or her last name (maximum of 20 characters), followed by a comma, followed by his or her first name (maximum of 10 characters). The next line contains his or her total sales (`int`) and expenses (`float`). Write a program that produces a report with a header line containing the total sales and total expenses. Following this header should be a table with each salesperson's first name, last name, percentage of total sales, and percentage of total expenses.

2. Only authorized shareholders are allowed to attend a stockholders' meeting. Write a program to read a person's name from the keyboard, check it against a list of shareholders, and print a message saying whether or not the person may attend the meeting. The list of shareholders is in a file `inFile` in the following format: first name (maximum 10 characters), blank, last name (maximum 20 characters). Use the end-of-file condition to stop reading the file. The maximum number of shareholders is 1000.

   The user should be prompted to enter his or her name in the same format as is used for the data in the file. If the name does not appear on the list, the program should repeat the instructions on how to enter the name and then tell the user to try again. A message saying that the person may not enter should be printed only after he or she has been given a second chance to enter the name. The prompt to the user should include the message that a *Q* should be entered to end the program.

3. Enhance the program in Problem 2 as follows:

   a. Print a report showing how many stockholders there were at the time of the meeting, how many were present at the meeting, and how many people who tried to enter were denied permission to attend.

   b. Follow this summary report with a list of the names of the stockholders, with either *Present* or *Absent* after each name.

4. A life insurance company has hired you to write a program to print a list of their customers and the premium that each customer pays. Premiums are based on the age the customer was when he or she became a customer. The following table is used to determine each customer's premium, but these rates are subject to change.

Age	Premium
25	$277.00
35	287.00
45	307.00
55	327.00
65	357.00

Each age listed in this table is the upper limit for the premium. For example, if a customer signed up for a policy when she was 37, she would pay $307.00.

Write a program that reads the table into parallel arrays, then reads in the customers' names and ages when they bought the policies into another pair of parallel arrays. The table and the customers' names and ages are stored in two files. Print out a formatted, labeled list showing each customer's name, his or her age when the policy was bought, and the customer's premium.

5. The local bank in Programming Problem 4, Chapter 11, was so successful with its advertising campaign that the parent bank decided to collect data on waiting times from banks all over the state and run a contest. However, this time they decided to assign frustration levels to wait times as follows:

Wait Time	Frustration Level
wait ≤ (mean - standardDev)	"Amazed"
(mean - standardDev) < wait < mean	"Pleased"
mean ≤ wait < (mean + standardDev)	"Calm"
(mean + standardDev) ≤ wait < (mean + 2 * standardDev)	"Irritated"
(mean + 2 * standardDev) ≤ wait	"Berserk"

where `mean` is the mean waiting time, `wait` is the wait time, and `standardDev` is the standard deviation of the waiting times. Calculate frustration levels for each recorded wait.

Input:

Same as in Programming Problem 4, Chapter 11, except that two digits have been added to the teller ID number to indicate at which bank the teller is located.

Output:

Same as for Programming Problem 4, Chapter 11, plus (1) a bar graph (histogram) showing frustration level distribution; and (2) a table sorted by three-digit ID numbers showing (a) ID number, (b) wait time, and (c) frustration level.

6. Complete the driver program described in the Testing and Debugging section. Use it to test the functions `Search`, `SearchOrd`, and `BinSearch` thoroughly. Choose your test data carefully, making sure that all cases are tested.

13 *Multidimensional Arrays*

GOALS

- To be able to declare a two-dimensional array
- To be able to access a component of a two-dimensional array
- To be able to perform fundamental operations on a two-dimensional array:
  Initialize the array
  Print the values in the array
  Process the array by rows
  Process the array by columns
- To be able to declare a two-dimensional array as a formal parameter
- To be able to view a two-dimensional array as an array of arrays
- To be able to declare and process a multidimensional array
- To be able to choose an appropriate array data structure for a given problem

Data structures play an important role in the design process. The choice of data structure directly affects the design, because it determines the algorithms used to process the data. We have discussed the one-dimensional array, which gives us the ability to reference a group of data objects by one name. This simplifies the design of many algorithms.

In many problems, however, the relationships between data items are more complex than a simple list. In this chapter, we begin by examining the two-dimensional array, which is useful when data are to be organized in the form of a table with rows and columns. Two-dimensional arrays are also useful for representing board games, like chess, tic-tac-toe, or Scrabble, and in computer graphics, where the screen is thought of as a two-dimensional array.

The definition of an array then is extended to allow arrays with any number of dimensions, called multidimensional arrays. Each dimension of such an array is used to represent a different feature of a component. For example, a three-dimensional array of sales figures might be indexed by (1) store number, (2) month, and (3) item number.

Two-Dimensional Arrays

A one-dimensional array is used to represent a list. A **two-dimensional array** is used to represent a table with rows and columns, provided each item in the table is of the same data type. A component in a two-dimensional array is accessed by specifying the row and column indices of the item in a table. This is a familiar task. For example, if you want to find a street on a map, you look up the street name on the back of the map to find the coordinates of the street, usually a letter and a number. The letter specifies a column to look on, and the number specifies a row. You find the street where the row and column meet.

Figure 13-1 shows a two-dimensional array that has 100 rows and 9 columns. The rows are accessed by an integer ranging from 0 through 99; the columns are accessed by an integer ranging from 0 through 8. Each component is accessed by a row-column pair—for example, 0, 5.

A two-dimensional array is declared in exactly the same way as a one-dimensional array, except that sizes must be specified for two dimensions. Below is an example of declaring an array with more than one dimension.

```
const int NUM_ROWS = 100;
const int NUM_COLS = 9;
     .
     .
     .
float alpha[NUM_ROWS][NUM_COLS];
              ↑           ↑
            First      Second
          dimension   dimension
```

FIGURE 13-1

A Two-Dimensional
Array

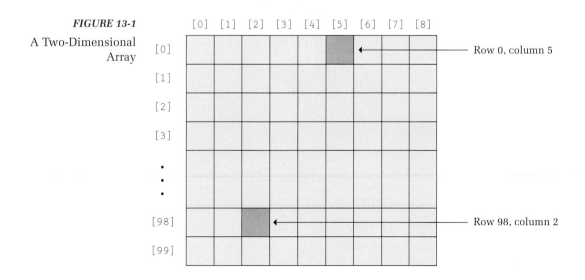

This example declares `alpha` to be a two-dimensional array whose components are `float` values. The declaration creates the array pictured in Figure 13-1.

To access an individual component of the `alpha` array, two expressions (one for each dimension) are used to specify its position. Each expression is in its own pair of brackets next to the name of the array:

```
alpha[0][5] = 36.4;
       ↗    ↖
Row      Column
number   number
```

As with one-dimensional arrays, each index expression must result in an integer value.

Let's look now at some examples. Here is the declaration of a two-dimensional array with 364 integer components:

```
int hiTemp[52][7];
```

We can think of `hiTemp` as a table with 52 rows and 7 columns. The contents of each place in the table (each component) can be any `int` value. Our intention is that the array contains high temperatures for each day in a year. Each row represents one of the 52 weeks in a year, and each column represents one of the 7 days in a week. (To keep the example simple, we ignore the fact that there are 365—and sometimes 366—days in a year.) The expression `hiTemp[2][6]` refers to the `int` value in the third row (row 2) and the seventh column (column 6). Semantically, `hiTemp[2][6]` is the temperature for the seventh day of the third week. The code fragment shown in Figure 13-2 would print the temperature values for the third week.

Another representation of the same data might be as follows:

```
enum DayType
{
    MONDAY, TUESDAY, WEDNESDAY, THURSDAY, FRIDAY, SATURDAY, SUNDAY
};

int hiTemp[52][7];
```

Here, `hiTemp` is declared the same as before, but we can use an expression of type `DayType` for the column index. `hiTemp[2][SUNDAY]` corresponds to the same component as `hiTemp[2][6]` in the first example. (Recall that enumerators such as MONDAY, TUESDAY, . . . are represented internally as the integers 0, 1,

FIGURE 13-2

hiTemp Array

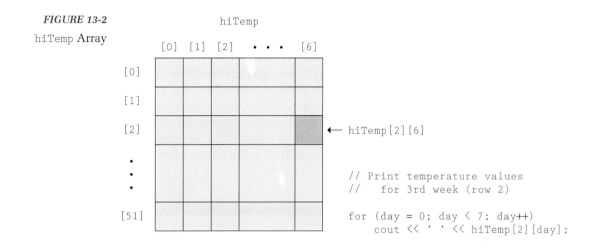

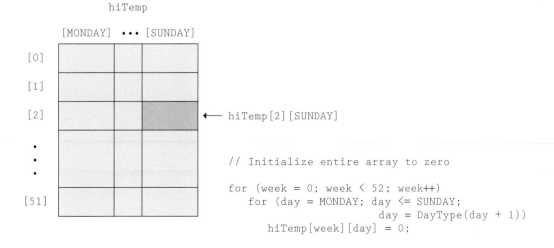

2, ...) If day were of type DayType and week of type int, the code fragment shown in Figure 13-3 would set the entire array to 0. (Notice that by using DayType, the temperature values in the array begin with the first Monday of the year, not necessarily with January 1.)

If the declaration of hiTemp listed the sizes of the two dimensions in reverse order, the rows and columns would be reversed; that is, the declaration

FIGURE 13-3 hiTemp Array (Alternate Form)

```
int hiTemp[7][52];
```

declares an array like that shown in Figure 13-4. Notice how the code fragment in this figure differs from the equivalent code in Figure 13-3: the two index expressions are reversed. The order in which we define the rows and columns doesn't matter to the computer as long as we're consistent. To help visualize a two-dimensional array, we always use the convention of letting the first dimension define the rows and the second dimension define the columns.

Another way of looking at a two-dimensional array is to see it as a structure in which each component has two features. For example, in the following code,

```
enum Colors {RED, ORANGE, YELLOW, GREEN, BLUE, INDIGO, VIOLET};
enum Makes
{
    FORD, TOYOTA, HYUNDAI, JAGUAR, CITROEN, BMW, FIAT, SAAB
};
const int NUM_COLORS = 7;
const int NUM_MAKES = 8;

float crashRating[NUM_COLORS][NUM_MAKES];   // Array of crash
                                            // likelihoods by color
                                            // and make
          .
          .
          .
crashRating[BLUE][JAGUAR] = 0.83;           // Blue Jaguars have a crash
                                            //   likelihood of 0.83
crashRating[RED][FORD] = 0.19;              // Red Fords have a crash
                                            //   likelihood of 0.19
```

FIGURE 13-4 `hiTemp` Array (Third Variation)

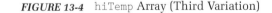

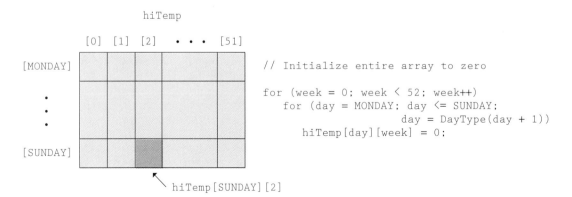

the data structure uses one dimension to represent the color and the other to represent the make of automobile. In other words, both indices have semantic content—a concept we discussed in Chapter 11.

Processing Two-Dimensional Arrays

Processing data in a two-dimensional array generally means accessing the array in one of four patterns: randomly, along rows, along columns, or throughout the entire array. Each of these may also involve subarray processing.

The simplest way to access a component is to look in a given location. For example, a user enters map coordinates that we use as indices into an array of street names to access the sought-after name at those coordinates. This process is referred to as *random access* because the user may enter any set of coordinates at random.

There are many cases in which we might wish to perform an operation on all the elements of a particular row or column in a table. Look back at the `hiTemp` array pictured in Figure 13-3, where the rows represent weeks of the year and the columns represent days of the week. The data represent the high temperatures for each day in a year. If we wanted the average high temperature for a given week, we would sum the values in that row and divide by 7. If we wanted the average for a given day of the week, we would sum the values in that column and divide by 52. The former case is access along rows; the latter case is access along columns.

Now, suppose that we wish to determine the average for the year. We must access every element in the array, sum them, and divide by 364. In this case, the order of access—by row or by column—is not important. (The same is true when we initialize every element of an array to 0.) This is access throughout the array.

There are situations when we must access every element in an array in a particular order, either by rows or by columns. For example, if we wanted the average for every week, we would run through the entire array, taking each row in turn. However, if we wanted the average for each day of the week, we would run through the array a column at a time.

Let's take a closer look at these patterns of access by considering four common examples of array processing.

1. Sum the rows.
2. Sum the columns.
3. Initialize the table to all zeroes (or some special value).
4. Print the table.

First, let's define some constants and variables using general identifiers, such as `row` and `col`, rather than problem-dependent identifiers. Then let's look at each algorithm in terms of generalized table processing.

```
const int NUM_ROWS = 50;
const int NUM_COLS = 50;

int table[NUM_ROWS][NUM_COLS];    // A two-dimensional array
int rowLength;                    // Data is in 0..rowLength-1
int row;                          // A row index
int colLength;                    // Data is in 0..colLength-1
int col;                          // A column index
int total;                        // A variable for summing
```

Sum the Rows   Suppose we want to sum row number 3 (the fourth row) in array `table` and
print the result. We can do this easily with a For loop:

```
total = 0;
for (col = 0; col < NUM_COLS; col++)
    total = total + table[3][col];
cout << "Row sum: " << total << endl;
```

This For loop runs through each column of `table`, while keeping the row index
equal to 3. Every value in row 3 is added to `total`. Suppose we wanted to sum
and print two rows—row 2 and row 3. We could add a duplicate of the preceding code fragment, but with the index set to 2:

```
// Sum row 2 and print the sum

total = 0;
for (col = 0; col < NUM_COLS; col++)
    total = total + table[2][col];
cout << "Row sum: " << total << endl;

// Sum row 3 and print the sum

total = 0;
for (col = 0; col < NUM_COLS; col++)
    total = total + table[3][col];
cout << "Row sum: " << total << endl;
```

or we could use a nested loop and make the row index a variable:

```
for (row = 2; row < 4; row++)
{
    total = 0;
    for (col = 0; col < NUM_COLS; col++)
        total = total + table[row][col];
    cout << "Row sum: " << total << endl;
}
```

The second approach is shorter, but its real advantage is that we can easily modify it to process any range of rows.

The outer loop controls the rows, and the inner loop controls the columns. For each value of `row`, every column is processed; then the outer loop moves to the next row. In the first iteration of the outer loop, `row` is held at 2 and `col` goes from 0 through `NUM_COLS-1`. Therefore, the array is accessed in the following order:

```
table[2][0]  [2][1]  [2][2]  [2][3] . . . [2][NUM_COLS-1]
```

In the second iteration of the outer loop, `row` is incremented to 3, and the array is accessed as follows:

```
table[3][0]  [3][1]  [3][2]  [3][3] . . . [3][NUM_COLS-1]
```

We can generalize this row processing to run through every row of the table by having the outer loop run from 0 through `NUM_ROWS-1`. However, if we want to access only part of the array (subarray processing), we write the code fragment as follows:

```
for (row = 0; row < rowLength; row++)
{
    total = 0;
    for (col = 0; col < colLength; col++)
        total = total + table[row][col];
    cout << "Row sum: " << total << endl;
}
```

Figure 13-5 illustrates subarray processing by row.

Sum the Columns Suppose we want to sum and print each column. The code to perform this task is given below. Again we have generalized the code to sum only the portion of the array that contains valid data.

```
for (col = 0; col < colLength; col++)
{
    total = 0;
    for (row = 0; row < rowLength; row++)
        total = total + table[row][col];
    cout << "Column sum: " << total << endl;
}
```

In this case, the outer loop controls the column, and the inner loop controls the row. All the components in the first column are accessed and summed before the

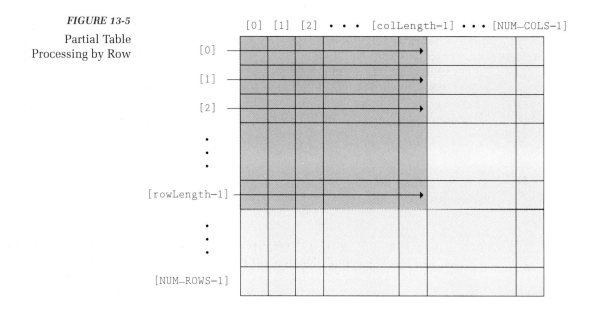

FIGURE 13-5

Partial Table
Processing by Row

outer loop index changes and the components in the second column are accessed. Figure 13-6 illustrates subarray processing by column.

Initialize the Table

As with one-dimensional arrays, we can initialize a two-dimensional array either by initializing it in its declaration or by using assignment statements. If the array is small, it is simplest to initialize it in its declaration. To initialize a 2-row by 3-column table to look like this:

```
14    3   -5
 0   46    7
```

we can use the following declaration.

```
int table[2][3] =
{
    {14, 3, -5},
    {0, 46, 7}
};
```

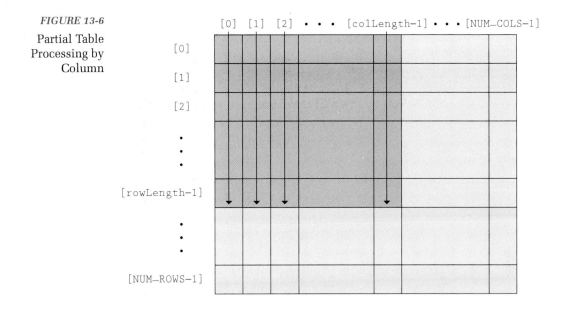

FIGURE 13-6

Partial Table
Processing by
Column

In this declaration, the initializer list consists of two items, each of which is itself an initializer list. The first inner initializer list stores 14, 3, and −5 into row 0 of the table; the second stores 0, 46, and 7 into row 1. The use of two initializer lists makes sense if you think of each row of the table as a one-dimensional array of three ints. The first initializer list initializes the first array (the first row), and the second list initializes the second array (the second row). Later in the chapter, we revisit this notion of viewing a two-dimensional array as an array of arrays.

Initializing a table in its declaration is impractical if the table is large. For a 100-row by 100-column table, you don't want to list 10,000 values. If the values are all different, you should store them into a file and input them into the table at run time. If the values are all the same, the usual approach is to use nested For loops and an assignment statement. Here is a general-purpose code segment that zeroes out a table with NUM_ROWS rows and NUM_COLS columns:

```
for (row = 0; row < NUM_ROWS; row++)
    for (col = 0; col < NUM_COLS; col++)
        table[row][col] = 0;
```

In this case, we initialized the table a row at a time, but we could just as easily have run through each column instead. The order doesn't matter as long as we access every element.

Print the Table   If we wish to print out a table with one row per line, then we have another case of row processing:

```
#include <iomanip.h>     // For setw()
   .
   .
   .

for (row = 0; row < NUM_ROWS; row++)
{
    for (col = 0; col < NUM_COLS; col++)
        cout << setw(15) << table[row][col];
    cout << endl;
}
```

This code fragment prints the values of the table in columns that are 15 characters wide. As a matter of proper style, this fragment should be preceded by code that prints headings over the columns to identify their contents.

There's no rule that we have to print each row on a line. We could turn the table sideways and print each column on one line simply by exchanging the two For loops. When you are printing a table, you must consider which order of presentation makes the most sense and how the table fits on the page. For example, a table with 6 columns and 100 rows would be best printed as 6 columns, 100 lines long.

Almost all processing of data stored in a two-dimensional array involves either processing by row or processing by column. In most of our examples the index type has been `int`, but the pattern of operation of the loops is the same no matter what types the indices are.

The looping patterns for row processing and column processing are so useful that they are summarized below. To make them more general, we use `minRow` for the first row number and `minCol` for the first column number. Remember that row processing has the row index in the outer loop, and column processing has the column index in the outer loop.

Row Processing

```
for (row = minRow; row < rowLength; row++)
    for (col = minCol; col < colLength; col++)
        .
        .
        .             // Whatever processing is required
```

Column Processing

```
for (col = minCol; col < colLength; col++)
    for (row = minRow; row < rowLength; row++)
        .
        .
        .                  // Whatever processing is required
```

Passing Two-Dimensional Arrays as Parameters

In Chapter 11, we said that when one-dimensional arrays are declared as formal parameters in a function, the size of the array usually is omitted:

```
void SomeFunc( /* inout */ float list[],
               /* in */    int   size  )
```

If you include a size in the square brackets, the compiler ignores it. As you learned, the base address of the actual parameter (the memory address of the first array element) is passed to the function. The function works for an actual parameter of any size. Because the function cannot know the size of the caller's actual array, we either pass the size as a parameter—as in `SomeFunc` above— or use a declared constant if the function always operates on an array of a certain size.

When a two-dimensional array is passed as a parameter, again the base address of the actual array is sent to the function. But you cannot leave off the sizes of both of the array dimensions. You can omit the size of the first dimension (the number of rows) but not the second (the number of columns). Here is the reason.

In the computer's memory, C++ stores two-dimensional arrays in row order. Thinking of memory as one long line of memory cells, the first row of the array is followed by the second row, which is followed by the third, and so on (see Figure 13-7). To locate `table[1][0]` in this figure, a function that receives table's base address must be able to know that there are four elements in each row— that is, that the table consists of four columns. Therefore, the declaration of a formal parameter must always state the number of columns:

```
void AnotherFunc( /* inout */ int arr[][4] )
```

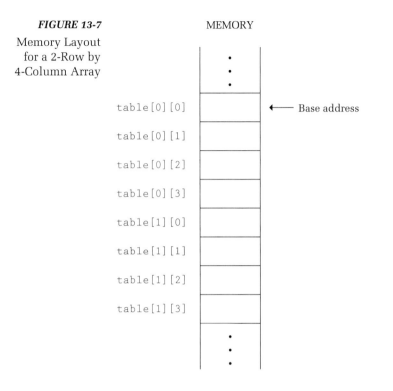

FIGURE 13-7

Memory Layout
for a 2-Row by
4-Column Array

Furthermore, the number of columns declared for the formal parameter must be *exactly* the same as the number of columns in the caller's actual array. As you can tell from Figure 13-7, if there is any discrepancy in the number of columns, the function will access the wrong array element in memory.

Our `AnotherFunc` function works for a two-dimensional array of any number of rows, as long as it has exactly four columns. In practice, we seldom write programs that use arrays with a varying number of rows but the same number of columns. To avoid problems with mismatches in formal and actual parameter sizes, it's practical to use a Typedef statement to define a two-dimensional array type and then declare both the actual and the formal parameters to be of that type. For example, we might make the declarations

```
const int NUM_ROWS = 10;
const int NUM_COLS = 20;
typedef int TableType[NUM_ROWS][NUM_COLS];
```

and then write the following general-purpose function that initializes all elements of an array to a specified value:

```
void Initialize( /* out */ TableType table,    // Array to initialize
                 /* in */  int       initVal) // Initial value

// Initializes each element of table to initVal

{
    int row;
    int col;

    for (row = 0; row < NUM_ROWS; row++)
        for (col = 0; col < NUM_COLS; col++)
            table[row][col] = initVal;
}
```

The calling code could then declare and initialize one or more arrays of type `TableType` by making calls to the `Initialize` function. For example,

```
TableType delta;
TableType gamma;

Initialize(delta, 0);
Initialize(gamma, -1);
    .
    .
    .
```

Another Way of Defining
Two-Dimensional Arrays

We hinted earlier that a two-dimensional array can be viewed as an array of arrays. This view is supported by C++ in the sense that the components of a one-dimensional array do not have to be atomic; they can also be structured. For example, we could declare an array of student names as follows.

```
const int MAX_LENGTH = 200;
typedef char String10[11];       // Room for 10 characters plus '\0'

String10 student[MAX_LENGTH];    // Array of student names
```

With this declaration, the components of the array `student` are one-dimensional arrays of type `String10`. In other words, `student` has two dimensions. We can access each row as an entity: `student[57]` accesses the name of student number 57. We can also access each individual component of `student` by specifying both indices: `student[57][0]` accesses the first letter in the name of student 57.

Now that you know how to declare a two-dimensional array, `student` can be redeclared as follows:

```
char student[MAX_LENGTH][11];
```

Does it matter which way we declare a two-dimensional array? Not to C++. The choice should be based on readability and understandability. Sometimes the features of the data are shown more clearly if both indices are specified in a single declaration. At other times, the code is clearer if one dimension is defined first as a one-dimensional array type.

Here is an example of when it is advantageous to define a two-dimensional array as an array of arrays. If the rows have been defined first as a one-dimensional array type, each can be passed to a function expecting as a parameter a one-dimensional array of the same type. The following function reads a student name into a variable of type `String10`, returning both the name and its length.

```
#include <string.h>    // For strlen()
   .
   .
   .

void GetAName( /* out */ String10 stuName,    // Input name
               /* out */ int&     length  )   // Length of name

// Inputs a student name

{
    cin.get(stuName, 11);      // Read at most 10 characters
    cin.ignore(100, '\n');
    length = strlen(stuName);
}
```

We can call `GetAName` using a component of `student` as follows.

```
GetAName(student[2], nameLength);
```

Row 2 of `student` is passed to `GetAName`, which treats it like any other one-dimensional array of type `String10` (see Figure 13-8). It makes sense to pass the

FIGURE 13-8

A One-Dimensional
Array of One-
Dimensional Arrays

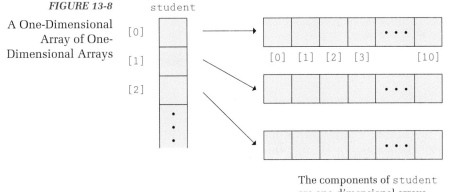

The components of student
are one-dimensional arrays
of type String10.

row as a parameter because both it and the formal parameter are of the same
named type, String10.

Declaring student as a one-dimensional array of strings is clearer than declaring it directly as a two-dimensional array. Whenever possible, we like to treat
a string as a single item rather than as an array of individual characters.

Multidimensional Arrays

array
*A collection of com-
ponents, all of the
same type, ordered
on N dimensions
(N ≥ 1). Each compo-
nent is accessed by N
indices, each of which
represents the com-
ponent's position
within that dimension*

C++ does not place a limit on the number of dimensions that an **array** can have.
We can generalize our definition of an array to cover all cases.

You should have guessed by now that you can have as many dimensions as
you want. How many should you have in a particular case? As many as there
are features that describe the components in the array.

Take, for example, a chain of department stores. Monthly sales figures must
be kept for each item by store. There are three important pieces of information
about each item: the month in which it was sold, the store from which it was purchased, and the item number. We can define an array type to summarize these
data as follows:

```
const int NUM_ITEMS = 100;
const int NUM_STORES = 10;

typedef int SalesType[NUM_STORES] [12] [NUM_ITEMS];
```

```
SalesType sales;    // Array of sales figures
int       item;
int       store;
int       month;
int       numberSold;
int       currentMonth;
```

A graphic representation of the array variable `sales` is shown in Figure 13-9.

The number of components in `sales` is 12,000 (10 × 12 × 100). If sales figures are available only for January through June, then half the array is empty. If we want to process the data in the array, we must use subarray processing. The following program fragment sums and prints the total number of each item sold this year to date by all stores.

```
for (item = 0; item < NUM_ITEMS; item++)
{
    numberSold = 0;
    for (store = 0; store < NUM_STORES; store++)
        for (month = 0; month <= currentMonth; month++)
            numberSold = numberSold + sales[store][month][item];
    cout << "Item #" << item << " Sales to date = " << numberSold
        << endl;
}
```

Because `item` controls the outer For loop, we are summing each item's sales by `month` and `store`. If we want to find the total sales for each store, we use

FIGURE 13-9

Graphical Representation of Array Variable `sales`

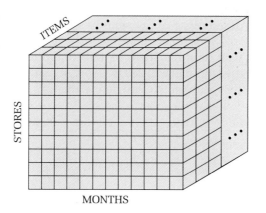

store to control the outer For loop, summing its sales by month and item with the inner loops.

```
for (store = 0; store < NUM_STORES; store++)
{
    numberSold = 0;
    for (item = 0; item < NUM_ITEMS; item++)
        for (month = 0; month <= currentMonth; month++)
            numberSold = numberSold + sales[store][month][item];
    cout << "Store #" << store << " Sales to date = " << numberSold
        << endl;
}
```

It takes two loops to access each component in a two-dimensional array; it takes three loops to access each component in a three-dimensional array. The task to be accomplished determines which index controls the outer loop, the middle loop, and the inner loop. If we want to calculate monthly sales by store, month controls the outer loop and store controls the middle loop. If we want to calculate monthly sales by item, month controls the outer loop and item controls the middle loop.

If we want to keep track of the departments that sell each item, we can add a fourth dimension.

```
enum Departments {A, B, C, D, E, F, G};
const int NUM_DEPTS = 7;
typedef int SalesType[NUM_STORES][12][NUM_ITEMS][NUM_DEPTS];
```

How would we visualize this new structure? Not very easily! Fortunately, we do not have to visualize a structure in order to use it. If we want the number of sales in store 1, during June, for item number 4, in department C, we simply access the array element

```
sales[1][5][4][C]
```

When a multidimensional array is declared as a formal parameter in a function, C++ requires you to state the sizes of all dimensions except the first. For our four-dimensional version of SalesType, a function heading would look either like

```
void DoSomething( /* inout */ int arr[][12][NUM_ITEMS][NUM_DEPTS] )
```

or, better yet, like

```
void DoSomething( /* inout */ SalesType arr )
```

The second version is the safest (and the most uncluttered to look at). It ensures that the sizes of all dimensions of the formal parameter match those of the actual parameter exactly. With the first version, the reason why you must declare the sizes of all but the first dimension is the same as we discussed earlier for two-dimensional arrays. Because arrays are stored linearly in memory (one array element after another), the compiler must use this size information to locate correctly an element that lies in the middle of the array.

▪ Choosing a Data Structure

We have now seen two different data structures that can be used to represent data arranged as a table: parallel arrays and two-dimensional arrays. We can always use parallel arrays instead of a two-dimensional array. How do we decide which is most appropriate?

Recall that, in an array, all the components are of the same type; they represent the same thing. But what if we want to process information on the number of items sold, the cost of each item, and the percent tax to be charged for each item? We can define a table with the following headings to hold this information:

> Item Number   Number Sold
> Cost per Item   Tax Rate

If we keep the item number and number sold as floating point numbers, we can define a two-dimensional array of type `float` with four columns, each corresponding to one of the headings; however, in this case, four parallel arrays are more appropriate. Even though the components are all of the same data type, they represent different things. The components in the Item Number column represent an identifying number; those in the Number Sold column represent

the quantity sold; the Cost per Item column contains prices; and the Tax Rate column holds percentages. Defining this structure as a set of four parallel arrays also allows us to represent Item Number and Number Sold with integers, which are a better choice for this type of information.

To decide whether to use parallel arrays or a multidimensional array, we can ask three questions:

1. Are all the components of the same data type?
2. Do all the components represent the same kinds of values?
3. Can a set of independent features be used as indices to select a component?

If the answer to all three questions is yes, a multidimensional array is appropriate. Otherwise, parallel arrays are a better choice.

In some cases, a single data structure is more appropriate than multiple arrays. In the next chapter, we look at a data structure called a record, a structure that allows us to group nonhomogeneous items. As we introduce more data structures, we provide additional guidelines on how to choose among them.

PROGRAMMING EXAMPLE

City Council Election

Problem: There has just been a hotly contested city council election. In four voting precincts, citizens have cast their ballots for four candidates. Let's do an analysis of the votes for the four candidates by precinct. We want to know how many votes each candidate received in each precinct, how many total votes each candidate received, and how many total votes were cast in each precinct.

Input: An arbitrary number of votes in a file `voteFile`, with each vote represented as a pair of numbers: a precinct number (1 through 4) and a candidate number (1 through 4); and candidate names, entered from the keyboard (to be used for printing the output).

Output: The following three items, written to a file `reportFile`: a table showing how many votes each candidate received in each precinct, the total number of votes for each candidate, and the total number of votes in each precinct.

www.jbpub.com/C++links

Discussion: The data are available in the form of a pair of numbers for each vote. The first number is the precinct number; the second number is the candidate number.

If we were doing the analysis by hand, our first task would be to go through the data, counting how many people in each precinct voted for each candidate. We would probably create a table with precincts down the side and candidates across the top. Each vote would be recorded as a hash mark in the appropriate column and row (see Figure 13-10).

FIGURE 13-10	Precinct	Smith	Jones	Adams	Smiley
	1	⊞⊞ ‖	‖	⊞⊞ ⊞⊞ ‖	⊞⊞
	2	⊞⊞ ⊞⊞	‖	⊞⊞	‖‖
	3	‖	⊞⊞ ‖‖	⊞⊞ ⊞⊞ ⊞⊞	‖‖
	4	⊞⊞	⊞⊞ ‖‖	⊞⊞ ⊞⊞	‖

PROGRAMMING EXAMPLE cont'd

When all of the votes had been recorded, a sum of each column would tell us how many votes each candidate had received. A sum of each row would tell us how many people had voted in each precinct.

As is so often the case, this by-hand algorithm can be used directly in our program. A two-dimensional array can be created where each component is a counter for the number of votes for a particular candidate in each precinct; that is, the value indexed by [2][1] would be the counter for the votes for candidate 1 in precinct 2. Well, not quite. C++ arrays are indexed beginning at 0, so the correct array component would be indexed by [1][0]. When we input a precinct number and candidate number, we must remember to subtract 1 from each before indexing into the array. Likewise, we must add 1 to an array index that represents a precinct number or candidate number before printing it out.

Data Structures:

A two-dimensional array `votes`, where the rows represent precincts and the columns represent candidates

A one-dimensional array of strings containing the names of the candidates, to be used for printing (see Figure 13-11).

FIGURE 13-11

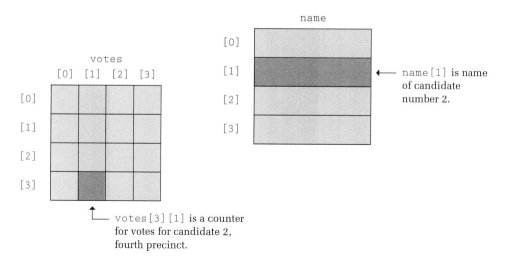

votes[3][1] is a counter for votes for candidate 2, fourth precinct.

name[1] is name of candidate number 2.

PROGRAMMING EXAMPLE cont'd

```
//*********************************************************************
// Election program
// This program reads votes represented by precinct number and
// ballot position from a data file, calculates the sums per
// precinct and per candidate, and writes all totals to an
// output file
//*********************************************************************
#include <iostream.h>
#include <iomanip.h>      // For setw()
#include <fstream.h>      // For file I/O
const int NUM_PRECINCTS = 4;
const int NUM_CANDIDATES = 4;

typedef char String10[11];        // Room for 10 characters plus '\0'

typedef int VoteTable[NUM_PRECINCTS][NUM_CANDIDATES];
                                  // 2-dimensional array type
                                  //   for votes
void GetNames( String10[] );
void OpenForInput( ifstream& );
void OpenForOutput( ofstream& );
void WritePerCandidate( const VoteTable, const String10[],
                        ofstream& );
void WritePerPrecinct( const VoteTable, ofstream& );
void WriteTable( const VoteTable, const String10[], ofstream& );
void ZeroVotes( VoteTable );

int main()
{
    VoteTable votes;           // Totals for precincts vs. candidates

    String10  name[NUM_CANDIDATES];   // Array of candidate names

    int       candidate;       // Candidate number input from voteFile
    int       precinct;        // Precinct number input from voteFile
    ifstream  voteFile;        // Input file of precincts, candidates
    ofstream  reportFile;      // Output file receiving summaries

    OpenForInput(voteFile);
    if ( !voteFile )
        return 1;
    OpenForOutput(reportFile);
    if ( !reportFile )
        return 1;
```

PROGRAMMING EXAMPLE cont'd

```
        GetNames(name);
        ZeroVotes(votes);

        // Read and tally votes

        voteFile >> precinct >> candidate;
        while (voteFile)
        {
            votes[precinct-1][candidate-1]++;
            voteFile >> precinct >> candidate;
        }

        // Write results to report file

        WriteTable(votes, name, reportFile);
        WritePerCandidate(votes, name, reportFile);
        WritePerPrecinct(votes, reportFile);

        return 0;
    }

//**********************************************************************

void OpenForInput( /* inout */ ifstream& someFile )  // File to be
                                                     // opened
// Prompts for name of input file and opens it

// Postcondition:
//     The user has been prompted for a file name
//  && IF the file could not be opened
//         An error message has been printed
// Note:
//     Upon return caller must test stream state

{
    char fileName[51];    // User-specified file name (max. 50 chars)

    cout << "Input file name: ";
    cin.get(fileName, 51);
    cin.ignore(100, '\n');

    someFile.open(fileName);
    if ( !someFile )
        cout << "** Can't open " << fileName << " **" << endl;
}
```

PROGRAMMING EXAMPLE cont'd

```
//*********************************************************************

void OpenForOutput( /* inout */ ofstream& someFile )    // File to be
                                                        // opened
// Prompts for name of output file and opens it
// Postcondition:
//     The user has been prompted for a file name
//  && IF the file could not be opened
//          An error message has been printed
// Note:
//     Upon return, caller must test stream state

{
    char fileName[51];    // User-specified file name (max. 50 chars)

    cout << "Output file name: ";
    cin.get(fileName, 51);
    cin.ignore(100, '\n');

    someFile.open(fileName);
    if ( !someFile )
        cout << "** Can't open " << fileName << " **" << endl;
}

//*********************************************************************

void GetNames( /* out */ String10 name[] )    // Array of candidate
                                              //    names
// Reads the list of candidate names from standard input

// Postcondition:
//     The user has been prompted to enter the candidate names
//  && name[0..NUM_CANDIDATES-1] contain the input names,
//     truncated to 10 characters each

{
    int  candidate;      // Loop counter

    cout << "Enter the names of the candidates, one per line,"
        << endl << "in the order they appear on the ballot."
        << endl;
    for (candidate = 0; candidate < NUM_CANDIDATES; candidate++)
    {
        cin.get(name[candidate], 11);  // At most 10 chars plus '\0'
        cin.ignore(100, '\n');
    }
}
```

PROGRAMMING EXAMPLE cont'd

```
//*********************************************************************

void ZeroVotes( /* out */ VoteTable votes )   // Array of vote totals

// Zeroes out the votes array

// Postcondition:
//     All votes[0..NUM_PRECINCTS-1][0..NUM_CANDIDATES-1] == 0

{
    int precinct;       // Loop counter
    int candidate;      // Loop counter

    for (precinct = 0; precinct < NUM_PRECINCTS; precinct++)
        for (candidate = 0; candidate < NUM_CANDIDATES; candidate++)
            votes[precinct][candidate] = 0;
}


//*********************************************************************

void WriteTable(
        /* in */    const VoteTable votes,      // Total votes
        /* in */    const String10  name[],     // Candidate names
        /* inout */ ofstream&       reportFile ) // Output file

// Writes the vote totals in tabular form to the report file

// Precondition:
//     votes[0..NUM_PRECINCTS-1][0..NUM_CANDIDATES] are assigned
//   && name[0..NUM_CANDIDATES-1] are assigned
// Postcondition:
//     The name array has been output across one line, followed by
//     the votes array, one row per line

{
    int precinct;       // Loop counter
    int candidate;      // Loop counter

    // Set up headings

    reportFile << "              ";
    for (candidate = 0; candidate < NUM_CANDIDATES; candidate++)
        reportFile << setw(12) << name[candidate];
    reportFile << endl;

    // Print table by row
```

PROGRAMMING EXAMPLE cont'd

```cpp
        for (precinct = 0; precinct < NUM_PRECINCTS; precinct++)
        {
            reportFile << "Precinct" << setw(4) << precinct + 1;
            for (candidate = 0; candidate < NUM_CANDIDATES; candidate++)
                reportFile << setw(12) << votes[precinct][candidate];
            reportFile << endl;
        }
        reportFile << endl;
    }

    //*******************************************************************

    void WritePerCandidate(
            /* in */     const VoteTable  votes,        // Total votes
            /* in */     const String10   name[],       // Candidate names
            /* inout */  ofstream&        reportFile )   // Output file

    // Sums votes per person and writes totals to report file

    // Precondition:
    //     votes[0..NUM_PRECINCTS-1][0..NUM_CANDIDATES] are assigned
    //  && name[0..NUM_CANDIDATES-1] are assigned
    // Postcondition:
    //     For each person i, name[i] has been output,
    //     followed by the sum
    //     votes[0][i] + votes[1][i] + ... + votes[NUM_PRECINCTS-1][i]

    {
        int precinct;      // Loop counter
        int candidate;     // Loop counter
        int total;         // Total votes for a candidate

        for (candidate = 0; candidate < NUM_CANDIDATES; candidate++)
        {
            total = 0;

            // Compute column sum

            for (precinct = 0; precinct < NUM_PRECINCTS; precinct++)
                total = total + votes[precinct][candidate];

            reportFile << "Total votes for"
                    << setw(10) << name[candidate] << ":"
                    << setw(3) << total << endl;
        }
        reportFile << endl;
    }
```

PROGRAMMING EXAMPLE cont'd

```
//******************************************************************

void WritePerPrecinct(
            /* in */      const VoteTable    votes,       // Total votes
            /* inout */ ofstream&            reportFile )  // Output file

// Sums votes per precinct and writes totals to report file

// Precondition:
//     votes[0..NUM_PRECINCTS-1][0..NUM_CANDIDATES] are assigned
// Postcondition:
//     For each precinct i, the value of i+1 has been output,
//     followed by the sum
//     votes[i][0] + votes[i][1] + ... + votes[i][NUM_CANDIDATES-1]

{
    int precinct;       // Loop counter
    int candidate;      // Loop counter
    int total;          // Total votes for a precinct

    for (precinct = 0; precinct < NUM_PRECINCTS; precinct++)
    {
        total = 0;

        // Compute row sum

        for (candidate = 0; candidate < NUM_CANDIDATES; candidate++)
            total = total + votes[precinct][candidate];

        reportFile << "Total votes for precinct"
                   << setw(3) << precinct + 1 << ':'
                   << setw(3) << total << endl;
    }
}
```

Testing: This program was run with the data listed on the next page. (We list the data in three columns to save space.) The names of the candidates were Smith, Jones, Adams, and Smiley. In this data set, there is at least one vote for each candidate in each precinct. Programming Warm-Up Exercise 10 asks you to outline a complete testing strategy for this program.

PROGRAMMING EXAMPLE cont'd

Input Data

```
1 1    3 1    3 3
1 1    4 3    4 4
1 2    3 4    4 4
1 2    3 2    4 3
1 3    3 3    4 4
1 4    2 1    4 4
2 2    2 3    4 1
2 2    4 3    4 2
2 3    4 4    2 4
2 1    3 2    4 4
```

The output, which was written to file `reportFile`, is shown below.

```
                    Jones      Smith      Adams      Smiley
Precinct    1         2          2          1          1
Precinct    2         2          2          2          1
Precinct    3         1          2          2          1
Precinct    4         1          1          3          6

Total votes for      Jones:   6
Total votes for      Smith:   7
Total votes for      Adams:   8
Total votes for      Smiley:  9

Total votes for precinct   1:  6
Total votes for precinct   2:  7
Total votes for precinct   3:  6
Total votes for precinct   4: 11
```

Testing and Debugging

Errors with multidimensional arrays usually fall into two major categories: index expressions that are out of order and index range errors. In addition, undefined-value errors may result from trying to access uninitialized components.

As the number of dimensions increases, so does the likelihood of a subtle logic error. The syntax of your nested loop structure may be valid, but what you intended to have happen may not be what you coded. Using meaningful identifiers for your loop control variables will help. If you were to use i, j, and k as the loop control variables in the department store example, it would be easy to interchange them by mistake. If you use item, store, and month, you are less likely to confuse the indices. Even if you have the index expressions in the correct order following the array name, you can end up with index range errors if you use the wrong upper (or lower) limits for an index variable that is controlling a loop.

Suppose we were to expand the Election program to accommodate 10 candidates and four precincts. Let's declare the votes array as

```
int votes[4][10];
```

The first dimension represents the precincts, and the second represents the candidates. An example of the first kind of error—incorrect order of the index expressions—would be to print out the votes array as follows.

```
for (precinct = 0; precinct < 4; precinct++)
{
    for (candidate = 0; candidate < 10; candidate++)
        cout << setw(4) << votes[candidate][precinct];
    cout << endl;
}
```

In the output statement we have specified the array indices in the wrong order. The loops march through the array with the first index ranging from 0 through 9 (instead of 0 through 3) and the second index ranging from 0 through 3 (instead of 0 through 9). The effect of executing this code may vary from system to system. The program may output the wrong array components and continue executing, or the program may crash with a memory access error.

An example of the second kind of error—an incorrect index range in an otherwise correct loop—can be seen in this code:

```
for (precinct = 0; precinct < 10; precinct++)
{
    for (candidate = 0; candidate < 4; candidate++)
        cout << setw(4) << votes[precinct][candidate];
    cout << endl;
}
```

Here, the output statement correctly uses `precinct` for the first index and `candidate` for the second. However, the For statements use incorrect upper limits for the index variables. As with the preceding example, the effect of executing this code is undefined but is certainly wrong. A valuable way to prevent this kind of error is to use named constants instead of the literals 10 and 4. In the program, we used `NUM_PRECINCTS` and `NUM_CANDIDATES`. You are much more likely to spot an error (or to avoid making an error in the first place) if you write something like this:

```
for (precinct = 0; precinct < NUM_PRECINCTS; precinct++)
```

than if you use a literal constant as the upper limit for the index variable.

Testing and Debugging Hints

1. Initialize all components of an array if there is any chance that you will attempt to access the entire array.
2. Use the proper number of indices with array names when referencing an array component, and make sure the indices are in the correct order.
3. Use meaningful identifiers for index variables.
4. In array-processing loops, double-check the upper and lower bounds on each index variable to be sure they are correct for that dimension of the array.
5. When declaring a multidimensional array as a formal parameter, you must state the sizes of all but the first dimension. Also, these sizes must agree exactly with the sizes of the caller's actual parameter.
6. To eliminate the chances of size mismatches referred to in item 5, use a Typedef statement to define a multidimensional array type. Declare both the actual parameter and the formal parameter to be of this type.

Summary

Two-dimensional arrays are useful for processing information that is represented naturally in table form. Processing data in two-dimensional arrays usually takes one of two forms: processing by row or processing by column. An array of arrays, which is useful if rows of the array must be passed as parameters, is an alternative way of defining a two-dimensional array.

A multidimensional array is a collection of like components, ordered on more than one dimension. Each component is accessed by a set of indices, one for each dimension, that represents the component's position on the various dimensions. Each index may be thought of as describing a feature of a given array component.

Data structures should be selected to reflect accurately the relationships inherent in the data values themselves. Two-dimensional arrays and parallel arrays can be used to hold the same data. An analysis of what the data mean can help you make the appropriate choice.

Quick Check

1. Declare a two-dimensional array, named `plan`, with 30 rows and 10 columns. The component type of the array is `float`. (pp. 419–423)
2. Assign the value 27.3 to the component in row 13, column 7 of the array `plan` from Question 1. (pp. 419–423)
3. Nested For loops can be used to sum the values in each row of array `plan`. What range of values would the outer For loop count through to do this? (pp. 423–425)
4. Nested For loops can be used to sum the values in each column of array `plan`. What range of values would the outer For loop count through to do this? (pp. 425–426)
5. Write a program fragment that initializes array `plan` from Question 1 to all zeros. (pp. 426–427)
6. Write a program fragment that prints the contents of array `plan`, one row per line of output. (p. 428)
7. Suppose array `plan` is passed as a parameter to a function in which the corresponding formal parameter is named `someArray`. What would the declaration of `someArray` look like in the formal parameter list? (pp. 429–431)
8. Given the declarations

   ```
   typedef int OneDimType[100];

   OneDimType twoDim[40];
   ```

   rewrite the declaration of `twoDim` without referring to type `OneDimType`. (pp. 431–433)
9. How many components does the following data type contain? (pp. 433–436)

   ```
   const int SIZE = 10;
   typedef char FourDim[SIZE][SIZE][SIZE][SIZE-1];
   ```

10. Write a program fragment that fills a variable of type `FourDim`, named `quick`, with blanks. (pp. 433–436)
11. Suppose you are writing a program to process a table of employee numbers, names, and pay rates. Is a two-dimensional array an appropriate data structure for this problem? Explain. (p. 436)

Answers 1. `float plan[30][10];` 2. `plan[13][7] = 27.3;`
3. `for (row = 0; row < 30; row++)` 4. `for (col = 0; col < 10; col++)`
5. `for (row = 0; row < 30; row++)`
        `for (col = 0; col < 10; col++)`
            `plan[row][col] = 0.0;`

```
6. for (row = 0; row < 30; row++)
   {
        for (col = 0; col < 10; col++)
            cout << setw(8) << plan[row][col];
        cout << endl;
   }
```
7. Either
```
       float someArray[30][10]
```
   or
```
       float someArray[][10]
```
8. `int twoDim[40][100];` 9. Nine thousand (10 * 10 * 10 * 9)
```
10. for (dim1 = 0; dim1 < SIZE; dim1++)
        for (dim2 = 0; dim2 < SIZE; dim2++)
            for (dim3 = 0; dim3 < SIZE; dim3++)
                for (dim4 = 0; dim4 < SIZE - 1; dim4++)
                    quick[dim1][dim2][dim3][dim4] = ' ';
```

11. A two-dimensional array is inappropriate because the data types of the columns are not the same. Parallel arrays are appropriate in this case.

Exam Preparation Exercises

1. Given the declarations

```
const int NUM_WEEKS = 5;
const int NUM_TEAMS = 6;

int tickets[NUM_TEAMS][NUM_WEEKS];
```

answer the following questions:
a. What is the number of rows in `tickets`?
b. What is the number of columns in `tickets`?
c. How many components does `tickets` have?
d. What kind of processing (row or column) would be needed to total the ticket sales by weeks?
e. What kind of processing (row or column) would be needed to total the ticket sales by teams?

2. Given the declarations

```
const int NUM_SCHOOLS = 10;
const int NUM_SPORTS = 3;
enum SportType {FOOTBALL, BASKETBALL, VOLLEYBALL};

int   kidsInSports[NUM_SCHOOLS][NUM_SPORTS];
float costOfSports[NUM_SPORTS][NUM_SCHOOLS];
```

answer the following questions:
a. What is the number of rows in `kidsInSports`?
b. What is the number of columns in `kidsInSports`?
c. What is the number of rows in `costOfSports`?
d. What is the number of columns in `costOfSports`?
e. How many components does `kidsInSports` have?
f. How many components does `costOfSports` have?
g. What kind of processing (row or column) would be needed to total the amount of money spent on each sport?
h. What kind of processing (row or column) would be needed to total the number of children participating in sports at a particular school?

3. Given the following code segments, draw the arrays and their contents after the code is executed. Indicate any undefined values with the letter *U*.

a.
```
int exampleA[4][3];
int i, j;

for (i = 0; i < 4; i++)
    for (j = 0; j < 3; j++)
        exampleA[i][j] = i * j;
```
b.
```
int exampleB[4][3];
int i, j;

for (i = 0; i < 3; i++)
    for (j = 0; j < 3; j++)
        exampleB[i][j] = (i + j) % 3;
```
c.
```
int exampleC[8][2];
int i, j;

exampleC[7][0] = 4;
exampleC[7][1] = 5;
for (i = 0; i < 7; i++)
{
    exampleC[i][0] = 2;
    exampleC[i][1] = 3;
}
```

4. a. Define enumeration types for the following:

   `TeamType` made up of classes (freshman, sophomore, etc.) on your campus.
   `ResultType` made up of game results (won, lost, or tied)

   b. Using Typedef, declare an integer array type named `Outcome`, intended to be indexed by `TeamType` and `ResultType`.
   c. Declare an array variable `standings` to be of type `Outcome`.
   d. Give a C++ statement that increases the number of freshman wins by one.

5. The following code fragment includes a call to a function named DoSomething.

```
typedef float ArrType[100][20];

ArrType x;
    .
    .
    .
DoSomething(x);
```

Indicate whether each of the following would be valid or invalid as the function heading for DoSomething.

a. `void DoSomething( /* inout */ ArrType arr )`
b. `void DoSomething( /* inout */ float arr[100][20] )`
c. `void DoSomething( /* inout */ float arr[100][] )`
d. `void DoSomething( /* inout */ float arr[][20] )`
e. `void DoSomething( /* inout */ float arr[][] )`
f. `void DoSomething( /* inout */ float arr[][10] )`

6. Given the following declarations

```
typedef char String20[21];

String20 oneName;
String20 nameList[50];
```

indicate whether each of the following is valid or invalid.

a. `strcpy(nameList[3], oneName);`
b. `nameList[14][27] = 'z';`
c. `nameList[3][7] = 'y';`
d. `cin >> nameList;`
e. `cin >> nameList[0];`
f. `cin >> nameList[0][5];`

7. Declare the array variables described below. Use proper style.
   a. A table with five rows and six columns that contains Boolean values. (Assume the Boolean type has been defined previously.)
   b. A table, indexed from 0 through 39 and 0 through 199, that contains float values.
   c. A char table with rows indexed by a type

   ```
   enum FruitType {LEMON, PEAR, APPLE, ORANGE};
   ```

   and columns indexed by the integers 0 through 15.
8. A logging operation keeps records of 37 loggers' monthly production for purposes of analysis, using the following array structure:

```
const int NUM_LOGGERS = 37;

int logsCut[NUM_LOGGERS][12];  // Logs cut per logger per month
int monthlyHigh;
int monthlyTotal;
int yearlyTotal;
int high;
int month;
int bestMonth;
int logger;
int bestLogger;
```

a. The following statement would assign the January log total for logger number 7 to
   `monthlyTotal`. (True or False?)

```
monthlyTotal = logsCut[7][0];
```

b. The following statements would compute the yearly total for logger number 11.
   (True or False?)

```
yearlyTotal = 0;
for (month = 0; month < NUM_LOGGERS; month++)
    yearlyTotal = yearlyTotal + logsCut[month][10];
```

c. The following statements would find the best logger (most logs cut) in March.
   (True or False?)

```
monthlyHigh = 0;
for (logger = 0; logger < NUM_LOGGERS; logger++)
    if (logsCut[logger][2] > monthlyHigh)
    {
        bestLogger = logger;
        monthlyHigh = logsCut[logger][2];
    }
```

d. The following statements would find the logger with the highest monthly production and the logger's best month. (True or False?)

```
high = -1;
for (month = 0; month < 12; month++)
    for (logger = 0; logger < NUM_LOGGERS; logger++)
        if (logsCut[logger][month] > high)
```

```
        {
            high = logsCut[logger][month];
            bestLogger = logger;
            bestMonth = month;
        }
```

9. Declare the `float` array variables described below. Use proper style.
   a. A three-dimensional array where the first dimension is indexed from 0 through 9, the second dimension is indexed by an enumeration type representing the days of the week, and the third dimension is indexed from 0 through 20.
   b. A four-dimensional array where the first two dimensions are indexed from 0 through 49, and the third and fourth are indexed by any valid ASCII character.

Programming Warm-Up Exercises

1. Write a C++ value-returning function that returns `true` if all the values in a certain subarray of a two-dimensional array are positive, and returns `false` otherwise. The array (of type `TableType`), the number of columns in the subarray, and the number of rows in the subarray should be passed as parameters.
2. A *square array* is a two-dimensional array in which the number of rows is the same as the number of columns. Write a C++ function to initialize the two diagonals of a square `char` array to a specified character. The array (named `data`, of type `DataType`), the row and column lengths of the array (`length`), and the specified character (`someChar`) should be passed as parameters.
3. Write a C++ function `Copy` that takes an array `data`, defined to be NUM_ROWS by NUM_COLS, and copies the values into a second array `data2`, defined the same way. `data` and `data2` are of type `DataType`. The constants NUM_ROWS and NUM_COLS may be accessed globally.
4. Write a C++ function that finds the largest value in a two-dimensional `float` array of 50 rows and 50 columns.
5. Using the declarations in Exam Preparation Exercise 1, write functions to do the following tasks. Use proper style. Only constants may be accessed globally.
   a. Determine the team that sold the most tickets during the first week of ticket sales.
   b. Determine the week in which the second team sold the most tickets.
   c. Determine the week in which the most tickets were sold.
   d. Determine the team that sold the most tickets.
6. Using the declarations in Exam Preparation Exercise 2, write functions, in proper style, to do the following tasks. Only constants may be accessed globally.
   a. Determine which school spent the most money on football.
   b. Determine which sport the last school spent the most money on.
   c. Determine which school had the most students playing basketball.
   d. Determine in which sport the third school had the most students participating.
   e. Determine the total amount spent by all the schools on volleyball.
   f. Determine the total number of students who played any sport. (Assume that each student played only one sport.)
   g. Determine which school had the most students participating in sports.

h. Determine which was the most popular sport in terms of money spent.

i. Determine which was the most popular sport in terms of student participation.

7. Given the following declarations

```
const int NUM_DEPTS = 100;
const int NUM_STORES = 10;
const int NUM_MONTHS = 12;

typedef int SalesType[NUM_STORES][NUM_MONTHS][NUM_DEPTS];
```

write a C++ function to initialize an array of type `SalesType` to 0. The constants `NUM_STORES`, `NUM MONTHS`, and `NUM_DEPTS` may be accessed globally. The array should be passed as a parameter.

8. Sales figures are kept on items sold by store, by department, and by month. Write a C++ function to calculate and print the total number of items sold during the year by each department in each store. The data are stored in an array of type `SalesType` as defined in Programming Warm-Up Exercise 7. The array containing the data should be passed as a parameter. The constants `NUM_STORES`, `NUM_MONTHS`, and `NUM_DEPTS` may be accessed globally.

9. Write a C++ value-returning function that returns the sum of the elements in a specified row of an array. The array, the number of filled-in columns, and which row is to be totaled should be passed as parameters.

10. Outline a testing strategy that fully tests the Election program.

Programming Problems

1. A group of playing cards can be represented as a two-dimensional array, where the first dimension is rank and the second dimension is suit. Read in a bridge hand (13 cards) and determine whether the player should pass or bid. Each card should be input on a line by itself, with the suit given first and the rank next.

The decision to pass or bid is based on the number of points the hand is worth. Points are counted as follows:

An ace is worth 4 points.
A king is worth 3 points.
A queen is worth 2 points.
A jack is worth 1 point.

Add up the points in the hand and print one of the following messages.

Below 13 points,	"Pass"
From 13 through 16 points,	"Bid one of a suit"
From 17 through 19 points,	"Bid one no trump"
From 20 through 22 points,	"Bid one of a suit"
Over 22 points,	"Bid two of a suit"

2. Write an interactive program that plays tic-tac-toe. Represent the board as a three-by-three character array. Initialize the array to blanks and ask each player in turn to input

a position. The first player's position will be marked on the board with an *O*, and the second player's position will be marked with an *X*. Continue the process until a player wins or the game is a draw. To win, a player must have three marks in a row, in a column, or on a diagonal. A draw occurs when the board is full and no one has won.

Each player's position should be input as indices into the tic-tac-toe board—that is, a row number, a space, and a column number. Make the program user-friendly.

After each game, print out a diagram of the board showing the ending positions. Keep a count of the number of games each player has won and the number of draws. Before the beginning of each game, ask each player if he or she wishes to continue. If either player wishes to quit, print out the statistics and stop.

3. Write a C++ program to read in two 2-dimensional arrays, and then multiply one by the other. This is called matrix multiplication. For example, if `firstArray` (a 2-row by 2-column array) appears as

```
2   7
9   3
```

and `secondArray` (a 2-row by 1-column array) appears as

```
8
6
```

then the product matrix is

```
productMatrix[0][0] = 2 * 8 + 7 * 6
productMatrix[1][0] = 9 * 8 + 3 * 6
```

Matrix multiplication can be done only if the number of columns in the multiplicand (the first array) equals the number of rows in the multiplier (the second array).

The program should read in the two arrays, test to see if multiplication is possible, and then multiply them if it is. The output will be a printout of the two arrays and will either output the product array or print a message saying that multiplication is not possible.

4. Photos taken in space by the Galileo spacecraft are sent back to earth as a stream of numbers. Each number represents a level of brightness. A large number represents a high brightness level, and a small number represents a low level. Your job is to take a matrix (a two-dimensional array) of the numbers and print it as a picture.

One approach to generating a picture is to print a dark character (like a $) when the brightness level is low, and to print a light character (like a blank or a period) when the level is high. Unfortunately, errors in transmission sometimes occur. Thus, your program should first attempt to find and correct these errors. Assume a value is in error if it differs by more than one from each of its four neighboring values. Correct the erroneous value by giving it the average of its neighboring values, rounded to the nearest integer.

Example:

	5		The 2 would be regarded as an error and would be given
4	2	5	a corrected value of 5.
	5		

Note that values on the corners or boundaries of the matrix have to be processed differently than the values on the interior. Your program should print an image of the uncorrected picture and then an image of the corrected picture.

5. In competitive diving, each diver makes three dives of varying degrees of difficulty. Nine judges score each dive from 0 through 10 in steps of 0.5. The total score is obtained by discarding the lowest and highest of the judges' scores, adding the remaining scores, and then multiplying the scores by the degree of difficulty. The divers take turns, and when the competition is finished, they are ranked according to score. Write a program to do the above, using the following input and output specifications.

Input:

Number of divers

Diver's name (10 characters), difficulty (`float`), and judges' ratings (nine `float`s)

There is a line of data for each diver for each dive. All the data for Dive 1 are grouped together, then all for Dive 2, then all for Dive 3.

Output:

The input data, echo printed in tabular form with appropriate headings—for example, Name, Difficulty, judge's number (1–9)

A table that contains the following information, sorted by final total, in descending order (highest diver first):

Name	Dive 1	Dive 2	Dive 3	Total

where Name is the diver's name; Dive 1, Dive 2, and Dive 3 are the total points received for a single dive, as described above; and Total is the overall total

14 Records (C++ Structs)

record (structure, in C++)
A structured data type with a fixed number of components that are accessed by name, not by index. The components may be heterogeneous (of different types)

In the last three chapters, we looked in depth at a homogeneous structured data type called an array. We discussed common algorithms that are applied to arrays: sorting, linear searching, and binary searching. We added a data structures section to our functional decomposition. Clearly, how we choose to represent our data is an important aspect of the programming process.

Although the array is an extremely useful data structure, it can be used only when the components are all the same data type. In this chapter, we examine a *heterogeneous* (nonhomogeneous) structured data type called a **record.** The components of a record do not have to be of the same data type, and they are accessed by name rather than by relative position.

The last chapter closed with a discussion of how to choose a data structure. We continue this discussion at the end of this chapter, adding the record data type to our list of possible choices.

Records

*field (member,
in C++)*
*A component of a
record*

Records allow us to group related components together, regardless of their data types. Each component in a record is called a **field** of the record, and each field is given a name called the *field name*. C++ uses its own terminology with records. A record is called a **structure,** the fields of a record are called **members** of the structure, and each member has a *member name*.

In C++, record data types are most commonly declared according to the following syntax:

StructDeclaration

```
struct TypeName
{
    MemberList
};
```

where TypeName is an identifier giving a name to the data type, and MemberList is defined as

MemberList

```
DataType MemberName ;
DataType MemberName ;
            .
            .
            .
```

The reserved word `struct` is an abbreviation for *structure,* the C++ term for a record. Because the word *structure* has many other meanings in computer science, we'll use `struct` or *record* to avoid any possible confusion about what we are referring to.

You probably recognize the syntax of a member list as being nearly identical to a series of variable declarations. Be careful: a `struct` declaration is a type declaration, and we still must declare variables of this type for any memory locations to be associated with the member names. As an example, let's use a `struct` to describe a student in a class. We want to store the first and last names, the

We have formatted the initializer list vertically but could just as well have arranged it horizontally. Each value in the initializer list corresponds to one member of the `struct`. The two strings are stored into the `firstName` and `lastName` members, 3.24 is stored into the `gpa` member, 320 is stored into the `programGrade` member, and so forth.

The struct component `student.lastName` is an array. We can access the individual elements in this component just as we would access the elements of any other array: we give the name of the array followed by the index, which is enclosed in brackets.

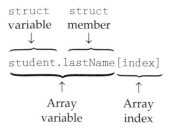

The expression `student.lastName[0]` would access the first letter in the last name, `student.firstName[1]` would access the second letter in the first name, and so on.

In addition to accessing individual components of a `struct` variable, we can in some cases manipulate `struct`s as a whole. C++ is more permissive about aggregate operations on `struct`s than on arrays, but there still are restrictions. The following table compares arrays and `struct`s with respect to aggregate operations:

Aggregate Operation	Arrays	Structs
I/O	No (except strings)	No
Assignment	No	Yes
Arithmetic	No	No
Comparison	No	No
Parameter passage	By reference only	By value or by reference
Return as a function's return value	No	Yes

According to the table, one `struct` variable can be assigned to another. However, both variables must be declared to be of the same type. For example, if `student` and `anotherStudent` are both declared to be of type `StudentRec`, the statement

overall grade point average prior to this class, the grade on programming assignments, the grade on quizzes, the final exam grade, and the final course grade.

```
// Type declarations

enum GradeType {A, B, C, D, F};

typedef char NameString[16];    // Max. 15 characters plus '\0'

struct StudentRec
{
    NameString firstName;
    NameString lastName;
    float      gpa;           // Grade point average
    int        programGrade;  // Assume 0..400
    int        quizGrade;     // Assume 0..300
    int        finalExam;     // Assume 0..300
    GradeType  courseGrade;
};

// Variable declarations

StudentRec firstStudent;
StudentRec student;
int        index;
int        grade;
```

Notice, both in this example and in the syntax template, that a `struct` declaration ends with a semicolon. By now, you have learned not to put a semicolon after the right brace of a compound statement. However, the member list in a `struct` declaration is not considered to be a compound statement; the braces are simply required syntax in the declaration. A `struct` declaration, like all C++ declaration statements, must end with a semicolon.

`firstName`, `lastName`, `gpa`, `programGrade`, `quizGrade`, `finalExam`, and `courseGrade` are member names within the `struct` type `StudentRec`. These member names make up the member list. Note that each member name is given a type.

`firstName` and `lastName` are of type `NameString`, which is a `char` array type. `gpa` is a `float` member. `programGrade`, `quizGrade`, and `finalExam` are `int` members. `courseGrade` is of an enumeration data type made up of the grades A through D and F.

None of these `struct` members are associated with memory locations until we declare a variable of the `StudentRec` type. `StudentRec` is merely a pattern for a `struct` (see Figure 14-1). The variables `firstStudent` and `student` are variables of type `StudentRec`.

FIGURE 14-1

Pattern for a struct

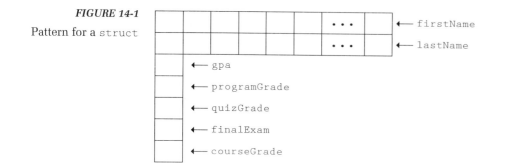

FIGURE 14-2

struct Variable
student with
Member Selectors

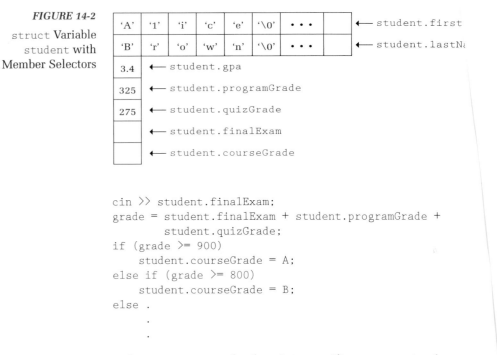

member selector
The expression used to access components of a struct *variable. It is formed by using the* struct *variable name and the member name, separated by a dot (period)*

The members of a struct variable are accessed by giving the name of the variable, followed by a dot (period), and then the member name. This expression is called a **member selector.** The syntax template is

MemberSelector

StructVariable . MemberName

Just as brackets ([ ]) are used to select individual components of an array, *dot notation* is used to select individual components of a struct. To access the grade point average of firstStudent, we would write

```
firstStudent.gpa
```

To access the final exam score of student, we would write

```
student.finalExam
```

The component of a struct accessed by the member selector is treated just like any other variable of the same type. Figure 14-2 shows the struct variable student with the member selector for each member. In this example, values are already stored in some of the components.

Let's demonstrate the use of these member selectors. Using our student variable, the following code segment reads in a final exam grade; adds up the program grade, the quiz grade, and the final exam grade; and then assigns a letter grade to the result.

```
cin >> student.finalExam;
grade = student.finalExam + student.programGrade +
        student.quizGrade;
if (grade >= 900)
    student.courseGrade = A;
else if (grade >= 800)
    student.courseGrade = B;
else .
     .
     .
```

Just as we can read values into specific components of an array, values into members of a struct. The statement

```
cin >> student.finalExam;
```

reads a value from the standard input device and stores the value finalExam member of student. As with arrays, we *cannot* read in struct as an aggregate; we must read values into a struct one m a time.

An alternative to reading in values is to initialize a struct in its dec The syntax is similar to the initialization of an array: you provide a list values, separate the values with commas, and enclose the whole list braces. Here's an example of declaring and initializing the variable stu

```
StudentRec student =
{
    "John",
    "Smith",
    3.24,
    320,
    290,
    95,
    B
};
```

```
anotherStudent = student;
```

copies the entire contents of the `struct` variable `student` to the variable `anotherStudent`, member by member.

An entire `struct` can also be passed as a parameter, either by value or by reference, and a `struct` can be returned as the value of a value-returning function. Let's define a function that takes a `StudentRec` variable as a parameter.

The task of this function is to determine if a student's grade in a course is consistent with his or her overall grade point average (GPA). We define *consistent* to mean that the course grade is the same as the rounded GPA. The GPA is calculated on a 4-point scale, where A is 4, B is 3, C is 2, D is 1, and F is 0. If the rounded GPA is 4 and the course grade is A, then the function returns true. If the rounded GPA is 4 and the course grade is not A, then the function returns false. Each of the other grades is tested in the same way.

The `Consistent` function is coded below. The formal parameter `aStudent`, a `struct` of type `StudentRec`, is passed by value. (Assume that the data type `Boolean` has been defined previously.)

```
Boolean Consistent( /* in */ StudentRec aStudent )

{
    int roundedGPA = int(aStudent.gpa + 0.5);

    switch (roundedGPA)
    {
        case 0: return (aStudent.courseGrade == F);
        case 1: return (aStudent.courseGrade == D);
        case 2: return (aStudent.courseGrade == C);
        case 3: return (aStudent.courseGrade == B);
        case 4: return (aStudent.courseGrade == A);
    }
}
```

Let's look at another example. A parts wholesaler wants to computerize her operation. Until now, she has kept the inventory on handwritten 8 × 10 cards. A typical inventory card contains the following data:

Part number: 1A3321
Description: Cotter pin
Cost: 0.012
Quantity on hand: 2100

A `struct` is a natural choice for describing a part. Each item on the inventory card can be a member of the `struct`. The relevant declarations look like this:

```
typedef char String6[7];
typedef char String20[21];

struct PartType
{
    String6  partNumber;
    String20 description;
    float    cost;
    int      quantity;
};


PartType part;
```

The left and right braces surround the member list, and a semicolon terminates the `struct` declaration.

Once the `struct` variable `part` has been declared, member selectors can be used in expressions such as

```
part.quantity = part.quantity + 24;
if (part.cost <= 5.00)
    cout << part.description << ' ' << part.cost;
```

If the parts wholesaler supplies inventory data that look like

```
2B3310Ring, piston       2.95   15
```

then the following program segment would read and store the data into the appropriate members.

```
cin.get(part.partNumber, 7);
cin.get(part.description, 21);
cin >> part.cost >> part.quantity;
```

To complete our initial look at C++ `structs`, we give a more complete syntax template for a `struct` type declaration:

StructDeclaration

```
struct TypeName
{
    MemberList
} VariableList ;
```

As you can see in the syntax template, two items are optional: TypeName (the name of the `struct` type being declared), and a list of variable names between the right brace and the semicolon. Our examples thus far have declared a type name but have not included a variable list. The variable list allows you not only to declare a `struct` type but also to declare variables of that type, all in one statement. In this book, we avoid combining variable declarations with type declarations, preferring to keep the two notions separate.

If you omit the type name but include the variable list, you create an anonymous type. All the arguments given in Chapter 10 against anonymous typing of enumeration types apply to `struct` types as well.

Arrays of Records

Although single records can be useful, many applications require a collection of records. For example, a business needs a list of parts records, and a teacher needs a list of students in a class. Arrays are ideal for these applications. We simply define an array whose components are records.

Let's define a grade book to be a list of students as follows:

```
const int MAX_STUDENTS = 150;

enum GradeType {A, B, C, D, F};

typedef char NameString[16];

struct StudentRec
{
    NameString firstName;
    NameString lastName;
    float      gpa;
    int        programGrade;
    int        quizGrade;
    int        finalExam;
    GradeType  courseGrade;
};

StudentRec gradeBook[MAX_STUDENTS];
int        length;
int        count;
```

This data structure can be visualized as shown in Figure 14-3.

An element of `gradeBook` is selected by an index. For example, `gradeBook[2]` is the third component in the array variable `gradeBook`. Each

FIGURE 14-3   Array `gradeBook` with Records as Elements

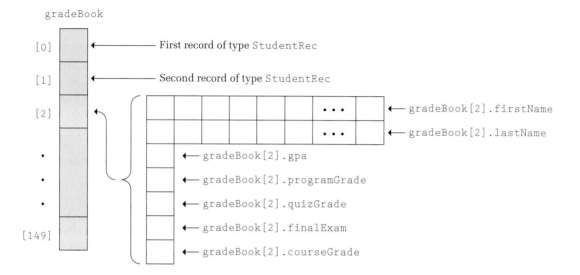

component of `gradeBook` is a record of type `StudentRec`. To access the course grade of the third student, we use the following expression:

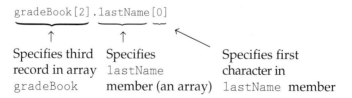

To access the first character in the last name of the third student, we use the following expression:

gradeBook[2].lastName[0]

Specifies third   Specifies   Specifies first
record in array   lastName   character in
gradeBook   member (an array)   lastName member

The following code fragment prints the first and last names of each student in the class:

```
for (count = 0; count < length; count++)
    cout << gradeBook[count].firstName << ' '
         << gradeBook[count].lastName << endl;
```

Hierarchical Records

We have seen examples where the components of a record are simple variables and arrays. A component of a record can also be another record. Records whose components are themselves records are called **hierarchical records.**

hierarchical records
Records in which at least one of the components is itself a record

Let's look at an example where a hierarchical structure is appropriate. A small machine shop keeps information about each of its machines. There is descriptive information, such as the identification number, a description of the machine, the purchase date, and the cost. Statistical information is also kept, such as the number of down days, the failure rate, and the date of last service. What is a reasonable way of representing all this information? First, let's look at a flat (nonhierarchical) record structure that holds this information.

```
typedef char String50[51];

struct MachineRec
{
    int       idNumber;
    String50  description;
    float     failRate;
    int       lastServicedMonth;  // Assume 1..12
    int       lastServicedDay;    // Assume 1..31
    int       lastServicedYear;   // Assume 1900..2050
    int       downDays;
    int       purchaseDateMonth;  // Assume 1..12
    int       purchaseDateDay;    // Assume 1..31
    int       purchaseDateYear;   // Assume 1900..2050
    float     cost;
};
```

Type `MachineRec` has 11 members. There is so much detailed information here that it is difficult to quickly get a feeling for what the record represents. Let's see if we can reorganize it into a hierarchical structure that makes more sense. We can divide the information into two groups: information that changes and information that does not. There are also two dates to be kept: date of purchase and date of last service. These observations suggest use of a record describing a date, a record describing the statistical data, and an overall record containing the other two as components. The following type declaration reflects this structure.

```
const int NUM_MACHINES = 25;

typedef char String50[51];
struct DateType
{
    int month;   // Assume 1..12
    int day;     // Assume 1..31
    int year;    // Assume 1900..2050
};
struct StatisticsType
{
    float     failRate;
    DateType lastServiced;
    int       downDays;
};
struct MachineRec
{
    int           idNumber;
    String50      description;
    StatisticsType history;
    DateType      purchaseDate;
    float         cost;
};


MachineRec inventory[NUM_MACHINES];
MachineRec machine;
int        counter;
```

The contents of a machine record are now much more obvious. Two of the components of the struct type MachineRec are themselves structs: purchaseDate is of struct type DateType, and history is of struct type StatisticsType. One of the components of struct type StatisticsType is a struct of type DateType.

How do we access a hierarchical structure such as this one? We build the accessing expressions (member selectors) for the members of the embedded structs from left to right, beginning with the struct variable name. Following are some expressions and the components they access.

Expression	Component Accessed
`machine.purchaseDate`	`DateType struct` **variable**
`machine.purchaseDate.month`	`month` **member of a** `DateType struct` **variable**
`machine.purchaseDate.year`	`year` **member of a** `DateType struct` **variable**
`machine.history.lastServiced.year`	`year` **member of a** `DateType struct` **variable contained in a** `struct` **of type** `StatisticsType`

Figure 14-4 is a pictorial representation of `machine` with values. Look carefully at how each component is accessed.

We can, of course, have an array of hierarchical records; `inventory` is such an array. We can access the year that the first machine was purchased using the following expression:

```
inventory[0].purchaseDate.year
```

And here is a code segment that prints out the ID number and the year of purchase of each machine that has a failure rate of more than 8 percent:

```
for (counter = 0; counter < NUM_MACHINES; counter++)
    if (inventory[counter].history.failRate > 0.08)
        cout << inventory[counter].idNumber << ' '
             << inventory[counter].purchaseDate.year << endl;
```

Unions

In Chapter 11, we presented a diagram (Figure 11-2) showing the structured types available in C++. We repeat this diagram in Figure 14-5.

So far we have discussed two of the four structured types: arrays and `structs`. We now look briefly at *union* types. The fourth structured type—the class—is the topic of Chapter 15.

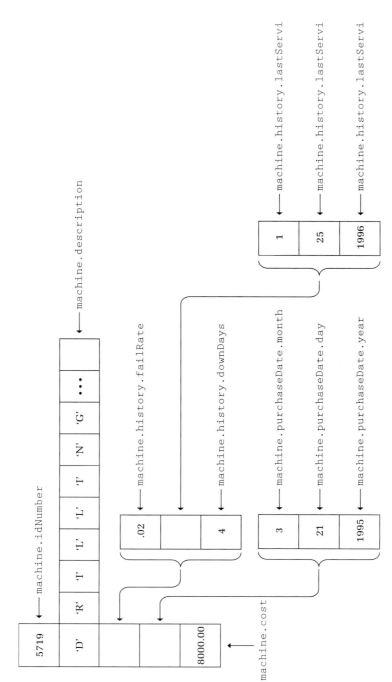

FIGURE 14-4 Hierarchical Records in machine Variable

FIGURE 14-5

C++ Structured
Types

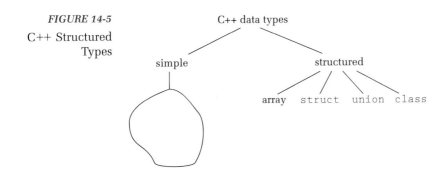

In C++, a union is defined to be a `struct` that holds only one of its members at a time during program execution. Here is a declaration of a union type and a union variable:

```
union WeightType
{
    long  wtInOunces;
    int   wtInPounds;
    float wtInTons;
};
WeightType weight;
```

The syntax for declaring a union type is identical to that of a `struct` type, except that the word `union` is substituted for `struct`.

At run time, the memory space allocated to the variable `weight` does *not* include room for three distinct components. Instead, `weight` can contain only one of the following: *either* a `long` value *or* an `int` value *or* a `float` value. The assumption is that the program will never need a weight in ounces, a weight in pounds, and a weight in tons simultaneously while executing. The purpose of a union is to conserve memory by forcing several values to use the same memory space, one at a time. The following code shows how the `weight` variable might be used.

```
weight.wtInTons = 4.83;
    .
    .
    .
// Weight in tons is no longer needed. Reuse the memory space.

weight.wtInPounds = 35;
    .
    .
    .
```

After the last assignment statement, the previous `float` value 4.83 is gone, replaced by the `int` value 35.

It's quite reasonable to argue that a union is not a data structure at all. It does not represent a collection of values; it represents only a single value from among several *potential* values. On the other hand, unions are grouped together with the structured types because of their similarity to `struct`s.

There is much more to be said about unions, including subtle issues related to their declaration and usage. However, these issues are more appropriate in an advanced study of data structures and systems programming. We have introduced unions only to present a complete picture of the structured types provided by C++ and to acquaint you with the general idea in case you encounter unions in other C++ programs.

More on Choosing Data Structures

Representing Logical Entities with Hierarchical Records

We have demonstrated how to design algorithms and data structures in parallel. We progress from the logical or abstract data structure envisioned at the top level through the refinement process until we reach the concrete coding in C++. We have also shown two ways of representing the logical structure of a machine record in a shop inventory. The first used a record where all the components in an entry were defined (made concrete) at the same time. The second used a hierarchical record where the dates and statistics describing a machine's history were defined in lower-level records.

Let's look again at the two different ways in which we represented our logical data structure.

```
typedef char String50[51];

// ** Version 1 **

struct MachineRec
{
    int       idNumber;
    String50  description;
    float     failRate;
    int       lastServicedMonth;   // Assume 1..12
    int       lastServicedDay;     // Assume 1..31
    int       lastServicedYear;    // Assume 1900..2050
    int       downDays;
    int       purchaseDateMonth;   // Assume 1..12
    int       purchaseDateDay;     // Assume 1..31
    int       purchaseDateYear;    // Assume 1900..2050
    float     cost;
};
```

```
// ** Version 2 **

struct DateType
{
    int month;   // Assume 1..12
    int day;     // Assume 1..31
    int year;    // Assume 1900..2050
};
struct StatisticsType
{
    float     failRate;
    DateType  lastServiced;
    int       downDays;
};
struct MachineRec
{
    int            idNumber;
    String50       description;
    StatisticsType history;
    DateType       purchaseDate;
    float          cost;
};
```

Which of these two representations is better? The second one is better for two reasons.

First, it groups elements together logically. The statistics and the dates are entities within themselves. We may want to have a date or a machine history in another record structure. If we define the dates and statistics only within `MachineRec` (as in the first structure), we would have to define them again for every other data structure that needs them, giving us multiple definitions of the same logical entity.

Second, the details of the entities (statistics and dates) are pushed down to a lower level in the second structure. The principle of deferring details to as low a level as possible should be applied to designing data structures as well as to designing algorithms. How a machine history or a date is represented is not relevant to our concept of a machine record, so the details need not be specified until it is time to write the algorithms to manipulate those members.

Pushing the implementation details of a data type to a lower level separates the logical description from the implementation. The separation of the logical properties of a data type from its implementation details is called **data abstraction,** which is a goal of effective programming and the foundation upon which abstract data types are built. (We introduced the concept of abstract data types briefly in Chapter 12 and explore them more fully in Chapter 15.)

www.jbpub.com/C++links

data abstraction
The separation of a data type's logical properties from its implementation

Eventually, all the logical properties have to be defined in terms of concrete data types and routines written to manipulate them. If the implementation is properly designed, we can use the same routines to manipulate the structure in a wide variety of applications. For example, if we have a routine to compare dates, that routine can be used to compare dates representing days on which equipment was bought or maintained, or dates representing people's birthdays. The concept of designing a low-level structure and writing routines to manipulate it is the basis for C++ class types, which we examine in Chapter 15.

PROGRAMMING EXAMPLE

Campaigning for a Candidate

Problem: A friend is running for City Council. It's down to the wire, and we want to call all those people who showed an interest in our friend and remind them to vote on election day. We have three different lists of people we should call. We don't want to annoy people by calling them twice—or worse still, three times—so we decide to merge the three lists and remove any duplicates.

Input: Three input files (`file1`, `file2`, and `file3`), each containing a sequence of lines in the form

```
Jones Arthur 612 374-6715
```

A person's last name (maximum 15 characters with no blanks), first name (maximum 15 characters with no blanks), area code (integer), and phone number (8 characters) are separated by one or more blanks. The people's records are in alphabetical order by last name. A sentinel record containing all Zs for the last name signals the end of each file. The values on the rest of this line can be anything:

```
ZZZZZZZZZZZZZZZ A 111 111-1111
```

Output: The records from `file1`, `file2`, and `file3` merged onto file `masterFile`, which should have the same form as the three input files.

Discussion: One of our problem-solving heuristics is to solve simpler problems first. Let's solve the problem for two lists, and then expand the solution to three lists.

How would we do this process by hand if we had two stacks of index cards? We would take the top card from each stack and compare the names. If they were the same, we would put one in a new stack and throw the other one away. If they weren't the same, we would put the card with the name that came first alphabetically in the new stack and take a replacement card from the stack that the card came from. We would repeat this process until one of the stacks of index cards became empty. Then we would move the rest of the other stack to the new one. Of course, the lists might both end at the same time with a duplicate name.

We can employ this same process to solve the problem using two computer lists. Rather than having two stacks of index cards, we have two computer files. Examining the next person's record is the equivalent of "take a replacement card from that stack."

Now that we have solved the problem for two files, we can expand the solution to three files. We can merge the first two files and store the result into a temporary list, then merge that list with the records from the third file.

Data Structures: We use a `struct` type to represent one person's information:

```
typedef char String15[16];        // Room for 15 characters plus '\0'
struct PersonRec
{
    String15  lastName;
    String15  firstName;
    PhoneType phone;
};
```

where `PhoneType` is itself a `struct` type.

```
typedef char String8[9];          // Room for 8 characters plus '\0'
struct PhoneType
{
    int     areaCode;      // Range 100..999
    String8 phoneNumber;
};
```

Notice that `PersonRec` is therefore a hierarchical record type.

To store the records from the input files and merge them, we use four one-dimensional arrays whose components are of type `PersonRec`:

PROGRAMMING EXAMPLE cont'd

```
const int MAX_RECS = 100;        // Max. no. of records in a file
                                 //   (including sentinel record)
PersonRec firstList[MAX_RECS];   // Records from an input file
PersonRec secondList[MAX_RECS];  // Records from an input file
PersonRec tempList[MAX_RECS*2];  // Temporary merged list
PersonRec masterList[MAX_RECS*3]; // Final merged list
```

Each of `firstList` and `secondList` holds the records from one input file. The `tempList` array must be large enough to hold the merged records from two input files, and `masterList` holds the merged records from all three files.

```
//*********************************************************************
// MergeLists program
// This program merges sorted data from three files
// onto a master file with no duplicates.
//*********************************************************************
#include <iostream.h>
#include <fstream.h>            // For file I/O
#include <string.h>            // For strcmp()

const char SENTINEL[] = "ZZZZZZZZZZZZZZZ";
const int MAX_RECS = 100;       // Max. no. of records in a file
                                //   (including sentinel record)

typedef char String8[9];        // Room for 8 characters plus '\0'
typedef char String15[16];      // Room for 15 characters plus '\0'

struct PhoneType
{
    int     areaCode;           // Range 100..999
    String8 phoneNumber;
};

struct PersonRec
{
    String15  lastName;
    String15  firstName;
    PhoneType phone;
};
```

PROGRAMMING EXAMPLE cont'd

```cpp
void Append( const PersonRec[], const PersonRec[], PersonRec[],
             int&, int&, int& );
void GetRecords( ifstream&, PersonRec[] );
void Merge( const PersonRec[], const PersonRec[], PersonRec[] );
void OpenForInput( ifstream& );
void OpenForOutput( ofstream& );
void Write( const PersonRec[], ofstream& );

int main()
{
    PersonRec firstList[MAX_RECS];      // Records from an input file
    PersonRec secondList[MAX_RECS];     // Records from an input file
    PersonRec tempList[MAX_RECS*2];     // Temporary merged list
    PersonRec masterList[MAX_RECS*3];   // Final merged list
    ifstream file1;                     // Input file
    ifstream file2;                     // Input file
    ifstream file3;                     // Input file
    ofstream masterFile;                // Output file

    OpenForInput(file1);
    if ( !file1 )
        return 1;
    OpenForInput(file2);
    if ( !file2 )
        return 1;
    OpenForInput(file3);
    if ( !file3 )
        return 1;
    OpenForOutput(masterFile);
    if ( !masterFile )
        return 1;

    GetRecords(file1, firstList);
    GetRecords(file2, secondList);
    Merge(firstList, secondList, tempList);
    GetRecords(file3, firstList);
    Merge(firstList, tempList, masterList);
    Write(masterList, masterFile);
    return 0;
}
```

PROGRAMMING EXAMPLE cont'd

```
//*********************************************************************

void OpenForInput( /* inout */ ifstream& someFile )    // File to be
                                                       // opened
// Prompts for name of input file and opens it

// Postcondition:
//     The user has been prompted for a file name
//  && IF the file could not be opened
//          An error message has been printed
// Note:
//     Upon return, caller must test stream state

{
    char fileName[51];   // User-specified file name (max. 50 chars)

    cout << "Input file name: ";
    cin.get(fileName, 51);
    cin.ignore(100, '\n');

    someFile.open(fileName);
    if ( !someFile )
        cout << "** Can't open " << fileName << " **" << endl;
}

//*********************************************************************

void OpenForOutput( /* inout */ ofstream& someFile )    // File to be
                                                        // opened
// Prompts for name of output file and opens it

// Postcondition:
//     The user has been prompted for a file name
//  && IF the file could not be opened
//          An error message has been printed
// Note:
//     Upon return, caller must test stream state

{
    char fileName[51];   // User-specified file name (max. 50 chars)

    cout << "Output file name: ";
    cin.get(fileName, 51);
    cin.ignore(100, '\n');
```

PROGRAMMING EXAMPLE cont'd

```
        someFile.open(fileName);
        if ( !someFile )
            cout << "** Can't open " << fileName << " **" << endl;
}


//*******************************************************************


void GetRecords( /* inout */ ifstream& inFile,    // Input file
                 /* out */   PersonRec list[] )  // List receiving
                                                 //   input records
// Reads people's records from inFile into array "list"

// Precondition:
//     inFile has been successfully opened for input
//   && inFile contains at least one record and at most MAX_RECS
//      records, including the sentinel record
//   && People's last names and first names are at most
//      15 characters each
// Postcondition:
//     Assuming inFile contains N records (including the
//     sentinel record), list[0..N-1] contain the input records

{
    int index = 0;   // Array index
    do
    {

        inFile >> list[index].lastName
               >> list[index].firstName
               >> list[index].phone.areaCode
               >> list[index].phone.phoneNumber;
        index++;
    } while (strcmp(list[index-1].lastName, SENTINEL) != 0);
}


//*******************************************************************


void Merge( /* in */ const PersonRec list1[],     // List to merge
            /* in */ const PersonRec list2[],     // List to merge
            /* out */      PersonRec mergedList[] ) // Resulting
                                                  //   merged list


// Merges list1 and list2 into mergedList
```

PROGRAMMING EXAMPLE cont'd

```
// Precondition:
//      The elements of list1 and list2 are in ascending order
//      of last name, and both contain sentinel records
//   && The size of mergedList is at least as large as the
//      length of list1 plus the length of list2
// Postcondition:
//      mergedList contains the elements of both list1 and list2
//      in ascending order of last name without duplicates
//   && The last element of mergedList is the (only) sentinel record


{
    int index1 = 0;   // Index variable for list1
    int index2 = 0;   // Index variable for list2
    int index3 = 0;   // Index variable for mergedList
    int strRelation;  // Result of comparing two last names


    while (strcmp(list1[index1].lastName, SENTINEL) != 0 &&
           strcmp(list2[index2].lastName, SENTINEL) != 0  )
    {
        strRelation = strcmp(list1[index1].lastName,
                             list2[index2].lastName);
        if (strRelation < 0)
        {
            // Assert: Last name in 1st list is less than in 2nd
            mergedList[index3] = list1[index1];
            index1++;
        }
        else if (strRelation > 0)

        {
            // Assert: Last name in 1st list is greater than in 2nd
            mergedList[index3] = list2[index2];
            index2++;
        }
        else
        {
            // Assert: Last names are the same in both lists
            mergedList[index3] = list1[index1];
            index1++;
            index2++;
        }
        index3++;
    }
    Append(list1, list2, mergedList, index1, index2, index3);
}
```

PROGRAMMING EXAMPLE cont'd

```
//*********************************************************************

void Append(
  /* in */    const PersonRec  list1[],      // List being merged
  /* in */    const PersonRec  list2[],      // List being merged
  /* inout */       PersonRec  mergedList[], // Resulting list
  /* inout */       int&       index1,       // Index for list1
  /* inout */       int&       index2,       // Index for list2
  /* inout */       int&       index3     )  // Index for mergedList

// Appends remainder of either list1 or list2 to mergedList

// Precondition:
//     Either list1[index1] contains the sentinel record
//     or list2[index2] contains the sentinel record, or both do
// Postcondition:
//     IF list1[index1@entry] contains the sentinel record
//         Remainder of list2 (except the sentinel) is
//         appended to mergedList@entry
//     ELSE
//         Remainder of list1 (except the sentinel) is
//         appended to mergedList@entry
//  && The last element of mergedList is the (only) sentinel record

{
    // Append rest of list1, if more exists

    while (strcmp(list1[index1].lastName, SENTINEL) != 0)
    {
        mergedList[index3] = list1[index1];
        index1++;
        index3++;
    }

    // Append rest of list2, if more exists

    while (strcmp(list2[index2].lastName, SENTINEL) != 0)
    {
        mergedList[index3] = list2[index2];
        index2++;
        index3++;
    }

    // Store sentinel record

    mergedList[index3] = list2[index2];
}
```

PROGRAMMING EXAMPLE cont'd

```
//*****************************************************************

void Write( /* in */    const PersonRec masterList[],  // Merged list
            /* inout */       ofstream& masterFile   ) // Output file

// Writes the contents of masterList to masterFile
// Precondition:
//     masterFile has been successfully opened for output
//  && masterList ends with a sentinel record
// Postcondition:
//     Contents of masterList have been written to masterFile

{
    int index = 0;   // Array index

    do
    {
        masterFile << masterList[index].lastName << ' '
                   << masterList[index].firstName << ' '
                   << masterList[index].phone.areaCode << ' '
                   << masterList[index].phone.phoneNumber << endl;
        index++;
    } while (strcmp(masterList[index-1].lastName, SENTINEL) != 0);
}
```

Testing: Because we have three input files, there are several cases to test.

1. `file1` is empty.
2. `file2` is empty.
3. `file3` is empty.
4. `file2` and `file3` are empty.
5. `file1` and `file3` are empty.
6. `file1` and `file2` are empty.
7. All three files are empty.
8. All three files have values.

There are data-dependent conditions that should be tested as well:

1. The files should be tested with each one containing the name that comes first in the alphabet.
2. The files should be tested with each pair containing duplicate names in the first position, an intermediate position, and the last position.
3. The files should be tested with each one containing the name that comes last in the alphabet.

PROGRAMMING EXAMPLE cont'd

It may be more trouble than it is worth to thoroughly test this program using the procedure outlined above. If the program is to be used only once, three short files with values might suffice. If this program is to be used more than once, however, it should be tested rigorously.

Before leaving this problem, we should talk about efficiency. When we input the data from a file into an array, the program stores the sentinel record into the array as well. Every loop that processes the array checks for the end of the list by invoking the strcmp library function. If each input file contains 100 people's records, the strcmp function is called hundreds of times. This is very time-consuming as strcmp itself uses a loop to compare characters in two strings. It would make more sense for the GetRecords function to return the integer length of the list instead of storing the sentinel record into the array. Thereafter, each loop could use the length of the list to control the number of loop iterations.

If this program were to be run several times, it would be worthwhile to re-code it so that function GetRecords returns the length of a list and the other functions make use of the appropriate list lengths. Programming Warm-Up Exercise 15 asks you to do this.

Testing and Debugging

As we have demonstrated in many examples in this chapter and the last, it is possible to combine data structures in various ways: structs whose components are arrays, structs whose components are structs, arrays whose components are arrays (multidimensional arrays), and arrays whose components are structs. When arrays and structs are combined, there can be confusion about precisely where to place the operators for struct member selection (.) and array element selection ([ ]).

To summarize the correct placement of these operators, let's use the StudentRec type we introduced at the beginning of the chapter:

```
typedef char NameString[16];

struct StudentRec
{
    NameString firstName;
    NameString lastName;
    float      gpa;
    .
    .
    .
};
```

If we declare a variable of type StudentRec

```
StudentRec student;
```

then what is the syntax for selecting the first letter of a student's last name (that is, for selecting element 0 of the lastName member of student)? The dot operator is a binary (two-operand) operator; its left operand denotes a struct variable, and its right operand is a member name:

StructVariable . MemberName

The [ ] operator is a unary (one-operand) operator; it comes immediately after an expression denoting an array:

Array [IndexExpression]

Therefore, the expression

```
student
```

denotes a struct; the expression

```
student.lastName
```

denotes an array; and the expression

```
student.lastName[0]
```

denotes a character—the character that is located in element 0 of the student.lastName array.

With arrays of structs, again you have to be sure that the [] and . operators are in the proper positions. Given the declaration

```
StudentRec gradeBook[150];
```

we can access the gpa member of the first element of the gradeBook array with the expression

```
gradeBook[0].gpa
```

The index [0] is correctly attached to the identifier gradeBook because gradeBook is the name of an array. Furthermore, the expression

```
gradeBook[0]
```

denotes a struct, so the dot operator selects the gpa member of this struct.

Another potential source of confusion when working with structs is the scope of member names. Member names must be unique within a struct. Additionally, we mentioned in Chapter 8 that there are three kinds of scope in C++: local scope, file (global) scope, and *class scope*. Class scope applies to the member names within structs, unions, and classes (the topic of Chapter 15). To say that a struct member name has class scope means that the name is local to that struct. If the same identifier happens to be declared outside the struct, the two identifiers are unrelated. For example, name is such a meaningful identifier that it might be used logically in more than one struct. Look at the following declarations:

```
const int CLASS_SIZE = 120;
const int NUM_CITIES = 1000;

typedef char String20[21];

enum YearType {FRESHMAN, SOPHOMORE, JUNIOR, SENIOR};

struct PersonType
{
    String20 name;
    YearType year;
    int      age;
};
struct CityType
{
    String20 name;
    String20 state;
    int      elevation;
};

PersonType oneStudent;
String20   name;
PersonType roster[CLASS_SIZE];
CityType   city[NUM_CITIES];
```

The declarations are valid, even though the identifier name is declared in three places: as a string variable, a member name in the PersonType struct, and a member name in the CityType struct. No ambiguities arise because name, oneStudent.name, roster[i].name, and city[i].name are all unique. No ambiguities arise for the compiler, that is; but ambiguities can arise for someone reading the program. Using the same identifier in several different contexts can lead to confusion or hard-to-detect errors. In general, it is wisest to create struct member names that are different from those in other struct types and that are different from non-struct variable names.

Testing and Debugging Hints

1. The declaration of a `struct` type must end with a semicolon.
2. Be sure to specify the full member selector when referencing a component of a `struct` variable.
3. When using arrays within `struct`s or arrays of `struct`s, be sure to attach the index to the array name when accessing individual components of the array.
4. Process each member of a `struct` separately, except when assigning one `struct` variable to another (of the same type), passing the `struct` as a parameter, or returning the `struct` as a function return value.
5. Be cautious about using the same member names in different `struct` types. It is allowed but may be confusing.
6. Do not use anonymous `struct` types.

Summary

The record is a data structure for grouping together heterogeneous data—data that are of different types. Individual components of a record are accessed by name rather than by relative position, as in an array. In C++, records are referred to as *structures* or as `struct`s. We can use a `struct` variable to refer to the `struct` as a whole, or we can use a member selector to access any individual member (component) of the `struct`. Entire `struct`s of the same type may be assigned directly to each other, passed as parameters, or returned as function return values. Comparison of `struct`s, however, must be done member by member. Reading and writing of `struct`s must also be done member by member. We can build quite complex structures made up of arrays of `struct`s, where the components of the `struct`s are themselves arrays and `struct`s.

Applying the top-down, defer-details principle to data structures is an example of data abstraction. The logical description of the data structure is at a higher level. The details of how the data structure is implemented are pushed down to a lower level.

Quick Check

1. Write the type declaration for a `struct` data type named `TimeType` with three members: `hour`, `minute`, and `second`. The hour member is intended to store integer values from 0 through 23. The other two members store values from 0 through 59. (pp. 458–459)
2. Assume a variable named `now`, of type `TimeType`, has been declared. Write the assignment statements necessary to store the time 8:37:28 into `now`. (pp. 460–462)
3. Declare a hierarchical record type named `Interval` that consists of two members of type `TimeType`. The members are named `past` and `present`. (pp. 467–469)

4. Assume a variable named `channelCrossing`, of type `Interval`, has been declared. Write the assignment statements necessary to store the time 7:12:44 into the `past` member of `channelCrossing`. Write the assignment statement that stores the contents of variable `now` into the `present` member of `channelCrossing`. (pp. 467–469)
5. Declare a variable `boatTimes` that is an array of `Interval` values to be indexed by an enumeration type named `BoatNames`:

```
enum BoatNames {LUCKY, MY_PRIDE, SWELL_STUFF};
```

Then write a statement that stores the contents of variable `now` into the `present` member of the `struct` for the boat named "Swell Stuff." (pp. 465–466)
6. Decide what form of data structure is appropriate for the following problem. A single card in a library catalog system must contain the call number, author, title, and description of a single book. (pp. 472–474)
7. What is the primary purpose of C++ union types? (pp. 470–472)

Answers
1. ```
struct TimeType
{
    int hour;   // Range 0..23
    int minute;   // Range 0..59
    int second;   // Range 0..59
};
```
2. ```
now.hour = 8;
now.minute = 37;
now.second = 28;
```
3. ```
struct Interval
{
    TimeType past;
    TimeType present;
};
```
4. ```
channelCrossing.past.hour = 7;
channelCrossing.past.minute = 12;
channelCrossing.past.second = 44;
channelCrossing.present = now;
```
5. ```
Interval boatTimes[3];
boatTimes[SWELL_STUFF].present = now;
```
6. A simple `struct` with four members is sufficient.   7. The primary purpose is to save memory by forcing different values to share the same memory space, one at a time.

## Exam Preparation Exercises

1. Define the following terms:

   record (`struct` in C++)
   member
   member selector
   hierarchical record
   data abstraction
```

2. Given the declarations

```
typedef char CodeString[26];    // Max. 25 characters plus '\0'

enum StyleType {FORMAL, BRIEF};

struct RefType
{
    CodeString token[2000];
    CodeString symbol[20];
};
struct MapType
{
    CodeString mapCode;
    StyleType  style;
    RefType    chart;
};

MapType    guide[200];
MapType    aMap;
RefType    aRef;
int        count;
CodeString aCode;
```

mark each of the following statements as valid or invalid. (Assume that all the valid variables have been assigned values.)

Statement	Valid	Invalid
a. `if (aMap.style == BRIEF)` `count++;`	___	___
b. `guide[1].chart.token[2] = aMap;`	___	___
c. `guide[6].chart = aRef;`	___	___
d. `strcpy(aMap.mapCode[0], aRef.token[0]);`	___	___
e. `guide[100].chart.token[1][2] = aCode[2];`	___	___
f. `guide[20].token[1] = aCode;`	___	___
g. `if (guide[20].style == FORMAL)` `guide[20].chart.token[0][0] = 'A';`	___	___
h. `aMap = guide[5];`	___	___
i. `aMap.chart = aRef;`	___	___

3. Using the declarations in Exercise 2, write a single statement to do each of the following:
   a. Assign the value of the `chart` member of the seventy-first element of `guide` to the variable `aRef`.
   b. Copy the first element of the `token` member of the `chart` member of the eighty-eighth element of `guide` to the variable `aCode`.
   c. Assign the value 'X' to the first element of the twenty-third element of the `token` member of the `chart` member of the ninety-fourth element of `guide`.
   d. Copy the fourth element of the `mapCode` member of `aMap` to the ninth element of the twentieth element of the `symbol` member of `aRef`.

4. What are the two basic differences between a record and an array?
5. A hierarchical record structure may not contain another hierarchical record structure as a member. (True or False?)
6. If the members of a record are all the same data type, an array data structure could be used instead. (True or False?)
7. For each of the following descriptions of data, determine which general type of data structure (array, record, array of records, or hierarchical record) is appropriate.
   a. A payroll entry with a name, address, and pay rate.
   b. A person's address.
   c. An inventory entry for a part.
   d. A list of addresses.
   e. A list of hourly temperatures.
   f. A list of passengers on an airliner, including names, addresses, fare class, and seat assignment.
   g. A departmental telephone directory with last name and extension number.
   h. A street name.
8. Given the declarations

```
typedef char String20[21];

struct DateType
{
     int month;
     int day;
     int year;
};
struct InfoType
{
     String20 firstName;
     String20 lastName;
     DateType birthDate;
};


DateType today;
String20 aName;
InfoType aFriend;
InfoType self;
```

show the value of each variable after the following program segment is executed.

```
strcpy(aName, " ");
strcpy(aFriend.firstName, aName);
strcpy(aFriend.lastName, aName);
today.month = 1;
today.day = 1;
today.year = 1996;
aFriend.birthDate = today;
self = aFriend;
```

9. Declare a `struct` type named `RecType` to contain two integer variables and one Boolean variable. (Assume a `Boolean` type has already been defined.)
10. Using the declarations in this chapter of the `MachineRec` type and the `inventory` array, the code below is supposed to count the number of machines that have not been serviced within the current year. The code has an error. Correct the error by using a proper member selector in the If statement.

```
DateType currentDate;
  .
  .
  .
machineCount = 0;
for (index = 0; index < NUM_MACHINES; index++)
    if (currentDate.year != lastServiced.year)
        machineCount++;
```

11. Given the declarations

```
typedef char String20[21];
typedef char String2[3];

struct NameType
{
    String20 first;
    String20 last;
};
struct PlaceType
{
    String20 city;
    String2  state;
    long     zipCode;
};
struct PersonType
{
    NameType  name;
    PlaceType place;
};

PersonType person;
```

write C++ code that stores information about yourself into `person`.

Programming Warm-Up Exercises

1. a. Write a `struct` declaration to contain the following information about a student:

Name (string of characters)
Social security number (string of characters)
Year (freshman, sophomore, junior, senior)
Grade point average (floating point)
Sex (M, F)

   b. Declare a `struct` variable of the type in part (a), and write a program segment that prints the information in each member of the variable.

   c. Declare `roll` to be an array of 3000 `struct`s of the type in part (a).

2. Write a program segment to read in a set of part numbers and associated unit costs. Keep the data sorted by part number as you read it in. Use an array of `struct`s with two members, `number` and `cost`, to represent each pair of input values. Assume the end-of-file condition terminates the input.

3. Write a hierarchical C++ `struct` declaration to contain the following information about a student:

Name (up to 30 characters)
Student ID number
Credit hours to date
Number of courses taken
Course grades (a list of up to 50 elements containing an integer course ID and the letter grade)
Date first enrolled (month and year)
Year (freshman, sophomore, junior, senior)
Grade point average

Each `struct` and enumeration type should have a separate type declaration.

4. a. Declare a `struct` type named `AptType` for an apartment locator service. The following information should be included:

Landlord (a string of up to 20 characters)
Address (a string of up to 20 characters)
Bedrooms (integer)
Price (floating point)

   b. Declare `available` to be an array of up to 200 `struct`s of type `AptType`.

   c. Write a function to read values into the members of a variable of type `AptType`. (The `struct` variable should be passed as a parameter.) The order in which the data are read is the same as that of the items in the `struct`.

5. Using the declarations given in Exam Preparation Exercise 2, write statements to do the following:

   a. Assign the contents of the `chart` member of `aMap` to `aRef`.

   b. Assign `aMap` to the fourth element of `guide`.

  c. Copy `aCode` to the `mapCode` member of the tenth element of `guide`.

  d. Compare the first character in `aCode` and the first character in the `mapCode` member of the second element of `guide`. If they are equal, then output the `mapCode` member and the `style` member of the second element of `guide`.

  e. Compare `aMap.chart` and `aRef` for equality. Show which elements (if any) are not equal by outputting the indices for the appropriate `token` members and/or `symbol` members. For example, if the second element of the `token` members of both `struct`s were not equal, you would output "1," and so on, for the remaining nonequal elements.

6. You are designing an automated library catalog system. The library contains 50,000 books. For each book, there is a catalog entry consisting of the call number (up to 10 characters), the number of copies in the library (an integer), the author (up to 30 characters), the title (up to 100 characters), and a description of the contents (up to 300 characters).

  a. Write the type declarations necessary to represent this information.

  b. Estimate how many characters of memory space are required to hold all the catalog information for the library. (Assume that an integer value occupies the equivalent of four characters in memory.)

  c. How many book records can a computer with 650,000 characters of memory hold?

7. Write a function that reads the information for a book into a `struct` of the type defined in Exercise 6. Write another function that prints the information contained in a `struct` of the type defined in Exercise 6. The `struct` should be passed as a parameter to each of these functions.

8. You are writing the subscription renewal system for a magazine. For each subscriber, the system is to keep the following information:

Name (first, last)

Address (street, city, state, zip code)

Expiration date (month, year)

Date renewal notice was sent (month, day, year)

Number of renewal notices sent so far

Number of years for which subscription is being renewed (0 for renewal not yet received; otherwise, 1, 2, or 3 years)

Whether or not the subscriber's name may be included in a mailing list for sale to other companies

Write a hierarchical record type declaration to represent this information. Each sub-record should be declared separately as a named data type.

9. You are writing a program that keeps track of the terminals connected to a company computer. The computer may have up to 30 terminals connected to it. For each terminal, the following information must be kept:

Brand and model (a string of up to 15 characters)

Data rate (an integer representing 10 through 19,200 characters per second)

Parity (an enumeration type representing Even, Odd, One, Zero, or None)

Echoplex (an enumeration type representing Half or Full)

Data bits (an integer representing 7 or 8)

Stop bits (an integer representing 1 or 2)

Design a data structure for this problem, and write the type declarations for all the data types that are needed to implement your design.

10. Write a `struct` declaration to contain a string of no more than 20 characters and the length of the string. Then write a value-returning function that returns the length of a string stored in this `struct`.

11. Write a function that concatenates (joins) two strings into a third string. Use the declaration you wrote in Exercise 10.

12. You are writing a program to keep track of a manufacturing company's inventory. For each part, the following information needs to be stored:

    Part number
    Part name
    Cost
    Quantity

    Write a function and the necessary declarations to read in a variable of `struct` type `Inventory`.

13. In Program MergeLists, we represented a person's area code as an `int` value. Printing an `int` area code works fine for North American phone numbers, where area codes are greater than 200. But international area codes may start with a zero. Our programs would print an area code of 052 as 52. Suggest two ways of accommodating international area codes so that leading zeros are printed.

14. Change the MergeLists program so that the sentinel line consists of 15 Zs only—no first name, area code, or phone number. Specifically, rewrite the `GetRecords` function so that input of the first name, area code, and phone number are not attempted if the last name is all Zs.

15. Recode the MergeLists program so that the sentinel records are not stored in any arrays in memory. Function `GetRecords` should input data until the sentinel record is encountered, returning both the list and its length. Thereafter, whenever a list is passed as a parameter to a function, its length should be passed also.

Programming Problems

1. The MergeLists program merges three lists by merging two lists, and then merging the third list with the result of the merger of the first two. Another way of solving the same problem is to merge three lists at the same time, storing the result into a fourth list. Design a solution to the problem using this second strategy. Code your design in C++. Test your program thoroughly.

2. The Emerging Manufacturing Company has just installed its first computer and hired you as a junior programmer. Your first program is to read employee pay data and produce two reports: (1) an error and control report, and (2) a report on pay amounts. The second report must contain a line for each employee and a line of totals at the end of the report.

Input:

Transaction File

Set of five job site number/name pairs
One line for each employee containing ID number, job site number, and number of hours worked

These data items have been presorted by ID number.

Master File

ID number
Name
Pay rate per hour
Number of dependents
Type of employee (1 is management, 0 is union)
Job site
Sex (M, F)

This file is ordered by ID number.

Note: (1) Union members, unlike management, get time and a half for hours over 40.
(2) The tax formula for tax computation is as follows: If number of dependents is 1, tax
rate is 15%. Otherwise, the tax rate is the greater of 2.5% and

$$\left[1 - \left(\frac{\text{No. of dep.}}{\text{No. of dep. } + 6}\right)\right] \times 15\%$$

Output:

Error and Control Report

Lists the input lines for which there is no corresponding master record, or where the
    employees' job site numbers do not agree with those in the master file. Continues
    processing with the next line of data
Gives the total number of employee records that were processed correctly during
    the run

Payroll Report (Labeled for Management)

Contains a line for each employee showing the name, ID number, job site name, gross
    pay, and net pay
Contains a total line showing the total amount of gross pay and total amount of
    net pay

3. The Emerging Manufacturing Company has decided to use its new computer for parts
inventory control as well as payroll. You are writing a program that is to be run each
night. It takes the stock tickets from the day's transactions, makes a list of the parts
that need ordering, and prints an updated report that must be given to the five job site
managers each morning. Note that you are not being asked to update the file.

Input:

Transaction File

Set of five job site number/name pairs
One line for each stock transaction containing part ID number, job site number, and
    number of parts bought or sold (a negative number indicates that it has been sold)

These data have been presorted by site number within part ID number.

Master File

Part ID number
Part name (no embedded blanks)

Quantity on hand
Order point (the minimum quantity on hand that will trigger a reorder of the part)
Job site

This file is also ordered by job site number within part ID number. If a part is not in the master file and the transaction is a sale, an error message should be printed. If the transaction is a purchase, the part should be listed in the proper place in the parts report. Note that there is a separate entry in the master file for parts at each job site.

Output:

Error and Control Report

Contains error messages
Lists the parts that need to be ordered (those for which quantity on hand is less than order point)

A Report for All the Parts in the Master File

Contains the part number
Contains the part name
Contains the job site name
Contains the number on hand

Remember, this report is for management. Be sure it is written so managers can read it.

4. Your assignment is to write a program for a computer dating service. Clients give you their names, phone numbers, and a list of interests. Your job is to maintain lists of men and women using the service and to match up the compatible couples.

Data Structures:

The problem requires you to maintain two lists, one for men and one for women. The lists must include the following information: name (20 characters), phone number (8 characters), number of interests (maximum number is 10), interests (10 characters each; must be in alphabetical order), and a variable that gives the position of the client's current match (-1 if not matched). When a new client is added to the list, his or her name is added to the bottom of the appropriate list. (You do not keep the names of the clients in alphabetical order.)

Input:

Number of current clients
Sex ('M' or 'F'), name (20 characters), phone number (8 characters), number of interests, list of interests (10 characters for each one, with no embedded blanks; interests are separated by blanks). There is a record like this for each of the current clients.

The rest of the file includes data lines that look like one of the following (all the lines start with a 10-character word as outlined below; □ indicates a blank):

NewClient □ sex ('M' or 'F'), name (20 characters), number of interests, interests (10 characters for each one; see above for description)

If the keyword NewClient occurs, you should add the client to the appropriate list by storing the required information. Match him or her with a member of the opposite sex. (A match occurs when at least three of the interests are the same. Interests are sorted, which makes the matching process easier. Use an insertion sort to sort interests.) Make sure you then designate both persons matched as described above. Print the name of the new client, his or her match, and both phone numbers. If no match is found, print an appropriate message.

OldClient □ name (20 characters)

Unmatch this name from its current match by setting the match variables for the name and its match to −1.

PrintMatch

Print a list of all matched pairs.

PrintNot□□

Print the names and phone numbers of clients who are not currently matched.

StopProg□□

This will be the last line in the file.

Output:

Information as described above, printed with appropriate titles.

5. A *sparse matrix* is a matrix (two-dimensional array) in which the great majority of elements are zero. It is inefficient to store these as two-dimensional arrays because most of the elements do not contain any useful information. Instead, the elements that are not equal to zero should be stored as an array of structs where the first two members of the struct contain the row and column number and the third member contains the element. For example, this matrix

0.0	0.0	7.0	0.0	0.0
0.0	0.0	0.0	0.0	8.0
0.0	0.0	0.0	0.0	0.0

would be stored as follows:

| 1 | 3 | 7.0 |
| 2 | 5 | 8.0 |

Write a C++ program that reads a sparse matrix and converts it into an array of structs of this form. The program should then output the structs (properly labeled).

15

Classes, Data Abstraction, and Object-Oriented Software Development

At the end of the last chapter, we introduced the concept of data abstraction, the separation of a data type's logical properties from its implementation. Data abstraction is important because it allows us to create data types not otherwise available in a programming language. Another benefit of data abstraction is the ability to produce *off-the-shelf software components*—pieces of software that can be used over and over again in different programs.

The primary tool for practicing data abstraction is the abstract data type, introduced briefly in Chapter 12. In this chapter, we examine abstract data types in depth and introduce the C++ language feature designed expressly for creating abstract data types: the *class*. We then examine how classes, which define *objects*, are used in *object-oriented programming*. We describe the basic principles, terminology, and programming language features associated with the object-oriented approach, and then consider their implications for the design phase of the software development process.

Abstract Data Types

We live in a complex world. To cope with complexity, the human mind engages in *abstraction*—the act of separating the essential qualities of an idea or object from the details of how it works or is composed.

With abstraction, we focus on the *what*, not the *how*. For example, our understanding of automobiles is largely based on abstraction. Most of us know *what* the engine does (it propels the car), but fewer of us know—or want to know—precisely *how* the engine works internally. Abstraction allows us to discuss, think about, and use automobiles without having to know everything about how they work.

www.jbpub.com/C++links

In the world of software design, it is now recognized that abstraction is an absolute necessity for managing immense, complex software projects. In introductory computer science courses, programs are usually small (perhaps 50 to 200 lines of code) and understandable in their entirety by one person. However, large commercial software products composed of hundreds of thousands—even millions—of lines of code cannot be designed without using abstraction in various forms. To manage complexity, software developers regularly use two important abstraction techniques: control abstraction and data abstraction.

Control abstraction is the separation of the logical properties of an action from its implementation. We engage in control abstraction whenever we write a function that reduces a complicated algorithm to an abstract action performed by a function call. By invoking a library function, as in the expression

```
4.6 + sqrt(x)
```

we depend only on the function's *specification,* a written description of what it does. We can use the function without having to know its *implementation* (the algorithms that accomplish the result).

Abstraction techniques also apply to data. Every data type consists of a set of values (the domain) along with a collection of allowable operations on those values. In Chapter 14, we described data abstraction as the separation of a data type's logical properties from its implementation details. Data abstraction comes into play when we need a data type that is not built into the programming language. We can define the new data type as an **abstract data type (ADT),** concentrating only on its logical properties and deferring the details of its implementation.

abstract data type
A data type whose properties (domain and operations) are specified independently of any particular implementation

As with control abstraction, an abstract data type has both a specification (the *what*) and an implementation (the *how*). The specification of an ADT describes the characteristics of the data values as well as the behavior of each of the operations on those values. The user of the ADT needs to understand only the specification, not the implementation, in order to use it. Here's a very informal specification of a list ADT:

TYPE
  IntList
DOMAIN
  Each IntList value is a collection of up to 100 separate integer numbers.
OPERATIONS
  Insert an item into the list.
  Delete an item from the list.
  Search the list for an item.
  Return the current length of the list.
  Sort the list into ascending order.
  Print the list.

Notice the complete absence of implementation details. We have not mentioned how the data might actually be stored in a program (for example, in an array) or how the operations might be implemented. Concealing the implementation details reduces complexity for the user and also shields the user from changes in the implementation.

Below is the specification of another ADT, one that might be useful for representing time in a program.

TYPE
  TimeType
DOMAIN
  Each TimeType value is a time of day in the form of hours, minutes, and seconds.
OPERATIONS
  Set the time.
  Print the time.
  Increment the time by one second.
  Compare two times for equality.
  Determine if one time is "less than" (comes before) another.

The specification of an ADT defines abstract data values and abstract operations for the user. Ultimately, of course, the ADT must be implemented in program code. To implement an ADT, the programmer must do two things:

data representation
The concrete form of data used to represent the abstract values of an abstract data type

1. Choose a concrete **data representation** of the abstract data, using data types that already exist.
2. Implement each of the allowable operations in terms of program instructions.

To implement the IntList ADT, we could choose a concrete data representation consisting of two items: a 100-element `int` array and an `int` variable that keeps track of the current length of the list. To implement the IntList operations, we must create algorithms—such as the searching and sorting routines we wrote in Chapter 12—based on the chosen data representation.

To implement the TimeType ADT, we might use three `int` variables for the data representation—one for the hours, one for the minutes, and one for the seconds. Or we might use three strings (`char` arrays) as the data representation, or even a three-element `int` array. The specification of the ADT does not confine us to any particular data representation. As long as we satisfy the specification, we are free to choose among alternative data representations and their associated algorithms. Our choice may be based on time efficiency (the speed at which the algorithms execute), space efficiency (the economical use of memory space), or simplicity and readability of the algorithms. Over time, you will acquire knowledge and experience that help you decide which implementation is best for a particular context.

C++ *Classes*

In previous chapters, we have treated data structures as passive quantities to be acted upon by functions. In Chapter 12, we viewed an integer list as an ADT, representing the list as an `int` array and implementing the list operations as functions that take an `int` array as a parameter (see Figure 15-1).

This separation of operations and data does not correspond very well with the notion of an abstract data type. After all, an ADT consists of *both* data values and operations on those values. It is preferable to view an ADT as defining an *active* data structure—one that combines both data and operations into a single, cohesive unit (see Figure 15-2). C++ supports this view by providing a built-in structured type known as a **class.**

class

A structured type in a programming language that is used to represent an abstract data type

In Chapter 14, we listed the four structured types available in the C++ language: the array, the `struct`, the union, and the class (Figure 14-5). A class is a structured type provided specifically for implementing abstract data types. It is similar to a `struct` but is nearly always designed so that its components (**class members**) include not only data but also functions that manipulate that data. Here is a C++ class declaration corresponding to the TimeType ADT that we defined in the previous section:

class member

A component of a class. Class members may be either data or functions

```
class TimeType
{
public:
    void    Set( int, int, int );
    void    Increment();
```

```
    void    Write() const;
    Boolean Equal( TimeType ) const;
    Boolean LessThan( TimeType ) const;
private:
    int hrs;
    int mins;
    int secs;
};
```

(For now, you should ignore the word const appearing in some of the function prototypes. We explain this use of const later in the chapter.)

The TimeType class has eight members—five member functions (Set, Increment, Write, Equal, LessThan) and three member variables (hrs, mins,

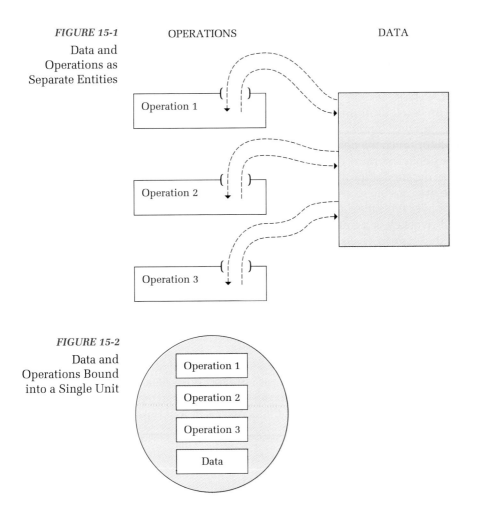

FIGURE 15-1

Data and Operations as Separate Entities

FIGURE 15-2

Data and Operations Bound into a Single Unit

secs). As you might guess, the three member variables form the concrete data representation for the TimeType ADT. The five member functions correspond to the operations we listed for the TimeType ADT: set the time, increment the time by one second, print the time, compare two times for equality, and determine if one time is less than another. Although the Equal function compares two TimeType variables for equality, its parameter list has only one parameter—a TimeType variable. Similarly, the LessThan function has only one parameter, even though it compares two times. We'll see the reason later.

Like a struct declaration, the declaration of TimeType creates a data type but does not create variables of the type. Class variables (more often referred to as **class objects** or **class instances**) are created by using ordinary variable declarations:

class object (class instance)
A variable of a class type

```
TimeType startTime;
TimeType endTime;
```

client
Software that declares and manipulates objects of a particular class

Any software that declares and manipulates TimeType objects is called a **client** of the class.

As you look at the preceding declaration of the TimeType class, you can see the reserved words public and private (each followed by a colon). Data and/or functions declared between the words public and private constitute the public interface; clients can access these class members directly. Class members declared after the word private are considered private information and are inaccessible to clients. If client code attempts to access a private item, the compiler will signal an error.

Private class members can be accessed only by the class's member functions. In the TimeType class, the private variables hrs, mins, and secs can be accessed only by the member functions Set, Increment, Write, Equal, and LessThan, not by client code. This separation of class members into private and public parts is a hallmark of ADT design. To preserve correctly the properties of an ADT, an instance of the ADT should be manipulated *only* through the operations that form the public interface. We have more to say about this issue later in the chapter.

Classes, Class Objects, and Class Members

It is important to restate that a class is a type, not a data object. Like any type, a class is a pattern from which you create (or *instantiate*) many objects of that type. Think of a type as a cookie cutter and objects of that type as the cookies.

The declarations

```
TimeType time1;
TimeType time2;
```

create two objects of the TimeType class: time1 and time2. Each object has its own copies of hrs, mins, and secs, the private data members of the class. At a given moment during program execution, time1's copies of hrs, mins, and secs might contain the values 5, 30, and 10; and time2's copies might contain the values 17, 58, and 2. Figure 15-3 is a visual image of the class objects time1 and time2.

(In truth, the C++ compiler does not waste memory by placing duplicate copies of a member function—say, Increment—into both time1 and time2. The compiler generates just one physical copy of Increment, and any class object executes this one copy of the function. Nevertheless, the diagram in Figure 15-3 is a good mental picture of two different class objects.)

Be sure you are clear about the difference between the terms *class object* and *class member.* Figure 15-3 depicts two objects of the TimeType class, and each object has eight members.

Built-In Operations on Classes

In many ways, programmer-defined classes are like built-in types. You can declare as many objects of a class as you like. You can pass class objects as parameters to functions and return them as function values. You can declare arrays

FIGURE 15-3   Conceptual View of Two Class Objects

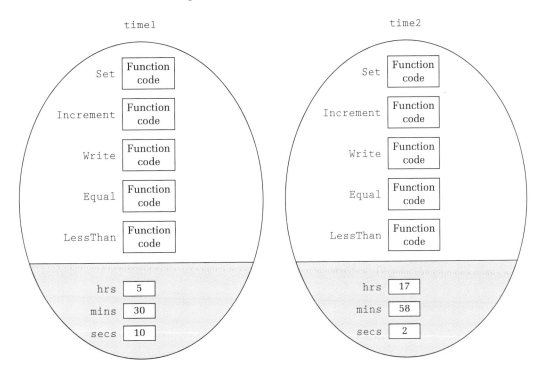

of class objects. Like any variable, a class object can be automatic (created each time control reaches its declaration and destroyed when control exits its surrounding block) or static (created once when control reaches its declaration and destroyed when the program terminates).

In other ways, C++ treats classes differently from built-in types. Most of the built-in operations do not apply to classes. You cannot use the + operator to add two TimeType objects, nor can you use the == operator to compare two TimeType objects for equality.

Two built-in operations that are valid for class objects are member selection (.) and assignment (=). As with structs, you select an individual member of a class by writing the name of the class object, then a dot, then the member name. The statement

```
time1.Increment();
```

invokes the Increment function for the time1 object, presumably to add one second to the time stored in time1. The other built-in operation, assignment, performs aggregate assignment of one class object to another with the following semantics: If x and y are objects of the same class, then the assignment x = y copies the data members of y into x. Below is a fragment of client code that demonstrates member selection and assignment.

```
TimeType time1;
TimeType time2;
int      inputHrs;
int      inputMins;
int      inputSecs;

time1.Set(5, 20, 0);
// Assert: time1 corresponds to 5:20:0

cout << "Enter hours, minutes, seconds: ";
cin >> inputHrs >> inputMins >> inputSecs;
time2.Set(inputHrs, inputMins, inputSecs);

if (time1.LessThan(time2))
    DoSomething();

time2 = time1;                      // Member-by-member assignment
time2.Write();
// Assert: 5:20:0 is output
```

Earlier we remarked that the Equal and LessThan functions have only one parameter each, even though they are comparing two TimeType objects. In the

If statement of the code segment above, we are comparing `time1` and `time2`. Because `LessThan` is a class member function, we invoke it by giving the name of a class object (`time1`), then a dot, then the function name (`LessThan`). Only one item remains unspecified: the class object that `time1` should be compared with (`time2`). Therefore, the `LessThan` function requires only one parameter, not two. Here is another way of explaining it: If a class member function represents a binary (two-operand) operation, the first operand appears to the left of the dot operator and the second operand is in the parameter list. (To generalize, an *n*-ary operation has $n - 1$ operands in the parameter list. Thus, a unary operation—such as `Write` or `Increment` in the `TimeType` class—has an empty parameter list.)

In addition to member selection and assignment, a few other built-in operators are valid for classes. These operators are used for manipulating memory addresses, and are not discussed in this book. For now, think of . and = as the only valid built-in operators.

From the very beginning, you have been working with C++ classes in a particular context: input and output. The standard header file `iostream.h` contains the declarations of two classes—`istream` and `ostream`—that manage a program's I/O. The C++ standard library declares `cin` and `cout` to be objects of these classes:

```
istream cin;
ostream cout;
```

(The actual declarations are slightly different from these, but the differences are not important to this discussion.)

The `istream` class has many member functions, two of which—the `get` function and the `ignore` function—you have already seen in statements like these:

```
cin.get(someChar);
cin.ignore(200, '\n');
```

As with any C++ class object, we use dot notation to select a particular member function to invoke.

You also have used C++ classes when performing file I/O. The header file `fstream.h` contains declarations for the `ifstream` and `ofstream` classes. The client code

```
ifstream dataFile;

dataFile.open("input.dat");
```

declares an `ifstream` class object named `dataFile`, then invokes the class member function `open` to try to open a file `input.dat` for input.

We do not examine in detail the `istream`, `ostream`, `ifstream`, and `ofstream` classes and all of their member functions. To study these would be beyond the goals of this book. What is important to recognize is that classes and objects are fundamental to all I/O activity in a C++ program.

Class Scope

As with members of a `struct`, the name of a class member has class scope—that is, the name is local to the class. If the same identifier happens to be declared outside the class, the two identifiers are unrelated.

The `TimeType` class has a member function named `Write`. In the same program, another class (say, `SomeClass`) could also have a member function named `Write`. Furthermore, the program might have a global `Write` function that is completely unrelated to any classes. If the program has statements like

```
TimeType    checkInTime;
SomeClass  someObject;
int        n;
    .
    .
    .
checkInTime.Write();
someObject.Write();
Write(n);
```

then the C++ compiler has no trouble distinguishing among the three `Write` functions. In the first two function calls, the dot notation denotes class member selection. The first statement invokes the `Write` function of the `TimeType` class, and the second statement invokes the `Write` function of the `SomeClass` class. The final statement does not use dot notation, so the compiler knows that the function being called is the global `Write` function.

Information Hiding

abstraction barrier
The invisible wall around a class object that encapsulates implementation details. The wall can be breached only through the public interface

Conceptually, a class object has an invisible wall around it. This wall, called the **abstraction barrier,** protects private data and functions from being accessed by client code. The barrier also prohibits the class object from directly accessing data and functions outside the object. This barrier is a critical characteristic of classes and abstract data types.

For a class object to share information with the outside world (that is, with clients), there must be a gap in the abstraction barrier. This gap is the public interface—the class members declared to be `public`. The only way that a client can manipulate the internals of the class object is indirectly—through the operations in the public interface. Engineers have a similar concept called a

black box. A black box is a module or device whose inner workings are hidden from view. The user of the black box depends only on the written specification of *what* it does, not on *how* it does it. The user connects wires to the interface and assumes that the module works correctly by satisfying the specification (see Figure 15-4).

In software design, the black box concept is referred to as **information hiding.** Information hiding protects the user of a class from having to know all the details of its implementation. Information hiding also assures the class's implementor that the user cannot directly access any private code or data and compromise the correct functioning of the implementation. In this chapter, you'll see how to hide the implementations of class member functions by placing them in files separate from the client code.

The creator of a C++ class is free to choose which members are private and which are public. However, making data members public allows the client to inspect and modify them directly. Because information hiding is so fundamental to data abstraction, most classes exhibit a typical pattern: The private part contains data, and the public part contains the functions that manipulate the data.

The TimeType class exemplifies this organization. The data members hrs, mins, and secs are private, so the compiler prohibits a client from accessing these members directly. The following client statement therefore results in a compile-time error:

```
checkInTime.hrs = 9;    // Prohibited
```

Because only the class's member functions can access the private data, the creator of the class can offer a reliable product, knowing that external access to the private data is impossible. If it is acceptable to let the client *inspect* (but not modify) private data members, a class might provide functions that return their values. The TimeType class has three such functions: Write, Equal, and LessThan.

black box
An electrical or mechanical device whose inner workings are hidden from view

information hiding
The encapsulation and hiding of implementation details to keep the user of an abstraction from depending on or incorrectly manipulating these details

www.jbpub.com/C++links

FIGURE 15-4
A Black Box

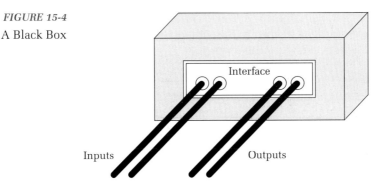

Because these functions are not intended to modify the private data, they are declared with the word const following the parameter list:

```
void    Write() const;
Boolean Equal( TimeType ) const;
Boolean LessThan( TimeType ) const;
```

C++ refers to these functions as *const member functions*. Within the body of a const member function, a compile-time error occurs if any statement tries to modify a private data member. Although not required by the language, it is good practice to declare as const those member functions that do not modify private data.

Specification and Implementation Files

An abstract data type consists of two parts: a specification and an implementation. The specification describes the behavior of the data type without reference to its implementation. The implementation creates an abstraction barrier by hiding the concrete data representation as well as the code for the operations.

The TimeType class declaration serves as the specification of TimeType. This declaration presents the public interface to the user in the form of function prototypes. To implement the TimeType class, we must provide function definitions (declarations with bodies) for all the member functions.

In C++, it is customary (though not required) to package the class declaration and the class implementation into separate files. One file—the *specification file*—is a header (.h) file containing only the class declaration. The second file—the *implementation file*—contains the function definitions for the class member functions. Let's look first at the specification file.

The Specification File Below is the specification file for the TimeType class. On our computer system, we have named the file timetype.h. The class declaration is the same as we presented earlier, with one important exception: We include function preconditions and postconditions to specify the semantics of the member functions as unambiguously as possible for the user.

```
//******************************************************************
// SPECIFICATION FILE (timetype.h)
// This file gives the specification
// of a TimeType abstract data type
//******************************************************************
#include "bool.h"
class TimeType
{
public:
```

```
    void Set( /* in */ int hours,
              /* in */ int minutes,
              /* in */ int seconds );
        // Precondition:
        //      0 <= hours <= 23  &&  0 <= minutes <= 59
        //  && 0 <= seconds <= 59
        // Postcondition:
        //      Time is set according to the incoming parameters
        // NOTE:
        //      This function MUST be called prior to
        //      any of the other member functions

    void Increment();
        // Precondition:
        //      The Set function has been invoked at least once
        // Postcondition:
        //      Time has been advanced by one second, with
        //      23:59:59 wrapping around to 0:0:0

    void Write() const;
        // Precondition:
        //      The Set function has been invoked at least once
        // Postcondition:
        //      Time has been output in the form HH:MM:SS

    Boolean Equal( /* in */ TimeType otherTime ) const;
        // Precondition:
        //      The Set function has been invoked at least once
        //      for both this time and otherTime
        // Postcondition:
        //      Function value == true, if this time equals otherTime
        //                     == false, otherwise

    Boolean LessThan( /* in */ TimeType otherTime ) const;
        // Precondition:
        //      The Set function has been invoked at least once
        //      for both this time and otherTime
        //   && This time and otherTime represent times in the
        //      same day
        // Postcondition:
        //      Function value == true, if this time is earlier
        //                              in the day than otherTime
        //                     == false, otherwise
private:
    int hrs;
    int mins;
    int secs;
};
```

Notice the preconditions for the Increment, Write, Equal, and LessThan functions. It is the responsibility of the client to set the time before incrementing, printing, or testing it. If the client fails to set the time, the effect of each of these functions is undefined.

In principle, a specification file should not reveal any implementation details to the user of the class. The file should specify *what* each member function does without disclosing how it does it. However, as you can see in the class declaration, there is one implementation detail that is visible to the user: the concrete data representation of our ADT that is listed in the private part. However, the data representation is still considered hidden information in the sense that the compiler prohibits client code from accessing the data directly.

The Implementation File   The specification (.h) file for the TimeType class contains only the class declaration. The implementation file must provide the function definitions for all the class member functions. In the opening comments of the implementation file below, we document the file name as timetype.cpp. Your system may use a different file name suffix for source code files, perhaps .c, .C, or .cxx.

We recommend that you first skim the C++ code below, not being too concerned about the new language features such as prefixing the name of each function with the symbols

```
TimeType::
```

Immediately following the program code, we explain the new features. We omit the Preconditions and Postconditions here to save space, although they would normally be repeated in the implementation file.

```
//*******************************************************************
// IMPLEMENTATION FILE (timetype.cpp)
// This file implements the TimeType member functions
//*******************************************************************
#include "timetype.h"
#include <iostream.h>

// Private members of class:
//      int hrs;
//      int mins;
//      int secs;

//*******************************************************************
```

```cpp
void TimeType::Set( /* in */ int hours,
                    /* in */ int minutes,
                    /* in */ int seconds )

{
    hrs = hours;
    mins = minutes;
    secs = seconds;
}

//*******************************************************************

void TimeType::Increment()

{
    secs++;
    if (secs > 59)
    {
        secs = 0;
        mins++;
        if (mins > 59)
        {
            mins = 0;
            hrs++;
            if (hrs > 23)
                hrs = 0;
        }
    }
}

//*******************************************************************

void TimeType::Write() const

{
    if (hrs < 10)
        cout << '0';
    cout << hrs << ':';
    if (mins < 10)
        cout << '0';
    cout << mins << ':';
    if (secs < 10)
        cout << '0';
    cout << secs;
}

//*******************************************************************
```

```
Boolean TimeType::Equal( /* in */ TimeType otherTime ) const

{
    return (hrs == otherTime.hrs && mins == otherTime.mins &&
            secs == otherTime.secs);
}


//*******************************************************************

Boolean TimeType::LessThan( /* in */ TimeType otherTime ) const

{
    return (hrs < otherTime.hrs ||
            hrs == otherTime.hrs && mins < otherTime.mins ||
            hrs == otherTime.hrs && mins == otherTime.mins
                                 && secs < otherTime.secs);
}
```

This implementation file demonstrates several important points.

1. The file begins with the preprocessor directive

```
#include "timetype.h"
```

Both the implementation file and the client code must #include the specification file. Figure 15-5 pictures this shared access to the specification file. This sharing guarantees that all declarations related to an abstraction are consistent. That is, both client.cpp and timetype.cpp must reference the same declaration of the TimeType class located in timetype.h.

2. Near the top of the implementation file we have included a comment that restates the private members of the TimeType class.

```
// Private members of class:
//      int hrs;
//      int mins;
//      int secs;
```

This comment reminds the reader that any references to these identifiers are references to the private class members.

3. In the heading of each function definition, the name of the member function is prefixed by the class name (TimeType) and the C++ *scope resolution operator* (::). As we discussed earlier, it is possible for several different classes to have member functions with the same name, say, Write. In addition, there may be a global Write function that is not a member of any class. The scope

FIGURE 15-5   Shared Access to a Specification File

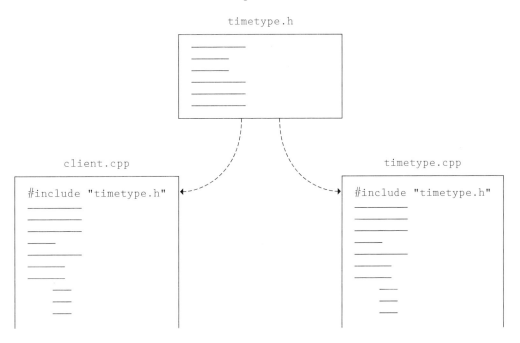

resolution operator eliminates any uncertainty about which particular function is being defined.

4. Although clients of a class must use the dot operator to refer to class members (for example, `startTime.Write()`), members of a class refer to each other directly without using dot notation. Looking at the bodies of the `Set` and `Increment` functions, you can see that the statements refer directly to the member variables `hrs`, `mins`, and `secs` without using the dot operator.

An exception to this rule occurs when a member function manipulates two or more class objects. Consider the `Equal` function. Suppose that the client code has two class objects, `startTime` and `endTime`, and uses the statement

```
if (startTime.Equal(endTime))
       .
       .
       .
```

At execution time, the `startTime` object is the object for whom the `Equal` function is invoked. In the body of the `Equal` function, the relational expression

```
hrs == otherTime.hrs
```

refers to class members of two different class objects. The unadorned identifier `hrs` refers to the `hrs` member of the class object for whom the function is invoked (that is, `startTime`). The expression `otherTime.hrs` refers to the `hrs` member of the class object that is passed as a function parameter: `endTime`.

5. `Write`, `Equal`, and `LessThan` do not modify the private data of the class. Because we have declared these to be `const` member functions, the compiler will prevent them from assigning new values to the private data. The use of `const` is both an aid to the user of the class (as a visual signal that this function does not modify any private data) and an aid to the class implementor (as a way of preventing accidental modification of the data). Note that the word `const` must appear in both the function prototype (in the class declaration) and the heading of the function definition.

Compiling and Linking a Multifile Program

Now that we have created a specification file and an implementation file for our `TimeType` class, how do we (or any other programmer) make use of these files in our programs? Let's begin by looking at the notion of *separate compilation* of source code files.

Earlier in the book we referred to the concept of a multifile program—a program divided up into several files containing source code. In C++, it is possible to compile each of these files separately. The compiler translates each source code file into an object code file. Figure 15-6 shows a multifile program consisting of the source code files `myprog.cpp`, `file2.cpp`, and `file3.cpp`. We can compile each of these files independently, yielding object code files `myprog.obj`, `file2.obj`, and `file3.obj`. Although each `.obj` file contains machine language code, it is not yet in executable form. The system's *linker*

FIGURE 15-6

Separate Compilation and Linking

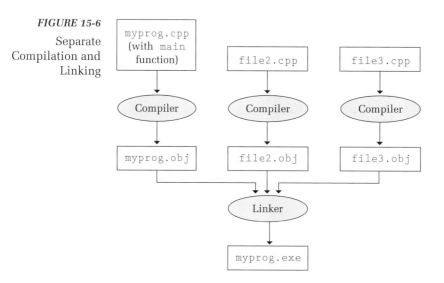

program brings the object code together to form an executable program file. (In Figure 15-6, we use the file name suffixes .cpp, .obj, and .exe. Your C++ system may use different file name conventions.)

Files such as file2.cpp and file3.cpp typically contain function definitions for functions that are called by the code in myprog.cpp. An important benefit of separate compilation is that modifying the code in just one file requires recompiling only that file. The new .obj file is then relinked with the other existing .obj files. Of course, if a modification to one file affects the code in another file—for example, changing a function's interface by altering the number or data types of the function parameters—then the affected files also need to be modified and recompiled.

Returning to our TimeType class, let's assume we have created the timetype.h and timetype.cpp files. Now we can compile timetype.cpp into object code. If we are working at the operating system's command line, we use a command similar to the following:

```
cc -c timetype.cpp
```

In this example, we assume that cc is the name of a command that invokes either the C++ compiler or the linker or both, depending on various options given on the command line. The command-line option -c means, on many systems, "compile but do not link." In other words, this command produces an object code file, say, timetype.obj, but does not attempt to link this file with any other file.

A programmer wishing to use the TimeType class will write code that #includes the file timetype.h, then declares and uses TimeType objects:

```
#include "timetype.h"
   .
   .
   .
TimeType appointment;

appointment.Set(15, 30, 0);
appointment.Write();
   .
   .
   .
```

If this client code is in a file named diary.cpp, an operating system command like

```
cc diary.cpp timetype.obj
```

compiles the client program into object code, links this object code with `timetype.obj`, and produces an executable program (see Figure 15-7).

The mechanics of compiling, linking, and executing vary from one computer system to another. The examples we gave using the `cc` command assume you are working at the operating system's command line. Some C++ systems provide an *integrated environment*—a program that bundles the editor, the compiler, and the linker into one package.

Whichever environment you use—the command-line environment or an integrated environment—the overall process is the same: You compile the individual source code files into object code, link the object files into an executable program, then execute the program.

Before leaving the topic of multifile programs, we stress an important point. Referring to Figure 15-7, the files `timetype.h` and `timetype.obj` must be available to users of the `TimeType` class. The user needs to examine `timetype.h` to see what `TimeType` objects do and how to use them. The user must also be able to link his or her program with `timetype.obj` to produce an executable program. But the user does *not* need to see `timetype.cpp`. The implementation of `TimeType` should be treated as a black box. The main purpose of abstraction is to simplify the programmer's job by reducing complexity. Users of an abstraction should not have to look at its implementation to see how to use it, nor should they write programs that depend on implementation details. In the latter case, any changes made to the implementation could "break" the user's programs.

FIGURE 15-7

Linking with the
TimeType
Implementation
File

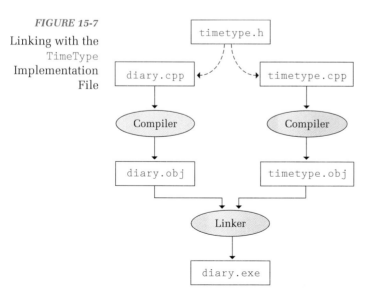

Avoiding Multiple Inclusion of Header Files

The TimeType *specification file contains the preprocessor directive* #include "bool.h". *But think about what happens if a programmer using the* TimeType *class already has included* bool.h *for other purposes, overlooking the fact that* timetype.h *also includes it:*

```
#include "bool.h"
#include "timetype.h"
```

The preprocessor inserts the file bool.h, *then* timetype.h, *and then* bool.h *a second time (because* timetype.h *also includes* bool.h). *The result is a compile-time error, because the identifiers* true *and* false *are defined twice.*

  The widely used solution to this problem is to write bool.h *this way:*

```
#ifndef BOOL_H
#define BOOL_H
typedef int Boolean;
const Boolean true = 1;
const Boolean false = 0;
#endif
```

The lines beginning with "#*" are directives to the preprocessor.* BOOL_H *(or any identifier you wish to use) is a preprocessor identifier, not a C++ program identifier. In effect, these directives say:*

  If the preprocessor identifier BOOL_H *is not already defined, then:*

1. *define* BOOL_H *as an identifier known to the preprocessor,*
and
2. *let the* typedef *and* const *declarations pass through to the compiler.*

If a subsequent #include "bool.h" *is encountered, the test* #ifndef BOOL_H *will fail. The* typedef *and* const *declarations will not pass through to the compiler a second time.*

Guaranteed Initialization with Class Constructors

The TimeType class we have been discussing has a weakness. It depends on the client to invoke the Set function before calling any other member function. For example, the Increment function's precondition is

```
// Precondition:
//      The Set function has been invoked at least once
```

If the client fails to invoke the Set function first, this precondition is false and the contract between the client and the function implementation is broken. Because classes nearly always encapsulate data, the creator of a class should not rely on the user to initialize the data. If the user forgets to, unpleasant results may occur.

C++ provides a mechanism, called a *class constructor*, to guarantee the initialization of a class object. A constructor is a member function that is implicitly invoked whenever a class object is created.

A constructor function has an unusual name: the name of the class itself. Let's change the `TimeType` class by adding two class constructors:

```
class TimeType
{
public:
    void    Set( int, int, int );
    void    Increment();
    void    Write() const;
    Boolean Equal( TimeType ) const;
    Boolean LessThan( TimeType ) const;
    TimeType( int, int, int );          // Constructor
    TimeType();                          // Constructor
private:
    int hrs;
    int mins;
    int secs;
};
```

This class declaration includes two constructors, differentiated by their parameter lists. The first has three `int` parameters which, as we will see, are used to initialize the private data when a class object is created. The second constructor is parameterless and initializes the time to some default value, such as 0:0:0. A parameterless constructor is known in C++ as a *default constructor*.

Constructor declarations are unique in two ways. First, as we have mentioned, the name of the function is the same as the name of the class. Second, the data type of the function is omitted. The reason is that a constructor cannot return a function value. Its purpose is only to initialize a class object's private data.

In the implementation file, the function definitions for the two `TimeType` constructors might look like the following:

```
//**********************************************************************

TimeType::TimeType( /* in */ int initHrs,
                    /* in */ int initMins,
                    /* in */ int initSecs )
// Constructor
```

```
{
    hrs = initHrs;
    mins = initMins;
    secs = initSecs;
}


//*********************************************************************

TimeType::TimeType()

// Default constructor

{
    hrs = 0;
    mins = 0;
    secs = 0;
}
```

Invoking a Constructor Although a constructor is a member of a class, it is never invoked using dot notation. A constructor is automatically invoked whenever a class object is created. The declaration

```
TimeType lectureTime(10, 30, 0);
```

includes a parameter list to the right of the name of the class object being declared. When this declaration is encountered at execution time, the first (parameterized) constructor is automatically invoked, initializing the private data of `lectureTime` to the time 10:30:0. The declaration

```
TimeType startTime;
```

has no parameter list after the identifier `startTime`. The default (parameterless) constructor is implicitly invoked, initializing `startTime`'s private data to the time 0:0:0.

Remember that a declaration in C++ is a genuine statement and can appear anywhere among executable statements. Placing declarations among executable statements is extremely useful when creating class objects whose initial values are not known until execution time. Here's an example:

```
cout << "Enter appointment time in hours, minutes, and seconds: ";
cin >> hours >> minutes >> seconds;

TimeType appointmentTime(hours, minutes, seconds);
```

```
cout << "The appointment time is ";
appointmentTime.Write();
    .
    .
    .
```

Revised Specification and Implementation Files for TimeType

By including constructors for the TimeType class, we are sure that each class object is initialized before any subsequent calls to the class member functions. One of the constructors allows the client code to specify an initial time; the other creates an initial time of 0:0:0 if the client does not specify a time. Because of these constructors, it is *impossible* for a TimeType object to be in an uninitialized state after it is created. As a result, we can delete from the TimeType specification file the warning to call Set before calling any other member functions. Also, we can remove all of the function preconditions that require Set to be called previously. Here is the revised TimeType specification file:

```
//*********************************************************************
// SPECIFICATION FILE (timetype.h)
// This file gives the specification
// of a TimeType abstract data type
//*********************************************************************
#include "bool.h"

class TimeType
{
public:
    void Set( /* in */ int hours,
              /* in */ int minutes,
              /* in */ int seconds );
        // Precondition:
        //     0 <= hours <= 23  &&  0 <= minutes <= 59
        //  && 0 <= seconds <= 59
        // Postcondition:
        //     Time is set according to the incoming parameters

    void Increment();
        // Postcondition:
        //     Time has been advanced by one second, with
        //     23:59:59 wrapping around to 0:0:0

    void Write() const;
        // Postcondition:
        //     Time has been output in the form HH:MM:SS
```

```
Boolean Equal( /* in */ TimeType otherTime ) const;
    // Postcondition:
    //      Function value == true, if this time equals otherTime
    //                     == false, otherwise

Boolean LessThan( /* in */ TimeType otherTime ) const;
    // Precondition:
    //      This time and otherTime represent times in the
    //      same day
    // Postcondition:
    //      Function value == true, if this time is earlier
    //                              in the day than otherTime
    //                     == false, otherwise

TimeType( /* in */ int initHrs,
          /* in */ int initMins,
          /* in */ int initSecs );
    // Precondition:
    //     0 <= initHrs <= 23  &&  0 <= initMins <= 59
    //  && 0 <= initSecs <= 59
    // Postcondition:
    //      Class object is constructed
    //  && Time is set according to the incoming parameters

TimeType();
    // Postcondition:
    //      Class object is constructed  &&  Time is 0:0:0
private:
    int hrs;
    int mins;
    int secs;
};
```

To save space, we do not include the revised implementation file here. The only changes are

1. the inclusion of the function definitions for the two class constructors, which we presented earlier.
2. the deletion of all function preconditions stating that the Set function must be invoked previously.

At this point, you may wonder why we need the Set function at all. After all, both the Set function and the parameterized constructor seem to do the same thing—set the time according to values passed as parameters—and the implementations of the two functions are essentially identical. The difference is that Set can be invoked for a class object whenever and as often as we wish, whereas the parameterized constructor is invoked once only—at the moment a class object is created. Therefore, we retain the Set function to provide maximum flexibility to clients of the class.

Guidelines for The class is an essential language feature for creating abstract data types in C++.
Using Class The class mechanism is a powerful design tool, but along with this power come
Constructors rules for using classes correctly.

C++ has some very intricate rules about using constructors, many of which relate to language features we have not discussed. Below are some guidelines that are pertinent at this point.

1. A constructor cannot return a function value, so the function is declared without a return value type.
2. A class may provide several constructors. When a class object is declared, the compiler chooses the appropriate constructor according to the number and data types of the parameters to the constructor.
3. Parameters to a constructor are passed by placing the actual parameter list immediately after the name of the class object being declared:

```
SomeClass anObject(param1, param2);
```

4. If a class object is declared without a parameter list, as in the statement

```
SomeClass anObject;
```

then the effect depends upon what constructors (if any) the class provides.

If the class has no constructors at all, memory is allocated for `anObject` but its private data members are in an uninitialized state.

If the class does have constructors, then the default (parameterless) constructor is invoked if there is one. If there is no default constructor, a syntax error occurs.

5. If a class has at least one constructor, and an array of class objects is declared:

```
SomeClass arr[10];
```

then one of the constructors must be the default (parameterless) constructor. This constructor is invoked for each element of the array. There is no way to pass parameters to a constructor when creating an array of class objects.

Before leaving the topic of constructors, we give you a brief overview of another special member function supported by C++: the *class destructor*. Just as a constructor is implicitly invoked when a class object is created, a destructor is implicitly invoked when a class object is destroyed—for example, when control leaves the block in which a local object is declared. A class destructor is named the same as a constructor except that the first character is a tilde (~):

```
class SomeClass
{
public:
    .
    .
    .
    SomeClass();    // Constructor
    ~SomeClass();   // Destructor
private:
    .
    .
    .
};
```

We won't be using destructors; the kinds of classes we'll be writing have no need to perform special actions at the moment a class object is destroyed. In more advanced coursework, you will learn about situations in which you need to use destructors.

Object-Oriented Programming

Throughout this text we have used functional decomposition (also called *structured design*), in which we decompose a problem into modules, where each module is a self-contained collection of steps that solves one part of the overall problem. The process of implementing a functional decomposition is often called **structured** (or **procedural**) **programming.** Some modules are translated directly into a few programming language instructions, whereas others are coded as functions with or without parameters. The end result is a program that is a collection of interacting functions (see Figure 15-8). In structured design and programming, data are considered passive quantities to be acted upon by statements.

structured (procedural) programming
The construction of programs that are collections of interacting functions or procedures

In building large software systems, structured design has two important limitations. First, the technique yields an inflexible structure. If the top-level algorithm requires modification, the changes may force many lower level algorithms to be modified as well. Second, the technique does not lend itself easily to code reuse. By *code reuse* we mean the ability to use pieces of code—either as they are or adapted slightly—in other sections of the program or in other programs. It is rare to be able to take a complicated C++ function and reuse it easily in a different context.

object-oriented programming (OOP)
The use of data abstraction, inheritance, and dynamic binding to construct programs that are collections of interacting objects

A second methodology that especially facilitates reuse is object-oriented design (OOD), which we introduced briefly in Chapter 4. OOD decomposes a problem into objects—self-contained entities composed of data and operations on the data. The process of implementing an object-oriented design is called **object-oriented programming (OOP).** The end result is a program that is a collection of interacting objects (see Figure 15-9). In OOD and OOP, data play

FIGURE 15-8

Program Resulting
from Structured
(Procedural)
Programming

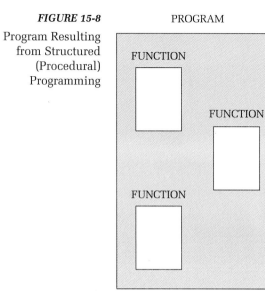

FIGURE 15-9

Program Resulting
from Object-
Oriented
Programming

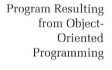

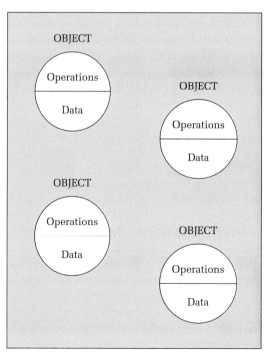

a leading role; the primary contribution of algorithms is to implement the operations on objects.

Several programming languages have been created specifically to support OOD and OOP: C++, Smalltalk, Simula, CLOS, Objective-C, Eiffel, Actor, Object-Pascal, recent versions of Turbo Pascal, and others. These languages, called *object-oriented programming languages,* have facilities for

1. data abstraction
2. inheritance
3. dynamic binding

You have already seen that C++ supports data abstraction through the class mechanism. Some non-OOP languages also have facilities for data abstraction. But only OOP languages support the other two concepts—*inheritance* and *dynamic binding.* Before we define these two concepts, we discuss some of the fundamental ideas and terminology of object-oriented programming.

Objects

The major principles of OOP originated as far back as the mid-1960s with a language called Simula. However, much of the current terminology of OOP is due to Smalltalk, a language developed in the late 1970s at Xerox's Palo Alto Research Center. In OOP, the term *object* has a very specific meaning: It is a self-contained entity encapsulating data and operations on the data. In other words, an object represents an instance of an ADT. More specifically, an object has an internal *state* (the current values of its private data, called *instance variables*), and it has a set of *methods* (public operations). Methods are the only means by which an object's state can be inspected or modified by another object. An object-oriented program consists of a collection of objects, communicating with one another by *message passing.* If object *A* wants object *B* to perform some task, object *A* sends a message containing the name of the object (*B*, in this case) and the name of the particular method to execute. *B* responds by executing this method in its own way, possibly changing its state and sending messages to other objects as well.

As you can tell, an object is quite different from a traditional data structure. A record is a passive data structure that contains only data and is acted upon by a program. In contrast, an object is an active data structure; the data and the code that manipulates the data are bound together within the object. In OOP jargon, an object can manipulate itself.

The literature of OOP is full of phrases such as "methods," "instance variables," and "sending a message to." But don't be put off by the vocabulary. Here are some OOP terms and their C++ equivalents:

OOP	C++
Object	Class object or class instance
Instance variable	Private data member
Method	Public member function
Message passing	Function call (to a public member function)

In C++, we define the properties and behavior of objects by using the class mechanism. Within a program, classes can be related to each other in various ways. The three most common relationships are:

1. Two classes are independent of each other and have nothing in common.
2. Two classes are related by *inheritance.*
3. Two classes are related by *composition.*

The first relationship—none—is not very "interesting." Let's look at the other two—inheritance and composition.

Inheritance

inheritance
A mechanism by which one class acquires the properties—the data and operations—of another class

base class (super-class)
The class being inherited from

derived class (sub-class)
The class that inherits

In the world at large, it is often possible to arrange concepts into an *inheritance hierarchy*—a hierarchy in which each concept inherits the properties of the concept immediately above it in the hierarchy. For example, we might classify different kinds of vehicles according to the inheritance hierarchy in Figure 15-10. Moving down the hierarchy, each kind of vehicle is more specialized than its *parent* (and all of its *ancestors*) and is more general than its *child* (and all of its *descendants*). A wheeled vehicle inherits properties common to all vehicles (it holds one or more people and carries them from place to place) but has an additional property that makes it more specialized (it has wheels). A car inherits properties common to all wheeled vehicles but also has additional, more specialized properties (four wheels, an engine, a body, and so forth).

The inheritance relationship can be viewed as an *is-a relationship.* Every two-door car is a car, every car is a wheeled vehicle, and every wheeled vehicle is a vehicle.

In OOP languages, **inheritance** is the mechanism by which one class acquires the properties of another class. You can take an existing class *A* (called the **base class** or **superclass**) and create from it a new class *B* (called the **derived class** or **subclass**). The derived class *B* inherits all the properties of its base class *A*. In particular, the data and operations defined for *A* are now also defined for *B*.

FIGURE 15-10

Inheritance
Hierarchy

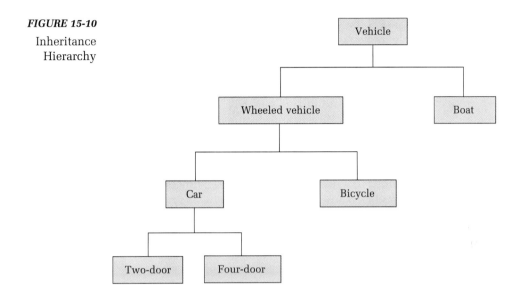

(Notice the is-a relationship—every *B* is also an *A*.) The idea, next, is to special-
ize class *B*, usually by adding specific properties to those already inherited from
A. Let's look at an example in C++.

Deriving One
Class from
Another

Suppose that someone has already written a `Time` class with the following
specification:

```cpp
class Time
{
public:
    void Set( /* in */ int hours,
              /* in */ int minutes,
              /* in */ int seconds );
    void Increment();
    void Write() const;
    Time( /* in */ int initHrs,          // Constructor
          /* in */ int initMins,
          /* in */ int initSecs );
    Time();                              // Default constructor,
                                         //    setting time to 0:0:0
private:
    int hrs;
    int mins;
    int secs;
};
```

This class is the same as our `TimeType`, simplified by omitting the `Equal` and `LessThan` member functions. Figure 15-11 displays a *class interface diagram* for the `Time` class. The public interface, shown as ovals in the side of the large circle, consists of the operations available to client code. The private data items shown in the interior are inaccessible to clients.

Suppose we want to modify the `Time` class by adding, as private data, a variable of an enumeration type indicating the (American) time zone—`EST` for Eastern Standard Time, `CST` for Central Standard Time, `MST` for Mountain Standard Time, `PST` for Pacific Standard Time, `EDT` for Eastern Daylight Time, `CDT` for Central Daylight Time, `MDT` for Mountain Daylight Time, or `PDT` for Pacific Daylight Time. We'll need to modify the `Set` function and the class constructors to accommodate a time zone value. And the `Write` function should print the time in the form

```
12:34:10 CST
```

The `Increment` function, which advances the time by one second, does not need to be changed.

To add these time-zone features to the `Time` class, the conventional approach would be to obtain the source code found in the `time.cpp` implementation file, analyze in detail how the class is implemented, then modify and recompile the source code. This process has several drawbacks. If `Time` is an off-the-shelf class on a system, the source code for the implementation is probably unavailable.

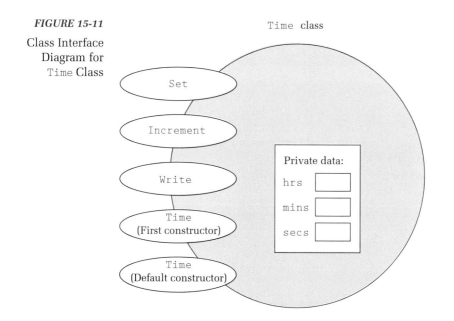

FIGURE 15-11

Class Interface Diagram for `Time` Class

Even if it is available, modifying it may introduce bugs into a previously de-bugged solution. Access to the source code also violates a principal benefit of ab-straction: Users of an abstraction should not need to know how it is implemented.

In C++ there is a far quicker and safer way in which to add time-zone fea-tures: Use inheritance. Let's derive a new class from the Time class and then spe-cialize it. This new, extended time class—call it ExtTime—inherits the members of its base class, Time. Here is the declaration of ExtTime:

```cpp
enum ZoneType {EST, CST, MST, PST, EDT, CDT, MDT, PDT};

class ExtTime : public Time
{
public:
    void Set( /* in */ int      hours,
              /* in */ int      minutes,
              /* in */ int      seconds,
              /* in */ ZoneType timeZone );
    void Write() const;
    ExtTime( /* in */ int      initHrs,        // Constructor
             /* in */ int      initMins,
             /* in */ int      initSecs,
             /* in */ ZoneType initZone );
    ExtTime();                                 // Default constructor,
                                               //   setting time to
private:                                       //   0:0:0 EST
    ZoneType zone;
};
```

The opening line

```cpp
class ExtTime : public Time
```

states that ExtTime is derived from Time. The reserved word public declares Time to be a *public base class* of ExtTime. This means that all public members of Time (except constructors) are also public members of ExtTime. In other words, Time's member functions Set, Increment, and Write can also be in-voked for ExtTime objects.* However, the public part of ExtTime specializes the

---

*If a class declaration omits the word public and begins as

```cpp
class DerivedClass : BaseClass
```

or if it explicitly uses the word private,

```cpp
class DerivedClass : private BaseClass
```

then BaseClass is called a *private base class* of DerivedClass. Public members of BaseClass are *not* public members of DerivedClass. That is, clients of DerivedClass cannot invoke BaseClass operations on DerivedClass objects. We do not work with private base classes in this book.

overriding

Reimplementing a member function inherited from a parent class

base class by reimplementing (**overriding**) the inherited functions Set and Write and by providing its own constructors.

The private part of ExtTime declares that a new private member is added: zone. The private members of ExtTime are therefore hrs, mins, secs (all inherited from Time), and zone. Figure 15-12 pictures the relationship between the ExtTime and Time classes.

This diagram shows that each ExtTime object has a Time object as a *subobject*. Every ExtTime is a Time, and more. C++ uses the terms base class and derived class instead of superclass and subclass. The terms superclass and subclass can be confusing because the prefix *sub* usually implies something smaller than the original (for example, subset of a mathematical set). In contrast, a subclass is often "bigger" than its superclass—that is, it has more data and/or functions.

In Figure 15-12, you see an arrow between the two ovals labeled Increment. Because Time is a public base class of ExtTime, and because Increment is not overridden by ExtTime, the Increment function available to clients of ExtTime is the same as the one inherited from Time. We use the arrow between the corresponding ovals to indicate this fact. (Notice in the diagram that Time's constructors are operations on Time, not on ExtTime. The ExtTime class must have its own constructors.)

◼ *Inheritance and Accessibility*

With C++, it is important to understand that inheritance does not imply accessibility. Although a derived class inherits the members of its base class, both private and public, it cannot access the private members of the base class. Figure 15-12 shows the variables hrs*,* mins*, and* secs *to be encapsulated within the* Time *class. Neither external client code nor* ExtTime *member functions can refer to these three variables directly. If a derived class were able to access the private members of its base class, any programmer could derive a class from another and then write code to directly inspect or modify the private data, defeating the benefits of encapsulation and information hiding.*

Specification of the ExtTime *Class*

Below is the specification of the ExtTime class. Notice that the preprocessor directive

```
#include "time.h"
```

is necessary for the compiler to verify the consistency of the derived class with its base class.

FIGURE 15-12   Class Interface Diagram for ExtTime Class

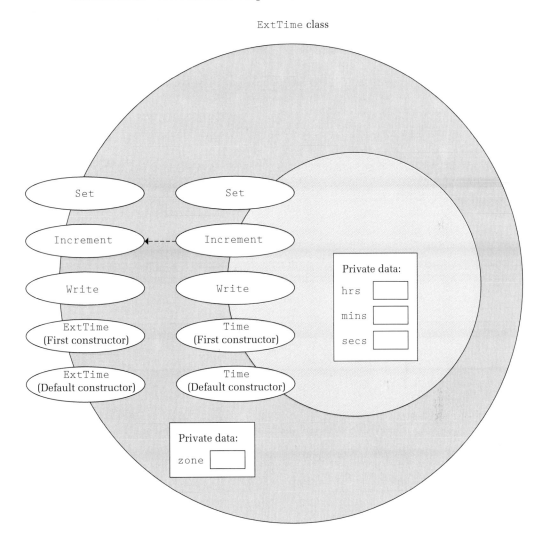

```
//*******************************************************************
// SPECIFICATION FILE (exttime.h)
// This file gives the specification of an ExtTime abstract data
// type.  The Time class is a public base class of ExtTime, so
// public operations of Time are also public operations of ExtTime.
//*******************************************************************
#include "time.h"

enum ZoneType {EST, CST, MST, PST, EDT, CDT, MDT, PDT};
class ExtTime : public Time
{
public:
    void Set( /* in */ int      hours,
              /* in */ int      minutes,
              /* in */ int      seconds,
              /* in */ ZoneType timeZone );

    void Write() const;

    ExtTime( /* in */ int      initHrs,
             /* in */ int      initMins,
             /* in */ int      initSecs,
             /* in */ ZoneType initZone );

    ExtTime();
private:
    ZoneType zone;
};
```

With this new class, the programmer can set the time with a time zone (via a class constructor or the overridden `Set` function), output the time with its time zone (via the overridden `Write` function), and increment the time by one second (via the inherited `Increment` function):

```
#include "exttime.h"
    .
    .
    .
ExtTime time1(8, 35, 0, PST);
ExtTime time2;                    // Default constructor called
time2.Write();                    // Outputs 0:0:0 EST
cout << endl;

time2.Set(16, 49, 23, CDT);
time2.Write();                    // Outputs 16:49:23 CDT
cout << endl;
```

```
time1.Increment();
time1.Increment();
time1.Write();                    // Outputs 08:35:02 PST
cout << endl;
    .
    .
    .
```

Implementation of the ExtTime **Class**

The implementation of the ExtTime class needs to deal only with the new features that are different from Time. Specifically, we must write code to override the Set and Write functions and we must write the two constructors.

With derived classes, constructors are subject to special rules. At run time, the base class constructor is implicitly called first, before the body of the derived class's constructor executes. Additionally, if the base class constructor requires parameters, these parameters must be passed by the derived class's constructor. To see how these rules pertain, let's examine the implementation file exttime.cpp (see Figure 15-13 on the next page).

In the first constructor in Figure 15-13, notice the syntax by which a constructor passes parameters to its base class constructor:

```
ExtTime::ExtTime( /* in */ int      initHrs,
                  /* in */ int      initMins,
                  /* in */ int      initSecs,
                  /* in */ ZoneType initZone )

    : Time(initHrs, initMins, initSecs)  ←—— Constructor initializer

{
    zone = initZone;
}
```

After the parameter list to the ExtTime constructor (but before its body), you insert what is called a *constructor initializer*—a colon and then the name of the base class along with the actual parameters to *its* constructor. When an ExtTime object is created with a declaration such as

```
ExtTime time1(8, 35, 0, PST);
```

the ExtTime constructor receives four parameters. The first three are simply passed along to the Time class constructor by means of the constructor initializer.

FIGURE 15-13

ExtTime
Implementation
File

```
//*******************************************************************
// IMPLEMENTATION FILE (exttime.cpp)
// This file implements the ExtTime member functions.
// The Time class is a public base class of ExtTime
//*******************************************************************
#include "exttime.h"
#include <iostream.h>


// Additional private members of class:
//      ZoneType zone;


//*******************************************************************


ExtTime::ExtTime( /* in */ int      initHrs,
                  /* in */ int      initMins,
                  /* in */ int      initSecs,
                  /* in */ ZoneType initZone )


    : Time(initHrs, initMins, initSecs)


// Constructor


{
    zone = initZone;
}


//*******************************************************************


ExtTime::ExtTime()


// Default constructor


{
    zone = EST;
}


//*******************************************************************


void ExtTime::Set( /* in */ int      hours,
                   /* in */ int      minutes,
                   /* in */ int      seconds,
                   /* in */ ZoneType timeZone )


{
    Time::Set(hours, minutes, seconds);
    zone = timeZone;
}
```

FIGURE 15-13
(*continued*)

```
//**********************************************************************

void ExtTime::Write() const

{
    static char zoneString[8][4] =
    {
        "EST", "CST", "MST", "PST", "EDT", "CDT", "MDT", "PDT"
    };

    Time::Write();
    cout << ' ' << zoneString[zone];
}
```

After the Time class constructor has executed (creating the base class subobject as shown in Figure 15-12), the body of the ExtTime constructor executes, setting zone equal to the fourth parameter.

The second constructor in Figure 15-13 (the default constructor) does not need a constructor initializer; there are no parameters to pass to the base class's default constructor. When an ExtTime object is created with the declaration

```
ExtTime time2;
```

the ExtTime class's default constructor first implicitly calls Time's default constructor, after which its body executes, setting zone to EST.

Next, look at the Set function in Figure 15-13. This function overrides the Set function inherited from the base class. Consequently, there are two distinct Set functions, one a public member of the Time class, the other a public member of the ExtTime class. Their full names are Time::Set and ExtTime::Set. In Figure 15-13, the ExtTime::Set function begins by "reaching up" into its base class and calling Time::Set to set the hours, minutes, and seconds. (Remember that a class derived from Time cannot access the private data hrs, mins, and secs directly; these variables are private to the Time class.) The function then finishes by assigning a value to ExtTime's private data, the zone variable.

The Write function in Figure 15-13 uses a similar strategy. It reaches up into its base class and invokes Time::Write to output the hours, minutes, and seconds. Then it outputs a string corresponding to the time zone. (Recall that a value of enumeration type cannot be output directly in C++. If we were to print the value of zone directly, the output would be an integer from 0 through 7—the internal representations of the ZoneType values. The Write function establishes an array of eight strings and selects the correct string by using zone to index into the array.)

Now we can compile the file exttime.cpp into an object code file, say, exttime.obj. After writing a test driver and compiling it into test.obj, we can obtain an executable file by linking three object files:

1. `test.obj`
2. `exttime.obj`
3. `time.obj`

We can then test the resulting program.

The remarkable thing about derived classes and inheritance is that modification of the base class is unnecessary. The source code for the implementation of the `Time` class may be unavailable. Yet variations of this ADT can continue to be created without that source code, in ways the creator never even considered. Through classes and inheritance, OOP languages facilitate code reuse. A class such as `Time` can be used as-is in many different contexts, or it can be adapted to a particular context by using inheritance. Inheritance allows us to create *extensible* data abstractions—a derived class typically extends the base class by including additional private data or public operations or both.

Composition

composition (containment)
A mechanism by which the internal data (the state) of one class includes an object of another class

Earlier we said that two classes typically exhibit one of the following relationships: They are independent of each other, they are related by inheritance, or they are related by **composition**. Composition (or **containment**) is the relationship in which the internal data of one class *A* include an object of another class *B*. Stated another way, a *B* object is contained within an *A* object.

C++ does not have (or need) any special language notation for composition. You simply declare an object of one class to be one of the data members of another class. Let's look at an example.

Design of a `TimeCard` Class

You are developing a program to manage a factory's payroll. Employees are issued time cards containing their ID numbers. When reporting for work, an employee "punches in" by inserting the card into a clock, which punches the current time onto the card. When leaving work, the employee takes a new card and "punches out" to record the departure time. For your program, you decide that you need a `TimeCard` ADT to represent an employee's time card. The abstract data consist of an ID number and a time. The abstract operations include Punch the Time, Print the Time Card Data, constructor operations, and others. To implement the ADT, you must choose a concrete data representation for the abstract data and you must implement the operations. Assuming an employee ID number is a large integer value, you choose the `long` data type to represent the ID number. To represent time, you remember that one of your friends has already written and debugged a `Time` class (we'll use the one from earlier in this chapter). At this point, you create a `TimeCard` class declaration as follows:

```
#include "time.h"
    .
    .
    .
class TimeCard
{
public:
    void Punch( /* in */ int hours,
                /* in */ int minutes,
                /* in */ int seconds );
    void Print() const;
    .
    .
    .
    TimeCard( /* in */ long idNum,
              /* in */ int  initHrs,
              /* in */ int  initMins,
              /* in */ int  initSecs );
    TimeCard();
private:
    long id;
    Time timeStamp;
};
```

In designing the TimeCard class, you have used composition; a TimeCard object is composed of a Time object (and a long variable). Composition creates a *has-a relationship*—a TimeCard object *has a* Time object as a subobject (see Figure 15-14).

Implementation The private data of TimeCard consist of a long variable named id and a Time
of the TimeCard object named timeStamp. The TimeCard member functions can manipulate id
Class by using ordinary built-in operations, but they must manipulate timeStamp through the member functions defined for the Time class. For example, you could implement the Print and Punch functions as follows:

```
void TimeCard::Print() const
{
    cout << "ID: " << id << " Time: ";
    timeStamp.Write();
}

void TimeCard::Punch( /* in */ int hours,
                      /* in */ int minutes,
                      /* in */ int seconds )
{
    timeStamp.Set(hours, minutes, seconds);
}
```

FIGURE 15-14 Class Interface Diagram for TimeCard Class

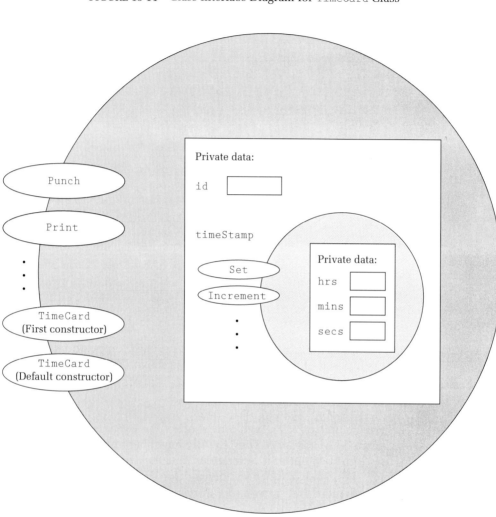

Implementing the class constructors is a bit more complicated to describe. Let's start with an implementation of the first constructor shown in the TimeCard class declaration:

```
TimeCard::TimeCard( /* in */ long idNum,
                    /* in */ int  initHrs,
                    /* in */ int  initMins,
                    /* in */ int  initSecs )

    : timeStamp(initHrs, initMins, initSecs)  ←——— Constructor initializer

{
    id = idNum;
}
```

This is the second time we've seen the unusual notation—the constructor initializer—inserted between the formal parameter list and the body of a constructor. The first time was when we implemented the parameterized ExtTime class constructor (Figure 15-13). There, we used the constructor initializer to pass some of the incoming parameters to the base class constructor. Here, we use a constructor initializer to pass some of the parameters to a member object's (timeStamp's) constructor. Whether you are using inheritance or composition, the purpose of a constructor initializer is the same: to pass parameters to another constructor. The only difference is the following: With inheritance, you specify the name of the *base class* prior to the actual parameter list:

```
ExtTime::ExtTime( /* in */ int      initHrs,
                  /* in */ int      initMins,
                  /* in */ int      initSecs,
                  /* in */ ZoneType initZone )

    : Time(initHrs, initMins, initSecs)
```

With composition, you specify the name of the *member object* prior to the actual parameter list:

```
TimeCard::TimeCard( /* in */ long idNum,
                    /* in */ int  initHrs,
                    /* in */ int  initMins,
                    /* in */ int  initSecs )

    : timeStamp(initHrs, initMins, initSecs)
```

Furthermore, if a class has several members that are objects of classes with parameterized constructors, you form a list of constructor initializers separated by commas:

```
SomeClass::SomeClass( ... )

    : memberObject1(param1, param2), memberObject2(param3)
```

Having discussed both inheritance and composition, we can give a complete description of the order in which constructors are executed:

Given a class X, if X is a derived class, its base class constructor is executed first. Next, constructors for member objects (if any) are executed. Finally, the body of X's constructor is executed.

When a `TimeCard` object is created, the constructor for its `timeStamp` member is first invoked. After the `timeStamp` object is constructed, the body of `TimeCard`'s constructor is executed, setting the `id` member equal to `idNum`.

The second constructor shown in the `TimeCard` class declaration—the default constructor—has no parameters and could be implemented as follows:

```
TimeCard::TimeCard()
{
    id = 0;
}
```

In this case, what happened to construction of the `timeStamp` member object? We didn't include a constructor initializer, so the `timeStamp` object is first constructed using the *default* constructor of the `Time` class, after which the body of the `TimeCard` constructor is executed. The result is a time card having a time stamp of 0:0:0 and an ID number of 0.

Dynamic Binding and Virtual Functions

Early in the chapter, we said that object-oriented programming languages provide language features that support three concepts: data abstraction, inheritance, and dynamic binding. The phrase *dynamic binding* means, more specifically, *dynamic binding of an operation to an object*. To explain this concept, let's begin with an example.

Given the `Time` and `ExtTime` classes of this chapter, the following code creates two class objects and outputs the time represented by each.

```
Time      startTime(8, 30, 0);
ExtTime   endTime(10, 45, 0, CST);

startTime.Write();
cout << endl;
endTime.Write();
cout << endl;
```

This code fragment invokes two different `Write` functions, even though the functions have the same name. The first function call invokes the `Write` function of the `Time` class, printing out three values: hours, minutes, and seconds. The second call invokes the `Write` function of the `ExtTime` class, printing out four values: hours, minutes, seconds, and time zone. In this code fragment, the compiler uses **static** (compile-time) **binding** of the operation (`Write`) to the appropriate object. The compiler can easily determine which `Write` function to call by checking the data type of the associated object.

static binding
The compile-time determination of which function to call for a particular object

In some situations, the compiler cannot determine the type of an object, and the binding of an operation to an object must occur at run time. One situation, which we look at now, involves parameter passage of class objects.

The basic C++ rule for passing class objects as parameters is that the actual parameter and its corresponding formal parameter must be of identical type. With inheritance, though, C++ relaxes the rule. You may pass an object of a child class *C* to an object of its parent class *P*, but not the other way around—that is, you cannot pass an object of type *P* to an object of type *C*. More generally, you can pass an object of a descendant class to an object of any of its ancestor classes. This rule has a tremendous benefit—it allows us to write a single function that applies to any descendant class instead of writing a different function for each. For example, we could write a fancy `Print` function that takes as a parameter an object of type `Time` or any class descended from `Time`:

```
void Print( /* in */ Time someTime )
{
    cout << "*************************" << endl;
    cout << "** The time is ";
    someTime.Write();
    cout << endl;
    cout << "*************************" << endl;
}
```

Given the code fragment

```
Time      startTime(8, 30, 0);
ExtTime   endTime(10, 45, 0, CST);

Print(startTime);
Print(endTime);
```

the compiler lets us pass either a `Time` object or an `ExtTime` object to the `Print` function. Unfortunately, the output is not what we would like. When `endTime` is printed, the time zone `CST` is missing from the output. Let's see why.

The Slicing Problem
Our `Print` function uses pass-by-value for the formal parameter `someTime`. Pass-by-value sends a copy of the actual parameter to the formal parameter. Whenever you pass an object of a child class to an object of its parent class using pass-by-value, only the data members they have in common are copied. Remember that a child class is often "larger" than its parent—that is, it contains additional data members. For example, a `Time` object has three data members (`hrs`, `mins`, and `secs`), but an `ExtTime` object has four data members (`hrs`, `mins`, `secs`, and `zone`). When the larger class object is copied to the smaller formal parameter using pass-by-value, the extra data members are discarded or "sliced off." This situation is called the *slicing problem* (see Figure 15-15).

(The slicing problem also occurs with assignment operations. In the statement

```
parentClassObject = childClassObject;
```

only the data members that the two objects have in common are copied. Additional data members contained in `childClassObject` are not copied.)

With pass-by-reference, the slicing problem does not occur because the *address* of the actual parameter is sent to the function. Let's change the heading of our `Print` function so that `someTime` is a reference parameter:

```
void Print( /* in */ Time& someTime )
```

Now when we pass `endTime` as the actual parameter, its address is sent to the function. Its time zone member is not sliced off because no copying takes place. But to our dismay, the `Print` function *still* prints only three of `endTime`'s data members—hours, minutes, and seconds. Within the `Print` function, the difficulty is that static binding is used in the statement

```
someTime.Write();
```

The compiler must generate machine language code for the `Print` function at compile time, but the type of the actual parameter (`Time` or `ExtTime`) isn't

FIGURE 15-15   The Slicing Problem Resulting from Pass-by-Value

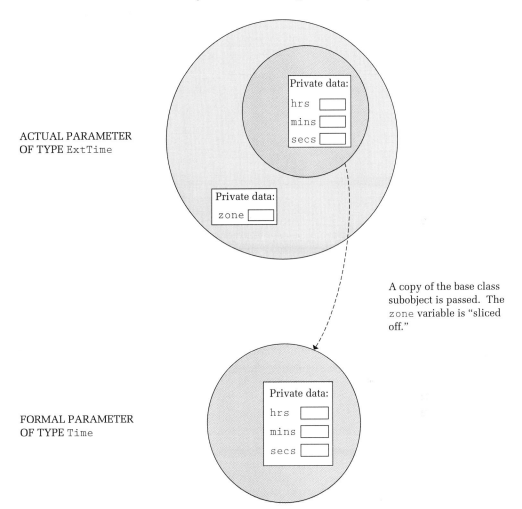

ACTUAL PARAMETER
OF TYPE ExtTime

A copy of the base class
subobject is passed. The
zone variable is "sliced
off."

FORMAL PARAMETER
OF TYPE Time

known until run time. How can the compiler know which Write function to use—Time::Write or ExtTime::Write? The compiler cannot know, so it uses Time::Write because the formal parameter someTime is of type Time. Therefore, the Print function always prints just three values—hours, minutes, and seconds—regardless of the type of the actual parameter. Fortunately, C++ provides a very simple solution to our problem: *virtual functions.*

Virtual Functions   Suppose we make one small change to our Time class declaration: We begin the declaration of the Write function with the reserved word virtual.

```
class Time
{
public:
    .
    .
    .
    virtual void Write() const;
    .
    .
    .
private:
    .
    .
    .
};
```

dynamic binding
The run-time determination of which function to call for a particular object

Declaring a member function to be `virtual` instructs the compiler to generate code that guarantees **dynamic** (run-time) **binding** of a function to an object. That is, the determination of which function to call is postponed until run time. (Note that to make `Write` a virtual function, the word `virtual` appears in one place only—the `Time` class declaration. It does not appear in the `Write` function definition that is located in the `time.cpp` file, nor does it appear in any descendant class—such as `ExtTime`—that overrides the `Write` function.)

Virtual functions work in the following way. If a class object is passed *by reference* to some function, and if the body of that function contains a statement

```
formalParam.MemberFunc( ... );
```

then

1. If `MemberFunc` is not a virtual function, the type of the *formal parameter* determines which function to call. (Static binding is used.)
2. If `MemberFunc` is a virtual function, the type of the *actual parameter* determines which function to call. (Dynamic binding is used.)

With just one word—`virtual`—the difficulties we encountered with our `Print` function disappear entirely. If we declare `Write` to be a virtual function in the `Time` class, the function

```
void Print( /* in */ Time& someTime )
{
    .
    .
    .
```

```
someTime.Write();
    .
    .
    .
}
```

works correctly for actual parameters either of type `Time` or of type `ExtTime`. The correct `Write` function (`Time::Write` or `ExtTime::Write`) is invoked because the actual parameter carries the information necessary at run time to choose the appropriate function. Deriving a new and unanticipated class from `Time` presents no complications. If this new class overrides the `Write` function, then our `Print` function still works correctly. Dynamic binding ensures that each object knows how to print itself, and the appropriate version will be invoked. In OOP terminology, `Write` is a **polymorphic operation**—an operation that has multiple meanings depending on the type of the object to which it is bound at run time.

polymorphic operation
An operation that has multiple meanings depending on the type of the object to which it is bound at run time

Here are some things to know about using virtual functions in C++:

1. To obtain dynamic binding, you must use pass-by-reference when passing a class object to a function. If you use pass-by-value, the compiler does not use the `virtual` mechanism; instead, member slicing and static binding occur.
2. In the declaration of a virtual function, the word `virtual` appears only in the base class, not in any derived class.
3. If a base class declares a virtual function, it *must* implement that function, even if the body is empty.
4. A derived class is not required to provide its own reimplementation of a virtual function. In this case, the base class's version is used by default.
5. A derived class cannot redefine the function return type of a virtual function.

Object-Oriented Design

We have looked at language features that let us implement an object-oriented design. Now let's turn to the phase that precedes implementation—OOD itself.

A computer program usually models some real-life activity or concept. A banking program models the real-life activities associated with a bank. A spreadsheet program models a real spreadsheet, a large paper form used by accountants and financial planners. A robotics program models human perception and human motion.

Nearly always, the aspect of the world that we are modeling (the *application domain* or *problem domain*) consists of objects—checking accounts, bank tellers, spreadsheet rows, spreadsheet columns, robot arms, robot legs. The computer program that solves the real-life problem also includes objects (the *solution domain*)—counters, lists, menus, windows, and so forth. OOD is based on the philosophy that programs are easier to write and understand if the major objects in a program correspond closely to the objects in the problem domain.

There are many ways in which to perform object-oriented design. Different authors advocate different techniques. Our purpose is not to choose one particular technique or to present a summary of all the techniques. It is to describe a three-step process that captures the essence of OOD:

1. Identify the objects and operations.
2. Determine the relationships among objects.
3. Design the driver.

In this section, we do not show a complete example of an object-oriented design of a problem solution. Instead, we describe the important issues involved in each of the three steps.

Step 1: Identify the Objects and Operations

Recall that functional decomposition begins with identification of the major actions the program is to perform. In contrast, OOD begins by identifying the major objects and the associated operations on those objects. In both design methods, it is often difficult to see where to start.

A good way to start to identify solution-domain objects is to look at the problem domain. More specifically, go to the problem definition and look for important nouns and verbs. The nouns (and noun phrases) may suggest objects; the verbs (and verb phrases) may suggest operations. For example, the problem definition for a banking program might include the following sentences:

. . . The program must handle a customer's savings account. The customer is allowed to deposit funds into the account and withdraw funds from the account, and the bank must pay interest on a quarterly basis. . . .

In these sentences, the key nouns are

Savings account
Customer

and the key verb phrases are

Deposit funds
Withdraw funds
Pay interest

Although we are working with a very small portion of the entire problem definition, the list of nouns suggests two potential objects: `savingsAccount` and `customer`. The operations on a `savingsAccount` object are suggested by the list of verb phrases—namely, `Deposit`, `Withdraw`, and `PayInterest`. What are the operations on a `customer` object? We would need more information from the rest of the problem definition in order to answer this question. In fact, `customer` may not turn out to be a useful object at all. The nouns-and-verbs technique is only a starting point—it points us to *potential* objects and operations.

Determining which nouns and verbs are significant is one of the most difficult aspects of OOD. There are no cookbook formulas for doing so, and there probably never will be. Not all nouns become objects, and not all verbs become operations. The nouns-and-verbs technique is imperfect, but it does give us a first approximation to a solution.

The solution domain includes not only objects drawn from the problem domain but also *implementation-level* objects. These are objects that do not model the problem domain but are used in building the program itself. In systems with graphical user interfaces—Microsoft Windows or the Macintosh operating system, for example—a program may need several kinds of implementation-level objects: window objects, menu objects, objects that respond to mouse clicks, and so on. Objects such as these are often available in class libraries so that we don't need to design and implement them from scratch each time we need them in different programs.

Step 2:
Determine the
Relationships
Among Objects

After selecting potential objects and operations, the next step is to examine the relationships among the objects. In particular, we want to see whether certain objects might be related either by inheritance or by composition. Inheritance and composition relationships not only pave the way for code reuse—as we emphasized in our discussion of OOP—they also simplify the design and allow us to model the problem domain more accurately. For example, the banking problem may require several kinds of savings accounts—one for general customers, another for preferred customers, and another for children under the age of 12. If these are all variations on a basic savings account, the is-a relationship (and, therefore, inheritance) is probably appropriate. Starting with a SavingsAccount class that provides operations common to any savings account, we could design each of the other accounts as a child class of SavingsAccount, concentrating our efforts only on the properties that make each one different from the parent class.

Sometimes the choice between inheritance and composition is not immediately clear. Earlier we wrote a TimeCard class to represent an employee's time card. Given an existing Time class, we used composition to relate TimeCard and Time—the private part of the TimeCard class is composed of a Time object (and an ID number). We could also have used inheritance. We could have derived class TimeCard from Time (inheriting the hours, minutes, and seconds members) and then specialized it by adding an extra data member (the ID number) and the extra operations of Punch, Print, and so forth. Both inheritance and composition give us four private data members: hours, minutes, seconds, and ID number. However, the use of inheritance means that all of the Time operations are also valid for TimeCard objects. A user of the TimeCard class could—either intentionally or accidentally—invoke operations such as Set and Increment, which are not appropriate operations on a time card. Furthermore, inheritance leads to a confused design in this example. It is not true that a `TimeCard` *is a* `Time`; rather, a `TimeCard` *has a* `Time` (and an ID number). In general, the best design strategy is to use inheritance for is-a relationships and composition for has-a relationships.

Step 3: Design the Driver The final step is to design the driver—the top-level algorithm. In OOD, the driver is the glue that puts the objects (along with their operations) together. When implementing the design in C++, the driver becomes the `main` function.

Notice that structured design *begins* with the design of the top-level algorithm, whereas OOD *ends* with the top-level algorithm. In OOD, most of the control flow has already been designed in steps 1 and 2; the algorithms are located within the operations on objects. As a result, the driver often has very little to do but process user commands or input some data and then delegate tasks to various objects.

◾ The Iterative Nature of Object-Oriented Design

Software developers, researchers, and authors have proposed many different strategies for performing OOD. Common to nearly all of these strategies are three fundamental steps:

1. *Identify the objects and operations.*
2. *Determine the relationships among objects.*
3. *Design the driver.*

Experience with large software projects has shown that these three steps are not necessarily sequential—step 1, step 2, step 3, then we are done. In practice, step 1 occurs first, but only as a first approximation. During steps 2 and 3, new objects or operations may be discovered, leading us back to step 1 again. It is realistic to think of steps 1 through 3 not as a sequence but as a loop.

Furthermore, each step is an iterative process within itself. Step 1 may entail working and reworking our view of the objects and operations. Similarly, steps 2 and 3 often involve experimentation and revision. In any step, we may conclude that a potential object is not useful after all. Or we might decide to add or eliminate operations on a particular object.

There is always more than one way to solve a problem. Iterating and reiterating through the design phase leads to insights that produce a better solution.

Implementing the Design

In OOD, when we first identify an object, it is an *abstract object*. We do not immediately choose an exact data representation for that object. Similarly, the operations on objects begin as *abstract operations*, because there is no initial attempt to provide algorithms for these operations.

Eventually, we have to implement the objects and operations. For each abstract object, we must

- choose a suitable data representation.
- create algorithms for the abstract operations.

To select a data representation for an object, the C++ programmer has three options:

1. Use a built-in data type.
2. Use an existing ADT.
3. Create a new ADT.

For a given object, a good rule of thumb is to consider these three options in the order listed. A built-in type is the most straightforward to use and understand, and operations on these types are already defined by the language. If a built-in type is not adequate to represent an object, you should survey available ADTs in a class library (either the system's or your own) to see if any are a good match for the abstract object. If no suitable ADT exists, you must design and implement a new ADT to represent the object.

Fortunately, even if you must resort to option 3, the mechanisms of inheritance and composition allow you to combine options 2 and 3. When we needed an `ExtTime` class earlier in the chapter, we used inheritance to build on an existing `Time` class. And when we created a `TimeCard` class, we used composition to include a `Time` object in the private data.

In addition to choosing a data representation for the abstract object, we must implement the abstract operations. With OOD, the algorithms that implement the abstract operations are often short and straightforward. We have seen numerous examples in this chapter in which the code for ADT operations is only a few lines long. But this is not always the case. If an operation is extremely complex, it may be best to treat the operation as a new problem and use functional decomposition on the control flow. In this situation, it is appropriate to apply both functional decomposition and object-oriented methodologies together. Experienced programmers are familiar with both methodologies and use them either independently or in combination with each other. However, the software development community is becoming increasingly convinced that, although functional decomposition is important for designing low-level algorithms and operations on ADTs, the future in developing huge software systems lies in OOD and OOP.

Testing and Debugging

Testing and debugging a C++ class amounts to testing and debugging each member function of the class. All of the techniques you have learned about—algorithm walk-throughs, code walk-throughs, hand traces, test drivers, verification of preconditions and postconditions, debug outputs, the `assert` function, and the system debugger—may be brought into play.

Consider how we might test this chapter's `TimeType` class. Here is the class declaration, abbreviated by leaving out the function preconditions and post-conditions:

```
class TimeType
{
public:
    void Set( /* in */ int hours,
              /* in */ int minutes,
              /* in */ int seconds );

    void Increment();

    void Write() const;

    Boolean Equal( /* in */ TimeType otherTime ) const;

    Boolean LessThan( /* in */ TimeType otherTime ) const;

    TimeType( /* in */ int initHrs,
              /* in */ int initMins,
              /* in */ int initSecs );

    TimeType();
private:
    int hrs;
    int mins;
    int secs;
};
```

To test this class fully, we must test each of the member functions. Let's step through the process of testing just one of them: the `Increment` function.

We implemented the `Increment` function as follows:

```
void TimeType::Increment()

{
    secs++;
    if (secs > 59)
    {
        secs = 0;
        mins++;
        if (mins > 59)
        {
            mins = 0;
```

```
            hrs++;
            if (hrs > 23)
                hrs = 0;
        }
    }
}
```

For test data we should pick values of `hrs`, `mins`, and `secs` that ensure code coverage. To execute every path through the control flow, we need cases where

1. the first If condition is `false`
2. the first If condition is `true` and the second is `false`
3. the first If condition is `true`, the second is `true`, and the third is `false`
4. the first If condition is `true`, the second is `true`, and the third is `true`

Below is a table displaying values of `hrs`, `mins`, and `secs` that correspond to these four cases. For each case we also write down what we hope will be the values of the variables after executing the algorithm.

Case	Initial Values			Expected Results		
	hrs	mins	secs	hrs	mins	secs
1	10	5	30	10	5	31
2	4	6	59	4	7	0
3	13	59	59	14	0	0
4	23	59	59	0	0	0

Finally, we write a test driver for the `Increment` function:

```
#include <iostream.h>
#include "timetype.h"

int main()
{
    TimeType time;
    int      hours;
    int      minutes;
    int      seconds;

    cout << "Enter a time (use hours < 0 to quit): ";
    cin >> hours >> minutes >> seconds;
    while (hours >= 0)
```

```
    {
        time.Set(hours, minutes, seconds);
        time.Increment();
        cout << "Incromonted time is ";
        time.Write();
        cout << endl;
        cout << "Enter a time (use hours < 0 to quit): ";
        cin >> hours >> minutes >> seconds;
    }
    return 0;
}
```

The `timetype.cpp` implementation file only needs to contain function definitions for the following member functions: `Set`, `Increment`, `Write`, and the default constructor. The other member functions do not need to be implemented yet. Now we compile the test driver and `timetype.cpp`, link the two object files, and execute the program. For input data we supply the four test cases discussed earlier. The program's output should match the desired results.

Now that we have tested the `Increment` function, we can apply the same steps to the remaining class member functions. We can create a separate test driver for each function or we can write just one driver that tests all of the functions. The disadvantage of writing just one driver is that devising different combinations of input values to test several functions at once can quickly become complicated.

Before leaving the topic of testing a class, we must emphasize an important point. Even though a class has been tested thoroughly, it is still possible for bugs to arise. Let's look at two examples using the `TimeType` class. The first example is the client statement

```
time.Set(24, 0, 0);
```

The second example is the test

```
if (time1.LessThan(time2))
    .
    .
    .
```

where the programmer intends `time1` to be 11:00:00 on a Wednesday and `time2` to be 1:20:00 on a Thursday. (The result of the test is `false`, not `true` as the programmer expects.) Do you see the problem? In each example, the client has violated the function precondition. The precondition of `Set` requires the first parameter to have a value from 0 through 23. The precondition of `LessThan` requires the two times to be on the same day, not on two different days.

If a class has been well tested and there are bugs when client code uses the class, always check the member function preconditions. You can waste many hours trying to debug a class member function when, in fact, the function is correct. The bug may lie in the client code.

When an object-oriented program uses inheritance and composition, the order in which you test the classes is, in a sense, predetermined. If class X is derived from class Y or contains an object of class Y, you cannot test X until you have designed and implemented Y. Thus, it makes sense to test and debug class Y before testing class X. The general principle is that if class X is built on class Y (through inheritance or composition), the testing of X is simplified if Y is already tested and is known to behave correctly.

Testing and Debugging Hints

1. The declarations of `struct` and class types both end with semicolons.
2. Regarding semicolons, the declarations and definitions of class member functions are treated the same as any C++ function. The member function prototype, located in the class declaration, ends with a semicolon. The function heading—the part of the function definition preceding the body—does not end with a semicolon.
3. When implementing a class member function, don't forget to prefix the function name with the name of the class and the scope resolution operator (: :).

```
void TimeType::Increment()
{
    .
    .
    .
}
```

4. The only built-in operations that apply to class objects are member selection (.) and assignment (=). To perform other operations, such as comparing two class objects, you must write class member functions.
5. If a class member function inspects but does not modify the private data, it is a good idea to make it a `const` member function.
6. A member function does not use dot notation to access private members of the class object for which the function is invoked. In contrast, a member function *must* use dot notation to access the private members of a class object that is passed to it as a parameter.
7. To avoid bugs caused by uninitialized data, it is good practice to always include a class constructor when designing a class.
8. A class constructor is declared without a return value type and cannot return a function value.
9. It is not possible to pass parameters to a class constructor when creating an array of class objects. The class either must have no constructors at all or

      must include a default (parameterless) constructor, which is then invoked for each element of the array.

10. If a client of a class has bugs that seem to be related to the class, start by checking the preconditions of the class member functions The errors may be in the client, not the class.

11. When using inheritance, don't forget to include the word `public` when declaring the derived class:

```
class DerivedClass : public BaseClass
{
    .
    .
    .
};
```

      The word `public` makes `BaseClass` a public base class of `DerivedClass`. That is, clients of `DerivedClass` can apply any public `BaseClass` operation (except constructors) to a `DerivedClass` object.

12. The header file containing the declaration of a derived class must `#include` the header file containing the declaration of the base class.

13. Although a derived class inherits the private and public members of its base class, it cannot directly access the inherited private members.

14. If a base class has a constructor, it is invoked before the derived class's constructor is executed. If the base class constructor requires parameters, you must pass these parameters using a constructor initializer:

```
DerivedClass::DerivedClass( ... )
    : BaseClass(param1, param2)
{
    .
    .
    .
}
```

      If you do not include a constructor initializer, the base class's default constructor is invoked.

15. If a class has a member that is an object of another class and this member object's constructor requires parameters, you must pass parameters using a constructor initializer:

```
SomeClass::SomeClass( ... )
    : memberObject(param1, param2)
```

```
{
        .
        .
        .
}
```

If there is no constructor initializer, the member object's default constructor is invoked.

16. To obtain dynamic binding of an operation to an object when passing class objects as parameters, you must

- pass the object using pass-by-reference.
- declare the operation to be `virtual` in the class declaration.

17. If a base class declares a virtual function, it *must* implement that function even if the body is empty.

18. A derived class cannot redefine the function return type of a virtual function.

Summary

Data abstraction is a powerful technique for reducing the complexity and increasing the reliability of programs. Separating the properties of a data type from the details of its implementation frees the user of the type from having to write code that depends on a particular implementation of the type. This separation also assures the implementor of the type that client code cannot accidentally compromise a correct implementation.

An abstract data type (ADT) is a type whose specification is separate from its implementation. The specification announces the abstract properties of the type. The implementation consists of (a) a concrete data representation and (b) the implementations of the ADT operations. In C++, an ADT can be realized by using the class mechanism. The members of a class are not only data but also functions. Class members can be designated as public or private. Most commonly, the private members are the concrete data representation of the ADT, and the public members are the functions corresponding to the ADT operations.

Among the public member functions of a class, the programmer often includes one or more class constructors—functions that are invoked automatically whenever a class object is created.

Separate compilation of program units is central to the separation of specification from implementation. The declaration of a C++ class is typically placed in a specification (`.h`) file, and the implementations of the class member functions reside in another file: the implementation file. The client code is compiled separately from the class implementation file, and the two resulting object code files are linked together to form an executable file. Through separate compilation, the user of an ADT can treat the ADT as an off-the-shelf component without ever seeing how it is implemented.

Object-oriented design (OOD) decomposes a problem into objects—self-contained entities in which data and operations are bound together. In OOD, data are treated as active, rather than passive, quantities. Each object is responsible for one part of the solution, and the objects communicate by invoking one another's operations.

OOD begins by identifying potential objects and their operations. Examining objects in the problem domain is a good way to begin the process. The next step is to determine the relationships among the objects using inheritance (to express is-a relationships) and composition (to express has-a relationships). Finally, a driver algorithm is designed to coordinate the overall flow of control.

Object-oriented programming (OOP) is the process of implementing an object-oriented design by using language mechanisms for data abstraction, inheritance, and dynamic binding. Inheritance allows any programmer to take an existing class (the base class) and create a new class (the derived class) that inherits the data and operations of the base class. The derived class then specializes the base class by adding new private data, adding new operations, or overriding inherited operations—all without analyzing and modifying the implementation of the base class in any way. Dynamic binding of operations to objects allows objects of many different derived types to respond to a single function name, each in its own way. Together, inheritance and dynamic binding have been shown to reduce dramatically the time and effort required to customize existing ADTs. The result is truly reusable software components whose applications and lifetimes extend beyond those conceived of by the original creator.

Quick Check

1. The specification of an ADT describes only its properties (the domain and allowable operations). To implement the ADT, what two things must a programmer do? (pp. 498–500)
2. Write a C++ class declaration for the following Checkbook ADT. Do not implement the ADT other than to include in the private part a concrete data representation for the current balance. All monetary amounts are to be represented as floating point numbers.

   TYPE
     Checkbook
   DOMAIN
     Each instance of the Checkbook type is a value representing one customer's current checking account balance.
   OPERATIONS
     Open the checking account, specifying an initial balance.
     Write a check for a specified amount.

Deposit a specified amount into the checking account.
Return the current balance.

(pp. 500–502)

3. Write a segment of client code that declares two `Checkbook` objects, one for a personal checkbook and one for a business account. (pp. 500–502)
4. For the personal checkbook in Question 3, write a segment of client code that opens the account with an initial balance of $300.00, writes two checks for $50.25 and $150.00, deposits $87.34 into the account, and prints out the resulting balance. (pp. 502–506)
5. Implement the following `Checkbook` member functions. (pp. 510–514)
   a. `Open`
   b. `WriteCheck`
   c. `CurrentBalance`
6. A compile-time error occurs if a client of `Checkbook` tries to access the private class members directly. Give an example of such a client statement. (pp. 506–508)
7. In which file—the specification file or the implementation file—would the solution to Question 2 be located? In which file would the solution to Question 5 be located? (pp. 508–514)
8. For the `Checkbook` class, replace the `Open` function with two C++ class constructors. One (the default constructor) initializes the account balance to zero. The other initializes the balance to an amount passed as a parameter. (pp. 517–520)
   a. Revise the class declaration.
   b. Implement the two class constructors.
9. Fill in the blanks: Functional decomposition results in a program that is a collection of interacting _____ , whereas OOP results in a program that is a collection of interacting _____ . (pp. 523–525)
10. Name the three language features that characterize object-oriented programming languages. (pp. 523–525)
11. What is the difference between static and dynamic binding of an operation to an object? (pp. 540–545)
12. Although there are many specific techniques for performing OOD, this chapter uses a three-step process. What are these three steps? (pp. 545–548)
13. When selecting a data representation for an abstract object, what three choices does the C++ programmer have? (pp. 548–549)

Answers 1. a. Choose a concrete data representation of the abstract data, using data types that already exist. b. Implement each of the allowable operations in terms of program instructions.

```
2. class Checkbook
   {
   public:
       void Open( /* in */ float initBalance );
       void WriteCheck( /* in */ float amount );
       void Deposit( /* in */ float amount );
       float CurrentBalance() const;
   private:
       float balance;
   };

3. Checkbook personalAcct;
   Checkbook businessAcct;
```

4. ```
personalAcct.Open(300.0);
personalAcct.WriteCheck(50.25);
personalAcct.WriteCheck(150.0);
personalAcct.Deposit(87.34);
cout << '$' << personalAcct.CurrentBalance() << endl;
```

5. a. ```
void Checkbook::Open( /* in */ float initBalance )
{
    balance = initBalance;
}
```

   b. ```
void Checkbook::WriteCheck(/* in */ float amount)
{
    balance = balance - amount;
}
```

   c. ```
float Checkbook::CurrentBalance() const
{
    return balance;
}
```

6. ```
personalAcct.balance = 10000.0;
```

7. The C++ class declaration of Question 2 would be located in the specification file. The C++ function definitions of Question 5 would be located in the implementation file.

8. a. ```
class Checkbook
{
public:
    void WriteCheck( /* in */ float amount );
    void Deposit( /* in */ float amount );
    float CurrentBalance() const;
    Checkbook();
    Checkbook( /* in */ float initBalance );
private:
    float balance;
};
```

   b. ```
Checkbook::Checkbook()
{
    balance = 0.0;
}
Checkbook::Checkbook(/* in */ float initBalance)
{
    balance = initBalance;
}
```

9. functions, objects    10. Data abstraction, inheritance, dynamic binding
```

11. With static binding, the determination of which function to call for an object occurs at compile time. With dynamic binding, the determination of which function to call for an object occurs at run time.   12. Identify the objects and operations, determine the relationships among the objects, and design the driver.   13. Use a built-in data type, use an existing ADT, or create a new ADT.

Exam Preparation Exercises

1. The specification of an abstract data type (ADT) should not mention implementation details. (True or False?)
2. Below are some real-world objects you might want to represent in a program as ADTs. For each, give some abstract operations that might be appropriate. (Ignore the concrete data representation for each object.)
   a. A thesaurus
   b. An automatic dishwasher
   c. A radio-controlled model airplane
3. Consider the following C++ class declaration and client code:

Class Declaration	*Client Code*

```
class SomeClass                SomeClass object1;
{                              SomeClass object2;
public:                        int      m;
    void Func1( int n );
    int Func2( int n ) const;  object1.Func1(3);
    void Func3();              m = object2.Func2(5);
private:
    int someInt;
};
```

   a. List all the identifiers that refer to data types (both built-in and programmer-defined).
   b. List all the identifiers that are names of class members.
   c. List all the identifiers that are names of class objects.
   d. List the names of all member functions that are allowed to inspect the private data.
   e. List the names of all member functions that are allowed to modify the private data.
   f. In the implementation of SomeClass, which one of the following would be the correct function definition for Func3?
      i. void Func3()
         {
               .
               .
               .
         }

ii. ```
void SomeClass::Func3()
    {
       .
       .
       .
    }
```

iii. ```
SomeClass::void Func3()
    {
       .
       .
       .
    }
```

4. Define the following terms:

instantiate
const member function
specification file
implementation file

5. To the TimeType class we wish to add three operations: CurrentHrs, CurrentMins, and CurrentSecs. These operations simply return the current values of the private data to the client. We can amend the class declaration by inserting the following function prototypes into the public part:

```
int CurrentHrs() const;
    // Postcondition:
    //      Function value == hours part of the time of day

int CurrentMins() const;
    // Postcondition:
    //      Function value == minutes part of the time of day

int CurrentSecs() const;
    // Postcondition:
    //      Function value == seconds part of the time of day
```

Write the function definitions for these three functions as they would appear in the implementation file.

6. Answer the following questions about Figure 15-6, which illustrates the process of compiling and linking a multifile program.
   a. If only the file myprog.cpp is modified, which files must be recompiled?
   b. If only the file myprog.cpp is modified, which files must be relinked?
   c. If only the files file2.cpp and file3.cpp are modified, which files must be recompiled? (Assume that the modifications do not affect existing code in myprog.cpp.)
   d. If only the files file2.cpp and file3.cpp are modified, which files must be relinked? (Assume that the modifications do not affect existing code in myprog.cpp.)

7. Define the following terms:

scope resolution operator
separate compilation
C++ class constructor
default constructor

8. The following class has two constructors among its public member functions:

```
class SomeClass
{
public:
    float Func1() const;
        .
        .
        .
    SomeClass( /* in */ float f );
        // Precondition:
        //      f is assigned
        // Postcondition:
        //      Private data is initialized to f
    SomeClass();
        // Postcondition:
        //      Private data is initialized to 8.6
private:
    float someFloat;
};
```

Write declarations for the following class objects.
a. An object obj1, initialized to 0.0.
b. An object obj2, initialized to 8.6.
c. An array arr1 of class objects, each initialized to 8.6. (If it cannot be done, explain why.)
d. An array arr2 of class objects, each initialized to 24.7. (If it cannot be done, explain why.)

9. The C++ compiler will signal a syntax error in the following class declaration. What is the error?

```
class SomeClass
{
public:
    void Func1( int n );
    int  Func2();
    int  SomeClass();
private:
    int privateInt;
};
```

10. Define the following terms:

    functional decomposition   method (of an object)
    code reuse   is-a relationship
    state (of an object)   has-a relationship
    instance variable (of an object)

11. In C++, inheritance allows a derived class to access directly all of the functions and data of its base class. (True or False?)

12. Given an existing class declaration

```
class Sigma
{
public:
      void Write() const;
        .

        .

        .

private:
      int n;
};
```

    a programmer derives a new class `Epsilon` as follows:

```
class Epsilon : Sigma
{
public:
    void Twist();
    Epsilon( /* in */ float initVal );
private:
    float x;
};
```

    Then the following client code results in a compile-time error:

```
Epsilon someObject(4.8);

someObject.Write();    // Error
```

    a. Why is the call to the `Write` function erroneous?
    b. How would you fix the problem?

13. Consider the following two class declarations:

```
class Abc
{
public:
    void DoThis();
private:
    void DoThat();
```

```
    int   alpha;
    int   beta;
};

class Xyz : public Abc
{
public:
    void TryIt();
private:
    int gamma;
};
```

For *each* class, do the following:
a. List all private data members.
b. List all private data members that the class's member functions can reference directly.
c. List all functions that the class's member functions can invoke.
d. List all member functions that a client of the class may legally invoke.

14. A class *X* uses both inheritance and composition as follows. *X* is derived from class *Y* and has a member that is an object of class *Z*. When an object of class *X* is created, in what order are the constructors for classes *X*, *Y*, and *Z* executed?

15. With parameter passage in C++, you can pass an object of an ancestor class to a formal parameter that is an object of a descendant class. (True or False?)

16. Define the following terms associated with object-oriented design:

    problem domain
    solution domain
    implementation-level object

17. Mark each of the following statements as True or False.
    a. Every noun and noun phrase in a problem definition becomes an object in the solution domain.
    b. For a given problem, there are usually more objects in the solution domain than in the problem domain.
    c. In the three-step process for performing object-oriented design, all decisions made during each step are final.

18. For each of the following design methodologies, at what general time (beginning, middle, end) is the driver—the top-level algorithm—designed?
    a. Object-oriented design
    b. Structured (top-down) design

19. Fill in each blank with either *is-a* or *has-a*.
    In general, the best strategy in object-oriented design is to use inheritance for _____ relationships and composition for _____ relationships.

Programming Warm-Up Exercises

1. The `TimeType` class supplies two member functions, `Equal` and `LessThan`, that correspond to the relational operators `==` and `<`. Show how *client code* can simulate the other four relational operators (`!=`, `<=`, `>`, and `>=`) using only the `Equal` and

LessThan functions. Specifically, express each of the following pseudocode statements in C++, where time1 and time2 are objects of type TimeType.

a. IF time1 ≠ time2
     Set n = 1
b. IF time1 ≤ time2
     Set n = 5
c. IF time1 > time2
     Set n = 8
d. IF time1 ≥ time2
     Set n = 5

2. In reference to Programming Warm-Up Exercise 1, make life easier for the user of the TimeType class by adding new member functions NotEqual, LessOrEqual, GreaterThan, and GreaterOrEqual to the class.
   a. Show the function specifications (prototypes and preconditions and postconditions) as they would appear in the new class declaration.
   b. Write the function definitions as they would appear in the implementation file. (*Hint:* Instead of writing the algorithms from scratch, simply have the function bodies invoke the existing functions Equal and LessThan. And remember: Class members can refer to each other directly without using dot notation.)

3. Enhance the TimeType class by adding a new member function WriteAmPm. This function prints the time in 12-hour rather than 24-hour form, adding AM or PM at the end. Show the function specification (prototype and precondition and postcondition) as it would appear in the new class declaration. Then write the function definition as it would appear in the implementation file.

4. Add a member function named Minus to the TimeType class. This value-returning function yields the difference in seconds between the times represented by two class objects. Show the function specification (prototype and precondition and postcondition) as it would appear in the new class declaration. Then write the function definition as it would appear in the implementation file.

5. a. Design the data sets necessary to thoroughly test the LessThan function of the TimeType class.
   b. Write a driver and test the LessThan function using your test data.

6. a. Design the data sets necessary to thoroughly test the Write function of the TimeType class.
   b. Write a driver and test the Write function using your test data.

7. a. Design the data sets necessary to thoroughly test the WriteAmPm function of Programming Warm-Up Exercise 3.
   b. Write a driver and test the WriteAmPm function using your test data.

8. Reimplement the TimeType class so that the private data representation is a single variable:

```
long secs;
```

This variable represents time as the number of seconds since midnight. *Do not change the public interface in any way.* The user's view is still hours, minutes, and seconds, but the class's view is seconds since midnight.

Notice how this data representation simplifies the `Equal` and `LessThan` functions but makes the other operations more complicated by converting seconds back and forth to hours, minutes, and seconds. Use auxiliary functions, hidden inside the implementation file, to perform these conversions instead of duplicating the algorithms in several places.

9. Below is the specification of a "safe array" class, which halts the program if an array index goes out of bounds. (Recall that C++ does not check for out-of-bounds indices when you use built-in arrays.)

```cpp
const int MAX_SIZE = 200;


class IntArray
{
public:
    int ValueAt( /* in */ int i ) const;
        // Precondition:
        //      i is assigned
        // Postcondition:
        //      IF i >= 0  &&  i < declared size of array
        //          Function value == value of array element
        //                              at index i
        //      ELSE
        //          Program has halted with error message


    void Store( /* in */ int val,
                /* in */ int i   );
        // Precondition:
        //      val and i are assigned
        // Postcondition:
        //      IF i >= 0  &&  i < declared size of array
        //          val is stored in array element i
        //      ELSE
        //          Program has halted with error message


    IntArray( /* in */ int arrSize );
        // Precondition:
        //      arrSize is assigned
        // Postcondition:
        //      IF arrSize >= 1  &&  arrSize <= MAX_SIZE
        //          Array created with all array elements == 0
        //      ELSE
        //          Program has halted with error message
private:
    int arr[MAX_SIZE];
    int size;
};
```

Implement each member function as it would appear in the implementation file. To halt the program, use the `exit` function supplied by the C++ standard library through the header file `stdlib.h` (see Appendix C).

10. a. Design the data sets necessary to thoroughly test the `IntArray` class of Programming Warm-Up Exercise 9.

   b. Write a driver and test the `IntArray` class using your test data.

11. The following class represents a person's mailing address in the United States.

```
typedef char String20[21];

class Address
{
public:
    void Write() const;
    Address( /* in */ const String20 newStreet,
             /* in */ const String20 newCity,
             /* in */ const String20 newState,
             /* in */ const String20 newZip    );
private:
    String20 street;
    String20 city;
    String20 state;
    String20 zipCode;
};
```

Using inheritance, we want to derive an international address class, `InterAddress`, from the `Address` class. For this exercise, an international address has all the attributes of a U.S. address plus a country code (a string indicating the name of the country). The public operations of `InterAddress` are `Write` (which overrides the `Write` function inherited from `Address`) and a class constructor that receives five parameters (street, city, state, zip code, and country code). Write a class declaration for the `InterAddress` class.

12. Implement the `InterAddress` class constructor.

13. Implement the `Write` function of the `InterAddress` class.

14. Write a global function `PrintAddress` that takes a single parameter and uses dynamic binding to print either a U.S. address or an international address. Make the necessary change(s) in the declaration of the `Address` class so that `PrintAddress` executes correctly.

Programming Problems

1. A rational number is a number that can be expressed as a fraction whose numerator and denominator are integers. Examples of rational numbers are 0.75 (which is ¾) and 1.125 (which is %). The value π is not a rational number; it cannot be expressed as the ratio of two integers.

   Working with rational numbers on a computer is often a problem. Inaccuracies in floating point representation can yield imprecise results. For example, the result of the C++ expression

```
1.0 / 3.0 * 3.0
```

is likely to be a value like 0.999999 rather than 1.0.

Design, implement, and test a `Rational` class that represents a rational number as a pair of integers instead of a single floating point number. The `Rational` class should have two class constructors. The first one lets the client specify an initial numerator and denominator. The other—the default constructor—creates the rational number 0, represented as a numerator of 0 and a denominator of 1. The segment of client code

```
Rational num1(1, 3);
Rational num2(3, 1);
Rational result;

cout << "The product of ";
num1.Write();
cout << " and ";
num2.Write();
cout << " is ";
result = num1.MultipliedBy(num2);
result.Write();
```

would produce the output

```
The product of 1/3 and 3/1 is 1/1
```

At the very least, you should provide the following operations:

- constructors for explicit as well as default initialization of `Rational` objects
- arithmetic operations that add, subtract, multiply, and divide two `Rational` objects. These should be implemented as value-returning functions, each returning a `Rational` object.
- a Boolean operation that compares two `Rational` objects for equality
- an output operation that displays the value of a `Rational` object in the form numerator/denominator

Include any additional operations that you think would be useful for a rational number class.

2. A complex ("imaginary") number has the form $a + bi$, where i is the square root of -1. Here, a is called the real part and b is called the imaginary part. Alternatively, $a + bi$ can be expressed as the ordered pair of real numbers (a, b).

Arithmetic operations on two complex numbers (a, b) and (c, d) are as follows:

$$(a, b) + (c, d) = (a + c, b + d)$$
$$(a, b) - (c, d) = (a - c, b - d)$$
$$(a, b) * (c, d) = (a*c - b*d, a*d + b*c)$$
$$(a, b)(c, d) = \left(\frac{a*c + b*d}{c^2 + d^2}, \frac{b*c - a*d}{c^2 + d^2} \right)$$

Also, the absolute value (or magnitude) of a complex number is defined as

$$| (a, b) | = \sqrt{a^2 + b^2}$$

Design, implement, and test a complex number class that represents the real and imaginary parts as double precision values (data type `double`) and provides at least the following operations:

- constructors for explicit as well as default initialization. The default initial value should be (0.0, 0.0).
- arithmetic operations that add, subtract, multiply, and divide two complex numbers. These should be implemented as value-returning functions, each returning a class object.
- a complex absolute value operation
- two observer operations, `RealPart` and `ImagPart`, that return the real and imaginary parts of a complex number

3. Design, implement, and test a countdown timer class named `Timer`. This class mimics a real-world timer by counting off seconds, starting from an initial value. When the timer reaches zero, it beeps (by sending the alert character, `'\a'`, to the standard output device). Some appropriate operations might be the following:

- Create a timer, initializing it to a specified number of seconds.
- Start the timer.
- Reset the timer to some value.

When the `Start` operation is invoked, it should repeatedly decrement and output the current value of the timer approximately every second. To delay the program for one second, use a For loop whose body does absolutely nothing; that is, its body is the null statement. Experiment with the number of loop iterations to achieve as close to a one-second delay as you can.

If your C++ standard library provides functions to clear the screen and to position the cursor anywhere on the screen, you might want to do the following. Begin by clearing the screen. Then, always display the timer value at the same position in the center of the screen. Each output should overwrite the previous value displayed, just like a real-world timer.

4. In Chapter 12, we introduced the list informally as an abstract data type. Design, implement, and test a class named `IntList`. Each `IntList` object is an unordered list of up to 100 `int` values. (Recall that an unordered list is one whose components are not assumed to be arranged in order of value.) Include at least the following operations:

- Create an initially empty list.
- Report whether the list is empty (`true` or `false`).
- Report whether the list is full (`true` or `false`).
- Insert a specified integer into the list.
- Delete a specified integer from the list.
- Search for a specified integer, returning `true` or `false` according to whether the item is present in the list.
- Sort the list into ascending order.
- Output all the items in the list.

Think carefully as you choose a precondition for each operation. For example, the precondition for the `Delete` operation should be that the list is not empty. Fortunately, the client can check this precondition by first invoking the operation that reports whether the list is empty. You should also decide whether it is allowed to delete a nonexistent integer from the list. If it is allowed, the `Delete` operation should silently have no effect (and the postcondition should make this clear to the user). If it is not allowed, you should say so in the precondition. The burden of error checking is then on the caller, not on the `Delete` operation.

For the concrete data representation of `IntList`, you might consider using two items: a 100-element `int` array to hold the list items, and a simple variable that stores the current length of the list.

5. Modify Programming Problem 4 by creating an *ordered* integer list class, `OrdIntList`. Keep the list in ascending order at all times when inserting and deleting items. Remove the `Sort` operation; it is no longer necessary. Notice that the algorithms for inserting, deleting, and searching are now different from those in Programming Problem 4. You may want to review the discussions of these operations in Chapter 12.

6. Your parents are thinking of opening a video rental store. Because they are helping with your tuition, they ask you to write a program to handle their inventory.

What are the major objects in a rental store? The items to be rented and people who rent them. You begin with the abstraction of the items to be rented—video tapes. To determine the characteristics of a video object, you jot down a list of questions.

- Should the object be one physical video, or should it be a title (to allow for multiple copies of a video)?
- What information about each title should be kept?
- Should the object contain a place for the card number of the person who has it rented?
- If there are multiple copies, is it important to keep track of specific copies?
- What operations should a video object be able to execute?

You decide that the basic object is the title, not an individual tape. The number of copies owned can be a data member of the object. Other data members should include the title, the movie stars, the producer, the director, and the production company. The system eventually must be able to track who has rented which videos, but this is not a property of the video object itself. You'll worry about how to represent the "has rented" object later. For now, who has which specific copy is not important.

The video object must have operations to initialize it and access the various data members. In addition, the object should adjust the number of copies (up or down), determine if a copy is available, check in a copy, and check out a copy. Because you will need to create a list of videos later, you decide to include operations that compare titles and print titles.

You decide to stop at this point, implement the video object, and test it before going on to the rest of the design.

7. Having completed the design and testing of the video object in Programming Problem 1, you are ready to continue with the original problem. Write a program to do the following tasks.
   a. Create a list of video objects.

    b. Search the list for a particular title.

    c. Determine if there are any copies of a particular video currently in the store.

    d. Print the list of video titles.

8. Now that the video inventory is under control, determine the characteristics of the customer and define a customer object. Write the operations and test them. Using this representation of a customer, write a program to do the following tasks.

    a. Create a list of customers.

    b. Search the list by customer name.

    c. Search the list by customer identification number.

    d. Print the list of customer names.

9. Combine the list of video objects and the list of customer objects into a program with the following capabilities.

    a. Check out a video.

    b. Check in a video.

    c. Determine how many videos a customer has (by customer identification number).

    d. Determine which customers have a certain video checked out (by title).

    (*Hint:* Create a `hasVideo` object that has a video title and a customer number.)

Recursion

GOALS

- To be able to identify the base case(s) and the general case in a recursive definition
- To be able to write a recursive algorithm for a problem involving only simple variables
- To be able to write a recursive algorithm for a problem involving composite variables

recursive call
A function call in which the function being called is the same as the one making the call

www.jbpub.com/C++links

In C++, any function can call another function. A function can even call itself! When a function calls itself, it is making a **recursive call.** The word *recursive* means "having the characteristic of coming up again, or repeating." In this case, a function call is being repeated by the function itself. Recursion is a powerful technique that can be used in place of iteration (looping).

Recursive solutions are generally less efficient than iterative solutions to the same problem. However, some problems lend themselves to simple, elegant, recursive solutions. Some programming languages are especially oriented to recursive algorithms—LISP is one of these. C++ lets us implement both iterative and recursive algorithms.

Our examples are broken into two groups: problems that use only simple variables and problems that use structured variables. If you are studying recursion before reading Chapter 11 on structured data types, then cover only the first set of examples and leave the rest until you have completed the chapters on structured data types.

What Is Recursion?

You may have seen a set of gaily painted Russian dolls that fit inside one another. Inside the first doll is a smaller doll, inside of which is an even smaller doll, inside of which is yet a smaller doll, and so on. A recursive algorithm is like such a set of Russian dolls. It reproduces itself with smaller and smaller examples of itself until a solution is found—that is, until there are no more dolls. The recursive algorithm is implemented by using a function that makes recursive calls to itself.

In Chapter 8, we wrote a function named `Power`, which calculates the result of raising an integer to a positive power. If X is an integer and N is a positive integer, the formula for X^N is

$$X^N = \underbrace{X * X * X * X * \ldots * X}_{N \text{ times}}$$

We could also write this formula as

$$X^N = X * \underbrace{(X * X * \ldots * X)}_{(N-1) \text{ times}}$$

or even as

$$X^N = X * X * \underbrace{(X * X * \ldots * X)}_{(N-2) \text{ times}}$$

In fact, we can write the formula concisely as

$$X^N = X * X^{N-1}$$

recursive definition
A definition in which something is defined in terms of smaller versions of itself

base case
The case for which the solution can be stated nonrecursively

general case
The case for which the solution is expressed in terms of a smaller version of itself; also known as recursive case

recursive algorithm
A solution that is expressed in terms of (a) smaller instances of itself and (b) a base case

This definition of X^N is a classic **recursive definition**—that is, a definition given in terms of a smaller version of itself.

X^N is defined in terms of multiplying X times X^{N-1}. How is X^{N-1} defined? Why, as $X * X^{N-2}$, of course! And X^{N-2} is $X * X^{N-3}$; X^{N-3} is $X * X^{N-4}$; and so on. In this example, "in terms of smaller versions of itself" means that the exponent is decremented each time.

When does the process stop? When we have reached a case where we know the answer without resorting to a recursive definition. In this example, it is the case where N equals 1: X^1 is X. The case (or cases) for which an answer is explicitly known is called the **base case.** The case for which the solution is expressed in terms of a smaller version of itself is called the **recursive** or **general case.** A **recursive algorithm** is an algorithm that expresses the solution in terms of a call to itself, a recursive call. A recursive algorithm must terminate; that is, it must have a base case.

Figure 16-1 shows a recursive version of the `Power` function with the base case and the recursive call marked. The function is embedded in a program that reads in a number and an exponent and prints the result.

Each recursive call to `Power` can be thought of as creating a completely new copy of the function, each with its own copies of the parameters `x` and `n`. The value of `x` remains the same for each version of `Power`, but the value of `n` decreases by one for each call until it becomes 1.

Let's trace the execution of this recursive function, with `number` equal to 2 and `exponent` equal to 3. We use a new format to trace recursive routines: We number the calls and then discuss what is happening in paragraph form.

Call 1: `Power` is called by `main`, with `number` equal to 2 and `exponent` equal to 3. Within `Power`, the formal parameters `x` and `n` are initialized to 2 and 3, respectively. Because `n` is not equal to 1, `Power` is called recursively with `x` and `n − 1` as parameters. Execution of Call 1 pauses until an answer is sent back from this recursive call.

FIGURE 16-1

Power Function

```
//****************************************************************
// Exponentiation program
//****************************************************************
#include <iostream.h>

int Power( int, int );

int main()
{
    int number;              // Number that is being raised to power
    int exponent;            // Power the number is being raised to

    cin >> number >> exponent;
    cout << Power(number, exponent);  ←——— // Nonrecursive call
    return 0;
}

//****************************************************************

int Power( /* in */ int x,    // Number that is being raised to power
           /* in */ int n )   // Power the number is being raised to

// Computes x to the n power

{
    if (n == 1)
        return x;  ←——————————————— // Base case
    else
        return x * Power(x, n - 1);  ←——— // Recursive call
}
```

Call 2: x is equal to 2 and n is equal to 2. Because n is not equal to 1, the function Power is called again, this time with x and n − 1 as parameters. Execution of Call 2 pauses until an answer is sent back from this recursive call.

Call 3: x is equal to 2 and n is equal to 1. Because n equals 1, the value of x is to be returned. This call to the function has finished executing, and the function return value (which is 2) is passed back to the place in the statement from which the call was made.

Call 2: This call to the function can now complete the statement that contained the recursive call because the recursive call has returned. Call 3's return value (which is 2) is multiplied by x. This call to the function has finished executing, and the function return value (which is 4) is passed back to the place in the statement from which the call was made.

Call 1: This call to the function can now complete the statement that contained the recursive call because the recursive call has returned. Call 2's return value (which is 4) is multiplied by x. This call to the function has finished executing, and the function return value (which is 8) is passed back to the place in the statement from which the call was made. Because the first call (the nonrecursive call in main) has now completed, this is the final value of the function Power.

This trace is summarized in Figure 16-2. Each box represents a call to the Power function. The values for the parameters for that call are shown in each box.

infinite recursion
The situation in which a function calls itself over and over endlessly

What happens if there is no base case? We have **infinite recursion,** the recursive equivalent of an infinite loop. For example, if the statement

```
if (n == 1)
```

were omitted, Power would be called over and over again. Infinite recursion also occurs if Power is called with n less than or equal to zero.

In actuality, recursive calls can't go on forever. When a function is called, the computer system creates temporary storage for the actual parameters and the

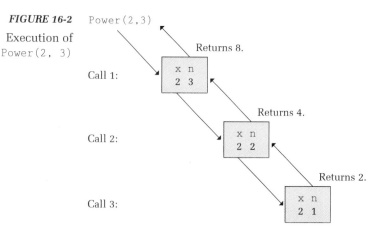

FIGURE 16-2

Execution of Power(2, 3)

function's (automatic) local variables. With infinite recursion, each time the function calls itself, a little more memory is used to store the new copies of the variables. Eventually, all the memory space is used. At that point, the program crashes.

Let's organize what we have done in our `Power` function into an outline for writing recursive algorithms.

1. Understand the problem. (We threw this in for good measure; it is always the first step.)
2. Determine the base case(s).
3. Determine the recursive case(s).

We used the power algorithm to demonstrate recursion because it is easy to visualize. In practice, one would never want to calculate this function using the recursive solution. The iterative solution is simpler and much more efficient because starting a new iteration of a loop is a faster operation than calling a function. If we compare the code for the iterative and recursive versions of the power problem we see that the iterative version has a local variable, whereas the recursive version has none. There are usually fewer local variables in a recursive routine than in an iterative routine. Also, the iterative version always has a loop, while the recursive version always has a selection statement.

In the next section, we examine a more complicated problem—one in which the recursive solution is not immediately apparent.

Towers of Hanoi

One of your first toys may have been three pegs with colored circles of different diameters. If so, you probably spent countless hours moving the circles from one peg to another. If we put some constraints on how the circles or disks can be moved, we have an adult game called the Towers of Hanoi. When the game begins, all the circles are on the first peg in order by size, with the smallest on the top. The object of the game is to move the circles, one at a time, to the third peg. The catch is that a circle cannot be placed on top of one that is smaller in diameter. The middle peg can be used as an auxiliary peg, but it must be empty at the beginning and at the end of the game.

To get a feel for how this might be done, let's look at some sketches of what the configuration must be at certain points if a solution is possible. We use four circles or disks. The beginning configuration is:

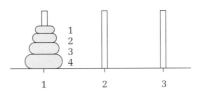

To move the largest circle (circle 4) to peg 3, we must move the three smaller circles to peg 2. Then circle 4 can be moved into its final place:

Let's assume we can do this. Now, to move the next largest circle (circle 3) into place, we must move the two circles on top of it onto an auxiliary peg (peg 1 in this case):

To get circle 2 into place, we must move circle 1 to another peg, freeing circle 2 to be moved to its place on peg 3:

The last circle (circle 1) can now be moved into its final place, and we are finished:

Notice that to free circle 4, we had to move three circles to another peg. To free circle 3, we had to move two circles to another peg. To free circle 2, we had to move one circle to another peg. This sounds like a recursive algorithm: to free the *n*th circle, we have to move $n - 1$ circles. Each stage can be thought of as beginning again with three pegs, but with one less circle each time. Let's see if we can summarize this process, using *n* instead of an actual number.

Get N Circles Moved from Peg 1 to Peg 3

Get n – 1 circles moved from peg 1 to peg 2
Move nth circle from peg 1 to peg 3
Get n – 1 circles moved from peg 2 to peg 3

This algorithm certainly sounds simple; surely there must be more. But this really is all there is to it.

Let's write a recursive function that implements this algorithm. We can't actually move disks, of course, but we can print out a message to do so. Notice that the beginning peg, the ending peg, and the auxiliary peg keep changing during the algorithm. To make the algorithm easier to follow, we call the pegs `beginPeg`, `endPeg`, and `auxPeg`. These three pegs, along with the number of circles on the beginning peg, are the parameters of the function.

We have the recursive or general case, but what about a base case? How do we know when to stop the recursive process? The clue is in the expression "Get *n* circles moved." If we don't have any circles to move, we don't have anything to do. We are finished with that stage. Therefore, when the number of circles equals 0, we do nothing (that is, we return).

```
void DoTowers(
    /* in */ int circleCount,    // Number of circles to move
    /* in */ int beginPeg,       // Peg containing circles to move
    /* in */ int auxPeg,         // Peg holding circles temporarily
    /* in */ int endPeg       )  // Peg receiving circles being moved
{
    if (circleCount > 0)
    {
        // Move n - 1 circles from beginning peg to auxiliary peg

        DoTowers(circleCount - 1, beginPeg, endPeg, auxPeg);
        cout << "Move circle from peg " << beginPeg
            << " to peg " << endPeg << endl;

        // Move n - 1 circles from auxiliary peg to ending peg

        DoTowers(circleCount - 1, auxPeg, beginPeg, endPeg);
    }
}
```

It's hard to believe that such a simple algorithm actually works, but we'll prove it to you. Following is a driver program that calls the DoTowers function. Output statements have been added so you can see the values of the actual parameters with each recursive call. Because there are two recursive calls within the function, we have indicated which recursive statement issued the call.

```cpp
//*********************************************************************
// TestTowers program
// This program, a test driver for the DoTowers function, reads in
// a value from standard input and passes this value to DoTowers
//*********************************************************************
#include <iostream.h>
#include <iomanip.h>    // For setw()

void DoTowers( int, int, int, int );

int main()
{
    int circleCount;    // Number of circles on starting peg

    cout << "Input number of circles: ";
    cin >> circleCount;
    cout << "OUTPUT WITH " << circleCount << " CIRCLES" << endl
        << endl;
    cout << "CALLED FROM  #CIRCLES" << setw(8) << "BEGIN"
        << setw(8) << "AUXIL." << setw(5) << "END"
        << "    INSTRUCTIONS" << endl
        << endl;
    cout << "Original  :";
    DoTowers(circleCount, 1, 2, 3);
    return 0;
}


//*********************************************************************

void DoTowers(
    /* in */ int circleCount,    // Number of circles to move
    /* in */ int beginPeg,       // Peg containing circles to move
    /* in */ int auxPeg,         // Peg holding circles temporarily
    /* in */ int endPeg     )    // Peg receiving circles being moved

// This recursive function moves circleCount circles from beginPeg
// to endPeg.  All but one of the circles are moved from beginPeg
// to auxPeg, then the last circle is moved from beginPeg to endPeg,
// and then the circles are moved from auxPeg to endPeg.
// The subgoals of moving circles to and from auxPeg are what
// involve recursion
```

```
{
    cout << setw(6) << circleCount << setw(9) << beginPeg
        << setw(7) << auxPeg << setw(7) << endPeg << endl;
    if (circleCount > 0)
    {
        cout << "From  first:";
        DoTowers(circleCount - 1, beginPeg, endPeg, auxPeg);
        cout << setw(58) << "Move circle " << circleCount
            << " from " << beginPeg << " to " << endPeg << endl;
        cout << "From second:";
        DoTowers(circleCount - 1, auxPeg, beginPeg, endPeg);
    }
}
```

The output from a run with three circles follows. "Original" means that the parameters listed beside it are from the nonrecursive call, which is the first call to DoTowers. "From first:" means that the parameters listed are for a call issued from the first recursive statement. "From second:" means that the parameters listed are for a call issued from the second recursive statement. Notice that a call cannot be issued from the second recursive statement until the preceding call from the first recursive statement has completed execution.

OUTPUT WITH 3 CIRCLES

CALLED FROM	#CIRCLES	BEGIN	AUXIL.	END	INSTRUCTIONS
Original :	3	1	2	3	
From first:	2	1	3	2	
From first:	1	1	2	3	
From first:	0	1	3	2	
					Move circle 1 from 1 to 3
From second:	0	2	1	3	
					Move circle 2 from 1 to 2
From second:	1	3	1	2	
From first:	0	3	2	1	
					Move circle 1 from 3 to 2
From second:	0	1	3	2	
					Move circle 3 from 1 to 3
From second:	2	2	1	3	
From first:	1	2	3	1	
From first:	0	2	1	3	
					Move circle 1 from 2 to 1
From second:	0	3	2	1	
					Move circle 2 from 2 to 3
From second:	1	1	2	3	
From first:	0	1	3	2	
					Move circle 1 from 1 to 3
From second:	0	2	1	3	

Recursive Algorithms with Structured Variables

In our definition of a recursive algorithm, we said there were two cases: the recursive or general case, and the base case. In the general case for all our algorithms so far, a parameter was expressed in terms of a smaller value each time. When structured variables are used, the recursive case is often in terms of a smaller structure rather than a smaller value; the base case occurs when there are no values left to process in the structure.

We examine a recursive algorithm for printing the contents of a one-dimensional array of *n* elements to show what we mean.

Print Array

```
IF more elements
    Print the value of the first element
    Print Array of n − 1 elements
```

The recursive case is to print the values in an array that is one element "smaller"; that is, the length of the array decreases by 1 with each recursive call. The base case is when the length of the array becomes 0—that is, when there are no more elements to print.

Our parameters must include the index of the first element (the one to be printed). How do we know when there are no more elements to print (that is, when the length of the array to be printed is 0)? We know we have printed the last element in the array when the index of the next element to be printed is beyond the index of the last element in the array. Therefore, the index of the last array element must be passed as a parameter. We call the indices `first` and `last`. When `first` is greater than `last`, we are finished. The name of the array is `list`.

```
void Print( /* in */ const int list[],   // Array to be printed
            /* in */       int first,     // Index of first element
            /* in */       int last  )    // Index of last element
{

    if (first <= last)
    {                                          // Recursive case
        cout << list[first] << endl;
        Print(list, first + 1, last);
    }
    // Empty else-clause is the base case
}
```

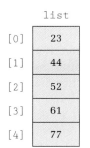

list

[0]	23
[1]	44
[2]	52
[3]	61
[4]	77

tail recursion
A recursive algorithm in which no statements are executed after the return from the recursive call

Figure 16-3 illustrates execution of the function call

```
Print(list, 0, 4);
```

using the array shown at the left.

Notice that once the deepest call (the call with the highest number) was reached, each of the calls before it returned without doing anything. When no statements are executed after the return from the recursive call to the function, the recursion is known as **tail recursion**. Tail recursion often indicates that the problem could be solved more easily using iteration. We used the array example because it made the recursive process easy to visualize; in practice, an array should be printed iteratively.

Notice that the array gets smaller with each recursive call (list[first]... list[last]). If we want to print the array elements in reverse order recursively, all we have to do is interchange the two statements within the If statement.

FIGURE 16-3

Execution of
Print(list,0,4)

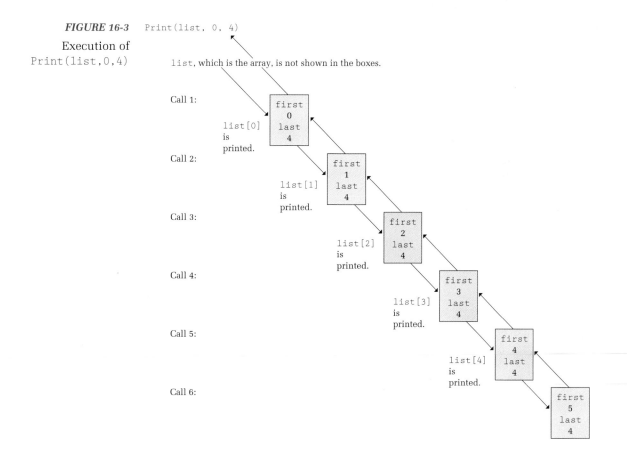

Recursion or Iteration?

www.jbpub.com/C++links

Recursion and iteration are alternative ways of expressing repetition in a program. Which is better to use: recursion or iteration? There is no simple answer to this question. The choice usually depends on two issues: efficiency and the nature of the problem being solved.

Historically, the quest for efficiency, in terms of both execution speed and memory usage, has favored iteration over recursion. Each time a recursive call is made, the system must allocate space for all (automatic) local variables and actual parameters. The overhead involved in any function call is time-consuming. On early, slow computers with limited memory capacity, recursive algorithms were slower than the iterative versions. However, studies have shown that on modern, fast computers, the overhead of recursion is often so small that the increase in computation time is almost unnoticeable to the user. Except in cases where efficiency is absolutely critical, then, the choice between recursion and iteration more often depends on the second issue—the nature of the problem being solved.

Consider the power algorithm we discussed earlier in the chapter. In this case, an iterative solution was obvious and easy to devise. We imposed a recursive solution on this problem only to demonstrate how recursion works. As a rule of thumb, if an iterative solution is more obvious or easier to understand, use it; it will be more efficient. However, there are problems for which the recursive solution is more obvious or easier to devise, such as the Towers of Hanoi problem. (It turns out that Towers of Hanoi is surprisingly difficult to solve using iteration.) Computer science students should be aware of the power of recursion. If the definition of a problem is inherently recursive, then a recursive solution should certainly be considered.

Testing and Debugging

Recursion is a powerful technique when used correctly. Improperly used, recursion can cause errors that are difficult to diagnose. The best way to debug a recursive algorithm is to construct it correctly in the first place. To be realistic, however, we give a few hints about where to look if an error occurs.

Testing and Debugging Hints

1. Be sure there is a base case. If there is no base case, the algorithm continues to issue recursive calls until all of memory has been used. An error message such as "STACK OVERFLOW" indicates that the base case is missing.
2. Be sure you have not used a While structure. The basic structure in a recursive algorithm is the If-Then-Else. There must be at least two cases: the recursive case and the base case. If the base case does nothing, the else-clause

is not present. The selection structure, however, must be there. If a While statement is used in a recursive algorithm, the While statement usually should not contain a recursive call.

3. As with nonrecursive functions, do not reference global variables directly within a recursive function unless you have justification for doing so.

4. Formal parameters that relate to the size of the problem must be value parameters, not reference parameters. The actual parameters that relate to the size of the problem are usually expressions. Arbitrary expressions can be passed only to value parameters.

5. Use your system's debugger program (or use debug output statements) to trace a series of recursive calls. Inspecting the values of parameters and local variables often helps to locate errors in a recursive algorithm.

Summary

A recursive algorithm is expressed in terms of a smaller instance of itself. It must include a recursive case, for which the algorithm is expressed in terms of itself, and a base case, for which the algorithm is expressed in nonrecursive terms.

In many recursive problems, the smaller instance refers to a numeric parameter that is being reduced with each call. In other problems, the smaller instance refers to the size of the data structure being manipulated. The base case is the one in which the size of the problem (value or structure) reaches a point where an explicit answer is known.

In the example for printing an array, the size of the problem was the length of the array being printed. When the array length became 0, the printing process was complete.

In the Towers of Hanoi game, the size of the problem was the number of disks to be moved. When there was only one left on the beginning peg, it could be moved to its final destination.

Quick Check

1. What distinguishes the base case from the recursive case in a recursive algorithm? (pp. 572–575)
2. What is the base case in the Towers of Hanoi algorithm? (pp. 575–579)
3. In working with simple variables, the recursive case is often stated in terms of a smaller value. What is typical of the recursive case in working with structured variables? (pp. 580–581)

Answers   1. The base case is the simplest case, the case where the solution can be stated nonrecursively.   2. When there are no more circles left to move.   3. It is often stated in terms of a smaller structure.

Exam Preparation Exercises

1. Recursion is an example of:
   a. selection
   b. a data structure
   c. repetition
   d. data-flow programming
2. A void function can be recursive, but a value-returning function cannot. (True or False?)
3. When a function is called recursively, the actual parameters and automatic local variables of the calling version are saved until its execution is resumed. (True or False?)
4. Given the recursive formula $F(N) = -F(N - 2)$, with base case $F(0) = 1$, what are the values of $F(4)$, $F(6)$, and $F(5)$? (If any of the values are undefined, say so.)
5. What algorithm error(s) lead to infinite recursion?
6. What control structure appears most commonly in a recursive function?
7. If you develop a recursive algorithm that employs tail recursion, what should you consider?
8. A recursive algorithm depends on making something smaller. When the algorithm works on a data structure, what may become smaller?
   a. Distance from a position in the structure.
   b. The data structure.
   c. The number of variables in the recursive function.
9. Given the following input:

   ```
   15
   23
   21
   19
   ```

   what is the output of the following program?

   ```
   #include <iostream.h>

   void PrintNums();

   int main()
   {
       PrintNums();
       cout << endl;
       return 0;
   }

   //*****************************************
   ```

```
void PrintNums()
{
    int n;

    cin >> n;
    if (cin)            // If not EOF...
    {
        cout << n << ' ';
        PrintNums();
        cout << n << ' ';
    }
}
```

Programming Warm-Up Exercises

1. Write a C++ value-returning function that implements the recursive formula $F(N) = F(N - 1) + F(N - 2)$ with base cases $F(0) = 1$ and $F(1) = 1$.

2. Add whatever is necessary to fix the following function so that Func(3) equals 10.

```
int Func( /* in */ int n )
{
    return Func(n - 1) + 3;
}
```

3. Rewrite the following DoubleSpace function without using recursion.

```
void DoubleSpace( /* inout */ ifstream& inFile )
{
    char ch;

    inFile.get(ch);
    if (inFile)             // If not EOF...
    {
        cout << ch;
        if (ch == '\n')
            cout << endl;
        DoubleSpace();
    }
}
```

4. Rewrite the following PrintSquares function using recursion.

```
void PrintSquares()
{
    int count;

    for (count = 1; count <= 10; count++)
        cout << count << ' ' << count * count;
}
```

5. Write a recursive value-returning function that sums the integers from 1 through *N*.
6. Rewrite the following function so that it is recursive.

```
void PrintSqRoots( /* in */ int n )
{
    int i;

    for (i = n; i > 0; i--)
        cout << i << ' ' << sqrt(double(i)) << endl;
}
```

Programming Problems

1. Use recursion to solve the following problem.

   A *palindrome* is a string of characters that reads the same forward and backward. Write a program that reads in strings of characters and determines if each string is a palindrome. Each string is on a separate input line. Echo print each string, followed by "Is a palindrome" if the string is a palindrome or "Is not a palindrome" if the string is not a palindrome. For example, given the input string

   ```
   Able was I, ere I saw Elba.
   ```

   the program would print "Is a palindrome." In determining whether a string is a palindrome, consider uppercase and lowercase letters to be the same and ignore punctuation characters.

2. Write a program to place eight queens on a chessboard in such a way that no queen is attacking any other queen. This is a classic problem that lends itself to a recursive solution. The chessboard should be represented as an 8 × 8 Boolean array. If a square is occupied by a queen, the value is `true`; otherwise, the value is `false`. The status of the chessboard when all eight queens have been placed is the solution.

3. A maze is to be represented by a 10 × 10 array of an enumeration type composed of three values: PATH, HEDGE, and EXIT. There is one exit from the maze. Write a program to determine if it is possible to exit the maze from a given starting point. You may move vertically or horizontally in any direction that contains PATH; you may not move to a square that contains HEDGE. If you move into a square that contains EXIT, you have exited.

   The input data consists of two parts: the maze and a series of starting points. The maze is entered as ten lines of ten characters (P, H, and E). Each succeeding line contains a pair of integers that represents a starting point (that is, row and column numbers). Continue processing entry points until end-of-file occurs.

- nonzero (`true`), if `ch` is an uppercase letter ('A'–'Z')
- 0 (`false`), otherwise

`tolower(ch)`

Parameter: A `char` value `ch`

Function return value: A character that is
- the lowercase equivalent of `ch`, if `ch` is an uppercase letter
- `ch`, otherwise

`toupper(ch)`

Parameter: A `char` value `ch`

Function return value: A character that is
- the uppercase equivalent of `ch`, if `ch` is a lowercase letter
- `ch`, otherwise

The Header File `float.h` This header file supplies named constants that define the characteristics of floating point numbers on your particular machine. Among these constants are the following:

`FLT_DIG`	Approximate number of significant digits in a `float` value
`FLT_MAX`	Maximum positive `float` value
`FLT_MIN`	Minimum positive `float` value
`DBL_DIG`	Approximate number of significant digits in a `double` value
`DBL_MAX`	Maximum positive `double` value
`DBL_MIN`	Minimum positive `double` value
`LDBL_DIG`	Approximate number of significant digits in a `long double` value
`LDBL_MAX`	Maximum positive `long double` value
`LDBL_MIN`	Minimum positive `long double` value

The Header File `limits.h` This header file supplies named constants that define the limits of integer values on your particular machine.

`CHAR_BITS`	Number of bits in a byte (8, for example)
`CHAR_MAX`	Maximum `char` value
`CHAR_MIN`	Minimum `char` value
`SHRT_MAX`	Maximum `short` value
`SHRT_MIN`	Minimum `short` value
`INT_MAX`	Maximum `int` value
`INT_MIN`	Minimum `int` value
`LONG_MAX`	Maximum `long` value
`LONG_MIN`	Minimum `long` value

APPENDIXES

APPENDIX A   *Reserved Words*

asm	double	new	switch
auto	else	operator	template
break	enum	private	this
case	extern	protected	throw
catch	float	public	try
char	for	register	typedef
class	friend	return	union
const	goto	short	unsigned
continue	if	signed	virtual
default	inline	sizeof	void
delete	int	static	volatile
do	long	struct	while

APPENDIX B   *Operator Precedence*

Precedence (highest to lowest)

Operator	*Associativity*
`::`	Left to right
`() [] -> .`	Left to right
Unary: `++ -- ~ ! + - & * new delete (cast) sizeof`	Right to left
`->* .*`	Left to right
`* / %`	Left to right
`+ -`	Left to right
`<< >>`	Left to right
`< <= > >=`	Left to right
`== !=`	Left to right
`&`	Left to right
`^`	Left to right
`|`	Left to right
`&&`	Left to right
`||`	Left to right
`?:`	Right to left
`= += -=` etc.	Right to left
`,` (the operator, not the separator)	Left to right

Note This book does not discuss all of the operators listed in the chart.

APPENDIX C   *C++ Library Routines*

The C++ standard library provides a wealth of functions, named constants, and specialized data types. This appendix details only some of the most widely used library routines (and several named constants). It is a good idea to consult the manual for your particular system to see what other routines the standard library provides.

This appendix is organized according to the header files your program must #include before accessing the listed items.

The Header File `assert.h`

`assert(booleanExpr)`

Parameter:	An int expression booleanExpr, usually written as a logical (Boolean) expression
Effect:	If booleanExpr is nonzero (true), execution continues. If booleanExpr equals 0 (false), execution terminates with a message stating the expression, the name of the file, and the line number.
Function return value:	None (a void function)
Note:	If the preprocessor directive #define NDEBUG is placed before the directive #include <asert.h>, all assert statements are ignored.

The Header File `ctype.h`

`isalnum(ch)`

Parameter:	A char value ch
Function return value:	An int value that is
	▪ nonzero (true), if ch is a letter or a digit character ('A'–'Z', 'a'–'z', '0'–'9')
	▪ 0 (false), otherwise

`isalpha(ch)`

Parameter:	A char value ch
Function return value:	An int value that is
	▪ nonzero (true), if ch is a letter ('A'–'Z', 'a'–'z')
	▪ 0 (false), otherwise

`iscntrl(ch)`

Parameter:	A char value ch
Function return value:	An int value that is
	▪ nonzero (true), if ch is a control character (in ASCII, a character with the value 0–31 or 127)
	▪ 0 (false), otherwise

`isdigit(ch)`

Parameter:	A char value ch
Function return value:	An int value that is
	▪ nonzero (true), if ch is a digit character ('0'–'9')
	▪ 0 (false), otherwise

`isgraph(ch)`

Parameter:	A char value ch
Function return value:	An int value that is
	▪ nonzero (true), if ch is a nonblank printable character (in ASCII, '!' through '~')
	▪ 0 (false), otherwise

`islower(ch)`

Parameter:	A char value ch
Function return value:	An int value that is
	▪ nonzero (true), if ch is a lowercase letter ('a–')
	▪ 0 (false), otherwise

`isprint(ch)`

Parameter:	A char value ch
Function return value:	An int value that is
	▪ nonzero (true), if ch is a printable character including the blank (in ASCII, ' ' through '~')
	▪ 0 (false), otherwise

`ispunct(ch)`

Parameter:	A char value ch
Function return value:	An int value that is
	▪ nonzero (true), if ch is a punctuation character (equivalent to isgraph(ch) && !isalnum)
	▪ 0 (false), otherwise

`isspace(ch)`

Parameter:	A char value ch
Function return value:	An int value that is
	▪ nonzero (true), if ch is a whitespace character (blank, newline, tab, carriage return, form)
	▪ 0 (false), otherwise

`isupper(ch)`

Parameter:	A char value ch
Function return value:	An int value that is

UCHAR_MAX	Maximum unsigned char value
USHRT_MAX	Maximum unsigned short value
UINT_MAX	Maximum unsigned int value
ULONG_MAX	Maximum unsigned long value

The Header File math.h

In the following math routines,

1. Error handling is system-dependent.
2. All parameters and function return values are technically of type double. However, float values may be passed to the functions.

acos(x)

Parameter: An expression x, where $-1.0 \leq x \leq 1.0$

Function return value: Arc cosine of x, in the range 0.0 through π

asin(x)

Parameter: An expression x, where $-1.0 \leq x \leq 1.0$

Function return value: Arc sine of x, in the range $-\pi/2$ through $\pi/2$

atan(x)

Parameter: An expression x

Function return value: Arc tangent of x, in the range $-\pi/2$ through $\pi/2$

ceil(x)

Parameter: An expression x

Function return value: "Ceiling" of x (the smallest whole number $\geq$ x)

cos(angle)

Parameter: An expression angle, measured in radians

Function return value: Trigonometric cosine of angle

exp(x)

Parameter: An expression x

Function return value: The value e (2.718 . . .) raised to the power x

fabs(x)

Parameter: An expression x

Function return value: Absolute value of x

floor(x)

Parameter: An expression x

Function return value: "Floor" of x (the largest whole number $\leq$ x)

log(x)

Parameter: An expression x, where x > 0.0

Function return value: Natural logarithm (base e) of x

`log10(x)`

    Parameter: An expression x, where x $>$ 0.0

    Function return value: Common logarithm (base 10) of x

`pow(x, y)`

    Parameters: Floating point expressions x and y. If x = 0.0, y must be positive; if x $\leq$ 0.0, y must be a whole number

    Function return value: x raised to the power y

`sin(angle)`

    Parameter: An expression `angle`, measured in radians

    Function return value: Trigonometric sine of `angle`

`sqrt(x)`

    Parameter: An expression x, where x $\geq$ 0.0

    Function return value: Square root of x

`tan(angle)`

    Parameter: An expression `angle`, measured in radians

    Function return value: Trigonometric tangent of `angle`

The Header File `stdlib.h`

`abs(i)`

    Parameter: An `int` expression i

    Function return value: An `int` value that is the absolute value of i

`atof(str)`

    Parameter: A string (null-terminated `char` array) str representing a floating point number, possibly preceded by whitespace characters and a '+' or '−'

    Function return value: A `double` value that is the floating point equivalent of the characters in str

    Note: Conversion stops at the first character in str that is inappropriate for a floating point number. If no appropriate characters were found, the return value is system-dependent.

`atoi(str)`

    Parameter: A string (null-terminated `char` array) str representing an integer number, possibly preceded by whitespace characters and a '+' or '−'

    Function return value: An `int` value that is the integer equivalent of the characters in str

Note: Conversion stops at the first character in `str` that is inappropriate for an integer number. If no appropriate characters were found, the return value is system-dependent.

`atol(str)`

Parameter: A string (null-terminated `char` array) `str` representing a long integer, possibly preceded by whitespace characters and a '+' or '−'

Function return value: A `long` value that is the long integer equivalent of the characters in `str`

Note: Conversion stops at the first character in `str` that is inappropriate for a long integer number. If no appropriate characters were found, the return value is system-dependent.

`exit(exitStatus)`

Parameter: An `int` expression `exitStatus`

Effect: Program execution terminates immediately with all files properly closed

Function return value: None (a void function)

Note: By convention, `exitStatus` is 0 to indicate normal program completion and is nonzero to indicate an abnormal termination.

`labs(i)`

Parameter: A `long` expression `i`

Function return value: A `long` value that is the absolute value of `i`

`rand()`

Parameter: None

Function return value: A random `int` value in the range 0 through `RAND_MAX`, a constant defined in `stdlib.h` (`RAND_MAX` is usually the same as `INT_MAX`)

Note: See `srand` below.

`srand(seed)`

Parameter: An `int` expression `seed`, where `seed` ≥ 0

Effect: Using `seed`, the random number generator is initialized in preparation for subsequent calls to the `rand` function.

Function return value: None (a void function)

Note: If `srand` is not called before the first call to `rand`, a seed value of 1 is assumed.

The Header `strcat(toStr, fromStr)`
File `string.h`

Parameters:	Strings (null-terminated `char` arrays) `toStr` and `fromStr`, where `toStr` must be large enough to hold the result
Effect:	`fromStr`, including the null character '\0', is concatenated (joined) to the end of `toStr`.
Function return value:	The base address of `toStr`
Note:	Programmers usually ignore the function return value, using the syntax of a void function call rather than a value-returning function call.

`strcmp(str1, str2)`

Parameters:	Strings (null-terminated char arrays) `str1` and `str2`
Function return value:	An `int` value < 0, if `str1` $<$ `str2` lexicographically
	The `int` value 0, if `str1` = `str2` lexicographically
	An `int` value > 0, if `str1` $>$ `str2` lexicographically

`strcpy(toStr, fromStr)`

Parameters:	`toStr` is a `char` array and `fromStr` is a string (null-terminated `char` array), and `toStr` must be large enough to hold the result.
Effect:	`fromStr`, including the null character '\0', is copied to `toStr`, overwriting what was there.
Function return value:	The base address of `toStr`
Note:	Programmers usually ignore the function return value, using the syntax of a void function call rather than a value-returning function call.

`strlen(str)`

Parameters:	A string (null-terminated `char` array) `str`
Function return value:	An `int` value ≥ 0 that is the length of `str` (excluding the '\0')

APPENDIX D *Character Sets*

The following charts show the ordering of the two most common character sets: ASCII (American Standard Code for Information Interchange) and EBCDIC (Extended Binary Coded Decimal Interchange Code). The internal representation for each character is shown in decimal. For example, the letter *A* is represented internally as the integer 65 in ASCII and as 193 in EBCDIC. The blank character is denoted by a "□".

APPENDIXES

APPENDIX A   *Reserved Words*

asm	double	new	switch
auto	else	operator	template
break	enum	private	this
case	extern	protected	throw
catch	float	public	try
char	for	register	typedef
class	friend	return	union
const	goto	short	unsigned
continue	if	signed	virtual
default	inline	sizeof	void
delete	int	static	volatile
do	long	struct	while

APPENDIX B   *Operator Precedence*

Precedence (highest to lowest)

Operator	*Associativity*
::	Left to right
() [] -> .	Left to right
Unary: ++ -- ~ ! + - & * new delete (cast) sizeof	Right to left
->* .*	Left to right
* / %	Left to right
+ -	Left to right
<< >>	Left to right
< <= > >=	Left to right
== !=	Left to right
&	Left to right
^	Left to right
|	Left to right
&&	Left to right
||	Left to right
?:	Right to left
= += -= etc.	Right to left
, (the operator, not the separator)	Left to right

Note   This book does not discuss all of the operators listed in the chart.

APPENDIX C   _C++ Library Routines_

The C++ standard library provides a wealth of functions, named constants, and specialized data types. This appendix details only some of the most widely used library routines (and several named constants). It is a good idea to consult the manual for your particular system to see what other routines the standard library provides.

This appendix is organized according to the header files your program must #include before accessing the listed items.

The Header File assert.h

assert(booleanExpr)

Parameter:	An int expression booleanExpr, usually written as a logical (Boolean) expression
Effect:	If booleanExpr is nonzero (true), execution continues. If booleanExpr equals 0 (false), execution terminates with a message stating the expression, the name of the file, and the line number.
Function return value:	None (a void function)
Note:	If the preprocessor directive #define NDEBUG is placed before the directive #include <asert.h>, all assert statements are ignored.

The Header File ctype.h

isalnum(ch)

Parameter:	A char value ch
Function return value:	An int value that is

- nonzero (true), if ch is a letter or a digit character ('A'–'Z', 'a'–'z', '0'–'9')
- 0 (false), otherwise

isalpha(ch)

Parameter:	A char value ch
Function return value:	An int value that is

- nonzero (true), if ch is a letter ('A'–'Z', 'a'–'z')
- 0 (false), otherwise

iscntrl(ch)

Parameter:	A char value ch
Function return value:	An int value that is

- nonzero (true), if ch is a control character (in ASCII, a character with the value 0–31 or 127)
- 0 (false), otherwise

isdigit(ch)

Parameter: A char value ch

Function return value: An int value that is

- nonzero (true), if ch is a digit character ('0'–'9')
- 0 (false), otherwise

isgraph(ch)

Parameter: A char value ch

Function return value: An int value that is

- nonzero (true), if ch is a nonblank printable character (in ASCII, '!' through '~')
- 0 (false), otherwise

islower(ch)

Parameter: A char value ch

Function return value: An int value that is

- nonzero (true), if ch is a lowercase letter ('a'–'z')
- 0 (false), otherwise

isprint(ch)

Parameter: A char value ch

Function return value: An int value that is

- nonzero (true), if ch is a printable character, including the blank (in ASCII, ' ' through '~')
- 0 (false), otherwise

ispunct(ch)

Parameter: A char value ch

Function return value: An int value that is

- nonzero (true), if ch is a punctuation character (equivalent to isgraph(ch) && !isalnum(ch))
- 0 (false), otherwise

isspace(ch)

Parameter: A char value ch

Function return value: An int value that is

- nonzero (true), if ch is a whitespace character (blank, newline, tab, carriage return, form feed)
- 0 (false), otherwise

isupper(ch)

Parameter: A char value ch

Function return value: An int value that is

- nonzero (`true`), if `ch` is an uppercase letter ('A'–'Z')
- 0 (`false`), otherwise

`tolower(ch)`

    Parameter: A `char` value `ch`

    Function return value: A character that is

- the lowercase equivalent of `ch`, if `ch` is an upper-case letter
- `ch`, otherwise

`toupper(ch)`

    Parameter: A `char` value `ch`

    Function return value: A character that is

- the uppercase equivalent of `ch`, if `ch` is a lower-case letter
- `ch`, otherwise

The Header File `float.h`

This header file supplies named constants that define the characteristics of floating point numbers on your particular machine. Among these constants are the following:

`FLT_DIG`	Approximate number of significant digits in a `float` value
`FLT_MAX`	Maximum positive `float` value
`FLT_MIN`	Minimum positive `float` value
`DBL_DIG`	Approximate number of significant digits in a `double` value
`DBL_MAX`	Maximum positive `double` value
`DBL_MIN`	Minimum positive `double` value
`LDBL_DIG`	Approximate number of significant digits in a `long double` value
`LDBL_MAX`	Maximum positive `long double` value
`LDBL_MIN`	Minimum positive `long double` value

The Header File `limits.h`

This header file supplies named constants that define the limits of integer values on your particular machine.

`CHAR_BITS`	Number of bits in a byte (8, for example)
`CHAR_MAX`	Maximum `char` value
`CHAR_MIN`	Minimum `char` value
`SHRT_MAX`	Maximum `short` value
`SHRT_MIN`	Minimum `short` value
`INT_MAX`	Maximum `int` value
`INT_MIN`	Minimum `int` value
`LONG_MAX`	Maximum `long` value
`LONG_MIN`	Minimum `long` value

UCHAR_MAX   Maximum unsigned char value
USHRT_MAX   Maximum unsigned short value
UINT_MAX   Maximum unsigned int value
ULONG_MAX   Maximum unsigned long value

The Header
File math.h

In the following math routines,

1. Error handling is system-dependent.
2. All parameters and function return values are technically of type double. However, float values may be passed to the functions.

acos(x)
Parameter: An expression x, where $-1.0 \leq x \leq 1.0$
Function return value: Arc cosine of x, in the range 0.0 through π

asin(x)
Parameter: An expression x, where $-1.0 \leq x \leq 1.0$
Function return value: Arc sine of x, in the range $-\pi/2$ through $\pi/2$

atan(x)
Parameter: An expression x
Function return value: Arc tangent of x, in the range $-\pi/2$ through $\pi/2$

ceil(x)
Parameter: An expression x
Function return value: "Ceiling" of x (the smallest whole number $\geq$ x)

cos(angle)
Parameter: An expression angle, measured in radians
Function return value: Trigonometric cosine of angle

exp(x)
Parameter: An expression x
Function return value: The value *e* (2.718 . . .) raised to the power x

fabs(x)
Parameter: An expression x
Function return value: Absolute value of x

floor(x)
Parameter: An expression x
Function return value: "Floor" of x (the largest whole number $\leq$ x)

log(x)
Parameter: An expression x, where x > 0.0
Function return value: Natural logarithm (base *e*) of x

```
log10(x)
```
    Parameter: An expression x, where x > 0.0

    Function return value: Common logarithm (base 10) of x

```
pow(x, y)
```
    Parameters: Floating point expressions x and y. If x = 0.0, y must be positive; if x ≤ 0.0, y must be a whole number

    Function return value: x raised to the power y

```
sin(angle)
```
    Parameter: An expression angle, measured in radians

    Function return value: Trigonometric sine of angle

```
sqrt(x)
```
    Parameter: An expression x, where x ≥ 0.0

    Function return value: Square root of x

```
tan(angle)
```
    Parameter: An expression angle, measured in radians

    Function return value: Trigonometric tangent of angle

The Header
File stdlib.h

```
abs(i)
```
    Parameter: An int expression i

    Function return value: An int value that is the absolute value of i

```
atof(str)
```
    Parameter: A string (null-terminated char array) str representing a floating point number, possibly preceded by whitespace characters and a '+' or '−'

    Function return value: A double value that is the floating point equivalent of the characters in str

    Note: Conversion stops at the first character in str that is inappropriate for a floating point number. If no appropriate characters were found, the return value is system-dependent.

```
atoi(str)
```
    Parameter: A string (null-terminated char array) str representing an integer number, possibly preceded by whitespace characters and a '+' or '−'

    Function return value: An int value that is the integer equivalent of the characters in str

Note:	Conversion stops at the first character in `str` that is inappropriate for an integer number. If no appropriate characters were found, the return value is system-dependent.

`atol(str)`

Parameter:	A string (null-terminated `char` array) `str` representing a long integer, possibly preceded by whitespace characters and a '+' or '−'
Function return value:	A `long` value that is the long integer equivalent of the characters in `str`
Note:	Conversion stops at the first character in `str` that is inappropriate for a long integer number. If no appropriate characters were found, the return value is system-dependent.

`exit(exitStatus)`

Parameter:	An `int` expression `exitStatus`
Effect:	Program execution terminates immediately with all files properly closed
Function return value:	None (a void function)
Note:	By convention, `exitStatus` is 0 to indicate normal program completion and is nonzero to indicate an abnormal termination.

`labs(i)`

Parameter:	A `long` expression `i`
Function return value:	A `long` value that is the absolute value of `i`

`rand()`

Parameter:	None
Function return value:	A random `int` value in the range 0 through `RAND_MAX`, a constant defined in `stdlib.h` (`RAND_MAX` is usually the same as `INT_MAX`)
Note:	See `srand` below.

`srand(seed)`

Parameter:	An `int` expression `seed`, where `seed` ≥ 0
Effect:	Using `seed`, the random number generator is initialized in preparation for subsequent calls to the `rand` function.
Function return value:	None (a void function)
Note:	If `srand` is not called before the first call to `rand`, a `seed` value of 1 is assumed.

strcat(toStr, fromStr)

    Parameters: Strings (null-terminated char arrays) toStr and fromStr, where toStr must be large enough to hold the result

    Effect: fromStr, including the null character '\0', is concatenated (joined) to the end of toStr.

    Function return value: The base address of toStr

    Note: Programmers usually ignore the function return value, using the syntax of a void function call rather than a value-returning function call.

strcmp(str1, str2)

    Parameters: Strings (null-terminated char arrays) str1 and str2

    Function return value: An int value < 0, if str1 $<$ str2 lexicographically

                          The int value 0, if str1 $=$ str2 lexicographically

                          An int value > 0, if str1 $>$ str2 lexicographically

strcpy(toStr, fromStr)

    Parameters: toStr is a char array and fromStr is a string (null-terminated char array), and toStr must be large enough to hold the result.

    Effect: fromStr, including the null character '\0', is copied to toStr, overwriting what was there.

    Function return value: The base address of toStr

    Note: Programmers usually ignore the function return value, using the syntax of a void function call rather than a value-returning function call.

strlen(str)

    Parameters: A string (null-terminated char array) str

    Function return value: An int value ≥ 0 that is the length of str (excluding the '\0')

APPENDIX D   *Character Sets*

The following charts show the ordering of the two most common character sets: ASCII (American Standard Code for Information Interchange) and EBCDIC (Extended Binary Coded Decimal Interchange Code). The internal representation for each character is shown in decimal. For example, the letter *A* is represented internally as the integer 65 in ASCII and as 193 in EBCDIC. The blank character is denoted by a "□".

Left Digit(s)	Right Digit	*ASCII*									
		0	1	2	3	4	5	6	7	8	9
0		NUL	SOH	STX	ETX	EOT	ENQ	ACK	BEL	BS	HT
1		LF	VT	FF	CR	SO	SI	DLE	DC1	DC2	DC3
2		DC4	NAK	SYN	ETB	CAN	EM	SUB	ESC	FS	GS
3		RS	US	□	!	"	#	$	%	&	'
4		(	)	*	+	,	−	.	/	0	1
5		2	3	4	5	6	7	8	9	:	;
6		<	=	>	?	@	A	B	C	D	E
7		F	G	H	I	J	K	L	M	N	O
8		P	Q	R	S	T	U	V	W	X	Y
9		Z	[	\	]	∧	_	`	a	b	c
10		d	e	f	g	h	i	j	k	l	m
11		n	o	p	q	r	s	t	u	v	w
12		x	y	z	{	|	}	~	DEL		

Codes 00–31 and 127 are the following nonprintable control characters:

NUL	Null character	VT	Vertical tab	SYN	Synchronous idle
SOH	Start of header	FF	Form feed	ETB	End of transmitted block
STX	Start of text	CR	Carriage return	CAN	Cancel
ETX	End of text	SO	Shift out	EM	End of medium
EOT	End of transmission	SI	Shift in	SUB	Substitute
ENQ	Enquiry	DLE	Data link escape	ESC	Escape
ACK	Acknowledge	DC1	Device control one	FS	File separator
BEL	Bell character (beep)	DC2	Device control two	GS	Group separator
BS	Back space	DC3	Device control three	RS	Record separator
HT	Horizontal tab	DC4	Device control four	US	Unit separator
LF	Line feed	NAK	Negative acknowledge	DEL	Delete

Left Digit(s)	Right Digit	*EBCDIC*									
		0	1	2	3	4	5	6	7	8	9
6						□					
7						¢	.	<	(	+	|
8		&									
9		!	$	*	)	;	¬	−	/		
10								∧	,	%	−
11		>	?								
12			`	:	#	@	'	=	"		a
13		b	c	d	e	f	g	h	i		

(continued on next page)

(continued)

Left Digit(s)	Right Digit	EBCDIC 0	1	2	3	4	5	6	7	8	9
14							j	k	l	m	n
15		o	p	q	r						
16			~	s	t	u	v	w	x	y	z
17									\	{	}
18		[	]								
19					A	B	C	D	E	F	G
20		H	I								J
21		K	L	M	N	O	P	Q	R		
22								S	T	U	V
23		W	X	Y	Z						
24		0	1	2	3	4	5	6	7	8	9

Nonprintable control characters—codes 00–63, 250–255, and those for which empty spaces appear in the chart—are not shown.

APPENDIX E   *Program Formatting*

Useful programs have very long lifetimes, during which they must be modified and updated. Good style and documentation are essential if another programmer is to understand and work with your program.

General Guidelines.   Style is of benefit only for a human reader of your program—differences in style make no difference to the computer. Good style includes the use of meaningful variable names, comments, and indentation of control structures, all of which help others to understand and work with your program. Perhaps the most important aspect of program style is consistency. If the style within a program is not consistent, then it becomes misleading and confusing.

Comments   You should include a comment anywhere the code is difficult to understand. However, don't overcomment. Too many comments in a program can obscure the code and be a source of distraction.

In our style, there are four basic types of comments: headers, declarations, inline, and sidebar.

1. *Header comments* appear at the top of the program and should include your name, the date that the program was written, and its purpose. It is also useful to include sections describing input, output, and assumptions. Think of the header comments as the reader's introduction to your program. Here is an example:

```
// This program computes the sidereal time for a given date and
// solar time.
//
// Written By: Your Name
//
// Date Completed: 4/8/96
//
// Input: A date and time in the form MM DD YY HH MM SS
//
// Output: Sidereal time in the form HH MM SS
//
// Assumptions: Solar time is specified for a longitude of 0
//      degrees (GMT, UT, or Z time zone)
```

Header comments should also be included for all user-defined functions. (See Chapters 7 and 8.)

2. *Declaration comments* accompany the constant and variable declarations in the program. Anywhere that an identifier is declared, it is helpful to include a comment that explains its purpose. For example:

```
const float E = 2.71828;    // The base of the natural logarithms

float deltaX;               // The difference in the x direction
float deltaY;               // The difference in the y direction
```

Notice that aligning the comments gives the code a neater appearance and is less distracting.

3. *In-line comments* are used to break long sections of code into shorter, more comprehensible fragments. It is generally a good idea to surround in-line comments with blank lines to make them stand out. For example:

```
// Prepare file for reading

scoreFile.open("scores.dat");

// Get data

scoreFile >> test1 >> weight1;
scoreFile >> test2 >> weight2;
scoreFile >> test3 >> weight3;

// Print heading

cout << "Test Score   Weight" << endl;
```

Even if comments are not used, blank lines can be inserted wherever there is a logical break in the code that you would like to emphasize.

4. *Sidebar comments* appear to the right of executable statements and are used to shed light on the purpose of the statement. Sidebar comments are often just pseudocode statements from the lowest levels of your design. If a complicated C++ statement requires some explanation, the pseudocode statement should be written to the right of the C++ statement. For example:

```
while (file1 && file2)   // While neither file is empty . . .
  {
      .
      .
      .
```

Identifiers

The most important consideration in choosing a name for a data item or function in a program is that the name convey as much information as possible about what the data item is or what the function does. The name should also be readable in the context in which it is used. For example, the following names convey the same information but one is more readable than the other:

```
datOfInvc    invoiceDate
```

Although an identifier may be a series of words, very long identifiers can become quite tedious and can make the program difficult to read. The best approach to designing an identifier is to try writing out different names until you reach an acceptable compromise.

Formatting Lines and Expressions

C++ allows you to break a long statement in the middle and continue onto the next line. (However, you cannot split a line in the middle of an identifier, a literal constant, or a string.) When you must split a line, it's important to choose a breaking point that is logical and readable. Compare the readability of the following code fragments.

```
cout << "For a radius of " << radius << " the diameter of the cir"
     << "cle is " << diameter << endl;

cout << "For a radius of " << radius
     << " the diameter of the circle is " << diameter << endl;
```

Indentation

The purpose of indenting statements in a program is to provide visual cues to the reader and to make the program easier to debug. When a program is properly indented, the way the statements are grouped is immediately obvious. Compare the following two program fragments:

```
while (count <= 10)        while (count <= 10)
{                          {
cin >> num;                    cin >> num;
if (num == 0)                  if (num == 0)
{                              {
count++;                           count++;
num = 1;                           num = 1;
}                              }
cout << num << endl;           cout << num << endl;
cout << count << endl;         cout << count << endl;
}                          }
```

As a basic rule in this text, each nested or lower-level item is indented by four spaces. Exceptions to this rule are formal parameters and statements that are split across two or more lines. Indenting by four spaces is a matter of personal preference. Some people prefer to indent by three, five, or even more than five spaces.

GLOSSARY

abstract data type (ADT) a data type whose properties (domain and operations) are specified independently of any particular implementation

abstraction barrier the invisible wall around a class object that encapsulates implementation details. The wall can be breached only through the public interface

abstraction (in OOD) the essential characteristics of an object from the viewpoint of the user

actual parameter a variable or expression listed in a call to a function

algorithm a step-by-step procedure for solving a problem in a finite amount of time

anonymous type a type that does not have an associated type identifier

arithmetic/logic unit (ALU) the component of the central processing unit that performs arithmetic and logical operations

array a collection of components, all of the same type, ordered on N dimensions ($N \geq 1$). Each component is accessed by N indices, each of which represents the component's position within that dimension.

assignment expression a C++ expression with (1) a value and (2) the side effect of storing the expression value into a memory location

assignment statement a statement that stores the value of an expression into a variable

automatic variable a variable for which memory is allocated and deallocated when control enters and exits the block in which it is declared.

auxiliary storage device a device that stores data in encoded form outside the computer's main memory

base address the memory address of the first element of an array

base case the case for which the solution can be stated nonrecursively

binary operator an operator that has two operands

black box an electrical or mechanical device whose inner workings are hidden from view

central processing unit (CPU) the part of the computer that executes the instructions (program) stored in memory; made up of the arithmetic/logic unit and the control unit

class a structured type in a programming language that is used to represent an abstract data type

class member a component of a class. Class members may be either data or functions.

class object (class instance) a variable of a class type

client software that declares and manipulates objects of a particular class

compiler a program that translates a high-level language into machine code

composite data type a collection of components whose organization is characterized by the method used to access individual components. The allowable operations on a structured data type include the storage and retrieval of individual components.

computer a programmable device that can store, retrieve, and process data

computer program a list of instructions to be performed by a computer

computer programming the process of planning a sequence of steps for a computer to follow

control structure a statement used to alter the normally sequential flow of control

control unit the component of the central processing unit that controls the actions of the other components

count-controlled loop a loop that executes a specified number of times

data information that has been put into a form a computer can use

data abstraction   the separation of a data type's logical properties from its implementation

data flow   the flow of information from the calling code to a function and from the function back to the calling code

data representation   the concrete form of data used to represent the abstract values of an abstract data type

data type   a specific set of data values along with a set of operations on those values

declaration   a statement that associates an identifier with a data object, a function, or a data type so that the programmer can refer to that item by name

demotion (narrowing)   the conversion of a value from a "higher" type to a "lower" type according to a programming language's precedence of data types

documentation   the written text and comments that make a program easier for others to understand, use, and modify

driver   a simple `main` function that is used to call a function being tested. The use of a driver permits direct control of the testing process.

editor   an interactive program used to create and modify source programs or data

encapsulation   hiding a module implementation in a separate block with a formally specified interface

encapsulation (in OOD)   the bundling of data and actions in such a way that the logical properties of the data and actions are separated from the implementation details

enumeration type   a user-defined data type whose domain is an ordered set of literal values expressed as identifiers

enumerator   one of the values in the domain of an enumeration type

event-controlled loop   a loop that terminates when something happens inside the loop body to signal that the loop should be exited

expression statement   a statement formed by appending a semicolon to an expression

external representation   the printable (character) form of a data value

field (member, in C++)   a component of a record

formal parameter   a variable declared in a function heading

function   a subprogram in C++

function call (function invocation)   the mechanism that transfers control to a function

function call (to a void function)   a statement that transfers control to a void function. In C++, this statement is the name of the function, followed by a list of actual parameters.

function definition   a function declaration that includes the body of the function

function prototype   a function declaration without the body of the function

function value type   the data type of the result value returned by a function

functional decomposition   a technique for developing a program in which the problem is divided into more easily handled subproblems, the solutions of which create a solution to the overall problem

general case   the case for which the solution is expressed in terms of a smaller version of itself; also known as *recursive case*

hardware   the physical components of a computer

hierarchical records   records in which at least one of the components is itself a record

hierarchy (in OOD)   structuring of abstractions in which a descendant object inherits the characteristics of its ancestors

identifier   a name associated with a function or data object and used to refer to that function or data object

infinite recursion   the situation in which a function calls itself over and over endlessly

information   any knowledge that can be communicated

information hiding   the encapsulation and hiding of implementation details to keep the user of an abstraction from depending on or incorrectly manipulating these details

inheritance   a mechanism for automatically sharing data and methods among members of a class and its subclasses

input/output (I/O) devices   the parts of the computer that accept data to be processed (input) and present the results of that processing (output)

interface   a shared boundary that independent systems permits to meet and act on or communicate with each other. Also, the formal description of the purpose of a subprogram and the mechanism for communicating with it

iteration   an individual pass through, or repetition of, the body of a loop

length   the actual number of values stored in a list

lifetime   the period of time during program execution when an identifier has memory allocated to it

list   a variable-length, linear collection of homogeneous components

literal value   any constant value written in a program

local variable   a variable declared within a block and not accessible outside of that block

loop   a control structure that causes a sequence of statements to be executed repeatedly

loop entry   the point at which the flow of control reaches the first statement inside a loop

loop exit   the point at which the repetition of the loop body ends and control passes to the first statement following the loop

loop test   the point at which the While expression is evaluated and the decision is made either to begin a new iteration or skip to the statement immediately following the loop

machine language   the language, made up of binary-coded instructions, that is used directly by the computer

member selector   the expression used to access components of a `struct` or `class` variable. It is formed by using the `struct` or `class` variable name and the member name, separated by a dot (period).

memory unit   internal data storage in a computer

mixed type (or mixed mode) expression   an expression that contains operands of different data types

modularity (in OOD)   meaningful packaging of objects

name precedence   the precedence that a local identifier in a function has over a global identifier with the same name in any references that the function makes to that identifier; also called *name hiding*

named constant   a location in memory, referenced by an identifier, where a data value that cannot be changed is stored

named type   a user-defined type whose declaration includes a type identifier that gives a name to the type

nonlocal identifier   any identifier declared outside a given block is said to be nonlocal with respect to that block

object-oriented design (OOD)   a technique for developing a program in which the solution is expressed in terms of objects—self-contained entities composed of data and operations on that data. Also, the bundling of data and actions in such a way that the logical properties of the data and actions are separated from the implementation details

object program   the machine language version of a source program

one-dimensional array   a structured collection of components, all of the same type, that is given a single name. Each component (array element) is accessed by an index that indicates the component's position within the collection.

operating system   a set of programs that manages all of the computer's resources

out-of-bounds array index   an index value that, in C++, is either less than zero or is greater than the array size minus one

parameter list   a mechanism by which functions communicate with each other

peripheral device   an input, output, or auxiliary storage device attached to a computer

polymorphism   the ability to overload the name of an action so that it is possible to determine at compile time or run time which action is appropriate for a particular instance variable

postcondition   an assertion that must be true after a module has executed

precision   the maximum number of significant digits

precondition   an assertion that must be true before a module begins executing

programming   planning, scheduling, or performing a task or an event

programming language   a set of rules, symbols, and special words used to construct a program

promotion (widening)   the conversion of a value from a "lower" type to a "higher" type according to a programming language's precedence of data types

range of values   the interval within which values of a numeric type must fall, specified in terms of the largest and smallest allowable values

record (structure, in C++)   a structured data type with a fixed number of components that are accessed by name, not by index. The components may be heterogeneous (of different types).

recursive algorithm   a solution that is expressed in terms of (1) smaller instances of itself and (2) a base case

recursive call   a function call in which the function being called is the same as the one making the call

recursive definition   a definition in which something is defined in terms of smaller versions of itself

reference parameter   a formal parameter that receives the location (memory address) of the caller's actual parameter

representational error   arithmetic error that occurs when the precision of the true result of an arithmetic operation is greater than the precision of the machine

reserved word   a word that has special meaning in C++; it cannot be used as a programmer-defined identifier

scope   the region of program code where it is legal to reference (use) an identifier

scope rules   the rules that determine where in the program an identifier may be accessed, given the point where that identifier is declared

self-documenting code   program code containing meaningful identifiers as well as judiciously used clarifying comments

short-circuit (conditional) evaluation   evaluation of a logical expression in left-to-right order with evaluation stopping as soon as the final truth value can be determined

side effect   any effect of one function on another that is not a part of the explicitly defined interface between them

significant digits   those digits from the first nonzero digit on the left to the last nonzero digit on the right (plus any zero digits that are exact)

simple (atomic) data type   a data type in which each value is atomic (indivisible)

software   computer programs; the set of all programs available on a computer

sorting   arranging the components of a list into order (for instance, words into alphabetical order or numbers into ascending or descending order)

source program   a program written in a high-level programming language

static variable   a variable for which memory remains allocated throughout the execution of the entire program

string   a collection of characters interpreted as a single item; in C++, a null-terminated sequence of characters stored in a `char` array

stub   a dummy function that assists in testing part of a program. A stub has the same name and interface as a function that actually would be called by the part of the program being tested, but it is usually much simpler.

switch expression   the expression whose value determines which switch label is selected. It cannot be a floating point expression.

tail recursion   a recursive algorithm in which no statements are executed after the return from the recursive call

termination condition   the condition that causes a loop to be exited

testing the state of a stream   the act of using a C++ stream variable in a logical expression as if it were a Boolean variable; the result is nonzero (`true`) if the last I/O operation on that stream succeeded, and zero (`false`) otherwise

two-dimensional array   a collection of components, all of the same type, structured in two dimensions. Each component is accessed by a pair of indices that represent the component's position in each dimension.

type casting   the explicit conversion of a value from one data type to another; also called type conversion

type coercion   the implicit (automatic) conversion of a value from one data type to another

unary operator   an operator that has just one operand

value parameter   a formal parameter that receives a copy of the contents of the corresponding actual parameter

value-returning function   a function that returns a single value to its caller and is invoked from within an expression

variable   a location in memory, referenced by an identifier, in which a data value that can be changed is stored

void function (procedure)   a function that does not return a function value to its caller and is invoked as a separate statement

Answers to Selected Exercises

CHAPTER 2   Exam Preparation Exercises

1. a. invalid   b. valid   c. valid   d. invalid   e. valid
   f. invalid   g. valid   h. invalid

4. program—15;   algorithm—14;   compiler—3;   identifier—1;
   compilation phase—12;   execution phase—10;   variable—11;   constant—2;
   memory—13;   syntax—6;   semantics—8;   block—7

5. a. Integer: 13   b. Floating point: −15.6   c. Floating point: 3.33333
   d. Integer: 3   e. Integer: 1   f. Illegal: Both operands of the % operator must
   be of integer type.   g. Integer: 0

7. a. reserved   b. programmer-defined   c. programmer-defined
   d. reserved   e. programmer-defined

11. ```
Cost is
300
Price is 30Cost is 300
Grade A costs
300
```

12. The named constants make the program easier to read and understand. Also, to
    change one of the constants, you only need to change one line (the constant
    declaration) instead of changing every occurrence of the literal constant throughout
    the program.

## CHAPTER 2   Programming Warm-Up Exercises

1. Only one line needs to be changed. In the constant declaration

   ```
   const int LBS = 10;
   ```

   change 10 to 15.
   ```

3. `cout << "The moon" << endl;`
`cout << "is" << endl;`
`cout << "blue." << endl;`

CHAPTER 3 Exam Preparation Exercises

1. a. Floating point: 13.3333   b. Integer: 2   c. Integer: 5
d. Floating point: 13.75   e. Integer: −4   f. Integer: 1
g. Illegal: 10.0 / 3.0 is a floating point expression, but the % operator requires integer operands.

5. a. `iostream.h`   b. `stdlib.h`   c. `math.h`   d. `iostream.h`
e. `iostream.h` and `iomanip.h`

9. `A rolling`
`stone`

← One blank line

`gathers`

← Three blank lines

`nomoss`

11. False

CHAPTER 3 Programming Warm-Up Exercises

1. `sum = n * (n + 1) / 2;`

4. `discriminant = sqrt(b * b - 4.0 * a * c);`
`denominator = 2.0 * a;`
`solution1 = (-b + discriminant) / denominator;`
`solution2 = (-b - discriminant) / denominator;`

7a. Declare a constant `ROUND_FACTOR` (defined to be equal to the desired rounding factor, such as 100.0 for hundredths) and replace every occurrence of 10.0 with `ROUND_FACTOR`.

CHAPTER 4 Exam Preparation Exercises

2. a. `int1` contains 17, `int2` contains 13, and `int3` contains 7.

b. The leftover values remain waiting in the input stream. These values will be read by subsequent input statements (or they will be ignored if no more input statements are executed).

6. True

8. `123 147`

11. Errors in the program are as follows:

    ▪ The declaration of outData is missing:

    ```
    ofstream outData;
    ```

    ▪ The opening of the input file is missing:

    ```
    inData.open("myfile.dat");
    ```

    ▪ The statement

    ```
    cin >> n;
    ```

    does not read from the input file. Change cin to inData.

12. With the corrected version of the program in Exercise 11, file inData will still contain the 144 after the program is executed. File outData will contain 144, followed by a newline character.

14. Prepare File for Reading, Get Data, Find Weighted Average, Print Weighted Average, and Print Heading are concrete modules. Print Data is an abstract module because it has a submodule below it.

CHAPTER 4   Programming Warm-Up Exercises

1. `cin >> ch1 >> ch2 >> ch3;`
3. `cin >> length1 >> height1 >> length2 >> height2;`
4. In the following, the value 100 is arbitrary. Any value greater than 4 will work.

```
cin.get(chr1);
cin.ignore(100, '\n');
cin.get(chr2);
cin.ignore(100, '\n');
cin.get(chr3);
cin.ignore(100, '\n');
```

8.
```
#include <iostream.h>
#include <fstream.h>

int main()
{
    int     val1;
    int     val2;
    int     val3;
    int     val4;
    ifstream dataIn;
    ofstream resultsOut;

    dataIn.open("myinput.dat");
    resultsOut.open("myoutput.dat");
```

```
dataIn >> val1 >> val2 >> val3 >> val4;
resultsOut << val1 << val2 << val3 << val4 << endl;
return 0;
}
```

9. Note that the problem statement said nothing about getting into the car, adjusting seatbelts, checking the mirror, or driving away. Presumably those tasks, along with starting the car, are subtasks of a larger design such as "Go to the store." Here we are concerned only with starting the car itself.

Main Module

　Ensure car won't roll.
　Disengage gears.
　Attempt ignition.

Ensure car won't roll

　Engage parking brake.
　Turn wheels into curb.

Disengage gears

　Push in clutch with left foot.
　Move gearshift to neutral.
　Release clutch.

Attempt ignition

　Insert key into ignition slot.
　Turn key to ON position.
　Pump accelerator once.
　Turn key to START position.
　Release after engine catches or 5 seconds, whichever comes first.

CHAPTER 5   Exam Preparation Exercises

2. a. No parentheses are needed.   b. No parentheses are needed.
　c. No parentheses are needed.   d. `!(q && q)`

6. a. 4   b. 2   c. 5   d. 3   e. 1

9. a. If-Then-Else   b. If-Then   c. If-Then   d. If-Then-Else

10. The error message is printed because there is a semicolon after the right brace of a block (compound statement).

13. Yes

CHAPTER 5   Programming Warm-Up Exercises

2. In the following statement, the outer parentheses are not required but are included for readability.

```
available = (numberOrdered <= (numberOnHand - numberReserved));
```

4. In the following statement, the parentheses are not required but are included for readability.

```
leftPage = (pageNumber % 2 == 0);
```

6. ```
if (year % 4 == 0)
    cout << year << " is a leap year." << endl;
else
{
    year = year + 4 - year % 4;
    cout << year << " is the next leap year." << endl;
}
```

**7.** ```
if (age > 64)
    cout << "Senior voter";
else if (age < 18)
    cout << "Under age";
else
    cout << "Regular voter";
```

9. ```
// This is a nonsense program
if (a > 0)
    if (a < 20)
    {
        cout << "A is in range." << endl;
        b = 5;
    }
    else
    {
        cout << "A is too large." << endl;
        b = 3;
    }
else
    cout << "A is too small." << endl;
cout << "All done." << endl;
```

**13.** ```
if (temperature > 85)
    cout << "swimming.";
else if (temperature > 70)
    cout << "tennis.";
else if (temperature > 32)
    cout << "golf.";
else if (temperature > 0)
    cout << "skiing.";
```

```
else
    cout << "dancing.";
cout << endl;
```

CHAPTER 6   Exam Preparation Exercises

3.
```
number = 1;
while (number < 11)
{
    cout << number << endl;
    number++;
}
```

4. Six iterations are performed.

9. Telephone numbers read in as integers have many different values that could be used as sentinels. In the United States, a standard telephone number is a positive seven-digit integer (ignoring area codes) and cannot start with 0, 1, 411, or 911. Therefore, a reasonable sentinel may be negative, greater than 9999999, or less than 2000000.

11. a. (1) Change < to <=. (2) Change 1 to 0. (3) Change 20 to 21.

b. Changes (1) and (3) make `count` range from 1 through 21. Change (2) makes `count` range from 0 through 20.

CHAPTER 6   Programming Warm-Up Exercises

1.
```
dangerous = false;
while ( !dangerous )
{
    cin >> pressure;
    if (pressure > 510.0)
        dangerous = true;
}

or

dangerous = false;
while ( !dangerous )
{
    cin >> pressure;
    dangerous = (pressure > 510.0);
}
```

2.
```
count28 = 0;
loopCount = 1;
```

```
while (loopCount <= 100)
{
    inputFile >> number;
    if (number == 28)
        count28++;
    loopCount++;
}
```

6.
```
positives = 0;
negatives = 0;
cin >> number;
while (cin)        // While NOT EOF . . .
{
    if (number > 0)
        positives++;
    else if (number < 0)
        negatives++;
    cin >> number;
}
cout << "Number of positive numbers: " << positives << endl;
cout << "Number of negative numbers: " << negatives << endl;
```

7.
```
sum = 0;
evenInt = 16;
while (evenInt <= 26)
{
    sum = sum + evenInt;
    evenInt = evenInt + 2;
}
```

8.
```
hour = 1;
minute = 0;
am = true;
done = false;
while ( !done )
{
    cout << hour << ':';
    if (minute < 10)
        cout << '0';
    cout << minute;
    if (am)
        cout << " A.M." << endl;
    else
        cout << " P.M." << endl;
```

```
minute++;
if (minute > 59)
{
    minute = 0;
    hour++;
    if (hour == 13)
        hour = 1;
    else if (hour == 12)
        am = !am;
    }
    if (hour == 1 && minute == 0 && am)
        done = true;
}
```

CHAPTER 7 Exam Preparation Exercises

4. 5 3 13
    3 3 9
    9 12 30

7. For pass-by-value, parts (a) through (g) are all valid. For pass-by-reference, only parts (a) and (c) are valid.

8. 13571 (the memory address of the variable `widgets`).

10. The answers are 12 10 3

11. Variables in `main` just before `Change` is called: a = 10 and b = 7. Variables in `Change` at the moment control enters the function (before any statements are executed): x = 10, y = 7, and the value of b is undefined. Variables in `main` after return from `Change`: a = 10 (x in `Change` is a value parameter, so the actual parameter is not modified) and b = 17.

CHAPTER 7 Programming Warm-Up Exercises

2.
```
void RocketSimulation( /* in */     float    thrust,
                       /* inout */  float&   weight,
                       /* in */     int      timeStep,
                       /* in */     int      totalTime,
                       /* out */    float&   velocity,
                       /* out */    Boolean& outOfFuel )
```

5.
```
void Halve( /* inout */ int& firstNumber,
            /* inout */ int& secondNumber )

// Precondition:
//     firstNumber and secondNumber are assigned
```

```
// Postcondition:
//      firstNumber == firstNumber@entry / 2
//   && secondNumber == secondNumber@entry / 2

{
    .
    .
    .
}
```

7. a. Function definition:

```
void ScanHeart( /* out */ Boolean& normal )

// Postcondition:
//      normal == true, if a normal heart rate (60-80) was input
//                        before EOF occurred
//              == false, otherwise

{
    int heartRate;

    cin >> heartRate;
    while ((heartRate < 60 || heartRate > 80) && cin)
        cin >> heartRate;
    normal = (heartRate >= 60 && heartRate <= 80);
}
```

b. Function invocation:

```
ScanHeart(normal);
```

8. a. Function definition:

```
void Rotate( /* inout */ int& firstValue,
             /* inout */ int& secondValue,
             /* inout */ int& thirdValue  )

// This function takes three parameters and returns their values
// in a shifted order

// Precondition:
//      firstValue, secondValue, and thirdValue are assigned
```

```
// Postcondition:
//     firstValue == secondValue@entry
//  && secondValue == thirdValue@entry
//  && thirdValue == firstValue@entry
{
    int temp;    // Temporary holding variable

    // Save value of first parameter

    temp = firstValue;

    // Shift values of next two parameters

    firstValue = secondValue;
    secondValue = thirdValue;

    // Replace value of final parameter with saved value

    thirdValue = temp;
}
```

b. Test program:

```
#include <iostream.h>

void Rotate( int&, int&, int& );

int main()
{
    int int1;    // First input value
    int int2;    // Second input value
    int int3;    // Third input value

    cout << "Enter three values: ";
    cin >> int1 >> int2 >> int3;

    cout << "Before: " << int1 << ' ' << int2 << ' '
         << int3 << endl;
    Rotate(int1, int2, int3);
    cout << "After: " << int1 << ' ' << int2 << ' '
         << int3 << endl;
    return 0;
}

// The Rotate function, as above, goes here
```

CHAPTER 8   Exam Preparation Exercises

1. True

5. 1 1
    1 2
    1 3

7. Yes

11. It is risky to use a reference parameter as a formal parameter of a value-returning function because it provides a mechanism for side effects to escape from the function. A value-returning function usually is designed to return a single result (the function value), which is then used in the expression that called the function. If a value-returning function declares a reference parameter and modifies the parameter, that function is returning more than one result, which is not obvious from the way the function is invoked. (However, an I/O stream variable *must* be declared as a reference parameter, even in a value-returning function.)

CHAPTER 8   Programming Warm-Up Exercises

3.
```
Boolean NearlyEqual( /* in */ float num1,
                     /* in */ float num2,
                     /* in */ float difference )
```

5.
```
float CompassHeading( /* in */ float trueCourse,
                      /* in */ float windCorrAngle,
                      /* in */ float variance,
                      /* in */ float deviation    )

// Precondition:
//     All parameters are assigned
// Postcondition:
//     Function value == trueCourse + windCorrAngle +
//                       variance + deviation

{
    return trueCourse + windCorrAngle + variance + deviation;
}
```

8. Function body for `Hypotenuse` function (assuming the header file `math.h` has been included in order to access the `sqrt` function):

```
{
    return sqrt(side1*side1 + side2*side2);
}
```

13. Below, the type of `costPerOunce` and the function return type are `float` so that cost can be expressed in terms of dollars and cents (e.g., 1.23 means $1.23). These types could be integers if cost is expressed in terms of cents only (e.g., 123 means $1.23).

```
float Postage( /* in */ int     pounds,
               /* in */ int     ounces,
               /* in */ float costPerOunce )

// Precondition:
//      pounds >= 0  &&  ounces >= 0  &&  costPerOunce >= 0.0
// Postcondition:
//      Function value == (pounds * 16 + ounces) * costPerOunce

{
    return (pounds * 16 + ounces) * costPerOunce;
}
```

14. Change the body of `GetData` so that it begins as follows:

```
{
    Boolean badData;    // True if an input value is invalid

    badData = true;
    while (badData)
    {
        cout << "Enter the number of crew (1 or 2)." << endl;
        cin >> crew;
        badData = (crew < 1 || crew > 2);
        if (badData)
            cout << "Invalid number of crew members." << endl;
    }

    badData = true;
    while (badData)
    {
        cout << "Enter the number of passengers (0 through 8)."
            << endl;
        cin >> passengers;
        badData = (passengers < 0 || passengers > 8);
        if (badData)
            cout << "Invalid number of passengers." << endl;
    }
}
```

Continue in this manner to validate the closet weight (0–160 pounds), baggage weight (0–525 pounds), and amount of fuel loaded (10–565 gallons).

CHAPTER 9   Exam Preparation Exercises

2. False

4. False

6. `Mary JoeAnneWhoops!`

9. 1

13. False

CHAPTER 9   Programming Warm-Up Exercises

1.
```cpp
switch (grade)
{
    case 'A' : sum = sum + 4;
               break;
    case 'B' : sum = sum + 3;
               break;
    case 'C' : sum = sum + 2;
               break;
    case 'D' : sum++;
               break;
    case 'F' : cout << "Student is on probation" << endl;
               break;    // Not required
}
```

2.
```cpp
switch (grade)
{
    case 'A' : sum = sum + 4;
               break;
    case 'B' : sum = sum + 3;
               break;
    case 'C' : sum = sum + 2;
               break;
    case 'D' : sum++;
               break;
    case 'F' : cout << "Student is on probation" << endl;
               break;
    default  : cout << "Invalid letter grade" << endl;
               break;    // Not required
}
```

5.
```cpp
do
{
    cout << "Enter 1, 2, or 3: ";
    cin >> response;
} while (response != 1 && response != 2 && response != 3);
```

6.
```
cin >> ch;
while (cin)
{
    cout << ch;
    cin >> ch;
}
```

10. This solution returns proper results only if the precondition shown in the comments is true. Note that it returns the correct result for $base^0$, which is 1.

```
int Power( /* in */ int base,
           /* in */ int exponent )

// Precondition:
//     base is assigned  &&  exponent >= 0
//  && (base to the exponent power) <= INT_MAX
// Postcondition:
//     Function value == base to the exponent power

{
    int result = 1;    // Holds intermediate powers of base
    int count;         // Loop control variable

    for (count = 1; count <= exponent; count++)
        result = result * base;
    return result;
}
```

CHAPTER 10   Exam Preparation Exercises

3. a. `sumOfSquares += x * x;`
   b. `count--;`
      or
      `--count;`
   c. `k = (n > 8) ? 32 : 15 * n;`
5. Notice that
   the character \ is a backslash.
6. a. 1.4E+12 (to 10 digits)   b. 100.0 (to 10 digits)   c. 3.2E+5 (to 10 digits)
9. a. valid   b. invalid   c. invalid   d. valid
12. False. The angle brackets (< >) should be quotation marks.

CHAPTER 10   Programming Warm-Up Exercises

2. `cout << "Hello\tThere\n\n\n\"Ace\"";`

6. enum CourseType {CS101, CS200, CS210, CS350, CS375, CS441};

8. enum DayType {MONDAY, TUESDAY, WEDNESDAY, THURSDAY, FRIDAY};

9. DayType CharToDay(/* in */ char ch1,
                         /* in */ char ch2)

```
// Precondition:
//     ch1=='M' OR ch1=='W' OR ch1=='F' OR
//     (ch1=='T' && ch2=='U') OR (ch1=='T' && ch2=='H')
// Postcondition:
//     Function value == MONDAY, if ch1=='M'
//                    == TUESDAY, if (ch1=='T' && ch2=='U')
//                    == WEDNESDAY, if ch1=='W'
//                    == THURSDAY, if (ch1=='T' && ch2=='H')
//                    == FRIDAY, if ch1=='F'
{
    switch (ch1)
    {
        case 'M' : return MONDAY;
        case 'T' : if (ch2 == 'U')
                        return TUESDAY;
                   else
                        return THURSDAY;
        case 'W' : return WEDNESDAY;
        case 'F' : return FRIDAY;
    }
}
```

13. A sample might be

```
void PrintJanuary()
{
    cout << "Tracy Anderson: 1/14" << endl;
    cout << "Dallas Lightfoot: 1/27" << endl;
}
```

CHAPTER 11   Exam Preparation Exercises

1. True

5. a. enum BirdType {CARDINAL, BLUEJAY, HUMMINGBIRD, ROBIN};
    b. int sightings[4];

7. 1 3 -2
    17 6 11
    4 2 2
    19 14 5
    11 15 -4

    52 40 12

9. sample [0][1][2][3][4][5][6][7]

10	9	8	7	6	5	4	3

CHAPTER 11 Programming Warm-Up Exercises

1.
```
void Initialize( /* out */ Boolean failing[],
                 /* in */  int      length   )

// Precondition:
//     length <= MAX_STUD
// Postcondition:
//     failing[0..length-1] == false

{
    int index;   // Loop control and index variable
    for (index = 0; index < length; index++)
        failing[index] = false;
}
```

3.
```
void SetPassing( /* inout */       Boolean passing[],
                 /* in */    const int     score[],
                 /* in */          int     length   )

// Precondition:
//     length <= MAX_STUD
//  && score[0..length-1] are assigned
// Postcondition:
//     For all i, where 0 <= i <= length-1,
//        IF score[i] >= 60, THEN passing[i] == true

{
    int index;   // Loop control and index variable

    for (index = 0; index < length; index++)
        if (score[index] >= 60)
            passing[index] = true;
}
```

6.
```
void SetPassing2( /* inout */       Boolean passing[],
                  /* in */    const int     score[],
                  /* in */          int     length,
                  /* in */          int     grade    )

// Precondition:
//     length <= MAX_STUD
//  && score[0..length-1] are assigned
// Postcondition:
//     For all i, where 0 <= i <= length-1,
//        IF score[i] > grade, THEN passing[i] == true
```

```
{
    int index;    // Loop control and index variable
    for (index = 0; index < length; index++)
        if (score[index] > grade)
            passing[index] = true;
}
```

CHAPTER 12   Exam Preparation Exercises

6. a. `typedef char NameType[41];`

    b. `NameType oneName;`

    c. `NameType employeeName[100];`

7. a. valid   b. valid   c. invalid   d. valid   e. valid   f. invalid
    g. invalid   h. valid

9. a. valid   b. invalid   c. valid   d. invalid   e. valid   f. invalid
    g. valid

CHAPTER 12   Programming Warm-Up Exercises

2.
```
int Count( /* in */ const ItemType numList[],
           /* in */       ItemType item,
           /* in */       int      length   )

// Precondition:
//      length <= MAX_LENGTH
//   && numList[0..length-1] are assigned  && item is assigned
// Postcondition:
//      Function value == number of occurrences of value "item"
//                        in numList[0..length-1]

{
    int index;          // Loop control and index variable
    int counter = 0;    // Number of occurrences of item
    for (index = 0; index < length; index++)
        if (numList[index] == item)
            counter++;
    return counter;
}
```

12. The `BinSearch` function remains the same until the last assignment statement. This statement should be replaced with the following code segment:

```
if (found)
    index = middle;
else
    index = first;
```

Also, the function postcondition should read:

```
//      IF item is in list
//          found == true  &&  list[index] == item
//      ELSE
//          found == false  &&  index is where item belongs
```

13. Assuming that BinSearch has been modified as in Exercise 12, simply replace the call to SearchOrd with a call to BinSearch.

CHAPTER 13   Exam Preparation Exercises

1. a. 6   b. 5   c. 30   d. column   e. row
5. a. valid   b. valid   c. invalid   d. valid   e. invalid   f. invalid
8. a. True   b. False   c. True   d. True

CHAPTER 13   Programming Warm-Up Exercises

```
2. void SetDiagonals( /* inout */ DataType data,
                      /* in */    int      length,
                      /* in */    char     someChar )

// Precondition:
//      length <= MAX_LENGTH  &&  someChar is assigned
// Postcondition:
//      All elements on both diagonals of the "data" array
//      contain someChar

{
    int i;         // Loop control and index variable

    for (i = 0; i < length; i++)
    {
        data[i][i] = someChar;
        data[i][length-i-1] = someChar;
    }
}
```

```
9. int RowSum( /* in */ const TableType table,
              /* in */       int       whichRow,
              /* in */       int       colLength )

// Precondition:
//      colLength <= NUM_COLS  &&  whichRow < NUM_ROWS
//   && table[whichRow][0..colLength-1] are assigned
```

```
// Postcondition:
//      Function value == table[whichRow][0] + ...
//                              + table[whichRow][colLength-1]

{
    int col;            // Loop control and index variable
    int sum = 0;        // Accumulating sum

    for (col = 0; col < colLength; col++)
        sum = sum + table[whichRow][col];
    return sum;
}
```

CHAPTER 14   Exam Preparation Exercises

2. a. valid   b. invalid   c. valid   d. invalid   e. valid   f. invalid
g. valid   h. valid   i. valid

3. a. `aRef = guide[70].chart;`
  b. `strcpy(aCode, guide[87].chart.token[0]);`
  c. `guide[93].chart.token[22][0] = 'X';`
  d. `aRef.symbol[19][8] = aMap.mapCode[3];`

5. False

7. a. hierarchical record   b. record   c. record   d. array of records
e. array   f. array of hierarchical records   g. array of records
h. array (string)

CHAPTER 14   Programming Warm-Up Exercises

1. a.

```
const int NAME_LENGTH = 21;

typedef char NameStr[NAME_LENGTH];
typedef char SSStr[12];

enum YearType {FRESHMAN, SOPHOMORE, JUNIOR, SENIOR};
enum SexType {M, F};

struct PersonType
{
    NameStr   name;
    SSStr     ssNumber;
```

```
        YearType year;
        float    gpa;
        SexType  sex;
};
```

b.

```
PersonType person;

cout << person.name << endl;
cout << person.ssNumber << endl;
switch (person.year)
{
    FRESHMAN  : cout << "Freshman" << endl;
                break;
    SOPHOMORE : cout << "Sophomore" << endl;
                break;
    JUNIOR    : cout << "Junior" << endl;
                break;
    SENIOR    : cout << "Senior" << endl;
}
cout << person.gpa << endl;
if (person.sex == M)
    cout << "Male" << endl;
else
    cout << "Female" << endl;
c. PersonType roll[3000];
```

3.
```
const int NAME_LENGTH = 31;
const int MAX_COURSES = 50;

enum YearType {FRESHMAN, SOPHOMORE, JUNIOR, SENIOR};
enum GradeType {A, B, C, D, F, INCOMPLETE};
struct DateType
{
    int month;
    int year;
};
struct GradeRec
{
    int      courseID;
    GradeType grade;
};
typedef GradeRec GradeArray[MAX_COURSES];
typedef char NameStr[NAME_LENGTH];
```

```
struct StudentType
{
    NameStr     name;
    long        studentID;
    int         hoursToDate;
    int         coursesToDate;
    GradeArray  courseGrades;
    DateType    firstEnrolled;
    YearType    year;
    float       gpa;
};
```

10.
```
struct String
{
    char str[21];
    int  length;
};
      .
      .
      .
int StrLength( /* in */ String aString )
{
    return aString.length;
}
```

13. Assuming a variable `areaCode` is of type `int`, one solution is to print a leading zero if the area code is less than 100:

```
if (areaCode < 100)
    cout << '0';
cout << areaCode;
```

Another solution is to declare an area code to be a string rather than an `int`, thereby reading or printing exactly three characters each time I/O takes place.

CHAPTER 15   Exam Preparation Exercises

3. a. `SomeClass` and `int`   b. `Func1`, `Func2`, `Func3`, and `someInt`
   c. `object1` and `object2`   d. `Func1`, `Func2`, and `Func3`
   e. `Func1` and `Func3`   f. part (ii)
6. a. Only `myprog.cpp` must be recompiled.   b. All of the object (`.obj`) files must be relinked.   c. Only `file2.cpp` and `file3.cpp` must be recompiled.
   d. All of the object (`.obj`) files must be relinked.
11. False

13. *Class Abc :*
    a. The private data members are `alpha` and `beta`.
    b. Functions `DoThis` and `DoThat` can reference `alpha` and `beta` directly.
    c. Functions `DoThis` and `DoThat` can invoke each other directly.
    d. Clients can invoke `DoThis`.
    Class Xyz :
    a. The private data members are `alpha`, `beta`, and `gamma`.
    b. Functions `TryIt` can reference only `gamma` directly.
    c. Functions `TryIt` can invoke the parent class's `DoThis` function directly. The syntax for the function call is `Abc::DoThis()`.
    d. Clients can invoke `DoThis` and `TryIt`.

17. a. False   b. True   c. False

CHAPTER 15   Programming Warm-Up Exercises

1. a. `if ( !time1.Equal(time2) )`
        `n = 1;`
   b. `if (time1.LessThan(time2) || time1.Equal(time2))`
        `n = 5;`
   c. `if (time2.LessThan(time1))`
        `n = 8;`
   d. `if ( !time1.LessThan(time2) )`
        `n = 5;`

   or

   `if (time2.LessThan(time1) || time2.Equal(time1))`
       `n = 5;`

3. Function specification (within the `TimeType` class declaration):

```
void WriteAmPm() const;
   // Postcondition:
   //      Time has been output in 12-hour form
   //         HH:MM:SS AM   or   HH:MM:SS PM
```

Function definition (omitting the postcondition to save space):

```
void TimeType::WriteAmPm() const
{
    Boolean am;        // True if AM should be printed
    int     tempHrs;   // Value of hours to be printed

    am = (hrs <= 11);
    if (hrs == 0)
        tempHrs = 12;
    else if (hrs >= 13)
        tempHrs = hrs - 12;
    else
        tempHrs = hrs;
```

```
    if (tempHrs < 10)
        cout << '0';
    cout << tempHrs << ':';
    if (mins < 10)
        cout << '0';
    cout << mins << ':';
    if (secs < 10)
        cout << '0';
    cout << secs;
    if (am)
        cout << " AM";
    else
        cout << " PM";
}
```

4. Function specification (within the `TimeType` class declaration):

```
long Minus( /* in */ TimeType time2 ) const;
    // Precondition:
    //     This time and time2 represent times in the same day
    // Postcondition:
    //     Function value == (this time) - time2, in seconds
```

Function definition (omitting the precondition and postcondition to save space):

```
long TimeType::Minus( /* in */ TimeType time2 ) const
{
    long thisTimeInSecs;   // This time in seconds since midnight
    long time2InSecs;      // time2 in seconds since midnight

    // Using 3600 seconds per hour and 60 seconds per minute...

    thisTimeInSecs = long(hrs)*3600 + long(mins)*60 + long(secs);
    time2InSecs = long(time2.hrs)*3600 + long(time2.mins)*60 +
                  long(time2.secs);
    return thisTimeInSecs - time2InSecs;
}
```

11.
```
class InterAddress : public Address
{
public:
    void Write() const;
        // Postcondition:
        //     Address has been output

    InterAddress( /* in */ const String20 newStreet,
                  /* in */ const String20 newCity,
                  /* in */ const String20 newState,
                  /* in */ const String20 newZip,
                  /* in */ const String20 newCountry );
```

```
            //  Precondition:
            //      All parameters are assigned
            //  Postcondition:
            //      Class object is constructed with private data
            //      initialized by the incoming parameters
    private:
        String20 country;
    };
```

CHAPTER 16   Exam Preparation Exercises

2. False. Both void functions and value-returning functions can be recursive.
4. $F(4) = 1$, $F(6) = -1$, and $F(5)$ is undefined.
6. A selection control structure—either an If or a Switch statement

CHAPTER 16   Programming Warm-Up Exercises

```
1. int F( /* in */ int n )
   {
       if (n == 0 || n == 1)
           return 1;
       else
           return F(n - 1) + F(n - 2);
   }
```

```
3. void DoubleSpace( /* inout */ ifstream& inFile )
   {
       char ch;

       inFile.get(ch);
       while (inFile)                  // While not EOF...
       {
           cout << ch;
           if (ch == '\n')
               cout << endl;
           inFile.get(ch);
       }
   }
```

INDEX